R. H. Cassen is serving as a Senior Economist on the Secretariat of the Independent Commission on International Development Issues (the 'Brandt Commission') in Geneva. He took up his post in 1978, on leave from the Institute of Development Studies, Sussex, and the Centre for Population Studies, London School of Hygiene and Tropical Medicine, where he holds joint appointments.

He had taught previously at the London School of Economics (1961–69). He was an Economic Adviser, Ministry of Overseas Development (1966–67); First Secretary (Economic), British High Commission, New Delhi (1967–68); and Senior Economist, World Bank, Washington, D.C. (1969–72); he has also served as an Adviser to the House of Commons Select Committee on Overseas Aid and Development (1973–74).

His publications include contributions to *World Development* and *Population & Development Review* and other papers on development and population topics, mainly with reference to India.

INDIA:
POPULATION, ECONOMY, SOCIETY

India:
Population, Economy, Society

R. H. Cassen

*Senior Economist, Secretariat of the Independent Commission on
International Development Issues, Geneva
Fellow, Institute of Development Studies, University of Sussex
Senior Research Fellow, Centre for Overseas Population Studies, London
School of Hygiene and Tropical Medicine*

HOLMES & MEIER PUBLISHERS, INC.
New York

First published in the United States of America 1978
by Holmes & Meier Publishers, Inc.
101 Fifth Avenue
New York, NY 10003

Printed in Great Britain

Library of Congress Cataloging in Publication Data

Cassen, Robert.
  India—population, economy & society.

  Bibliography: p.
  1. India—Population. 2. India—Economic
conditions—1947–   3. India—Social conditions
—1947–   I. Title.
HB3639.C37 1978 330.9'54'05   77–16217
ISBN 0–8419–0300–X

*To my mother and father
and my brother*

Contents

Figures and Tables

Preface

My main purpose in writing this book has been to give an intelligible account of India and its contemporary problems, seen mainly from a population point of view. I have been particularly motivated by a number of common views about India which have repeatedly been expressed to me. How often, returning from a stay there, I have been asked, 'Don't you find India terribly depressing?' – A question impossible to answer; naturally there are in India scenes of appalling human deprivation to be witnessed and, if one has followed the country's fortunes over the years, one cannot feel enthusiasm about the pace of change. Yet a person who knows only the miseries of India does not know India. I fear I may add something to this false picture since the other things that make the experience of India vivid, indeed moving, have little place here.

Another question I often face is, 'Isn't India hopeless?' This question is posed sometimes by people whose interest in India is merely casual. But I have also encountered it in governmental circles and international agencies among people concerned with aid. I usually ask what the question really signifies; after all India is going to continue to exist. When pressed those who put the question often admit that they really mean they do not wish to contemplate India's problems for any length of time. Readers of this book will not be given any easy reassurance; but I hope they will derive a sense that, while the problems are great, they can be made less so. I am not in the business of feeding the public's appetite for nightmares which so many books on population themes do. India's situation calls for, and repays, analysis, not alarmism. A further purpose is to clarify some of the issues about the population question itself. What is the point of making efforts at development when everything is absorbed by the growth of numbers? Or, why bring down the death rate, it only means more people? These misconceptions are put in their place. Family planning is often said to have 'failed' in India – that too is a misconception, even if 'success' has not been conspicuous either.

The book has five parts. The first chapter gives some background to the problem of population change and the way it has occurred, mainly outside India. The second looks at current and future characteristics of India's population. The third examines the family planning programme. In the fourth the interrelationships between economic development and population change are explored, the character of economic progress in India and how population has affected it and been affected by it. In the last chapter the subject is the prospect for social and political development; some reflections on China have been included for comparative purposes. I have tried to pursue three aims at once: cover a wide range of topics, satisfy scholarly opinion, and be read by the non-specialist. Inevitably any particular reader will find an excess of material on one topic and not enough on another. My three aims were practically irreconcilable, but reflected an ambition I feel was worthwhile even if finally out of reach. I have avoided economic jargon wherever possible. The use of demographic terms proved unavoidable but they are explained in an appendix. Throughout I have tried to keep up some sort of narrative pace, frequently confining qualifying statements or statistical evidence to the notes if they would otherwise have made the text indigestible – this is especially true of Chapter 4, the notes to which are often substantive, unlike the other chapters, where they mainly supply references and points of detail.

The list of people whose help I must acknowledge is lengthy – not surprisingly; I have covered a range of subject matter which no individual could master and have frequently relied on others. Those who have read parts of my manuscript, supplied materials, answered queries or reduced my ignorance in helpful discussions include the following: J. Baneth, P. K. Bardhan, A. Barnett, B. Berelson, J. N. Biraben, J. G. Blacker, A. Bose, R. Briggs, T. Byres, D. N. Chaudhry, P. Chaudhuri, S. Cole-King, B. Dasgupta, M. Das Gupta, P. Demeny, R. P. Dore, O. Gish, P. Isenman, H. Joshi, S. Lateef, J. Mellor, J. W. Miller, R. Miller, M. Moore, R. Muscat, D. Nayyar, P. R. Payne, N. Perlman, V. Raleigh, S. Ramalingaswamy, N. Ruck, W. G. Runciman, A. K. Sen, I. Sutherland, C. Taylor, P. Visaria, J. Wyon. I owe a still greater debt to four people who have changed my mind or helped me to clarify my views over a period of years: Clive Bell and Michael Lipton of the Institute of Development Studies, Ronald Freedman of the University of Michigan and Ron Gray of the London School of Hygiene and Tropical Medicine. Four people, Helen Moody, Mohinder Puri, Bhanwar Singh and Penelope Sanger have most efficiently given me bibliographical and other assistance. Tim Dyson, who started as my research assistant, but has become my colleague and collaborator in various enterprises, deserves a special vote of thanks for putting his demographic expertise generously at my disposal. Pauline Baxter, Dorothy Boyes, Betty Dodson, Francine Spencer and Sandra Yelf are only some of the many who have struggled with my handwriting and turned it into typescript; I am grateful to each of them, but most of all to Ethel Royston who not only did her share of that but took cheerful care of many troublesome parts of my life. I also wish to thank the library staffs of the Institute of Development Studies – Sheila Howard most of all – and of the London School of Hygiene and Tropical Medicine for prolonged and unfailing assistance.

In an entirely special category I must place Lavraj and Dharma Kumar who had nothing to do with the contents of this book but much to do with my well-being while I worked on it. They almost became my family in New Delhi and, if I have any sense of not being a complete stranger in India, I owe it above all to their repeated kindness and generosity.

I must express my gratitude to the Centre Culturel Internationale at Cerisy-la-Salle and the Wingspread Foundation of Racine, Wisconsin for their hospitality – a conference organised by the latter proved a valuable occasion for meeting with others interested in India. Naturally my greatest institutional debt is to the Institute of Development Studies at the University of Sussex which provided me with facilities for work, intellectual stimulus, and a rewarding sense of commitment rare in the academic world. I should add that the Institute under its Director, Richard Jolly, tolerated my absorption in my own work to a degree that I did not, perhaps, entirely deserve. I have left two people to the last: one to whom, above all, I owe a considerable share of such merit as this book possesses, is David Glass of the London School of Economics and Political Science. He read most of the manuscript prior to its completion, a good deal of it when he was heavily burdened with other things. Throughout my writing of it the thought of presenting it for his formidable scrutiny has raised my sights and forced me to attempt to overcome my deficiencies. At an early stage, when I told him of the book's intended scope, he warned me that what I was trying to do was 'impossible'. I believe he meant by this that I would never satisfy his standards of scholarship in tackling so many subjects. I am certain that he must now think his warning was fully justified; I have not even satisfied my own standards. But while I have been writing I have had the frequent benefit of his help, his encouragement and occasionally some salutary discouragement, all of which have been invaluable to me. Lastly someone who has inspired any number of people working on India and whose early death in 1973 was a painful blow: Pitambar Pant. One could not be in the vicinity of the Indian Planning Commission without being aware of him as one of its major intellects whose drive and enthusiasm acted as a constant challenge. I shall not forget the occasion when I defended some argument I had advanced with the remark that he had asked for my opinion, not for a scientific treatise. 'You must be objective', he replied 'even in your dreams'. He too would undoubtedly have found this book wanting and not only for my inability to follow that injunction. It only remains for me to reflect that, despite the distinguished help I have received, I doubt that I have eradicated all error; I have certainly persisted in some opinions against good advice. Writing about India, it seems, one may never do more than provide 'just enough light to see the darkness by'.

1 Background

Nature's vast frame, the web of human things,
Birth and the grave, that are not as they were.
Shelley, Alastor

India defeats most of those who try either to understand or to change it. Part of the difficulty of trying to understand it is the legacy of past writing. The more you read, the more you must doubt the very possibility of taking a genuinely objective view of the country. There is a curious unchangingness about the sub-continent; even visually it seems to look as it has always been portrayed. The eighteenth and nineteenth century paintings of Daniell or Chinnery convey impressions of an India almost completely familiar to one who comes to it a hundred or more years later. Does it really change so little? Or are our perceptions conditioned? Such questions come particularly to mind in relation to India's population. Consider the following quotation:

> Before I quit the subject of *Delhi*, I will answer by anticipation a question which I am sensible you wish to ask, namely, what is the extent of the population of that city, and the number of its respectable inhabitants, as compared with the capital of *France*? When I consider that *Paris* consists of three or four cities piled upon one another, all of them containing numerous apartments, filled, for the most part, from top to bottom; that the streets are thronged with men and women, on foot and horseback; with carts, chaises, and coaches; and that there are very few large squares, courts, or gardens; reflecting, I say, upon all these facts, *Paris* appears to me the nursery of the world, and I can scarcely persuade myself that *Delhi* contains an equal number of people. On the other hand, if we take a review of this metropolis of the *Indies*, and observe its vast extent and its numberless shops; if we recollect that, besides the *Omrahs*, the city never contains less than thirty-five thousand troopers, nearly all of whom have wives, children, and a great number of servants, who, as well as their masters, reside in separate houses; that there is no house, by whomsoever inhabited, which does not swarm with women and children; that during the hours when the abatement of the heat permits the inhabitants to walk abroad, the streets are crowded with people, although many of those streets are very wide, and, excepting a

few carts, unincumbered with wheel carriages; if we take all these circumstances into consideration, we shall hesitate before we give a positive opinion in regard to the comparative population of *Paris* and *Delhi*; and I conclude, that if the number of souls be not as large in the latter city as in our own capital, it cannot be greatly less. As respects the better sort of people, there is a striking difference in favour of *Paris*, where seven or eight out of ten individuals seen in the streets are tolerably well clad, and have a certain air of respectability; but in *Delhi*, for two or three who wear decent apparel, there may always be reckoned seven or eight poor, ragged, and miserable beings, attracted to the capital by the army. I cannot deny, however, that I continually meet with persons neat and elegant in their dress, finely formed, well mounted, and properly attended. Nothing, for instance, can be conceived much more brilliant than the great square in front of the fortress at the hours when the *Omrahs*, *Rajas*, and *Mansebdars* repair to the citadel to mount guard, or attend the assembly of the *Am-Kas*. The *Mansebdars* flock thither from all parts, well mounted and equipped, and splendidly accompanied by four servants, two behind and two before, to clear the street for their masters. *Omrahs* and *Rajas* ride thither, some on horseback, some on majestic elephants; but the greater part are conveyed on the shoulders of six men . . .

This was written by a French doctor, François Bernier, who lived and travelled a great deal in India.[1] Exchange a detail or two, and the description would fit Delhi today; certainly the feel of much of the passage is remarkably close to contemporary India. It was written in 1663.

One could cite any number of sources to show that India has for long struck the observer as being both crowded and poor. Forty years before Bernier, a Dutch commercial agent named Pelsaert living in India wrote of 'the utter subjection and poverty of the common people – poverty so great and so miserable that the life of the people can be depicted and accurately described only as the home of stark want and the dwelling place of bitter woe'.[2] Two hundred and twenty years later, in 1842, a writer in the Calcutta Review described the peasantry of Bengal as 'trembling on the remotest verge of human misery and brutalisation'.[3] The point of drawing attention to this historical sense of India's problems is not to suggest that there is no truth in it. Far from it. It is rather to induce a certain caution. It is evident that the way the mass of Indians live, and have always lived, presents itself to European observation with particular vividness. The 'swarming cities', 'teeming native quarters', the 'poor and silent millions' were the commonplaces of eighteenth and nineteenth century writings on India, literary and administrative. There may indeed be something in the life-style of the Indian poor, particularly the proximity in which they lived, which peculiarly affronted the *bourgeois* European sensibility of the past and made conditions appear even worse than they were. But one can go back to earlier times and find the same sort of comments. Thus the Russian divine, Afanasiy Nikitin, who travelled in India in the 1460s, noted that 'the country is very populous; the rural inhabitants are very [poor and] naked, while the nobles are strong and sated with luxuries'.[4]

Such comments can be found for still earlier periods; but little purpose would be served by quoting them. What we would like to know, but cannot, is the extent of this poverty and whether it got less over time. Poverty was the lot of the majority of mankind in all countries until the modern era; it still is in all but a few countries and, even in these few, poverty is far from being eradicated. But perhaps no country is so clearly associated with the concept of poverty as India. That this has apparently always been so may provide a sense of perspective when we come to examine the present.

PRE-CENSUS POPULATION ESTIMATES

We have only the sketchiest idea of the population size before the nineteenth century. Going back to earliest known times, there were quite advanced civilisations at Harappa and Mohenjodaro in the third and fourth millennia B.C., with well developed city life and technology comparable to that of Egypt. Contemporary sources describe numerous cities and extensive trade from 800 B.C. onwards. The unreliable Arrian, who wrote his *Indica* in the second century A.D., but borrowed from sources from the fourth century B.C., wrote of cities 'too numerous to count'. The population of India in those times must have been numbered in tens of millions – but whether there were 100 million or more in 300 B.C., as has been suggested,[5] one might reasonably doubt. A possibly more plausible estimate of about 37 million in the seventh century A.D. has been made on the basis of the observation of Hiuen Tsang, a Chinese Buddhist who travelled in India at that time.[6]

The first tolerably reliable population figure for India is for 1881, though the first census was taken between 1867-72. (In what follows, references to 'India' are to the India of today's boundaries, which were established at partition in 1947, with one or two subsequent adjustments.) Prior to that an estimate for 1600 gives a population of 115 million. This is a reworking by Das Gupta[7] of an old estimate by Moreland.[8] Moreland estimated North India by looking at cultivated area and other data; for South India he only had figures of army complements and army-to-population ratios for European countries. Das Gupta has improved on the North India figures but, while properly doubting those for South India, could not improve on them. Thus, while 115 million is of the right order of magnitude for 1600, it should be treated sceptically. In the nineteenth century there were a number of enumerations conducted by the British authorities prior to 1871 but the first census, faulty though it was, showed them up as too small. Das Gupta and his colleagues have made an estimate of the pre-1871 growth rate by looking at sections of India for which some data were available and combining them into an overall rate. Figures of 154 million for 1800 and 189 million for 1850 were thus arrived at – more reliable techniques than Moreland's, but still to be regarded as only a little better than orders of magnitude.

From 115 million to 154 million in two hundred years is an extremely slow rate of growth, but it is consistent with what we know of India and with the experience of European populations. There were numerous famines in India in those two centuries – mortality caused by them is not known, but one in Bengal in 1770 – 72 is thought to have killed eight to ten million people – about a third of the province's population.[9] Given what we know of poverty and disease, it is perfectly plausible to assume the same pattern of high birth and death rates and periodic visitations of *la mort extraordinaire*, with which we shall become familiar when we turn to pre-industrial Europe. An extremely slow rise up to the 1600 figure would also plausibly account for the circumstantial evidence indicating a very large population in the pre-Christian era.

It would be possible to spend fascinating hours attempting to refine estimates of the pre-census population but, in terms of the purposes of this book, it would advance us little. If anything, the estimates are mostly too low. But, if the population was anything like 115 million in 1600, we cannot but conclude that Bernier and Pelsaert and others must have been correct in the picture they give of historical poverty on a wide scale. Most of the people lived in small rural settlements, then as now; irrigation and cultivation techniques were little developed, so the food supply must have been scanty and even more subject to climatic fluctuations than it is today. The vast building programmes of the Mogul emperors and other princes and the retinues of servants in the pay of people even of relatively modest means bear witness to a seemingly inexhaustible supply of ill-paid labour.

One should not exaggerate the reliability of such informal evidence. In times past Europeans seeing relatively undressed people may have had a tendency to think them ill-dressed and therefore poor. There were some travellers who found parts of India quite paradisal.[10] The building programmes of the Moguls show there was wealth to be taxed; India was known as a wealthy country where fortunes could be made and plunder taken. The probable explanation of the contrast in these images of poverty and riches is the character of income distribution. The population of India was huge as compared with any European country of the seventeenth century; a small amount taken from a very large number of people can provide very substantial revenues. The image of India's wealth derives, in any case, from the country's products, from tales of the jewels of maharajas, the silks worn by the rich, the sumptuousness in general of the life of the few and not from any picture of the well-being of the many. Perhaps the last word should be left to an Indian source, a verse from the Subhasitaratna kosa, an anthology of Sanskrit verse dating from the eleventh century A.D.[11]

> Often the pauper's children go to others' houses. With their little hands leaning against the doorways, hungry, but with voices hushed by shame, they cast half glances at those who eat within.

THE FIRST CENSUS AND AFTER

Even more so than with European populations estimates of India's total numbers or vital rates prior to the census era are highly tentative. Once the censuses begin estimates rest on firmer ground, though one should continue to treat them with a certain amount of reservation. The first Indian census was taken from 1867 – 72; on the basis of its evidence and supplementary observations the 1871 population within India's present boundaries may be taken to have been about 209 million. Even that figure is not too reliable.[12] The far more sophisticated censuses of today are not a hundred per cent secure. In those earlier days there was under-reporting of female children, invention of non-existent sons and possibly, as hearsay has it, such curiosities as the inclusion of domestic cattle as countable members of the household. The extent of such errors and others is unknown though it is thought[13] that even the areas covered by the first censuses were under-estimated by 12 million. Further problems are created by the fact that the territory then enumerated was not the India of today – and, even for the India of 1871, some regions were omitted by the count.

The actual total recorded by the 1867 – 72 census was 203 million for the whole of what was then India. Kingsley Davis[14] has adjusted that figure to 255 million in the light of the considerations mentioned above. The figure of 209 million which is given here for 1871 is 255 million, reduced by 18 per cent to allow for the areas of what are now Pakistan and Bangladesh which were of course part of India in those days. The 18 per cent proportion is taken from the 1941 Census, in which 70 million out of the total 389 million, or 18 per cent were in the Pakistan and Bangladesh areas. This proportion, as a rough but reasonable approximation, is also used to reduce Davis's 1881 and 1891 estimates of the population of pre-partition India to that of India within its present boundaries. From 1901 onwards the official Indian figures are used.

To say that Indian censuses are variable in quality does not in the least reflect on the Census Commissioner and his organisation. On the contrary the achievements of the census organisation are remarkable for their coverage and the range of studies assembled under the wing of the census itself. The problems lie in the intractable character of the material – the size and diversity of the country, the prevailing low standards of literacy, the difficulty of recruiting skilled enumerators. The total staff of the 1971

Census numbered somewhere in the region of $1\frac{1}{2}$ million, including enumerators and tabulators. The count in each village – and India has over 600,000 villages – starts with a map on which every dwelling is identified; the enumerator then has to visit each household individually and record the data, usually taken verbally. Obviously the skill and thoroughness with which this is done, or can be done, must vary from one enumerator to another. And anyone who has seen an urban slum in India would despair of the possibility of making a definitively accurate assessment of the numbers and other population characteristics. Added to this one should not forget political disruption – the Non-Cooperation Movement interfered with the 1921 Census; the Civil Disobdience campaigns affected those of 1931 and 1941.[15] Even in 1971 the census in West Bengal is alleged to have been troubled by the political upheaval there at the time.

Despite all these difficulties the censuses, especially those of 1951, 1961 and 1971 are obviously fairly reliable. There is a good deal of internal consistency, particularly on a State-by-State basis, and the intercensal rates of growth in the states correspond approximately with what is known about conditions affecting births and deaths. If the errors were constant from one census to another, the rate of growth could be accurate even if the estimate of numbers were not: this may apply for the male population. What are known to be particularly defective in the censuses are the age distribution and, to a lesser and (over time) diminishing extent, the counting of female children. Most Indians do not know their own age with any accuracy. Birthdays are not celebrated and records are not extensively kept. Enumerators are given calendars of significant historical events, nationally or locally, and respondents who do not know their date of birth are asked to place it in relation to these events. Such techniques are better than nothing but the age data in the censuses are useable for research purposes only after considerable manipulation. This is sad since it reduces the scope of demographic inference, so much of which depends on reliable age data. The under-enumeration of female children stems from the general relative lack of esteem which greets a female addition to the family – this will be discussed below under fertility.

With these qualifications about the censuses in mind we can now examine the growth of India's population in the census period. The picture that emerges is one of unsteady growth with one decade of actual decline from 1871 – 1921, and an accelerating growth rate from 1941 – 71 as shown in Table 1.1

The total growth from 1871 – 1941 was 52 per cent; during the same period the British Isles, Germany and Europe as a whole grew somewhat faster. Of course these periods in the different countries are not comparable in terms of social change. More relevant would be, say, the fifty years from 1921 – 71 in which India's population grew by 118 per cent, compared with the seventy years of rapid growth in the British Isles from 1821 – 91

TABLE 1.1 Population of India

(millions)	
1871	209·1
1881	210·9
1891	231·4
1901	238·4
1911	252·1
1921	251·3
1931	279·0
1941	318·7
1951	361·1
1961	439·2
1971	547·8

SOURCE Davis (1951); Census reports.

when the population grew by only 79 per cent; or Japan which took seventy, rather than fifty, years to grow by 120 per cent between 1879 and 1940. In other words, while India's population growth prior to World War II was nothing unusual compared with what was happening simultaneously

FIG. 1.1 Growth of the population of India and rate of growth, 1800 to 1971. The figures before 1947 refer to the region within the present boundaries of India
SOURCE Das Gupta (1972); Davis (1951); Census reports.

elsewhere, the last fifty years in India have been remarkable compared with similar stages in countries where the transition to modern low levels of births and deaths has occurred. The same would be true of other developing countries. Indeed in terms of rate of growth as opposed to growth in absolute members, India is relatively modest by the standards of many countries of Africa and Latin America. The decade 1961 – 71 showed an annual rate of population growth of 2.23 per cent in India, higher than ever before; but rates of 3 per cent and more have been quite common elsewhere.

In absolute terms however the growth of India's population is decidedly impressive. The meaning of this growth to India's economy and society is the subject of the last two chapters. But the last decade has brought India into a new demographic era. The fifty years after 1921 added 300 million to India's numbers; but more than 100 million of those arrived in the ten years prior to the 1971 Census. It is this momentous absolute rise in numbers which has given new cause for concern.

The distinctive demographic feature of the last fifty years has been the gradual rise in the annual growth rate – by an average of a quarter of one per cent every decade in the last forty years, from 1.25 per cent for 1931 – 41 to 2.23 per cent for 1961–71. Population growth from 1871 to 1921 is akin to that of pre-modern Europe, with high birth and death rates, producing a barely positive rate of growth, except for the years of major famines and epidemics – as the table shows it was a population of over 200 million, growing by less than one million a year. The slight decline of population between the 1911 and 1921 Census is due largely to the influenza epidemic of 1918 in which at least 16 million people are believed to have died. The last major famine deaths occurred in the decade 1891–1901 apart from the uncharacteristic events of 1943 (see below) – altogether a pattern familiar from the study of Europe's population history.

After 1921 mortality began to decline; indeed it is the extent and swiftness of mortality decline that has produced India's accelerated population growth; the birth rate may have been falling somewhat in recent decades but mortality has fallen much faster. The 1971 Census total of 548 million came in fact as a surprise to most demographers – something nearer to 560 million had been anticipated. Whether this resulted from a failure of mortality to decline as much as was expected or from a further fall in the birth rate, is a question which will be gone into in the next sections. But clearly continuation of the growth rate of the 1961 – 71 decade would confront India with a most serious situation; any further acceleration of the rate would be even more serious.

Before we turn to the examination of population change in India and what causes it, we will take an extended detour. Its purpose is to provide the reader with a general background of understanding of the phenomenon of population growth and particularly of the behaviour of mortality and fertility. The history of population change in Britain, France and

Japan will be looked at in some detail and the general situation in the developing countries today. But first come two more abstract discussions – Malthus, unavoidably; and the theory of the 'demographic transition'.

MALTHUS

Quite the most famous theory about human populations is to this day that of Thomas Robert Malthus, the son of an eighteenth century English clergyman. The word 'Malthusian' has passed into the language having become synonymous with the pressures leading to poverty or increased mortality which result from excessive population growth. The historical influence of Malthus was really immense. Keats' lines 'Thou wast not born for death, immortal Bird: No hungry generations tread thee down' are a case in point – many people to whom these lines are as well-known as the face of the Mona Lisa may never have stopped to reflect on the curiosity of the image employed. Keats was undoubtedly familiar with Malthus's works and nineteenth century literature is full of conscious and unconscious references to them.[16]

It is no exaggeration to say that Malthus's ideas, since they were first published in 1798, coloured the imagination of social thinkers and literary men contributing to a pessimistic view of the prospects of human society. Even John Stuart Mill – who described himself as in some respects a socialist – felt constrained to refer to them in his autobiography[17] as a 'great doctrine'; and, although he did not agree with Malthus on many issues, he went so far as to get himself arrested as a young man for distributing birth control literature and retained throughout his life a belief that excessive population was a cause of poverty. Only in the third edition of Mill's *Principles of Political Economy* (1852) did he publish his conviction that Malthus was wrong about the impossibility of benefiting the poor. Mill in fact never refuted Malthus completely but, before the middle of the nineteenth century, the opponents of Malthus were more numerous and more distinguished than the adherents and Malthus before his death in 1834 had been forced himself to qualify his theory substantially.

The basis of the theory can really all be found in the familiar proposition that 'Population, when unchecked, increases in a geometrical ratio. . . . Subsistence increases only in an arithmetical ratio.' (The distinction between 'geometrical' and 'arithmetical' here is the same as that between compound and simple interest. Any rate of compound interest, however small, will eventually overtake a given rate of simple interest however large. The view that food output could only grow by an 'arithmetical ratio' is in fact quite arbitrary.) From this it followed that the numbers of people would ultimately outstrip the available means of support; the cutting back of the growth of population by food-shortage was the chief of what Malthus called 'the positive checks'. To sustain this argument two assumptions were needed: that the food supply could not be made to grow faster by technical improvements; and that population growth would not be limited by other means than starvation.

Malthus did in fact believe that people could limit their families but he attributed the ability to do so – which he called 'the preventive check' – mainly to the educated classes who had both the wit to perceive the limits to their ability to keep large families and the self-discipline to control sexual desire. The poor were improvident – the more they prospered, the more they would add to their numbers. From this followed the 'iron law of wages' – the subsistence level was the ultimate labour wage as the lower classes would breed more if wages rose above that level and be cut down by poverty when numbers expanded above the limits society could support. There was little point in poor relief therefore; it would encourage improvidence and could not conceivably alleviate poverty.

The views generally characterised as 'Malthusian' should properly be attributed to the first edition of the *Essay on Population*. These were the ones with which his name is associated, which his followers propagated and which were taken by many as intellectual support for conservative views of society. In fact, in subsequent editions of the *Essay*, Malthus modified his more extreme views and yielded to many criticisms. In the last (1826) edition Malthus advocated universal education as a means of countering the 'population principle'. The postponement of marriage was the way to limit population growth; education would give the ordinary man 'a portion of that knowledge and foresight which so much facilitates the attainment of this object in the educated part of the community'.[18]

Malthus did not wholly oppose the population principle which he sometimes saw as a spur to economic development in the minds of men and society. But, by the time he came to write his *Principles of Political Economy* (2nd ed. 1836), he even retreated from the 'iron law of wages', admitting that improved living standards could lead to the formation of 'new and improved tastes and habits' before the rising standards induced a self-defeating increase in population; 'after the labourers have once acquired these tastes, population will advance in a slower ratio, as compared with capital, than formerly.' Thus, with suitable policies, it would be possible to have economic growth with rising levels of living. It is ironical that while people used to say of the poor in rich countries such as Britain or still do say of the developing countries, that there is no point in working for their prosperity as the result would only be more children, they would not find an intellectual ally in Malthus – not the later Malthus at any rate.

To adopt a term from the discussion of reproduction in animals, the 'Malthusian' view amounts to the proposition that man, though potentially capable of limiting his numbers by other means, will reproduce up to the point where 'density-dependent' factors take control. As we shall see two of Malthus's important assumptions turned out to be false in nineteenth century Europe and elsewhere. However a subtler version of the Malthusian theory, based on twentieth century evidence in the developing world, will still remain to be dealt with. But, in nineteenth century Europe, the death rate declined, prosperity gradually increased and, after an interval, the birth rate began to fall, ushering in the modern era of low rates of population growth and – after millennia of poverty – the beginnings in the twentieth century of reasonable living standards for the majority. This sequence has acquired the name of the 'demographic transition' to which we now turn.

THE DEMOGRAPHIC TRANSITION

A full understanding of the process known as the 'demographic transition' is essential before the important questions about India's population can be answered. If all the societies which have become 'developed' have acquired low population growth rates, will not the development of India solve India's population problem? The answer to that question depends on the interactions between population growth and social and economic change as they occurred in the countries which are now industrialised and whether a process similar in relevant respects is likely to occur in India.

The general character of the process in the industrialised countries used to be described in elaborate detail with various 'stages' at which mortality and fertility behaved in particular ways. Prolonged historical research has left little of this more elaborate account intact. The 'demographic transition' is now just a term to describe the passage societies make from high birth and death rates to low ones.[19] The passage has of course typically been the experience of countries going through a process of modernising economic and social development. This experience finally disposed of the early Malthusian theory as a depiction of inevitable necessity. Prosperity, far from bringing improvidence with it, seems eventually to lead to reduced fertility. And technical improvements – even if there is some ultimate limit to them, a point which will be examined later – have enabled the means of sustenance to grow rather faster than population. The 'arithmetical' versus the 'geometrical' rates of growth turned out to be a misdescription. Food and incomes generally grew at compound rates higher than the population growth rate.

The reasons for this pattern of population change are however much more uncertain. There is no simple and continuous relationship between the rise in living standards and the decline in mortality and fertility. There were periods in each country while incomes rose when mortality did not fall significantly, others when it did, with or without significant increases in incomes. And all the influences working to reduce fertility were in operation for some time without much effect. The present state of knowledge is that the factors which account for the changes in mortality and fertility can be listed but it is not possible to demonstrate quantitative relationships between these factors and their results. Mortality declined as a result of improved health and nutrition and we can produce a large set of causes for the decline in fertility, most of which we know to have been important. What we cannot, or can only rarely, do is to say 'this much of the decline in the death rate in years x is due to these health measures taken in years y.' But what we do know is quite adequate to provide valuable insights into the process of change, insights which will be helpful to understand the present position in India.

THE HISTORICAL DEMOGRAPHIC TRANSITION: ENGLAND

The demographic transition is a historical process and has to be seen in history. We shall treat it at its greatest length in the case of England and then consider briefly certain other countries. England was the first country to experience the social and economic transformation associated with industrial development – most of the features of the demographic transition can be discussed in the context of this experience although, as will be seen, the precise course of many relevant events is uncertain.

The period prior to the transition need not detain us – if we had no evidence that it had the character which has been observed, we would have to postulate it. England and Wales had less than 10 million people by the end of the eighteenth century. Had that number been arrived at by any rapid rate of growth, projecting the rate backwards would get to Adam and Eve far too quickly. (A population of 100 people would grow to 10 million in just over 2300 years at a rate of only $\frac{1}{2}$ per cent per year.) Such a low level of population in 1800 after centuries of recorded history must have been approached extremely slowly. In fact quite a lot is known about pre-transition populations in Britain and Europe generally and growth rates were very slow.[20]

Parish registers and a broad range of other evidence show fluctuating birth rates and high death rates, punctuated with periods of literal decimation by one scourge or another all over Europe until the eighteenth or nineteenth centuries. Denmark for example lost more than one fifth of its population between 1650 and 1660.[21] The Black Death may have carried off something like 30 per cent of the population of London in 1348-9, or over 15,000 out of a total of about 52,000; the bubonic plague of 1665-6 may have taken 80,000 out of a population of under half a million, something like four times London's normal death rate at that period.[22]

The generally accepted figure for the population of England and Wales in 1695 in 5.2 million, a modern revision by David Glass of Gregory King's contemporaneous estimate.[23] Prior to the first census in 1801 estimates for the years after 1695 are based on parish registers and other incompletely reliable materials but they seem to agree on very little growth between

1700 and 1750. The second half of the eighteenth century showed a clear acceleration of growth though its magnitude, and the question of whether it started just in the last two decades of the century or earlier, are uncertain.[24] Few of the estimates place the 1750 population much above 6 million though one outside estimate gives seven million. But the 1801 Census gave a figure of 8.9 million for England and Wales and that may be an under-estimate by as much as 5 per cent.[25] In the last two decades of the eighteenth century the population was probably growing by only a little less than one per cent annually.

Unless all the figures are completely wrong there was definitely a considerable acceleration of growth in the last quarter of the eighteenth century – how considerable depends on what estimate is accepted for earlier years but it must exceed by a large margin the average for the first half of the century. Needless to say opinions differ about growth in the 1700 – 50 period; and some have claimed that the growth in the second half of the century was only getting back onto the path of expansion of the late seventeenth century. More troublesome for our purposes is that the causes of this late eighteenth century growth are obscure. The majority opinion favours a declining death rate as the main factor though there have been some who believe that fertility also rose importantly.

In 1841 the birth rate was 35 per thousand and the death rate 23. The timing of the move to these rates from the much higher ones of the eighteenth century is not established. Some evidence suggests birth rates upwards of 40 per thousand prior to 1781 implying death rates of 35 per thousand or more. The more commonly accepted view is that the birth rate rose gradually to about 35 by 1790 and death rates were correspondingly lower.

The demographic transition began with a decline in mortality, particularly with a smoothing out of the high peaks in the mortality curve. This undoubtedly started in England and Wales in the mid eighteenth century. But whether the fall in mortality was a continuous process interrupted by reversals we do not know. We are also ignorant of the precise course of fertility. The factors which reduced mortality in the late eighteenth and early nineteenth centuries – improved nutrition, health and incomes – should also have increased fertility. But other factors were working in the opposite direction. The most probable course of fertility from 1781 – 1841 was a slight rise followed by a somewhat greater fall while mortality was decreasing fairly steadily.

The main reason for our ignorance about the early nineteenth century is the discrepancy between the data from the registration of births and deaths and that derivable from retrospective inferences from the censuses. The commonly accepted view, resting on the former evidence, keeps a lower and relatively stable level of fertility up to 1841; this has been challenged by Hollingsworth.[26] Using the reverse survival method[27] and other assumptions he arrives at far higher birth rates for the turn of the century and is forced to postulate a steep decline in fertility between 1821 and 1841, attributing the accelerating growth of population after 1750 solely to the decline in mortality. It would be an extremely complex task to sort out the true course of vital events for this period and it certainly cannot be attempted here. Both the registration data and the census age distributions are faulty: and the assumptions used by Hollingsworth to manipulate the census data are also subject to errors of unspecifiable dimensions. The conclusion reached at the end of the previous paragraph above rests on the observation that the forces reducing mortality should also have raised fertility and it would be odd if these were precisely cancelled out by other factors. It has been suggested that the available accounts of declining mortality do not explain enough of the acceleration in growth so that increased fertility must be postulated; it has been counter-claimed that fertility was already high and could hardly have risen and the mortality decline *is* adequate to explain the acceleration. But such arguments are no substitute for unassailable fact which regrettably is simply not available.

From 1841 onwards we are on steadily firmer ground as both the censuses and registration become more reliable. The death rate shows little movement from 1841 until the 1860s when it continues its descent. The birth rate does not start to fall until the second half of the 1870s. The century before that is thus one of relatively rapid growth which only begins to be curtailed after 1910; both mortality and fertility level off in the 1930s. Thus, for England and Wales, the timing of the mortality decline in the demographic transition cannot be precisely identified but major fertility decline follows it only after a considerable interval. The explanations which follow concentrate mainly on England and Wales and are analytical rather than purely chronological.

MORTALITY

It is hardly surprising that explaining the events of the demographic transition is so difficult, if it is not certain exactly when they occurred. When it comes to accounting for the decline in mortality in England and Wales for the transition period there are extra difficulties. Not only are the trends in mortality prior to 1841 uncertain, the course of the standard of living during the Industrial Revolution, to which we might wish to relate those trends, happens to be the most controversial single issue in the whole of British economic history. The British gross national product certainly rose; but who benefited from this rise, whether the mass of the poor got richer or poorer, and, if so, when – these questions are the subject of a whole library full of books and articles of academic debate.[28] So even if we had accurate figures for the trends in mortality, we could not assess the contribution to mortality reductions of increases in material prosperity.

Of course the general reasons why mortality goes down are well known – improvements in diet, in public health measures and sanitation, in medical care and in general environmental conditions, including the conditions of work. What is not known precisely – and would be very useful if it were known – is how much of the reduction in the death rate can be attributed to each of these things. The great killers of the pre-industrial era – famine, pestilence and the sword as the Bible called them – were gradually tamed. Famine yielded to the introduction of new crops – especially, in Europe, the potato – and the improvement of old ones and of farming practices generally. Better transport also permitted faster distribution of food to famine areas – though famine deaths were still occurring in Russia in the 1890s, both because of Witte's harsh economic policies and as a reflection of the country's relative backwardness at that time, as was also the terrible Irish famine of 1845.

The plague ceased its major visitations in England in 1667 but continued in Europe – the Balkans last of all – up to 1850, although odd cases occurred in East Anglia as late as 1918. According to the old theory we owe our preservation to *Rattus norvegicus*. He was thought to have displaced the domestic black rat and, because of his outdoor habits of life, he harboured mainly the flea *N. fasciatus* rather than *X. cheopis*, the most efficient carrier of the plague *bacillus*.[29] This view has however been challenged: *Rattus norvegicus* arrived about 1722, too late for the theory, and the black rat was not in fact so comprehensively displaced. Attention is now given to other possible carriers such as the human flea.[30]

There were important epidemics other than plague – typhus and cholera could also kill in large numbers. Epidemics were in fact nearly always the immediate cause of the 'dismal peaks' in mortality: famine, and war for that matter, often brought more deaths by disease than directly by food shortage or the sword. (Though a study[31] has been made for pre-industrial Finland showing that the epidemic mortality peaks were not connected with starvation.) By the end of the eighteenth century the dismal peaks were more or less smoothed out in the more advanced countries of Western Europe though the pattern differed in each country. The mortality curve for Norway for example shows fluctuations around a very gradually declining trend of about 30 per thousand in 1740 to 17 per thousand in 1850. There are two very large upward bumps in the graph in the eighteenth century and several quite large ones; then, with two bad spots on either side of 1810, it trickles slowly downwards towards modern levels. This is very different from England and Wales.

For Britain, once the inroads of the years of extraordinary mortality are at an end, explanations of mortality decline have to cover two rather different periods – from the last decades of the eighteenth to the mid nineteenth century and from then until the twentieth century. In the first of these periods there is really only one major innovation of medical importance which can have influenced mortality significantly and that was smallpox vaccination. Vaccination against smallpox, which began on a wide scale in Britain in the first years of the nineteenth century, was undoubtedly important and must have saved large numbers of lives in the cities. Watt (1888)[32] estimated that between 1783 and 1800 in Glasgow, 19 per cent of all deaths, and more than a third of deaths of children under ten, were caused by smallpox. These percentages fell to 4 and 9 respectively by 1818 after the introduction of vaccination – the city had a policy of free vaccination for poor children by 1801. The evidence concerning the weight of this factor in the explanatory account of mortality reduction for the early nineteenth century is inconclusive. Smallpox vaccination was made compulsory in England and Wales in 1854 but not enforced until 1871. In the second half of the nineteenth century the decline of smallpox only accounted for 6 per cent of the reduction in mortality. But, in the early decades of the century, its contribution must have been considerable.[33]

Many commentators do not believe that the opening of hospitals had much impact on mortality as they were quite likely to spread disease among the patients. There is a common observation that it is only relatively recently that one could be sure, on entering a hospital, of dying from the disease with which one came in. It was in 1859 after all that Florence Nightingale published her celebrated observation that the first thing one should ask of a hospital is that it 'do the sick no harm.' However very few people ever entered hospitals and until the end of the nineteenth century, those with infectious diseases were excluded. Their existence was thus of little consequence for the course of mortality. Another possibility to consider is changes in the organisms responsible for disease: in some cases a particular organism may have lost its virulence – scarlet fever was once a lethal illness and ceased to be so in the nineteenth century. The frequency of other such changes is however judged to be low. Nor was curative medicine, again until well on into the nineteenth century, all that good at saving lives.[34] One is left with environmental improvements, public health measures and better nutrition as the main explanatory factors in the earlier period.

The most important sanitation measures had to wait till the mid nineteenth century in England when the outbreaks of cholera, and the understanding of their cause, made the treatment of sewage and purification of the water-supply a matter of urgency: the medical knowledge which made hospitals more than isolation centres came even later, starting in the 1870s. Nevertheless there were environmental changes in the earlier half of the century which made some contribution. One of the most important of them was the gradual replacement of other forms of clothing by cotton cloth which was easy to wash. The advent of soap and of brick houses, to replace wooden ones more likely to harbour vermin, no doubt played a part.[35] One cannot help feeling though that improved nutrition must have been an important factor in any decline in mortality in the first half of the nineteenth century or before.

Nutrition did improve from the mid eighteenth century onwards. There is a good deal of evidence concerning increased consumption, not only of the potato, but of green vegetables, fruit, meat and so forth. But the change was most probably in the quality of nutrients rather than greatly increased real expenditure on food by the mass of the poor. There is no need to get involved in the controversy about living standards during the Industrial Revolution. We know from various studies that poverty was still fairly acute at the end of the nineteenth century in Britain. Thus Rowntree's famous study of York in 1889 showed that 10 per cent of the people were in primary poverty which Rowntree defined as incomes insufficient for purchase of the minimum necessary caloric intake, and a further 18 per cent were in secondary poverty, scarcely less wretched. (Secondary poverty denoted, for Rowntree, the failure through defect of education or character to purchase the minimum physical necessities where income just sufficed.)[36] Similar statements could be made about most of the industrial cities in the nineteenth century.[37] This is after a century of industrial growth: so even if those who argue that the Industrial Revolution benefited the poor are right, we can only surmise that the depths of poverty before these benefits came must have been quite profound. Quite recently a rural labourer from Suffolk could recall even about 1921 'I remember when I was about twelve we boys were so hungry we used to get together, crouch down in the corn and bark . . . Barking like dogs, imagine!'[38]

But a major source of mortality decline in the later nineteenth century was the relief of tuberculosis and McKeown and Record,[39] after excluding other agencies of improvement, attribute this to a rise in the standard of living. Indeed if one is uncertain about how much of the reduction in death rates can be ascribed to improved living standards, it does at least seem respectable to turn the argument round and claim the decline of mortality as evidence for – and an important feature of – substantial improvement of the conditions of life. In fact the gains in material conditions even among the working class in the second half of the nineteenth century are not disputed; real wages rose and height and weight data may provide evidence of nutritional improvement, at least for those periods where little else can be claimed to have influenced mortality extensively.

McKeown and Record's case about tuberculosis in support of this conclusion however must be qualified. Any simple explanation of the decline in tuberculosis is bound to fail and, although nutritional improvements played a part, the commonly accepted account omits in particular the role of immunity. Most European countries demonstrate a similar pattern of the rise and fall of tuberculosis mortality. The biggest city reaches its mortality peak before the rest of the country: London in the mid eighteenth century, Stockholm at the turn of the century. Most West European capitals went through their peak in the mid nineteenth century and were followed by the rest of their respective countries after an interval of several decades. There appears in fact to be a wave motion of tuberculosis which has three important critical points of mortality, epidemiology and immunity. The first of these is simply the maximum of mortality; the second, the point of change from epidemicity to endemicity, and the third when immunity in the population is so widespread that the disease ceases to be a major public health problem.[40]

Tuberculosis is the work of a micro-organism transmitted by contact. The degree of contagiousness depends on the prospective host and the 'reactability' of his tissues. This in turn depends on genetic, nutritional and other factors. Immunity has both genetic and acquired factors – immunity will rise as reactable individuals are weeded out; but improved nutrition also obviously helps to develop immunity. It is the nature of reactability itself which destroys any simplistic theory. Urbanisation and poverty produce many of the conditions for tuberculosis but so do stress – which induces hormonal changes–and alterations in environment. Contemporary studies find that the proximity of infected individuals is not necessarily the main factor in the disease; in urban slums single people may be more prone to tuberculosis than families living in greater densities and stress is taken to be the reason for this.[41] Altogether therefore the decline in tuberculosis mortality in the absence of direct preventive and curative measures seems to require not only improvement in living conditions but the passage of time while immunity to the disease runs its historical course.

Some faint light is shed on the causes of mortality decline when looked at from the point of view of geographical distribution and age distribution. The declines in mortality coincided with rapid urbanisation and the urban-industrial tenements of the nineteenth century are proverbial for the atrocity of their living conditions and known to have been subject to much higher than average death rates in many European countries[42] for obvious reasons. All that can be said about this – and intellectually it is not terribly incisive – is that the adverse effect on mortality as a whole was outweighed by other factors. Only a proportion of the population lived in these conditions and many of them, rural migrants or descendants of the urban poor, must have come from sections of the population already subject to the highest mortality in the country. The combination of multiplying urban slums and declining death rates for the population as a whole is therefore only superficially paradoxical. The rise in rural living standards also compensated somewhat for any worsening of urban conditions.

An important characteristic of the decline in mortality was its age distribution; in England, and indeed in most of Europe, it was children, the younger age groups generally, that benefited most in the nineteenth century, with the significant exception of infant mortality. The chances of survival for men and women over forty-five hardly improved at all before the turn of the century. There is a common demographic observation that cohorts carry their own mortality conditions with them through life. There are two main kinds of explanation for this pattern of change. One is that of nutrition – the nutritional status of the child, and indeed of its mother during pregnancy, has a lasting effect on the growth of the child and its potential health throughout life. Those who have reached their mid-forties have already passed the test of fitness for survival and general nutritional improvements are not likely to effect their chances of further survival to any great degree. Similarly with the types of infectious disease which were effectively controlled in nineteenth century England – children, and especially ill-nourished children, were most likely to be carried off by typhus, diphtheria and the like and it was they who most benefited from their control.

It was not however until the very end of the nineteenth century that infant mortality – death in the first year of life – began to be affected. Infant mortality rates were still as high as 247 per 1000 live births in the poorest parts in York in 1898.[43] The child depends mainly on the mother's milk in the early months of life, a sound and relatively hygienic nutritional source. The kinds of diseases from which infants died were rather specialised and little understood until the turn of the century; thus infants profited little from the control of the common diseases though they may have suffered more than others from the insanitary conditions of urban life. The survival of the new-borm is affected by midwifery practices and prevailing customs of child care for which new knowledge is an important aspect of change.

Thomas Smout in his *History of the Scottish People* gives an interesting account of medical work in Scotland. In the matter of child care he cites William Buchan's *Domestic Medicine* as a valuable source of sensible practices and quotes a gruesome passage from Moncrief's *Poor Man's Physician* (1712), the previous popular manual. (Cure for falling sickness: 'Take a little black sucking puppy (but for a girl take a bitch-whelp), choke it, open it, and take out the gall which hath not above three or four drops of pure choler; Give it all to the child in the time of the fit, with a little tiletree flower water, and you shall see him cured as it were by a Miracle . . .') Buchan was published in 1769 and ran to twenty-two editions by 1826; its precepts, if followed, could undoubtedly have saved innumerable infant deaths – but evidently his readership was confined to the educated *bourgeoisie*; and, for the poor, the recommendation that babies should have 'warm, clean, loose clothing (frequently changed) and dry accommodation' was hardly a practicable suggestion even had they known of it. Petersen (1960) reports a peculiarly odious-sounding habit in the Netherlands of parents giving babies chewed bread with sugar wrapped in cloth to suck when they cried, a practice which continued until the end of the nineteenth century. Mortality from such causes would decline only with the spread of education, knowledge of hygiene and the incomes to adopt new methods. Similarly with midwifery – advances in knowledge were made and published in the late eighteenth century, but 'as long as there were few doctors or trained midwives in the parishes and as long as puerperal fever (the great slayer of women in childbirth) was misunderstood, the saving of life would be restricted to a narrow and mainly upper class section of society.'[44]

If there is any summary statement to be made of the historical relationships between economic change and mortality in Europe, it is that, once the sporadic visits of *la mort extraordinaire* are ended, the gradual improvement of diet is the main background factor but knowledge and its application become in some sense the most potent and most autonomous forces. Working to reduce mortality, apart from medical science and deliberate public health measures, were nutrition and certain environmental factors such as the materials used for clothes and house building or the methods of food distribution; working to increase it were the other conditions of urban-industrial life and work. Both these sets of influences are clearly related to economic development. It was the control of the great lethal diseases which really made the difference. Of course these advances are themselves dependent on economic change – not only the improvements in the environment, and the ability to afford major public works for sanitation, but even society's capacity to devote resources to medical research. Nevertheless the history of Europe in the late nineteenth century to some extent bears out the possibility of major changes in mortality with no other substantial improvement or even some worsening of the general conditions of life of the ordinary man. There are also periods when incomes rise and mortality does not decline. One could elaborate the distinction between knowledge whose application costs relatively little and that which only becomes available to people when incomes rise sufficiently. Smallpox vaccination on the one hand for example; the general availability of good medical practitioners or improved methods of child care on the other. But it is undoubtedly the impact of medical science which renders uneven the correspondence over time between improvements in the death rate and in economic conditions generally. The separation of sewage from water-supplies in the 1860s, consequent on John Snow's work on cholera, obviously had a major impact on mortality. Equally obviously the timing of these changes was only remotely connected with industrial progress.

The explanation of the European experience of mortality is valuable for comparison with that of the developing countries altogether, and of India in particular. In the latter countries those of them at least where substantial progress has been made, death rates have gone down much faster than in Europe but with a more marked divorce of mortality decline from the other conditions of life of ordinary people. Nineteenth century Europe needed both material progress and the application of new knowledge which was simultaneously being acquired. In developing countries the knowledge began to be applied while material conditions were often still at the level of mediaeval Europe. Indeed it is arguable that in some countries, and India is probably one of them, the economic effects of population pressure have been disguised by the decline in mortality brought about largely by public health measures. Further improvements in mortality may now depend more completely on raising the level of living of the mass of the people.[45] But this begins to anticipate Chapter 2. We must now look at fertility.

FERTILITY

The great reductions of fertility which occurred in nineteenth century Europe have been studied at great length by scholars from a large range of disciplines – demography, sociology, economics, geography, biology, medicine. That each of these disciplines has a contribution to make is a reflection of the complexity of the process of change in fertility. The number of children parents are likely to want depends on a great number of factors; and the relation between the number they may want and the number they actually have is not automatic.

Even to speak of the number of children parents want may introduce unwarranted assumptions especially when the eighteenth and nineteenth centuries are under discussion. Looking at the determination of family size in this way implies the presence of a degree of conscious decision which simply may not have been there. Of course deliberate family-limitation was practised at that time; contraceptive measures were used by the ancient Romans for that matter.[46] But even today there are people in Britain who just have children as they come, and only *decide* to stop them coming quite late in the day, if ever. By no means all or even most parents today set out on married life with a precise idea of the number of children they would like; on the other hand the majority do set out conditioned against large families. Two hundred years ago that was not at all the case. One of the significant features of economic and social development is in fact the gradual diffusion of the understanding that the number of children one has can be a matter for rational choice – or for conscious choice at least. In what follows a distinction will be made between factors which affect fertility without necessarily impinging on the conscious decision of parents and those which act at least in part through influencing deliberate choice. The distinction is faint and somewhat artificial but the reasons for attempting it will be apparent at the end of the section.

As far as we can tell fertility in pre-industrial Britain never approached the biological maximum levels. A common standard for the highest known birth rates is taken from the Hutterites in the 1920s. The Hutterites are a religious group in the north-western United States and Canada: living in prosperous family communities, they enjoy excellent health and place a high premium on having large numbers of children with the result that birth rates of 50 or more per thousand have been reached. In any society where birth rates are below these levels fertility is in effect being restrained by one circumstance or another.

An important factor among the determinants of fertility is the age at marriage. One of the features of economic and social development does seem to be a considerable rise in the average age at marriage. Hajnal (1965) has distinguished what he calls the 'European pattern' of marriage, comprising a high age at marriage and a high proportion of men and women who never marry at all. He illustrates the prevalence of this pattern in Western Europe in 1900, contrasting it with that of Eastern Europe. More generally Matras (1965) has formulated a 'typology' of marriage and fertility patterns consisting of early or late marriage with controlled or uncontrolled fertility – his approach treats marriage and fertility as a subcomplex of the demographic transition, examining the history of countries as they progress from early marriage and uncontrolled fertility (the least sophisticated state) to late marriage and controlled fertility. In very recent times America and many European countries have of course experienced a decline in the marriage age – fulfilling perhaps what have been the ambitions of young people throughout history to marry early, now made possible by economic progress and reliable contraception.

Prior to this modern period in the West, one could presume that, where marriage was postponed or impossible because of economic austerity, increases in income should have permitted earlier marriages and more marriages. The spread of education and perception of the advantages of continuing education would operate in the other direction tending to raise the age at marriage as would also the need for greater mobility, both social and geographical, in rapidly changing societies. Such forces are at work in many developing countries today, where a tendency for the marriage age to rise can be observed.

However in so far as we are concerned with demographic change as it was influenced by industrialisation specifically (as opposed to social change more broadly considered), it must be noted that the basic 'European' marriage patterns were established in England before the end of the seventeenth century as both Hajnal and Laslett[47] have claimed. Laslett examined a thousand marriage licenses issued by the diocese of Canterbury between 1619 and 1660 and found the average age of the brides to be about 24 and that of the grooms nearly 28. In the pre-industrial world of the seventeenth century, which Laslett described, an apprentice could not set up his household until he was established as an income-earner and his master would permit him to move – often until a house in the village was vacated by the departure or death of the existing householder. Certainly birth rates rose and fell in pre-industrial England and demographers have speculated that an important cause of these changes was variation in the age at marriage which probably went down when times were good and up when they were not.[48] But the fluctuations were around a pattern of late marriages and low marriage rates relative to those such as can be observed in today's developing countries.

From the seventeenth to the mid-nineteenth century in Britain there is no evidence to suggest anything other than a gradual, if slight, rise in the age at marriage. Thus, if any of the population increase between 1750 and 1850 was due to a rise in fertility, it was unlikely to have been caused by declines in marriage age though it may have been due to increases in the marriage rate, if only to a minor extent. The conditions of seventeenth century England, when poverty really did prevent or postpone marriage, were gradually replaced by a situation in which, while people could materially afford to marry earlier, other considerations in fact led them not to do so. One of the innumerable unsolved problems of British historical demography is to give an account of the factors which produced a rise in the average age at marriage, consistent with what we know of changing economic conditions since the seventeenth century. Between 1851 and 1891, the crucial period prior to fertility decline, both the age at marriage and the proportions marrying were pretty constant. The proportions of men and women marrying before the age of 24 began to decline somewhat after 1871, up to the first decades of the twentieth century, though the proportion of men ever marrying rose through the period while that of women changed very little.[49] In the later nineteenth century and after, it must be added, there is no necessary relationship between age at marriage and fertility – once contraception is practised indeed people may embark on marriage which they might otherwise have postponed. Thus in France, Switzerland, Belgium and Netherlands women's mean age at first marriage declined from 1850 to 1960 but so did fertility after 1870, if not before.[50]

The theory of the demographic transition has many instruments besides the marriage age for explaining the fall in fertility. Urbanisation, education and economic change are the chief of these together with the change in mortality itself which we will consider last of all. Unlike the age at marriage and the age distribution these factors work on fertility through the process of conscious choice. But, before we come to them, there are further factors at a more purely non-conscious level, namely physiological ones. Of these the most important are nutrition, medical care and the physical character of domestic life, travel and work.

We are confident that nutrition improved in the nineteenth century – as well as reducing mortality, this would also have had the effect of increasing fertility, in particular the proportion of live-births to total births. (Babies which die after birth, however soon, are recorded in both fertility and mortality statistics; still-births only lessen fertility.) Improved nutrition advances the age of puberty and may in general be taken to enhance fecundity. (Though fertility is not necessarily affected by the advance of puberty itself; when few marriages are contracted at fourteen years of age the onset of puberty at twelve and a half is unlikely to affect fertility.) Similarly, with medical care, any general improvements in health are likely to increase fertility, if for no other reason than that they permit greater frequency of sexual intercourse. The reduction of malaria is known also to improve the ratio of live to total births. The author is not aware of any work examining the effect on fertility of the main diseases whose ravages were repelled in England in the nineteenth century but it is likely that they had some harmful effect and their reduction a beneficial one. Lastly the other physical conditions to which reference was made. There is medical evidence of hard physical labour affecting live-births quite significantly.[51] Prior to the Industrial Revolution women had done agricultural work; but such work is seasonal and the gradual spread of continuous female employment in factories and elsewhere may have had some effect on fertility. It cannot be said with any certainty that this effect was in the downward direction – to do that one would have to assess the quantity and nature of work previously done by women and the way it changed with the Industrial Revolution. Of course much of the main work done by women – in the home – did not change significantly but, if there was an addition of strenuous employment outside the home, the result could have been a reduction in fertility. However any such reductions are unlikely to have been very great or to have outweighed the increases caused by better diet and the lower incidence of disease. The net result of physiological factors therefore was to increase fertility.

If this is so, then the sources of the observed reduction in fertility lie elsewhere – and must have been sufficiently powerful to counteract the other influences which tended to increase fertility. In fact it is commonly accepted among demographers that the most important causes of fertility decline in the transition period were education, urbanisation and the social change which accompanied them – all related to the decline in mortality. These processes act far more on the conscious wishes of parents about the numbers of children they should have than did the other influences considered so far. It is necessary to keep this in mind as we shall find that on the whole such urbanisation as has been taking place in India did not have much impact on fertility there until the 1960s – not at least on marital fertility.

England's urban population grew rapidly over a very long period with London playing a major role. At the end of the seventeenth century it is estimated that London was absorbing most of the natural increase of the 2 million population of England. In 1650 London already had 350,000 people. By 1700, despite the plague of 1665 and the Great Fire, it had 550,000 and was already the largest city in Europe; by 1800 it had reached 900,000, twice the size of Paris at the time.[52] The city gentleman, familiar today, who thinks of himself as separated from his natural life in the country, was prevalent in the seventeenth century except that in those days his return to country life was more likely to be real than imagined.[53] With early industrialisation and the enclosure movement urban population absorbed an increasing proportion of total numbers and this continued through the nineteenth century. The consequences for fertility were important. In a common English household of the seventeenth century, there were the master and two generations of his family and apprentices and servants all living together. The change from this to the nuclear family of parents and children which became prevalent in the nineteenth century was a slow one; the break-up of these earlier large households may indeed have removed a constraint on fertility in that the master of the house had a major say in the marriage plans of his family and other householders – plans which, as has been noted, were also affected by economic stringency. But the pattern of life which the Industrial Revolution imposed ultimately became unfavourable to having very large numbers of children.[54]

The formation of urban industrial society affects fertility in a number of ways. One of these is the cost of additional children in the fullest sense of the word 'cost'. Even in the limited sense of the direct expenses of raising an additional child, urban life tends to inhibit the generation of large families. Urban housing is expensive and, because of the constriction of space, not easily extendable; food which has to be bought in the local shop both costs more and makes the parents more aware of the cost than is the case for the husbandman who grows it himself. But there are other 'costs' to children. In the country children could accompany their parents in the fields or could be left to play in the village without much danger; children could in general be a part of the rhythm of their parents' life at work and leisure. When one or both parents work long hours in a factory children, requiring attention when the parents come home, are more likely to be seen as making inroads on rare hours of leisure. Similarly for mobility – the farmer or farm-labourer may expect to live in the same place doing the same work fairly indefinitely. Urban industrial man may see jobs coming and going; it is in his interest to be less rooted to one spot and the larger his family, the harder it is for him to take advantage of new opportunities. As long as child labour continued on the other hand children were by no means wholly burdensome after their early years. Indeed it is quite possible that the early years of industrialisation stimulated the demand for children. They could, and did, also accompany their parents to the place of work.

No contrast is intended here between some sprawling, easy-going rural life and a harsh, clock-bound city one – for the great majority of people, for nearly all indeed except the gentry themselves, rural life in England was equally harsh and continued to be so into the twentieth century. But there undoubtedly were features of country life which made children less of a burden to their parents. It should not be suggested either that urbanisation produces lower birth rates with any speed – on the contrary England had a century of urban-industrial development before the steep decline in fertility which began in the 1870s. There is a good deal of evidence that in the first decades of their existence many of the major industrial areas of Europe experienced increases in fertility[55] – though this evidence needs care in its interpretation to disentangle the complex of simultaneously operating influences. It may be for example that such areas initially attract a disproportionate number of young married couples and only slowly acquire the age distribution of the whole population. The only thing which this argument establishes is that the slow process of change from a rural-agricultural to an urban-industrial society will ultimately, by the fact of urbanisation alone, produce something of a tendency towards smaller families.

The proposition is hard to test in a single country; as urban-industrial life becomes the pattern so many other things are changing as well. If any one feature of this process of societal change can be said to reinforce the tendency towards smaller families, it is education. This happens in a number of ways. The first and least important is the actual time spent in school or college preventing people from marrying – this is a relatively unimportant historically because only recently has a fair proportion of children remained in education beyond the age at which they might be expected to start families. Even by 1938, only one in seven of labour force entrants in Britain had had *any* education beyond the minimum age.[56] Much more important is the effect on the parents of the realisation that education brings benefits to the children. The wider the spread of such realisation and the more pervasive the parents' sense of obligation to have their children schooled, the greater the cost to the parents and the smaller the number of children they will wish to have.

But possibly more important still is the effect on potential parents of their own education. This is the hardest of all things to assess – the contribution of education to fertility decline not just by the alteration of parents' aspirations, but by the spread of rationality itself. The basic differentiator of those for whom babies just come and those for whom the number that come is a result of more or less deliberate choice seems so often to be education. The decline of superstition and fatalism, the dawning in the individual of the sense that many of the important matters affecting his life are subject to his own control and decision – these are the material of social progress and not just the gifts of formal education.

But certainly statistical studies investigating low fertility in the twentieth century show better connections with education of one form or another than most other variables. This is certainly true looking at cross-sections of population in a given country at a given time as demographic surveys for many a rich country will demonstrate.

A suggestive study by Adelman (1963), comparing a group of thirty-seven countries at a single point of time, took a very crude index of education and found that this variable was negatively correlated with fertility when the effect of income and other variables was separately accounted for. Similar studies by Weintraub (1962) and Heer (1966) come to the same sorts of conclusions – across countries, income by itself may be associated with higher fertility but other variables, associated with higher incomes, are negatively related to fertility, particularly education or literacy. One cannot properly infer from observations across countries at a point of time what will happen in one country over time.[57] Nevertheless this is part of a broad spectrum of evidence that the more educated people are, other things being equal, the fewer children they will have. Though it may well be commonly true that, *for a given level of education*, the richer you are, the *more* children you will have – the evidence from cross-section studies in a given country at a given point of time is inconclusive about the effect of income on fertility.[58]

Be that as it may for societies as a whole, as incomes rise during and after industrialisation, fertility declines; the rise in incomes may of itself permit larger families but the changes associated with rising incomes counterweigh this influence. It is however just because the spread of education over time is universally a product of a changing society with rising incomes that the prime importance of education on its own in reducing fertility is so hard to establish beyond all doubt, however strongly and for whatever good reasons we may believe it. Nevertheless the evidence and the arguments are so powerful that to doubt the importance of education in the reduction of fertility is scarcely possible.

This is of course the standard situation of the social sciences when causal inferences are made from statistics in a non-experimental situation. The phrase 'other things being equal' is introduced but these 'other things' are held constant by mathematical manipulation, not by laboratory controls, and the variations are difficult to interpret when one knows that one thing cannot change without the others. Such difficulties are even more powerfully present when we come to the major influence on fertility remaining to be considered, that of mortality itself. There are few historical cases of a country where fertility has declined over a long period without a prior or at least concomitant decline in mortality. There are also substantial reasons why this might be expected. But quantifiable support for the relationship between mortality and fertility is even harder to produce than in the case of education.

First the reasons: the basic ground for postulating a relationship between mortality and fertility is that what people want is not just children but surviving children. When children are known to be likely to die – and it must be remembered that we are thinking of situations in early nineteenth century Europe and before, when a quarter or more of all babies born alive did not even survive their first year – the whole psychological nature of child-bearing is likely to be far removed from the careful consideration of supportable numbers. Adam Smith (1776) observed that women in Scotland might have twenty children and remain with but two alive – an extreme no doubt. But the frame of mind of parents in such circumstances is likely to be to go on having children up to a largish number and, in so far as stopping is deliberate at all, to stop when several are on their way to maturity. The gradual decline in mortality might have played a part in inducing parents to have fewer children – not probably because they consciously perceived that their children were more likely to survive and they therefore did not need to have so many, but rather because it was gradually found that more of them were surviving and were thus harder to support, or one generation had memories of the privations of the numerous families in which they grew up and resolved to make things easier for their own children. Such a process must be an inter-generational one and is therefore bound to be a matter of several decades where mortality decline is slow. But the relation of mortality to fertility is clearly significant and forms the last important link in the causal chain of the events we have been trying to explain, as far as concerns the *desire* for smaller families (there will still be the question of how the desire was fulfilled). The inter-connections matter; the survival of more children would not have had so considerable an effect without the other changes that have been discussed, as a result of which children cost more financially and came more into competition with the other wishes and ambitions of parents. Similarly it is quite possible that education would not have had the impact it did had mortality not been declining.

These relationships between mortality and fertility deserve particular emphasis: apart from the Malthusian case itself, they are probably the least well understood aspect of population change, among people at least who have no familiarity with the demographic literature. Just as in 1845 distinguished statesmen wondered – on Malthusian grounds – whether it was really in the interest of the Irish poor to receive assistance after the 1845 famine,[59] so today many well-meaning people suffer unnecessary agonies over the question of whether medicine should really be encouraged to save lives in the developing countries since it will only add to the population problem. Such a view is erroneous. Were there no other grounds for saving lives, the study of population seems to show that a decline in mortality may today be virtually a necessary condition for major and sustained reductions in fertility – as long as family limitation is voluntary at least.

This point will recur in the discussion of India – but it is so important that we must pause here to make sure it is not left in any obscurity. There are a number of problems about the relations between mortality and fertility decline. In nineteenth century Europe most countries experienced substantial mortality decline before the onset of continuous fertility decline but not all of them did – France is a counter-example. And if one looks at small regional units, further counter-examples are not hard to find. Perhaps the *locus classicus* is Demeny's study of Austria-Hungary,[60] where some provinces exhibited significant reductions in marital fertility in the later nineteenth century without prior mortality decline, supplying, as Demeny observed, 'remarkable proof for a possible adoption of increasing degrees of voluntary control of marital fertility in the absence of any fundamental modernisation of the underlying socio-economic structure.' In fact by the beginning of the twentieth century 'reproductive perfor-mance in a large number of villages was well under replacement levels, and birth rates sank below twenty or even fifteen per thousand, consistently remaining below the level of crude death rates. The evidence indicates that an increasing proportion of the families sought to raise only a single child.' And this with no modern methods of contraception and even in the face of official disapproval.

These observations are a valuable corrective to any simplistic notions of the conditions of fertility decline. But we should make it clear that these provinces of Austria-Hungary (and there are other places where similar trends have been found) are by means typical. Except in times of unnaturally high mortality, birth rates below replacement levels have been extremely rare and for whole countries since the nineteenth century, practically unknown until very recently. Also, although the historical experience of the rich countries provides valuable analogies for looking at the developing countries of today, it does not provide a blueprint for their future; as we shall see below major fertility decline in these countries is most uncommon in the absence of declining mortality.

Many studies have made observations concerning the possible influence of mortality on fertility but regrettably few have examined the actual mortality experience of those particular groups whose fertility was declining – they mostly deal in average levels of mortality and fertility. Thus, in countries or smaller geographical units where average mortality decline has not preceded fertility decline, it might still be the case that those classes whose fertility was declining were subject to lower than average mortality. The whole problem turns on the way reduced mortality at large is experienced within the family. As we have suggested above the effect was likely to be an inter-generational one in nineteenth century society. It was unlikely to be by direct observation of families about them that parents perceived an increase in the probability of survival of their children. Nowadays parents in rich countries may count with fair certainty on the survival into their own old age of any children born alive to them but the process by which that perception over the decades gradually replaced the opposite one that preceded it is not well understood.

Finally on this point some comfort even in Demeny's study may be found for those fearful for the loss of all support for 'modernisation' theories of fertility decline. While the main correlates of fertility decline in his provinces were ethnic, religious and cultural and, while among the groups whose birth rates were falling, economic aspirations (particularly the accumulation of land) seem to have been of especial importance, *within* each province early fertility decline 'does tend to show an association with both lower infant mortality and higher literacy' though infant mortality levels were quite high even by present developing country standards. Even in England infant mortality was about 150 per 1000 live births from 1840 to about 1910 – but it was lower among higher income groups whose fertility was the first to decline.

The longer one studies fertility the less one would care to attribute alterations in it to any simple single cause. Rather there is a set of mutually interacting causes all of which are part of a broad process of societal change. As was found in the discussion of mortality, the conditions for fertility decline are associated with industrialisation and the kinds of social change it brings with it among which education and urbanisation are of exceptional importance. But, because it is most unusual for any one of these changes to occur at all sweepingly without the others, it is to the process as a whole that we must attribute the transition, understood in terms of its relevant parts. And it must not be forgotten that a critical factor in the English transition – the rise in the age at marriage – began well before industrialisation took place.

This discussion of fertility in nineteenth century England and Europe has deliberately omitted the question of birth control. Since an entire chapter of this book is devoted to the Indian family planning programme we shall not discuss theories of contraception and its relation to historical fertility here. But some mention is necessary now. Most of the influences on fertility that have been considered here relate to the number of children people may want – but what about the relation between the number they want and the number they actually have? Just to raise this question is to open another controversy; an important aspect of controlling births is the existence of knowledge about, and attitudes to, means to control them. There is a school of thought, associated particularly with the name of Kingsley Davis, which holds that knowledge (or more particularly new knowledge) of contraceptive techniques is not the significant factor. According to this view, there is always a body of knowledge about how to limit births, including *coitus interruptus*, abortion or the use of primitive spermicides – when people want to limit their families, they will.

The best historical case for this view is that of France, where fertility began to decline in the eighteenth century. The case of France will be discussed at some length below. But, from the point of view of the 'transition' in England, there is a problem: if all the factors we have been discussing were at work throughout the nineteenth century, why should fertility only start to decline importantly in the second half of the 1870s? Of course the answer could lie in just these other factors. There is a time-lag between the reduction of mortality and that of fertility: and, while the experience of improved survival is being absorbed, education, urbanisation and social change are playing their part. The threshold of the effect of these measures on fertility has to be reached at some point and that point happened to be, for nineteenth century England, the late 1870s. Were demography an exact science, and had we reliable data for all relevant variables, it might have been predicted.

This argument cannot be refuted, even if it is not very convincing. But there was a significant happening in 1876 which may plausibly have had a connection with the beginnings of the fall in fertility. In 1832 an American called Charles Knowlton published in America a book called *The Fruits of Philosophy* – it was a calmly written guide to contraceptive practice directed to young married couples and was first published in England in 1834. But the book got into trouble. In 1876 Annie Besant, who was perhaps the first prominent woman in England to propagate birth control, decided to re-publish it in conjunction with Charles Bradlaugh, both of them knowing what they were in for. *Regina v. Charles Bradlaugh and Annie Besant* was heard before the Queen's Bench in 1876 and the defendants were found guilty; but the decision was reversed in 1877. The case attracted tremendous attention and public debate, as might be expected in late Victorian England and the issues of birth control were given a more spirited airing than they had ever received there before.

Whether or not the publicity attaching to this trial had any real impact on the practice of family planning is conjectural. The coincidence in time is intriguing. On the other hand the trial was not really an isolated event but part of a general movement towards female emancipation and questioning of Victorian morality, particularly tht part of it which affected contraception.[61] It is because questions such as this cannot be conclusively answered that demography cannot be an exact science. One cannot measure the climate of moral opinion; but it matters.

It is unlikely that this famous trial – if it was as influential as has been surmised – would have been nearly so important without the other factors already discussed. If we were to look for other influences which became particularly powerful in the mid 1870s, changes in education would be the most likely to claim one's attention. The discussion above of the general relationships between education and fertility reflects the accepted doctrine of demographers; as far as concerns late nineteenth century Britain – and perhaps for any period anywhere – it is in fact excessively imbued with middle class biases. At the time in question many British children of poor families were not in school at all and, for many, education was far from being perceived as an advantage. The 1870 Education Act neither made school attendance compulsory nor provided for free schooling but it enabled school boards to pass by-laws to those effects and the boards were quite active: it was mainly for this reason that school attendance rose rapidly during the subsequent years.

Curiously enough it was the year 1876 which saw the passing of Lord Sandon's Act to improve attendance and prescribe it as the parents' duty to get their children instructed in basis educational skills. School attendance was made legally compulsory by Mundella's Act in 1880 though *free* education was not enacted until 1901. It is unclear whether this movement during the critical period of the late 1870s had an influence on desired family size. The cost to parents may have been considerable – even if school fees were paid by grants, children's earnings were lost; child labour was still common and only partly reduced by restrictive legislation. Parents certainly opposed compulsory schooling for their children and connived at truancy (in 1870 there were 1·5 million children on the books of inspected day schools; average attendance was less than 1·17 million[62]).

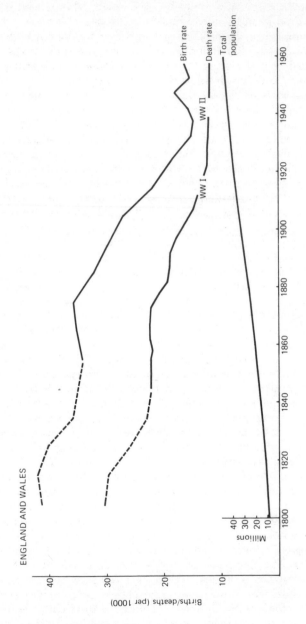

FIG. 1.2 England and Wales

Sources: 1840–1960 – Cox, 1970
              1800–1840 – Razzell, 1874
Note: Some of the apparent rise in birth rate after 1850 may be due to under-registration in the 1840s.

Even if therefore the more inspiring aspects of education played their part in British fertility decline, it is possible that the speed and timing of the process were influenced by the move to make education compulsory. The question which is difficult to answer is who was affected by this movement and whose fertility was declining. There is some evidence that, until the early twentieth century, it was mainly the middle classes whose fertility was declining;[63] but mainly working class families were being forced to educate their children – the middle classes had already been doing so for some time.

However tempting the explanations look it cannot finally be established beyond all doubt that these events were responsible for the timing of the decline in fertility. The fact that fertility in general in European countries also began to decline in the late 1870s and the 1880s under similar but by no means identical circumstances must make one pause for reflection. On this inconclusive note the decline of fertility will be left until the cases of France and Japan have been briefly described, after which will follow a short summary of the demographic transition related to the current situation in the developing countries as a whole.

FRANCE

An account of the European demographic transition would be incomplete without France. Any generalisations about the demographic transition in nation states would be a lot easier without this awkward example, though work on small regions within nation states would serve the same function.[64] The troublesome irregularity of France is that it seems to have begun its fertility decline about a hundred years before any other country without the benefit of urbanisation, industrialisation or other modern amenities.

We must therefore start from the seventeenth century, the age of Louis XIV, 1643 – 1715. The situation will be depicted here in crude colours and with bold outlines; it should be said right at the outset that we do not really *know* all these things. The picture has been built up by decades of painstaking work by demographers and historians relying on parish records and other fragmentary evidence – nothing which could satisfy a statistician as proper sampling for the country as a whole, however tantalisingly accurate may be each glimpse of the parts. What is presented here is what the parts suggest, not what they prove. And it borrows very heavily from the superb *Histoire Economique et Sociale de la France*, edited by Braudel and Labrousse, whose account is both spacious and subtle.

The first tolerably reliable count of the French population dates from just before the Revolution of 1789 when there were something of the order of 26 million. None of the previous counts were satisfactory. In 1700 the best that can be said is that the population numbered somewhere between 17 and 21 million, perhaps 19 million.[65] It was far bigger than that of any other country of Western Europe – this alone would indicate that something unusual happened. If England and Wales had only 10 million in 1800, while today Britain and France have populations of the same order of magnitude, somethings must have occurred to slow down France's rate of growth.

In the seventeenth century, the French population was controlled by the typical conditions of mortality – famine, epidemics and the general hazards of poverty without sanitation. Thus in 1661 – 3, 1691 – 4, 1709 – 10 parish records show an excess of burials over baptisms for most of France. There were other dark years including 1720 – 21, the last major plague episode.[66] The worst individual years 1662, 1694 and 1710 correspond with widespread evidence of higher than normal prices, especially food prices.

The effect of these years of '*cherté*', a concept preserved in the English word 'dearth', are graphically surmised in Braudel:

> Those who could not afford corn and bread at three times their normal price had recourse to cereals of poor quality, rotten, fermented, even ergot-ridden (rye); or they would unearth seeds that had just been sown, steal unripened grain, make bread from oats or fernroots (Burgundy, Velay), cook weeds from the roadside or the fields, eat tainted meat from dead animals, collect blood and offal from abattoirs, and so forth. One can guess what diseases were caused by such vile fare. The prevailing dirt, the crowding and promiscuity of cramped quarters and the weakness of undernourished and badly malnourished bodies did the rest. First came the high prices, then epidemics, transmitted by parasites, by the growing hordes of beggers, by soldiers and traded goods. To persevere in the view that the subjects of the *Grand Roi* died only of epidemics would be closing one's eyes to reality: the unavoidable cause of these massacres were the high prices. . . . And it was the people who felt them, even if the ensuring epidemics moved across social frontiers, despite the attempts – frequently too late – of the rich, including most doctors and far too many priests, to escape them.[67]

The authors warn against taking this explanation of mortality too far. But they also note that the *chertés* were commonly accompanied or followed by lower numbers of births than usual, the prevailing conditions having their effect on the marriage rate and on the mother's ability to conceive or bring the child successfully to term as also on her own life too. (This phenomenon, of simultaneous mortality and fertility 'crises', is quite a common one.)

In this same period, the late seventeenth and early eighteenth centuries, marriage rates were high – higher than the nineteenth century; celibacy was rare and first marriages took place at the same sorts of ages observed in England – at about twenty-four for women, twenty-seven or twenty-eight or later for men. The birth rate is thought to have been about 40 per 1000, apart from the cities where there were concentrations of single people. Illegitimacy, or births less than eight months after marriage, were rare – little more than one or two per cent of all births. There appears to have been some spacing of births, most likely as a result of temporary sterility during lactation. But otherwise there is no evidence of widespread family limitation prior to 1750. Women bore children up to their forty-fifth year, if they reached it, at intervals of two to two and a half years – or more as they grew older, less if a child died very young. 'In short, the number of children born to a fertile couple was determined principally by the number of fertile years the marriage lasted.'[68]

With the birth intervals observed and the typical female period of fertile years of marriage being seventeen years (from age twenty-five to forty-two), there would be a maximum of about eight confinements. More than nine births was a rarity – less than 5 per cent of families in Crulai.[69] The common deaths of husband or wife within the fertile period and the proportion of still-births produced an average of something closer to four or five children per family. This would have been enough to double the population in each generation. But infant mortality removed a quarter of all children and only half of those born would reach the age of marriage. The population thus moved at about the replacement level – 'near the danger mark' as Braudel puts it. A wave of earlier marriages or a surge in the death rate could produce growth or decline.

We have been speaking of rough trends – these are themselves as we have said not statistical averages for the whole country but a generalisation from all the existing reliable observations of individual places at particular times. And within France there were of course considerable variations in these 'average' conditions, from region to region and over time. Thus Brittany exhibited very high birth and infant and child mortality rates, little starvation and relatively rare if serious outbreaks of epidemic disease. The temperate climate, the variety of crops and the fact that bread was not the only staple food, reduced the influences of the *cherté*; but epidemics struck with force – Breton hygiene was no better than anyone else's. The south-west of France, the *Midi*, showed rather lower birth rates and lower infant and child mortality, the climate being offered as a partial explanation for the latter. In these and certain other areas the population had fairly consistent positive rates of growth, the main explanation being the relative avoidance of the terrible famines of the age. At the same time there were areas where deaths considerably exceeded births – the Paris region, most cities and some rural areas where population was only kept from declining by migration.

There is suggestive – but not conclusive – evidence in the parish records that the last years of the reign of Louis XIV were in fact a period of demographic decline or at least of negligible growth within the frontiers of 1643. But after the plague outbreak of 1720, the population as a whole with relatively minor local exceptions entered an era of expansion. No more plague, wars on a briefer and smaller scale with insignificant losses and, at last, a gradual reduction of famines. These improvements could scarcely have been discernible at the time; the approaching storm of 1789 had its social and economic background after all.[70] Widespread poverty and terrible living conditions continued to be the lot of the majority – all that was occurring was the ironing out of the years of extraordinary national mortality with the result that the normal death rate of about 36 per 1000 and the birth rate of 40 began to produce persistent growth. As late as 1771 serious famines and *chertés* of a kind comparable to those described above still produced regional distress. They were only less prolonged and less widespread. It is probable too that most of the growth in the eighteenth century occurred after 1750 and was particularly strong in the two decades up to 1770.[71]

It would appear that the weather had much to do with these improvements: the late seventeenth and early eighteenth centuries have been called 'a little ice age' in France, and the records show improved climatic conditions for much of the eighteenth century. Later in the century there were also improvements in grain varieties and in agricultural productivity generally. Certainly for France, as for England, no one credits medicine for any of the improvement. As the distinguished Montyon – an important name in the population literature – wrote in 1778 'It is difficult to know whether medicine does not destroy more people than it saves.'[72] (Though many observers, then and later, gave more credit to administrative action than to shifting rat ecology for the disappearance of the plague.)[73]

At any rate as well as the overall growth in numbers, there are signs in the parish records of a slight reduction of infant and child deaths and a more than slight increase in the numbers living to sixty or seventy or beyond. French cities do not seem to have had much part in this improvement; low birth rates, due particularly to the large numbers of single people, and high death rates continued. But the cities were only a fifth of the population and grew little – apart from migration – during the whole century compared with rural populations.

We now come to one of the most celebrated moments in population history – the decline of natality in France. But what do we genuinely know about it? Downward fluctuations in French fertility occur after 1770; the downward *trend* which sets in until World War II begins unambiguously in the 1790s.[74] Much of this in its later stages is clearly related to deliberate family limitation; the question is when the practice of family planning began to spread beyond the upper strata of society. The latter exhibited fertility decline at least from 1680 – 1700 onwards. The classier courtesans were known also to be capable of avoiding this set of occupational hazards. But in 1778 Montyon wrote the following famous and remarkable sentence: '*Les femmes riches . . . ne sont pas les seules qui regardent la propagation de l'espèce comme une duperie du vieux temps . . . dèjà les funestes secrets inconnus á tout animal autre que l'homme ont pénétré dans les campagnes: on trompe la nature jusque dans les villages.'*[75]

Such a distinguished authority deserves some credence and there is a certain amount of evidence to substantiate his view. As the exploitation of parish records by France's demographers deepens there will be more. But at least three studies support Montyon's observation though only one of them actually in villages. In the town of Châtillon-sur-Seine, for marriages contracted after 1770, there were 26·3 per cent of *completed* families (i.e. wives living to forty-five with living husbands) with only three children – this was the commonest number of children.[76] In Meulan, marriages contracted from 1660 – 1739 showed 503 live births per 1000 women aged thirty to thirty-four; those contracted between 1765 and 1789, 385– indeed, age specific fertility was lower at all ages for women married between 1765 and 1789 compared with those married from 1740 – 64.[77] In three villages of Ile-de-France age specific fertility rates of post-1780 marriages are some 16 – 20 per cent below those of pre-1780. The average number of births per household moved from 6·7 to 5·3. Poor people also exhibited this decline (though the evidence quoted is for 1790 and after).[78] Each of these studies claims – rightly it appears – to show these changes as indubitable evidence of deliberate family limitation. But none of them offers an explanation. Châtillon-sur-Seine had had no demographic crisis for several decades; both here and in the villages in question the authors speculate that prolonged growth unrestrained by the usual decimations may have made families feel the pinch. But speculation it remains.

It is interesting to have established the beginnings of deliberate limitation of families prior to 1789. Fertility went on declining – and more rapidly – after the Revolution and there have not been lacking explanations attributing the fact to that event and its aftermath. But, if the process had begun before, the subsequent changes must be seen as working on motives already brought into being by other forces. The most commonly adduced of these changes is that in the laws of inheritance which were revised to abolish the unique privilege of the eldest child. A family concerned to preserve its estate intact through the generations would have a motive to keep the number of children small under laws of equal inheritance. A second factor alleged is 'dechristianisation' – the anti-clericalism unleashed by the Revolution reduced the influence of the Church opposed to contraception. This of course implies that parents already wanted less children and only needed to be released from religious inhibition in order to satisfy the want. One might note that several of the places where fertility was below average even earlier in the eighteenth century were ones in which the clergy were held less in awe. Thirdly the massive troop levies of 1893 are credited with introducing large numbers of rural males to the *mores* of the towns and most particularly to contraception.[79] This explanation too implies – as do all which rely on the spread of contraceptive knowledge – that motivation for smaller families existed and awaited only the means in order to be acted on.

It should be said that French demographers are very sparing of explanations of the decline in fertility in the last third of the eighteenth century – in all the works referred to in this section not more than half a dozen sentences altogether – and most of those end in question marks. It is hard to leave this highly significant occurrence, for which the rest of Europe waited another hundred years, without another word. But where they have feared to tread, one knows that will be thought of anyone who rushes in. We shall content ourselves with the thoroughly tentative view that it may have had some of its origins in local population pressure after the deflection of the major instruments of death. Possibly no less important was the spread of new ideas characteristic of the age, of man as the master of his fate replacing the view that children – among other things – were the gift of divine providence: perhaps the French deserve their reputation for rationality and acquired it before the rest of us. The eighteenth century was also a time of rising social and economic ambitions for *bourgeois* and peasant alike who recognised the liability of large families.[80] Given underlying sources of motivation for smaller families, the weakening of religious attitudes towards contraception, the spread of contraceptive knowledge, the economic depression of the 1770s and after, the turbulence and uncertainty – and the legislation – of the Revolution could all have added to the momentum of change. None of this is, or is likely to become, conclusive; every part of the account is open to question. For example there were parts of France which had equal inheritance prior to 1789 and fertility no lower than elsewhere. Many parents read the philosophers of the Enlightenment without suddenly taking up *coitus interruptus*. Economic depressions are by no means universally correlated with fertility decline. The reasons adduced are therefore at best compatible with the facts; no stronger claims can be made for them.

The decline of fertility in the 1770s and after is attested not only by parish registers, but also by retrospective calculations based on older studies and on the censuses which began in 1801 (though age data were not recorded until 1851).[81] The precise magnitude of the early stages of the decline is of course open to question, since calculation of the age distribution for the period has to make use of dubious data. In the nineteenth century the decline of fertility is slow but reasonably steady, except for the 1850s when there is a deceleration. As in so many other countries in Europe a period of more rapid decline ensued after 1881. The wars of the Revolution and the Empire removed a sufficient number of men before 1815 to affect the trends. In the middle of the century a fall in nuptiality explains part of the decline. But from 1870 marital fertility too is in decline – apart from a modest rise between 1930 – 50 – right up to 1960. This is the age of really widespread birth control as the age of women at first marriage also shows a downward trend on average from the mid 1850s onwards.[82]

We shall not dwell on the explanation of fertility decline in the nineteenth century. To the momentum already established by 1800 were applied forces similar to those found in England. There continued of course to be considerable regional variations: in 1866 there were several departments with mean age of women's first marriage at twenty-seven or over and equally several where it was less than twenty-three. The indices of marital fertility in the latter are frequently 40 or 50 per cent below those of the former – birth control obviously acting as a permissive agent to the natural desires of the young.[83]

We shall not either spend much time on mortality decline in France. It was in general very slow, from about 30 per 1000 at the beginning of the nineteenth century to about 20 by the end, with only minor fluctuations on either side of the trend. After 1850 the most important mortal events, to coin a phrase, were the World Wars. France's huge losses in World War I are well-known. Indeed the French population declined during both World Wars. (Of course this was due to reduction of births as well as increase of deaths.) But no demographic issues of principle are at stake in France in the later period which have not already been raised in the discussion of England. It is all the same instructive to look at the graph on page 40. Unlike other European countries the curves of births and deaths are quite close to each other all the way. There is no long period where death rates are falling while births continue at a high level, such as provided other countries with rapid population growth.

The downward slope of the birth rate is not atypical. What is is its position. The birth rate drops permanently below 30 per 1000 in the 1830s; apart from Ireland in the 1840s no other country was to pass that point until Belgium and Switzerland in the 1880s followed by a group of countries including England and Wales in the 1890s. It is this that explains how France's population size became unexceptional in Western Europe, having previously overshadowed all others. It also goes a long way to explain the prolonged concern in France about insufficiency of numbers and the presence even today of a large body of French opinion favouring high birth rates for the good of the country. Ironically enough, Malthus had numerous intellectual predecessors in France.[84] Robespierre went so far as to believe that wars and the terror had demographic as well as other justifications. In his view France could not support more than 25 million. Perhaps he would have appreciated that just as the high price of bread brought people out on the streets in 1789, whereas previously they lay down and died, so in the 1770s they began to control births which previously were determined mainly by the duration of marriage. The parallel may be more than accidental, but we shall probably always be better informed about the reasons for the revolt than those for birth control. And in neither case are the reasons ever likely to be known for certain.

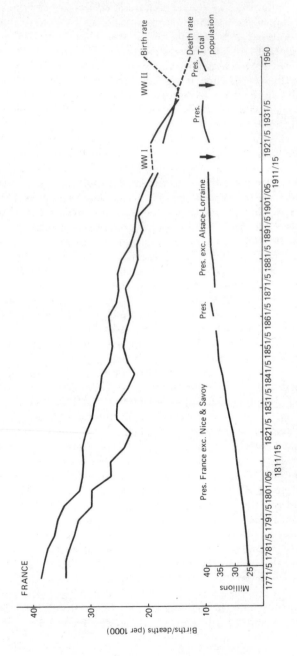

Fig. 1.3 France

Data: Bourgeois-Pichat, 1951.

JAPAN

Naturally great interest must attach to the transition in Japan, an Asian country whose industrialisation occurred later than that of the advanced European countries. As in its economic development, and indeed in many other respects, so too in the history of its population change, Japan turns out to have been highly idiosyncratic at least in the time-path of change. Nevertheless, several features of its history resemble what was observed elsewhere.

Because of the paucity of data we shall confine ourselves mainly to the period after 1920 when the first census was taken. Prior to that mortality appears to have declined slightly from 1885 onwards, though there may have been some significant increase in the years just before 1920 probably related to the almost world-wide influenza epidemic. The birth rate appears to have risen somewhat over the same period. An important feature of the period was an attempt by the authorities to reduce the prevalence of abortion and infanticide. In the case both of births and of deaths the situation is uncertain as the registration system, from which much of the evidence comes, was constantly being improved.[85] The pre-1920 birth rates in our diagram (p. 44) do look on the low side; the 1920 death rate on the other hand was almost certainly higher than had been common in the first decades of the twentieth century. Undoubtedly the population was growing, at a rate in excess of one per cent a year – a rate which was to increase fairly continuously up until 1948.

The decade from 1948 – 58 saw a decline in the natural rate of growth from 2·16 per cent to 1·06 per cent – truly remarkable in that the death rate was still declining during the period. Births per 1000 women aged fifteen to forty-nine actually fell by 41 per cent between 1950 and 1957. This extremely rapid reduction of fertility is virtually without parallel elsewhere. But the rapidity of it can only be understood in the light of the preliminary experience which began thirty years earlier. The 1920s saw both a more distinctive downward trend in mortality than before and the first signs of declining fertility – even marital fertility. One cannot explain the trend in fertility with great confidence. Nevertheless certain aspects of it are clear enough.

A cross-section taken in 1950 showed late marriages to be more prevalent in cities than in rural areas for women aged fifty to fifty-four, i.e. women who had married at the turn of the century. Similarly completed family size was lowest in the great cities, intermediate in the small cities, highest in rural areas. Fertility was lower among women with husbands in non-agricultural than in agricultural employment – this was the case even in rural areas considered alone. Early marriage was less frequent the more educated the husband. Indeed fertility was 'related inversely to the education levels, whatever the ages of the women, the durations of the marriages, the area of residence, or the regions'.[86] The history of these women examined for 1950 when their families were complete shows the beginnings of the demographic transition occurring between 1925 and 1937. After the interruption of the war and immediate post-war years the patterns of past relationships continued in the further decline of fertility. Altogether the Japanese case provides a clear example of education, urbanisation and industrialisation combining to produce a desire for smaller families. The fact that a continuous spectrum of fertility rates is to be found over time from the largest cities to the countryside, across the categories of lesser cities and towns, suggests that it was in part a process of the gradual diffusion of sophisticated behaviour from the urban *élite* throughout the society, under the impact of these forms of social change.

This spread of 'educated' behaviour should not however be regarded by any means as the only force. Why after all was urbanisation taking place? The success in reducing mortality put pressure on rural as well as urban families. Kingsley Davis (1963) sees the rural-urban migration in nineteenth and twentieth century Japan as a response to population pressure. He cites evidence from various countries that owners of larger landholdings had more numerous children. To maintain income and status with rising numbers of children and no possible acquisition of additional land, rural families must send their children to the cities. Unlike many developing countries of today Japan's cities at the end of the nineteenth and in the twentieth centuries had jobs to offer – there was both a rural 'push' and an urban 'pull'. However it should be noted that much of this migration was of educated men from the upper strata of rural society so it was by no means a purely poverty-induced movement.[87]

Another powerful influence on the birth rate was the rise in the age at marriage. In 1920 nearly 18 per cent of women aged fifteen to nineteen, and over two-thirds of women aged twenty to twenty four, were married. By 1955 the figure was only 1.8 per cent of women fifteen to nineteen, and only one-third of women aged twenty to twenty-four.[88] The postponement of marriage was quite pronounced even in rural areas where the rise in age at marriage was almost as fast as the urban. Education played an important part in this movement. By 1955 half the female school-age group were in school until the age of eighteen, and nearly 10 per cent until twenty-one; the motivation for this was as much (perhaps more) a matter of social prestige and making a better marriage as the desire for economic gain. This was all part of a gradual improvement in the status of women which accelerated in the pre-war period.

Once again however it is easier to say that fertility declined under these influences than to explain the particular pattern of change over time. As so often the underlying factors responsible for change seem to operate over a long period, while the changes themselves are quite concentrated in time. Urbanisation focussed on industrial growth had been in progress for at least thirty years before significant decline in the birth rate started to occur.

This process did in fact accelerate after 1920. Japanese records were kept for *shi*, incorporated municipalities usually of more than 30,000 population and *gun*, smaller towns, villages and rural areas. The population of the *gun* was 45.9 million in 1920, 59.0 million in 1930 and 45.5 million in 1940. Had all the estimated natural accrual of population in the *gun* from 1920 – 40 remained there, it would have grown by more than a third rather than fallen slightly.[89] This represents a massive population transfer.

The process continued in the post-war period. By 1965 over 57 million people, or 58 per cent of the whole population, lived in cities of 50,000 people or more with nearly 20 million in the seven major cities over one million in size.[90] By 1960 the major cities had already lost their drawing power with migrants increasingly being absorbed in smaller cities. The period 1950 – 68 also saw a vast change in occupational structure with a decline of households engaged solely in agriculture from 50 per cent in 1950 to 20 per cent in 1968. Since agricultural productivity was high and constantly increasing these movements of population, both geographically and occupationally, lend weight to Davis's assertion (cited above) that the maintenance of status and the desire to profit from new economic opportunity were powerful motives.

To revert to the birth rate – we have already referred to its incipient decline in the 1920s and to some of its presumed causes. But not only birth rates were showing a tendency to decline, particularly as a result of postponement of marriage; age specific fertility rates of women in their middle and late thirties also fell. As well as the influences of development, to which we have already alluded, there were some more specific events. Margaret Sanger, a celebrated American proponent of birth control, visited Japan in the early 1920s and her visit was followed by a whole series of newspaper and magazine articles. There was a left wing movement at the time which took the form of middle class intellectuals going among the people with a message of socialism, birth control and abstinence from alcohol. Also, in the wake of the 'rice riots' of 1918, there had been a good deal of discussion of the population issue culminating in a government commission to investigate the population and food situations, which started work in 1927 and reported three years later.[91]

Some or all of these factors promoted a desire for smaller families but little in the way of modern contraception was available. And after 1930 pro-natalist propaganda began to work in the opposite direction. The crude birth rate, steady around 32.5 from 1929 – 32, still declined slowly thereafter going below 30 in the last years of the decade. The rise in the birth rate after 1939 may well have been due to the stated Government policies to increase population which began to prevail in the World War II period; certainly all birth control programmes were suspended. After the end of the war overpopulation became a public issue again and 'the need for birth limitation was voiced vigorously among the general public'.[92] Certainly birth control – mainly abortion – began to be extensively prac-

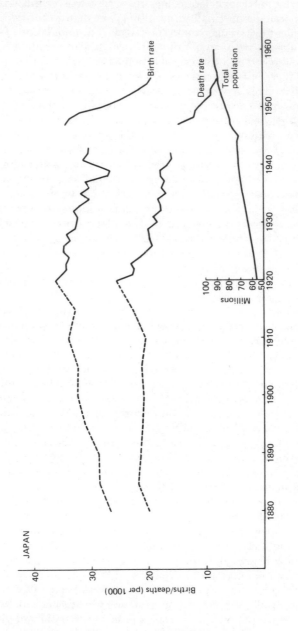

Fig. 1·4 Japan

tised once more. A national survey found one-fifth of all couples employing contraceptive methods in 1950.[93] In 1948 an amendment to the Eugenic Protection Law had been passed, liberalising induced abortion, and the annual number of reported abortions reached a peak of 1.17 million in 1955; after that other forms of contraception, particularly condoms, began to be substituted though even in 1969 reported abortions exceeded 740,000. (And the reported figures may understate the truth.) From the birth rates of 34.3 in 1947 and 33.0 in 1949, the figure of 28.1 was reached in 1950 and by 1955 it was 19.3 — remarkable years.

Thus Japan presents its own unusual version of the demographic transition. While the typical factors of social change play their part a high degree of social control is apparent with a public seemingly responsive to the needs of national welfare as stated by the political leadership. The widespread acceptability of abortion as a means of birth control is quite atypical among countries we have examined. Though to some extent Japan *seems* more abortion-prone than other countries simply because the Japanese are more open about it. But it is evident that when the Japanese wish to limit their families they will do so. The year 1966 saw a birth rate nearly 30 per cent lower than 1965 or 1967. This remarkable event is widely attributed to the fact that 1966 was the year of 'fire and horse' in the Japanese zodiac, regarded as unfavourable for the birth of female children. If the figures and the explanation are right, voluntary control of fertility, as Muramatsu (1971) has said, can now be regarded as complete.[94] Though with birth rates of the order of 19 per thousand (somewhat higher than the European average) and death rates of 7 per thousand the population in 1974 was still growing by more than a million a year, or over one per cent per annum, creating problems by no means negligible.

THE DEMOGRAPHIC TRANSITION TODAY

In order that a higher standard of living may affect the rate of reproduction it is apparent that not only is an increase in education and culture involved, since it seems definitely established that intellectual activity acts as a check upon fertility, but also the psychological appreciation of a higher probability of survival.
Census of India, 1931, Vol. 1, Part 1 (Report).

Our brief review of some case histories of the demographic transition substantiates the general view that not much is left of its characterisation in detailed 'stages'. It seems that little more can be said as a generalisation than that societies go through a phase in which birth and death rates decline, a phase rather loosely associated – as far as concerns birth rates – with economic development, urbanisation, the spread of education and changes in attitudes towards contraception. The pattern differs very considerably from one society to another and the broad trends in individual nation states conceal much local variation. Some fairly pervasive features can be observed such as for example the importance of rising economic aspirations, or the tendency for family limitation to begin earlier among the more prosperous social classes and gradually to spread to the rest of the population. But there is little uniformity in the timing of birth and death rate declines among countries and virtually none when considered statistically in relation to changes in various indices of social and economic development.[95]

Where have the world's countries come to now? One way of looking at the situation is provided by Figure 1.5 on which each country is represented by a number. The complete list of countries and their birth and death rates is given in Appendix B (pp. 343–5). The position of each country shows its crude birth and death rates – the figures are the most recent easily available, which is not all that recent in some cases as the Appendix makes clear. But the basic picture conveyed by the diagram would be little altered if all the information were more up to date or even more accurate. The rich countries cluster over on the left with low birth and death rates and low rates of population growth; the poor countries exhibit a wide scatter on the right with much higher rates of growth and high birth and death rates. The parallel diagonal lines represent population growth rates – thus the zero population growth line connects all the points at which birth and death rates are equal, the one per cent line connects the points at which the birth rate exceeds the death rate by 10 per 1000 (one per cent) and so forth. One country is growing faster than another if the parallel on which it lies is to the right of that on which the other lies. (The effect of international migration is ignored.)

In view of the discussion under the heading of fertility above we must make clear that the figure is not intended to suggest a *causal* relationship between birth and death rates. Although we may believe a declining death rate is almost a necessary condition for sustained fertility decline, it is certainly not a sufficient condition and there are many purely statistical reasons why birth and death rates should be to some degree correlated, in developing countries at least – in particular, where mortality is heavy in the early years of life, there is bound to be some statistical association between births and deaths. Finally it should be noted that the rates measured are slightly misleading as between countries of different age distributions – in particular the low death rates for some developing countries in so far as they are accurate (and some of the very low ones are suspect) would not really be lower than those in the rich countries if they did not have such young populations: as a rough guide one can raise the mortality level in a developing country by about 3 per thousand to allow for the difference in age distribution in comparison with developed countries.

The diagram should be thought of simply as a convenient way of presenting the data. Most rich countries are growing at less than one per cent and only one country – East Germany – has attained 'zpg' (though

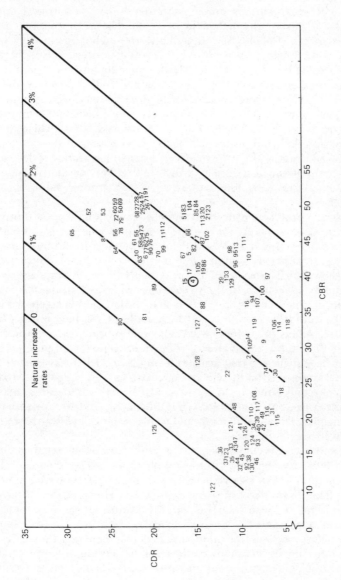

Fig. 1.5 The World's countries – crude birth and death rates per 1000 (1970).

since these data were assembled, mainly by the U.N., one or two countries such as Britain or West Germany have touched the line at least for a single year). The wide variety among the developing countries is quite apparent.[96] The majority of them lie in the band between 2 per cent and 3 per cent growth of population though a distressingly large number have growth rates exceeding 3 per cent. Many of the countries in the upper right hand corner of the scatter are in Africa – a continent where the highest birth and death rates are often found together. India, circled on the the diagram, is a little below average for birth and growth rates and about average in mortality. Perhaps the greatest interest attaches to the countries which are as it were in the neck of the hour-glass – those which on the diagram lie below and on the left of the great scatter of the developing countries and to the right of the relatively small concentration of developed countries.[97] Will the next decade or two see a number of countries moving into that small concentration? Is there a new demographic transition in the offing?

As far as mortality is concerned there is plainly ample opportunity for further decline, especially for the age group 0–5 where it is still high in many countries. But it is very difficult to predict the future course of mortality: certainly the simple view that economic development would bring about continuing rapid improvements in death rates no longer stands up to inspection. In the developing world as a whole the rate of mortality decline seems to have fallen off in the last decade compared with the 1950s and 1960s: in some countries fairly low levels have already been reached, in others the failure of development to bring relevant improvements to those subject to high risk of death has interrupted progress.[98] It has even been suggested that death rates in the mid 1970s have been rising in several countries,[99] although the evidence for this is slender. Modern Malthusians may continue to predict disaster and their warnings may be useful if they prevent complacency, but the general tendency of death rates in the high mortality countries should be to continue downwards, if not as fast as was once anticipated.

A number of developing countries with reasonably reliable demographic data have birth rates in the low 30s or the 20s per thousand. They include in the Western Hemisphere the Bahamas, Chile, Guyana, Jamaica, Puerto Rico, Trinidad; in Asia Sri Lanka, Hong Kong, Malaysia, Singapore and Taiwan, and Fiji and Mauritius. In some of them the decline in birth rates has been spectacular; in Mauritius for example fertility halved between 1963 and 1972. There is more generally a decline in couple-fertility in very many countries of the developing world – indeed the birth rate figures somewhat mask this decline as developing countries have had a growing proportion of their populations in the child-bearing age groups. But this more general decline in birth rates has been relatively modest in the last twenty years, from the high or middle 40s down to the middle 40s or just into the high 30s. The large, populous countries, Brazil, the Indian sub-continent, Indonesia and Nigeria, still have very high birth rates.[100] (China – coded 127 in our diagram – very probably is now an exception to this though the figures for birth and death rates there are rather uncertain.[101])

Examination of the low birth rate countries referred to in the previous paragraph is not immensely revealing. They are mostly small and nearly all islands. In Asia the importance of Confucian culture is noticeable. Both of these features may be significant: the latter because of the oft-remarked capacity for social control in countries where this culture is dominant. And it is not beyond the bounds of possibility that population pressure is peculiarly vivid on small islands from which migration is difficult; the relative ease of communications within these small areas and small populations may also be a factor – it almost certainly is for control of mortality. But the general level of various indicators of social and economic development in these countries is well above the Third World average; the more interesting question is the extent to which development brings reduced fertility in its train.

The short answer to that question is 'It depends on what you mean by development'. In looking at countries as units of observation one has first to group them in areas of cultural similarity – attempts to explain in-ternational differences in fertility by social and economic variables in all countries at once have not been very successful.[102] But, when grouped in cultural regions, countries do exhibit some relationship of their birth rates with the sorts of variables discussed in this chapter.[103] Various factors such as education, health, per cent of population employed outside agriculture or urbanisation together account statistically for a good deal of the variation in birth rates among countries of a given region. But interest today centres on the relation between fertility and those variables in particular which reflect not so much the growth of average incomes as the distribution of the gains of development.[104]

The growth of average incomes used often to be employed as the chief index of success in development. But we have learnt so often in recent years that income per head can rise very substantially in developing countries while the distribution of incomes worsens or improves only a little so that the mass of the poor benefit barely from this growth, if at all. Not surprisingly this is important for population change since, if the incomes of the mass of the people are not increasing, it is unlikely that they will experience improvements in the things which correlate with reduced fertility, particularly education and health. Rich (1973) has suggested for example how much stronger is the relationship between countries' birth rates and the average incomes of the poorest 60 per cent of their populations than between their birth rates and the average incomes of the populations as a whole. He has also assembled an interesting table of data for the developing countries of the Western Hemisphere. Countries such as Mexico or Venezuela which have experienced considerable economic growth and have high levels of income per head ($670 and $931 in 1970 respectively), but where the poor have not benefited much, have high birth rates (42 and 41 respectively in 1970) which have come down only a little in the last decade. Literacy rates correlate better (negatively) with birth rates in the Western Hemisphere than does income per head.

Looking within countries one sees the same forces at work. Various studies have shown strong relationships between the familiar variables and fertility.[105] The role of religion is especially interesting. It seems to be true that there is a general association of higher fertility with religions which do not favour contraception, such as Catholicism, or which favour high natality, such as the Muslim religion. And, at given levels of income or education, the more religious may have more children.[106] But it is also frequently true that *among* Catholics or Muslims the better-off, the urbanised, the better educated, those whose mortality is lower, have fewer children. Thus within a country, even one whose cultural values imply a predisposition to high fertility, we may have some faith that the spread of the advantages of modern development allied to family planning pro- grammes will lead to fertility decline – a decline which as we have seen can be very rapid once it starts, far more rapid than in nineteenth century Europe. Any comfort to be derived from that last sentence will be diminished by two observations – that for many, indeed most, countries we have little idea of when the onset of rapid fertility decline will occur. And that even if the decline were to occur instantaneously tomorrow the world could not avoid substantial population growth as a result of the existing age distribution in developing countries. The latter is a point which will be explored in the next chapter when we come to our projections of India's future population. As regards the former, we are prepared by our brief excursion into historical demography not to expect any mechanical relation between development and fertility. But it is adequately clear that what matters for population trends is not just economic growth but a strategy of development which benefits the poor: a fact with which much of the remainder of this book will be occupied.

This strategy may not involve swift industrialisation or urbanisation on a large scale – indeed for many developing countries industrialisation must be, on grounds of sheer economic infeasibility, ruled out for many years to come. But modernising rural development coupled with whatever in- dustrial growth is possible can bring to the mass of the people in the Third World the improvements in incomes, employment, education and health which should be theirs by right. These improvements are the main necessities in the long run for reducing fertility. There is also an obvious message here for the rich countries – if they are really concerned about rapid population growth in the world, their first priority should be to pursue policies far more radical than those of the past to assist the elimination of developing country poverty.

2 Fertility, Mortality, Migration and Projections

> It appears to be the general opinion of Indian economists who discuss the population problem of this country that the only practical method of limiting the population is by the introduction of artificial methods of birth control, though it is not easy to exaggerate the difficulties of introducing such methods in a country where the vast majority of the population regard the propagation of male offspring as a religious duty and the reproach of barrenness as a terrible punishment for crimes committed in a former incarnation.
>
> *Census of India, 1931*, Vol. i, Part i (Report).

FACTORS AFFECTING FERTILITY

In 1976 the Government of India launched a new National Population Policy designed to achieve a rapid reduction in the birth rate. Much of it involved direct intervention attempting to cut across traditional fertility behaviour. To provide an understanding of those traditions is the aim of this section and the whole subject of family planning is left until Chapter 3. Indian society is so complex that no one would expect any straightforward account of fertility there – difficult as it is to account for the level of fertility anywhere. Most of our explanations derive from studies of differential fertility. As we have seen Indian fertility is not above average, internationally speaking, among developing countries. But it has been high relative to India's needs in recent decades as well as to levels prevailing in rich countries. A standard account would run as follows: 'Fertility has its basis in history – a response to past high levels of mortality. If it has not declined much in the recent past, that is because a number of other contributory factors continue to favour high fertility: the age at marriage is low; Hindus need sons to light their funeral pyres; various religions in India, while not prohibiting contraception, may give a disposition to high fertility; parents need children to look after them in old age; they often see immediate economic or social advantage in large families. And in situations where life offers little but hardship to the majority, sexual pleasure and the joy children can bring are one of the few sources of satisfaction. Other factors tend to reduce fertility. But fertility is dominated by traditional attitudes and perceptions of supposed advantage; while there is some excess of births over those desired by parents, perhaps considerable in some sections, it is not the case that most parents are having vastly more children than they desire and are only waiting for the family planning programme to save them from unwanted burdens.' We shall consider the veracity of this account in detail.

Age at Marriage

The average age at marriage for females in the 1971 Census was 17.1[1]. It has changed only slowly since 1921 when it was 13.89 years, rising to 15.83 in 1961. For males the 1971 figure was 22·5 years. Analysis of the effect of alterations in the age at marriage is made difficult by the fact that early marriages are usually not consummated for a period of years – indeed a separate ceremony (in Hindi, *gauna*) is celebrated when cohabitation begins. The average age at this point – often referred to as the age at effective marriage – was estimated to have risen from 15.29 to 16.49 over the forty years prior to 1960. Obviously it is the age at effective marriage that matters – for this reason small increases in the age at marriage may have little effect on fertility. The aim of raising the age at marriage is an old one. In 1956 the Hindu Code Bill raised the minimum age for legal marriage to 15; the Sarda Act of 1929 had placed it at 14. P. K. Wattal, writing in 1916,[2] said he had sat at meetings of various worthy bodies during the previous thirty years (i.e. since 1886) discussing this difficult goal of social policy. 1976 brought new measures as we shall see; but legislation does not seem to be the way ahead – the old law was so unpopular and widely ignored that it proved impossible to enforce. Few attempts were made to enforce it: the author in 1972 watched a wedding taking place in full view of any passer-by – the groom was 12 years old and the bride 8.

Everyone agrees that a rise in the age at marriage is desirable; opinions vary on the impact a given change could be expected to have on overall fertility. Assuming unaltering age specific marital fertility rates, Malaker[3] estimated the birth rate reduction for a rise from 15 to 17 to be insignificant: if it rose to 19, the birth rate would fall by 11 per cent and to 21, by 24 per cent; in the last case the net reproduction rate would be down by 9 per cent and the total fertility rate by 10 per cent – all this based on 1961 data. Agarwala[4] estimated that, if age at marriage rose to 19–20, the expected decline in birth rate would be 30 per cent. Most authors would put the figure rather lower – some suggest that a rise of 2–3 years might reduce the reproductive period so little as to leave fertility barely altered.[5] One claims on the basis of empirical study that women marrying between 20 and 24 have similar fertility to that of those marrying before age 20; only if the marriage age reached 25 or over would there be a significant reduction of fertility.[6] There is some ground for believing this in the measurements of fecundity: one study[7] suggests that 40 per cent of married women at age 15 are non-fecund, 29 per cent at age 16 and 22 per cent at age 17 – if such figures are representative, only a reduced share of total fertility can be contributed by these very early years of marriage and a correspondingly limited reduction of fertility is to be expected from small rises in the age at marriage.

The average duration of marital unions is currently only a little less than 25 years.[8] Even if we had accurate information on parity by age, we could not without making questionable assumptions assess the likely impact of a small shortening of that span. It is evident that, if the average number of children born to women of completed fertility is in the region of six (see below), their fertility is already subject to restraint within that 25 year period. Much therefore depends on the reasons why people are marrying later – presumably it is at least in part out of a desire to start their families later which, as we know from Chapter 1, is usually related to a desire for smaller families. Were this not so, one could argue that a small rise in marriage age would just be offset by an increase in fertility at later ages. There is a further influence in the well-known syndrome of 'shame at grandmother pregnancy'.[9] It seems to be a well observed phenomenon that women object to becoming pregnant when their own daughters are having children. So if women began to have children later, might their mothers respond by doing so also? The answer again depends on who is marrying later and why – if it is mainly educated women from educated families, the effect on mothers' fertility might be minimal. In general the burden of the evidence points to a distinct negative association between marriage age and fertility despite the numerous offsetting effects;[10] but it may simply reflect the fact that those with a tendency to have less children marry later rather than providing a measure of the impact of marriage age itself. The one thing we can be sure of is that a rise in the age at marriage will postpone some births and thus at least for a time reduce measured fertility over all. The importance of the fact that it also reduces exposure to the risk of pregnancy remains difficult to assess as long as there are already so many years when exposure to that risk is present, and fails to result in pregnancy, for reasons that we do not fully understand.

Since every assumption affects the results the least objectionable way to examine the effect of a changing marriage age is to do so in the context of a population projection in which everything is changing. To illustrate, we have done this for one of the projections later in this chapter which employ a fertility schedule with a parameter representing age at marriage. Below are given the results of raising the age at marriage by four years (from 18 to 22) between 1971 and 1976 and 1976 and 1981. As can be seen the difference in birth rates is not enormous but the effect on total population is considerable especially in the longer run. (See Table 2.1)

This is only an illustrative calculation but we would recommend further exploration by such techniques rather than use of methods commonly employed hitherto. Only in this way can one examine the simultaneous effects of mortality and fertility change: in particular the combined effects of later marriage, changes in age specific fertility and duration of marital unions with their consequent implications for the length of the generation and measured fertility.

TABLE 2.1 Effect of raising age at marriage

	Projection F_3M_1*		Same projection with more rapid increase in age at marriage	
	Population	Birth rate	Population	Birth rate
1976	619·1	38·07	615·3	36·46
1981	681·5	35·23	669·2	32·66
1986	745·0	33·00	725·1	30·88
1991	807·9	30·67	781·1	29·18
1996	867·7	27·29	883·9	26·98
2001	921·9	25·09	881·7	24·24

* See section on population projections below

What determines the age at marriage? Agarwala[11] observed the distinct regional differentials in India with the South having the highest and the North and West the lowest ages at marriage. There are also differentials by religion and by caste but they conform to some extent to the regional patterns – thus Hindus, who tend to marry youngest of the main religious groups, marry later in States where the average age at marriage is higher. Urban men and women marry later than rural as do the educated relatively to the less educated.[12] Education or literacy emerge as the strongest variables for explaining differential female age at marriage. They explain much of the regional differentials. Undoubtedly the continuing rise in the age at marriage has to do with the spread of education. Where opportunities for female employment exist parents may also prefer to keep their daughters' incomes longer in their own families or, even if it is the family farm or growing household demands, they may similarly wish to keep their daughters at home. The slowness of the rise in marriage age reflects the persistence of tradition and the modest pace and impact of modernising trends.

Son Preference

One of the most common explanations of high fertility is the alleged preference of Indian parents for male children. The son can improve his father's fate in the afterworld by performing certain rites after his death.[13] Yet, as Mandelbaum[14] has pointed out, the performance of these rites can be carried out by someone other than a son and in any case is not important among many Indians, especially the poor; and the giving of a daughter in marriage is also an act of 'high religious merit'. There certainly is evidence that sons are more highly prized when born in some communities – giving birth to a son may be an occasion for celebration and a daughter almost for commiseration.[15] It is also obvious that, when times are difficult, male children are much better treated than female, as witness the excess of female over male mortality and the disproportionate frequency of appearance of malnourished female children in nutrition surveys. But there is precious little evidence of any influence on fertility of this favouring of the male.

What might such evidence be? Not the proportion of male children actually born: if the sex of any child born to a particular couple were independent of the sex of children previously born, then even if parents were more likely to curtail fertility after the birth of male children, no difference would be observed in the sex distribution of births; while if sex of children were not independent – that is if it were more likely that parents who had produced children of one sex would produce subsequent children of the same sex – the effect of parents' curtailing fertility after a number of male births would curiously be to reduce the number of male children who would otherwise have been born, since it would be couples with a tendency to produce female children who had the larger families. Individual fertility histories might provide some clues – if we knew the birth order by sex of children for couples of completed fertility, we could observe whether those who had sons first curtailed their fertility sooner than those who did not. The only study known to the author (other than that referred to in the next paragraph) that has examined such evidence found no effect of the kind.[16]

Further evidence is available from survey data. The Operations Research Group (O.R.G.) in Baroda questioned an India-wide sample of about 25,000 couples in 1970 on various aspects of fertility and contraception[17] – we shall return to the O.R.G. survey in Chapter 3. It supports the view that the majority of Indian couples want children of both sexes as well as suggesting a modest preference for sons. Women were asked how many additional children they wanted and of what sex, and the answers were tabulated against their past fertility history. Most of those who wanted an even number of children wanted an equal number of sons and daughters while those who stated a desire for an odd number generally wanted sons one more than the number of daughters. 'Parity progression ratios' – the probability of going on to parity $x + 1$ from parity x – were little influenced by the sex of children already born, though it was found that couples who had only daughters were the least likely to want any more children and wanted the largest number of additional children (especially sons).[18] Altogether whatever people believe, or say they believe, about the desirability of sons those 'ideals' do not very greatly affect reproductive performance although, among contraceptive users, there is some correlation between the number of surviving sons and acceptance of terminal methods.[19] It would make sense to expect the effect to be observable only where there is a high level of contraceptive practice as indeed has been found to be the case in Taiwan.[20]

Religion

No doubt, as with most religions, statements can be found in the holy texts of Indian religions supporting many views and their opposites. In the case of contraception however prevailing opinion is that neither the Hindu nor the Muslim religion is expressly opposed to it: on the other hand those texts will certainly yield plentiful examples of revered persons extolling the virtues of procreation – though many authorities of Hinduism also express asceticism and disgust with the body and its functions.[21] It is virtually impossible to assess the part played by the content of religion in fertility. Even if we could state what is the net impact of encouragements and discouragements to procreation in scripture and teachings, we would not know how influential they are, and whether that influence is waning.

More important than the actual teachings of religion may be the behaviour patterns of groups in the population belonging to different religions which may or may not derive closely from the teachings themselves. Muslims were 10.7 per cent of the total population in the 1961 Census, 11.2 per cent (61.4m) in 1971. The vast majority of the population – 82.7 per cent (453.3m) in 1971 – being Hindus, particular interest attaches to the relative rates of growth of the two groups. The decade growth rate was 30.8 per cent for Muslims, 23.7 per cent for Hindus or, in compound annual terms, 2.7 per cent as against 2.2 per cent. A part, though not a large part, of this differential is explained by migration – ever since the major population transfers at Independence there has been a small net immigration of Muslims. Since there is little reason to suspect lower mortality among Muslims than Hindus, there must be somewhat higher fertility to account for their more rapid growth – if the figures pointing that growth are reliable.

The evidence does show higher fertility among Muslims. Muslim age at marriage is on the whole higher than Hindu but so are marital fertility, completed fertility, child/women ratios and so forth in most studies.[22] The difference in fertility rates is small, ranging from 5 – 15 per cent. Thus in the National Sample Survey (N.S.S.) 18th Round (1963 – 4) Muslim women married 22 years or more had a completed fertility some 6 – 7 per cent higher than their Hindu counterparts. Muslim urban fertility is much the same as rural while for Hindus urban fertility is lower. Especially evident are differentials in Muslim fertility for women aged 30 and over where the effect of negative attitudes to widow remarriage on the part of many Hindus may be a partial explanation.[23] In the family planning programme, as we shall see, the participation of Hindus is proportionately slightly greater than that of Muslims, though the latter have been increasing their share of the total clientele: in the third Ernakulam vasectomy camp for example both Muslims and Hindus participated according to their proportions in the local population.

Three observations are in order: firstly there are areas – mainly in Central India – where the Muslim population shows *lower* fertility than the

Hindu. These are areas where the Muslim share of the population is lower than average – of the order of 4 per cent of the total – and where possibly for that reason community relations are more consistently amicable: it is where Muslims are numerically strongest on the whole that communal feeling is aroused and perhaps there is some connection between that fact and the relatively higher Muslim fertility in these areas. Secondly both Muslim and Hindu fertility are declining. Thirdly a good deal of the differential between Muslim and Hindu fertility may be explained by socio-economic differences. The difference between the fertility of educated, well-off, urban Muslims and Hindus is relatively small; but the average socio-economic and educational status of Muslims is lower than that of Hindus.

Assuming Hindus and Muslims to have the same age distribution and to be subject to the same death rate, and ignoring migration, the relative rates of growth between the last two censuses imply a difference of five points in the crude birth rates of Hindus and Muslims. If these rates are say 39 and 44 respectively, then Muslim fertility is where Hindu fertility was ten years ago. Assume now that the Hindu population will grow at an annual rate declining 0.5 per cent each decade and the Muslim population does the same but with a ten-year lag until both are growing at 0.2 per cent annually – that is assume that the Hindu population grows at 1.7 per cent annually, 1.2 percent, 0.7 per cent, 0.2 per cent and 0.2 per cent annually for the decades 1971–81, 1981–91 etc. up to the decade 2011–21 while, over the same five decades, the Muslim population grows annually at 2.2 per cent, 1.7 per cent, 1.2 per cent, 0.7 per cent and 0.2 per cent respectively; assume also that the rest of the population, non-Hindu and non-Muslim, remains a constant 6 per cent of the total. Then the population would stabilise after the year 2021 with over 80.7 per cent Hindu and 13.3 per cent Muslim compared with the current 82.7 per cent to 11.2 per cent. These sets of growth rates are improbably low even by comparison with our low projections (q.v.), but they illustrate the point that, if one group has a rate of growth half a per cent higher than that of the other consistently for forty years, the change in the ultimate population proportions may be relatively small. Even if the 'Hindu' growth rate declined as indicated for the 50 years and the 'Muslim' rate remained at 2.2 per cent throughout the period, in 2021 the proportions would be 74.05 to 19.95 per cent. And that assumption is tantamount to saying that all benefits of development associated with fertility decline will accrue to Hindus only during the period and none to Muslims.

In fact as Hindu opposition to widow remarriage declines and the practice of family planning spreads, the relative rates of growth of the two groups are likely to approach each other much more rapidly than assumed here. Under most plausible demographic assumptions therefore the relative weight of Hindus and Muslims in the population is unlikely to alter a very great deal. For that to happen one would have to assume a discrepancy between the decline in one rate of growth and the other which seems quite unrealistic. Thus if, as is sometimes alleged, Hindus maintain high fertility or oppose family planning because they fear being numerically overtaken by Muslims, such fear seems to have little empirical or quantitative basis.

The Correlates of Fertility Decline

The demographic transition as we have seen usually accompanies some form of socio-economic change which includes to varying degrees the spread of education, urbanisation, improved health and lower mortality and new economic expectations. We shall examine how each of these is related to fertility in India. In doing so for each factor separately we must bear in mind that in reality all such changes are interconnected as is their influence on fertility; no less important than each of them may be an alteration in attitudes towards the use of contraception and towards the desirability of large families and such attitudes are only loosely related to any particular dimension of social change.

There is no dearth of evidence for the negative correlation between education and fertility in India. Opinions vary as to the influence of the very earliest years of education – in some studies women with only one or two years of education have little lower, or even higher, fertility than women with no education.[24] Where this is so a part of the explanation may be that the very early years of education are not very educative; also to some extent those who go to school at all are likely to be of a higher income level than those who do not – at these very low levels of poverty, that difference may be enough to affect fecundity positively. Developing countries seem to divide into those where the negative correlation between education and fertility is 'continuous', every additional year of schooling of mothers being associated with a lower level of their fertility, and those where this association begins mainly *after* primary education. The latter group of countries tend to be the poorer among the developing countries.[25] However at least one study[26] in India – based on well over 4000 households in Lucknow city in 1966–67 – has shown the 'continuous' type of correlation: illiterates had a general fertility rate of 163·9, those with incomplete primary education 145.2, and with completed primary education, 102.0. The O.R.G. survey also shows a continuous negative relationship between educational status and desired number of children.[27]

All the studies cited show a negative correlation between children born and female post-primary education, the sharpest drop usually occurring, as one might expect, at the level of college education. There is also evidence that birth rates are in general lower and family planning more successful in States of India where education and literacy are more widespread.[28] It is impossible to attribute more than a share of these differences to education itself. One of the troubles of any study of inter-State differentials in India is that the States where one indicator is 'better' than elsewhere typically are better in several other things, as we shall see. One study[29] notes interestingly that the better performance of family planning in the better-educated States is only partially explained by the higher incidence of education itself; in those States fertility is lower and the practice of family planning more widespread even among the illiterate. As the authors note this more rapid transmission of favourable attitudes to family planning may be due either to the influence on the behaviour of illiterate groups of the example of the educated or the greater success of the family planning programme in reaching the poorest people in these States. (The States or Union Territories in question are Delhi, Gujarat, Kerala, Maharashtra, Punjab, Tamil Nadu and West Bengal. These States have literacy rates of 56.6, 35.8, 60 1, 39.2, 33.7, 39.5 and 33.2 per cent respectively compared with the national average of 29.5 per cent.)

The reader may recall the discussion in Chapter 1 of the potential reasons for a relationship between educational progress and fertility decline. Similar reasons appear to prevail in India. Mandelbaum[30] adds one important consideration missing from our account. In village India a woman owes much of her status to the children she bears; 'the educated wife,' as he puts it, 'is not as likely to want to keep proving herself through obstetrical channels.' There are few societies on earth other than the world of Islam where ordinary women are so constrained to a life of child-bearing, domestic toil and menial labour. Even their legal status is often one of deprivation.[31] We have quoted the figure for the average literacy rate of 29.46 per cent in India. This is in fact composed of a male literacy rate of 39.45 per cent and female of 18.72 per cent. Given the importance attached to female education in relation to fertility there can be no more telling sign of the persistence of non-development. In terms of percentage growth the advances since Independence have been greater for females than males. The proportions literate in 1951 were, males 24.95 per cent and females 7.93 per cent. But post-Independence development has still favoured males, whose literacy rate has risen 14.5 percentage points (including their growth in numbers) from a larger original base since 1951 compared with an addition of only 10.8 per cent for females. This trend was modestly reversed between 1961 and 1971 when females gained slightly more than males. But perhaps the most terrible indictment of this feature of society are the female literacy rates for Bihar and Uttar Pradesh – 8.72 per cent and 10.7 per cent respectively in 1971.[32] Bihar had a total population of 56.35 million in 1971 and Uttar Pradesh 88.34 million, together a quarter of the population as a whole but contributing more than a quarter of total births.

As a source of fertility decline there is not a great deal to be expected from urbanisation, both because the rate of urbanisation is low and because it has not so far been strongly associated with reduced fertility. Urban crude birth rates are lower than in rural areas but most of this is for arithmetical reasons – in particular the very high ratio of males to females which results from the pattern of migration. Until recently comparisons of marital fertility showed little urban/rural differential. Data of the early 1960s showed marital fertility in urban areas for most States comparable to that of their surrounding rural areas.[33] More recently however some fertility surveys have begun to show distinctly lower urban fertility of a non-arithmetical nature.[34] The probable explanation of this is the common observation that urbanisation in India has not been accompanied for most people with forms of social change that lead to reduced fertility; rather the social character of rural life is reproduced in the urban setting to a considerable degree. However if modernisation is taking place anywhere in India, it is mainly in the bigger cities and this is at last beginning to show – the combination of better educational facilities, higher age at marriage, lower mortality and latterly, with little doubt, the family planning programme which has had its greatest successes in urban areas.

In most countries the historical pattern of fertility decline began in cities, the centres almost everywhere from which the diffusion of new social norms begins; even with modern communications cities are still likely to give people the greatest exposure to new forms of behaviour. But the pace of urbanisation in India is slow: in the last two censuses the 'proportion urban' has risen by only 2 percentage points per *decade*. Thus even if urbanisation produced an automatic and major decline in fertility among the urbanised it would have to proceed at a greatly accelerated rate to have any appreciable impact on average fertility in the country as a whole. Experience suggests however that it is not urban residence itself but the adoption of a 'modern' life-style in terms of employment, education and social relations which influences fertility. As we demonstrate in Chapter 4,[35] there are no prospects that such a life-style will absorb any fast-increasing proportion of the population for many years to come – it is economically impossible.

Even if the rate of fertility-reducing urbanisation is unlikely to speed up, there is every prospect that urban fertility will continue to decline; but if we ask about the potential for diffusion of the urban example to the countryside we are back with all the determinants of fertility, including mortality itself, which we must now discuss. Our review of the historical demographic transition in Europe and elsewhere suggested that there were some examples – if on the whole the exceptions rather than the rule – of substantial fertility decline without major prior mortality decline or while mortality levels were still high. Most contemporary developing country studies stress the need for mortality decline as a pre-condition for reduced fertility. An author who has done much to investigate these relationships is Paul Schultz who has found a clear statistical relationship between mortality and fertility for several developing countries after allowing for the influence of other factors.[36] There are two separate effects one might expect: we shall call them the 'replacement' and the 'risk' effect. If parents actually decide to have an additional child in the event of the death of a child already born, then a lessening of child mortality should lessen the incidence of this 'replacement' behaviour. That such behaviour takes place has been shown by Schultz who found a statistically significant tendency of parents to have an additional child in the late years of the reproductive span.[37] But the 'replacement' effect is of relatively little significance for the demographic transition; if mortality decline only impinges on replacement births, little difference is made to population growth, the reduced number of deaths being matched by the reduced number of births.

If a reduction in mortality is to be (causally) succeeded by a more than offsetting reduction in births, a number of things are necessary. Parents must previously have been aiming at a given number of surviving children allowing for the risk of mortality; when mortality declines they must become aware of it, and they must at some point have been over-compensating for the true risk – or alternatively their fertility behaviour must have been invariant to some decline in risk. There must also be no net positive effect of reduced mortality on fertility. As noted earlier the non-fulfilment of a combination of such considerations made it unlikely in nineteenth century Europe that there would be any rapid follow-on of fertility decline after the declines in mortality. Schultz however has claimed[38] that the sequence is more swift nowadays. Possibly modern communications enhance the appreciation by parents of the improving survival prospects of their children. Certainly in some attitude surveys it has been found that those indicating a desire for smaller numbers of children are also more likely to give a positive answer when asked whether they believe current child mortality is lower than in the past.[39]

It may well be that the whole psychological setting of procreation is affected by mortality conditions. If parents feel that having children is like sending a platoon into battle in the knowledge that only some will survive, they hardly dwell in an atmosphere conducive of prudent foresight in fertility behaviour. Studies in India commonly show that parents of completed fertility in the past had only two-thirds or less of their children still alive. In the Khanna Study for example a survey in 1959 showed only a little over 60 per cent of live-born children surviving until their mothers passed 45 years of age.[40] Even today the probability of a child's surviving to age ten in India is less than 75 per cent and infant mortality is still about 150 per thousand live births. Thus even though mortality declined considerably in the last fifty years, the risks for parents are still high. It is extremely difficult to estimate the offsetting positive effects of mortality decline on fertility which are due to the increased duration of marital unions, and the rise in fecundity associated with the control of communicable diseases and improvement in nutrition (to the extent there have been any) – one must recall at least one further offsetting effect in the opposite direction, namely the increase in birth interval ascribable to the improved survival of infants and the consequent prolongation of lactation and post-partum amenorrhea as well as other reasons for reduced exposure to pregnancy risk.[41]

TABLE 2.2 Rural birth and death rates by States (average 1970–72)

State	Birth Rate	Death Rate
Kerala	31·6	9·2
Maharashtra	33·1	13·8
Manipur	33·1	8·8
Tamil Nadu	33·5	17·5
(Bihar	33·6	16·0)
Karnataka (Mysore)	34·1	14·2
Jammu & Kashmir	35·0	12·4
Himachal Pradesh	35·1	16·3
Punjab	35·2	12·0
Andhra Pradesh	35·7	16·5
Orissa	36·0	17·7
Tripura	36·4	17·5
Assam (incl. Meghalaya)	38·7	18·0
Madhya Pradesh	40·4	18·0
Haryana	41·5	10·9
Gujarat	42·2	17·6
Rajasthan	42·5	18·1
Uttar Pradesh	45·9	23·6

NOTE As we observe in the text many if not most of these figures are under-estimates. There are none for West Bengal, and those for Bihar are of such doubtful accuracy that we print them in parentheses. Figures for 1973 were published in 1975 but were stated to be unreliable owing to administrative difficulties in the Sample Registration System.

SOURCE Government of India (1974a).

Altogether the likelihood is that some of the recent decline in fertility is to be seen as a delayed response to falling mortality. At the very least it has made contraception more acceptable, especially the 'terminal' methods. One must however be extremely cautious in attributions of causal connection. If one takes the Sample Registration data for rural birth and death rates by States,[42] they correlate well – suspiciously well: see Table 2.2. There are three reasons for this which have nothing to do with any implied causal connection between mortality and fertility decline – since infant and child mortality is a high proportion of all mortality there are bound to be less deaths where there are less births; where statistical collection of birth data is better so is that of mortality data in all probability, and the levels of births and deaths are related to a range of other variables many of which, such as education or degree of urbanisation, have a downward influence on both births and deaths. Looking to the future we may expect some further fertility decline for a period in part as a response to the mortality decline which has already occurred even if mortality has stopped falling (see below). But we find it difficult to believe that there will be a spontaneous transition in fertility to rich country levels until mortality falls so far as to assist a fundamental change in what we have termed – perhaps a shade grandiosely – the psychological setting of procreation.

The economics of family formation

Allegedly important motives for high fertility in India are the contributions of children to the family's income, while the parents are themselves working, and in old age when they can no longer work. This is a subject of major importance, not least for the Indian family planning programme, which has tried to persuade people to have less children on the grounds that they will be better off if they do. But would they really be better off? Are people acting against their own best interests? Or are they in fact having many children because they believe they will thereby become richer, not poorer? One author who claims the last to be the correct view is M. Mamdani, whose *The Myth of Population Control*[43] attracted attention when it was published in 1971. He was examining a part of the same area as the *Khanna Study*,[44] that is, a village in a relatively prosperous region of the Punjab. 'Had they practised contraception,' he concluded, 'most of the villagers would have wilfully courted economic disaster.'

Mamdani was able to quote interviews with parents in a range of occupational groups. With the exception of high-caste non-agricultural families and some big landowners, most of those interviewed attributed such well-being as they possessed to their large families. Hence – in part – his conclusion and his title. We do not believe his position is wholly incorrect. But it is not wholly correct either. His criticism of the Government's family planning programme and its conflict with the values of village society has a good deal of weight. Curiously, though one would hardly realise it from reading his book, the *Khanna Study* which Mamdani violently attacks comes to many of the same conclusions. But we are concerned here solely with the economic argument. A significant point is that most of Mamdani's interlocutors owed, or said they owed, their economic advantage not to their children in general but to their sons. Yet half their children were daughters; and more than one of those interviewed said he would have no more children as he could 'not afford another daughter.' Since some parents have only daughters may they not be courting economic disaster by having children at all? There is something puzzling here.

Let us start with the question whether a surviving child is a good investment seen purely from the point of view of the parents. We have in mind mainly poor families, small landholders or labourers. The child must be supported up to the age at which it becomes economically useful and we assume at first that its earnings above these support costs accrue to the

TABLE 2·3 Discounted present value of child earnings

	Rate of Discount	'FAO' Age			'Poverty' Age			'Malnutrition' Age			Earnings schedule (% above cost)
		15	30	40	15	30	40	15	30	40	
Earnings start at age 5	5%	−	−	−	−	−	−	−	+	+	10%
		−	+	+	−	+	+	+	+	+	20%
		+	+	+	+	+	+	+	+	+	40%
	10%	−	−	−	−	−	−	−	−	−	10%
		−	−	−	−	+	+	+	+	+	20%
		−	+	+	+	+	+	+	+	+	40%
Earnings start at age 7	5%	−	−	−	−	−	−	−	−	−	10%
		−	−	−	−	−	+	−	+	+	20%
		−	+	+	+	+	+	+	+	+	40%
	10%	−	−	−	−	−	−	−	−	−	10%
		−	−	−	−	−	−	−	−	+	20%
		−	−	−	−	+	+	+	+	+	40%

Cost Schedules (% of Adult Consumption Unit)

	Age	0	1	2	3	4	5	6	7	8	9	10	11	12	13	14	15
'FAO'		·27	·39	·45	·52	·57	·62	·67	·71	·75	·79	·83	·87	·9	·93	·97	1
'Poverty'		·1	·2	·3	·4	·5	·58	·65	·71	·75	·79	·83	·87	·9	·93	·97	1
'Malnutrition'		·05	·1	·15	·2	·25	·35	·45	·55	·65	·73	·8	·85	·9	·93	·97	1

(For explanation see text)

parents. The economist would assess the life-time costs and earnings by taking their 'discounted present value'. In Table 2.3, we show the results of such a procedure under a variety of assumptions. There are three schedules of 'costs': what we have called 'F.A.O.', 'Poverty', and 'Malnutrition'. For the first of these we took the F.A.O./W.H.O. estimate of calorie requirements by age[45], gave the value of 1 to the adult norm, which is assumed here to be reached at age 15 and calculated the result for the earlier ages as proportions of 1. This does not involve a belief that calories are the only costs but rather that the costs of child support are proportional to calorie requirements. (Major educational costs and so forth could of course change the shape of this age-cost profile considerably.) Since the calculation is sensitive to the gradient of the curve and the F.A.O./W.H.O. provisions in the early years are on the generous side, we explore two further cost schedules: one which is called 'Poverty' rising by a much shallower slope in the early years; and a third, 'Malnutrition', shallower still – a child receiving only 35 per cent of adult needs in its sixth year, especially with the low provisions of earlier years, would definitely be suffering from malnutrition.

Three separate schedules for 'earnings' are tried: for each set of costs, at 10 per cent, 20 per cent and 40 per cent in excess of costs. We are not presuming at first that these are typical or likely but simply exploring the cc﹏sequences of such figures. The earnings may take any form – money wages or the imputed value of a child's assistance with domestic or other tasks. Earnings begin at age 5 or age 7 and the percentage earned in excess of cost is unchanged with age once earnings start. Discount rates of 5 per cent and 10 per cent are employed and the present value is calculated for ages 15, 30 and 40 – we do not present the actual figures in the table but simply whether the sum is positive or negative by the time those ages are reached. (For the non-economist this procedure is somewhat like comparing the net earnings of the child with the income which would accrue if, instead of being spent on the child, the support costs were invested at 5 per cent or 10 per cent compound up to the age at which earnings start; the present value being negative is equivalent to the parents being better off with the fixed interest investment; if the present value is positive, the child is the better investment.) The table should be read as follows: consider the ninth line of pluses and minuses under the 'Poverty' cost heading – the table says that if the child starts earning at age 7 and provides for its parents 40 per cent in excess of 'Poverty' costs, the present value of its earnings minus costs, discounted at 5 per cent, is negative at age 15 but positive by age 30.

As can be seen the calculations are very sensitive to changes in the age at which earnings start. This is hardly surprising: if the child starts earning at age 7, compared with age 5, the parents incur an additional 0·8–1·3 Adult Consumption Units of costs uncovered by earnings, depending on the cost assumption, while later earnings are only a fraction of a unit. The calculations are also sensitive to the rate of discount used and the assumption about the rate of earnings above cost. But only the 'Malnutrition' schedule of costs makes more than a small difference to the result – and then not a great deal. With 'Malnutrition' costs and earnings 40 per cent above them starting at age 7, discounted at 10 per cent, the parents are only in the black investing in a child after waiting about 30 years; though, if the child starts at age 5 with the same support costs, it pays off as an investment by age 15 even earning 20 per cent above costs.

How realistic are these figures? It certainly is possible that a child can start to be economically useful to the family in his sixth year, even if it is only by minding cattle or other minor tasks. Indian children are even to be found in (unorganised) manufacturing at the age of six or seven. Whether earnings as much as 40 per cent above support costs in the early years are at all common is another question; it is rather unlikely that that is the average experience. (And for someone as acutely underfed as in the 'Malnutrition' cost schedule it must be considered extremely unlikely.) But the assumption made in some other calculations of this kind that children do not earn until much later,[46] or that when they do their earnings are negligible, is far from being universally valid. Unfortunately we have nothing like adequate information of *actual* costs and earnings by age. One or two published surveys suggest rather low child participation in the labour force. This has possibly to do with definitional criteria and response bias as considerable evidence exists to the opposite effect; also to the extent that we are concerned particularly with poor families child participation is likely to be above average.[47]

At later ages we are probably under-estimating earnings for many groups. It is more likely that actual earnings, rather than being a constant percentage over costs, rise to a peak from the late teens to the early fifties and decline thereafter. One study[48] suggests the appropriate figure is 65 per cent above costs from 15 – 19, and 120 per cent above from 20 – 54. Obviously very many workers must earn substantially more than 40 per cent above personal consumption costs at some stages in their life – families with substantial numbers of children in school, and no relatives to provide additional support, for example. But estimates of consumption and incomes in India, which we review in Chapter 4, do not suggest that such figures are representative for poor rural families, most of whom must work in order for the family to achieve a bare sufficiency. As we note there, a large proportion of families cannot afford to forego child earnings by leaving their children in school – a finding which casts doubt both on the validity of the allegedly low labour force participation rates for children just mentioned, and on the often presumed insignificance of child earnings. One or two of the adult household members may earn at rates 120 per cent or more above their consumption costs. Data on daily wages and family budgets suggest this; but for it to be true in general the daily wage must be earned 365 days a year. We suggest however that the earnings figures be interpreted not as actual percentages earned above consumption costs, but as the percentage above costs *which parents may actually receive from their children*; the reasons for this are explained below.

The question of the appropriate rate of discount presents yet further difficulties. The relevant issue is the practical opportunities the individual faces. He may not be able through any formal savings institution to put his money away at 10 per cent or better in real terms. (1975 Post Office deposit rates in India were in the region of 9 per cent depending on terms – and not proof against inflation.) On the other hand vast numbers of the poor borrow at 20 per cent or substantially higher rates from the local money lender – Rural Credit Surveys suggest a high proportion of such borrowing is for consumption purposes. So even if the individual could not find an institutional investment at 10 per cent for money which would otherwise go in child support, he could use it to pay off his own debts which were costing him much more than 10 per cent; or, if he had no debts, he might lend to other individuals – though presumably a part of the high rate of interest in the village reflects the risk of default. Altogether most observers would agree that 10 per cent is on the low side for calculations such as these; but at discount rates substantially above 10 per cent most of the few pluses in our table would disappear.

If one tries to summarise all these thoughts, it seems at first sight that a child is not a very good investment. If we agree that a discount rate of 10 per cent or more is appropriate and that 'earnings' 20 per cent above costs are more common than those at 40 per cent above, even if they start in the sixth year, the child only pays as an investment under the third and lowest schedule of costs which are so low as to make it doubtful that the child would live, let alone earn 20 per cent or more above costs. In other words if the parent took the resources necessary to raise a child at a level above 'Malnutrition' costs and invested them at 10 per cent or more (or paid off debts that cost more than 10 per cent), income from the investment would be higher than from the child except under 'Poverty' costs after 40 years – and then only just. (It may be interesting to note that slave owners in the Southern States of ante-bellum America did not recoup their investment on a slave raised from infancy until he or she reached 27 years of age.[49]) If earnings do not start until the eighth year, not even with 'Malnutrition' costs is there a positive return to investing in a child. Clearly, if a child is a good investment, it must be on some basis other than this – we really have chosen numbers that favour a positive result for 'child-investment' compared with what many would consider appropriate.

In fact there is such a basis – indeed more than one. We have already noted that there is some doubt whether the poor always or often have investment opportunities yielding 10 per cent – and if they have them, whether they regard them as sufficiently reliable. What is still more doubtful is whether they would take advantage of such opportunities even if they existed. The necessities of child support make powerful and direct claims on the family's resources – resources however meagre which moreover may need no connection with the money economy. If the child were not there, the family would have to make daily efforts to reduce already stringent consumption standards and invest them farsightedly. Thus an important effect of the child as an economic entity may be to force the parents to forego their own consumption on its behalf – a kind of forced saving from the parents' point of view. (This is obviously not 'savings' in the national accounting sense.) Finally, there is the important issue of risk and old age. So far we have treated the child as a potential earner on the labour market or within the family's economic activity. But the son or daughter may have a much greater value substituting for father or mother when one or other falls sick, is too old to work or dies; even though the son earns very little outside the family economy, if the father operates a small farm which only needs one man's labour, the son's value is transformed if his father is out of action for any reason. Alternatively when the parents are in trouble the child may be able to contribute considerably more than usual. In terms of our analysis above this is equivalent to saying that there may be periods when the child's value to parents may be very considerably in excess of its own costs – much more than 40 per cent; or when – as in the parents' old age – the reliability of the child is, or is believed to be, greater than that of institutional or other investment alternatives.

There are however other factors pointing in the opposite direction. In the first place we assumed that the parents would receive a significant share of the child's income in excess of its consumption. This depends in part on the child's goodwill and the strength of custom or moral obligation – but obviously the child may not itself be a reliable investment (a reason, if some children are essential, for having several). Further after a period of say twenty-five years the child will begin to have children of his or her own to support; this is why we interpret the earnings schedules in Table 2.3 as the share of the child's earnings parents may have prospects of receiving. It is for such reasons that, while the child's earnings are not likely to be a constant fraction above support costs throughout its life, it may not be too misleading an approximation of the pattern of contributions parents are likely to receive since, as the children's actual earnings rise, so do their own responsibilities.

When we speak of risk we have so far considered only the risk of the parent being unable to work or of one parent dying leaving the other alive. Clearly the parent will be willing to pay dearly to cover him or herself against the risk of unsupported sickness or old age. But there are other risks which adversely affect the calculated value of child-investment. The child may die after imposing substantial costs on the family and before it has yielded a substantial return. And, if the child has to seek work on the general labour market, there is a risk that he or she may be unemployed and never yield any considerable income to the parents at all. (The probability of this, if small, may be balanced by the opposite (small) probability that the child will be a very high earner.) Depleting the costs and earnings schedule in our table for mortality reduces the return on child-investment, even though child death is most likely in the years before parents have incurred major costs in child-support.[50]

We have so far not distinguished between male and female children as far as concerns their earnings prospects. This obviously cannot remain unquestioned. There are parts of India where female children are, for some strata of society at least, more likely to be a burden than a benefit. They may be unable to earn much or, if they do, the earnings are lost to the family on marriage. Quite probably the first daughter is something of an asset – she will be able to look after younger siblings and free the mother for work; but a subsequent daughter may only be valuable if her elder sister dies or gets married. (As we have suggested above preference for sons seems to be little reflected in fertility behaviour, but it may underlie the treatment of daughters which is responsible, in some parts of India, for the excess of female over male mortality at younger ages.) We shall revert to this matter below. But we should also note that, once the daughter is married, in most Indian families her economic contribution will be transferred to the husband's family; though there must be many instances of the son-in-law working for his wife's family if they have land and need him and he has no land. As we have seen the expected investment value of a child may be on the low side, if due allowance is made for mortality, poor employment prospects and the possibility that daughters' economic usefulness may be considerably less than sons'. But we have also seen that the outcome of the calculation can be positive or negative depending on relatively small changes in the assumptions. In the actual calculations that underlie Table 2.3, the present value, positive or negative, is mostly quite small. Thus even where it is negative, provided it is not enormously so, we may regard the cost of children as insurance taken out by parents against future risks. An important feature of this anlysis is thus the parents' evaluation of the risks they would face in a life without children – and it will not do to say that this is measured by what they pay for insurance against it since the problem is to assess whether it is worth what they pay.

Let us first note that old age is not something to be contemplated with equanimity by most Indians, especially women. The vast mass of people have no pensions and their own children are the family members who can be most counted on. Given the pattern of mortality, between 50 and 60 per cent of married women who live to age 50 – 55 will be widows.[51] Almost all women marry. Those who have been supported solely by their husbands and have no other person to support them will find it extremely difficult to find work at the age of 50. One must remember also that although mortality is high in general it is particularly so in the early years of life, so that a married woman of 20 has an expectation of life of a further 43 years. She can expect to survive but she cannot expect all her children to. In a well-known study, May and Heer showed that an Indian couple had to have an average of 6.3 children to be 95 per cent certain that one son would survive to the father's 65th birthday.[52] This is more than we estimate them to have currently, in fact, even if only slightly more. But May and Heer's calculation was based on a 1950–61 life-table with expectation of life at birth of 37.7 years: with today's mortality their calculation would come out lower. Also if parents waited to see whether their children survive and adjusted their fertility accordingly rather than expecting *average* mortality to prevail, they could achieve the same objective with fewer children.

We may consider the risk of being incapable of supporting themselves as the only risk at issue for parents; it has some probability at any point in their life, and is a virtual certainty in the last years, unless they die early, or succeed in securing an income for themselves from some source other than their family. It need not be solely due to sickness or old age; it might be drought ruining the crop or loss of employment for any of a multiplicity of reasons. Since these circumstances involve the strong possibility of starvation the individual clearly has a strong incentive to provide against them. Our question now is, suppose having a child is an investment with a negative rate of return, if we consider only the average stream of contributions parents can expect; but at some point in their life parents are vulnerable to a disastrous drop in their own earnings and then children can raise their contributions and ensure that their parents survive: does this alter the economic value of children?

Once again part of the answer lies in thinking about the alternatives. If the crisis occurs in mid-life, the parents can borrow money for a short period – though probably at an interest rate compared with which the child will be a rather good investment; and one must remember that, if someone is not in a position to save much and borrows to cover a substantial period without earnings, when earnings do resume he will have difficulty in paying off the debt and may be saddled with interest payments for a long period. Many people buy gold bangles or bury valuables under the floor – one should realise that at any positive real rate of discount this too is a negative return investment. (The fact that people do save in this way – unless they are compensated by the 'consumption' satisfactions of wearing bangles or having gold under the bed – is an index of their lack of faith in savings institutions or price stability.) But once they can no longer work, they will not be able to borrow, and they have no way of knowing how long they will live and therefore whether the sale of any valuables they have stored up will yield enough to help them through their old age. Of course what we have said about the availability and reliability of alternative investments still holds; if there were alternatives with satisfactory yields and if, as discussed, parents did actually forego consumption to provide for their future by them, investment in children might not be a wise choice. (And if only a son could support parents in old age and six children were really necessary to ensure the survival of a son into the parents' late 60s, the calculation would be still clearer: the support costs of six children up to the children's earning age – even subject to mortality – all invested at 10 per cent till the parents were 65 would provide them with a handsome income thereafter.) But a crisis in mid-life could still force parents to use up their savings even if these alternatives existed. One of the miseries of this topic is that the closer we approach an analysis of the economics of child-bearing that would satisfy economic theory, the further we seem to be from anything that might conceivably be going through the mind of an Indian villager. It is distasteful enough to talk of children as investments; to go into the further sophistications of decision theory takes us into realms of even more remote abstraction. Let us bear with them for a few moments more. We may say that parents have children in part as an insurance against risk – the risk of being unsupported at some point in life. But in fact there are two elements of risk: one their own which they may hope that their children will compensate for; the other that their children, far from contributing to their parents income in times of need, may impose unrequited costs on their parents. Let us make an illustrative calculation. Suppose the probability of being born male or female is 0.5; the probability of living beyond earning age is 0.75; the probability of a surviving child making a positive contribution to parental income is 0.8 in the case of males, 0.6 in the case of females; if the child dies before earning age, or survives but fails to make a contribution, he or she imposes costs on the parents. The position can be set out as follows:

TABLE 2.4 Probabilities for child contribution to parental income

	Male				Female		
	0·5				0·5		
	Survive 0·75		Die 0·25		Survive 0·75		Die 0·25
	Contribute 0·8	not 0·2			Contribute 0·6	not 0·4	
Joint Probabilities	0·3	·075	0·125		0·225	0·15	·125

Now the probabilities of various possible outcomes can be seen; they are called 'joint probabilities' in the table. Thus the probability of a child being male, surviving beyond earning age and making a contribution is 0.5 × 0.75 × 0.8 = 0.3. The probability of parents receiving a contribution as a result of having a child is 0.3 + 0.225 = 0.525, and there is a complementary probability of 0.475 that the child will impose costs. If we call the contributions 'y' and the costs 'c', the expected benefit from a child is 0.525y − 0.475c. (Implicitly y and c are weighted sums of different

amounts of contribution and cost.) But this is not the sum parents –
theoretical parents that is – are concerned with; they have to balance the
expected *utilities* of the contributions and costs. Gains and losses in money
terms may not have an equal weight: someone just on the margin of
survival will be much more concerned about losing Rs. 100 which would
drive him below the margin than about gaining the same sum – the
disutility of that particular loss is greater than the utility of the same
monetary gain.

To take this analysis further we would have to construct utility functions
for parents – but to do this would be to add further flimsy storeys to the
numerical house of cards we have already constructed. Given our
ignorance about actual contributions and costs it does not seem
worthwhile to attach 'plausible' utility values to 'plausible' present values
of children's net earnings in order to see whether parents' fertility decisions
are economically rational. But whatever sorts of numbers the reader thinks
appropriate in Table 2.4, the probability of loss on a child will remain
substantial even if due to mortality alone. And since so many parents are
on the margin of survival, the disutility of loss must be very great. The risk
parents are insuring against however, being potentially the risk of
starvation, also has a high disutility and the utility of child contributions in
such an eventuality is correspondingly high.[53] In general a decision-
theoretic approach to family formation appears to be a potentially useful
line of enquiry but one that is unlikely to yield results until there is much
more data available on the actual costs and earnings of children, the
fluctuations in parents' incomes and the nature of transfers within the
family. But this discussion does make one thing clear: even if it were
reasonable for parents to *expect* to profit from the number of children they
have – and we have not been able to demonstrate either that it is or that it is
not – the probability that they will not benefit is sufficiently great to
guarantee that the expectations of many will be defeated. If having
children has some probability 'p' of benefiting parents, there is a
probability of 1-p that they will not; if every family faced the same
probabilities, then, over a large enough number of families, a proportion
equal to 1-p would lose as a result. Thus it can be perfectly rational on
economic grounds for people to have the number of children that they do
while many will regret the decision after the event.

We may now widen the analysis beyond the framework of the welfare of
one generation of parents related to a single child. Looking again at the
cost schedules in Table 2.3 one can see that, if parents have children at
fairly short intervals, they could incur a substantial volume of costs
uncovered by child earnings if those earnings begin late. A different way of
examining the economics of family formation is to consider the family
budget and whether it will suffice to cover parents' and children's needs
under various assumptions about the timing of child-bearing, mortality
and family earnings. This approach was first suggested by Frank Lorimer

and further work has gone on with computer simulations of the possible patterns.[54] The period of stress for the family comes when there is a bunching of non-earning children. Such 'stress' models for some assumptions show substantial periods of ten years or more when the family budget cannot cope on a straight consumption-production basis. But they do not take account of the possibilities of borrowing or of transfers from the previous generation. While parents are having their first children their own parents may well contribute to their support – they must in many cases be still of working age. (This would alter the analysis above of the single generation, single child case, since we assumed that parents captured some or all of their children's income while it is now apparent that, on the contrary, they may have to support their children when the latter are starting their families.)

These life-cycle models are no substitute for estimating the economic contribution of children; the notion of discounting is absent from them and therefore that of economic alternatives to children. But they do serve to show the economic difficulties families may face with large numbers of children, and possibly they reflect the way poor parents contemplate the future. As with the one-generation single-child case we are hampered by lack of information – not only on age earnings and consumption profiles but also on transfers within the family. Clearly one virtue of the large – and the extended – family is the coverage provided by some members for periods when others are in deficit. But very little is known about how the arrangements actually work, how strong are the obligations on members of each kinship-relation and generation to assist other members at different times of life. It is commonly believed that the security-giving capacity of the extended family reduces any inherent economic disincentive which might otherwise limit fertility – though there is no evidence in India that the fertility of parents in extended families is significantly different from that of parents in nuclear families.[55]

As we have seen the economic considerations which could explain why people have large families are many and various; and there are others which must be added. We concluded that, while the balance of expectations might favour large families, many parents are bound to find their expectations defeated. This is what seems so one-sided in Mamdani's account – he does not appear to have interviewed anyone whose children died before making an economic contribution, whose children were unemployed or who had too many daughters. (If the probability of being male or female at birth is 0.5, 6 per cent of all couples would find their first four children all girls.) And as we have seen much of the argument in favour of children as investments lies not so much in their bringing prosperity to their parents as in protecting them against disaster. From Mamdani's point of view it is difficult to explain why hundreds of thousands of Punjabi couples have taken to family planning – why indeed fertility is declining in the Punjab. But, further to all of this, we have so far not countenanced the possibility that parents are mistaken in some aspect of these hypothetical calculations: they may over-estimate the chances of their children making a contribution – or, if they are right about that, they may over-estimate mortality and consequently the number of children needed to guarantee support in later life.

Most important of all if the 'costs' are too high, parents may not bear them: if they or their children cannot fend for themselves, it is often the children – especially as we have noted female children – who suffer. So far the analysis has concentrated on the parents acting in their own interests. But, if the main concern of parents were for the average welfare of their *children*, they would almost certainly have fewer rather than more. The landowner would have fewer sons among whom to divide his land, the poor family fewer children to feed. (Each child is likely to affect adversely the survival prospects in early years of those born shortly before it.) We have noted elsewhere the nutritional consequences of large families, and the evidence from a variety of studies that the children of large families tend to perform less well in education and other departments of life. If an additional child benefits the whole family, presumably existing children benefit too; a female child may well benefit from having a brother – we are not suggesting that *every* additional child reduces the economic welfare of those already born, rather that the fifth and sixth are likely to, if not the third and fourth as well. High fertility in circumstances of poverty displays a degree of disregard for the well-being of children: it is one of the humanising benefits of economic development that parents are able to give due weight to their children's nurture, instead of being forced, or rather feeling themselves forced, to procreate largely in their own selfish interests.

The last major point is the relations between families in the wider economy and society. If any of the arguments in Chapter 4 about the macroeconomics of population are correct, and the rapid growth of population makes it more difficult to increase the rate of growth of average incomes, then while each family is having several children in what it thinks are its own interests, it is in fact worsening the prospects not only of its own children, but of other families and of future generations.[56] Even if parents were 'courting economic disaster' for themselves by practising contraception, they are courting it for others by not doing so. Particularly when they are adding to the supply of agricultural labour, their own children make a negligible contribution to reducing the average wage; but the contribution of all families' children has a tremendous effect. (This is not a new argument; it is at least as old as 1833, and has been called the 'tragedy of the commons'.[57]) The interest of each is not the interest of all; in fact the interest of each may be quite opposed to the interest of all, or of most at any rate. Such situations have been examined in economics under the general title of the 'isolation paradox'.[58] Each individual in isolation will act to the detriment of his fellows unless he knows that his fellows will act in a manner that serves the general well-being – and even then he may not act in the public good himself. The individual may like the idea of a large family but he may have little incentive to act with self-restraint on his own, if he knows that others are not being similarly restrained – and, even if they are, he may still have a large family himself. Thus while he would prefer everyone other than himself to have small families, or, if all were required to do the same, he would prefer all having small families to all having large ones, unless everybody enforceably agrees (or is compelled) to have small families, he will have a large one – and so, if they think as he does, will everybody else. (One must add '*enforceably* agrees' since, if any agreement is unenforceable, the individual benefits, economically if not morally, from breaking it.) In the good old days of the 'invisible hand' economists enjoyed demonstrating how each individual could pursue his own selfish interests and the result would benefit one and all. The isolation paradox describes one class – there are others too – of situations in which this is not so and family formation in India is clearly among them. So, even if the country would be better off with everyone having smaller families, parents, even those who grant that this is so, will not themselves limit their fertility as long as they believe large families are valuable to them personally. Putting together the points of these last paragraphs we might say that if parents had their way, many of them would wish to limit the fertility of others and, if children had their way, many of them would wish to limit their own parents' fertility.

So much discussion of the economics of family formation may leave the reader with the impression that we believe fertility to be subject to economic determinism. We do not. The economist would only claim that the *net* effect of economic factors should be perceptible while allowing the importance of the non-economic. (The thorough-going economic determinist would assert that even the non-economic factors have their basis in economics – this too we cannot wholly believe.) This net effect is in fact very difficult to discern; there are too many other roles of children, from giving pleasure to parents and grandparents or giving status to the mother among her new relatives, to adding numerical weight to the family in factional disputes in the village. There are various hypotheses that could be tested with adequate data: that improved savings possibilities provide a substitute for the pensions motive in fertility for example. In some cases one is not even sure what to expect: if there were two groups of families with the same levels of parental income and subject to the same incidence of child mortality, but one group's children faced worse earnings prospects than the other's, would they have less children because the economic advantage is less, or more because they would 'need' more to reach a given income? Less, possibly, though it could hardly be predicted with confidence. In general parents seem to go on having children up to a certain point for all manner of economic, social and traditional reasons and leave off after that point for another complex of reasons, including an assessment of the situation they have reached, the mother's health and all the influences referred to earlier in this chapter. Fertility behaviour in India may be affected by the hope of economic advantage but to interpret it as the result of universally well-informed prior estimation of that advantage is hardly consistent with the evidence or with *a priori* analysis.

The key to any view of parents – or more particularly poor parents – as procreating for motives of economic gain is that they must be prepared for their children to suffer if times are hard and to suffer particularly if they are females. Their attitude must be one of hoping that things will turn out well and of being resigned to the consequences if they do not. They must also understandably pay little attention to the welfare of others beyond their own family or that of future generations. In this Indian parents are little different from parents anywhere else; in so far as their fertility behaviour is marked by such characteristics, it should perhaps be judged not to their detriment but as a mark of their desperation. In a society lacking in communal supportiveness, where the powerful use and perpetuate their advantages in every conceivable way, the family becomes for most people· the only source of security. It is an inefficient and in some ways a cruel one; it will continue so until an alternative appears.

The demographic transition in India

As we can see from Table 2.2 above there are States in India where even rural birth rates are quite low. These are States which are above average in India in many respects but with worse conditions than some countries where birth rates are higher. This alone suggests that birth rate reductions are possible in India without high income levels, a high degree of urbanisation, industrialisation, all the accompaniments of most of the 'transitions' in the nineteenth and early twentieth centuries. Were this not so India's case would indeed be dreadful to contemplate since it will be many decades before these aspects of development are widely shared in India, even under a radically more egalitarian and successful political system. But the transition in India does seem to depend on providing certain minimum conditions of education, health and employment for the mass of the people. In the last two chapters we discuss India's record and prospects in these and related dimensions.

Our conclusions there indicate the necessity of providing higher incomes for the deprived. But we shall end this section by noting that income by itself, like everything else, is not enough. There certainly is evidence that average rich families have fewer children than the poor,[59] but the rich are commonly also better educated, healthier and more exposed to features of the culture and of communications which promote fertility decline. Where incomes rise without bringing changes in attitudes and objectives there may be no negative effect on fertility – not initially at any event. One study, admittedly based on limited data, has suggested that when incomes rise among occupational groups such as truck-drivers, masons, mechanics, factory workers and so forth, because they are concerned to raise their status among their caste and community peers – rather than, as with many middle class groups, their status in the society at large – they will continue to have big families and indulge a taste for such ostentatious expenditure as their means permit. Only changing aspirations and opportunities – especially for women – in the company of material improvement will alter attitudes to family size.[60]

The 'status of woman' question, as touched on briefly above, lies behind many of the factors affecting fertility discussed here. Whether one thinks of the age at marriage, education or indeed almost any relevant social or economic variable, one could place them all in the dimension of the role of women in Indian society. In many parts of India girls are not educated because parents do not believe it necessary if they are 'only' destined for marriage. Women commonly live in the home of the husband's family after marriage and have no status there until they have borne a son. They may have few contacts outside the home and their work may be wholly confined to household tasks and labour in the fields. Such lives are scarcely open to modernising influences. The foreigner may often be misled by the prominence of women in professional and public life into thinking that India is unusually emancipated in its treatment of women. Nothing could be further from the truth. While middle class women can reach the highest positions and often without the disabilities which women suffer in other countries, at the other end of the social scale women are as oppressed as anywhere in the world. This is not just a 'Western' view; a recent report by a governmental commission cited extensive evidence that women of all classes resented their treatment and hoped for change.[61]

The view that fertility decline depends on improvements in the status of women cannot precisely be substantiated by evidence in India or elsewhere. While quite a number of studies in other developing countries have shown that this may be the case,[62] it is possible both for status to improve and fertility remain high or for fertility to decline without change in status. Nevertheless several commentators have expressed a belief that improvements in female status may be influential for the promotion of fertility decline,[63] and logic is on their side. Some surveys show women desire smaller families than men and family planning studies have observed husbands over-ruling their wives' desire for birth control.[64] And as we have suggested many of the features of social change which are associated with declining fertility are strongly related to conceptions of women's role. We commented above on the slow progress of female education; yet there is not much point in some parts of India in calling for accelerated female education as an element of population policy. Much else will have to change, even if better facilities for girls' education are provided, before parents – especially poor parents – take advantage of them.

This serves as a valuable reminder of something which may have receded from view while we considered individual influences on fertility:

the interdependence of so many of the factors involved in fertility decline, more complex than we have been able to illuminate even in a treatment of this length. We shall have more to say on these matters when we come to examine the family planning programme. For now we shall leave the subject of the determinants of fertility on a note that anticipates later discussion: apart from the family planning programme there are forces at work in India which can lead to further fertility decline; urbanisation, mortality decline, the spread of education, increasing land shortage and the gradual undermining of traditional attitudes.[65] But these forces are operating far too slowly to produce a fundamental change in the rate of population growth in the next fifteen years, perhaps in the next thirty. This will continue to be so as long as the process of development yields so little for the great mass of the people and as long as social relations are such as to leave the family as the main institution in the competitive struggle for a better life.

MORTALITY: DISEASE AND MALNUTRITION

Just as the death of him who is born is certain; so the rebirth of him who is dead is inevitable; therefore it behoves you not to grieve over an inevitable event.
Bhagavad Gita.

In several countries of the world the 1961 round of censuses surprised demographers – and others – with higher population totals than were expected. In 1971, possibly because the experts were trying to avoid making the same mistake twice, forecasts were often higher than the censuses found; in India the main reason was the failure of mortality to decline as rapidly as had been anticipated. The common explanation of this failure is that the swift decline of mortality in the 1950s and early 1960s was due to the control of communicable diseases; towards the end of the 1960s the control programmes had either succeeded, so that further mortality decline could not be expected from them, or in one or two instances the diseases were actually on the way back. As we have seen in Chapter 1 reductions in mortality are scarcely less troublesome to explain than those in fertility. While the common explanation does appear to be convincing it would be the more so if we had a clearer idea about what has been happening to nutrition, hygiene, sanitation, water supplies and medical care which in the opinion of many are just as important as the control of individual diseases.

Even for the 1970s information about mortality in India is quite deficient. As has been noted the age data in the censuses are not sufficiently accurate to permit detailed inferences. Censuses in European countries are supplemented by the registration of births and deaths; India has a registration system but its coverage is very far from complete. This is quite understandable – the average Indian villager rarely has any need for a birth certificate or a certificate of death of a relative. As a result the registration system is resorted to largely in times of need rather than as a matter of course. There has even been legislation to make birth and death registration compulsory, but the law is so widely overlooked that the penalties are rarely if ever exacted. As long as social life does not demand frequent documentary proof of identity, this situation will continue despite considerable official efforts to improve it.

If mortality is ill-served with information, cause of death is still more so: even if all deaths were recorded, it would be too much to expect the cause of death to be accurately reported as well. Urban India is not always adequately supplied with doctors; in rural areas, where most of the population lives, there is often one doctor to tens of thousands of people and without a qualified observer the cause of death cannot be accurately established.

Nevertheless it is possible to say a good deal about mortality. There are sufficient survey data and studies of villages and urban areas to convey a reasonably clear picture of the present and of the main sources of mortality decline in the last thirty years. As with European populations the first steps are the removal of famine and epidemics and then reduction of the incidence of the major diseases; unlike much (though not all) European experience however there appears in India to be a considerable independence of mortality reduction from improvements in other aspects of the conditions of life of the ordinary man. The main sources of mortality in the past and their decline in the twentieth century will be discussed at some length, not only because they are important in themselves in relation to possible future mortality but also because doing so provides an opportunity to include descriptive material about certain aspects of India which deserve attention.

Famines

Though there were some famine deaths in the terrible successive droughts of 1966–7 the last famine which occasioned deaths on a very large scale was the severe Bengal famine of 1943 which is thought to have taken between 1.5 and 3 million lives. This appears to have been due in part to the complications of war and the (British) administration's incompetence, but little to do with crop failure. Rather, after a fairly normal crop, a combination of food hoarding and speculation led to very large increases of food prices at a time of more than usually poor employment conditions.[66] Certainly throughout the twentieth century there had been a continuous improvement in irrigation and road and rail communications and the Bengal famine was something of an anachronism. The monsoon failed in 1938 and 1939 in the Punjab, but deaths did not occur on such a scale. Indeed one has probably to go back to the turn of the century for comparable disasters.

The decade of 1891 – 1901, for example, was distinguished by the occurrence of terrible famines in its closing years. Despite the intial outbreak of plague in the decade, deaths from epidemic disease seem to have been, if anything, fewer than usual, and no other causes of death stand out as of peculiar importance. The fact that the population grew only one per cent during this decade is therefore attributable to the occurrence of famines. How much might the population have grown otherwise? Well, in the previous decade it grew 9.4 per cent, and in the following decade 6.1 per cent. If the 1891 – 1901 decade had experienced the average rate of growth shown by these two decades, it would have grown by 7.8 per cent instead of one per cent. The difference is a matter of some 19 million persons, which may be taken as a rough estimate of loss due to famines.

It should be borne in mind, however, that relief measures were functioning at this time and that this saved the lives of millions of persons who otherwise would have died. 'In ancient times the occurrence of a severe famine was marked by the disappearance of a third or a fourth of the population of the area afflicted.' By the decade under consideration the relief measures had reached the point not of nullifying the effects of famine, but of greatly reducing the mortality resulting from it. After the turn of the century both relief and preventive measures became more effective.[67]

By 1966 – 7 they had become so effective that one of the most severe crop failures in recent history passed off – one can by no means say without suffering but at least with a very small number of starvation deaths even in Bihar, one of the worst hit States, and among the very poorest regions of India at the best of times. When the second drought struck in Eastern India while food stocks were already depleted from the first one, it was feared that a tragedy involving millions of deaths was on hand. In the end starvation deaths were numbered at most in thousands, epidemics were contained and the episode demonstrated the capacity of the Indian bureaucracy, given strong leadership and reasonably adequate resources, to cope with the most appalling circumstances. The relief operation required the transport and distribution not only of 20 million tons of food, but of water to thousands of villages and the establishment of at least temporary economic rehabilitation programmes for millions of people whose livelihood had been wiped out. The lessons of 1967 proved to have been well learned in 1971 when the Government of India coped with notable success with the vast influx of refugees in Bengal – in many ways an even more difficult situation than 1967, and also in the appalling droughts in Maharashtra in 1972 and 1973. These three episodes give one to believe that famine deaths in millions are a thing of the past unless, owing to unprecedented calamity, a food shortage were to arise of such dimensions that massive imports of food were required and these were not available.

Such a view of course also depends on the long run average balance between the food supply and the growing population. This will be discussed below in Chapter 4. The abolition of famine – if it has been abolished – still leaves the problem of malnutrition which is examined in this Chapter.

Plague

The first severe outbreak of the plague in the last century occurred in Bombay in 1896. From Bombay it spread rapidly and became endemic in the Punjab, Mysore and Madras provinces. The worst year in India was 1904–5 when there were 1.3 million recorded deaths. It declined thereafter and remained relatively quiescent then until 1922 and, after brief spasms in 1923 and 1924, gradually faded away. The worst affected area was the Punjab where over 2 million plague deaths were reported between 1901 and 1911.[68] But hardly anywhere in India did the plague reach the calamitous intensities experienced in fourteenth or seventeenth century Europe. The worst year in any province was the Punjab in 1906 – 7 when there were over 650,000 plague deaths or 27 per 1000.[69] In Calcutta, where one might have thought conditions ripe for the plague, deaths from it were of the order of 1000 – 3000 a year during the period in question. Grain transport, which often transmitted the disease in other countries, did not spread it in India much beyond the areas mentioned. There were no cases in Madras city in 1905 although the plague was to be found in nearby rural areas.

Once again there is a rat-based theory of the disease in India namely that Indian rats typically harboured *X. astia* rather than the more dangerous *X. cheopis* especially in Southern and Eastern India. Undoubtedly the effect of the climate on rat and flea populations was significant. Another frequently alleged feature is that the plague *bacillus* was so virulent when it was at work that it killed off rats as well as humans and therefore did not last long – this may have been the case in the Punjab.[70]

However if the further factor of human-borne carriers is important (as suggested in Chapter 1 above), this would fit in well with observations of India. In the centuries when the plague was rife the average European, not greatly given to washing, was commonly verminous and flea-ridden. Although India does not display a very high standard of environmental hygiene the average Indian is given to habits of personal cleanliness. Gandhi was shocked during his stay in England by the infrequency with which the British took baths; he was probably less exceptional among his countrymen in this than in most of his other attributes and he would probably still be moderately shocked today. The poorest workman washing himself under a tap is a common sight in India. The quality of the water-supply available to the average man may nowadays render his efforts somewhat vain, but certainly it is entirely plausible to suggest that the human flea has been far less common in India during the past hundred years than it was in seventeenth century Europe. Indeed Parkinson, in a not particularly frivolous moment, has suggested with some evidence that such habits of personal cleanliness as the British acquired in earlier times they brought home from India.[71] That pre-industrial European man was a rather unsavoury creature has been documented by McLaughlin.[72]

This relative freedom from human fleas may help to explain the general relatively low incidence of plague deaths in India even when the plague was about. Its virtual disappearance since 1924 has been attributed to changes in the rat population, improved sanitation and housing, acquired immunity in the rat population and the effect on fleas of the malaria spraying of DDT which began in Bombay in 1946 and was nationwide by 1953.[73] The true situation is in fact exceedingly complex. Thus it is known that *X. cheopis* will soon cease to transmit plague at temperatures higher than 26°C since the plague *bacillus* is then rapidly eliminated from the flea's alimentary tract.[74] There are also climatic variations influencing the life cycles of fleas common to India. But the geography of plague does not follow any obvious climatic or other patterns – no doubt because micro-climatic variations are as important as the broader features of temperature and humidity[75] – the temperature, humidity and liability to flooding of rat burrows for example.

Researchers have generally found *X. astia* or *X. brasiliensis* to be more common in most parts of the country since 1960 but recent studies have turned up high concentrations of *X. cheopis* in Poona for example or parts of Mysore and Tamil Nadu.[76] In the Mysore District studied *X. cheopis* prevailed in domestic rodents and *X. astia* in wild rodents. But in those cities where *X. cheopis* is found the rats are commonly immune as a result of previous infections. Generally speaking *X. astia* flourishes in warm and humid climates and is intolerant of low temperatures, *X. brasiliensis* favours temperate regions; high temperatures and low humidity are unfavourable to these and *X. cheopis*. Nevertheless the vectors are found in areas of generally unsuitable climate; when this is so the explanation is commonly in terms of the type of settlement and differential rat prevalence. It is possible that what importantly arrived in Bombay in 1896 was not so much the plague pathogen as *X. cheopis* which spread to the focal areas and then gradually was replaced by his more congenial predecessors – the nature of pre- and post-1896 outbreaks supports such a view, conjectural though it is. Until the late 1950s, *X. cheopis* was still the most prevalent rat flea in India.[77]

It is only to be expected that a disease which can be spread by a variety of fleas and a variety of rats, or even without rats during intense outbreaks, and which can remain latent for long periods in its non-human hosts will not behave with discernible uniformity in the Indian sub-continent. Fortunately there is one significant uniformity today and that is its rarity. Actual deaths from the plague are now likely to be extremely few in number, other than in remote areas, since plague is curable by sulpha drugs and antibiotics – indeed, by the early 1960s, deaths were occurring only in ones and twos – even if the endemic areas of Mysore and Tamil Nadu[78] and none has been recorded thereafter. Since rats, fleas and *Y. pestis* are still to be found in India it is just possible that new, resistant forms of the flea or the *bacillus* could bring back the disease on a dangerous scale. But given both the vigilance of the health authorities and the practicability of cure when cases occur it would appear that plague in India has been laid to rest.[79]

Cholera

Like plague cholera can be a frightening disease, spreading rapidly and killing profusely. Unlike plague cholera through much of history has been regarded as having its home in India and particularly the Bengal delta. *Vibrio cholerae* is one of a number of water bacteria called *vibrios* because of their 'darting movements, propelled by a single *flagellum*'.[80] It is transimitted usually in food or water, through contact with faecal material from infected persons. People can carry the organism without any other manifest symptoms of the disease so that they can spread it without suffering from it. This both makes it difficult to eradicate and may partially explain the observed cyclicity of outbreaks in endemic areas – it can lie dormant in the human carrier for a month or more.

The life-cycle of *v. cholerae* explains its persistence in India where food handling outside the home or the better hotels and restaurants is without elementary precautions, regulation or inspection; where water supplies – particularly in rural areas – are unprotected, if periodically chlorinated, and defecation commonly takes place on the soil through which the water percolates; and where lake and riverside populations in no way protect the water courses in which they wash and from which they take water for drinking. These conditions provide favourable ground for the transmission of many diseases besides cholera. The success of public health measures in restraining cholera in such conditions is remarkable.

In twentieth century India cholera has been a major endemic source of mortality in some areas and continues to threaten epidemic danger. It did not reach the level of plague mortality at the latter's height. (In 1907 plague accounted for over 500 deaths per 100,000 population and 14 per cent of all deaths. 1900, the worst cholera year, reached in the region of 360 deaths per 100,000 and 10 per cent of all deaths. But after 1925, when plague deaths were relatively insignificant, cholera in certain years passed 100 per 100,000 people, and 5 per cent of all deaths.[81]) But even today it can kill thousands when floods or famines occur. A major historical focus of epidemics were the great religious fairs of India, where as many as 5 million people might congregate to bathe in some sacred place – the *Kumbh Mela* of Allahabad is one such occasion. Health measures at melas are now strict and cholera inoculation has usually been compulsory since 1954 so that these phenomenal gatherings are no longer a dangerous cholera hazard.[82]

In 1966 and 1967 cholera accounted for only 0.4 per cent of all deaths, if the data of the Model Registration Survey are to be trusted (see below).[83] This same source gives plague deaths at rather less than one tenth of one per cent in 1966 and the 1967 rate one quarter of that. But, unlike plague, cholera must be considered an ever present danger. *V. cholerae* may be carried for more than twelve months by healthy carriers with mild diarrhoea – an epidemic can occur without new importation.[84] It can be cured when it strikes provided antibiotics and intravenous drips are made available. It is possible that a simple pill will be developed to cure the disease at its onset now that the physiology of the rapid fluid-depletion induced by cholera is understood.[85] But as long as insanitary water supplies and food handling continue in India – and that is likely to be for many years – cholera will not disappear and, when the cure does not materialise quickly, it will cause deaths. But epidemics, once identified as such, can be cut short and are unlikely to recur on the scale of earlier years.

Smallpox

On an India-wide basis smallpox has not been a major killer in the twentieth century. It is an old disease in India and in the nineteenth century was responsible for very large numbers of deaths – in the 1880s it killed more than 75 per 100,000 population and only 27 people in every thousand were vaccinated. The disease declined until recently, except for a resurgence in 1944–5 to the levels of the 1890s (despite a continuous increase in vaccinations). The fact that smallpox in 1967 still accounted for approximately one per cent of all deaths[86] testified to the difficulty of ensuring universal vaccination – though this was of course one per cent of a much lower overall death rate. If the overall death rate of 1971 was 16 per 1000, one per cent of that represents 16 deaths per 100,000 population. The final elimination of smallpox was once considered difficult to achieve in India but now appears to be in prospect, if not already achieved. There used to be an important smallpox goddess who required propitiation. The Khanna Study[87] has a photograph of one of her shrines crumbling in disuse outside a Punjab village.

There was a disquieting episode in the early 1970s when smallpox reappeared in Eastern India most probably as a consequence of the tremendous refugee movements during and after the Bangladesh War. In 1973 smallpox cases in India were up to six figures with about three-quarters of the cases reported in Bihar. Smallpox deaths probably exceeded 15,000. This represented some laxity in reporting procedures since epidemics are supposed to be declared when smallpox deaths exceed specified levels and this did not happen. Indeed the extent of the outbreak in Bihar was only discovered by a search instituted during a new campaign against the disease; the local administrations, not wonderful at their best, were in disarray due to political instability.[88] But even in Calcutta political considerations appear to have muffled the medical authorities' disquiet and kept it hidden. However in 1975 the W.H.O. was still maintaining its ambition of removing the last traces of the disease from the world in a fairly short time. This is now hoped for. In September 1975 it was reported that there had been no cases of smallpox in India during the year. A reward of Rs. 1000 was offered to anyone who reported a case, but no one had claimed it.[89]

Malaria
Another major disease for which the picture has changed radically since Kingsley Davis wrote in 1951 is malaria. It was still killing nearly 500 per 100,000 population and he quoted an estimate that as many as 100 million people might suffer from the disease each year. DDT only became available in 1945 but its effectiveness had been demonstrated and so he wrote: 'It seems within reason, therefore, to think that by a combination of cheap and powerful insecticides and drugs, India and Pakistan will eventually solve their malaria problem. Complete elimination by whole-sale spraying of outdoor breeding grounds . . . does not at present look feasible for a whole sub-continent; but even without this it appears that rigid control is possible.'

In fact Davis was wrong only in under-estimating the distance India would go towards complete elimination. Statistics for malaria are less reliable than those for plague, cholera or smallpox as there are more diseases with similar manifest symptoms; and while records were often kept for those three great scourges, record-keepers uncertain of the cause of death would commonly write down simply 'fever', a category within which malaria often disappears. Nevertheless the surveys for 1966 and 1967 to which we have referred give deaths specifically attributed to malaria in those years at less than a fifth and about a half of one per cent of all deaths respectively. Whatever the validity of these estimates, we do know that malaria deaths were down to very low levels by the mid 1960s. Indeed it was thought that complete eradication was not far off.

The control of malaria is of exceptional importance to the general behaviour of mortality in a country where it is endemic. The death rate will decline when malaria is reduced not only because malaria is lethal but because those whom it does not kill it leaves debilitated and a prey to other forms of death. The argument is sometimes heard in demography that a given cause of death, when eliminated, may not be the explanation of an observed reduction in mortality as those who die of it would have died of something else – such an argument (implausibly in the present writer's view) is directed against those who claim that the control of smallpox in the early 1800s accounted for an important share in the decline of English mortality at the time. There are of course what are known medically as competing risks – classes of people may be subject to one or other of a group of illnesses all of which flourish in similar conditions. But ordinarily, although obviously *some* of those who die of a particular cause would have died anyway, the elimination of a major lethal disease with a distinctive epidemiology must usually be credited with reductions of mortality. In the case of malaria this is doubly true: in Ceylon for instance prior to the introduction of DDT spraying the prevalence of malaria was significantly correlated with all the principal lethal diseases except typhoid and paratyphoid and infant deaths from gastric disorders; there was an 'especially strong relation with nephritis' – malaria affects the kidneys particularly.[90]

Ceylon is in fact a test case for this general argument. The contrary view to that just stated would hold that, when malnutrition is rife and general sanitary conditions are poor, most causes of death are competing risks. Thus in the 1940s and after Ceylon's death rate underwent a spectacular decline of which Newman[91] attributed a large share to malaria eradication. This was challenged by Frederiksen,[92] who claimed that the trends in mortality after DDT spraying was introduced were not dissimilar to those prevailing earlier and that the improvements in mortality could be explained by increased supplies of food. Newman[93] finally demonstrated beyond reasonable doubt that malaria eradication *did* account for a large proportion of mortality decline; though not perhaps as much as he claimed – 42 per cent of the decline which occurred between 1930 and 1945 and 1946 and 1960; as he admits the impact of malaria eradication on the death rate was over by 1949. This famous controversy has swung convincingly in favour of Newman's general position since the publication of Dr. R. H. Gray's analysis, which attributed about 23 per cent of Ceylon's post-war mortality decline specifically to malaria control.[94] In general it is now accepted by demographers that death rates in today's developing countries can be brought down by public health measures with considerable – though not total – independence from other improvements in living conditions. Whether this was to any extent the case in nineteenth century Europe is as we have seen rather more uncertain.[95]

The reason for the relationships between malaria and other health problems lies in the characteristic pattern of the disease: 'The initial attack generally takes the form of an acute febrile illness, but among those long resident in a malarious area the typical state is a chronic one, characterised by intermittent and remittent bouts of fever, an enlarged spleen, anaemia and often weakness, malnutrition, lethargy and irritability'.[96] In India in 1939, at a time when the average annual death rate was of the order of 31 or 32 per thousand people, malaria deaths were at the rate of about 5 per thousand. Today's overall death rates are in the range of 16–17; a substantial share of the decline in mortality since World War II must thus be attributed to malaria control which saved millions of lives, not only from malaria, but also from the diseases which afflicted those whose defences malaria had lowered.

The battle with malaria in India is unfortunately not yet won. Total eradication in India will always prove difficult as mosquitoes can breed anywhere where there is stagnant water, and DDT resistant mosquitoes are increasingly to be found. The disease requires, besides the vector, a number of infected people who carry *Plasmodium* in the blood, and a population of susceptible people. Although today people can be cured or made more or less immune to malaria by drugs, to achieve this for the entire population is obviously a lengthy job. Nevertheless substantial progress has been made. By 1958 several endemic areas had been cleared[97] and the success of the malaria organisation was demonstrated. By 1961 malaria units were in operation virtually throughout the country. The programme faltered in 1963–4 perhaps due to excessive optimism regarding the results achieved. One wonders whether it is significant that the *Indian Journal of Malariology* ceased publication after 1963. The incidence of malaria was decreasing up to that year but appeared (as measured by blood tests) to have returned to 1961 levels by 1966[98] – though of course these levels were far lower than before the start of the campaign.

The self-explanatory World Health Organisation terminology for anti-malaria operations describes the eradication units as being in the phases of 'attack', 'consolidation' and 'maintenance'. After 1963 there were criticisms of imprudent economies[99] and administrative shortcomings.[100] In the Punjab and Haryana for example 1965 was the lowest year ever for malaria prevalence but there was a rapid increase in cases from 1966–70. To some extent this may have been due to a loss of acquired immunity, but blame must also attach to reduced effectiveness in the control programme.[101] An outbreak of malaria in 1968–9 in Tumkur District, Mysore after eight years of the maintenance phase underlines the same point. Since the outbreak was rapidly restricted by insecticide spraying and treatment it was not attributable to resistant strains of mosquitoes.[102] Such examples are fairly numerous. They bear witness to the troubles of the anti-malaria campaign – though one should not forget the extent to which they also bear witness to the technical difficulties of the last stages of eradication and of the maintenance of 'maintenance'. It must be said though that these difficulties were multiplied by the setbacks of the mid 1960s.

By April 1969 only 220 out of 400 malaria control units were in the maintenance phase; a further ten units moved into that phase in 1970. This represented only a modest improvement in five years over the situation in 1966 when more than half the population was already covered by units in the maintenance phase. By 1972 large areas had reverted to the attack phase; in most of them the common vector, *A. culicifacies*, had become resistant to DDT and malathion had to be used instead.[103] Reports have also come in of malaria cases, both *falciparum* and *vivax*, resistant to treatment by the commonly used drugs such as chloroquine.[104] In 1971 1.3 million and in 1972 1.2 million cases of malaria were identified by laboratory test suggesting that the actual incidence was even greater.[105]

The number of reported cases rose to several millions by the mid 1970s (4.2 million in 1975), but malaria mortality did not appear to be great.

It is interesting to compare India's recent experience of malaria with that of other countries; there are remarkable similarities. The tendency to slacken 'maintenance', reduce funds and relax administration generally has been very common. DDT resistant vectors have also been common. The returning malaria being predominantly *vivax* rather than *falciparum* also seems to be part of the pattern; *vivax* being the milder strain the case fatality rates are usually low.[106] No doubt many of the better 'malaria men', thinking the disease was disappearing in the 1960s, began to seek alternative careers. Finally many of the areas where control has not yet been achieved are difficult terrain or border districts where eradication presents special problems. And wherever internal migration takes place on a large scale, as in India, it too will hamper the control programme since the reduction of infection is made much harder. In 1973 the target date for transferring all units in India to maintenance was 1976. But medical opinion is now dubious that the target can be reached by the early 1980s. Malaria has certainly come back to India in quite a big way. It may however prove only a temporary setback and does not as yet threaten a major increase in mortality.

Tuberculosis

Tuberculosis probably causes more deaths in India today than any single specific disease. Kingsley Davis described it as second in lethality only to malaria which has, as we have noted, declined rapidly since he wrote. On general principles one would expect tuberculosis to be seriously entrenched in India – low levels of nutrition, high densities of housing and patterns of migration which favour the spread of the disease. In the late nineteenth century the disease was comparatively rare in rural areas though established in the cities. Dr. Arthur Lankester, who conducted a tuberculosis survey in India between 1914 and 1916, found that prevalence had increased in the larger cities in the previous forty years and that the disease had gained ground in smaller towns and villages connected to them by rail and main roads. The rural population had little immunity and, where the disease struck, mortality was high.[107]

Today tuberculosis has been diffused more comprehensively. A sample survey conducted between 1955 and 1958 found rural morbidity only slightly below urban.[108] In urban or rural areas it is, as might be expected, highest among the poorer sections. The migration pattern has done its work. As we shall see from the discussion of migration below it is a common practice for males to leave their villages in search of employment in towns and cities and to return to the village periodically; they have a particular habit of returning home when ill. The overall result is a very heavy incidence of the disease; for various reasons tuberculosis is even less likely to be correctly identified as the cause of death than the other diseases – it was nevertheless found to account for about 7 per cent and 6 per cent of all deaths in 1966 and 1967 respectively in the survey already referred to[109] and this may well be an under-estimate.

If the 'wave theory' of tuberculosis referred to in Chapter 1 has any validity, we can identify India as having passed the mortality critical point and the epidemiological critical point. But the state of information is insufficient for further assessment. It is doubtful that the stage of widespread immunity has been reached. As with tuberculosis and mortality generally in the developed countries there is a disagreement in the literature about the relative importance of malnutrition and lack of immunity in the susceptibility of the people of India to tuberculosis. The new programme of domiciliary treatment is having some success in reducing deaths among tuberculosis sufferers. But in so far as the fundamental circumstances in which the disease flourishes are unlikely to improve rapidly it will not disappear. In fact any extent to which it does diminish will probably be an argument for the immunity-and-treatment school against those who believe in the greater importance of improvements in living conditions.

The difficulties of conducting a tuberculosis campaign in India are formidable. In his pioneering research Wallace Fox demonstrated that bad living conditions are not necessarily an obstacle to *curing* the disease: he treated two samples of acute cases with the same chemotherapy, one group in a sanatorium with well-regulated diets and hygienic conditions, the other in their homes in the poorest parts of Madras city with no diet supplement or other interventions. The treatment was highly successful – and the response rates to the chemotherapy almost identical in the two groups.[110] As a result of this work tuberculosis sanatoria have ceased to be a major part of health programmes in India and elsewhere. But there is one major difficulty of treatment programmes in poor conditions and that is ensuring the continuation of treatment: current drugs require a six-month course of chemotherapy but the patient often feels that he has been cured before he actually has been and is very likely to discontinue the course unless he is supervised strictly. Since the incompletely cured can still spread the disease – and indeed, if they believe themselves cured, may be more likely to spread it than those who know they are not – incomplete curative programmes may be positively harmful.

Preventive programmes also have their difficulties: there are problems in ensuring that adequate numbers of people are vaccinated. And the evidence does not show all that high a degree of effectiveness of the vaccine. Tuberculosis *bacilli* are more common than the disease: far more people are infected with the organism than have the disease and what will contribute to progress towards active disease or resistance to it is not entirely clear. Other *bacilli* may give protection against tuberculosis – in parts of South India its relatively low incidence may partly be explained by this; and in parts of India the *bacillus* itself appears to be less virulent than in Europe.

In Europe the diminishing spread of the disease – in the sense that every 100 cases identified generated less than 100 new cases – was observed by 1910 and it is believed that improvements in living conditions were what tipped the balance. Poor diet and housing provide the *milieu* in which tuberculosis flourishes; given the painful slowness with which the material life of most Indians improves and given also the difficulties of both prevention and cure – difficulties which are a function of socio-economic organisation – mortality from the disease is unlikely to release its hold in India with any speed. The latest data known to the author suggest no change in incidence in the fifteen years from 1958 to 1973.[111] The movement towards better provision of primary health care which we discuss in Chapter 3 is the one thing that could make a big difference. It is claimed that most tuberculosis sufferers spontaneously present themselves with the disease at dispensaries and health centres but are treated (if at all) for simple coughs. If health workers at these levels were trained to test for the disease, they could at least dispense appropriate chemotherapy: if they were able to maintain contact with the patients, they might even persuade them to continue with the treatment for a sufficient time.[112]

Nutrition and malnutrition

It seems clear that a substantial part of post-Independence mortality decline up to the mid 1960s was due to the more or less successful control of malaria and cholera, but one must also doubt whether these items alone can account for the whole of the decline. It is however extremely difficult to account for the remainder of it. Most students of demographic history find it difficult to attribute mortality decline in conditions of widespread poverty merely to reasons of control of individual diseases. But there is little reliable evidence concerning other factors. The known government-funded improvements in village water supplies have been very limited – though unrecorded improvements from tube-well sources may be more widespread. The trend in quantity and quality of urban water-supply is also hard to document though no doubt purification has made considerable progress. But there is some question about the efficacy of improved water-supply in the absence of other changes.[113] We know little about trends in sanitation and hygiene in village or city though clearly not all the efforts at introduction of better methods have been in vain. The progress of education must also have made its contribution to teaching personal hygiene and nutritional efficiency in food purchasing and preparation. What would best help us to understand changes in mortality is some knowledge of the trends in nutrition.

Unfortunately, although we can make some inferences about the current nutritional situation, there is nothing like a time series of information adequate to assess the change in nutritional level over the last thirty years. The one place from which we are not likely to get help is the figures for average availability of food. A careful study by Blyn has suggested that between 1891 and 1947 the per capita availability of foodgrains declined.[114] But the death rate was declining in the pre-Independence period also when there were even fewer public health measures in evidence. Even if the average availability was declining, its distribution over time and space was improving as has already been suggested. And the figures in Blyn's study are not above suspicion: one author has examined the foodgrains figures in the Punjab in some detail and concluded that the errors in Blyn's estimates are likely to be very large indeed.[115] For the 1925–47 period it appears that we must believe in an improvement in the distribution of food and the diminution of previously epidemic diseases – influenza, plague – as the main sources of mortality decline.[116]

There is no obvious trend in availability of foodgrains on an average basis for the post-Independence period. (For a discussion see Chapter 4, pp 256ff.) After a poor start the 1950s and early 1960s were an improvement on the 1940s–in the 12 years between 1953/4 and 1964/5 there was only one when per capita food production fell below 170 kg per head. But, in the decade which followed, there were at least four such years (figures for the end of the period are as yet uncertain). We know little however about the *distribution* of food during the whole post-Independence era. The earlier period had greater stability in food prices so that the distribution of food may have been more even prior to the mid 1960s. This would be consistent with our estimate that gains in expectation of life at birth were relatively modest in the decade 1961–71 – as they were also in 1941–51 though greater in 1951–61. However, given the doubts attaching to the figures for average food availability and its distribution and for the level of mortality and the timing and magnitude of its changes and also the differential movements in all the variables in different parts of the country, there is little point in attempting to account in this way for mortality decline on an India-wide basis. We have besides even less quantitative data for the impact on mortality of factors other than the food supply. It is even doubtful that one would have much success in trying to explain mortality decline on this basis for areas more limited than the country as a whole.

In what follows we concentrate on the present nutritional situation in India. While confident statements are often published to the effect that twenty, thirty or even higher percentages of the population are suffering from malnutrition, the truth is more awkward: there is much evidence of widespread malnutrition but its extent cannot be measured on a national basis given current knowledge and techniques. There are three fundamental methods of measuring the extent of malnutrition: (1) by observing the prevalence of clinical signs of malnutrition; (2) by anthropometric measurement; and (3) by assessing food intake in relation to nutritional norms. Of the first of these the main source of unreliability is that estimates will vary widely from one clinician to another. Anthropometric measurement, though possessing its own problems, is beginning to be considered the most reliable method but is not yet systematically or widely carried out in India. Most published estimates of malnutrition in India are based on intake assessment and are subject to extremely wide margins of error.

Clinical signs

Examples of the first method were the Gurgaon (Haryana) study of 1966–8 and one in rural areas near Hyderabad at about the same time. The former[117] showed 1.7 per cent of pre-school children exhibiting 'frank marasmus', 4·6 per cent 'mild to severe' muscle-wasting, 4·1 per cent vitamin A deficiency. The Hyderabad survey[118] showed only 0.6 per cent exhibiting kwashiorkor but 40 per cent showed 'some sign of malnutrition', i.e. one or another of some 20 clinical conditions of varying severity. Gurgaon is a fairly well-off district by Indian standards but the survey was conducted in and just after the drought years of the mid 60s; income distribution in the survey seems to have been about average. The Hyderabad study was (deliberately) biased towards poorer families – 50 per cent of the sample were landless labourers. There are several further studies of this type;[119] they all have fairly similar results but it is not clear how representative they are or, even if they are representative, how accurate are their findings. Their two fairly common features worth noting are, firstly that malnutrition is much more prevalent among female than male children (bearing out the facts about female mortality observed above) and in higher compared with lower birth orders. Indeed Gopalan (1969) found in one study that while children born fourth and later constituted 32 per cent of his sample, 62 per cent of those with nutritional deficiencies came from them: malnutrition was almost twice as common among the later as among the earlier birth orders. Secondly the percentages showing the most severe forms of malnutrition, such as kwashiorkor or marasmus, are almost always rather small. The most comprehensive recent study, the I.C.M.R.'s *Studies on Pre-school Children*, observes rates mostly in the range of 1–4 per cent at any age (except for marasmus between ages 12–18 months, where rates in three of the six studies were above 5 per cent). This is partly because the acute states of malnutrition are in any case relatively rare and partly because mortality is so high among the sufferers that only relatively small numbers will be found alive at the point of time of the survey.[120] Some participants in this I.C.M.R. study believe that one of its findings – that 40 per cent of pre-school children exhibit some sign or other, more or less severe, of malnutrition – may be of general validity for middle and low income families.[121]

Anthropometric measures

Examples of estimates based on anthropometric measures also exist but again not on any all-India basis. Thus the Punjab Nutrition Development Project (P.N.D.P.)[122] found 8·39 per cent of infants (6–12 months), 10·97 per cent of 'toddlers' (13–24 months) and 5·45 per cent of pre-school children (2–6 years) to be in the category 'severely malnourished'. Their procedure was to define reference weights from a sample of 'well-nourished' children from better-off families. ('Severe malnutrition' was less than 60 per cent of the reference weight.) The complete findings were as follows:

TABLE 2.5

| | Per cent of reference weight for age | Per cent of age groups Age in months | | |
		6–12	13–24	25–72
Severe malnutrition	< 60	8·39	10·97	5·45
Moderate	60–70	21·01	27·37	24·75
Mild	70–80	27·46	34·98	38·38
Normal	80	43·13	26·68	31·43
		100	100	100

SOURCE P.N.D.P. (1974).

The breakdown of these figures by sex is revealing: in virtually all the classifications of malnutrition females exceed males. Among the 'severely malnourished' infants the female percentage is 8 times that of the male; among toddlers almost 100 per cent more and over 50 per cent more in the pre-school age group. Just as malnutrition in general drops off with age so does the male-female differential. (Only in the pre-school, 'mild malnutrition' group do females have a lower representation than males and then only minutely lower.)

The difficulty of interpreting such figures is that very little is known about the significance of the criterion employed. The P.N.D.P. improved on other studies which employ the common 'Harvard Standards', a set of weight, height and age tables derived from an American population in that they tried to use healthy children from the study area as a reference. But little is known about the *consequences* of a child being at a given percentage of the reference weight. Very few studies have been done anywhere in the world, let alone in India, following up children whose anthropometric data have been recorded to examine their subsequent health experience. In other words while the range 'less than 60 per cent' is labelled 'severe malnutrition' and that between 60–70 per cent 'moderate malnutrition' nothing is known of the relative health risks of belonging to these as opposed to other categories.

There are of course a large number of studies of the consequences of malnutrition at early ages.[123] But these are almost all based on follow-up studies of small numbers of acutely malnourished children, i.e. suffering from kwashiorkor or marasmus or with extreme low weight or height (etc.)

measurements who are then compared with healthy children. The health significance of a child being at other points in the measurement range is obscure. This is not a deficiency of nutrition studies in India in particular but rather of the present state of work on nutrition in the world at large. A rare exception is a study carried out in Bangladesh fairly recently, which took height and arm circumference measurements on nearly 9000 children and conducted a subsequent mortality survey on the same children two years later: this is one of extremely few studies which attempt to develop anthropometric measurement as a device for predicting future health experience.[124] It was shown that children within certain ranges had much higher risk of mortality than others. Much remains to be done to develop for each country the particular anthropometric measure which is sensitive to its nutritional conditions and which is also inexpensive and easy to use. Until this is done the value of anthropometric data will remain limited.[125]

There has only been one attempt at assembling a set of anthropometric data for India as a whole, published by the I.C.M.R.in 1972.[126] Over 125,000 children were examined. The sample frame, and the nature of the socio-economic groups into which the data are classified, are not stated. Another survey provided data on 9000 well-to-do children from 14 public schools.[127] The difference between rich and poor comes out clearly, the fiftieth percentile of the 'low income' groups in the former study corresponded to the fifth percentile in the latter and only the ninety-fifth percentile of the low income children reached the fiftieth percentile of the well-to-do. But without the further analysis described in the previous paragraph it is not really possible to use the data for a meaningful assessment of the extent of malnutrition. While it is clear that children with extremely low weight or height for age, or weight for height, are malnourished, there is some shortfall from the reference heights or weights which represents smallness of stature that may be perfectly healthy rather than a dangerous condition of retarded growth. On the basis of present knowledge the boundaries between these states are indeterminate.

Food intake

Finally there are the food-intake measures. They take on particular importance in India as the cost of the 'minimum adequate diet' is often used in the determination of a 'poverty line' and hence has played a major part in the whole discussion of poverty. As with anthropometric measurement problems arise both concerning the quality of the data on intakes and their assessment against standards of desirable consumption. Three important points stand out: firstly whenever both anthropometric and intake measurements are made the results do not correspond. Secondly the data on intakes are often defective, and thirdly the standard by which they are usually assessed is not, and cannot be, a unique and objective test of nutritional adequacy.

On the first point two cases may be cited as examples. The following table is from the Punjab study just referred to:

TABLE 2.6 Intake of calories as per cent of I.C.M.R. recommended allowances:

Per cent of rec. allowance	*Age in months*			*Pregnant mothers*	*Lactating mothers*
	6 – 12	*13 – 24*	*25 – 72*		
50	42·82	35·33	17·56	18·64	15·17
51 – 75	36·61	29·22	30·82	39·43	45·84
76 – 99	11·52	19·60	23·89	28·33	28·12
100	9·02	15·83	27·70	13·58	10·85

SOURCE P.N.D.P. (1974).
(For I.C.M.R. Allowances: I.C.M.R. (1968).)

As can be seen comparison of the intake and the weight tables suggests something is odd about the measurements or standards employed since, in each child age group, the proportion with less than 50 per cent of the recommended dietary allowance is three or more times the proportion at less than 60 per cent of the reference weight. It is a common feature of such studies however that it is hard to match intake and weight data where both are collected. Clearly a child less than 60 per cent of the weight of a healthy child may lack an adequate diet; but whether or not the I.C.M.R. recommended dietary allowances are on the generous side (as is discussed below) they appear from this study to be more than is required to reach the reference weights employed. The same problem arose in the Morinda study[128] where children meeting over 90 per cent of reference weight for age received only 65 per cent of the I.C.M.R. recommended calories. The author of that study speculated – without conclusions – whether caloric intakes were underestimated (especially for breast milk), the allowances were too generous or children compensated for low intake by reduced energy expenditure without foregoing weight gain. As we have observed if malnourished means 'failing to reach a reference weight or caloric intake', such tables as the above indicate malnutrition. But the precise implications of failing to meet these standards are unclear.

The general quality of intake data for India is extremely variable. Attempts have been made to base estimates of the extent of malnutrition on National Sample Survey household food consumption data. These are of uncertain reliability. A recent study suggests that in at least one State (Kerala) the N.S.S. may have under-estimated per capita caloric intake for the state as a whole by more than 40 per cent.[129] The measurement problem in Kerala seems peculiarly acute and estimates for other States are possibly less unreliable. However even if the household data are not too inaccurate, what counts for measuring malnutrition is the distribution within the household which the N.S.S. does not supply. Statistical techniques have been used for getting round this problem; they do not however go further than suggesting by assumption some lower limit to the number who must be deficient in calories – about 25 per cent of the population according to some studies.[130] Actual intake surveys have also been conducted, by questionnaire or by direct weighing of food prior to consumption, but these are generally for small samples whose representativeness is not known. Once again the only relatively systematic data collection (apart from the N.S.S.) is that provided by the I.C.M.R.'s *Studies on Pre-school Children* already cited. The publication gives mostly average figures which are of little interest; but from a diagram on the Hyderabad (low income, rural) study it can be seen that the lowest quintile receives between 40 per cent and 55 per cent of the I.C.M.R. recommended allowances for calories, the second quintile from 55–67 per cent, the next two quintiles between 67 per cent 85 per cent. Only the highest 7 per cent or so receive 100 per cent or more of the allowance. There is little reliable data with anything resembling national coverage for people above the age of 5, but aggregate data on food supplies and income distribution, together with N.S.S. data on food expenditure, suggest that the proportion of the school-age and adult population well below the I.C.M.R. recommended allowances is substantial.

Unfortunately, as with the anthropometric standards, the significance of departures from the I.C.M.R. intake recommendations is obscure, especially in the middle ranges of deficiency. The laying down of definitions of dietary adequacy has a long history. One can go back for example to the nineteenth century Bombay Famine Relief Code (based on estimates employed in the Bengal and Orissa famines of 1867) which established minimum diets for an adult male of 16 oz of flour made of bajra and jowar (*atta*), 2 oz of dal, $\frac{1}{2}$ oz of vegetables and condiments, 1/3 oz of clarified butter (*ghee*) and of salt.[131] These allowances seem rather generous today: one of the features of 'minimum necessary diets' is that they seem to get smaller over time. A more modern approach starts by estimating calorie and protein requirements. The standards currently employed in India as we have noted were established by the Indian Council of Medical Research in 1968 (themselves somewhat lower than those of ten years earlier).[132]

There is some doubt nowadays as to whether these standards are really appropriate. It is as much a question of the actual numbers as of the principles involved though the latter have become more precisely understood and widely known in recent years especially since the publication in 1973 of *Energy and Protein Requirements*, the report of a joint F.A.O./W.H.O. committee set up to examine the matter.[133] This work divides calorie needs into three categories 'maintenance', 'growth' and 'activity' – all of them related to body weight. The requirement for maintenance is related to basal metabolism but makes an allowance for certain essential bodily functions so that the requirement comes to one-and-a-half times the basal metabolic rate; there is not a constant rate per kg of bodyweight – it varies with size and is somewhat less for females compared with males.[134] The requirement for growth is not uniform at different stages of body development, but 5 kcals per gram of tissue gain is considered a good approximation.[135] Finally activity: four levels are described 'light', 'moderate', 'very active' and 'exceptionally active' – these are in turn derived from the energy requirements of time spent in a variety of activities during an average day, from sleeping to weight-lifting. 'Moderate activity' is the norm for a person with a standard daily programme of activities at work and leisure; 'light activity' would be more appropriate for the unemployed and the other categories are for people who spend considerable portions of their day in more demanding physical labour or athletic pursuits.

Let us first perform the exercise of applying the F.A.O./W.H.O. 1973 standards to India. While each of these requirements in calorie terms is founded on objective measurement of energy consumption, working out a nutritional standard involves choice in two of the three categories. Obviously everyone must meet the maintenance requirement. But it is not so obvious that children should be fed as if they were to grow into an adult population with mean weight for males of 65 kg. And the desirable level of activity is even more open to question. In an ideal society the desirable level of activity is just what every individual desires (subject of course to the desire of each being compatible with the good of all). But that would hardly give one a nutritional standard such that whoever falls below it would generally be called malnourished. It might be nice if everyone had the energy for a game of tennis after work but we will not necessarily think it nutritional deprivation if they have not; it is more a question of privilege for those who have. It has become customary in fact to take moderate activity as the norm though it must be recognised that any level chosen is a compromise between the actual, the desirable and the possible. We might know the actual levels of activity in India but recognise that they are constrained by poor diets; even if Indians had more energy, the level of employment would constrain them also. But it does not seem over-generous to specify a standard which would permit a life of moderate activity for all.

Accepting the level of activity, to generate standards of caloric requirements we would need data on the weights of the Indian population by age and sex – actually, as we shall see, for the adult population, for knowing that, we would know the growth pattern by which a well nourished child population would reach those or greater adult weights. Data from two sources give an average weight for males aged 20–21 just below 50 kg.[136] *Energy and Protein Requirements* gives a table for a population with an adult male mean weight of 53 kg, and we think this is a more appropriate reference figure.[137] The sources for the Indian weight data are ten years old or more, and one would expect the current population to be taller and heavier; the actual measured average weight is in any case on the low side, and we wish to err on the side of generosity. The question of appropriate weight is often misunderstood. One author has coined the term 'nutritional dwarfism' to refer to those whose weight is appropriate to their height, but height and weight are low for their age as a result of earlier malnutrition.[138] But such a measure is highly evaluative; if people have adjusted to poor availability of food by being small in stature and requiring less food, that would seem to be a sensible state of affairs, if no other negative consequences ensue. The term 'dwarfism' has achieved some currency; to use it, with its associations of abnormality, is misleading not to say distasteful. We do know that Indian children given the same diet as others will grow to European sizes;[139] they are not genetically a small race. But for adult populations, provided weight is appropriate to height, there is no point in speaking of nutritional standards appropriate for larger people.

In fact the weights achieved by Indians are very low for their height: the mean height of males aged 20–21, in the same source which gave the mean weight already cited, was just over 164 cm; a weight of 53 kg at that height is less than that implied by the height/weight ratios of the smallest 3 per cent in the Harvard Standards. And in the same source weights at that age of 51.3–52.6 kg are recorded for social classes I–III whose heights are only a little greater compared with just below 50 kg for classes IV–VI.[140] If one wishes to make a generous allowance for the adult male, basing it on a weight of 53 kg seems reasonable. On similar grounds we accept the average weight for adult females in the *Energy and Protein Requirements* table of 46 kg – this is the weight of females in the higher social classes in the source for India. When it comes to *pre-adult* ages, we have to discard the actual heights and weights recorded for India; while it makes little sense to have nutritional standards for those who have stopped growing based on a stature greater than they have attained, for those who are still growing the standards must be adequate for appropriate growth. The F.A.O./ W.H.O. report recommends that after the thirteenth birthday intake should be 'corrected for body weight in both sexes in the same way as for adults.' Prior to that age higher allowances in later years will assist 'catch-up growth' even if there has been inadequate nutrition and growth in earlier years. We may now examine side by side the Indian Council of Medical Research (1968) standards, and those of the F.A.O./W.H.O. report (Table 2.7).

A number of things emerge from the comparison. The I.C.M.R. allowances are lower than those of the F.A.O./W.H.O. report up to age twelve and higher thereafter. The F.A.O./W.H.O. figures may be on the generous side, but the I.C.M.R. figures are related more closely to actual weights of Indian children rather than what they desirably should be. The I.C.M.R. adult allowances are on the high side and appropriate for greater body weights than exist in India; they also do not decline with age as do the F.A.O./W.H.O. figures after thirty-nine years and as seems right that they should. Altogether the F.A.O./W.H.O. allowances seem the better reasoned with one very minor exception. They incorporate the pregnancy and lactation allowance for mothers in the figure for children under one year which, in a population with heavy infant mortality, will under-estimate the need; it seems better to estimate the number of pregnant and lactating mothers and make the allowance on that basis directly. Weighting the estimates by age and sex the I.C.M.R. figures come out at 2200 kcals per capita and F.A.O./W.H.O. figures at 2000. If we were to combine the I.C.M.R. child allowances with the F.A.O./W.H.O. allowances for ages above twelve per capita 'requirements' would come down still further. Possibly this would give us a more 'appropriate' set of standards – as was noted above even the I.C.M.R. standards for children appeared to be quite generous perhaps allowing more for activity than is necessary. One additional point – it may be objected that the F.A.O./W.H.O. allowances do not take note of climate: the truth is that climatic

TABLE 2.7 Calorie allowances for moderately active populations

| I.C.M.R. India | | F.A.O./W.H.O. | Adult Male 53 kg |
Age	Calories per day	Age	Adult Female 46 kg Calories per day
0 – 6 months	120 per kg weight	< 1 year	1090[1]
7 – 12 months	100 per kg weight		
1 – 3 years	1200	1 – 3 years	1360
4 – 6 "	1500	4 – 6 "	1830
7 – 9 "	1800	7 – 9 "	2190
10 – 12	2100	Males 10 – 12	2600
Males 13 – 15	2500	Females 10 – 12	2350
Females 13 – 15	2200	Males 13 – 15	2370
Males 16 – 18	3000	Females 13 – 15	2080
Females 16 – 18	2200[2]	Males 16 – 19	2490
Males 19 –	2800	Females 16 – 19	1932
Females 19 –	2200[2]	Males 20 – 39	2440
		Females 20 – 39	1840
		Males 40 – 49	2318
		Females 40 – 49	1748
		Males 50 – 59	2196
		Females 50 – 59	1656
		Males 60 – 69	1952
		Females 60 – 69	1472
		Males 70 –	1708
		Females 70 –	1288
Per capita for India 2200[1]			2000[1]

SOURCES I.C.M.R. (1968); F.A.O./W.H.O. (1973) Table 27, col.1.
1. Includes allowance to mothers for pregnancy and lactation.
2. Not including allowance for second half of pregnancy (300 kcals/day) and lactation (700 kcals/day).

variation is deliberately omitted as there is 'no quantifiable basis' for including it; climate may however affect activity and it is there that adjustment should be made.

Comparison of these I.C.M.R. figures with actual intakes elsewhere is revealing. Intake of 120 kcals per kg weight is higher than that received by the fiftieth percentile of infants aged 0–6 months in the U.S.A. British children aged 4–5 were found to have an average intake of 1325 kcals in one recent study, rather less than the 1500 prescribed here. Girls aged 7–9 in the U.S.A. also averaged less than 1800 kcals in a recent study. Indeed in the United Kingdom in 1973, per capita intakes for a household containing two adults and two children averaged 2300 kcals – but for a 2-adult, 4-child household the figure was 2100.[141] Evidently while the I.C.M.R. allowances are perfectly proper recommendations, in that they are desirable of attainment, they cannot be regarded as nutritional minimum necessities for the average Indian in the sense that, if average intakes fall below them, consequences deleterious to health will inevitably follow.

The I.C.M.R. makes it clear that there is a distribution of individual requirements around the mean at each age, and the 'recommendation' may be as much as two standard deviations above that mean to ensure that 98 per cent of those who receive the allowance will be adequately nourished. Others have misinterpreted the allowances as constituting a 'minimum' for everybody. The 'recommended allowance' is a composite standard reflecting the norms of those who specify it in terms of growth and activity and a safety margin above the mean of such requirements. Several scholars who have contributed to the poverty debate in India have employed the cost of purchasing a diet satisfying the I.C.M.R. standards as a 'poverty line'. That is quite legitimate. But one can summarise much of the above discussion by listing the errors involved if one were to posit that the proportion of the population malnourished was equal to the proportion of household who, by this criterion, 'cannot afford an adequate diet.' (1) Even if the household data are accurate, within a household which on average cannot afford the recommended intakes some actual intakes may be above and some below the recommendations. In households which can afford the recommended levels, there may be (and often are) individuals deficient in calories by this criterion. (2) Individuals may be below the recommended intakes and not be malnourished for all the reasons stated above. There is no substitute for comparisons of individual intakes with the same individuals' requirements.

It is not widely recognised how much of the territory of the nutritionist's world remains uncharted – it is a feature of the subject of nutrition as much as of the work done in any particular country. India needs systematic data collection on intakes, anthropometric measurement and clinical signs of malnutrition. A National Nutrition Monitoring Bureau has recently been set up which is intended to do just that.[142] But without further research on the assessment of intake and anthropometric measures – and some studies to design better nutritional indicators specific to India's circumstances have been or are being conducted – the gathering of better data is only half the battle.

So far we have referred mainly to intakes of pre-school children. The average availability of food in India has been variously estimated to yield 1964 kcals per person per day (average for the years 1964–6), 2000 kcals/day (average 1963–5), 1900 (average 1963–7), 2100 (1970–71) and 2000 (1971).[143] Thus on the basis of the F.A.O./W.H.O. allowances, there would be just about enough food for the whole population in all except bad years provided it were distributed according to need. It must be remembered though that the F.A.O./W.H.O. allowance figures are only *an* estimate; they are not *the* estimate. And of course food is very far from being distributed according to need. To assess the number of people lacking adequate calories we require knowledge of the actual distribution of food consumption. Various attempts at assessment have been made in the absence of such knowledge and the authors have done what can be done. They come up with figures in the region of 25 per cent of the population lacking adequate calories.[144] We know the proportion must be substantial; if total food availability is very close to being adequate to need, it may only take a small number with consumption above the necessary level to leave a large number below it. But what that number is, the data do not tell us. Most of the existing information is in the nature of food expenditure by households as estimated by the National Sample Survey. These data are of uncertain usefulness as we observed. We may be no worse off, for average intakes for India as a whole, to calculate estimates from independently derived calorie-income relationships which give the following table:

TABLE 2.8 Distribution of calories calculated from income shares

	Decile	% Total income	Per capita income US$	Per capita calories (1)	Per capita calories (2)
Lowest	1	3·3	34·98	1360	1671
	2	4·4	46·64	1551	1767
	3	5·3	56·18	1674	1828
	4	6·1	64·66	1767	1875
	5	6·9	73·13	1848	1916
	6	8·1	85·86	1955	1969
	7	9·0	95·40	2025	2004
	8	10·0	114·48	2146	2065
	9	16·1	170·66	2411	2197
Highest	10	30·0	318·00	2823	2404
Average			106·00	1970	1956

SOURCE See text.

The table has been estimated from calorie-income relationships derived for an average Asian country in a study based on calculations of the income-elasticity of calorie purchases.[145] They accord moderately well with observations in India and the elasticities used (0·30 in the case of col. (i) and 0·15 in col. (2)) probably do span the range of possible cases without either impossibly low intakes at low income levels or too small a variance between the highest and lowest intakes. (One might suspect that India is closer to the less even distribution of col. (1) than col. (2): the figures from the Calcutta survey cited below, or those of the N.S.S., certainly suggest a substantial proportion of households with intakes below 1500 calories per head per day.[146])

Some clues about the distribution of caloric consumption within the family are available from a few sources. The most detailed data are given in the Tamil Nadu Nutrition Project,[147] which show a very interesting pattern relating the percentage of caloric need met at each age to the percentage of the need met for the family as a whole. The standards employed are the I.C.M.R. (1968) ones already discussed. It is noteworthy that the standard is not met below age two even for families consuming 112 per cent of requirement on average, suggesting at all the intake levels covered an almost exclusive reliance on breast milk in the first year. The age pattern of percentage of requirement met is remarkably similar at all levels of average family consumption, rising between age one and age 7–8, falling to about age 16, and rising again. Later in adulthood family members receive a percentage of the requirement above the average percentage for the family – the higher the family's average consumption, the earlier the age at which they do so. If the F.A.O./W.H.O. standard were employed, this skewness of percentage-of-requirement-met within the family would increase since, while the average (per head) requirement differs only by 200 calories as between the two sets of standards, the F.A.O./W.H.O. requirements are considerably greater than the I.C.M.R. at younger ages and considerably less at older ages. Evidently the distribution of food within the family is the result of 'deep seated cultural behaviour' as the report of the Tamil Nadu project observes.[148] It is important to remember however that the shape of the distributions is related to the I.C.M.R. allowances: if these are especially over-generous in the 0–2 and 10–16 age groups, that could at least in part account for the deficiencies observed for most ages.

Let us note that the Tamil Nadu is based on a survey of 2800 households which makes it reasonably representative for Tamil Nadu but not for India since food habits may differ from State to State. In fact such evidence as there is from elsewhere suggests that similar age patterns of consumption may not be uncommon. The Punjab study already referred to shows the particular nutritional disabilities of the very young. A study in Calcutta in 1969 showed less of a discrepancy between age groups: among the poorest third of families children aged 2–4 years received 55 per cent of needed calories, those aged 12–16 56 per cent and adults 22–56 years 59 per cent.[149] The study also indicates that higher incomes are associated with some redistribution of food within the family though at a rate which requires quite high family incomes before children are adequately nourished. A study by the Operations Research Group also showed lower proportions of I.C.M.R. requirements met for children than adults in Kerala and Tamil Nadu while in Andhra Pradesh and Mysore there was little difference at various ages.[150] But once again, if we only have average figures, it is extremely difficult to tell from the extent of average requirements met how many individuals there are for whom they are or are not met. In the Tamil Nadu study only where the percentage of family requirements met exceeds 90 per cent do some individuals – over age 35 – obtain more than 100 per cent of requirements; in our age distribution for India, the proportion of the population over 35 is 26 per cent. On the other hand children below 2 years do badly even in groups where the per capita requirement is exceeded on average. In yet another study, of 6 cities in various parts of India, in fact 92 per cent of all children aged 0–5 were found deficient in calories by the I.C.M.R. standards.[151] But that may tell us as much about the standards as it does about the extent of malnutrition.

The real problem of estimating the extent of calorie deficiency by these methods is the matching of the distribution of intakes against the distribution of requirements. Given data for average intakes, we do not usually know how they are distributed around the average. We might have information that so many households have an average intake of so many calories; but we do not know very often how it is distributed – not only between different age groups (for which we have information in the Tamil Nadu study for example) but, within age groups, the distribution between people of different weight, height, or activity. But there is a further and equally troublesome difficulty – the tremendous variation in individual requirements. Nutrition surveys in rich countries show very large variations in intake between individuals even of the same age, sex and weight or height. It does truly seem that individuals even of very similar physiological characteristics in those respects, and with very similar activity patterns, may have very different nutritional needs. With data for average intakes, but without detailed information about the dispersal around the average along all relevant dimensions, we do not have enough to go on. If in addition we have little knowledge of the variation in individual requirements around the average requirements in each age group, it can readily be seen that any methods of estimating the extent of calorie deficiency among individuals from these types of data are seriously unreliable.

All the estimates we referred to earlier – that approximately 25 per cent of the population were deficient in calories – employed a cut-off limit of one kind or another below which the average man was said to be malnourished. With no adjustment this would be tantamount to assuming that all these considerations produce errors which cancel each other out. The authors in question have attempted to make some provision for this by using cut-off points lower than the per capita requirement they thought appropriate, usually by taking a figure two or three standard deviations below the average requirement. Thus Sukhatme (1973) used 1900 or 2100 and Clark (1972) between 1650 – 1790 calories. But then the standard may really be too low except for providing a minimum figure, i.e. we can say that *at least* so many are calorie-deficient by an exceptionally low standard. But there is really no substitute for decent data. When one adds the uncertainties of the magnitudes of the per capita intake data themselves, quite apart from questions of distribution among individuals and the doubt attaching to the standards of requirement, one must conclude that this whole approach to estimating the extent of malnutrition is too crude to be of much help. This is not to say that 25 per cent of the population is *not* calorie-deficient by the I.C.M.R. standard; on the contrary income and price data suggest that such a figure at least, if not a higher one, is extremely plausible.[152] We are only criticising the approach that attempts to be more precise about the number of individuals deficient based on household or per capita data.

Questions of what to do about India's nutrition problems are addressed in Chapter 3; but even the diagnosis would be left incomplete without some further comment. The reader might be left with the impression that lack of purchasing power is the only issue. In fact a number of other features are important, particularly disease and unsatisfactory food habits. It is well-known that disease contributes to malnutrition and diminished nutrient-retention in the body. Controlling the sources of infection is an important part of nutritional improvement. The high incidence of gastro-intestinal disease is only one of the factors; nitrogen loss is also associated with malaria and other diseases. A great deal could also be done to improve nutrition especially among infants and young children, by changes in food habits that are financially within the means of most Indians. Well documented and common undesirable food practices include the following:

(i) Non-supplementation of breast milk: perhaps the most important single cause of malnutrition in the first two years of life. A large number of studies have demonstrated that the growth curve of infants is commonly satisfactory for the first six months, the period during which breast milk is usually adequate for all the infant's needs. These curves tend to flatten out over the following year or 18 months; it is extremely common for no supplementation to be given until the first birthday or later.[153]

(ii) Unsatisfactory weaning foods. When supplementation is given it is often food of the wrong type: portions from adult meals, often highly spiced, flour and water preparations etc. Small children are often fed by an older child in the mother's absence.

(iii) Specific nutrient deficiencies. The most serious are iron, vitamin A and vitamin B due to absence of green vegetables and other foods in the diet which contain the missing items.

(iv) Other deleterious food habits, especially the rejection of certain types of foods on non-rational grounds. Certain nutritious foods are regarded as 'cooling' or 'heat-producing' and are only eaten at certain times or may be rejected altogether. In particular under-feeding during pregnancy is common to avoid what is considered to be excessive foetal growth and difficult delivery; diet during illness is often reduced and foods consumed are frequently the opposite of what would be medically suitable.

(v) Loss of nutrients in food preparation. It is well-known that rice is more nutritious unpolished than polished. There are many other ways in which the nutritive value of purchased food is lost – for example the water in which rice is cooked contains valuable nutrients but is often thrown away. (Though, because of tastes and lack of nutritional education, food purchases are often nutritionally inefficient in the first place.)[154]

Little mention has so far been made of the protein problem. This is because it is now widely regarded that protein deficiency in India is rarely a separate problem on its own. Most Indian dietaries contain an adequate proportion of protein and – infant problems apart – if people simply ate more of their customary diet they would receive adequate proteins. It is the protein proportion in the diet that counts. Protein deficiency in a diet adequate in calories is found most commonly where starchy roots are the staple food (e.g. yam and cassava in West Africa). In Indian diet studies it is rare to observe in the same individual both caloric adequacy and protein inadequacy.[155] If calories are deficient, signs of protein deficiency will often be observed: proteins are utilised for energy instead of cell growth and maintenance. Hence the current phrase 'protein-calorie malnutrition' (P.C.M.) and its corollary the prescription of higher calorie intake as a remedy provided the 'net dietary protein-calories percentage' is satisfactory. This may give rise to bulk problems for small children but that can commonly be met by more frequent feeding of smaller amounts of food.

The problem of malnutrition goes beyond those found living with low nutritional levels; it also includes the dead and the still-born. Poor nutritional status of expectant mothers is responsible for congenital malformations, still-births or the birth of very small babies who, even if they live, have relatively poor chances of survival.[156] One study cites an average birth weight of Indian babies of 2771 g, with 28 per cent less than 2500 g; in Poland the average weight was 3380 g and the proportion below 2500 g, 6·8 per cent. (Comparative figures were Lebanon, 3150 g and 7·4 per cent; Japan 3029 g and 11·3 per cent; Malaysia 2986 g and 16·8 per cent – data for 1961.)[157] Two local studies have shown average caloric intake of mothers in the region of 1600 in the last months of pregnancy, levels which almost guarantee that infants start life with incipient malnutrition.[158] If the mother's nutrition does not improve after her baby is born, her ability to feed the child is also affected. And the surviving child of a malnourished mother is likely to perform less well in numerous ways later in life. More than half of all deaths in India occur in the first five years of life and a very large proportion of those deaths are associated with malnutrition. One of the few really careful studies of child mortality was conducted in an area of the Punjab by the Khanna project.[159] It showed that deaths in the first month of life were due particularly to tetanus and birth-associated diseases. For the remainder of the first two years acute diarrhoeal disease was the largest single cause of death. From 1 – 11 months the actual rates for the main causes of death were: diarrhoea, 27·8 deaths per 1000 live births; pneumonia, 10·7; prematurity, 10·7; measles, 5·7; typhoid, 2·8 and tuberculosis, 2·1. In the second year diarrhoea was again the cause of one-third of all deaths with measles, tuberculosis, typhoid fever, whooping cough and pneumonia contributing another third.

These patterns of mortality are the common consequences of malnutrition. In a famous series of studies in Guatemala, Gordon, Scrimshaw *et al.* showed the effects of what they called the 'synergism of malnutrition and infection.'[160] Children were dying of infections but ones whose virulence was greatly increased by malnutrition; the diarrhoeas in particular, part symptom and part cause of malnutrition, killed mainly by dehydration or sometimes by depleting the level of nutrition below the limit necessary for life. It was often not even possible to identify specific organisms causing gastric disorder. Deaths from other causes among those weakened by malnutrition were also obviously greater than would be expected in a well-nourished population, due not only to the greater prevalence of infections but also to diminished resistance. *The Khanna Study* shows an essentially similar pattern. Thus not only is it difficult to measure the prevalence of malnutrition – it is also almost impossible to measure its consequences owing to the complexity of its interactions with other causes of death and disease. But wherever infant and child mortality is perennially present on the scale found in India it is virtually impossible that malnutrition does not play a major part.

Conclusions

Since the last paragraphs have stressed the uncertainties of our knowledge of the extent of malnutrition it may be helpful to reiterate what is moderately well established:

(i) The finding in some surveys that some 40 per cent of pre-school children in middle and low income groups have been found to exhibit at least one of a variety of clinical signs of malnutrition is a matter of extreme seriousness. In the 1976 population, if generally correct, it would amount to at least 25 million children aged 0 – 5. This age group has been the most studied because it is the most vulnerable and because some results of early malnutrition in its more severe forms have irreversible consequences.

(ii) The probability of survival from birth to age 10 in India is currently little more than 75 per cent. But out of every hundred births of the 25 who die by the tenth birthday about 22 succumb by age 5, and of those perhaps 15 by the age of 1.[161] In all countries where such heavy tolls of infant and child mortality are observed the combination of malnutrition and infection has been found to explain a majority of deaths. In Latin America for example it is believed that 57 per cent of infant and child deaths are associated with malnutrition.[162]

(iii) At other ages information does not permit national assessment but, if the N.S.S. food expenditure data are any guide, while the I.C.M.R. recommended allowances may not be in any precise sense 'nutritional minima', a large proportion of households cannot afford even a small fraction of the allowance. It may be that a major reflection of caloric deficiency at later ages is reduced activity rather than ill-health or other consequences of malnutrition. But this too is a serious matter; the energy requirements of what is formally defined as 'moderate activity' are not over-generous, and their fulfilment is an important condition for leading a decent life.

The pattern of cause of death

We have discussed some of the major causes of death in India and how they have been changing in recent decades in so far as we know. We have omitted others – either their prevalence, history or aetiology is harder to trace or they are less important from a quantitative point of view: typhoid fever, filariasis, dengue fever are examples – considerable diseases in India but not on the scale of those reviewed above. A major omission is gastro-enteric disease; while the quantity of death and illness from this source is very great, it would be an enterprise beyond the scope of this book to examine it in all its variety. We have noted that the severity of such disease is in the main a function of nutrition; given its provenance in the general conditions of hygiene, sanitation and water supply, it is difficult to prevent.

There has been a system for recording cause of death in operation in India since 1966. Known as the Model Registration Scheme it employs paramedical staff under the supervision of a medical officer in a sample of villages and urban areas and has recorded the cause of death for over 20,000 deaths on an annual basis. There are nine basic categories: 'violence and injuries', 'childbirth and complicated pregnancy', 'diarrhoea', 'cough', 'swelling', 'fevers', 'other infant deaths', 'other clear symptoms', and 'extreme old age and others'. These categories are further sub-divided into individual sub-causes but about one quarter of all deaths were not classifiable by sub-cause; data are also given by age and in some cases by State. We give below some details from the 1969 figures.

It is not easy to assess the usefulness of these figures. We have presented them here indicating a few interesting sub-categories; in each of the groups

TABLE 2.9 Death by Cause – Model Registration Sample Data, 1969

Group	% of total	Total members	Of which (by sub-cause)	(by age 0–4)	% in Group unclassified by sub-cause
I *Violence & Injuries*	3·5	736		74	13·6
Suicide			73		
II *Childbirth &*					
Complicated Pregnancy	1·3	276		0	0
Abortion			27		
III *Diarrhoeas*	9·2	1929		925	
Cholera			118		–
IV *Cough*	24·5	5145		1761	12·5
Bronchopneumonia			1600		
Pneumonia			489		
Bronchitis			880		
Respiratory tb			1235		
V *Swellings*	8·0	1666		221	11·0
VI *Fevers*	20·6	4315		662	25·1
Typhoid			837		
Measles			487		
Smallpox			151		
Other tb			233		
VII *Other Infant*					
Deaths	11·1	2326		2326	17·9
Prematurity			565		
VIII *Other Clear*					
Symptoms	5·0	1058		391	
Tetanus			449		
IX *Extreme old age*					
& other causes	16·8	3513		0	36·4
Old age			2234		
Totals	100·0	20,964		6,839	27·21

SOURCE Government of India, 1972.

there is a longish list of sub-causes each accounting for a small percentage of the total in the group and we have not reproduced all this information. The groups as a whole may well have some approximate correspondence with the true pattern of cause of death, but the more detailed information is of doubtful value except possibly for the more clearly recognisable diseases. Thus in Group III, as well as cholera, there are separate entries for 'dysentery' and 'gastro-enteritis' and 'not classifiable' so that only the cholera figure is conceivably valuable; it is very doubtful that dysentery and gastro-enteritis have been accurately distinguished. Similarly in Group IV–we doubt that bronchopneumonia, pneumonia and bronchitis have been diagnosed with precision but tuberculosis may have been, relatively speaking; with a quarter of 'Fevers' unclassified in Group VI it is hard to know what to make of the figures from the ones that are listed, and one can note that 36·4 per cent of Group IX ascribed to 'other causes' means that 6·0 per cent of the deaths in the sample as a whole would not even be placed in any of the groups. Finally a sample of 20,000 is not adequate to provide detailed information about 10 million deaths; when it comes down to individual States, there were only 1685 deaths examined for Uttar Pradesh and 227 for West Bengal.

We have elicited from the tables classifying deaths by age (not reproduced here) a count of all deaths in the sample occurring in ages 0 – 4: since they come to one-third of all deaths there is further cause to be unhappy with the data, since we have good reason to believe from other sources that they should comprise more than half of all deaths. Thus while the Model Registration data provide some rough breakdown of causes of death they do not take us much further forward than we can go on the basis of information about the age distribution of mortality, nutrition surveys and studies of individual diseases such as we have discussed above. They do not, either, give one any stronger basis for the formulation of health programmes since it is clear that, apart from communicable disease control, the main need is for a combined attack on nutrition, sanitation and hygiene together with improved primary medical care; the lack of more detailed knowledge of causes of death is not, at this stage, a major obstacle to programmes for the reduction of mortality.

It is interesting to compare these figures with those of *The Khanna Study* which, though covering a very small population, covered it exhaustively and with high standards of observation. The first ten causes of death, in order of quantitative significance, were diarrhoeal disease, pneumonia, tuberculosis, tetanus, heart disease, birth injuries, cancer, typhoid fever, accidents and measles, with an incidence ranging from 49·5 per 100,000 population in the case of the last mentioned, rising to 187·2 per 100,000 for diarrhoeal disease. Between the ages of 15   44 tuberculosis was the chief cause of death; notable also was the volume of deaths due to accidents – none of them due to motorcars. After the age of five the authors found the expectation of life in these Punjab villages similar to that of the United States, which is probably better than average for India, and before age five, a large share of deaths were preventable – particularly by early supplementation of mother s milk with solid foods and by more hygienic procedures with the umbilical cord at birth as well as better nutrition, hygiene and sanitation generally. The Government has announced plans to improve the Model Registration data; it would do better to have a few centres doing continuous work of the quality of the *Khanna Study* in selected areas – there is little to be gained from extending the broader analysis of causes of death unless *all* deaths in the sample are medically examined, and the representativeness of the sample in various dimensions is adequate and is known.

THE LEVEL AND TREND OF FERTILITY AND MORTALITY

The average couple in India today surviving through the child-bearing years has probably only slightly fewer than six children. The 1971 crude birth rate was in the region of 40 per thousand and the current (1977) rate is likely to be about 36 – 37 per thousand. The foundation of these statements is a marsh of statistical inconclusiveness – but we believe them to be supported by a variety of evidence and calculations. There are two sources of such estimates – the census, and direct sample surveys of fertility. The basic problem with census-derived estimates is the age distribution. The 1971 Census counted distinctly less children in the age group 0 – 4 than in the 5 – 9 group.[163] If true this would reflect either a rise in child mortality or a fall in fertility in the second half of the 1960s vastly greater than is credible. The question is how to reassess the numbers in these early age groups. Were the 0 – 4s under-enumerated? Or were they moved into the 5 – 9s by age misreporting? And what is to be done with the other age groups?

Low estimates of the age group 0 – 4 were present in the 1961 and earlier censuses: indeed the numbers aged 10 – 14 in the 1971 Census are larger than those aged 0 – 4 in 1961 which is impossible (unless international migration could explain it, which it cannot). One can see what the correct order of magnitude should be: run the 1971 population back to 1966 at the intercensal growth rate of 2·24 per cent per year, calculate the number of births in the years 1966 – 70 and deplete them by appropriate mortality figures. This gives a figure for the 1971 0 – 4s of 84·8 million assuming a crude birth rate as low as 39 for the calculation. This figure compares with the Census enumeration of 78·3 million.[164] If correct it would raise the proportion aged 0 – 4 in the 1971 population from 14·36 per cent to 15·45 per cent. But we would be leaving out one important item – the last calculation assumes that the numbers aged 0 – 4 are to be inflated at the expense of other age groups as counted in the Census. Yet, if we have any reason to believe that the Census as a whole is under-enumerated, a larger than average share of the under-enumeration is likely to be precisely in the age group 0 – 4 – this is the experience of many censuses elsewhere.[165] In that case the numbers aged 0 – 4 must be inflated in part from the over-estimate for the 5 – 9 age group but also in part from those completely omitted. This implies a bigger 1971 population than the estimated 547·9 million of the Census. By a more sophisticated technique than that above (described elsewhere),[166] we place the numbers aged 0 – 4 at 90·3 million, 16·2 per cent of the (larger) population and corresponding to an average crude birth rate of 42 per thousand in the years 1966 – 70.

Any fertility estimates based on smoothing the 1971 Census age distribution without raising the figure for the total population cannot be entirely above suspicion. Some very careful work has however been done on this basis and deserves mention here. Rele and Sinha,[167] observing that the unsmoothed age data for 1971 are similar to those for 1961, used a technique they had found satisfactory for the 1961 Census to obtain a smoothed age distribution for 1971. Employing the reverse survival method with a variety of life-tables and mortality levels – in the region of expectation of life at birth of 45 years – they estimated the birth rate during the decade 1961 – 70 at 42 – 40 per thousand. In our view, while such birth rates are of the right order of magnitude for 1971 and the years immediately preceding it, as an average for the whole decade they are probably a little on the low side.

Interestingly enough another set of estimates by Adlakha and Kirk[168] come to almost the same conclusions as Rele and Sinha although they used slightly different estimation techniques. They first smooth the 1971 recorded age distribution by the percentage of over- or under-estimation of the first three age quintiles found by Coale for the 1961 Census (Coale used a new method for this purpose, derived from demographic theory and appropriate for circumstances of declining mortality with fertility assumed approximately constant).[169] Adlakha and Kirk then estimate the birth rate by the reverse survival method and place it between 42·0 – 40·5 for the 1961 – 70 decade. Given that they used a different technique for smoothing the 1971 data, and a different life-table, the correspondence with Rele and Sinha ought to create confidence. And they have attempted yet further confirmation by making an independent estimate of the death rate and adding it to the intercensal growth rate to yield birth rates – depending on different assumptions about expectation of life, they range in this case from 40·4 to 41·2.

What distinguished scholars have independently found by reasonable assumptions and impeccable technique we should not expect to upset. But there are other assumptions equally reasonable. We would suggest a slightly different assessment based on the following considerations: first the best survey data for India, the Sample Registration data, give birth rates for India of 36·9 for 1971 and 36·6 for 1972.[170] If these estimates are accurate, they accord very well with the estimates quoted above. But if they are under-estimates, the 1961 – 70 rates must be higher. In fact careful follow-up of the Sample Registration System suggests that births may be under-estimated by about 8 per cent;[171] but that yields 1971 birth rates only minutely below 40 per thousand: if, as everyone agrees, the birth rate has been declining during the 1960s, the average for the decade could not be 40. It must be closer to 42 or more if the decline has been of the order of 7 – 10 per cent; if, that is, the birth rate was in the region of 44 in 1961. Second there is further evidence that the Census as a whole was under-enumerated: the Sample Enumeration Check[172] suggested an under-count by 1·7 per cent or approximately 9·3 million – if that is right, the arithmetic of birth rate estimation by the techniques employed by the authors under discussion could be affected, depending on how the 9·3 million were distributed among the age groups. And the intercensal growth rate would be altered too: the 1961 Census was estimated to be under-counted by 0·7 per cent. Raising both Census totals by these respective amounts, the intercensal growth rate rises from 2·24 per cent per year to 2·34 per cent. This alone increases by one point any estimate of the birth rate derived from a death rate.[173]

Further to question Adlakha and Kirk's estimate there is no particular reason to expect the enumeration errors estimated by Coale for 1961 to be identical with the errors of 1971. On the contrary if there is more under-enumeration in general in 1971 than in 1961, under-enumeration in the 0–4 age group in particular is likely to be proportionately greater in 1971. Coale estimated in fact an under-count of males aged 0 – 4 of 9·6 per cent and females of 6·0 per cent and an over-count of males aged 5 – 9 of 11·0 per cent, females 12·6 per cent. All the 'missing' 0 – 4s were subtracted from the 5 – 9s. Few published estimates of vital rates based on the 1971 Census countenance the possibility that the whole population is under-enumerated and in particular that the number may be added to the enumerated 0 – 4s not from the 5 – 9 age group, but from those not counted at all. Of course we do not claim to know for certain that this possibility is more likely than the assumptions made by the authors we refer to. The Sample Enumeration Check is itself not to be exempted from doubt; neither its percentage of under-enumeration, nor that which we cite from the Sample Registration data, can be applied with confidence to the reported figures to give more reliable estimates. Nevertheless there is a very strong case for increasing the Census estimate of the 1971 population both to derive a consistent age distribution, and for other reasons.[174] To raise it by 1·7 per cent may well be too little rather than too much; but it is the only figure for which there is any direct justification.

Some additional work confirms the plausibility of an alternative view. Veena Soni has applied two entirely separate methods to the fertility data of the 1970 O.R.G. Survey: the Brass method, based on survey data for births in a current period and for total live-births, classified by ages of women in the reproductive age span, and the Coale-Trussell theoretical model of fertility which yields fertility schedules on the basis of a small number of parameters and has given excellent results for a range of countries with good data.[175] These techniques show a birth rate of the order of 42·0 for 1970 and a total fertility rate of a little more than 6·0. This coincides with the total fertility rate generated by the assumptions employed in the work underlying our population projections.[176] We wish to emphasise that we are not making any strong claim that such estimates of the birth rate at the end of the 1960s have greater validity than the somewhat lower ones reached in other estimates. We only wish to guard against the belief that fertility may be lower than it actually is – a belief reached on the basis of assumptions no more plausible than others which show it to be higher. If these other assumptions are correct, then the

Sample Registration birth rate estimates of 36·9 for 1971 and 16·6 for 1972 are also optimistically low and should be raised by at least 2 points. It seems controversial to suggest that the 1971 population was higher than 547·9 or the birth rate higher than 37; but the grounds for revising upwards both the census population estimate and the Sample Registration birth rates are rather stronger than the grounds for accepting them as they stand.

The one thing which no plausible assumptions disturb is the apparent fact that fertility is declining. One would expect this on the basis of observations of a modest rise in the age at marriage apparent in the 1971 Census, changes in the age distribution, the successes – however partial – of the family planning programme and the persistent, if slow, movement in other conditions related to fertility such as education and urbanisation. The main factor which might operate in the opposing direction is improvement in health and nutrition, increasing fecundity and reducing the number of pregnancies ending in still-births. It is quite possible that such changes were important in 1950s and early 1960s; there is a well-attested impact of malaria control on fertility.[177] Conceivably they have also been acting to slow down the fertility decline of more recent years but our conviction discussed above is that improvements in health and nutrition have themselves fallen off. A further factor would be mortality decline in the reproductive age groups increasing the duration of marital unions exposed to pregnancy. Adlakha and Kirk[178] estimate a decline of 3 to 4 points in the birth rates of 1961 – 71 relative to those of 1951 – 61 and attribute two-thirds of it to reductions in marital fertility, the other third being due to changes in age and marital status. In Chapter 3 we discuss our own guess that the family planning programme has accounted for prevention of approximately one million births a year on average since the mid 1960s, which is roughly equivalent to two points off the birth rate (a birth rate of 40 gives 22 million births for a population of 550 million) and thus in the same area as Adlakha and Kirk. Rele and Sinha[179] find the same 3 to 4 point decline in the birth rate between 1951 and 1960 and between 1961 and 1970 as do Adlakha and Kirk but assess 'a major part' of the decline as due to changes in age and marital status. (It is extremely difficult to be precise about this; Adlakha and Kirk derive their estimate from applying an age specific marital-fertility schedule to a standardised age distribution, yielding the result that, with no change in marital fertility, the birth rate would have declined by only one point between the two periods. However this assumes no change in the age pattern of fertility. Without knowing anything about such possible changes, there is no way to improve on their analysis.)

Once fertility has been estimated, at least on an intercensal basis, mortality estimates are confined to a fairly small range. There is a virtually negligible amount of net international migration (see below), a fairly secure intercensal growth rate and a limit to the amount of juggling one can do with the age distribution and with the age pattern of mortality. If the birth rate averaged 42 in the decade of 1961 – 70 and the population grew at 2·24 per cent, then the death rate averaged 19·6. Most estimates of the decade rates are in this region and since rates estimated for the previous decade are considerably higher, there has very clearly been considerable mortality decline. In our population projections we have taken the expectation of life at birth to be 48 years for males, 46 for females, during 1966 – 70, corresponding to our belief in a slightly higher birth rate for that period than others have estimated and a slightly higher intercensal growth rate allowing for under-enumeration in the censuses. This compares with Adlakha and Kirk's estimates of 46 – 47 years (males) and 45 – 44 years (females) for the whole decade 1961 – 71 or estimates by Rele and Sinha for 1966 – 70 ranging from 45·7 – 49·6 (males) and 45 – 47·5 (females).

There is not a tremendous amount of difference among these various estimates. They depend on the assumed or estimated age pattern of mortality which depends in turn either on the model life-table chosen or on survivorship ratios which in turn derive from the estimated sizes and age distributions of the 1961 and 1971 populations. We are unhappy about the use of standard model life-tables in this case, both for the sorts of reasons advanced by Adlakha himself,[180] and because no model life-tables take account of certain special features of Indian mortality, in particular the pattern of male and female mortality differentials. We have produced our own life-table (Table 2.12 below) to take account of these adjustments and others; in particular it incorporates infant mortality at 150 per thousand live births for males and 162 for females for the period 1961–70.

We have made a special point of correcting for the implications of female mortality. The male/female ratios found by successive censuses have been slowly and consistently rising, to reach 1075 males per 1000 females in 1971 (in 1911 it was 1038). Although other reasons have been alleged, such as abnormal ratios of male to female births and poor enumeration of females in the census, there is little doubt that the main factor is excess female over male mortality due fundamentally, as we point out elsewhere, to worse malnutrition among young females than males and the risks of maternity. Excess female mortality is present both in the infant and childhood years and in the reproductive ages. In the Sample Registration data for 1968 and 1969 – the only years for which age specific mortality is given – female mortality exceeds male up to age 34.[181] Not surprisingly if women pass the late reproductive years and their weaker sisters have been taken off then or earlier, their capacity to survive is greater than that of men. (In most countries of the world, women have a longer expectation of life at birth than men.)

What then of current mortality? In our view it has reached a plateau around which it fluctuates; there seems to be little or no downward trend and if there were one, as we have said above, it would be hard to explain. With no major progress in the extension of medical facilities or other services conducive to better health and the end – for the time being – of the mortality decline due to control of quantitatively important communicable diseases, the trend in mortality must now depend to a large extent on the availability and distribution of food and, as we show in Chapter 4, while the per capita availability of foodgrains fluctuates with hardly any upward trend, the proportion of people with incomes inadequate for satisfactory material existence is not falling. The only source of current mortality estimates is the Sample Registration System which has given combined urban and rural death rates per thousand as follows: 1970, 15·7; 1971, 14·9; 1972, 16·9; 1973, 15·5; 1974, 14·5; 1975, 15·2. This exhibits the fluctuations; it is impossible to tell though how far they are due to real changes in mortality or to changes in coverage and the quality of recording. The system has been continuously extended and presumably some of the areas of higher mortality have come in last. Rural mortality rates average over 70 per cent above urban. Some States are not covered for mortality (West Bengal); others have recorded rates which are frankly not credible (compare rural Bihar, 14·5 with rural Uttar Pradesh, 22·7 for 1970: the figures for Bihar are no longer printed). As with the birth rate figures from the same source, analysis referred to above has found underreporting of deaths also.[182]

Four tables appear below: the Sample Registration age specific death rates to which reference has already been made; a selection of published

TABLE 2.10 Age specific death rates average 1968 – 9 (Rural) per 1000 population

Age	Male	Female
0 – 4	58·72	68·49
5 – 9	5·66	6·84
10 – 14	2·63	2·66
15 – 19	2·04	3·78
20 – 24	3·27	5·32
25 – 29	3·46	6·21
30 – 34	3·92	6·17
35 – 39	6·39	6·07
40 – 44	8·10	7·76
45 – 49	12·93	9·27
50 – 54	17·78	14·97
55 – 59	25·36	19·04
60 – 64	41·88	39·43
65 – 69	56·04	52·25
70 –	118·43	115·50
All ages	17·85	19·54

SOURCE G.O.I (1972), Tables 20(b) and 20(c). All these figures are undoubtedly underestimates (see text) but they exhibit clearly the probable age pattern of differential male-female mortality.

birth and death rates; two estimated age distributions and the mortality assumptions used in our life-table for the intercensal period.

TABLE 2.11 Crude birth and death rates and expectation of life at birth

Year(s)	per 1000		Years $e^0_{|0}$		Source
	CBR	CDR	M	F	
1951 – 61	45	25·9	37·5	36·8	Coale and Demeny (1967)
1951 – 61	44·9	25·7	37·8	37·0	Visaria (1969)
1951 – 61	41·7	22·8	41·9	40·6	G.o.I. (1962) (?)
1961 – 71	42·0 – 40·4	18 – 19	46 – 47	44 – 45	Adlakha and Kirk (1974)
1961 – 70	42±	20±	45±		Rele and Sinha (1973)
1966 – 70	42·0	18·6	48	46	Cassen and Dyson (1976)
1970	36·8	15·7			G.o.I. (1974a)
1971	36·9	14·9			”
1972	36·6	16·9			”
1968 – 70	40·0	18·0			G.o.I. (1974c)
1961 – 70			47·1	45·6	”

NOTE G.o.I. (1974c) is a more authoritative source than 1974a; indeed the former comments on the latter, observing that they are under-estimates. The birth and death rates are an average of different rates derived in G.o.I. 1974c by different methods, all extremely close to these figures – which are still described by the document as 'provisional'.

TABLE 2.12 Male and female baseline life-tables (survivors to age x) adopted for India (1966 – 70)

Age x	Males	Females			
0	10,000	10,000			
1	8,499	8,378	*Infant Mortality*	*Life Expectation*	
5	7,769	7,513			
10	7,512	7,208	150	Males	48 years
15	7,414	7,092	162	Females	46 years
20	7,254	6,902			
25	7,048	6,658			
30	6,845	6,420			
35	6,628	6,184			
40	6,382	5,946			
45	6,091	5,693			
50	5,748	5,408			
55	5,328	5,056			
60	4,820	4,627			
65	4,176	4,069			
70	3,413	3,396			

SOURCE Cassen and Dyson (1976).

TABLE 2.13 1971 population of India: distribution by Age and Sex (1000s)

Age	A					B				
	M	F	M+F	%	M/F	M	F	M+F	%	M/F
0–4	44,827	41,920	86,747	15.8	107	46,697	43,630	90,327	16.2	107
5–9	38,835	36,449	75,284	13.7	107	39,487	37,241	76,728	13.8	106
10–14	33,488	31,548	65,036	11.9	106	34,278	32,328	66,606	12.0	106
15–19	27,942	26,616	54,558	10.0	105	27,654	26,031	53,735	9.6	106
20–24	23,555	22,884	46,439	8.5	103	23,986	22,411	46,397	8.3	107
25–29	20,768	20,201	40,969	7.5	103	20,741	19,379	40,120	7.2	107
30–34	18,693	17,754	36,447	6.7	105	18,345	16,825	35,170	6.3	109
35–39	16,714	15,173	31,887	5.8	110	16,378	14,751	31,129	5.6	111
40–44	14,506	12,602	27,108	4.9	115	14,201	12,676	26,877	4.8	112
45–49	12,138	10,278	22,416	4.1	118	12,201	10,989	23,190	4.2	111
50–54	9,787	8,284	18,071	3.3	118	10,235	9,302	19,537	3.5	110
55–59	7,663	6,628	14,291	2.6	116	8,352	7,660	16,012	2.9	109
60–64	5,746	5,097	10,843	2.0	113	6,379	5,905	12,284	2.2	108
65–69	3,956	3,562	7,518	1.4	111	4,636	4,332	8,968	1.6	107
70–	5,318	5,017	10,335	1.9	106	5,194	4,993	10,187	1.8	104
Total	283,936	264,013	547,949	100	107.5	288,763	268,502	557,265	100	107.5

SOURCES A Raghavachari (1974); B Cassen and Dyson (1976).

The 'A' distribution was evolved on the one per cent sample data (G.o.I. 1971) for a population of 546.953 million and has been pro-rated here to correspond to the Census total of 547.949 million.

It is really with the last two of these tables that our picture of the 1971 population can be seen in coherent relationship with as many partial observations as can be consistently fitted together. The 'B' distribution in Table 2.13 is our assessment of the 1971 population; it is contrasted with the 'A' distribution which has been employed in official work, particularly the Draft *Fifth Five Year Plan*. The life-table used in its derivation is based on a model life-table adjusted for the peculiarities of India's age-sex pattern of mortality already discussed: the 'survivors to age x' values of the life-table are given in Table 2.12.[183] Population 'B' and its age distribution thus permits a reconciliation of various inferences from a number of sources; the size of the 1971 population, the pattern of mortality and the level of fertility as already discussed. The size of the 0 – 4 age group is realistically enlarged accounting for under-enumeration; over all ages the proportion of females has been left virtually unchanged relative to the Census proportion although it is rather likely that female under-enumeration was greater than male. A further feature of the 'B' population is an intelligible age progression of the sex ratio. It is a little hard to account for the pattern in distribution 'A' with its very high ratios at some ages. Distribution 'B' is consistent with some improvement of female relative to male mortality over recent decades, at the same time as an increase in the male/female ratio and with the observed age-sex pattern of mortality. Perhaps one has no overwhelming reason to expect the age progression of the sex-ratio to be quite so smooth as in the 'B' population, but it should make sense in relation to these conditions.

Late in 1975 the Registrar General's provisional *Age and Life Tables* for the 1971 Census became available.[184] The age distribution, though derived by different methods, was very close to our own as were its conclusions on fertility and mortality in the decade prior to 1971. We nevertheless prefer our 'B' population and age distribution for various reasons. A fuller discussion appears elsewhere;[185] some of the considerations are relatively minor such as that in the Registrar General's distribution, the age progression of the sex-ratios is rather erratic without obvious cause. But the main consideration is that we cannot make sense of the figures without raising the census total, while the document in question, clearly stating that the population was under-enumerated, nevertheless follows, as presumably it must, 'the practice of keeping the already published census total population fixed.'[186]

To conclude we would place the birth and death rate in the mid 1970s in the region of 37 and 17 respectively and the total fertility rate between 5 and 6. The Government in official publications gave figures of 35 and 15 for 1975; there was some danger that these might be believed simply through being often repeated. Yet they are taken from Sample Registration data which repeated surveys have shown to under-estimate vital events by anywhere from 5 to 13 per cent. There is no reason to believe that this performance had improved by 1975 or indeed later. Figures of 37 and 17 are consistent with raising the Sample Registration estimates by something resembling the degree of observed under-estimation. The birth rate is also consistent with a continuation of fertility decline in the first half of the 1970s akin to that in the 1960s (most of which was concentrated in the second half of the decade) and accords with estimates of births prevented by family planning activities. The death rate figure is consistent with some slowing down of the rate of mortality decline which, besides being observed in the Sample Registration data, is borne out by our account of the sources of current mortality change. Having said all that we must confess that any one of the landmarks in relation to which these consistencies or shifts are judged might itself be insecure, and certainty is beyond our grasp. Some confidence however may be placed in the view that fertility in the 1970s has been and is falling faster than mortality and that the decade rate of growth should be closer to 2·0 per cent than the 2·2 per cent of the 1960s – indeed the latter decade should prove to have had the fastest population growth in India's history.

MIGRATION AND URBANISATION

To stand on the Howrah bridge at any time is to feel that you are in the middle of some colossal refugee movement struggling to make headway against an impending doom; and these refugees are so bewildered by their plight that they are attempting to move in both directions at once.

G. Moorehouse, *Calcutta.*

The literature on migration in India is considerable – there are many dozens of items relating just to the two decades 1951 – 71. It would not be possible to give a comprehensive treatment of the subject here. Rather we will pick out certain themes relevant to the main concerns of this book. India is a country of tremendous movement; migration is constantly in progress from one rural area to another, from one urban area to another, from rural to urban and *vice versa*. The movement is daily, weekly, seasonal, long term; roads and railways carry endless streams of humanity across the country. And yet for most Indians home is the village where they were born. The major pattern of long term movement, especially for men, is out of the village to the town or city in the early years of working life and a return in the late years. This is born out by the sex and age distributions in urban areas, where males outnumber females by even more than they do in the population at large and where people aged 15 – 50 constitute a higher proportion of all age groups than they do for India as a whole.

The chief source of information on migration is the census which records where people were born as well as where they are enumerated and the duration of residence there. In 1961 only 3·3 per cent were enumerated outside the *State* in which they were born; but 30·7 per cent were born outside the *place* of enumeration. A large share of that 30·7 per cent is accounted for by female 'marriage migration' – about three-quarters of all female migration is of women moving within the same District; that figure is one-half for male migration.[187] The amount of rural to urban migration is relatively small – astonishingly small to those who are familiar with migration rates in Africa and Latin America.

During 1951–61 India's urban population grew by 18·5 million but of this 13·3 million were contributed by natural increase of the urban population itself. An estimated 3·1 million people were net immigrants or returning migrants into India from other countries in that period.[188] We do not know what proportion of the immigrants ended up in urban areas, but if either none of them did or all of them did, we have a maximum of 5·2 million and a minimum of 2·1 million of net internal rural-urban migrants in the decade. Making less extreme assumptions about the distribution of foreign or returning migrants a plausible range might be of the order of 3 – 4 million rural-urban migrants. Thus, in a period where the average annual increase in the total population was about 7·5 million, net rural to urban migration of the indigenous population amounted to an average of something of the order of 300,000–400,000 annually. Whatever else may have been going on in 1951–61 the rural areas were not generating the intolerable volumes of migrants to urban areas witnessed in other developing countries.

The 1971 Census showed an increase in the rate of urbanisation. The proportion of population urban was 16·73 in 1951, 17·98 in 1961 and 19·87 in 1971. The population as a whole grew faster in 1961 – 71 than in the decade before and it is possible that part of the acceleration of growth of the urban population is due to a more rapid rate of decline of mortality in urban than in rural areas. Nevertheless when the results on migration of the 1971 Census are known we may expect an increase in rural-urban migrants not only in absolute terms but in proportion to the (increased) population. Since urban birth rates were probably also declining faster than rural it is highly unlikely that all the additional 2 per cent of the population urban in 1971 were contributed by a more rapid rate of natural increase in urban areas. With the exception of the transitory influx of Bangladesh refugees the volume of international immigration was lower than in the decade 1951 – 61, when post-partition resettlement was still important. Something was happening in the 1960s to quicken the pace of migration from village to town and city.[189]

Any attempt to explain this phenomenon runs into the bewildering variety of studies of causes of migration – there are surveys of villages and urban areas, of migrants and migrant communities and almost everything and its opposite seem to have been observed. If we look just at male migration, which avoids the issue of marriage migration, accounting for a large share even of rural-urban migration for females, we would expect to find and indeed do find a large economic component in the explanation. But even that is far from universal – in one survey of migrants the number of males saying they came to find employment, or better employment, accounted for only 57·4 per cent of the sample – and that was for the four major cities, Bombay, Calcutta, Delhi and Madras; for the smaller cities and towns the proportion was lower.[190] This estimate does seem a little on the low side. One of the reasons for a general sense of puzzlement about the pattern of migration is that urban growth seems to have been slower in 1951 – 61 than in the previous or subsequent decade while that was the decade of the most rapid acceleration of industrial growth – even adjusting to 1961 definitions the decade rate of urban population growth was 41·4 per cent for 1941 – 51 and 37·8 per cent for 1961 – 71 while it was only 34·0 per cent for 1951 – 61.

If rural-urban migration is a product not only of urban but of rural conditions also, one should not expect any simple correspondences. This is also a case where the aggregate figures for India as a whole conceal so much difference in the experience of individual States that it is not worth struggling too hard to explain them on an aggregate level. One or two things may however deserve comment: when the great spurt in industrialisation began in the 1950s there was a considerable unemployed urban population already in existence and rural distress was on the whole greater in the 1960s than in the 1950s. In terms of current theories of migration it is not necessarily actual earnings differentials which explain rural-urban migration but expected earnings.[191] Thus past growth may give rise to expectations of earnings which are later disappointed – in such circumstances the pattern of migration would only slowly adjust to current economic realities.

Some light is shed on these matters by studies of migration at village level and by the pattern of urban development. One thing we learn from the former is that on the whole migrants do not come from the poorest sections: the educated and the slightly better-off predominate among migrants – it is they who have connections in the city, prospects of employment and some capital to tide them over the resettlement period. The very poor, such as the scheduled castes, have more incentive to leave the village but smaller prospects of benefiting by so doing – they will be discriminated against when they seek work and they have little if any capital. On the other hand the poorer villages do tend to send out more migrants and among villages the ones where land is poor and most unequally distributed. Migrants also tend to come from larger families and are often the younger sons of the family.[192] There are thus unmistakable signs of rural-urban migration being in some measure the product of population pressure on the village, but it more commonly affects those in a position to respond. And as our reflections on the economics of family formation indicated, many parents have such migration in mind for their children. In relatively well-to-do families in the Punjab it is quite common for the eldest or two eldest sons to be given no education 'because' they are destined to farm their parents' land; the younger sons are equipped as best the family can afford to earn their living by other means. Cultural factors are also involved: there is a considerable out-migration from the rural Punjab and considerable in-migration to it from neighbouring Uttar Pradesh – both migration streams seek better prospects but the Punjabi migrants are not content with the opportunities at home which satisfy the incoming migrants.[193] This reflects both the higher economic expectations of the Punjabi and his determined character, derived from a long tradition of self-improvement. One might expect the extent of migration to increase as sub-division of family land reaches the feasible limit; but there has also to be a prospect for the potential migrant to improve his lot when he moves.

The lack of such prospects has no doubt helped to contain rural-urban migration. Accounts of this migration usually talk of 'push' factors, pressures from the rural areas, and 'pull' factors, the attractions of urban areas. But in India, as Ashish Bose has said, one must reckon with the 'push-back' factor: the migrant arrives but fails to find employment and eventually goes home. For this and other reasons a large share of migration has the character of 'turnover migration' – people who come to an urban area but leave within a year of arrival. The volume of such migration is unknown; but the indirect evidence that it exists lies in the large number of rural-urban migrants in the 1961 Census who had arrived less than a year before the census – some 2·44 million; unless this figure is unusually large for reasons peculiar to the particular year 1960/61 – and there are no obvious reasons – it suggests a considerable volume of short-term migration since total urban population growth in 1951 – 61 was less than 20 million, i.e. less than ten times 2·44 million;[194] and the total growth, as we know, is not due to migrants alone.

Until we learn more about the components of urban growth in 1961 – 71 there is little purpose in attempting to explain its acceleration. There certainly was an unusual amount of rural distress in the 1960s which may have been a contributory factor, but there was also a slowing down of industrial growth and, in some areas, a considerable increase in rural employment due to the improvements in agricultural output. The overall picture is not a happy one: growing pressure on the land, relieved to a degree by technical progress; sons and daughters sent to towns and cities when the family's land has become too small to employ them all or when those without land can find no livelihood; whole families migrating when debt or natural disaster makes rural life finally impossible. But employment growth in cities is too slow to absorb all those who seek it. We may not know the magnitudes or all the intricate mechanisms of these processes but their results can be seen in towns and cities all over India. Migration also contributes to the problems of the educated unemployed: the educated migrant has chances of work in part because he will be hired for a job for which he is over-qualified, but he thus assists the escalation of qualification to the detriment of the qualified and the less qualified alike.[195]

What then of India's urban future? There are few topics on which naive extrapolation has done so much to damage understanding as that of urban growth in developing countries. Predictions are made of vast urban agglomerations containing several tens of millions of suffering human beings; these urban populations are forecast to build up to densities at which, sometimes on dubious analogies with laboratory studies of animals, violence and chaos break out and result in cataclysm. The history of urban development in India does not suggest such a future; and even if extrapolation of some trends did suggest it, it could still be forestalled by policy. In fact the processes described in the previous paragraph make clear that urban growth depends on a large number of things, but most particularly the relative growth rates of urban and rural employment. And when densities in a city reach intolerable levels people cease to migrate there and those born there may well leave.

The recent history of Calcutta bears this out. Whilst the population of the Calcutta urban agglomeration grew by about 1·8 per cent, the Calcutta Metropolitan Corporation (C.M.C.) grew by 0·7 per cent annually, from 2·9 million to 3·1 million. Both the larger city and the Metropolitan Corporation experienced their most rapid growth of population between 1931 and 1941, a decade in which the C.M.C. population grew by 77·9 per cent; it grew by 24·4 per cent in the next decade, 8·5 per cent in the next and, as we have seen, even slower in the decade ending in 1971. Some of the central wards of the C.M.C. actually lost population in 1951 – 61 and have continued to do so. Calcutta has been in the first half of this century the great magnet of India, its hinterland containing the country's largest concentrations of coal, iron and steel making and industry generally; in 1964 it was calculated that 42 per cent of India's exports and 25 per cent of imports went through the port of Calcutta.[196] But the troubles of the city in the 1960s and the industrial slowdown of recent years, together with the growing attractions of other centres, have turned the tide. While the city continues to spread slowly outwards it is no longer a place where the multitudes – save for the most desperate – go to seek a better lot. Even the five Districts in which the urban agglomeration is situated – Calcutta, Hooghly, Howrah, Nadia and 24-Parganas – have slowed down their population growth, from 32 per cent in 1951 – 61 to 26·7 per cent in 1961 – 71. But in that latter decade there was still an increase from 15·2 million to 19·2 million representing a large reservoir to fill any new jobs created in the city.

India's next nine largest cities are all growing rapidly: Greater Bombay by 43·8 per cent between 1961 and 1971, Delhi by 54·6 per cent, Madras by 63·0 per cent, Hyderabad 43·9 per cent, Ahmedabad 44·4 per cent, Bangalore 37·8 per cent, Kanpur 31·3 per cent, Poona 43·5 per cent. These are all the cities over one million in population varying from Greater Bombay, about 6 million, to Poona at 1·14 million in 1971. (The Census figures are for the urban agglomerations; the respective Metropolitan Corporations grew at comparable rates except – not surprisingly – that of

Madras which grew at 42·8 per cent.) These rapid increases have in the main been in response to the development of industry and small scale manufacturing. But annual rates of growth of these magnitudes (they lie in the range from 2·7 per cent, Kanpur to 4·4 per cent, Delhi and 5 per cent, Madras) cannot continue for very long. When these cities lose their impetus as employment centres their rates of growth will tail off just as did that of Calcutta. Thus while there may be a logistic curve for urban population as a whole, to understand the way people are going to live in urban areas one must look at the curve for each urban place. Calcutta has already passed the hump at the end of the steep slope of increasing growth and is on the flat part where the growth rate is slowly diminishing.

It seems that Bombay is still on the steeply sloping segment of the curve. The population of Greater Bombay grew from 4·15 million in 1961 to almost 6 million in 1971 – an annual increase of 3·7 per cent. The interesting part of this growth is a falling off in the share of it which is due to net immigration and an acceleration of the rate of natural increase, as the following table indicates.

TABLE 2.14 Population of Bombay 1951 – 71

Year	Population	Annual growth in prev. dec.	Natural increase	Annual rate of natural increase in prev. dec.	Net Immi.	Migrants in Population	Males per 1000 females
1951	2·994m	5·2%	0·243m	1·3%	0·950m	72·1%	1659
1961	4·152m	3·3%	0·558m	1·7%	0·600m	64·2%	1507
1971	5·971m	3·7%	1·000m	2·2%	0·819m	54·1%	1396

SOURCES Census data; Zachariah (1968); Joshi and Joshi (1975).[197]

The rising rate of growth of the resident population together with an increasing share of females among migrants is bringing the sex ratio into balance which promises a continuation of the high rate of natural increase. The death rate is unlikely to fall substantially further with any speed since, with the relative decline in immigration, the proportion of the population in the young and old high-mortality age groups is rising, but the increase in the proportion of females in the population will to a considerable degree offset the fertility decline which has been occurring.

The effects of population growth in Bombay will depend particularly on the success or failure of the proposed 'New Bombay', an attempt to provide an alternative focus for economic activity away from the increasingly congested centres of Bombay proper – indeed its failure will assist its eventual success since the continuing location of new jobs in the older part of the city will eventually lead to overcrowding on the Calcutta scale and thus force development to move elsewhere. At present fashion and convenience lend prestige to the older city and attract new investment, despite the fact that the public costs of alternative locations would be much lower.[198] It is to be hoped that the Bombay authorities will succeed where Calcutta failed – the fate of Calcutta is an object lesson for urban planners of the costly consequences of neglect. At the same time there is a limit to their ability to forestall the consequences of population growth without complementary action beyond the city, most particularly in the field of employment.[199] Since much of the existing expansion has been achieved by reclaiming land from the sea, which is becoming increasingly expensive, there is fortunately also a limit to the physical space for expanding the older parts of Bombay. It appears that the vested interests of the old city are having a more and more difficult time influencing municipal decisions to finance the developments they would like.

Bombay's geography – and economics – will prevent gargantuan expansion. In the light of its history and that of Calcutta one need not expect therefore either that a large number of India's cities will reach the size of some super-megalopolis containing 40 or 50 million people or that unheard-of densities will be reached. Suppose India's population grows to 2 billion over the next hundred years and stabilises there with 40 per cent of the population urban – that would give an urban population roughly seven times the present one at 800 million. If the existing size distribution of urban places were kept, that would result in a Calcutta of 50 million, Bombay 42 million, Delhi 25 million and so on downwards. In fact it is far more likely that the existing size distribution will alter and that the major cities will stabilise at levels well below 50 million, while growth gradually shifts to places currently further down the size rankings. As far as concerns densities, the experience of Calcutta indicates that they do not go on increasing indefinitely: the maximum density of urban population likely to be reached in India may already have been experienced in Calcutta. There is a definite prospect however that vastly increased numbers will be living at or near this maximum density in various urban centres as decades of further population growth go by – the implications of that are part of the subject matter for the final chapter.

The actual pattern of urban development throws some light on these matters. Between 1961 and 1971 the total urban population grew from 78·9 million to 108·8 million – an increase of 30 million, or 38 per cent; but nearly two-thirds of that additional urban population in 1971 – 19 million in fact – were to be found in urban places of more than 100,000 people and 7·7 million of these were in the nine one-million-plus cities. That means there was substantial growth on average in the 100,000 plus class – indeed this size class increased its share of the total urban population from 48 per cent to 52 per cent; the next class down (50,000 – 99,999) also minutely increased its share; the remaining size classes declined in their share – indeed the two smallest classes recorded hardly any absolute increase in population. This confirms a trend apparent in the 1951 – 61 period, the stagnation of small towns and the tendency for most growth to occur in the largest places[200] – not surprisingly existing centres of employment attract new enterprises because of their complementary facilities. The smaller towns are market centres and such like with little if any 'modern sector' activity.

TABLE 2.15 Size Class of towns and population in 1961 and 1971

Population size	1961		1971	
	Number of towns	Population (in millions)	Number of towns	Population (in millions)
Class I	113	38·18	142	57·02
(100,000 and over)				
Class II	138	9·37	198	13·22
(50,000 – 99,999)				
Class III	484	14·63	617	18·89
(20,000 – 49,999)				
Class IV	748	10·29	931	13·10
(10,000 – 19,999)				
Class V	760	5·71	756	5·70
(5,000 – 9,999)				
Class VI	218	0·75	277	0·87
(Below 5,000)				
Total	2,461	78·93	2,921	108·79

SOURCE Census 1961 and 1971 cited in Bose (1973).

We can probably expect this pattern of urban growth to continue for some time, but as has been suggested a number of what are currently the largest urban places with the highest rates of population growth will gradually slow down their growth as new centres take over when the older ones become excessively large and congested. Although we have tried to counter some of the worst fears about urban growth in India – the proliferation of dozens of giant cities with intolerable densities higher than anything yet seen – we do not wish to minimise the present and future urban problems of the country. Even if the population of Calcutta stopped growing altogether, there would be several decades of work to make the city an agreeable place to live for the mass of its inhabitants. The prospect that many other cities may reach the state of Calcutta before migrants become discouraged from heading towards them is not appealing and Bombay is well on the way to becoming a second Calcutta.

Ashish Bose quotes effectively the Kannada proverb 'After ruin, go to the city.'[201] A large part of the solution of India's urban problems undoubtedly lies in rural development; the quotation of this proverb has point because it alludes realistically to a reluctance to leave the village except under dire necessity. But as we have seen much migration is not due to ruin and many of those to whom ruin has come are forced to face it in the village. Even with the most successful conceivable programmes of rural development cities will continue to grow rapidly and, in a country where resources for everything are scarce, the needs of urban development will remain low in the scale of priorities. One might observe that virtually no countries have developed without a period of grossly deficient urban living conditions and further, that there are few cities even today, in countries however rich, where some part of the population does not live in distressing circumstances. Yet there was nothing inescapable in the arrival of circumstances quite so distressing as those of Calcutta, which had been the victim of undue neglect in the 1960s as well as of rapid growth.[202] With the setting up of the Calcutta Metropolitan Development Authority in 1970 it was fairly quickly shown that an agency with some powers and even relatively modest resources could do much to arrest the decay of the city and plan for its improvement. Perhaps the most notable feature of current plans for Calcutta is their pragmatism. Urban planning in many developing countries often suffers from one particular fault: the false standard. By this we refer to the notion incorporated in plans of what is considered 'desirable' in housing, water-supply or transport. Existing shortfalls in urban services are measured in relation to standards quite inappropriate for the country's resources; a plan is drawn up to remedy the situation; the funds required are not available; some fraction of the planned improvements are carried out at considerable expense, and the bulk of the problem – the living conditions of the urban poor – is left untouched. Planning in Calcutta has not in the past been immune to such failings; indeed they are still to be seen in the estimates for 'housing requirements'. But there is a move towards regarding slum settlements as the only form of shelter the poor are likely to have and therefore not as things to be 'cleared', but to be provided with essential services so that they will be minimally tolerable. Whatever one may think of the economics of the subway system now being constructed, traffic planning is at least not being permitted to revolve around the needs of the car-owning few and measures are at last being started to make up for almost a century of neglect of sanitation and water-supply.[203] 'The results by 2001 would be neither uniform nor aesthetically pleasing', as one commentator[204] has put it, 'but, hopefully, human and more livable.'

POPULATION PROJECTIONS

In this part projections for India are presented. But it will be useful first to review some of the projections made by others, past and present. As is observed in Chapter 4 the early years of planning in India were marked by expectations of population growth lower than the 1961 Census was to show. The 1971 Census showed a smaller population than was commonly forecast although the decade rate of population growth was higher than ever. But the components of that growth were incorrectly estimated even though the total figure officially projected for 1971 was only a little above the Census estimate; indeed if one allows for under-numeration in the Census, it was not far off at all. The first main exercise in projection was carried out for the Planning Commission in 1958; it was revised in 1961 after the provisional Census figures were released and in 1964, when the final totals and life-tables were available, the Expert Committee carried the projections forward to 1981.[205]

In the 1964 projections mortality was assumed to decline rapidly: the expectation of life at birth, thought to have been 41.9 for males 40.6 for females in 1956, was to rise by 0.9 years annually up to 1970 and 0.75 years during 1971–80. International migration was assumed to be negligible. Three different assumptions were made about fertility decline; the 'Medium' assumption was chosen for the 'recommended' projection – according to it fertility (the general fertility rate) would decline by 5 per cent during 1966–70, 10 per cent in 1971–5 and 20 per cent in 1976–80. The population totals arrived at are shown in Table 2.16 below. With present hindsight it is easy to point out that the mortality decline incorporated in the projection was too rapid, as was also the fertility decline. At least one author correctly criticised the mortality assumptions before the 1971 Census;[206] he claimed that the base figures for expectation

TABLE 2.16 Projections

Author	Year	Projection		1971	1981	1986	2001
Expert Committee	1964			560	695	–	–
	1967	(see text)		560	695	747	–
		(see text)		560	680	723	–
Fifth Plan	1973			547	658	705	
Raghavachari	1974	High – 2		547	677	754	1032
		Medium – 2		547	668	734	945
		Low – 2		547	649	700	846
IBRD	1973	Series C		550	713	823	1288
		Series B		550	696	782	1108
		Series A		550	681	748	871
Frejka	1973	NRR = 1	2040 – 2045	547	697	789	1124
		"	2020 – 2025	547	692	776	1069
		"	2000 – 2005	546	680	753	959
		"	1980 – 1985	545	642	676	799
		"	1970 – 1975	539	590	626	728

of life in 1956 were optimistically high and the life-table used incorporated excessively low levels of infant mortality. The mortality assumptions in the projection yield a death rate of 14 per 1000 for 1966–70, a rate which is still some way from attainment. The fertility assumptions were also optimistic but not as excessively so as the mortality assumptions, with the consequence that the 1971 figures were on the high side – only the rapid fertility decline variant gave a figure close to the actual findings: 555 million for 1971 compared with the Census 547.9 million. In 1967 the Expert Committee's working group made a further set of projections based on 'the highly intensive programme of fertility control envisaged in the Fourth Plan'; we reproduce in Table 2.16 the projection to 1986 based on a further 25 per cent decline in the general fertility rate and a rise of expectation of life of 0.4 years annually from the 'Medium' projection of 1964, and also the new projection, which lay between the 'Medium' and 'Rapid' fertility decline projections with lower fertility after 1971.[207]

If a forecasting prize were to be awarded for the last twenty years of projecting India's population, it should probably go to Coale and Hoover who estimated the 1971 population at 550 million in 1958, assuming little fertility decline and basing mortality expectations interestingly on the expected impact of the malaria programme and a linear relationship between general mortality and infant mortality.[208] True they covered themselves with alternative estimates, but in general their realism compares well with the wishful thinking which has pervaded so much official work.

The habit of optimism in projections has not yet died. The Draft Fifth Plan contained projections up to 1986; they are based on a 10 per cent decline in the 1971–6 general fertility rate relative to that of 1966–71, and 20 per cent declines in each of the two succeeding quinquennia. The increases in life expectancy are 0.5 years annually for males and 0.6 years annually for females (slightly less in both cases for 1981–6). The annual rate of growth thus declines from 2.03 per cent in 1971–6 to 1.68 per cent in 1976–81 and 1·37 per cent in 1981–6. By our calculations the starting level of expectation of life was a little high at 51·3 (males) and 49·6 (females) for 1971–6, the mortality decline somewhat on the rapid side and fertility decline optimistically so. The result is a population estimate for the five years of the Plan that is almost certainly too low – 581·2 million for 1974 rising to 636·8 million in 1979. The final Fifth Plan repeated the assumptions of the Draft: a birth rate of 25 and a death rate of 11 by 1984, the end of the Sixth Plan – these were to result from the 1976 National Population Policy, to which we will refer below.

The next set of projections of major interest are those of Raghavachari[209] – these are based on the smoothed age distribution of the 'one per cent sample' of the 1971 Census, referred to above as the 'A' distribution. Although these were not 'official' projections, they emanated from the Registrar General's staff; they also contain figures used in official documents which have no other source – for example the Draft Fifth Plan gives the population aged 0–4 as 15·8 per cent of the total, the same figure used by Raghavachari and so far not yet published elsewhere. The life expectations of the Fifth Plan projection are also taken from this source. The difference lies in the assumptions about fertility: Raghavachari has six, two 'High', two 'Medium' and two 'Low', all based on varying degrees of success of the family planning programme; printed in Table 2.16 are the ones to which he gives particular weight, High-2 and Low-2 representing the 'possible range of population', and Medium-2 which he darkly observes is 'considered' for 'any discussion on specific issues regarding the trends over the future years.' The Fifth Plan projection lies below his Medium-2 variant – though, for the Plan period 1974–9, the difference is relatively small: the Draft Plan gives 636·8 million for 1979 as opposed to Raghavachari's Medium-2 which, by interpolation, gives 642·7 million.

There are two further sets of projections which deserve examination – those of the World Bank[210] and Tomas Frejka.[211] The Bank started work before the 1971 Census was available and used a base figure for India of 537 million in 1970 taken from the U.N. *Demographic Yearbook*: this figure is actually one million more than the 1970 total one would derive from the 1971 Census and the intercensal growth rate. The Bank assumed that the rate of increase of expectation of life at birth was a function of its level: it would rise by 0·2 years annually when the level was 30 – 34·9 years, going up to 0·6 years when it was 50 – 59·9 and then falling off to 0·4 years at levels 60 – 64·9, 0·2 years at 65 – 69·9 and 0.1 years thereafter. Similarly with fertility, which is assumed to fall by 2 per cent annually when the Gross Reproduction Rate lies between 1·5 and 2·0, 3 per cent between 2.0 and 2·5, 2 per cent between 2·5 and 3·0; below 1·5 and above 3·0 it falls at 1 per cent annually – these hold for the Series A projections of 'fast' fertility decline which the authors describe as 'rather optimistic'. Their Series C assumes constant fertility, and Series B an intermediate fertility assumption between A and C; all three have the same assumptions about expectation of life. These assumptions were used for all countries; their implications for India are summarised for the three series in Table 2.17. Table 2.16 gives the population totals for all three series approximately interpolated to give 1981, 1986 and 2001 figures.

Lastly the projections by Frejka; his particular interest is the very long term – the period over which populations cease to grow and the levels they will then reach. We have given some consideration to this question for India, to which we will refer later, but we record in the table Frejka's projections of India's population up to 2001. He employs only one set of mortality assumptions: life expectation rises from 49·0, 1965 – 70 to 62·5, 1995 – 2000 – that is by 0·5 years annually. The fertility assumption, dictated by the long term problem, is of the form of a linear decline in the Net Reproduction Rate until the point where it reaches the value of 1, where it remains indefinitely. There are five projections depending on whether

TABLE 2.17 I.B.R.D. projections: assumptions as applied to India

	1970	1980	1990	2000
Expectation of life at birth	50·3	53·3	61·4	64·68
Series A CBR	38·8	30·7	27·2	23·8
CDR	15·4	11·1	9·0	8·1
Series B CBR	38·8	34·6	32·7	30·4
CDR	15·4	11·4	9·1	7·8
Series C CBR	38·8	38·9	38·9	38·3
CDR	15·4	11·7	9·2	7·6

N.R.R. = 1 is reached in 0, 10, 30, 50 or 70 years – these correspond to Projections 1 – 5 respectively. They are mainly illustrative – the N.R.R. reaching one is roughly equivalent to the situation of the average couple having two children; while it is quite impossible that this should happen in India at once or in ten years' time – and is rather unlikely even in thirty years' time – the projections indicate the growth momentum in the population even after the two-child family becomes the norm. (As with the Bank projections, we have had to interpolate for the individual years as Frejka's results are given for 5-year intervals starting in 1970. Since he has started with a 1970 population of 534.3 million, but growing at different rates in each projection, the 1971 population differs in each.) Thus even if the two-child family was the norm by the early 1980s, India's population would rise to about 800 million in 2001, if Frejka's assumptions about mortality are right.

It might be wondered why, with all these projections available, anyone should go to the trouble of preparing yet more. In fact there are several reasons for being unhappy with the existing projections. In the first place they are each based on a single schedule of mortality decline. As we have observed there is reason to question whether mortality is currently falling at all; it seems more sensible to explore the consequences of different assumptions about future mortality. Secondly they are all based on starting populations which may be too low – it is at least worth examining the consequences of the possibility that the 1971 Census has under-estimated the true population and examining also the consequences of an age distribution for 1971 consistent with the population being larger than 547·9 million in that year. And thirdly most of the projections are rather optimistic about the initial levels of fertility and expectation of life. (We have already discussed our own conclusions about the situation prior to 1971 and given the life-table and age distribution which seem best to reconcile all the findings for the 1961 – 71 period.) We have presented a new set of projections based on the 'B' initial population and age distribution (Table 2.13). In these projections we explore the possibility of several different time paths of fertility decline. The present decline seems to be rather slow and the first four assumptions about fertility continue the existing decline at different rates: they are based on the period after which a total fertility rate of 2.5 is reached – in the case of these four assumptions, which we label $F_1 - F_4$, that rate is reached after 60, 50, 40 and 30 years respectively starting from 6·1 in 1965 – 70. It does not seem unreasonable to think of the years 1996 – 2000, twenty years from the present, as the earliest point by which the average number of children will reach 2·5 per couple in India. However some countries have experienced extremely rapid fertility decline in recent decades – Japan, Mauritius – and although India's circumstances do not appear similar in relevant respects, two further fertility declines were tried, F_5 and F_6, which depart from the trajectory of F_4 to reach the 2·5 level by 1991 – 5 and 1986 – 90 respectively. In $F_1 - F_4$, the total fertility rate declines logarithmically from the initial to the terminal level, that is faster at first, and gradually decelerating.

Mortality is made to decline by letting the male expectation of life at birth increase by a constant annual amount until it reaches 70 years: the amounts in the three time paths $M_1 - M_3$ are 0·2 years, 0·5 years and 0·7 years increase per year respectively. The annual increase in female expectation of life at birth is made slightly greater so that both male and female expectation reach 70 years at the same time: under M_1 this occurs beyond the 50-year horizon of the projection; under M_2 it occurs in 2011–15 and under M_3 in 2001–05. We adopt this approach in part because most projections assume unwarrantably large increases in expectation of life; the possibility that mortality will decline very slowly at least deserves exploration. Also there seems to be an unspoken belief among demographers that fertility is the dominant factor in such populations – it is hard to explain otherwise the rarity of projections containing more than one assumption about the path of mortality. As we shall see this is not the case. (The assumptions concerning fertility and mortality are given in Table 2.18. Permuting all of them gives us eighteen projections, from F_1M_1 to F_6M_3. These result in a wide range of population totals over the fifty years to 2021 for which the projections run: they are set out in Table 2.19 and the resulting crude birth and death rates in Table 2.20.)

With so many projections one ends up with an indigestible amount of data. In fact we originally made rather more, including a further eighteen for comparative purposes, based on the 'A' population – the reader interested in further details of the projections and their methodology is referred to Cassen and Dyson (1976). The complete set of 'B' projections is given here for the reader interested in the results of this wide variety of permutations of assumptions, though we cannot consider them all equally valid, some for logical and some for empirical reasons. Thus we believe that the early 1970s gave no basis for expecting mortality declines in the following years as fast as M_2 – an additional half-year added annually to

TABLE 2.18 Assumed courses of fertility decline ($F_1 - F_6$) in terms of total fertility, India 1971 – 2020

Period	1971–75	1976–80	1981–85	1986–90	1991–95	1996–2000	2001–05	2006–10	2011–15	2016–20
Fertility decline										
F_1	5·662	5·257	4·879	4·530	4·206	3·904	3·624	3·364	3·123	2·899
F_2	5·580	5·104	4·669	4·271	3·906	3·573	3·269	2·990	2·735	2·500
F_3	5·456	4·881	4·366	3·906	3·494	3·125	2·796	2·500	2·500	2·500
F_4	5·258	4·532	3·906	3·368	2·903	2·500	2·500	2·500	2·500	2·500
F_5	5·258	4·532	3·707	3·049	2·500	2·500	2·500	2·500	2·500	2·500
F_6	5·258	4·104	3·203	2·500	2·500	2·500	2·500	2·500	2·500	2·500

Assumed courses of male and female mortality decline ($M_1 - M_3$) in terms of life expectation (years)

Mortality decline		1971–75	1976–80	1981–85	1986–90	1991–95	1996–2000	2001–05	2006–10	2011–15	2016–20
M_1	Males	49·1	50·2	51·2	52·3	53·4	54·4	55·5	56·5	57·5	58·5
	Females	47·2	48·4	49·6	50·8	52·0	53·2	54·4	55·5	56·6	57·6
$M_{1·5}$	Males	50·0	51·9	53·8	55·6	57·4	59·1	60·8	62·4	64·0	65·5
	Females	48·2	50·3	52·4	54·4	56·4	58·3	60·2	62·0	63·8	65·5
M_2	Males	50·8	53·6	56·2	58·8	61·3	63·6	65·9	68·0	70·0	70·0
	Females	49·1	52·2	55·2	58·1	60·9	63·5	65·9	68·0	70·0	70·0
M_3	Males	51·6	55·1	58·4	61·6	64·6	67·4	70·0	70·0	70·0	70·0
	Females	50·0	53·9	57·6	61·2	64·5	67·4	70·0	70·0	70·0	70·0

TABLE 2.19 Projected population totals (millions) of India, 1971 – 2021

Projection	1976	1981	1986	1991	1996	2001	2006	2011	2016	2021
F1 M1	622·5	692·1	766·2	844·3	924·1	1004·2	1083·4	1160·8	1235·2	1304·5
F1 M2	625·9	702·5	787·6	881·0	981·1	1087·3	1198·4	1313·3	1430·7	1543·5
F1 M3	627·4	707·0	796·6	896·0	1004·0	1119·8	1242·3	1365·2	1487·0	1604·9
F2 M1	621·2	687·8	757·6	829·4	900·8	969·7	1035·0	1095·4	1149·7	1196·3
F2 M2	624·6	698·1	778·5	865·1	955·8	1049·0	1143·3	1237·1	1328·9	1412·1
F2 M3	626·1	702·5	787·3	879·8	977·9	1080·0	1184·6	1285·5	1380·6	1467·5
F3 M1	619·1	681·5	745·0	807·9	867·7	921·9	969·0	1008·2	1048·2	1086·8
F3 M2	622·4	691·6	765·3	842·1	919·8	995·8	1068·3	1135·8	1208·6	1280·3
F3 M3	623·9	695·9	773·8	856·2	940·7	1024·8	1106·3	1179·6	1254·9	1329·8
F4 M1	615·9	671·9	725·6	775·6	818·9	853·2	887·9	921·6	952·5	978·9
F4 M1·5	617·7	677·8	736·3	792·5	843·4	886·7	925·1	964·2	1002·4	1037·4
F4 M2	619·2	681·7	744·9	807·6	866·7	919·5	976·6	1036·2	1096·6	1151·7
F4 M3	620·6	685·9	753·1	820·8	885·9	945·6	1010·7	1075·5	1137·8	1195·4
F5 M1	615·9	671·9	721·4	763·4	796·0	831·0	865·3	896·5	922·8	944·0
F5 M2	619·2	681·7	740·4	794·5	841·6	894·8	951·2	1007·6	1061·8	1110·1
F5 M3	620·6	685·9	748·5	807·4	860·1	920·1	984·2	1045·6	1101·6	1152·0
F6 M1	615·9	663·6	701·9	730·8	764·5	798·5	828·9	853·4	872·8	889·4
F6 M2	619·2	673·0	720·0	759·7	807·4	859·2	910·6	958·5	1003·6	1045·3
F6 M3	620·7	677·1	727·6	771·6	824·8	883·2	942·1	994·5	1041·0	1084·5

TABLE 2.20 Projected crude birth rates (CBR) and crude death rates (CDR) of India, 1971–2020.

Projection		1971–75	1976–80	1981–85	1986–90	1991–95	1996–2000	2001–05	2006–10	2011–15	2016–20
F1 M1	CBR	39·4	37·5	36·0	34·3	32·2	30·0	28·0	26·1	24·3	22·6
	CDR	17·2	16·4	15·6	14·9	14·1	13·4	12·8	12·3	11·9	11·7
F1 M2	CBR	39·3	37·3	35·6	33·7	31·6	29·5	27·6	25·8	24·1	22·4
	CDR	16·1	14·3	12·7	11·3	10·1	9·0	8·2	7·5	7·0	7·3
F1 M3	CBR	39·3	37·2	35·4	33·5	31·4	29·4	27·5	25·8	24·2	22·5
	CDR	15·6	13·4	11·5	10·0	8·6	7·6	6·8	6·9	7·1	7·3
F2 M1	CBR	38·9	36·6	34·8	32·8	30·5	28·0	25·7	23·6	21·6	19·7
	CDR	17·2	16·2	15·5	14·7	14·0	13·3	12·7	12·2	11·9	11·7
F2 M2	CBR	38·8	36·4	34·4	32·3	29·9	27·6	25·4	23·4	21·5	19·6
	CDR	16·0	14·2	12·6	11·2	10·0	9·0	8·2	7·6	7·1	7·5
F2 M3	CBR	38·8	36·3	34·2	32·1	29·7	27·4	25·3	23·3	21·5	19·7
	CDR	15·5	13·3	11·4	10·0	8·6	7·6	6·8	7·0	7·2	7·5
F3 M1	CBR	38·1	35·3	33·0	30·7	28·0	25·2	22·5	20·1	19·9	19·5
	CDR	17·1	16·0	15·2	14·5	13·8	13·1	12·6	12·2	12·2	12·3
F3 M2	CBR	38·0	35·0	32·6	30·2	27·5	24·8	22·3	20·0	19·9	19·4
	CDR	15·9	14·0	12·4	11·1	9·9	8·9	8·2	7·7	7·4	7·9
F3 M3	CBR	38·0	34·9	32·5	30·0	27·3	24·7	22·2	19·9	19·9	19·5
	CDR	15·4	13·1	11·3	9·8	8·5	7·6	6·9	7·1	7·5	7·9
F4 M1	CBR	36·9	33·1	30·2	27·4	24·3	21·0	20·7	20·1	19·3	18·2
	CDR	16·9	15·7	14·8	14·1	13·4	12·8	12·7	12·7	12·7	12·8
F4 M1·5	CBR	36·8	33·3	30·0	27·2	24·0	20·8	18·8	18·4	17·8	16·9
	CDR	16·3	14·8	13·5	12·5	11·6	10·8	10·3	10·1	10·0	10·0

(*Table 2.20 contd.*)

Projection		1971–75	1976–80	1981–85	1986–90	1991–95	1996–2000	2001–05	2006–10	2011–15	2016–20
F4 M2	CBR	36·8	32·9	29·9	27·0	23·9	20·7	20·5	20·0	19·2	18·2
	CDR	15·8	13·7	12·1	10·8	9·8	8·9	8·4	8·1	7·9	8·4
F4 M3	CBR	36·8	32·8	29·7	26·8	23·7	20·6	20·4	19·9	19·2	18·3
	CDR	15·2	12·9	11·1	9·6	8·5	7·6	7·1	7·5	7·9	8·4
F5 M1	CBR	36·9	33·1	28·9	25·1	21·5	21·6	21·0	19·9	18·6	17·5
	CDR	16·9	15·7	14·7	13·8	13·1	13·0	12·9	12·8	12·8	12·9
F5 M2	CBR	36·8	32·9	28·5	24·7	21·1	21·3	20·8	19·8	18·5	17·4
	CDR	15·8	13·7	12·0	10·7	9·6	9·0	8·6	8·2	8·0	8·5
F5 M3	CBR	36·8	32·8	28·4	24·6	21·0	21·2	20·7	19·7	18·5	17·5
	CDR	15·2	12·9	10·9	9·5	8·3	7·7	7·2	7·7	8·1	8·6
F6 M1	CBR	36·9	30·2	25·4	21·4	22·3	22·0	20·6	18·8	17·5	17·0
	CDR	16·9	15·3	14·1	13·4	13·3	13·3	13·1	13·0	13·0	13·2
F6 M2	CBR	36·8	30·0	25·1	21·1	22·0	21·7	20·4	18·7	17·4	17·0
	CDR	15·8	13·4	11·6	10·4	9·8	9·3	8·8	8·4	8·2	8·8
F6 M3	CBR	36·8	30·0	25·0	21·0	21·8	21·6	20·3	18·6	17·4	17·1
	CDR	15·3	12·6	10·6	9·2	8·5	7·9	7·4	7·8	8·3	8·9

life expectancy – let alone the faster ones of M_3. Also even someone who believed strongly in the dissociation of fertility and mortality rates would probably agree that some combinations of assumptions are implausible, if only because many of the factors which are related to fertility decline are also concomitants of mortality decline. Thus F_1M_3 or F_6M_1 are extremely unlikely combinations and several others are not much less so: for example even moderate fertility declines may not continue indefinitely in company with very slow mortality declines and projections such as F_3M_1 do not look very realistic beyond the next 25 years.

If forced to a choice for the immediate future we would probably select F_3M_1 nevertheless as reflecting a continuation of the trends of the early 1970s; however, since many could consider those assumptions unduly pessimistic, we have made yet a further projection employing F_4 and a mortality decline in between M_1 and M_2 which has life expectancy rising by 0·35 years annually; we label it $M_{1.5}$. It is difficult to imagine a more difficult time to make a population forecast than the late 1970s. The effect of the 1976 family planning activities could be to accelerate fertility decline considerably or, if the alleged 'backlash' proved powerful, to interrupt the decline which was already in progress. From the mortality point of view the situation is perhaps less difficult – there seem to be few grounds for positing anything other than a continuing modest decline; though the rate at which it is proceeding must be conjectural. In the hope that the net effect of the population policies of 1976 will be some speeding up of fertility decline, or at least no slowing down of the past trend, we would expect the immediate future to be bracketed by projections F_3M_1 and $F_4M_{1.5}$.

A virtue of our complete set of projections is that it caters for most conceivable scenarios. Thus the Fifth Plan projections correspond very closely to F_6M_2. Table 2.21 gives the summary results of this projection up to the year 2001:

TABLE 2.21 Projection (a) Ultra-fast fertility decline, fast mortality decline

	1971	1976	1981	1986	1991	2001
Total Population (millions)	557·3	619·2	673·0	720·0	759·7	859·2
(Per 1000) Crude Birth Rate	36·8	30·0	25·1	21·1	21·8	
(Per 1000) Crude Death Rate	15·8	13·4	11·6	10·4	9·5	
(Per cent) Annual Growth Rate	2·1	1·7	1·4	1·1	1·2	

SOURCE Projection F_6M_2.
NOTE The C.B.R. rises slightly in the 1991 – 2001 decade owing to age distribution changes; the total fertility rate is declining as assumed.

If projection (a) approximately reflects official aspirations, one can only comment that both fertility and mortality declines look very fast indeed. The fertility decline was predicated on success for the sterilisation drive which began in 1976; but, as Chapter 3 indicates, it was clear by early 1977 that the momentum of the campaign could not be sustained. However a growth rate of 1·4 per cent by the end of the Sixth Plan is not unattainable though it is more likely to occur as a result of failure of mortality to fall as anticipated than as a result of the dramatic fertility reduction of projection (a). In fact that growth rate of 1·4 per cent is slightly higher than would result from a combination of F_3 with no mortality decline, which illustrates the importance of the mortality assumption.

Our 'preferred' range of projections is summarised in the following table:

TABLE 2.22 Projection (b) Medium fertility decline, slow mortality decline

	1971	1976	1981	1986	1991	2001
Total Population (millions)	557·3	619·1	681·5	745·0	807·9	921·9
	1971 – 75	1976 – 80	1981 – 85	1986 – 90	1991 – 2000	
(Per 1000) Crude Birth Rate	38·1	35·8	33·0	30·7	26·5	
(Per 1000) Crude Death Rate	17·1	16·0	15·2	14·5	13·4	
(Per cent) Annual Growth Rate	2·1	1·9	1·8	1·6	1·3	

SOURCE Projection F_3M_1

Projection (c) Medium-fast fertility and mortality declines

	1971	1976	1981	1986	1991	2001
Total Population	557·3	617·7	677·8	736·3	792·5	886·7
CBR	36·8	33·0	30·0	27·2	22·4	
CDR	16·3	14·7	13·5	12·5	11·2	
Growth Rate	2·1	1·8	1·7	1·5	1·1	

SOURCE Projection $F_4M_{1.5}$

A few small points may be noted. First in these and other projections here a base population of 557·3 million is adopted for 1971. As argued above, and as conceded in at least one official publication cited there, the 1971 Census was under-counted by a modest amount; 557·3 million is 1·7 per cent more than the actual Census count of 547·9 million – the degree of under-count estimated in the Census Post Enumeration Check: (For purposes of comparison with projections based on 547·9 million for 1971, the total population for any projection year may be reduced by 1·7 per cent as a very close approximation.) Second, as is customary in projections, the parameters change smoothly and in one direction whereas in fact they may swing sharply and change direction.

Population trends for India may not be predictable, but projection (c) represents what might be described as 'balanced optimism' – a rate of fertility decline faster than that of the early 1970s and a respectable rate of mortality decline. If the family planning programme were to meet with reverses however only the failure of mortality to fall could keep the population from growing at the uncomfortably fast rates of projection (b). The scenario of projection (b) cannot be ruled out as a practical possibility. We would thus suggest a range of 736–45 million for the population of 1986, and of 886–920 million for the year 2001. The final Fifth Five Year Plan gave point estimates of the population in 1988/89 (725·4 million) and 1991 (744·8 million). Allowing for the 1·7 per cent lower starting population, these correspond very closely to projection (a); but they are clearly too low by the standards of projections (b) and (c), which even when reduced by 1·7 per cent – i.e. related to a base of 547·9 million for 1971 instead of 557·3 million – yield a range of 779–795 million for 1991. If the population estimate in the Plan had any significance, it would surely have been wiser not to rely on a single estimate and that a highly optimistic one.

If F_3M_1 proves to be the true path in the immediate future, the difference from the Fifth Plan projection is considerable even after one

TABLE 2.23. Projected population for 1986 (millions)

Age Group	F_3M_1	$F_4M_{1.5}$	Draft Fifth Plan
0 – 4	99·1	91·2	74·2
5 – 14	172·8	168·1	160·0
15 – 59	422·4	425·0	426·6
60 +	50·7	52·0	43·8
Total	745·0	736·3	705·2

decade. By 1986 the population totals diverge by 40 million. F_3M_1 starts with a slightly larger and younger population than the Fifth Plan, but the main difference is made by the fertility assumption. Our projection contains heavier mortality; but, in the Plan projection, the birth rate has fallen below 25 per thousand by 1981 – 5 which does not seem at all likely. (The figure of 25 was adopted solely because it was the target birth rate of the family planning programme.) We believe our mortality path and the starting population and age distribution also to be more realistic than the Plan. The differences are apparent in the 1986 age distributions as well as the totals, as Table 2.23 shows. Despite its larger total, F_3M_1 even has a smaller population of 'working' age (15–59) as a result of all the assumptions. F_3M_1 may be pessimistic, one might add, but it is at least plausible. Even $F_4M_{1.5}$ presents a picture for 1986 significantly different from that of the Plan, with a population total only 9 million less than that of F_3M_1. $F_4M_{1.5}$ is about as 'optimistic' as legitimate expectations permit.

The age distributions in a projection are often of interest in themselves. For that reason we reproduce the age pyramids for the years 1971, 2001 and 2021 from $F_4M_{1.5}$ (Figure 2.1). The programme employed in our projections not only reduces fertility and mortality but changes its pattern: women's peak fertility both declines and moves from ages 20–4 to ages 25–9 reflecting a rise in the age at marriage and increasing use of contraception, as found in most low-fertility countries. The mortality pattern obviously enough reduces mortality most in the age groups in which there is most room for reduction, young and old.[212] Female mortality also

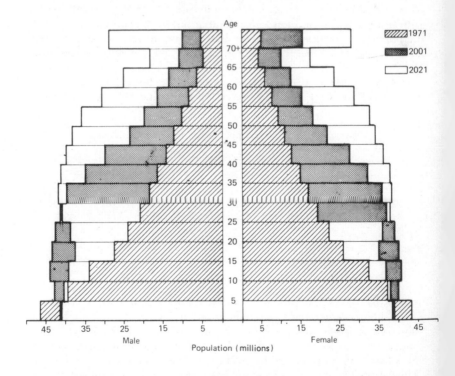

Fig. 2.1 Population Pyramids for India, for 1971, 2001 and 2021 (Projection $F_4M_{1.5}$)

SOURCE Tables 2.13 (B) and 2.24

improves faster than male, in part because fertility decline reduces maternal mortality, in part because one expects that the other factors leading to excess female mortality may gradually diminish in importance. Of course these alterations in behaviour are part assumption and part the inner logic of population arithmetic; in so far as they are assumptions one can only claim that they are well-founded in past experience. An interesting aspect of the age pyramids in Figure 2.1 is the very modest expansion of the base over time: most of the growth in population occurs in the adult age groups as one would expect with the assumed decline in fertility.

The most conspicuous feature of any projections for India is the enormous scope for population increase in the long run even with very rapid fertility decline. As is now well-known this is the result of the age distribution common to most developing countries, with a high proportion of women of child-bearing age that results from their demographic history. The most effective way to show this is by projections based on reaching a net reproduction rate (N.R.R.) of 1 at given points. When the N.R.R. is equal to 1, the level of fertility – usually a little over two children per couple – is such that the population will eventually just replace itself, given no changes in age specific mortality. But it takes some time for the stationary population to be reached. We have made such N.R.R. projections for India. There are nine projections in all, with N.R.R. = 1 reached after 50, 40 and 30 years and the mortality assumptions $M_1 - M_3$ already employed. They show the ultimate population of the distant future stabilising anywhere from 1·2 billion to 1·8 billion. But the impressive thing is the length of time it takes for the stationary state to be reached: even with N.R.R. = 1 reached by 2001, population is still growing with some pace until 2051 and comes to a complete halt only in the twenty-second century. (See Figure 2.2.) (It must be emphasised that such projections are even more artificial than our others; the condition N.R.R. = 1 is unlikely to be precisely met over long periods. One could of course just tell the computer to produce zero growth by a certain date but that can lead to very peculiar results.[213])

Many people cannot believe that India's population will ever reach these large figures. Before it happens they must presume some terrible famine or pandemic disease or war will intervene. We do not regard such things as probable. However to explore their consequences we made a further projection which we christened 'mediaeval mortality'. In this exercise mortality fluctuates randomly, within limits, around a constant trend, but for one year in every fifteen there is a great upward leap in mortality to double the trend level. This means an addition of upwards of 17 million deaths in each of these exceptional years; that is to say mortality experience vastly worse than anything in recent history. It results in a reduction in the terminal year, relative to the trend without the mortality peaks, of about 100 million – the population reaches one billion instead of

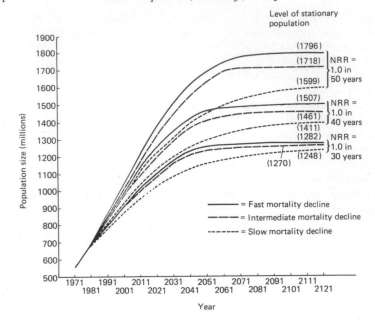

FIG. 2.2 Net reproduction rate projections

1·1 billion in 2061. (See Figure 2.3.) Evidently those who believe in smaller populations for a future India must have in mind mortality episodes of apocalyptic magnitude, vastly greater even than those projected in 'mediaeval mortality'. Of course such episodes cannot be categorically ruled out, but we do not think those depicted in 'mediaeval mortality' are at all likely, let alone still worse ones.

The population of 2021 is of somewhat academic interest; not only is its size uncertain but, even if it were known, the effect on current decisions would be limited. But it is as well to be aware that very considerable population growth is in store for a very long time to come, if only to have some sense of the kind of future society which lies ahead. In the nearer term there must be no self-deception or wishful thinking about sudden reductions in the rate of growth, even if 'radical change' is contemplated: and not just contemplated, but achieved. Perhaps the most practical lesson to be learned from attempts at projection is their uncertainty. Many decisions do have to be made in the present which should relate to the population fifteen years ahead; yet it is possible to be 40 million out in a population forecast for India over that period. This indicates the need for forms of planning which consist not of targets of provision related to numbers in the population, but of institutions capable of responding to

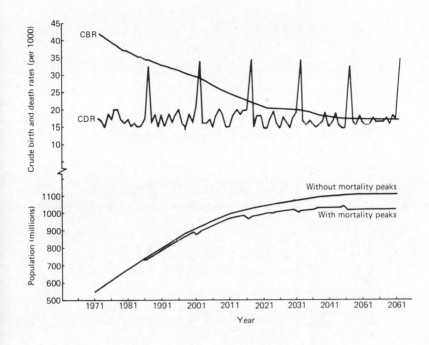

Fig. 2.3 Mediaeval mortality projection

whatever numbers turn out to be the true ones. 705 million is an implausibly low number for 1986; but 745 million may be too high or too low and what planners should be thinking about is a population in 1986 between, say, 720 and 760 million. They should be asking themselves what is implied for their plans by the fact that they do not know anything more precise than that.

TABLE 2.24 2001 and 2021 population of India: distribution by age and sex ('000s)

Age	2001					2021				
	M	F	M+F	%	M/F	M	F	M+F	%	M/F
0 – 4	41,505	38,971	80,476	9·08	106·5	41,127	38,795	79,922	7·70	106·0
5 – 9	42,918	39,935	82,853	9·34	107·5	40,272	37,792	78,064	7·52	106·6
10 – 14	44,013	40,717	84,730	9·56	108·1	39,244	36,698	75,942	7·32	106·9
15 – 19	43,673	40,165	83,838	9·46	108·7	37,652	35,080	72,732	7·01	107·3
20 – 24	42,765	39,025	81,790	9·22	109·6	38,762	35,937	74,699	7·20	107·9
25 – 29	41,041	37,109	78,150	8·81	110·6	41,030	37,813	78,843	7·60	108·5
30 – 34	39,853	35,987	75,840	8·55	110·7	41,921	38,388	80,989	7·74	109·2
35 – 39	35,037	32,248	67,285	7·59	108·6	41,200	37,503	78,703	7·59	109·9
40 – 44	30,004	27,718	57,722	6·51	108·2	39,975	36,213	76,188	7·34	110·4
45 – 49	23,549	21,873	45,422	5·12	107·7	37,884	34,199	72,083	6·15	110·8
50 – 54	19,783	18,387	38,170	4·30	107·6	36,056	32,747	68,803	6·63	110·1
55 – 59	16,345	15,402	31,747	3·58	106·1	30,750	28,696	59,446	5·73	107·2
60 – 64	13,453	12,652	26,105	2·94	106·3	25,109	23,720	48,829	4·71	105·9
65 – 69	10,795	10,116	20,911	2·35	106·2	18,264	17,533	35,797	3·45	104·2
70+	10,050	15,621	25,671	3·57	102·7	28,781	28,301	57,082	5·50	101·7
Total	460,734	425,928	886,662	100	108·2	538,028	499,415	1037,443	100	107·7

SOURCE **Projection** $F_4 M_{1.5}$

3 Health and Family Planning

> The most distressing experience for a writer is when he approaches his readers with a problem. Visits for subscriptions to charities are not half so irritating as the intrusions on the peace of mind of an occupied and self-satisfied public by faddists who put up their umbrellas and insist that it is raining when every good man of the world knows that the sun is shining.
>
> P. K. Wattal, *The Population Problem in India* (1916).

BACKGROUND

Many national family planning programmes have two strands in their history: a concern for health, in particular the health of mothers and children, and a concern for the socio-economic effects of rapid population growth. Until recently proponents of family planning, feeling reticent about the latter, often tended to disguise their views by speaking in public mainly about the former. Both these strands have been present in India's family planning history. The very first family planning clinic in India was opened in Bombay in 1925 by Prof. R. D. Karve who lost his post at the Christian Missionary College because of his 'advanced' views; but the first well-known public advocacy of family limitation was due to Pyare Kishen Wattal in 1916, to whose far-sighted book we have already referred. He put the argument in both health and socio-economic terms, as did the National Planning Committee of the Indian National Congress which, under Nehru's chairmanship, also supported family planning. These early days were marked by one particular debate, namely how family limitation was to be achieved. Gandhi favoured abstinence; but those who supported contraception rapidly gathered strength.[1]

The Mysore government, first in this as in many other welfare measures, established birth control clinics in State hospitals in 1930; Madras agreed to open clinics in 1933. But these initiatives were not copied extensively elsewhere, except by private agencies. World War II interrupted such developments as were going on – there was a certain amount of discussion in government committees in the early 1940s, but it was not until the Planning Commission was established after Independence that the first substantial sums were allocated by the Central Government for a family planning programme. Unsuccessful attempts to promote the rhythm-method were the main feature of the First Plan period, though 21 rural and 126 urban family planning clinics were opened. There were tremendous shortages of trained personnel and it was thought that the main needs were for educational advances so that people could be motivated to adopt family planning measures. In 1956 after limited progress under the First Plan, and the widely noticed remarks of the 1951 Census Commissioner about 'improvident maternities', the Central Family Planning Board was set up and the State Family Planning Committees were gradually appointed in each State. Bihar had had one in 1954; by 1958 all States had them except Jammu and Kashmir where one was only appointed in 1960.

Between 1956 and 1961, the Second Plan period, over 1030 rural and 400 urban family planning clinics were established and contraceptives were made available at a further 1865 rural and 330 urban health centres. Training schemes were set in motion but only a small number of thousands were trained. It was the Family Planning Committee of the Third Five Year Plan which began to establish norms for family planning centres of various types to be set up according to specific population ratios. But staff shortages were still a major constraint and little besides condoms and foam tablets were to be offered to clients. Sterilisation was just beginning but between 1956 and 1961 only 122,000 men and women underwent operations. The Third Plan offered 100 per cent financial assistance to State governments for training, staff and facilities for sterilisation which it suggested should be offered free to all regardless of income. It was still hoped that the Community Development network would play a major part in motivational work and there were extensive plans for giving C.D. personnel family planning education.

The Third Plan, which began in 1961, stated clearly that the objective of stabilising the growth of population within a reasonable time-period should be a central feature of planning, with major emphasis on the family planning programme. What gave particular impetus to government family planning measures was the 1961 Census which showed a higher rate of population growth than had been expected. It was in the early 1960s, before the first United Nations Mission had examined the programme in 1964, that a more comprehensive strategy began to be elaborated. The main feature was to be the system of clinics and sub-centres: in urban areas all hospitals and maternity homes were to incorporate family planning centres and further separate clinics would serve the urban population centres. In rural areas, the Primary Health Centres (P.H.C.s), the main unit of the health service at the local level, were to have two doctors, one of whom would be mainly occupied with family planning duties. The P.H.C. was supposed to cover all or most of a 'block', the administrative unit of the older Community Development organisation. (Indian States are divided into districts, which number some 320 in all, and then into Blocks, numbering about 5500. The district population averages from 1 – 1½ million, the block in the region of 100,000.) Certain mobile services were also provided for. Then extending from the P.H.C. there would be health/family planning sub-centres, one for every 10,000 people.

Fully staffed, the Primary Health Centre would have as its family planning personnel, besides one of the two doctors (probably a lady doctor, if the ideal staffing of one male and one female doctor was in post), Auxiliary Nurse Midwives (A.N.M.s), extension educators and health assistants (one for each 20,000 population), Lady Health Visitors (L.H.V.s, one for each 40,000) as well as statistical and other staff. The sub-centres would have a staff of an A.N.M. and an attendant, with additional provision for a male health assistant for every two sub-centres. The A.N.M., supervised by L.H.V.s, was to be infantry of the programme. It was recognised that an A.N.M. could only plausibly manage to serve a population of 3–4000; but the initial goal of 1:10,000 took note of the shortage both of trained staff and of funds. (One must not forget that 1:4000 for the 1971 rural population comes to about 110,000 A.N.M.s.) The Central Government decided to bear all the family planning costs in the States, though the rest of the P.H.C. staffs remained on the States' health budgets. This was the Government of India pattern of services, sanctioned for all States under the 'Extended Programme', although States were permitted to take initiatives of their own and minor variations on the 'G.o.I pattern' were permitted. Private voluntary agencies – such as the Family Planning Association of India, which under Lady Rama Rau has had a long and venerable history – operated side by side with the official programme; increasingly they have adapted their services to the G.o.I. pattern and received official assistance. Most of their work has been in urban areas.

The programme as a whole was centrally coordinated by a new Department of Family Planning in the Ministry of Health and Family Planning. The administrative structure ran through State family planning departments to the district level. This then was the perspective of the programme: a series of service points in parallel with and sharing the functions and facilities of the health service, aided by an extension system of male and female family planning workers. Each service point was in theory to deliver as many as possible of the contraceptive methods offered: the so-called 'cafeteria approach'. To increase the motivational effect a separate mass media campaign was organised spreading the message on posters, on the radio, in newspapers, films, puppet shows, even, for a time, on banners carried by live elephants. The inverted red triangle became extremely well known as the family planning symbol; indeed it has been adopted outside India too.

In successive plans the family planning programme was allocated increasing amounts of money. In the early 1970s in fact some States were not able to spend all the money allowed them – they could not construct centres and sub-centres fast enough, they could not fill the posts sanctioned, and some of the money was to cover incentives and other payments on a 'per client' basis – and the clients did not materialise. Nevertheless the programme managed to spend very large sums, rising from Rs. 134 million ($18 million) in 1966/7 to a peak of Rs. 797 million ($100 million) in 1972/3 after which the budget was cut during the economic crisis in and after the following year.[2] partly because of the great expenditure and the disappointing volume of clients, the programme prior to 1976 came under tremendous critical fire. It was accused of insufficient urgency, and excessive haste. It attracted political opposition. It was criticised for its inadequate administration. Service points were chosen without adequate selectivity.[3] The target orientation of the programme at all levels was counter-productive.[4] The communication effort was not directed with sufficient care to particular groups, and in any case promoted unacceptable notions, such as that parents were economically better-off with two or three children.[5] Unpleasant forms of persuasion were used to push clients into the clinics. In any case India was 'not ready' for family planning – the socio-economic conditions for widespread voluntary acceptance of birth control did not exist.

All these criticisms of the pre-1976 programme had considerable validity, as we shall see. But just as the Government at times had a tendency to exaggerate the programme's successes, so the critics exaggerated its failings. It had not been all bad by any means. And the real lesson of its history is that there is a considerable desire for family-limitation in India and even that was not being met. The desire was not so widespread that the birth rate would have declined to anywhere near replacement level if it were satisfied; but it was adequate to keep busy a more effective programme than existed on a scale within the country's means. As is well-known however the debate in 1974–5 over where family planning should go next ended up with the 1976 National Population Policy which assumed that much stronger measures were required to bring clients into the programme and that the government could carry them out. In the penultimate part of this chapter we assess the 1976 activities. But in the belief that the lessons of the programme up to 1975 have not been made widely known, we first review that experience in some detail. We shall do so method by method – for all the talk of the cafeteria approach, the programme has tended to concentrate its energies on one or another contraceptive method from time to time. Looking at it in this way also has the merit of giving adequate weight to the unsatisfactory character, for India's purposes, of existing contraceptive technology, a fact often forgotten. The truth about family planning in India prior to 1976 lies in the Government's attempts to introduce the I.U.D., sterilisation and the condom to a population who – even if some of them did want fewer children – knew little of birth control and its modern methods, with an administration that did not realise quite how far beyond its experience was the problem it was tackling, nor how inadequate to its needs were the services on which it intended to rely.

THE I.U.D.

When the Government of India pattern was sanctioned and the beginnings of the modern programme had been made, the major emphasis, as far as contraceptive techniques were concerned, was on the intra-uterine device – the I.U.D., sometimes called I.U.C.D. (where the 'C' stands for 'contraceptive'), or simply the 'loop' or the 'coil'.[6] Considerable hopes were placed on this device. It was inexpensive, consisting of a small piece of plastic; it could possibly be inserted by trained auxiliaries; and its contraceptive efficiency was quite high, though known to be less than 100 per cent even when it remained securely in place. The designer of the model of the I.U.D. which was employed at the outset, Mr Jack Lippes, and other foreign experts visited India and were instrumental in persuading the Government that it was suitable for widespread use.[7] The first U.N. Mission, which examined the family planning programme in 1964, had a major role in this respect.[8]

Enthusiasm at first ran high. Wherever personnel were available – for the most part the presence of a female doctor has been regarded as essential for loop-insertion – women were encouraged to use the I.U.D. The response seemed to be good; in 1966/7, only one year after the campaign had really started, over 900,000 women were fitted with I.U.D.s. People were already beginning to calculate how many years this accelerating programme needed to continue in order to resolve India's population problem. At the same time there were warning signs from observers in the field that all was not quite well. In the following year, 1967/8, the number of I.U.D. acceptors declined to 669,000, and from there the decline continued quite drastically up till 1970 when the annual acceptance rate stabilised just below the half-million mark, a point from which it began a slow but not substantial recovery up till 1971/2, after which it remained in the vicinity of 400,000 until 1975/6 when it rose to 594,000.[9]

The explanation of the ups and downs of this part of the family planning programme has little to do with the commonly expressed belief that the strongly motivated women got what they wanted and the programme then had to make headway among less interested clients and thus was bound to fall off. This 'creaming-off' theory is as inadequate to explain the I.U.D. history as it is in the case of vasectomies as we shall see below. The evidence of performance data from the clinics, of surveys of I.U.D. retention rates, of numerous observers and commentators on the operation of the programme at the field level, is much more consistent with the view that only a small segment of the demand had been touched when trouble began to be caused by difficulties attendant on the use of the loop in the setting of the Indian programme.

To understand this history it is worth taking a look at the experience of the I.U.D. in the rich countries of Europe and North America. The first appearance of the I.U.D. in anything like its modern form was in a paper by R. Richter in the *Deutsche Medizinische Wochenschrift* of September 1909: the 'Grafenburg ring' was introduced in the 1920s but did not do very well. Widespread use did not begin until after the invention of improved forms of the device in the late 1950s. To this day there is no settled account of its physiological action. A leading hypothesis at the moment is that the contact of the device with the endometrium leads to local changes in the uterine *milieu* which are gametotoxic, that is capable of destroying ova and spermatozoa. This is supported by most animal studies on the I.U.D. It would be valuable if this could be established beyond doubt, since another current theory holds that the role of the I.U.D.[10] is to inhibit implantation of the fertilised ovum; if that were true, the device would be an abortifacient and thus ethically unacceptable to many. The inherent difficulties of all research in this field make it hard to reach a final conclusion, but currently the first account given above seems to be as commonly believed as others which have been put forward hitherto.[11] It is by no means impossible that these and other effects are all present and weakly operative.

Just as a great deal is being learned of the physical functioning of the I.U.D., so we know vastly more of its operation in use and of how to make that use more effective. Different versions of the I.U.D. have been tried, many of whose names give an idea of their shape. The Lippes device, which comes in four different sizes, is serpentine in form with diminishing curves. It is still the most common in current use. There is the M or 'butterfly'; the Copper-T or Copper-7 and others. Most are made of inert plastic; the T or 7 versions have a copper filament, precipitations from which are said to increase contraceptive effectiveness. A later generation version of the I.U.D. which now appears to be going out of use is the Dalkon Shield. None of the devices seems superior to all others in all respects. The Copper-7 and Copper-T, which at one time appeared to be contending to replace the Lippes Loop, are not now judged to possess major advantages,[12] though they may do for India because they can be presented as a new device.

Several tens of thousands of women with I.U.D.s have now been surveyed in the United States and elsewhere, most exhaustively in the 'Cooperative Statistical Program'.[13] Experience has been gathered on a wide range of features affecting performance. A standard language has even grown up to describe various aspects of performance. 'Expulsion' is the term given to spontaneous ejection of the loop, 'removal' to the deliberate taking out of the device by the women herself or by a doctor. (Many I.U.D.s are fitted with a tiny thread which can be grasped with relative ease so that the device can be pulled out.) Removal, expulsion and pregnancy are the three main forms of failure of the I.U.D., known as 'events'. Translocation and perforation, which occur infrequently, are usually recorded separately. No cancer or other uterine malignancy has been found associated with the older I.U.D.s, nor ill-effects on fecundity after removal. (It is too soon for conclusions about these last features regarding the 'second generation' I.U.D.s discussed below.)

The general results of the Cooperative Statistical Program, completed in 1970, showed that no I.U.D. was consistently better than any other for all 'events'. The smaller sizes of loop had higher pregnancy rates and expulsions but were better tolerated if they remained in place; the larger sizes had better contraceptive efficiency but were more uncomfortable. (In some studies their retention rates are better, but that may be connected with the fact that they have to be removed by medical personnel.) Removals were the biggest single cause of discontinuation, even after excluding removals resulting from a desire for pregnancy. Removals are usually classified as being requested because of 'pain or bleeding', 'medical reasons' or 'other reasons' – the latter including desired pregnancy. At least three-fifths of the women surveyed (who number just under 24,000 and were from U.S.A., England, Sweden, Fiji and Puerto Rico) were still continuing with the device two years after first insertion. The risk for all 'events' was highest in the first year. Expulsions were less frequent, the greater the age of the women or the higher her parity. Bleeding and pain removals declined as parity rose. Other studies have confirmed these results in a general way for other countries though the individual performance figures differ.[14] It must be borne in mind that when these surveys are made, the I.U.D. clients are often under better medical supervision than they would be outside such surveys so that the event rates may be somewhat better than normal.

This is particularly true for early field trials of new I.U.D.s. Thus Davies's results with the Dalkon Shield (his own invention)[15], like Zipper's with the Copper-T[16], have given exceptionally low event-rates, lower than other researchers have been able to obtain even with the same devices. Davies's study claimed a total of 5 per cent for all events; this is among the lowest ever obtained. Its non-repeatability by other researchers does not necessarily cast doubt on its validity. But it does suggest that performance of this high standard is most unusual. A continuation rate of 80 per cent – that is 80 per cent of women fitted with the I.U.D. still retaining it after one year – would be considered a high level in a developed country; such a figure may represent an attainable maximum under ordinary conditions with the standards of health care prevailing in Europe or North America and figures in the region of 70 – 75 per cent first year continuation are more common.

It may be worth noting the opinions of researchers and practitioners in one or two other countries. Thus Soviet researchers have concluded after obtaining results similar to those mentioned above: 'We consider the I.U.D. an effective method of birth control. But the frequency of expulsions and removals and the related necessity for continuous medical observation limit their widespread application'. They observed that further research could reduce the incidence of these problems.[17] Similar conclusions were reached by a French practitioner who thought – as have others – that more attention to relating the size and shape of the device to each woman's uterus would minimise side effects. He claimed 96.2 per cent of his patients were contented with the device, partly as a result of his use of systematic hysterography.[18] It must be repeated that such a result is quite exceptional.

A fair amount of sophistication has entered into the accounts given of differential performance of the I.U.D. Thus obviously the care in examining women for contra-indications will affect performance. So too will follow-up care, the attention given to complaints of any nature presented by women with I.U.D.s. The skill of doctors fitting the loop seems to increase with practice but after a time attentiveness may decline out of sheer boredom – loop-insertion does not seem to keep its hold on the doctor's enthusiasm for more than a limited period. But many other things have also been claimed as affecting performance – from X-ray examination and measurement of the uterus as already mentioned to the quality of doctor-patient relationships, cultural characteristics of acceptors and even the tiredness of doctors fitting the device.[19] Medical opinion is sceptical about the precise significance of these. Much of the woman's ability to retain the I.U.D. may depend on her commitment and the degree to which she will tolerate initial discomfort if it occurs. For this reason it is always hard to tell whether something which correlates statistically with improved retention does so because it is physiologically beneficial or because it acts on the woman's psyche. Doctor-patient relationships have been shown to be important in the treatment even of wholly 'physiological' conditions such as virus infections.

Bearing this in mind the reader may note the conclusion of one of the authorities cited above. The I.U.D. is not a universal panacea. 'Every physician is not skilled in the use of the devices, nor is every woman a suitable candidate for the method. Observance of contra-indications, careful timing of insertions and meticulous insertion technique are important factors in obtaining first-class results with this, as with other birth control methods.'[20] This was the conclusion of a paper mainly based on U.S. experience and very enthusiastic about the I.U.D. As we have noted the usual situation requires even further qualification. But the general conclusion remains: possibly after some initial discomfort in the first months of use, 75 per cent or thereabouts of women in good health and with reasonable access to medical services should find the I.U.D. a highly satisfactory form of contraception. And it must be remembered that the 25 per cent or so who may not find it satisfactory do not necessarily reject it because of physiological malfunction. Especially if women adopt it early in marriage they will wish to remove it when they want a further child. People do also change their contraceptive choices from time to time trying out alternatives to find what suits them best, and no doubt some of the

I.U.D. performance figures reflect this ordinary volatility. Finally one must remember that new versions of the I.U.D. are constantly being tried out, in some cases with modestly improved results. The bulk of the studies referred to above, and of the experiences which have formed the views of many practitioners and family planning experts, were based on older models of the I.U.D. and also lacked the benefits of some of the experience now documented.

It is somewhat easier to understand what happened in India in the 1960s in the light of this experience elsewhere. Something definitely went wrong in the Indian programme – though all these years afterwards we can still not be absolutely sure of what went wrong or why. We have already alluded to the initial rise and fall in the annual number of acceptors with a high of 0·9 million in 1966/7 and a low of 0·46 million in 1969/70. (Even this is uncertain – the reporting of numbers of acceptors may have been on the optimistic side particularly in the early years.) The I.U.D. acquired a sufficiently unhappy reputation that the 'failure' of the programme was openly spoken of.

The first thing to ask is whether the I.U.D. really did 'fail' and if so in what sense. During the late 1960s a very large number of follow-up studies of the I.U.D. were carried out and they reported a very broad range of results. Continuation rates after one year varied from 50 per cent or even less to 80 per cent; after two years, 60 per cent retention was a common figure with rates as low as 40 per cent or even less observed occasionally, as well as figures above 60 per cent. It is very difficult to judge the accuracy of any of the studies. Most of them are based on case cards collected in clinics and do not make clear what sampling techniques were used, or whether those who came to the clinics were typical of the population. Some of the studies have continuation rates higher than the normal levels observed in rich countries. While that is not impossible for India it may be considered suspect. Altogether a review of published studies does not enable one to reach any settled quantitative conclusions about continuation rates for the I.U.D. in India.

The Director's Report of the National Institute of Family Planning for 1970/71 presents pooled data for a four-year follow-up study of the I.U.D. from seventy clinics. They show continuation rates of 75 per cent for the first year, 60 per cent after two years, dwindling to just over 30 per cent after four years.[21] If these results are characteristic of the programme as a whole, they certainly cannot be classed as 'failure' by any standards, as we have seen for the rich countries. By developing country standards, such results are excellent. Thus a Turkish study for 1969 showed 38·7 per cent terminating after one year,[22] or a continuation rate of 61·7 per cent. A study for Taiwan showed termination rates of 30–40 per cent after one year, 50 per cent after two years.[23] The Taiwanese programme is usually regarded as successful in international circles though not solely because of I.U.D. performance.

There are however a number of studies for India showing fairly catastrophic results, such as terminations after one year as high as 60 per cent, and over 70 per cent after two years.[24] There was also a survey taken in Delhi in 1966 to try and account for a wave of loop removals. The survey gave a fairly colourful picture of the state of mind of many Indian couples with the loop, wives believing all manner of strange things about it, including even the possibility that it could travel round the body and end up in the heart or lungs, and husbands fearing such things as penile injury during intercourse or even death.[25] And the loop clearly became very unpopular in India, for a time at least. A major 1970 study based on a sample of the population at large (i.e. not a clinic-based study) showed as few as 5 per cent of current users of any contraceptive method employing the I.U.D.; and 'current users' were only 13.6 per cent of couples at risk.[26] On all questions asked in the study concerning attitudes towards use of various methods of contraception – convenience, contraceptive effectiveness, lack of side effects – the I.U.D. was in each case at the bottom of the poll compared with condoms, orals or sterilisation.

A number of questions remain to be answered concerning the I.U.D. programme in India. What has the volume of cases of side effects actually been? If this is at all different from elsewhere in the world, what is the explanation? Have the numbers of women having their I.U.D. removed been greater than those actually experiencing side effects and, if, so why? What is the proper place of the I.U.D. in India's family planning programme? We will take up these questions in turn. Inevitably the answers to them are somewhat speculative for reasons which will become clear.

The evidence referred to so far has displayed an enormous variety of results. There are easily a hundred and fifty studies of I.U.D. performance in India.[27] They are variable not only in their findings but also in quality, the latter in ways which are often impossible to judge on the basis of the published reports. It is worth remembering too that a women's experience of the I.U.D. is a highly complex matter, with psychological factors playing a major part. The I.U.D. in its first months of use very commonly provokes discomfort or worse. One person's discomfort is another person's pain. Certainly a woman's tolerance of the I.U.D. through this early period will be partly a matter of her pain threshold and her commitment to the I.U.D. and everything it means. This helps to explain the potential importance of the doctor-patient relationship referred to above; it may also explain the great variability of results obtained in the studies which are carried out, after all, in a great variety of circumstances as well as employing different methodologies and definitions.

When it comes to the question of the volume of side-effects therefore we must confess that we do not know. What are measured are most commonly expulsions, removals and pregnancies – the 'events'. We do not know whether the rates found in clinic surveys are true for the clinic population since the characteristics of those lost to follow-up are unknown; it is probably correct to suspect that this biases measured performance upwards relative to the true since it seems plausible that a major reason for non-reappearance at the clinic is dissatisfaction with the I.U.D. We do not know how many expulsions are in fact removals since often it is only the word of the client that distinguishes between the two. (It must be remembered that many I.U.D. acceptors in India have had to be persuaded to take the device; they may prefer to tell the doctor that it came out rather than say that they removed it.) Most importantly we do not know whether women who have had the loop removed have done so because they have had side-effects or because they know that others have had them. Statements about reasons for removal are similarly suspect – women may state bleeding or pain as their reasons because they know those are the common symptoms whether they personally have experienced them or not.

So in the first place it is hard to tell on the basis of all the studies published what has been the event-rate for the I.U.D. in India. The widespread dissatisfaction with the I.U.D., together with the other arguments just referred to, point to an average performance for the programme as a whole somewhat worse than the 75 per cent first year and 60 per cent second year retention rates reported by the National Institute of Family Planning study referred to above. As already indicated these would be respectable figures in Britain or America and, if true for the whole programme in India, would not justify the official beliefs that the I.U.D. has failed there. It is very much more likely that the overall average figures are closer to 65 per cent and 50 per cent, or less, for first and second year continuations – somewhere between the best and the worst performance found in Indian surveys and comparable to other developing country programmes.

Much more difficult even to guess at is the volume of actual sufferers of side-effects as compared with the volume of terminations. One of the few studies which tried to establish this found that while 20 per cent of women terminated use of the loop after six months, and 60 per cent after two years, the 'true' failure rate looked very different on closer inspection. 55 per cent of the cases required no attention; of the 45 per cent who did need attention, 31 per cent had it successfully, 5 per cent did not accept the treatment offered – only 8 per cent took the treatment but without relief.[28] If this study is at all representative (some of the acceptors were from relatively prosperous urban areas), it shows that with reasonable care the number of unsatisfactory cases can be kept quite low, and it allows one to infer how much of what happens may be due to the deficiency of care. This is an important corrective to a common theme in I.U.D. studies all over Asia – it has often been found that one or two persuasive women in a village can induce large numbers of others to get rid of their loops whether or not the others have themselves suffered unduly. For that reason attempts to correlate I.U.D. retention with various characteristics of acceptors often come to grief. We shall refer again to this phenomenon, which we may christen the 'rumour effect' – it requires a name as it seems so often to have disturbed India's family planning effort. But for the present we shall just conclude that the 'true' proportion of sufferers from irremedial side-effects in the I.U.D. programme is unknown, while almost certainly less than the proportion of terminations.

There are however one or two things on which virtually all the studies agree. Symptoms of bleeding associated with the I.U.D. are by far the most common reasons for dissatisfaction with the device[29] and there is every sign that this aspect of I.U.D. performance in India has been more important than in most other countries. It is worth quoting the World Health Organisation on this subject:

> A certain amount of bleeding is so common immediately after insertion that it should be considered as the usual event. Intermittent slight bleeding ('spotting') or a sero-sanguineous discharge frequently continues after the initial period of bleeding associated with insertion. This pattern is thought to be particularly common in women suffering from iron deficiency and requires suitable medication; it can be a serious personal burden. Bleeding may also become manifest as menorrhagia or metrorraghia. These constitute probably the most troublesome symptoms and may be intense enough to alarm both patient and physician. Severe bleeding requires active treatment and usually calls for removal of the device.[30]

This although written in 1966 remains highly pertinent for India and certainly for the first generation I.U.D.s still in common use. If bleeding 'can be a serious personal burden' for women in general, it is particularly so for Indian women a very large proportion of whom – perhaps the majority – are malnourished or anaemic or both. Even if the I.U.D. only increased the menstrual flow – as it does in a moderate proportion of cases all over the world – it would be a sufficient disability for women in critical states of anaemia. Many Indian women have the additional religious problem that menstrual bleeding makes them ritually unclean – in particular they may be forbidden to cook and, since men rarely cook in the home, even 'spotting' can be a serious matter. Thus it appears both that Indian women are more than normally susceptible to problems of bleeding caused by the I.U.D. and that the consequences of it are more than normally insupportable. That is quite possibly the factor above all others responsible for the troubles of the I.U.D. programme. But a number of additional ones need to be brought out.

An important question is the skill of insertion: the second U.N. Mission[31] which examined India's family planning programme recommended more widespread use of paramedical staff to fit I.U.D.s – a recommendation whose wisdom was uncertain and in any case not extensively followed.

Nevertheless some paramedicals were permitted to insert the loop and there is evidence that they *can* do it as well as anyone else[32], and certainly doctors in training commonly did so. On the whole the programme has relied on qualified female doctors for loop insertion – but there is some doubt whether a high standard of insertion technique has universally prevailed.

There is also a question of the detection of contra-indications. It is commonly believed that prolonged and careful medical examination of women before insertion has not been a feature of the programme and that many women with say pelvic inflammation have been given I.U.D.s when they should not have been. Given the standard of medical care obtaining, and likely to obtain, in so poor a country and given also the premium on obtaining maximum numbers of insertions this cannot be wondered at. In fact the low level of medical attention has probably had a more important effect on retention rates for a different reason: the treatment or reassurance of women experiencing side-effects, which has been noted as a significant element in the achievement of high performance levels, has only been available to a limited extent in India particularly in rural areas. A woman may travel several miles to the clinic to receive her I.U.D.; when she is in pain or bleeding a few days or weeks later she may prefer simply to remove it rather than make the journey again. In general a programme striving for results at speed, and rewarding its personnel for numbers of insertions, is unlikely to constitute a recipe for good performance.

Altogether it can be seen that most of the conditions for high continuation rates have not existed in India or certainly not everywhere in India. And there have been features peculiar to India and perhaps certain other countries which have contributed further to poor performance. One other which may deserve consideration is the size of uterus of Indian women – there seems to be some evidence that Indian women differ in various respects from other races and therefore the sizes and shapes of devices appropriate for them (in so far as appropriateness depends on the uterine configuration) may require sophisticated exploration.[33] In fact the various studies do not seem to have determined even today which devices and sizes are most suitable for India.

It is difficult to believe that the low levels of health, nutrition and education prevailing in India have not affected continuation rates with the I.U.D.; on the other hand one can only believe in them as overall general factors. Virtually no evidence has been published on differential retention by income, educational or nutritional status.[34] It is rather sad that only one or two of the numerous studies which present both retention rates and socio-economic characteristics of the acceptors in the sample have attempted to relate the two. Given the widespread belief in an association between malnutrition or anaemia and poor tolerance of the loop, it is rather astonishing that the association has been so rarely tested in India. There are though good physiological and other reasons for postulating such an association. For what it is worth, and it is worth extremely little, the author has examined the *average* level of literacy, years of education or income in about twenty surveys and related these to the average retention rates in the same surveys. Some faint positive association can be discerned, but there is a preponderance of the lower figures among the rural surveys and it may well be that insertion has been less skilful, just as post-insertion care is less available, in the rural areas.

The one thing which emerges from Indian studies identically with those elsewhere is the positive relationship of retention with age and parity. This is partly for physiological and partly perhaps also for psychological reasons – the woman who wants no more children will be more committed to keeping the loop. The correlative of this is that younger women who use the loop for spacing children, even if they tolerated it physically as well as older women, would show lower retention rates. But also since the average age and parity of Indian loop-acceptors is higher than in many other countries some of the average performance figures look better by international standards than they actually are.

We must ask what lessons have been learned apart from these. An important feature which we have not so far mentioned is the question of advance warning of side-effects . On the whole in the early stages of the programme women were not told to expect difficulties; it was felt that it was sufficiently hard to persuade women to adopt the I.U.D. at all and would be even harder if they had to be told that they might experience pain or bleeding. It has now become customary to give such warnings and the failure to have done so in the past now looks like being a mistake. Another lesson has been the importance of the 'rumour effect' – there have been innumerable cases of severe impairment of local programmes by the spread of stories about supposed or actual side-effects, stories which influence both potential clients and otherwise satisfied clients. Un-doubtedly the low opinion in which the I.U.D. is held by Indian women is exaggerated. Yet it is a very sophisticated notion to advance anywhere, let alone among an ill-educated population, that women should adopt a contraceptive device with a certain probabilistic liability to malfunction, much but not all of which can be medically ameliorated. (Male readers are invited to contemplate how they would respond to the offer of a contraceptive device which could be painlessly inserted in the genital region, which might cause pain or other adverse symptoms that may or may not be prone to alleviation and which could be painlessly removed if dissatisfaction were irremediable.) One is tempted to infer that the introduction of any contraceptive with known liability to side-effects should be very gradual and should be based on extending proven popular successes in normal operational conditions. If there are risks, the client should know about them and know how they can be dealt with.

There is no doubt that the liability to side-effects *was* known in India before the mass programme was launched. Not only were there to hand all the published pre-1966 studies of I.U.D. performance elsewhere, some of which we have noted. The G.o.I. also conducted fifty clinical trials of the I.U.D. all over the country between 1962 and 1964. The results of these trials were not dissimilar to later experience. In a survey of thirty-one of them,[35] fairly typical retention rates were reported. Medical and other conferences took place discussing the incidence and treatment of side-effects. Nevertheless the Advisory Committee on Scientific Aspects of Family Planning met in Aurangabad in January 1965 and on the basis of these clinical trials concluded as follows: firstly that the Lippes Loop should be the I.U.D. of choice; secondly, that 'the I.U.C.D. is safe, effective and acceptable and should be made available through all medical and health centres having the requisite facilities. No paramedical personnel should be permitted to insert the I.U.C.D.: only the physicians may do the insertion for the present.'[36]

It is far easier to see now what went wrong than it was to foresee it at the time. While it is valuable to observe that the decisions were taken fairly deliberately in India, and thus to qualify the often-held view that everything was the fault of foreign advisers, we should also observe that the voices calling for caution and a slow build-up of the programme were very few. Those behind cried 'Forward' and most of those in front cried 'Forward' too – in the atmosphere of the mid 1960s, amid the talk of the population 'crisis' and the terrible droughts in Bihar and elsewhere which seemed to justify it, anyone suggesting that the family planning programme should lay deep and careful foundations was unlikely to hold out against those counselling bold action.

This history has shown that the I.U.D. was not suitable for universal distribution in the India of the mid 1960s. While mistakes were undoubtedly made, and the programme could have been more effective, the inherent problems of the loop suggest a more restricted role. This is, of course, not to say that it had, and has, no role at all. On the contrary – for those women who tolerate the device well there is no more satisfactory contraceptive technique available at present. The task is to deliver the I.U.D. to those women, while minimising the distress of those who do not tolerate it well, so that the latter do not broadcast their dissatisfaction and destroy the reputation of the device and the momentum of the family planning movement. This means in effect confining distribution first and foremost to women who have convenient access to medical follow-up care and also to situations where the other conditions of good performance, described above, are likely to prevail. It means also taking the precaution of warning women of the potential hazards of use as is now becoming common practice. In other words the prospects for success are greatest in urban areas, in hospital and maternity clinic programmes,[37] and in rural areas where medical care is readily available. The I.U.D. should not be offered to women who live at any distance from access to modern medical attention – 'can you come back here, or get medical attention near where you live if something goes wrong?' should be a standard question asked of all acceptors by doctors distributing the I.U.D. This is very different from the spirit of all-out promotion which underlay the beginnings of the I.U.D. programme.[38]

STERILISATION

Vasectomy had been practised in India in family planning clinics for some time before it became a major part of the official programme – it was available in Madras State in 1955. In the expanded programme with its policy of offering a variety of methods, vasectomy and tubectomy were to be made available in hospitals and rural Primary Health Centres whenever the presence of qualified staff permitted. But the first initiatives cannot be said to have been a sweeping success. A certain publicity was gained early on by the gift of a transistor radio to each patient (a practice which was in fact never common nor long continued) but, except in one or two areas, vasectomy and tubectomy did not achieve widespread use by Indian standards. The annual number of sterilisations did not reach 0·5 million prior to 1965, though of course even to get near this figure in the early stages demanded major efforts.

With the Expanded Programme, there was a considerable increase in the number of sterilisations, reaching a first peak of 1·8 million in 1967–8, undoubtedly assisted by the introduction of payment of a fee to the patient in 1966. From then on the programme declined fairly steadily until 1970. A host of reasons were given at the time: the programme had 'reached' most of those interested and was bound to fall off; the fee became less attractive once the hard times of 1967 receded; vasectomy had become unpopular because of the number of cases of post-operative pain and illness; there was opposition to vasectomy in the villages for a number of social reasons – vasectomised men were laughed at as 'eunuchs'; they could be the object of great shame if their wives became pregnant; vasectomy led to loose morals as men could indulge in sexual licence without fear of the consequences. No doubt each of these reasons was at some time believed by some people. The Gandhian precept that the man who is master of himself practises abstinence may also have played its part in opposition to vasectomy.[39] Yet none of those reasons, save a qualified version of the first, is at all convincing.

In normal circumstances vasectomy is an extremely safe procedure, relatively free of physiological side-effects. The most common are post-operative discoloration, swelling and pain – they may occur in as many as 50 per cent of cases but are nearly always of minor significance and short duration and very easily treated. Other problems such as haematoma, infection, sperm granuloma, epididymitis and so forth are rare – i.e. in the region of one per cent of cases in most studies. Recanalisation of the vas, or even failure to cut it, are not unknown; there are also obscurer complications such as the formation of sperm antibodies – obscure both in its causation and its consequences.[40] Various psychological sequelae have been observed, most frequently without objective basis, and commonly related to psychological attributes of the patient prior to the operation – doubts about masculinity, hypochondria and the like – which are almost contra-indications for having the operation at all and indeed, in some countries such as the U.K., are often so regarded. But, with proper screening of patients and good post-operative relations with the physician, most of these problems can be taken care of; and the vast majority of cases, apart from the temporary initial discomforts, are quite trouble free.

The programme has not been quite so trouble free in India, in part because both prior screening and follow-up care are not well-established. It may also be that under-nourished men working long hours at hard physical labour in high temperatures are more prone to suffer from post-operative side effects than the average well-nourished man in a rich country, but there is no hard evidence of this. It certainly is true that a large proportion of men complained of pain and other side effects after vasectomy,[41] and this may have contributed to a 'rumour effect' as with the I.U.D.; even if pain has psychological origins, it may be none the less painful for that. Some operations may well have been clumsily or unhygienically performed. And just as with the I.U.D., causal mis-attributions of the *post hoc ergo propter hoc* variety may have played a part. Thus in one village the author was told on a field trip in 1970 that there had been no more vasectomies in the village after the one vasectomy patient there had died – though on further enquiry it emerged that he had died one year after the operation and with symptoms not conceivably related to it. On this same field visit however we also verified locally what was shown in the aggregate statistics – in one Primary Health Centre after another in several rural districts, where previously several hundred sterilisations had been performed in a month, the level of monthly operations was down to single figures.

Some of the suggested causes of the early downturn in vasectomies have already been listed (it was mostly these rather than sterilisations as a whole – tubectomy has pursued a fairly consistent upward or at least constant course). There were others too and some would stress a certain loss of administrative momentum after the early progress. Our tendency – and the true causes will never be certain – is to believe a version of the 'creaming-off' theory: not that the programme had reached all those in the population who might be interested in having a vasectomy, but that the institutions offering the operation had reached, at least in many parts of the country, a high proportion of those *within geographical range* who were sufficiently highly motivated to undergo the operation. Take for example one of the most successful of the early programmes, that organised by Dr D. N. Pai[42] in the main Bombay railway station. Dr Pai had the ingenious notion of setting up a clinic at the main station and, with a passenger traffic of the order of 200,000 or more people daily, it was not long before vasectomies were being carried out at a rate of thousands per month. But the great majority of the passengers were regular travellers; the rate of operations was therefore bound to decline.

The same may perhaps be said of the rural health centres; while ostensibly the population served by each centre was 80–100,000, in practice the P.H.C. is effective only within a radius of say five miles.[43] If one assumes that only the husbands of women aged 25–44 are potential vasectomy clients, and such women are about 11.5 per cent of the population, then out of each 100,000 there may be a maximum of 11,500 potential clients. If the P.H.C. were accessible to 75 per cent of these, and only 25 per cent of husbands of women in the age range were sufficiently strongly motivated to have the operation, then performance would be likely to fall off once the P.H.C. had achieved about 2250 operations. There certainly were health centres that achieved such numbers and considerably higher. But the overall performance figures in each State are built up from such individual units. Only some of them were fully staffed and equipped to carry out vasectomies initially. The aggregate figures are thus compatible with a micro-history of the programme, in which facilities were gradually extended to more and more centres, but in each centre the number of operations soon reached a level from which it was likely to decline. It must be remembered that even today P.H.C.s are not fully staffed and equipped in all of India's 5500 blocks and also that the first to be so prepared were for the most part in the socially and economically more advanced areas so that the programme was to some degree pushing into progressively more difficult territory. Some 'backlash' effect from the kinds of real or imaginary complaints to which we have referred must also have exerted an influence. These two sets of factors seem to be the main causes of the fall-off in the programme.

That the vasectomy campaign had not yet contacted all its potential clients, even without more powerful attempts to raise the general level of demand, was effectively demonstrated with the advent of the so-called vasectomy 'camps'. These were the invention of S. S. Krishnakumar, collector of Ernakulam District in Kerala–inspired perhaps by Pai's imaginative work in Bombay. But where the latter had brought vasectomy to the crowds – and not just on the railway station (the Bombay programme went on from that to employ mobile clinics at markets and other occasions for large gatherings) – the former's feat was to bring the crowds to the operation. In December 1970 the town hall of Ernakulam was taken over and equipped with forty booths and trained doctors. An extensive publicity campaign had previously been mounted in the surrounding areas and transport was provided to bring clients to the town. A fairly large incentive was offered, worth Rs. 100 to each patient, including gifts in kind, and a 'lucky dip' with substantial prizes. The whole thing had something of a festive atmosphere. But the medical arrangements were under the supervision of the Surgeon General of Kerala and appear to have been virtually faultless – extremely few cases of untoward side-effects were notified. The result of this enterprise was a most remarkable achievement – in one month, over 15,000 vasectomies were performed in Ernakulam.[44]

The experiment was due to the imagination and enthusiasm of the collector but also to a great deal of voluntary assistance from local organisations, firms and individuals. The Government was not involved; indeed it took little notice of this first vasectomy 'camp'. Krishnakumar was determined to prove the value of his method and in July 1971 another camp was organised. In the same place, though drawing from a wider region for clientele, this one carried out over 63,000 vasectomies. It was a striking event in India's family planning history which had reached a state of near-despondency. It put paid to the stronger version of the 'creaming-off' theory; no one could claim any longer that all those interested in vasectomy had had one. (While most of the 15,000 in the first camp came from Ernakulam District, a large proportion of the second camp did not; but nearly 20,000 did. The previous peak for vasectomies in Ernakulam District was 10,662 in 1968/9.) Ernakulam had produced in one month 42 per cent of the vasectomies for the whole of Kerala in a year; in the three camps held between 1970–72 approximately 14 per cent of the couples of reproductive age in the district (about 50,000 out of 350,000) were protected by vasectomy from future births, the same proportion as achieved in Kerala as a whole in the six years 1965–71.[45]

The Department of Health and Family Planning in New Delhi was now becoming convinced of the efficacy of the camp approach and the States were encouraged to hold camps of their own. The first was held in Gujarat in 1971/2 where (at several centres rather than just in one in Ernakulam) 223,060 sterilisations were performed over two months – an increase of 122 per cent over the previous annual maximum in 1968/9. This seemed to give final proof of the value of the camp. By 1972–3 most States had held them and in almost all cases the numerical results were much higher than in any previous years. But then in several States where attempts were made to hold repeat camps performance was disappointing. Stories began to circulate of various malpractices connected with the camps. At one in Gorakhpur (U.P.) in 1972, eleven vasectomised men died of tetanus. By 1974, despite earlier statements from various government sources in favour of them, suitably modified,[46] the Department had abandoned major emphasis on the camp approach – partly as a result of the problems experienced, partly owing to the financial stringency of the period which affected all government programmes. In 1972/3, 3·1 million sterilisations were performed in India, a new peak greatly exceeding previous years and two-thirds accounted for by camps. In 1973/4 the figure was down to 0·94 million and by 1974/5 to 1·3 million, of which more than half were tubectomies, though the total rose again to 2·6 million in 1975/6.[47]

'This problem of hasty and enthusiastic adoption of a new strategy, leading to excessive preoccupation with it and followed soon after by a total rejection of it, is not a new phenomenon in the Indian family planning programme.'[48] We have indeed already discussed a similar problem in the I.U.D. experience. The similarity is perhaps greatest of all in one feature – the difficulty of containing the repercussions of a small proportion of adverse side-effects. But, in the case of vasectomies, the actual side-effects of the operation itself were more limited and the most potent factors in bringing it into disfavour seem to have been abuses associated with organisational features of the programme. Of these, in our opinion, the most damaging was the payment of fees to the 'motivator'. The payment of some form of compensation to the patient himself is justifiable – he may lose several days from work as a result of the operation and at the very least it seems proper to make up this loss, together with travel or other expenses. Though there is something ethically disturbing in the payment of a high incentive fee to the very poor in times of abnormal economic difficulty – this issue was certainly a factor in governmental decisions before 1976. But paying a fee to someone who brings in a client is another matter and it was this which led to trouble.

'Motivators' not only brought in men who were old, unmarried, impotent or with sterile wives (and of course some of these volunteered of their own accord);[49] they also brought in young men and others who may not have wanted the operation but whom they misled about its nature. They were not above bullying, blackmail and taking not only their own fee but a share of that due to the patient. The situation was sometimes even worse when persons in authority were doing the 'motivating'; thus a village headman might be offered some facility for the village if he 'delivered' fifty clients – those who know India might guess who were most likely to be delivered. Even some farmers were being refused credit or fertiliser supplies unless they would consent to having a vasectomy. In general such strong-arm measures were very limited before 1976; they also frequently arose from the behaviour of unscrupulous individuals. Nevertheless they created resentment and they stemmed, once again, from a government policy to raise the number of clients with an urgency which many, both inside and outside India, promoted and approved.

It was unfortunate that the camps were thus discredited. They offered many advantages compared with the local clinic. They had proven their ability to attract large numbers of clients which was achieved largely by major publicity efforts concentrated on a forthcoming camp in a manner difficult (and expensive) to achieve for a regularly operating clinic. Doctors who perform large numbers of vasectomies improve by experience. A high standard of hygiene and operative practice can be maintained for the short duration of the camp. Mass participation itself appeared to overcome some of the fears and hesitations of the individual who might well have been embarrassed at the idea of going alone into a clinic for the operation with members of his community looking on, while going in the company of a number of his peers, often in a festive atmosphere, seemed to overcome inhibition. In general the cost-effectiveness of camps compared well with other methods of providing vasectomy.

Most of the defects of the camps were in principle remediable. The majority of abuses were connected with the motivator system which could have been dropped or at least very substantially modified. There are risks in large-scale activities and these call for proportionate care. The tetanus deaths at Gorakhpur appear to have been caused by men putting cow-dung – a traditional specific – on their incisions rather than any lapse of hygiene by the camp staff.[50] Such possibilities can at least sometimes be foreseen, though as a matter of course unusual infections and other problems cannot be eliminated. Follow-up care has not always been well organised at camps and this too is something which requires special forethought. As world-wide experience of the operation is studied however it becomes safer and safer and practices which give rise to side-effects can be discarded. The most promising method of conducting a voluntary vasectomy programme in the absence of well-developed health services need not have been set aside in 1974. To do so was virtually to abandon vasectomy as a major technique in family planning. Given the paucity of reliable alternative techniques, it was not obvious that the moment for such a decision had come. There were risks and problems with the camp approach but they were worth facing. One problem was less remediable than many of the others – that the camps interrupted the working of the 'normal' programme. But where the normal programme was achieving little even this criticism did not have much weight. Of course ultimately it is much more desirable that family planning should become a part of local life and vasectomy be provided within an integrated health and family planning programme; but the camps had a continuing role in the interim period before such an integrated programme became a reality.

THE CONDOM, ABORTION AND OTHER METHODS

The most successful technique of the family planning programme in India, from many points of view, has been the *condom*. It has not aroused fear or mistrust; it has not had harmful effects ascribed to it and the number of users rose continuously until 1973/4 at least. Indeed the main difficulty in the programme recently has been a shortage of supplies. The condom had been offered free within the family planning organisation for some time up to 1969. But this placed limits on the volume which could be distributed since the number of outlets was itself limited – only about 40,000 within the official family planning network. In 1963 the Indian Institute of

Management (Calcutta) first explored the proposal to market condoms commercially on behalf of the Government, inspired by Peter King, a marketing specialist from M.I.T. A new name was chosen, Nirodh, from the Sanskrit ('prevention'). The first firms approached were Brooke Bond and Liptons which distributed tea through 600,000 retailers; eventually other firms – India Tobacco, Hindustan Lever, Tata Oil Mills, Union Carbide – were included bringing the total of potential retail outlets to over 2 millions.[51] After trials of the marketing system in 1967 and 1968 the programme was launched nationwide in September 1968.

The retailer sold condoms in packets of three for 15 paise (= Rs. 0.15, about U.S. 2 cents); the wholesaler sold them to him for 12 paise having bought them at a (subsidised) price of 8 paise. Thus it was profitable to all concerned while the price was kept within range of almost anyone. An imaginative advertising campaign supported the sales effort – indeed in 1971/2 the cost of advertising was eight times the sales revenue.[52] The results have been impressive; while only 15·75 million condoms were sold annually in 1968/9, and 43·4 million distributed free, by 1973/4 more than 225 million were distributed and more than half of those were bought from the commercial network. Were supplies available on a larger scale – and investments are going ahead to increase domestic production – this figure would undoubtedly be larger still, demonstrating both the success of the distribution system and the real interest in family planning on the part of a significant number of Indian men.

The Nirodh Marketing Programme has really been a remarkable success. The public (free) distribution system by itself could never have opened up the supply of condoms in this way and the costs of the commercial distribution (apart from the subsidy of the item itself) are met out of sales revenue. There is still a considerable way to go in further extension of the scheme especially in rural areas. The O.R.G. survey, already referred to, gave us the first statistical picture of condom use: to quote Anrudh Jain, who based himself on this survey:

> 'The profile of the average condom user is as follows: the wife is about 28 years old; the couple has about 3 living children; the wife has secondary schooling; the family income is 200 – 500 rupees per month; three-fifths live in urban areas. This profile includes all users of condoms and may differ slightly from the profile of couples who buy Nirodh from the market. Unfortunately we cannot separate the groups due to the small number of condom users in the sample.[53]

(The number of users in the sample was only 2.6 per cent of all couples.) Condom distribution in 1973/4 reached almost double the level of the period of the O.R.G. survey so no doubt it has extended somewhat to other sections of the population.

It is unfortunate that the condom is not the most satisfactory of contraceptives. Pregnancy rates of the order of 6 – 12 per 100 years of exposure are common even in developed countries and higher rates have been found in some studies in India.[54] Rates are higher in developed countries than for any of the other main methods – sterilisation, oral pills, I.U.D. or diaphragm. However the acceptability of the condom in India is a great advantage. Surveys show the great majority of users of the device – and their wives – reasonably content with it on most considerations,[55] the largest element of dissatisfaction being with its aesthetic, or perhaps one should say anaesthetic, properties. There are obvious logistical problems in supply and disposal if this is to become the main method of birth control in India. But it is in some countries – in Japan, as we have noted in Chapter 1, it was the choice of 70 per cent of contracepting couples until recently. Until the health service back-up needed for most other methods is more widely available in India the condom can certainly become a more important part of the programme. Given the low levels of adoption of other methods it accounted for a very large share of annual acceptors prior to 1974. Unfortunately the programme suffered a setback after 1973/4; in 1974/5 advertising expenditure was cut and the price of commercially distributed condoms raised; the result was a 40 per cent drop in sales.

Abortion is officially available in the family planning programme but it was not actively promoted or offered on a large scale upto 1975: the number of abortions carried out in 1974/5 was of the order of 97,000. The level of unofficial abortions is unknown. Estimates based on surveys of small populations multiplied up for the population as a whole – in this case a more than usually unreliable technique – give figures from 2 to 4 million a year in India.[56] No doubt the number is quite substantial; even if it is closer to the lower rather than the higher of those figures, it may be compared with the total number of births in India which currently exceeds 20 million. Most folk methods of abortion are dangerous; the name of one of the commonest ones in India, 'green stick abortion', speaks for itself. If any proportion of pregnancies of the order of 5 or 10 per cent or more are terminated by abortion, it is clearly preferable that these be carried out by qualified practitioners. But that is a very different thing from promoting abortion, as some have proposed, as a method of family planning.[57]

The legal situation was altered in 1971 by the Medical Termination of Pregnancy Act which legalised abortion carried out by recognised practitioners on medical grounds. The inclusion among the allowable grounds of 'failure of a contraceptive device' makes abortion more or less available on demand, but little change at first occurred in practice after passage of the Act, either because few newly trained and equipped doctors entered service or because their presence was not advertised. The Government of India was understandably moving with the greatest caution on this most controversial of subjects – there was enough emotion already surrounding the family-planning programme. But there are countries where abortion plays a major part (legally) in family planning and this remains an option for India. New techniques of abortion are exceptionally safe – provided it is carried out in the first trimester of pregnancy it may indeed be safer to have an abortion by aspiration than to have a baby.[58]

The family planning programme has not yet made extensive use of the *oral pill*. The reasons for this are not entirely clear. It is true that trials of the pill have not been tremendously encouraging – not because of any unusual incidence of side effects but because of the apparent difficulty for Indian women of keeping to the regimen. To take a pill daily with interruptions for precise intervals, month after month, is quite a sophisticated procedure and one not easy to follow accurately anywhere, let alone in a country where illiteracy is widespread and understanding of modern medicine limited. At any rate such studies as have been published[59] show rather poor continuation rates except among better educated, higher income groups. Possibly the prospects for the pill are dim in India. Nevertheless one might have expected to observe greater efforts on the part of the Department of Family Planning to encourage the use of the pill and educate people to take them efficiently. Perhaps the best defence one could make of the absence of such efforts lies in the history of the I.U.D. and vasectomy – since the pill is almost the only remaining contraceptive method of proven efficacy not widely promoted in India, it may be wise to wait for its introduction until there can be greater confidence in success. It has been said that the pill is too expensive for India though at about $5 for an annual cycle – especially with aid-support which would probably be available – the cost would not be prohibitive as one method among many. A more solid reason may be that the pill can have the effect of reducing or suppressing lactation and must therefore be offered with care to recently delivered mothers, but that too is not an insuperable problem. In fact it appears that, in the past at least, senior officials of the Department have not been convinced of the appropriateness of the pill for India for reasons which remain obscure. As a result little has been done to prepare for any large-scale introduction of the pill.

Other proven methods have had little impact in India, nor are most of them likely to. Neither the diaphragm nor the various chemical forms of vaginal contraception are really suitable for mass use, given the climate and prevailing standards of hygiene and even, for many poor people, the simple absence of an appropriate place to keep the requisite articles. These items have all been made available in the official programme but not on any major scale. More could undoubtedly have been made of such techniques. However it is apparent that, if the ideal contraceptive is inexpensive, reliable, simple, aesthetically and ethically satisfactory, reversible, safe and suitable for use in the absence of easily accessible professional medical cure, the methods currently available are far from ideal. What then are the prospects for new contraceptive methods?

New Methods

Some doubt was expressed above whether improved contraceptive methods would 'solve' India's population problem. But it is abundantly clear that more suitable methods would be of considerable assistance. What does current contraceptive research promise for India? To begin with there is quite a range of improvements of existing methods under examination. New techniques of vasectomy[60] and tubectomy are constantly being tried and the effectiveness of these methods, and their freedom from side-effects, will undoubtedly increase; for example there is scope for further development of operations for female tubal ligation *per vaginam* which do not require abdominal incisions. Similarly, as already indicated, a good deal of work is going on to improve the I.U.D. For reasons mentioned however it is not likely that small improvements in these methods, welcome though they will be, will have any major impact. The same is true of possible improvements of the oral pill.

The particular need in India is for a reversible method which requires neither medical follow-up nor meticulous procedures on the part of the user. A long-acting chemical would meet this need and there are several such under development. At least one is already in limited use in some countries – Depo-Provera, a progestin compound, which is given to women in intra-muscular injections; its use is spreading, and it seems to be reasonably free from side-effects but it has not been in use long enough for research to have dismissed all doubts. Clinical trials have been conducted in India on the basis of which it has been decided not to go ahead – a decision which may in fact be premature.[61] At the laboratory stage, or under theoretical examination, are various preparations which it is hoped will prove less drastic than the pill and its variants; the new methods would intervene at some point in the female reproductive process instead of affecting the hormonal system as a whole. Indian laboratories such as the Central Drug Research Institute, Lucknow are involved in such work and periodic announcements in the press suggest that breakthroughs are not far away.[62] Male chemicals are also being examined – a promising synthetic hormone was reported by Australian scientists in *Nature* late in 1974 which had been developed for other purposes but turned out to have (temporary) sterilising properties.[63] Other possibilities at various stages of development are numerous: they include new devices for insertion in various parts of the male and female anatomy to release contraceptive chemicals; cryogenic surgery for sterilisation; chemical methods to induce tubal occlusion; new abortifacients and so forth.[64] There is even an anti-pregnancy vaccine undergoing clinical trial in India – some would say dangerously early as the drug's properties will take several years to understand fully.[65]

Yet other possibilities outside the field of birth control include the sex selection of babies: in China apparently a test has already been developed to determine the sex of an unborn child and abortion is offered to parents when the sex is not in accordance with their wishes.[66] Obviously there may

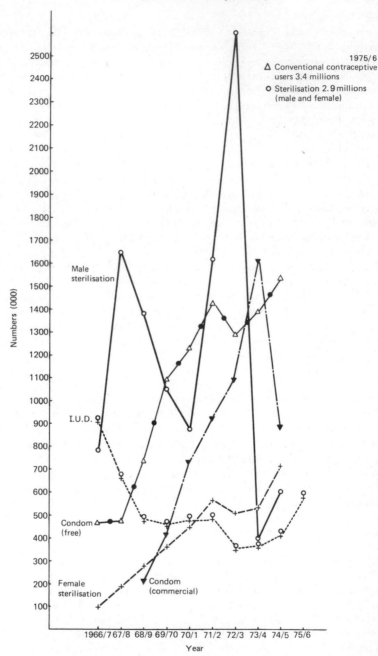

FIG. 3.1 All-India family planning performance by method

SOURCE Table 3.1

TABLE 3.1 All-India family-planning performance – by method

Year	Sterilisation Male	Sterilisation Female	Sterilisation Total	I.U.D.	Conventional Contraceptive Users* Government distribution	Conventional Contraceptive Users* Conventional distribution	Conventional Contraceptive Users* Total	Medical termination of pregnancy (M.T.P.)
1966–67	785,400	102,000	887,400	909,700	464,600		464,600	
1967–68	1,648,100	191,700	1,839,800	669,000	475,200		475,200	
1968–69	1,383,000	281,800	1,664,800	478,700	742,400	218,500	960,900	
1969–70	1,055,900	366,200	1,422,100	458,700	1,098,400	411,000	1,509,400	
1970–71	878,800	451,100	1,329,900	475,800	1,230,300	732,100	1,962,400	
1971–72	1,620,000	567,300	2,187,300	488,400	1,429,900	924,300	2,354,200	
1972–73	2,612,700	508,700	3,121,400	353,100	1,295,100	1,092,800	2,387,900	24,100
1973–74	400,400	535,600	936,000	367,200	1,394,800	1,614,300	3,009,100	44,200
1974–75	608,200	719,700	1,327,900	417,800	1,541,400	887,600	2,429,000	97,000
1975–76			2,627,300	594,400			3,358,000	181,000

* Refers to number of contraceptives distributed divided by coefficient of 'equivalent users', e.g. 72 condoms per year is one equivalent condom user.

SOURCE G.o.I. 1975(d) for figures up to 1974–5; figures for 1975–6 were supplied by Ministry of Health, New Delhi and are provisional as are those for 1973–4 and 1974–5.

be many scientific advances in the future which will assist parents to have the children they want. In 1970 the author was told by a distinguished researcher at the Karolinska Institute in Stockholm that all contraceptives then in use would be replaced by better ones within fifteen years. Perhaps he would now wish to put the date beyond 1985, but there is little doubt that the large volume of resources now going into contraceptive research will sooner or later yield useful results. Fortunately chemical sterilants that can be added to water supplies still exist only in Malthusian imaginations. But voluntary birth control should be made progressively simpler as time goes on.

FAMILY PLANNING AND FERTILITY

Although demographers lay most stress on social developments as the determinants of fertility decline, family planning programmes and changes in individual attitudes towards birth control are also important. Many commentators would cite the Besant-Bradlaugh trial as a key factor in British fertility decline in the 1870s; abortion legislation in twentieth century Japan and Rumania are other well-known instances. One should beware of claiming either too much or too little for family planning. It tends to be most successful where fertility is already beginning to go down, as in Taiwan, or where social conditions are ready for it. The extraordinarily rapid decline in birth rates in Mauritius for example could hardly have occurred without a family planning programme, but such a programme introduced twenty years earlier would not have found the public nearly so receptive. Many delegates at the 1974 World Population Conference in Bucharest attacked the view that family planning could bring down birth rates in the absence of social change – a view hardly held by anyone these days as Berelson has pointed out.[67] Much of the 'family planning debate' seems rather a sham. At any time in most societies there are some unwanted births, and family planning meets a need by helping parents to prevent them. Where fertility is high and most births are wanted by parents it is mainly to changes in social and economic conditions that we must look for reductions in desired family size; though until satisfactory means of contraception are available to all, and people have no objections to their use, it is often difficult to tell which births are desired and which are not. In these circumstances too family planning programmes have a role in providing information, overcoming prejudices, in making clear to parents at the least that the number of children they have can easily be limited, or even offering empirical grounds for believing in the benefits of small families, to the extent that family size norms may be based on false beliefs about the advantages of large families.

Nevertheless the Bucharest Conference may have served a useful purpose in emphasising the low priority many governments attach to family planning, especially in international debate, as compared with other means of improving the lot of their peoples – means which in some cases are unlikely to be popular with Western governments. But it would be really unfortunate if the extreme version of that case were to gain currency – that family planning is ineffective or unimportant. Countries differ considerably in their ability to accommodate rapid population growth and in the enthusiasm of their governments for policies to control it. But at least where the ability to accommodate growth is low, willing governments should not be discouraged from taking such steps as are practical. In the short run family planning is the only thing which makes much impact on fertility, and even if conditions are unpropitious and fundamental social and economic change is essential for major fertility decline, programmes are not so expensive as to make much difference to the pace of development, whereas they can make a difference, albeit limited, to fertility. To our way of thinking India exemplifies such a case perfectly.

Our account of the family planning programme so far has concentrated exclusively on the main techniques of contraception offered by it. We have emphasised this aspect because it has received too little attention. People speak of the slow progress of family planning in India prior to 1976 as if it demonstrated the absence of any widespread desire for family limitation; whereas what had in fact been demonstrated was the low level of acceptability of the I.U.D. and vasectomy *as offered within the Government's programme*. This is not to say that better contraceptives would solve India's population problem – far from it. Somebody once said that if there were a magic word in all Indian languages that could be uttered to prevent conception, and every couple knew it, fertility would not be greatly diminished. There is some truth in that. But the history of family planning in India, together with the incidence of abortion and child neglect, is also an expression of a considerable volume of unwanted pregnancies and frustrated desires to avoid them. Voluntary family planning in India has two problems; the main one is to create the demand for further limitation of family size, but there is also still that of satisfying the demand which already exists. It is quite right to say that major fertility decline without coercion awaits widespread improvements in living conditions, but wrong to conclude that voluntary family planning could not make headway in the meantime.

In 1974 the family planning programme had reached a state of financial and even philosophical disarray. Not only were budgets cut; with the Nirodh programme as the only successful element, it is not obvious what would have been done had more money been available. The newspapers were full of comment that India was not yet ready for family planning. Less publicity was given to the political problems of the programme but they were much discussed in private. Particularly in Northern India, it was said to be widely believed by Hindus that Muslims did not practise family planning and that if Hindus did they would eventually be outnumbered.

(For a discussion of this argument, see Chapter 2, pp. 56–8.) In fact the figures suggest that Muslims constitute a proportion of 'acceptors' not much smaller than their proportion in the population. A prestigious Hindu religious leader, Jagatguru Shankaracharya of Puri, even went so far as to suggest that the problem of 'genocide of Hindus' by family planning should be referred to the United Nations.[68] The real importance of this factor is obscure. Certainly family planning was a subject on which few politicians liked to speak – it seemed to be something which could damage but not enhance a political reputation. Even the Prime Minister, known to be sympathetic in private to the family planning movement, only rarely went out of her way to support it in public prior to 1976.[69] With the total number of acceptors in 1973/4 down 27 per cent on the previous year, things looked gloomy for the programme. In this context the appointment of a new Health Minister was welcomed by the family planning community – Dr. Karan Singh, not only an attractive and able personality, but someone relatively senior in the Congress hierarchy and a Cabinet member, unlike previous Ministers who had been more junior. It must be confessed however that his first year or two in office were not marked by notable advances.

In 1975 the new Minister announced the details of the strategy to be pursued which had already been outlined in the Fifth Plan. Some of the emphasis was not novel – the integration of family planning with health services had long been a stated ambition of the programme. But he placed the role of family planning within the framework of the Plan's overall attack on poverty and he spoke of a new committee, the Media Board, which would coordinate the propagation of what he called 'the new package' – it would include officials of the Ministries of Information, Education, Agriculture and Social Welfare.[70] A multi-purpose health worker at the village level was to be an important agent of the new approach and other organisational changes were hinted at. As far as specific methods were concerned the Minister emphasised the Nirodh programme as the most suitable one for major expansion. Sterilisation and abortion would still be on offer but, while it would be open to individual States to run vasectomy camps, they would not be pushed by the Centre. Pill use was to be liberalised and it was hoped that the introduction of lower-dose pills would reduce side-effects. Incentive payments were not going to be extended, but if anything limited to pure compensation for the client's costs and foregone earnings. Family planning must become 'something which the people demand for themselves.'[71]

This approach was very much in line with the Indian delegation's stand at the Bucharest Conference, where Karan Singh's statement that 'development is the best contraceptive' was widely noted. In 1975 it looked like a praiseworthy attempt to avoid the excessive urgency of the past and to relate the practice of family planning to social conditions, its organisation more closely to village experience and coordinated development.

Building the programme slowly on a basis of trust might not bring quick results, but it might be the only way to create a durable and effective movement. But it was not cynical to remark that such things had been heard before – ever since the days of the Community Development movement – even the Auxiliary Nurse Midwife, after all, was supposed to create willing demand for birth control by her intimate and understanding contact with mothers. If the complementary measures had been put into action, particularly the Minimum Needs programme of the Draft Fifth Plan and a new system of medical auxiliaries to provide primary care, there would have been hope for the 'new package'. But in mid, 1975 the Minimum Needs programme was still in abeyance; the stage was being set for the drastic moves of 1976 though this could not be seen at the time. Before we come to them a thorough assessment of the pre-1976 experience is required.

It follows from much of our analysis above that one should not conclude that family planning had failed in India; what failed had been certain well-intentioned initiatives. To reach a balanced conclusion about the results achieved we should look at the programme not method by method for India as a whole but State by State for the programme as a whole. It becomes apparent that some States did rather well. There are two main sources of data – figures for acceptors from the Department of Family Planning and a survey of contraceptive use conducted by the Operations Research Group (Baroda) on a sample of the public at large. Both sources show that in several States family planning had gone quite far: in Delhi, Gujarat, Haryana, Kerala, Maharashtra, Punjab, Tamil Nadu and West Bengal the level of contraceptive use was well above 20 per cent of couples with wives in the age group 15–44, according to the O.R.G. survey – and that was in 1970/1, before the vasectomy camps; in Kerala and Maharashtra indeed it was over 30 per cent. In Assam, Bihar, Madhya Pradesh, Mysore, Rajasthan and Uttar Pradesh the levels were 12·5 per cent or less – the average for India was 18·3 per cent. The figures include 'traditional methods' which is why they are higher than those for couples 'protected' by the official programme. But the official programme has also done well or badly in more or less the same groups of States.

Various attempts have been made to explain the differentials by States in contraceptive use. Three studies [72] (by Agarwala, Misra and Vig) have analysed the official data in relation to what might loosely be called development variables (levels of education, per capita income and so forth) and programme variables (expenditure on family planning, field staff appointed etc.). All the studies show a high proportion of the variations explained by all the variables together; they mostly show a higher proportion explained by the input variables than the development variables. To some extent however this is misleading – since programme performance is what is being explained and one cannot have programme outputs without the inputs, they are bound to be correlated. There cannot be I.U.D.s without female doctors or vasectomies without trained vasectomy surgeons. And if family planning expenditure is used as an explanatory variable, when it includes incentive payments to clients, it too is logically connected with the number of clients. A fourth study,[73] employing some of the material in the other three and additional variables, has shown the interaction of the development and input variables to be more important than either set of variables alone. A strong believer in the pure 'input' theory would also have to explain the large number of facilities which are grossly under-utilised.

A more interesting analysis by Jain and Sharma[74] has avoided some of the data problems by using the results of the O.R.G. survey though it sheds no light on the 'programme input' question since it did not use this explanatory variable for want of appropriate data. Both percentage of wives with secondary or higher education and degree of urbanisation were significant explanatory variables of State differentials (urbanisation, as the authors point out, to some extent serving as a proxy for input variables as the number and accessibility of programme 'service points' is higher in urban areas). Family income was not in general related to contraceptive use, but it was found to be positively related with I.U.D., condom or pill use, vasectomy and tubectomy being more common with lower income groups. As one might expect the education variable was of exceptional importance at the micro-level: 'Wife's education is the only factor which stands out and significantly increases the use of specific methods as well as all methods together.'[75] Even more interesting, in the better-performance States not only was education more advanced, but there was higher than average contraceptive use among the less educated – indeed in these States the level of use among illiterates is equal to or above the level of use among all couples in India. In the States where performance was relatively poor, contraceptive use was low even among educated couples.

All these studies simply bear out what one might in any case have expected. Family planning is relatively advanced in the States where education is more widespread, death rates are lower, economic development by most criteria further ahead. It is also most advanced where the level of family planning inputs is highest. But since all the factors are strongly related with each other, no amount of statistical sophistication at this level of aggregation can sort them out. As is usual with studies of inter-State variations in any field, each thing seems to do well where everything else does well. Not only are conditions more propitious for family planning in these 'good' States, nor is there only a higher degree of provision of programme inputs; the quality of personnel at all levels, especially management, is likely to be better and the State as a whole is better administered so that complementary services function better as well. Unfortunately the States listed above where the level of contraceptive use was 12·5 per cent or less of specified couples together comprised 253·4 million people or 46 per cent of the total population in 1971 – 144·7 million of those in Bihar and U.P. alone. The 'good' States comprised 211·6 million or 38·6 per cent of the total. (The remainder, the biggest being A.P. and Orissa, had use levels above 12·5 per cent but below 20 per cent.)

Examination of inter-State performance does not bear out the notions that voluntary family planning had failed or that India was not ready for it. What failed were the attempts to spread mass use of the I.U.D. where medical consultation was not easily accessible, and parts of the vasectomy programme – some of the camps, and the normal programme in places – most particularly because of abuse of the 'motivator' system and consequent adverse reactions and to a lesser extent shortcomings in follow-up care. By implication not all parts of India are ready for the same kind of programme; and obviously further socio-economic progress, especially in the poorer States, will facilitate the adoption of family planning. But the States which did well, while economically advanced by India's standards, were not so by international ones; the achievements of family-planning in Kerala and Maharashtra bear comparison with those in countries of considerably superior material conditions. Much therefore remained to be done by a voluntary family planning programme both in satisfying existing demand for services and in encouraging further demand even in the absence of the longed-for abolition of poverty.

Effectiveness
Many people have queried the economic value of family planning on general grounds – the Government seems to be spending large sums with comparatively small results. Would the money not be better spent on other things? Those who have read the literature of the cost-benefit analysis of family planning are often – rightly – sceptical of some of the extravagant claims which have been made on its behalf. Notoriously Stephen Enke once assessed the return to investment in family planning to be one hundred times the return to other investments.[76] Later studies, both for India and elsewhere, have made more sober but still impressive calculations.[77] We have reviewed this literature elsewhere,[78] and so have others.[79] In general some of the higher estimates have come from making implausibly low assumptions of the costs of preventing births and implausibly high ones about their value. Methodological difficulties abound, the most common being the presumption of an automatic connection between family planning expenditure and the prevention of births on the cost side, and, on the benefit side, a variety of arguments leading to a low estimate of the product of additional labour or its present value, and a high estimate of the value of preventing the arrival of an additional child.

A proper evaluation of family planning should contain two parts – an assessment of the demographic effectiveness of the family planning programme and an economic analysis of its results. Even the first of these is difficult enough. It requires accurate knowledge of the number of couples protected by various family planning methods, as provided by the programme, and some means of estimating the number of births thereby prevented. Most evaluations of the Indian programme rely on official performance statistics for the former, although it is recognised that they are not above suspicion. And one needs the faith of a true believer to follow to the end the trail of assumptions required for estimating the latter.

The Department of Family Planning employs the following method for estimating 'couples currently protected' by each method. It first assumes an age distribution for clients of each method and survives them by appropriate mortality figures to determine the numbers remaining protected by the method within the reproductive age group. In the case of sterilisations the rate of 'attrition' depends solely on aging or death; for I.U.D.s, it depends additionally on pregnancies and the proportion of I.U.D.s expelled or rejected. (Obviously in the case of condoms only current users are currently protected.) From the number protected each year and their age distribution and information on age specific marital fertility it is then possible to derive the number of births averted.[80] By February 1973 the programme was believed on one estimate to have averted 12·6 million births cumulatively since inception or to have reduced fertility by 10 per cent.[81]

The pitfalls in this method are numerous. One might begin by noting that, while the figure of fertility decline corresponds approximately to that which we believe to have occurred, most observers attribute a considerable share of the decline to changes in age at marriage and in the population age distribution. Further the computations assume that, had the couples not entered the programme, they would not have limited their fertility by other means. There is very little solid information on the age distribution of couples entering the programme. The study in question employs two alternative age distributions and finds the result quite sensitive to the choices. As far as concerns the actual figures used, the 'young' age distribution for sterilisation acceptors looks extremely optimistic, and the discontinuation rate for I.U.D. acceptors employed (24 per cent) is, as we have seen, also too low. Numbers protected by condoms are estimated simply by dividing the total number of condoms bought or distributed by seventy-two, that being the generally assumed figure for annual coital frequency – but this too is likely to over-estimate numbers protected: there is little certainty about the actual number of condom users and, even if seventy-two were the correct figure for coital frequency, it would make a considerable difference to the number of births prevented if a given number of men used condoms at each occasion of coitus, or a larger number used them only on some occasions. In general the only figures employed that tend to under-estimate the effectiveness of family planning are the survival rates used to calculate attrition, which are on the low side though not perhaps very greatly so. Otherwise the method and the figures tend to over-estimate performance.

The most careful attempt we have seen to estimate couples protected by sterilisation is by Veena Soni[82] which shows that about 10 per cent of the country's 97 million eligible couples were protected by sterilisation in March 1973. (Her figures do not differ substantially from those of the Department of Family Planning but they are considerably more reliable; her work contains further detailed criticisms of the Department's methodology.) Soni's work sensibly avoids the problematic question of the number of births prevented by these sterilisations but, as she estimates, '51 per cent of the wives were over 35 years of age and 78 per cent were over 30 years.' The potential impact on fertility can thus only be moderate. There is as usual a big variation by States: thus she finds only 3·3 per cent of eligible couples in 1973 were protected by sterilisation in Uttar Pradesh and 6·3 per cent in Karnataka (Mysore), while for Kerala the figure was over 20 per cent.

To go from couples protected to births prevented requires further numerical manipulation. First of all one needs figures for the use-effectiveness of the contraceptive method among protected couples: the Department plausibly assumes this is 100 per cent for sterilisation, 95 per cent for the I.U.D., and 60 per cent for conventional contraceptives. But then comes the more troublesome question of the number of children couples would have if they were not in the programme (which is slightly different from the question already raised, namely whether they might practise some other form of birth control outside the programme). If one knew that couples entering the programme at a given age had the same parity for age as the average couple, it might be reasonable to assume that the number of births prevented was the number common to couples outside the programme after that age – though couples entering the programme might be precisely those who would have lower than average fertility outside it. As we know neither the age nor the parity of couples entering the programme (nor for that matter age specific marital fertility in the population as a whole with any accuracy) it does indeed seem wise to forego estimation of prevented births by the sophisticated methods that are available.[83]

Nevertheless the programme has obviously had an impact – even allowing for possibly exaggerated numbers of clients, the demographic ineffectiveness of much family planning work owing to age and sterility of many clients and the possibility that the programme in part substitutes for traditional means of birth control, it is difficult to believe that family planning has not prevented something like an average of at least one million births annually, especially since the sterilisation programme got under way in 1967/8. Such an estimate would be consistent with discounting the official figures for numbers of clients of all methods, doubling the I.U.D. discontinuation rate, assuming a fairly old age distribution for sterilisation clients, reducing the estimated number of couples protected by conventional contraceptives and assuming that induced abortion or other methods would have been resorted to in a proportion of cases in the absence of the programme. One million births represents about 5 per cent of all births or two points off the birth rate: this too is consistent with the estimates of fertility decline referred to in Chapter 2 which show the birth rate to have fallen by about four points with varying accounts of the proportion of that fall attributable to declining marital fertility. We do not suggest this is an 'estimate' of births prevented – the figures involved are quite arbitrary – only that it is hard to believe the actual figure is less than that.

As noted above we have discussed the cost-benefit analysis of birth prevention elsewhere. We have little faith in the received methodology, particularly on the question of benefits. However there is a rough and ready way of judging the worthwhileness of family planning expenditure. Independently of any of the complex interactions of population with the economy, reducing the rate of population growth will increase the growth of income per head simply by reducing the number of heads. Since on balance the impact of population growth on the economy is negative, if all we are concerned with is to provide a lower limit to the worthwhileness of family planning expenditure, we may properly ignore these interactions. Then all we have to do is to compare the cost of raising income per head by reducing the rate of population growth with the cost of raising it by other means. This comparison is reasonable if we can assume that the births prevented are unwanted births. For the years 1967/8 to 1972/3 family planning expenditure averaged about Rs. 435 million annually; if this expenditure did prevent one million births annually for six years, then the population was 6 million, or about one per cent, smaller than it would otherwise have been. Per capita N.N.P. is estimated at Rs. 698·3 in 1972/3 in 1972/3; if the population had been one per cent larger, per capita N.N.P. would have been one per cent smaller or Rs 691·3. So the question is, had there been no family planning programme, and had the population grown by one million a year more, would that Rs. 435 million invested in other things have generated Rs. 7 per head for the larger population?

The answer is, No. If the Rs. 435m were invested every year in the rest of the economy instead of the family planning programme, the capital stock would be about Rs. 3,000 million bigger after six years which on very generous assumptions would yield an extra Rs. 1500 million of income in 1972/3 or about Rs. 2·5 per head.[84] Every assumption we have made favours non-family planning investment, including the low estimate of number of births prevented at high cost and the thoroughly optimistic figures for the income yielded by alternative investment. Yet per capita income is higher by preventing a million births annually than by investing generally in development – though not all that much higher. Various authorities have estimated the value of a prevented birth in India – the highest estimate was Rs. 7,800, the lowest Rs. 690.[85] All we have tried to do is to show that funds expended on family planning would not have made a bigger impact on income per head if spent elsewhere. Notice that the cost of a prevented birth works out at Rs. 435, or getting on for $60, much larger than many authors have sometimes assumed. This results in part from taking all programme costs as current costs which they are not – but separate figures are not published for capital and current costs in the Indian programme. Many would think also that our estimates of numbers of births prevented are rather low.

We made a remark above whose significance is worth bringing out, namely that the births prevented must be *unwanted* births – otherwise the logic of our calculation would apply equally to morally unacceptable ways of reducing population growth. There may be concerns about the distribution of gains from alternative investments, though presumably if family planning assists those who do not want further children to avoid having them the programme brings gains to them. Of course if only the rich patronised the programme and the poor benefited from the alternative investments, the distributional effect of having the programme would be regressive; but such is not the case. Finally we are not driven to the implication that vast additional sums should necessarily be spent on family planning – it will only be worth spending such sums as will achieve results at comparable costs on this argument. No light is shed on the question of the maximum it might be worth spending to prevent a birth – for that one really does need an estimate of the benefit of a prevented birth with all that implies. But we hope our calculation is adequate to reassure those who question whether it is worthwhile for India to spend such large sums on family planning. This is not either the only way of justifying such expenditure; it could be argued that even if the results have so far been moderate in terms of births prevented, an important feature of the programme has been to spread awareness and knowledge of birth control, the rewards of which will be reaped in the future.

THE 1976 'NATIONAL POPULATION POLICY' AND BEYOND

'When you really stopped to ask them – look, has this happened to you – to anybody you know, anybody in your village, they said – no, but we hear it's happening.'

Mrs. Gandhi, BBC Television, 21 July 1977.

India began in 1976 an extraordinary experiment in family planning – not entirely without precedent in other countries but particularly surprising in India because of the moderation of previous policies and the statements of the Health Minister and others as late as 1975. It seemed to be accepted at one point that development and family planning had to go hand in hand; at the next it was being said that the population problem could not wait on the slow processes of development and a more decisive approach was needed. We have already referred to some of what happened in between – in particular the receding of the prospects for those particular forms of development which were to have accompanied family planning in the philosophy of 1975 as well as the downturn in family planning performance after 1972/3. But undoubtedly also the suspension of the normal political processes under the Emergency of 1975 was a factor. (These events are discussed in Chapter 5.) There had always been a strand of Indian politics which took a nationalistic view of development – the view that development was essential not just for the welfare of its citizens but to enable India to enhance its international standing. When this view was coupled with the belief that development was thwarted by excessive population growth it provided a motive additional to the usual ones for greater activism in family planning. What was crucial were the limitations imposed on opposition politics and the press, which made possible the taking of unpopular steps.

On 16 April 1976 the new National Population Policy was announced. It contained a comprehensive range of measures. At the most general level, representation in Parliament and the allocation of Central resources to the States was no longer to be made on a current population basis but on the fixed basis of the 1971 Census figures; family planning performance would become one of the new criteria of financial allocation. The Policy also stressed the importance of female education, nutrition and basic health services. But the change in attitude was made clear: 'To wait for education and economic development to bring about a drop in fertility is not a practical solution. The very increase in population makes economic development slow and more difficult of achievement. The time factor is so pressing, and the population growth so formidable, that we have to get out of this vicious circle through a direct assault upon this problem as a national commitment.'[86] Not surprisingly therefore most attention has centred on the components of this 'direct assault'.

The policy statement reiterated the Government's Fifth Plan commitment to reach a birth rate of 25 per thousand by 1984, the end of the Sixth Plan period. Direct measures to achieve this included raising the legal minimum age at marriage to eighteen for females and twenty-one for males; introducing 'population values' in the education system; drawing all government departments into the 'motivation of citizens to adopt responsible reproductive behaviour'; increasing the monetary incentive for sterilisation patients, on a graduated scale depending on the number of children – from Rs. 150 for parents with two children to Rs. 70 with four or more; offering group incentives to Zila and Panchayat Samitis (elected rural councils), teachers, cooperatives, labour in the organised sector; drawing more voluntary agencies, including youth and women's organisations, into the family planning movement and the development of new media strategies. In addition there were the two measures which attracted the most comment: the permission to State legislatures to pass legislation for compulsory sterilisation; and the measures for government employees – the States were encouraged to prepare their own directives for rewarding those who observed fertility norms or penalising those who failed to do so. 'Employees of the Union Government will be expected to adopt the small family norm and necessary changes will be made in their service/conduct rules to ensure this.'[87]

While the possibility of compulsory sterilisation by law struck many as the most drastic of all these proposals, the course of events immediately following the announcement of the policy suggested that the political and administrative processes would overshadow possible legal changes. In 1976 only one State legislature – Maharashtra – actually passed a compulsory sterilisation bill which early in 1977 still awaited presidential assent. (A small number of other States prepared legislation but awaited the outcome in Maharashtra; several States declared they would not pass such legislation.) But sterilisations began to be performed in the country in very large numbers and in a wholly new atmosphere. Targets for sterilisation were set at various administrative levels, perhaps most importantly at the District level, where the collector was charged with pursuing the new family planning goals. Simultaneously the political authorities let it be known that they would welcome high levels of sterilisation performance. For the first time senior politicians went out of their way in speeches on major public occasions to express the Government's commitment to birth control; previously such speeches had been rather rare and, when they happened at all, had usually been confined specifically to family planning events.

The initial results were a high level of recorded numbers of sterilisations. The original target of four million for 1976/7 was ostensibly reached by September 1976. It began to appear that the key element of the new policy was not any legislated compulsion but the involvement of all government agencies in family planning motivation. This took various forms. For government workers the new rules were adopted fairly rapidly, most States as well as the Central Government introducing measures to deprive state employees of some benefits – loans, subsidised housing, travel allowances, free hospital treatment and the like – or grant them others – early increments, various forms of preferential treatment – depending on their willingness to undergo sterilisation after three children.[88] But for others the pressures were more varied.

In fact some parts of India in 1976 appeared to have embarked on a policy of maximum sterilisation by a great variety of means, ranging from the requirement of a vasectomy or tubectomy certificate before a government permit could be granted, to straightforward collection of sterilisation patients, willing or unwilling, by police or other transport. 'Some parts of India' is said advisedly, since there was genuinely a great variety of practice. In Delhi for example applicants for driver's licences, telephones, school places for their children and a host of other government or city administration controlled services or permits – were told that a certificate of sterilisation was necessary before the request could be granted. Such practices were becoming common all over India by the end of 1976. In many parts of the country school teachers were expected to report for sterilisation once they had three children or suffer various penalties, possibly including transfers to unpopular postings; in other places they were offered salary increments if they 'motivated' a certain number of clients per year or even – in Uttar Pradesh for example – threatened with non-payment of salary if they failed to 'motivate' their quota.

It is not easy to arrange these measures on a spectrum of degrees of compulsion. None of the features of the 1976 policy statement other than the legal issue amounted to forcible sterilisation, but some of the more severe economic sanctions actually imposed left the individual with little real choice. Other items not yet mentioned were just as harsh or harsher: thus some municipal authorities during slum clearance programmes had a policy of offering rehousing only to those who accepted sterilisation[89]; similar conditions were placed on offers of rural credit, power connections for tubewell pumps or fertiliser supplies. All the measures so far discussed were publicly known and officially supported. But there were others, not publicly or officially avowed, but occurring in some instances nevertheless. Here a senior police officer would take an initiative and personally 'motivate' cases by raiding villagers' houses and taking men away for vasectomy: elsewhere a District collector would give instructions as to how his targets would be reached – Block Development Officers for example would be told to find a number of clients each and they in turn would first seek volunteers, or if they were not forthcoming, put pressure on individuals or community leaders to provide them. Police detachments were employed to take clients away; on occasion there were confrontations resulting in police firings and even deaths. Towards the end of 1976 there was a major episode in the town of Muzaffarnagar in Western Uttar Pradesh; the foreign press estimated the number of deaths at between 50 and 150. The Prime Minister in a statement in Parliament admitted there had been 'some' deaths but claimed also that some people who had nothing to do with family planning had been killed by 'violent groups'.[90]

The Muzaffarnagar affair was an extreme case although other confrontations in which lives were lost were not unknown. Even by mid-1977 it was not possible to tell how many of them there were, or indeed what was the overall conduct of the family planning programme during 1976 and early 1977. Sterilisations were certainly performed at an unprecedented level, even if the numbers reported and their demographic quality are inevitably open to doubt. (In a drive of this kind there are strong incentives for officials to record cases which did not take place or for many of those to be sterilised who have least to lose – widows, the old, the sterile.) From many parts of the country there were no reports of untoward incidents; from others, not only violent confrontations when parents with three children were obliged to submit to sterilisation, but even cases of sterilisation of unmarried men leading to attacks on family planning units.

Officials during 1976 were at pains to stress that incidents of this kind were rare, the occasional consequences of over-zealous individuals going too far in the pursuit of targets. The Health Minister more than once claimed to deplore such 'abuses' and expressed his opposition to compulsion: only 'gentle and civilised pressure' was to be employed in the programme.[91] Yet it is difficult to see how episodes of this kind could be avoided under the practices of 1976. The programme offered group incentives at many points – for example Panchayats in Bihar were offered large cash sums for village development if they fulfilled even one-third of sterilisation targets.[92] It is impossible to believe that these incentives could be won entirely with voluntary clients; on the contrary it was predictable in the social circumstances of contemporary India that many people would be dragooned into sterilisation whether they wanted it or not and that this would happen particularly among the weaker sections of society.

Wherever incentives are offered to anyone other than the client, the door is open for coercion. The Government did not define what it meant by 'abuse' nor establish a code of conduct for family planning motivation or any policing system to ensure that such a code would be observed. Clearly if a young unmarried person was forcibly sterilised, that was an abuse; but what about non-payment of salaries to school teachers who failed to motivate their quota of patient? The 1976 National Population Policy with its political backing implied compulsion in practice whatever happened in the way of legislation. What is unknown however is the balance in the programme between compulsion and voluntarism. Without a doubt a large share of clients in the first period of the new policy actually wanted to limit their families or were attracted by the positive incentives offered; it would be helpful to know how large as compared with those who for one reason or another had little or no choice.

One of the difficulties of assessing the 1976 programme is precisely such ignorance as to how it was conducted. This affects both ethical and practical judgements. The ethical case for such a programme must be based on balancing the rights of today's parents to procreate as they wish against the rights of future generations to lead a decent life in so far as the latter is threatened by high current fertility. (This last proviso raises a further difficulty since there must be debate about how much the threat comes from population growth, how much from other things. In the analysis of this book, at least some of India's development problems are exacerbated by population growth and would be eased by its reduction.) But even if one accepts the right of governments to intervene in this way for the social good, the policy, to be just, must be fair – in particular that means universal in application. Indeed if there should be any departures from universality, a case could be made that they ought to be precisely among those less privileged members of the general public most likely to be caught in the net of compulsion – those among whom child mortality is highest and who most depend for security on their children.

It would take more than a paragraph or two to go further into the ethical issues raised by India's 1976 programme and that will not be attempted here. In several ways the practical assessment is equally important for there are many who would say that India's situation is so grave as to justify the most draconian measures. But to make that argument one must believe that the measures will succeed. Here obvious doubts arise. One might assume that elements of the authoritarian part of the programme could have operated indefinitely and without significant opposition: particularly the sanctions to which state employees were subject, or the establishment of family limitation as a *quid pro quo* for various forms of government permissions and services. But some of the methods employed to bring in poor men and women in large numbers were not viable. The more coercive of them, which were the main cause of the violent episodes noted above, created something of a dilemma even for the Emergency Government: either to continue an unpopular programme backed by threats of enforcement or to give it up in an atmosphere which posed difficulties for the pursuit of voluntary family planning.

There was much informal evidence by the end of 1976 that at least in some areas the family planning programme had become the object of popular fear. In many rural areas of Haryana, Rajasthan or Uttar Pradesh there were reports of villagers attacking or fleeing from official vehicles which were suspected of being connected with the sterilisation campaign. Field reports from a World Food Programme nutrition project in Rajasthan indicated that few people were coming to its nutrition centres and fear of sterilisations was the main reason. Cholera inoculators in South Bihar were unable to approach people at risk for the same reason. In December parents in Delhi suddenly started keeping their children back from school believing (obviously wrongly) that the school's inoculation programmes were for sterilising children – the Prime Minister had to make a statement before parents could be reassured. Even economic researchers found villagers suddenly becoming uncooperative, especially if their questionnaires contained enquiries about family size. More than one member of the population community made the ironic comment to the author that the 1981 Census would show the new policy to have succeeded as the number of children was likely to be more than usually under-recorded.

Once again it was hard to know in the first year of the programme what such reports meant. There was no way of telling how widespread were the phenomena mentioned – the press gave little coverage to negative features of family planning; during the Emergency there was a gazetted government order to the effect that articles on family planning had to be submitted for pre-censorship. The optimist could say that there would always be a certain amount of volatile public opinion, but it would all settle down and people would come to accept the programme. The arch-defender of the Government could say that the phenomena did not even exist but arose from mere 'rumour mongering'. The pessimist could say that the programme was unsustainable in its 1976 form and would have to be relaxed, but that serious damage had already been done to the image of family planning.

Perhaps the aspect of the so-called family planning 'backlash' most vexatious to the Government lay in the relations between India's Hindu and Muslim communities. We have already noted this as a cause of political reticence about family planning prior to 1976. Under the new policy major efforts were made to counter possible communal feeling about family planning. Muslim leaders went out of their way to endorse the new programme, were photographed in the press after undergoing sterilisation and made positive statements about the religious acceptability of birth control. The Government was also at pains to emphasise that the new policies applied to everyone and would be implemented without regard to caste or community. Yet inevitably, however even-handed the Government was in fact, members of the various communities might not be persuaded that such was the case. One or two of the more serious confrontations did take place during sterilisation drives in Muslim communities. If ever high-pressure methods are employed, governments will always find it difficult to convince Muslims that they are not being victimised, or Hindus that Muslims are not being 'let off' even if neither is true. Community relations are likely to remain no less of a problem in an authoritarian programme than they are under a voluntary one. (Hindu-Muslim relations are not the only relevant ones for family planning politics; similar things could be said about caste, tribal and other community fears of differential treatment.)

The Government obviously did not want its new policy to be a source of conflict; there were indications early in 1977 that some relaxation of the campaign might become unavoidable and not only because it was election year. There were further reasons for a slowdown in addition to the hostility which was building up in some areas. A key factor was the effect of the family planning drives on other government programmes. It will be recalled that the vasectomy camps of the early 1970s were criticised for disrupting other health work; that was even more true of the new policy which was absorbing a large amount of the country's health manpower. Apart from everything else the Government had a major task on its hands coping with the resurgence of malaria and was also trying to redesign the whole of its health services – it was not only the additional work that was causing disruption but also, as noted above, the suspicion in which many government workers unrelated to family planning began to be held. Such things can create pressure within the government machine for slowing down family planning, especially from departments whose work is being interfered with. Besides there were further reasons for believing that the 1976 levels of activity could not continue. A concern for demographic quality was bound to materialise, as it had with vasectomy camps before; if the programme was to confine itself to clients whose sterilisation would make a real difference to overall fertility rather than to anyone who would simply inflate the number of cases, its pace would be almost certain to fall off.

By the summer of 1977 it could not be said that the full extent of this family planning disaster was clearly known. But a stream of articles in the press supplemented the information which had during the Emergency mainly to be inferred from official statements or gathered privately from eyewitnesses. It became evident that cases of forcible sterilisation and undue pressure were very widespread. Another alarming feature was the large number of deaths due to hasty and unhygienic procedures on the operating table. There can be no doubt that sterilisation was a major factor in the election which defeated Mrs Gandhi's Congress Party. This matter is discussed in Chapter 5. Historians will perhaps trace the first step in this programme to the Turkman Gate episode early in 1976. During a sudden move to clear the hutments in the Jama Masjid area of old Delhi, rehousing was offered only to those who would submit to sterilisation. A riot followed which was not reported in detail at the time, but during which deaths were said to have reached three figures. This 'slum clearance' event, together with the fact that the greatest volume of sterilisation excesses occurred in North India in States where he was influential, linked the Emergency sterilisation drive very much with the name of Sanjay Gandhi.

It is the political authority behind the sterilisation drive which is the main undocumented feature of the 1976 events. The Centre continued to deny its backing for, even to deplore, coercive measures, at the same time as such measures were in full swing. As we have already indicated, the policies themselves gave scope for coercion especially wherever incentives were offered to those other than the clients themselves. But the fact that the policies were pushed much harder in some States than in others points to the influence of political factors. Sanjay Gandhi had publicly identified himself very clearly with the sterilisation drive. It is a moot point whether individual officers were acting on direct instructions or seeking personal advancement by collecting large numbers of sterilisations. But it was certainly disingenuous of defenders of the Emergency regime (and not least of the ex-Prime Minister herself) to blame the excesses on over-zealous individuals.[93] After all, perhaps the greatest number of excesses occurred in Haryana, and there is little doubt that they had the full backing of Bansi Lal, one of the exclusive inner circle of the Emergency regime.

While the main responsibility for the drive and its excesses belongs firmly to this inner circle, attention should not be completely distracted from other elements in the situation. The occasionally coercive features of the pre-1976 programme were noted earlier. Indeed one might say that family planning in India (and not only family planning) was often characterised by a modicum of insensitivity, if not contempt, on the part of those in authority towards ordinary people. Sporadic cases of compulsory sterilisation were not unknown, and in some States sterilisation camps had acquired clients by a variety of unsavoury means. Perhaps some officials of the Maharashtra programme above all bear independent blame as leaders in both the practice and advocacy of compulsion. The programme in Bombay was once a model of imaginative (and voluntary) family planning work, but well before 1976 the back streets of that city had become somewhat unsafe for men who did not wish to be sterilised. It was the Maharashtra spokesmen at a National Family Planning Council meeting in 1975 who proposed compulsory sterilisation for their own State, and, as already discussed, Maharashtra later passed the first Bill to that end. By mid-1976, D. N. Pai, the once praiseworthy architect of the early Bombay programme, was making the most grossly authoritarian statements describing women as 'baby factories'.[94] Maharashtra, it must be concluded, played a certain part in the move to compulsion. It was not, either, a State in which Sanjay Gandhi had any great influence, at least in the early months of the Emergency.

How then should one judge the 1976 National Population Policy? Foreign observers have long lectured the Indian Government to take more effective steps in family planning; had they any right to criticise it? One must start by saying that no such observers or official agencies, to our knowledge, ever advocated the more drastic aspects of the 1976 policy. (Indeed foreign agencies involved in giving aid to India's family planning programme began to be nervous about continuing it and some, such as the International Planned Parenthood Federation, publicly dissociated themselves from compulsion in any form.) The same considerations arise if the question is, did the Government have any viable alternative? If the 1976 policy was never going to succeed, it makes no sense to say there was no other course. It is conceivable, that after a period of restraint, the impact of the policy in bringing home the issues to the public will outweigh any 'backlash'; but the poor performance in 1977 showed that the excesses committed would make family planning difficult for some time. It was impossible under any political circumstances for the programme to continue as it was in 1976—backed by force, in an atmosphere of considerable unpopularity. We have called it a disaster, and such it was—disastrous for family planning in the short term, and a disastrous exercise in inhumanity.

What were the alternatives? First let it be said that many features of the 1976 policy were thoroughly desirable: some were renewals of earlier initiatives, others could—and should—have been started even earlier: the arrangements for State allocations of finance, the marriage age proposals, the increased incentives to clients, the greater involvement of all government agencies, the emphasis on female literacy, use of the media, incorporation of population materials in the educational system, above all the explicit support for family planning by national leaders. It is arguable that the positive and negative incentives to State employees for limitation of their own families are also justified (though not the harsh and selective manner in which they were implemented in 1976). These measures were not – with some exceptions perhaps – the ones that created hostility to the programme. What led to trouble was the setting of targets at various administrative levels without any clear advice as to what was permissible in the pursuit of those targets and indeed with general encouragement to maximise sterilisations. The administrator could expect to be rewarded by promotion or otherwise if he succeeded, and the opposite if he failed. It was . this which led to penalties on individuals not only if they refused sterilisation themselves, but if they failed to 'motivate' others.

Such administrative compulsion is bound to lead to malpractices, whether it be only false returns in the statistics, the development of a black market in sterilisation certificates or, at the extreme, forcible sterilisation with its attendant possibility of reactive violence. The existence of group incentives, where there is a possibility that the powerful impose their will on the powerless, also creates the possibility of abuse. A further issue under any family planning programme which attempts to impose a fertility norm is the definition of the norm and the sensitivity of its interpretation. The Government always made clear that it wanted three children to be the limit – though not all the agencies of government observed that rule faithfully. There are questions too about whether attention should be paid to the age and health of existing children: a father with two young children suffering from malaria and a third newly born would have some right to complain if treated on a par with the father of three older children all in good health. Many would suggest also, that if there is to be compulsion however 'gentle and civilised' to observe a fertility limit, more choice should be given to individual couples over the means they adopt to do so.

Family planning 'hawks' would counter with the view that considerations of this kind are all very well but it is only the fiercer measures which promise any fertility reduction in India in the short term. One can only agree that, apart from the increased client incentives, most of the other features of the 1976 Policy would be likely to operate relatively slowly. (Raising the age at marriage, as we indicated in Chapter 2, could have a significant effect, but it is hard to believe that the new legislation will in any short space of time be much more effective than the old.[95]) The measures involving state employees affect only a relatively small number of people and ones whose fertility is in any case lower than average. How are the great rural masses to be brought in to the programme? Unfortunately, as we have seen, even if faith in the voluntary approach had begun to be lost, it was not obvious that the more forceful measures were going to prove any more effective. It may well be that gradual progress is the only kind possible. Certainly the three major campaigns in the past – the I.U.D., the first mass promotion of vasectomies and the later vasectomy camps – were all damaged by going too fast. Tempering proper urgency with the patience of experience is the problem of India's family planning, and 'more haste, less speed' its trite but ineluctable rule.

This is not to say that there are no other things for family planning to do. The analysis above of the programme up to 1975 suggested that an important element both for improving family planning delivery and for improving the health of mothers and children – thereby encouraging birth control – is the development of a network of basic health workers with genuine outreach into the villages. Safe abortion could be made much more widely available. The pill could not only be made more widely available, greater efforts could be made to discover the conditions for its effective use and more instruction given on the basis of such enquiries. Depo-provera could be re-examined (see above, p. 169) and introduced where appropriate. The harmful economies and shortages which afflicted the Nirodh programme could be eliminated.

Above all family planning as a whole could be better managed. Too often considerable waste of resources has resulted from mechanical following of an established pattern. What has rarely been attempted is the matching of services to local circumstances. In many areas the family planning programme just *is* the P.H.C. doctor and supporting health workers and whatever they are able to do in the prevailing conditions, which is often very little. A more selective approach would be highly desirable, concentrating resources and choosing particular activities where they would be most effective. At the least different strategies are required for the more advanced and the more difficult areas. A great need currently is for progress in the States where birth rates are highest and large sections of the population scarcely touched by the family planning programme; yet there has been no evidence of any measures specifically designed for those conditions. Without them one can foresee a future in which fertility continues to decline relatively rapidly in the 'successful' family planning States while the current levels of fertility continue with little change in the others, leaving an India divided into demographically advanced and backward areas. What is needed in the more difficult conditions is the establishment by research and action programmes of the elements of an effective approach and its launching on a step-by-step basis until it covers the whole area. This is not a process which has to start from scratch as a great deal is known already.

An unusually careful study by Piers Blaikie[96] has examined the extension and communications organisation of the pre-1976 programme in a poor area of India. He observed the tendency of extension workers to contact mainly those who were likely to become 'acceptors' – naturally enough in a target-oriented programme. But it has the effect of reinforcing rather than altering existing patterns of contraceptive behaviour and of leaving largely untouched groups in the population who should be being approached – in this case lower caste groups and Muslims. Family planning workers hardly contacted such people at all – or did so only on the occasion of big vasectomy camps when they brought in clients who had little previous knowledge of or interest in vasectomy and who mostly regretted their hasty decisions on subsequent reflection. The author studied decision-making in family planning at the individual, Block, District and regional level and the interconnections between them. He was careful not to generalise his findings to less backward parts of the country but his broad conclusions are valid far beyond the parts of Bihar in which he worked. Specifically a good deal of information is fairly easily available at the local level which could be used to improve decisions about the location of services and select the most appropriate means of communication. With a pattern of services laid down in conformity with centrally devised norms, and bearing no relation to locally ascertainable circumstances, it is hardly surprising that the author was able to observe Blocks where the number of clients was so low in relation to services provided that the cost of preventing a birth was anywhere from Rs. 600 to over Rs. 860 ($80 – 115). His message is clear – even for so unpromising an area as North Bihar – that even a programme of the existing type could do very much better for the resources spent if greater selectivity were pursued together with other modest reforms.

It may well be for example that until a very different kind of health service has been extended, the extension approach is not likely to do any better in say Bihar or eastern Uttar Pradesh than it has in the past and that, for the time being, the 'old' kind of sterilisation camps, suitably modified to avoid past problems, are the best hope until better health services are available. (Assuming that is that the prospects for voluntary camps have not been ruined by the 1976 activities.) The condom programme is also suitable in areas where medical facilities are limited. But in the end family planning cannot be divorced from other forms of development and particularly from effective health services and the promotion of these must be the long term ambition everywhere in India.

Some of the above measures are at least partially already under way – as far as both abortions and the pill are concerned there was considerably more activity planned or already started by 1977 than ever before. But if the 1976 programme was to prove as shortlived as some of the previous dramatic initiatives, it was not at all clear what sort of policies would or could be continued in its wake. Our overall practical judgement of that programme is that it was not necessitated by the lack of viable alternatives and that it was simply too risky. If it succeeded it would possibly bring down the birth rate faster than the alternatives – but not necessarily very much faster than could have been achieved by a more cogent application of the lessons of experience of the programme up to 1975, together with the less controversial parts of the 1976 Policy. The risk was that if it failed, it might render any sustainable programme almost impossible to set in train for many years. That risk seems too great for what might have been gained. Perhaps authoritanarianism can succeed and the verdict of history will be that India's population problem, if at some human cost, would have been solved by it and that there was no other way. We have disagreed entirely with that verdict. In the light of what happened afterwards it is hard to imagine that others might accept it. Certainly the evidence up to 1977 hardly supports them.

HEALTH SERVICES AND HEALTH

The conclusions above about the desirable directions for family planning lay some stress on new kinds of health services. These are obviously important for purposes other than family planning. The extent of the problem can be seen from a description of the past; for this, the Government's medical and public health budgets provide a suitable framework. The country's curative medical services in the state sector come under the medical budget, and consist of a network of urban and rural hospitals, dispensaries, P.H.C.s and sub-centres and their associated staffs. There are also a substantial number of private facilities and doctors and, in rural areas especially, a great number of traditional practitioners. Table 3.2 gives some information about the availability of a variety of services. As is readily apparent their levels are fairly low in most places and some of the figures disguise the nature of the situation. Thus only five States have one doctor for less than 4000 population, but the majority of doctors everywhere are concentrated in urban areas. Census data on doctors showed the coverage for India to be one doctor per 5900 population in 1961 but the ratio was 1 : 1400 in urban areas and 1 : 18,000 in rural areas. (This did improve somewhat by 1971 when the urban ratio had actually risen slightly to 1 : 1500, and the rural decreased to 1 : 12,000.)[97] The same is true of hospital beds, of which only 30 per cent are in rural areas. Undoubtedly the intended thrust of current policies is to redress this imbalance, but there is still a long way to go.

The position in rural areas is somewhat better reflected by the distribution of P.H.C.s and sub-centres. Most States have approximately one P.H.C. functioning per Block and for that reason the number of P.H.C.s is not given; instead Col. (3) shows the percentage of P.H.C.s which have their official complement of two doctors – a proportion which varies from 100–93 per cent in Kerala, Tamil Nadu, Madhya Pradesh, Maharashtra, Punjab and Jammu and Kashmir to 16–2 per cent in Himachal Pradesh, Orissa and Uttar Pradesh. Figures for sub-centres are also given, since the P.H.C. serves a dispersed population of upwards of 100,000 people and the accessibility of services depends to a degree on the sub-centres from which auxiliary workers operate. As the table shows there is considerable variation in provision in this matter also. There is also a

TABLE 3.2 Health Indicators by States

	Population per doctor (1)	Hospital beds per 1000 pop. (2)	% PHCs with 2 doctors (3)	Sub-centres. per PHC (4)	Med. expenditure per head Rs. (5)	Public Health Exp. per head (Rupees) (6)	Population 1976 (millions) (7)
Andhra Pradesh	4416[a]	0·63	99	7·26	6·16	3·44	47·7
Assam	2631[a]	0·46	28	3·56	5·32	1·73	17·2
Bihar	6083[b]	0·20	70	6·00	3·20	2·19	61·5
Gujarat	4900[b]	0·54	62	7·12	6·50	4·28	30·0
Haryana	6702[a]	0·54	49	8·35	16·11	5·17	11·1
Himachal Pradesh	9026[a]	0·93	16	4·28	13·23	11·19	3·7
Jammu & Kashmir	1810[a]	0·73	83	3·55	12·86	9·25	5·8
Karnataka	5300[b]	0·77	74	7·44	7·71	4·09	23·8
Kerala	3981[a]	0·88	100	10·80	10·90	2·92	46·8
Madhya Pradesh	21663[b]	0·30	95	5·96	4·68	3·85	56·0
Maharashtra	2592[a]	0·72	93	7·13	6·45	11·64	32·3
Orissa	7008[b]	0·40	15	5·32	4·85	2·70	24·2
Punjab	5863[b]	0·58	87	6·74	8·93	3·92	14·9
Rajasthan	12662[b]	0·52	38	6·82	7·30	7·00	28·8
Tamil Nadu	3511[a]	0·54	98	7·58	8·33	1·90	45·2
Uttar Pradesh	7672[a]	0·39	2	6·52	3·61	1·16	95·8
West Bengal	1747[b]	0·77	30	4·56	8·41	2·59	49·4
All-India		0·55	58	6·36	6·98	3·76	605·6

SOURCE Col. (1) *Pocket Book of Health Statistics*, Table 31, Ministry of Health and Family Planning, New Delhi (1975). [a] Figures for January 1973
       [b] Figures for 1970.

SOURCE Col. (2) *Pocket Book*, Table 35, *ibid.* Includes public and private beds. Figures for Jan. 1973.

SOURCE Cols (3) *Pocket Book*, Table 37, *ibid.* Figures for 1974.
and (4)

       Col. (5) Budget data for 1975/76, all medical expenditures including medical education, from *An Analysis of Expenditures on Social Sectors*, Institute of Economic & Market Research, for I.B.R.D., New Delhi (1976).

       Col. (6) Budget data for 1975/76, all public health expenditures, *ibid.*

       Col. (7) *Pocket Book*, Table 6, *op. cit.* The figures are Expert Committee projections revised in the light of the 1971 Census. State population figures employed to derive cols (1) and (2) are for appropriate years from the same source.

considerable variation in medical expenditures, two of the poorest and most populous States, Bihar and Uttar Pradesh, spending only half the national average at Rs. 3·20 and 3·61 per head per year respectively. This of course reflects policy as well as poverty; Kerala is also one of the poorest States but manages Rs. 10·90 per head despite having one of the larger populations.

Even after the adverse rural/urban distribution of services has been noted, the true picture of the state of India's health services does not emerge. While it has been customary to measure progress in health services in terms of improvement in doctor and hospital-bed/population ratios these particular indicators mean very little as far as concerns health. This is not only because of restricted access to such services on the part of the mass of the people, but because curative medicine itself has only a limited impact on health. It has been repeatedly shown that, in populations suffering from widespread malnutrition and multiple sources of infection, curative medicine makes only a negligible difference to mortality and morbidity in the absence of simultaneous action on other health fronts. Maternal and child health (M.C.H.) services may have some impact on maternal and infant mortality especially if combined with nutritional assistance and education. Thus P.H.C. and sub-centre staffs engaged in M.C.H. work can make a greater contribution to mortality reduction than other curative workers. However the main worker in this field for rural areas, the A.N.M., is still relatively thin on the ground. Table 3.3 indicates the distance still to be travelled in further provision of rural A.N.M.s. It is accepted that an A.N.M. cannot satisfactorily serve a population of more than about 3000. Of course to reach such a level will require a vast number of workers who take time to train and the training programmes only got under way in the late 1960s. But plans for further developments were still in a state of flux in the mid 1970s.

The ultimate ambition of rural health manpower provision was stated in 1975 to be one sub-centre per 5000 population each staffed by one male and one female worker. Both would be 'multi-purpose health workers' responsible for treatment of minor ailments, nutrition education, M.C.H. and family planning, and some preventive work; the female worker's duties would not differ much from those of the A.N.M. In 1974 that would have required about 93,000 workers of each sex as compared with the actual level of about 20,000 A.N.M.s in Table 3.3. The training capacity of A.N.M. schools in that year was about 8400 admissions a year. Very clearly a considerable expansion of training facilities would be required to meet the 2-per-5000 target in any reasonable length of time to allow both for further population growth and exits from posts. The present period however is one of considerable ferment over the whole question of health delivery systems and past official statements about proposed staffing of health facilities are probably to be considered inoperative. Certainly they did not promise a great deal. The Draft Fifth Plan envisaged reaching a

TABLE 3.3

	ANMs in post, 1974	1974 rural population (millions)	000's rural per ANM
	(1)	(2)	(3)
Andhra Pradesh	2146	37·1	17·3
Assam	199	14·8	74·6
Bihar	1086	53·5	49·2
Gujarat	1146	20·6	18·0
Haryana	437	8·8	20·2
Himachal Pradesh	104	3·2	30·9
Jammu & Kashmir	97	4·0	41·1
Karnataka	921	19·1	20·7
Kerala	1333	33·8	25·4
Madhya Pradesh	2069	45·0	21·7
Maharashtra	1985	37·0	18·6
Orissa	921	21·3	23·2
Punjab	590	10·9	18·5
Rajasthan	1117	22·7	20·3
Tamil Nadu	(360)a	30·4	–
Utter Pradesh	3826	79·7	20·8
West Bengal	1260	35·6	28·2
All-India	19928b	465·7	23·3b

SOURCES Col (1) *Family Welfare Planning in India–Year Book 1974–75*, Table G–3, Ministry of Health & Family Planning, New Delhi (1975).
a. The figure for Tamil Nadu does not include sub-centre staff.
b. Includes an average for Tamil Nadu.

Col (2) Figures for rural population are derived from the 1974 totals in *Pocket Book* op.cit. adjusted by the 1971 Census rural/urban proportions by State.

Col (3) Col (2) ÷ Col (1)

target of one male and one female multi-purpose worker for every 8000 population by its terminal year (1979). A government report in 1975 noted: 'It is however anticipated that to complete the re-orientation training all over the country, keeping in view such other issues as the need to tackle any specific communicable diseases programme on a priority basis, it may take ten to twelve years unless there is augmentation of training facilities.'[98] As will be seen below the revised Fifth Plan did not appear to have retained the targets of the Draft version.

So far mainly the curative services of India's health programme have been covered. These of course are only a part of overall health activities and take up about half of the overall health budget, identified as 'medical' expenditure. The other parts are public health and family planning. These budget headings do not (indeed could not) perfectly correspond to the designated areas of activity; the work of many parts of the programme is interconnected, and much that is really 'curative' is carried on the family planning budget, while many 'medical' budget health workers engage in family planning work. Some preventive work is also carried out under budgets outside that of public health. A separate look at some aspects of the public health budget and activities under it is however revealing.

The total public health budget for 1975/6 was Rs. 2,278 million (Centre and States, including capital and revenue items).[99] Of this just over half, Rs. 1,172 million, was (mainly) for communicable disease programmes. Of the remainder some Rs. 50 million went towards sewage schemes, Rs. 687 million for urban and Rs. 369 million for rural water supply. A great deal of the communicable disease expenditure goes into rural areas; but in the water and sewage budgets, the 'urban bias' seen in medical expenditure is clearly visible. The low level of rural water supply expenditure may be judged in relation to the magnitude of the problem: in 1973 it was estimated[100] that there remained at the end of the Fourth Plan some 125,000 villages with either especially difficult water supply problems (water at greater than 50 feet depth or one mile distant) or acute health problems requiring water improvement. The cost of supplying those villages was put at Rs. 6,527·50 million; a further Rs. 12,228 million was needed for other villages whose problems were less severe. This makes a total of Rs. 18,755·5 million or $2,500 million at the exchange rate then prevailing ($1 = Rs. 7·5). In 1967/8 (the last year for which data are available) a sample of 8544 villages[101] showed 3·4 per cent of villages with tap water in the village; 7·4 per cent with a tube-well; 48·0 per cent with wells; 9·4 per cent with ponds or tanks. The remaining 32 per cent divided into 8 per cent with 'other sources', another 8 per cent had sources 'not recorded', about 3 per cent had some source or other outside the village but less than one kilometre away; the remaining 13 per cent had sources more than one kilometre distant. By the end of the Fourth Plan only 5·0 per cent of villages had reached the tap-water category; faster development undoubtedly took place with tube-well installation. No data exist for other improvements but, wherever the source is not tap-water or tube-wells, the probability that drinking water is both safe and in adequate supply is low.

Recent Plan estimates have taken to providing only for the 'difficult' villages. The Draft Fifth Plan allocated Rs. 5,730 million for the 116,000 villages identified as 'no source' or 'problem' villages;[102] the revised Plan[103] estimated that 57,800 of such villages would have been covered by 1977 at a cost of Rs. 2,011 million and the remaining 53,900 villages would be covered in the last two years of the Plan at a cost of Rs. 1,801 million, or Rs. 3,812 million for the Plan period as a whole. The constant downward trend in current rupees in the estimated cost of supplying the problem villages is remarkable – from Rs. 52,220 per village in 1973 to Rs. 33,413 per village in 1978 and 1979. Part of the explanation appears to be that the original cost estimates were made by State governments in the expectation of Central resources; but the Centre finally instructed the States that rural water supply was a State responsibility. But it is also likely that the target of 116,000 problem villages covered will not be met. And the needs of the 'non-problem' villages currently appear to receive no allocation at all; yet if the proportion of tap-water or tube-well supplied villages has doubled between 1967/8 and 1976, i.e. to say 22 per cent of all villages, even if only 10 per cent of the total are still problem villages as defined, there must be at least 68 per cent of villages without safe or adequate water. (It may be noted that the Plan figures for expenditure on rural water supply do not correspond to the Budget[104] figures which total only Rs. 1,182·5 million for 1974–7 against the revised Plan's Rs. 2,011 million. Presumably some rural water supply is carried under other programmes – e.g. minor irrigation.) By comparison the Draft Fifth Plan's Rs. 4,310 million for urban water supply (which has long been considerably better than supply in rural areas) was raised to Rs. 5,391·7 million in the revised Plan.[105]

Examination of planned health expenditures as a whole suggests a considerable sluggishness – especially on the part of State governments – in rural health work other than the malaria campaign and family planning. The per capita expenditures on the medical budget reported in Table 3.2 have doubled in terms of current rupees since 1970/71 but have risen by 25–30 per cent (depending on the price deflator used) in real terms. Per capita public health expenditures have increased only by 28 per cent in current rupees and have declined in real terms. The Draft Fifth Plan proposed an outlay of Rs. 7,960 millions on health services other than family planning. Its main objectives were (i) to make up the backlog in rural health facilities and personnel and increase the priorities of drugs to P.H.C.s, and sub-centres; (ii) to improve communications and other infrastructure so that these facilities would become more accessible; (iii) to extend various communicable disease programmes – not only malaria, but T.B., cholera, leprosy, filaria and so forth. The targets were not particularly ambitious: that for sub-centres for example was only 1 per 10,000 population. Yet the provision for such activities was reduced in the revised Fifth Plan from Rs. 7,960 millions to Rs. 6,817 millions. And *within* the latter total an additional Rs. 1,000 million was shifted to the malaria programme, which was allocated Rs. 1,964·4 million in the revised Plan as compared with Rs. 967·1 million in the Draft. Finally it may be noted that the modest nutrition activities proposed in the Draft, at a cost of Rs. 4,000 million for the Plan period, were reduced to an outlay of Rs. 1,156·7 million in the revised Plan.

These movements in Plan allocations took place in a Plan revision which, it will be recalled, actually increased the volume of total Plan outlay by Rs. 20,375 million. Most of the modest targets of the Draft Fifth Plan must be regarded as unattainable under the financial provision finally adopted. Further in 1976 a large proportion of existing facilities and manpower in the health sector were being drawn into the rapidly expanding sterilisation programme. Altogether the trends in the health sector gave cause for concern: while the malaria programme and family planning absorbed large share of health resources, per capita expenditures on most other health activities were seriously retarded. This is especially disturbing in a period when the fall in mortality has undergone a fairly sharp pause and when it is widely regarded that further reductions in infant and child mortality are a desirable condition for fertility decline and the voluntary practice of family planning.

It is important to realise that adjustments in Plan finance do not necessarily reflect alterations of the priorities of the Central Government. Many of the activities in the health sector are the responsibility of State governments and several of the downward Plan revisions noted above reflect the actual or expected achievements in construction of buildings, training of personnel and so forth which proved to be on the low side for the 1974–7 period. It is the State governments which have failed to meet many of the targets, for a number of reasons, ranging from shortages of building materials to difficulties of recruiting personnel. At the same time performance reflects the priorities in the States: if the Plan provision for urban water supply has risen, that is to a considerable extent because States have made more progress in urban water supply schemes. The Centre made a mild attempt to rectify this by making expenditure under minimum needs programme activities (such as rural water supply) 'earmarked expenditures', i.e. State expenditures in one year on the basis of which Central allocations are calculated for other programmes in the following year. But the States had not been putting rural health high on their list. Most of the reduction in the revised Plan relative to the Draft is for the States' expenditures as the following table shows:

TABLE 3.4 Health sector: Draft and Revised Fifth Plan outlay
(Rs. millions)

	Draft	Revised
1. Central	757·8	676·6
2. Centrally sponsored	1770·1	2681·7
of which malaria programme	(967·1)	(1964·4)
3. States/Union Territories	5432·1	3458·3
4. Total	7960·0	6816·6

SOURCE *Draft* and Revised *Fifth Five Year Plans*, op. cit.

Within the Central and centrally-sponsored schemes the increased allocation to the malaria programme was mainly accommodated by an increase of Rs. 830 million in the proposed outlay. The reduction of States' expenditures was bound to affect the deployment of rural health services relative to the anticipated targets.

A component of India's health services important for many people – especially in rural areas – are the traditional medical practitioners. These are practitioners of indigenous systems of medicine and known as vaids, hakims, unanis, homoeopaths and others. According to the 1971 Census (one per cent sample data) among traditional practitioners there were 48,900 Ayurvedics, 29,600 homoeopaths, 4700 unanis and 35,000 'others'. This same source gave a figure of 108,200 for allopathic (i.e. Western-style) doctors of whom almost exactly two-thirds were in urban practice; the vaids were about two-thirds rural and the other non-allopathic doctors were above or just below 60 per cent rural. These data conform fairly well to the proportions of rural and urban allopathic and non-allopathic 'licentiates and graduates' observed in the N.S.S. 22nd Round,[106] in which allopathic outnumber non-allopathic practitioners by about 2 to 1 in the urban sample and the position is reversed in the rural sample. The latter source also suggests that allopaths charge more for their services in rural than in urban areas; if that is explained by supply and demand, non-allopaths presumably charge less than allopaths in rural areas.

As with most other proposals concerning health in India the idea that traditional practitioners should be incorporated in one way or another in official health services has been promoted for some time. They have the great advantage of being trusted medical authorities in rural areas. There have been proposals, and some action, to enlist them for family planning and other rural health work. Their medical knowledge and medicaments have been under study for some time (including some W.H.O. assisted research) and various committees which have in the past pronounced on medical matters have recommended that their interests and their potential usefulness should not be neglected. At the same time studies of the ability of traditional practitioners to cooperate with modern health services in India and other countries are inconclusive. Some are willing and able to take on new roles, dispense modern drugs as well as their own and so forth, but others have proved unwilling or unable to adopt new activities. The *Draft Fifth Plan* (p. 237) announced a number of programmes for the development of 'indigenous systems of medicine and homoeopathy', but they were designed rather to strengthen existing activities than to draw traditional practitioners more firmly into official rural health-worker programmes. The Rs. 45 million (Central funds) allocated for the programmes was cut to Rs. 19·7 million in the Plan revision.

The health problem and steps to meet it
Other parts of this book have pointed to the nature of India's health problem. High levels of infant and child mortality related to malnutrition and infection; adolescent and adult mortality at more moderate levels, and due to a variety of causes – among the major sources of mortality are a

number of communicable diseases such as T.B. and malaria, tetanus and death in childbirth. Much of this mortality is described as preventable, that is, reducible by public health measures; most of it is related to poverty and lack of education – the death rate, like the birth rate, is commonly found to be negatively correlated with educational level other things being equal. But the difficulty of making progress is compounded by a number of cultural and traditional habits and beliefs surrounding diet practices, childbirth, illness and hygiene.

The allocation of resources in India's health programmes has never, as far as can be ascertained, been the subject of published research of high quality – hence the unsatisfactory nature of the foregoing account of the government sector. Nevertheless India's health system shares several features of the pattern of health services in other developing countries whose professional medical structures and distribution of major facilities are inherited from a colonial past. These features include a large share of health budgets devoted to major hospitals in urban centres and a consequent relative neglect of the rural health infrastructure and a medical profession whose orientation is towards high technology, curative medicine and an urban style of life. Increasingly the international health community has been looking at ways of doing better for health in developing countries. Since resources are limited, the emphasis has been on low cost alternatives, especially for rural areas. There is a growing consensus that the major sources of mortality can be controlled – with some exceptions – by relatively simple and inexpensive measures. The major problems at the village level do not require sophisticated medicine or costly equipment, but they do require concerted action on several fronts – studies have shown that curative medicine, improved water supply, better hygiene, even nutrition intervention, when pursued singly, may have modest or even negligible effects.

The combination of scarce resources and the need for concerted action has given rise to intellectual enthusiasm for popular participation in health work at the village level led by a basic health worker (B.H.W.). A few socialist countries and a number of pilot projects in several developing countries – including India – have demonstrated the potential effectiveness of this approach.[107] Above this level there has to be a network of referral facilities from local clinics to major hospitals but these can be developed without necessarily following the high cost technologies of the rich countries. At all levels appropriate training can be designed to provide health workers competent to do what is required at costs suited to a country's budget. In particular medical auxiliaries of various skill levels are needed; so too is the university-trained doctor but his or her training should be directed away from currently common orientations with far greater emphasis on management of lower level health facilities and supervision of auxiliaries and B.H.Ws. This whole approach is sometimes branded by medical conservatives as the recommendation of 'inferior' medicine for developing countries. Of course if the test of 'superior' medicine is the extent to which it employs high-cost technology, it is indeed inferior. But if the test is the improvement of health of the greatest number of people for a given expenditure, then such a health system is greatly superior to what currently exists in most developing countries. Many indeed would claim that these lessons of developing-country health services are not without applicability in the rich countries.

India too is currently undergoing a re-examination of its health system. Perhaps the most prestigious analysis was made by the Group on Medical Education and Support Manpower[108] whose members included the heads of the Indian Council of Medical Research, the All-India Institute of Medical Sciences, the Indian Council of Social Science Research, the Post-Graduate Institute of Medical Education and Research and officials of the Health Ministry, with the Director General of Health Services in the chair. The introduction of this report deserves quotation in full:

> The Government of India, in the Ministry of Health and Family Planning, have invited attention to some of the pressing problems and needs of medical education and support manpower and especially to:
> – the essentially urban orientation of medical education in India which relies heavily on curative methods and sophisticated diagnostic aids with little emphasis on the preventive and promotional aspects of community health,
> – the failure of the programmes of training in the fields of nutrition, family welfare planning and maternal and child health to subserve the total needs of the community because of their development in isolation from medical education,
> – the deprivation of the rural communities of doctors in spite of the increase of their total stock in the society,
> – the need to re-orient undergraduate medical education to the needs of the country with emphasis on community rather than on hospital care, and
> – the importance of integrating teaching of various aspects of family planning with medical education,
> and have expressed the view that the structure of medical education has to be modified to meet the changing requirements and to provide adequately for future needs, particularly of the rural community. Government have also stressed the need to improve the delivery of health services by better trained and more qualified personnel working under the supervision of fully-equipped medical doctors.

The Group expressed itself most forthrightly about the existing health system and its distortions, many of which were quite properly attributed to the origins overseas of India's present health 'model' and the nature of the international medical manpower market. 'The huge cost of the model and its emphasis on over-professionalisation is obviously unsuited to a developing country like ours. It is therefore a tragedy that we continue to persist with this model even when those we borrowed it from have begun to have serious misgivings about its utility and ultimate viability. It is . . . desirable that we . . . abandon this model and strive to create a viable and economic alternative. . . . The new model will have to place a greater emphasis on human effort (for which we have a large potential) rather than on monetary inputs (for which we have severe constraints).'

There were four main recommendations: (1) The creation of 'bands of para-professional or semi-professional health workers from the community itself to provide simple promotive, preventive and curative health services which are needed by the community.' (2) The development of two cadres of health workers between the community level and the Public Health Centre. This was one of the sources of the recommendation, referred to above, for one male and one female health auxiliary per 5000 population. The P.H.C. itself, the Group also recommended, should be strengthened with a third doctor and an additional nurse, particularly for M.C.H. work and its financial allocation for drugs increased; senior doctors from hospitals and medical colleges should be seconded to P.H.C.s for extended periods. (3) The 'Referral Services Complex': the P.H.C.s should develop links with their local communities and the whole complex of P.H.C.s, local, district, regional and medical college hospitals should work more closely together. A key proposal for this purpose was to change the character of the internship period in medical education to include terms of residence in institutions throughout the complex. (4) The establishment of a Medical and Health Education Commission to take forward a series of proposals – spelled out in the report – to 'restructure the entire programme of medical education' in the direction of greater relevance to India's needs and also perform grant-giving functions similar to those of a University Grants Commission.

The immediate reaction of the Government to these recommendations was not overly enthusiastic. In 1975 the Health Minister set up a committee under the Health Secretary to prepare a plan of action related to the Group's report. Its findings, referred to as the Action Plan,[109] were released in 1976. The committee felt that recommendation (1) 'bristles with a large number of practical difficulties'. Appropriate training facilities did not exist on an adequate scale to cope with substantial new demands for para-professional training. It was suggested that primary and middle school teachers, village postmasters and some community develop-ment workers might be trained in basic family planning, preventive, promotive and curative work. Recommendation (2) was more or less accepted being in line with other activities to be described below. On recommendations (3) and (4), the Action Plan proposed a scheme in which medical colleges should take responsibility for 3 or 4 rural Blocks, and eventually an entire District, as a means of combining some of the organisational and educational proposals. But it turned down the suggestion of a Medical and Health Education Commission on grounds mainly of absence of funds.

What would come out of all this was obscure. As far as concerns basic health workers the Action Plan's proposals fell far short of the idea of village level para-professionals chosen by and serving their own communities after appropriate (if modest) training. But current activities go beyond this. The government has launched its Integrated Child Development Scheme (I.C.D.S.) in Blocks in thirty-three different Districts, with an 'anganwari' (or 'courtyard') worker in each village or centre responsible for M.C.H. and educational work supported by supplemental services from the P.H.C. (which include the third doctor recommended by the Group and rather more additional personnel and facilities than the Group proposed). These pilot I.C.D.S. schemes will be evaluated by the Programme Evaluation Organization of the Planning Commission after two years, and 'if . . . successful, the Government . . . intend extending this project gradually to other blocks in the country'.[110] At the same time a considerable number of smaller schemes throughout the country are attempting to develop para-professional services at the village level. Some of them are working mainly on health and nutrition, others are pursuing health objectives within a context of integrated rural development projects. They are financed by national or foreign voluntary agencies, local firms, foreign aid; in many cases, where parts of the facilities provided are within recognised official patterns, they receive government support.[111] There is an officer in the Health Ministry who has the responsibility of keeping himself informed about the progress of these schemes and assessing their suitability for possible wider promotion in the governmental health service system.

There is no doubt that India is looking for new initiatives in rural health. At a 1976 conference in Hyderabad on health delivery systems most of the papers presented were about methods depending on basic health workers. But where that delivery system is actually heading is currently hard to judge for a number of reasons. In the first place promoting health at the village level is extremely hard to do. Villagers have strong beliefs about the causes of ill-health and do not easily come to trust new methods or the individuals who promote them. An important part of the development of a new health orientation is the establishment of rapport between health workers and the community – a process which often requires considerable time and patience (and one might add skilled supervision). Partly as a result of this, trial projects promoting health through B.H.W.s will take a long time to assess. The nature of most of these projects is that of the action programme, not the careful scientific study with baseline surveys and controls, so that the ingredients of success or failure cannot easily be identified. A key ingredient often seems to be the project leader or team – almost universally people of high calibre and dedication. When questions of 'replicability' are asked, the dependence of apparently successful schemes on remarkable individuals is the greatest single cause of scepticism.

Uncertainty about current directions also has more fundamental sources. The call for basic health workers is – like many 'new' initiatives in India – not all that new. 'The huge task that faces us could never be solved on a routine or bureaucratic basis. Thus the cornerstone of the scheme we recommend is a health worker. The health worker will be one of the villagers themselves only somewhat better trained than themselves. He will not appear to the villagers as a strange imposition of a strange system but their kith and kin who desires to help them. These health workers should be given elementary training in practical, community and personal hygiene, first aid and simple medical treatment, stress being laid on the social aspects and implications of medical and public health work.' The quotation is from the Report of the National Health Sub-Committee of the National Planning Committee of the Congress Party, set up in 1938.[112] What seems different today is a widespread acceptance, at the highest levels, that the existing health system has not brought even minimal health services to a vast section of the rural population and indeed cannot do so at reasonable cost. Simultaneously by an intellectual sea-change, similar to those observed in other fields, what was once the critical outsiders' view of health has become almost the conventional wisdom of the national and international health community. There is now a considerable impetus behind the search for alternatives in health. What is in question however is how far this is just an intellectual wave and how far the circumstances which have caused the health system to be as it is have really shifted.

Medical sociologists see health systems as products of the social structures – national and international – within which they arise. If the health system has an urban and middle class bias, it is because it is dominated by professionals who are themselves urban and middle class, often relating themselves more comfortably to international medical practice (itself similarly dominated) than to national needs, within an overall social and political system which itself does not reflect the numerical preponderance of the rural poor. Yet even if this view is true, it does not logically follow that the health system cannot be changed without changing the social fabric in which it has arisen any more than it follows, from the fact that T.B. is a disease of poverty, that T.B. cannot be cured or substantially prevented without eradicating poverty. Nevertheless past experience must restrain undue confidence in any early prospect of a 'new deal' in health for the rural poor. As noted, even if backed by more adequate resources and political will, the new approaches to health care are not easy to set in motion. And the historically minded will wonder how pervasive amongst decision-makers throughout the health hierarchy is any real commitment to change. The quotation above from the 1938 Congress sub-committee is not an isolated instance; there have been several committees and government bodies in the past forty years issuing proposals similar to those of the Group on medical education. Will there be any 'reorientation' of medical education? And if there is – and it is the main thing on which the Group rested its hopes – will it lead to changes throughout the health system?

The pessimist can point to a number of negative considerations. The incentives for doctors to work in rural areas are weak compared with the attractions of high-income (especially if 'foreign-returned') urban medical practice. Various government measures to compel rural service have not seriously been implemented. What is mainly staffing the rural P.H.C.s with doctors is the insufficiency of demand for their services in urban areas relative to supply – though many doctors still prefer to wait unemployed in hope of urban rewards rather than accept a rural posting from which they fear they may not return. If they do go to rural areas, all the attractions – psychological and financial – lie in curative work; indeed there are many complaints about government-salaried doctors in P.H.C.s spending disproportionate amounts of their time on fee-paid work for better-off private patients. If newly-trained doctors are to be re-oriented, who is being trained to teach them in a new manner?

All this said it remains true that many influential members of the medical profession are aware and ashamed of the failure of India's health system to make greater progress and the government is looking for new ways forward. It is to be hoped that these will include major efforts to correct the rural/urban imbalances. There is a danger that even if additional resources in future are disproportionately allocated towards rural work, the difficulties of achieving progress with B.H.W.s and the 'referral complex' will be allowed to excuse poor performance and the result really will be inferior services for the rural areas. The government's determination to make changes in the health field will test the significance of current declarations of intent by the political authorities to bend the instruments of the State to the service of all the people. A particular worry in 1977 was the conflict of such ambitions with the intensified family planning drive, which as noted was drawing personnel and facilities away from health and other development work. There is a constant danger that the 'correlates of fertility decline' other than family planning – especially the reduction of infant and child mortality – will receive insufficient attention.

Perhaps the strongest argument for the 'new approach' is that there is no feasible alternative. The figures above show how vast is the investment needed to improve village water supplies by the agency of the Public Works Department; but if villages were taught the necessary elements of safe and adequate water provision, much could be done by their own efforts at much lower cost to the public purse.[113] The incidence of T.B. has not come down in the last fifteen years and, while a large proportion of T.B. sufferers present themselves at clinics, they are more often than not given cough mixture and sent away, but conducting sputum tests and doing curative and preventive T.B. work is easily within the competence of a community health worker. Even malaria control needs B.H.W.s; while the early stages of control may be satisfactorily handled by a vertical campaign against the disease, the last stages of eradication require case-finding and treatment, as well as residual insecticide spraying, at the local level.[114]

As indicated in Chapter 2 India's greatest single health problem lies in the realm of nutrition. In coping with it too the B.H.W. could fulfil a valuable function. But the overall needs are more comprehensive than that. There are three main parts to the official nutrition programme in so far as concerns the direct provision of food: the Applied Nutrition Programme is the most ambitious in intent since it was designed to organise (i) supplementary feeding for women and children; (ii) nutrition education and (iii) programmes to increase local production of nutritious foods. The comprehensive nature of this integrated set of activities sounds like just what many might think is needed, but it has foundered, as so many such initiatives, on the failure to perform of numerous administrative organisms which were supposed to play a variety of interconnected parts at higher and lower levels[115] – the only element of the three that has gone forward at all has been the feeding programme. Then there is the Special Nutrition Programme aimed at assisting women and pre-school children in urban slums and backward rural areas through the establishment of 'balwadis' or nurseries and with the help of schools and various private and public agencies. Finally State Education Departments have for many years been running school meals programmes. These activities are believed to reach about 17 million women and children, the school meals accounting for about two-thirds of that number. In addition to these major programmes there have been widespread campaigns to fortify bread, flour, salt or other common foods with items such as vitamin A and iron which are deficient in many diets. There have also been commercial developments of various enriched foods only two of which, 'balahar' and 'sukhadi', have been taken up on any scale outside the higher income groups. (These are specially prepared foods made up from cereals, pulses and other ingredients to form high-protein compounds; they are used in feeding programmes and under special circumstances such as the Maharashtra drought relief operation of 1973.)

These various initiatives, or at least the major feeding programmes, have assisted a very small fraction of the malnourished in India and by no means only the poorest of those – on the contrary, since so much is distributed through school programmes and the poorest children are not in school, few of the extreme poverty groups are affected at all. No doubt all those assisted welcome, and most of them need, the extra food and one should not argue that small efforts are wasted because they fail to solve the larger problem. To some extent even these programmes do not reach their intended targets – children fed at school may receive less at home or take the food home and share it out with the family; nevertheless the children appear to receive some benefit;[116] and at the least the family as a whole does, so that there is an overall redistributive effect. But feeding India's population is not a matter for such 'programmes'. Apart from anything else they cannot be afforded on the necessary scale. The lowest estimate of the daily cost of a feeding programme for pre-school children is 25 paise,[117] or say only $10 a year; take only the low estimate in Chapter 2 of 25 million such children in need and an annual cost of $250 million results. The additional food needs in the population as a whole must be at least twice that figure – compared with a proposed annual expenditure on nutrition programmes of $25 million in the Fifth Plan.[118] Even if India had a spare $500 million worth of food, the Government could not afford to give it away; it would have to be the wages of useful employment.

The food problem is a macroeconomic problem. Growing – or importing – adequate amounts of food has first to be achieved by appropriate resource allocation. That is only the first step; the next is to ensure that those without sufficient food have the incomes to buy it. In India, or any really poor country, one's suspicions should immediately be aroused by plans which suggest the elimination of malnutrition by special feeding programmes. They are unlikely to be more than a palliative, a selective form of charity. The main 'nutrition programme' in India indeed is the rationed and subsidised sale of grain through the Fair Price Grain Stores but that too is inadequate for the population's needs. The real solution is agricultural expansion and rural development bringing more food and incomes and employment to those who cannot afford to buy it. Nevertheless reliance on income growth would be a slow path to ending malnutrition since, as we have seen earlier, people are nutritionally inefficient in their food expenditures and; without nutritional education, very considerable extra income would be needed by poor families before nutritional adequacy was reached. The problems of bad food habits and feeding practices would remain. It is here that the B.H.W. comes in, with a very large part to play in educating mothers on the subject of appropriate nutrition of infants and children.

Yet another function for the B.H.W. would be to provide instruction for community sanitation work. Most Indians in rural areas defecate in the fields and various disease organisms have little difficulty in finding their way into the water supply and back into the human body. A great deal of research has gone into the design of latrines for rural use including tests of acceptability to the users, and a good deal of energy has gone into attempting to encourage their use. According to a government report, a 'determined effort' is needed to press this programme to success. 'The improvement that this single measure will bring about in the mortality and morbidity statistics of bowel diseases will be considerable. The face of the countryside will change and a new era of sanitation will dawn in India villages.'[119] These stirring words were written in 1966. Little has happened.

The main sources of mortality in India are malnutrition, malaria, tuberculosis and tetanus and a variety of other air-borne or fecally transmitted and water-borne diseases. The main measures to reduce their incidence require control, prevention, environmental improvements, especially water-supply and sanitation, and curative work. These can be – and have been – pursued by expensive separate programmes with limited effectiveness. It seems logical to try to unite these separated functions in the activities of basic health workers under a participating rural health scheme with genuine outreach into the villages. This can also provide the follow-up care and instruction necessary for voluntary family planning. Both the costs and the organisational difficulties of other approches – as has been demonstrated most clearly in the case of water-supplies and nutrition – put the benefits of better health beyond the reach of most Indians for decades in the absence of such a scheme.[120] Whatever its difficulties – and they are, as noted above, numerous – there seems to be no other way.

4 Population and the Economy

My lord, since you have banished Poverty
From this fair land, I feel it is my duty
To lay an information that the outlaw
Has taken refuge in my humble home.

Anon, 1st Millennium A.D.
Poems from the Sanskrit, tr. J. Brough, Penguin, 1968.

RECENT ECONOMIC HISTORY

India at Independence inherited an economy whose main features reflected two centuries of subservience to British interests and, particularly in the twentieth century, the development of its own capitalism. The economic task of the new Congress government was to set India on the path of a different style of economic progress which would at long last relieve its people from millennia of poverty and make India internationally respected and truly independent. The years prior to Independence witnessed many political conflicts on economic policy both within and outside the Congress party – the relative roles of the state and the private sector, of heavy and small scale manufacturing (on which Nehru and Gandhi were in some degree of opposition), of industry and agriculture. Most of these conflicts were unresolved when the first moves towards planning were made – and to some extent they still are.

Immediately after 1947 the country was in the throes of upheaval caused by partition and its aftermath but the movement towards the five year plans as the centre of economic policy continued, along lines foreshadowed by many pre-Independence developments – not least the involvement of Congress in provincial government under the British.[1] In 1950 the Planning Commission was established and in 1951 the First Five Year Plan (F.Y.P.) appeared. There followed the second in 1956, the third in 1961 and the fourth, after a hiatus of three years, in 1969. None of these plans were fulfilled in detail or to the extent projected; but, guided by them, economic policy pursued certain fundamentals of economic transformation as a result of which India is, with whatever complications, a major industrial power capable of producing any but the most ultra-sophisticated of modern manufactures. A high proportion of output is of capital and intermediate goods – two-thirds of all manufactures compared with one-third at Independence. The public sector has a dominating role in the economy. And agriculture has just about been able to keep pace with the growth in population. All these were ambitions of planning, but there were many other ambitions which have not been attained. The overall rate of growth and of industrialisation has not been sufficient to raise average living standards a great deal or to initiate a concerted trend or increasing employment in industry fast enough to draw people off the land. The economy is not really self-sufficient; that is to say while it can survive without concessional borrowing from abroad, or at least reached a position where it could, both prior to the 1973–4 oil crisis and also in the last year or two, it cannot guarantee a continuing rate of growth which promises an end to domestic difficulties. Agricultural development has not been as thorough-going as was once hoped, with only the irrigated wheat areas so far benefiting from the 'green revolution'. Perhaps more fundamentally the social character of India's economy has altered only a little since Independence. Caste is still a dominant factor in employment and social relations, and strongly associated with income differentials. And land ownership has not been greatly affected by three decades of legislation except for the remedying of some of the worst abuses of the land-tenure system left by the British.

Perhaps one should not expect to see removed in three decades features of society which have existed for hundreds or even thousands of years. Nevertheless many have been disappointed in the hopes they once held. 'In order to remove the poverty and misery of the Indian people and to ameliorate the conditions of the masses, it is essential to make re-volutionary changes in the present economic and social structure of society and to remove gross inequalities.' This is not a modern criticism of gradualist approaches to development, though the sentiment is com-monplace enough in contemporary discussions of India. It is a quote from the Congress resolution made in Lahore in 1929.[2]

The First Five Year Plan, covering the period 1951–6, is commonly regarded as a documentary dressing up of an assortment of projects, most of which had been prepared and contemplated prior to the Plan's formulation. Nevertheless the policies enunciated in the Plan were an important statement of objectives – and of confusion between objectives. Everything and its competitor was accorded its due place, agriculture and industry, the state and the private sector, cottage industries and modern manufacturing, egalitarianism and little interference with the *status quo*. Everyone was to be consulted, all sections of opinion harmonised. The lack of decisiveness is seen in the Plan's vagueness over finance; while the resources were not adequate to cover the targets of expenditure, taxation was not to be greatly raised and deficit finance was thought dangerous; additional aid might be forthcoming, but little was said with any conviction about what would happen if it were not.

In the event the Plan appeared to have turned out reasonably well until its final year. There was an excellent harvest in 1952/3, after the drought of 1950/51 and not much better in 1951/2, and a spectacular one in 1953/4, almost repeated in the following year. These years created a certain euphoria; food imports in 1954/5 were down to 0·6 million tons and the foreign exchange position was not uncomfortable. Encouraged by the situation the Government had increased public expenditure in the absence of any significant rise in savings, private or public, and the good harvests kept inflation at bay; private industry moved ahead. The year 1955/6 produced a warning note in the shape of a poor harvest and consequent inflation as deficit financing continued and in the subsequent year the strain on the balance of payments became visible. But the warning was barely heeded.

The Second Plan was conceived in the optimistic period when it still seemed that the economy could stand the pace of forced expansion and the proponents of a bolder and larger Plan were listened to with respect. But this was not to be just a larger plan – it was to incorporate for the first time the explicit notion of a 'socialist pattern of society' and to emphasise further certain features of the economy already foreshadowed in the First Plan. And some emphases changed considerably – in particular the amount of resources allocated to the development of heavy industry in the state sector. This followed the working-out of the 'Mahalanobis model', a mathematical simulation of the economy under a set of particular assumptions which purported to show the superiority over the long-run of a growth pattern which restrained consumption in the early stages and maximised the output of investment goods.[3] The Second plan was even more notable than the First for confusion about the likely availability of resources to carry it out. A prolonged debate attended the early years of the Plan; the foreign exchange problem of 1956/7 deepened in 1957/8 after another bad harvest and the Plan had to retreat to a 'core' list of projects: the critics of the excessive size of the original Plan were vindicated.

However the foreign exchange situation eased, partly as a result of the industrial recession engendered by domestic problems, partly with an increase of aid receipts, and there was a much improved crop in 1958/9 even if there was little improvement in the two subsequent years; so the last two years of the Second Plan proved a calm after the storm, to some extent masking all the shortcomings of the progress made during the five years – the widening of the foreign exchange gap and loss of reserves; the low levels of domestic investment; the dependence of the harvest on the weather and the economy on the harvest; severe bottlenecks in power and transport. Only private sector industry had gone ahead faster than expected. But overall expansion in employment was modest compared with the growth of the labour force.

The Third Plan was mainly conspicuous, by comparison with the Second, for a renewed emphasis on the priority to be given to agriculture; it was also, both intellectually and administratively, very much more sophisticated than its predecessors. Committees were formed to examine the production possibilities for each major product or sector and attempts were made to reconcile their findings: a more sophisticated model was elaborated to investigate the framework of the Plan responding to some of the criticisms of previous models. Yet for all the improvements within months the Third Plan was in trouble; by its third year it was obvious that its targets were impossible to attain – the national income had grown by only 5 per cent in total at the mid-point of the Plan period instead of the planned 5·4 per cent annually. By the end of the Plan numerous downward revisions had been made and the events of the last year of the Plan were a plain disaster. Some of the Plan's troubles had nothing to do with its faults: the war with China, which necessitated some diversion of resources into defence spending, and the weather, which was not very good for agriculture in 1962/3 or 1963/4, and appalling later. But most of the problems were all too familiar from the experience of the Second Plan – the over-estimation of the capacity of the economy and the administration to perform in various respects, and the wishful thinking, if not deliberate avoidance of thought or at least of clarity, about the likely magnitude of available resources.

In 1965 there began the series of calamities which struck like hammerblows at the economy and at the principles and conduct of fifteen years of economic policy under planning. There was a brief but unpleasant conflict with Pakistan. The crop year of 1965/6 suffered from the acute drought and food production fell to the levels of the late 1950s necessitating heavy imports of food. Despite large volumes of aid (temporarily cut off during the war period) the balance of payments was in chronic crisis and India came under great pressure to devalue the rupee. Devaluation occurred in June 1966; it was politically traumatic as there was great debate about its advisability and the politicians of the day saw themselves, and were seen by others, to be submitting to the influence of the World Bank and I.M.F. and other forces in the international community, particularly the views of the major aid-giving countries. The devaluation, though necessary for long term rectification of structural problems in the economy, was also badly timed – industrial recession and shortages of domestic agricultural products are not the conditions for profiting from reduced export prices and more expensive imports. The production conditions in many export industries were also of a kind that would respond only slowly to improved opportunities. The Aid-India Consortium attempted to guarantee an aid package to see India through the devaluation, including an annual $900 million of non-project aid. The package fell apart after the first year, particularly owing to American defections.[4] *Pour comble des malheurs* 1966/7 was another year of severe drought; coming on top of that of the previous year, when stocks were already depleted, it was a calamity of a magnitude unparalleled since

Independence. Only a major inflow of food aid in these two years saved India from famines in which hundreds of thousands, if not millions, might have died.

What had gone wrong with planning? The main recurring malady of the Plans was the need to announce large ambitions – it was a political need, designed to generate optimism and enthusiasm although it is not obvious why politicians thought it better repeatedly to announce grandiose targets, and then go through 'crises' when these had to be revised, than to produce realistic programmes in the first place. Of course this was to some extent deliberate; greater efforts at domestic resource mobilisation were possible under large plans. There was plainly bound to be some inhibition hindering the adoption of targets which promised little progress, even if nothing more were manageable. And there was a dual presupposition, in the minds of some of those involved, about the response of aid-givers: they too would make greater effort to support a larger plan and aid acted as a kind of safety net, to be relied on if things went badly. Without the aid-community India could never have adopted a strategy of development so vulnerable to agriculture failure. (We shall argue below that it should not have done so anyway.) These and other considerations however suggest that it is not very fruitful to assess Indian economic performance by the extent to which the plans were fulfilled since they were not fulfillable in the first place We discuss them here as a convenient framework for a narrative of economic events since Independence and as reflecting the debates between and preoccupations of those responsible for economic policy.

The mid 1960s not only buried the Third Plan; they forced the abandonment of preparations for the Fourth. For three years, from 1966/7 to 1968/9, the main lines of economic policy were set out in Annual Plans. The Fourth Plan, which should have begun in 1966, finally emerged in 1969 to cover the period up to 1974. While it was both more realistic and more flexible than earlier Plans those who know India well will not be surprised by the fact that many of the faults of previous Plans, exposed, documented and criticised though they had been, were in evidence once more. The Fourth Plan was after all the product of much the same forces and interests which had produced the compromises of the last three. There was greater inner consistency than in previous plans, relatively modest assumptions about foreign aid and less exaggeratedly optimistic expectations concerning savings and taxation. There was also the most explicit statement of the importance of agriculture yet contained in any plan.[5] There were new emphases on social justice and economic equality. But in almost every field the targets for physical achievement looked difficult both financially and organisationally. What was missing was any indication of how the social and economic circumstances which had obstructed that achievement in the past were now to be removed.

By the early 1970s certain weaknesses of economic performance began to present a picture of intractable difficulty. All these weaknesses had been present – and widely discussed – for many years, but hopes that they might soon be overcome began to look optimistic. Agriculture, despite the 'green revolution', was very far from being insulated from adverse weather and, after an excellent start to the decade in 1970/71, there were disappointing crop years in 1971/2, 1972/3 and to some extent 1973/4 as well. The shortage of food caused rapid inflation – food prices doubled over the decade of the 1960s, but rose by a further 50 per cent between 1971 and 1973, leading to considerable unrest throughout the country. The inflation was not of the kind that benefits industry; indeed industrial production practically stagnated – it grew by 3 per cent in 1970/71 and 1971/2, by 5·3 per cent in 1972/3 and 0·5 per cent in 1973/4. Only the continuing progress in exports gave any hint of cheer – and that was more than cancelled out by the steep rise in oil and oil-product prices after 1973.[6]

It is important to appreciate the reasons for India's disturbingly sluggish industrial progress. A significant one is the structural imbalance related to the pattern of past investments. A large amount of capital is incorporated in heavy industry; plants which make heavy machine tools, electric generator sets, boilers, industrial equipment – the legacy of the philosophy of 'machines to build machines' which pervaded the early Plans. It takes a high level of overall output elsewhere in the economy and a high level of investment to keep these plants occupied – levels which India has had almost permanent difficulty in sustaining since 1965. Partly agriculture itself is to blame for this – the size of the crop affects the overall level of demand, prices and permissible magnitude of government expenditure; agriculture also supplies important raw materials for industry. Thus when the crop fails it is not only the rural economy that suffers.[7]

Another major factor is foreign exchange. India's export and imports in the early 1970s were of the order of \$2,500 million (about 5–6 per cent of total G.N.P.) – but a very large share of that is claimed by raw materials, fertilisers, oil, food (even food grains when necessary) and other essentials. India imports almost no manufactured consumption goods. But the strictness of the foreign exchange regime made life difficult for industrialists. Most imports are – or were until recently – obtained under licence; licences were difficult to get and the very fact of uncertainty and delay puts a considerable curb on activity, as do the shortages of necessary imports.[8] There is also a sense in which import controls make life easier for manufacturers – most of them do not have to face foreign competition in the domestic market and so – when they can produce and sell at all – they often make easy profits. The overall effects are profoundly negative for the whole economy; manufacturers are at a disadvantage in foreign markets because they cannot buy their inputs from the cheapest source; they cannot easily make long-term contracts for such things as they do import; necessities of production may be unavailable for lengthy periods: in a word, industry – and in particular exports – operates with the brakes on.

Added to these problems are the difficulties caused by the lack of coordination in the economy. Power fails because rainfall is deficient, the grid is overloaded, coal is not delivered to power stations, technical breakdowns occur. Transport is unreliable and supplies arrive at the factory late or damaged – or the products are not taken away and delivered to the purchaser. Technical failures in the more complex processes are common, due to faulty maintenance or poor design. These five factors – lack of demand, foreign exchange shortage, power, transport and technical failure – are responsible for a good deal of India's industrial difficulties. And when one of these is not the cause there are often labour problems. Indian labour has a good deal to complain about in the way of low wages and poor working conditions (even if industrial labour is well off by comparison with labour in agriculture or the less organised parts of the urban labour market); in addition unions are highly political, often organised by political forces opposed to the ruling party. Much industrial action in India has motives other than the ostensible grounds on which it takes place.

Various permutations of these factors have affected most sectors of industry during the last decade. After 1956, when the second Industrial Policy Resolution was declared, private sector investment and industry generally moved strongly forward, but since 1965 progress has been stilled. In the early 1970s, as we have noted, industry was barely able to grow at more than 2–3 per cent a year. This might have appeared to be only a temporary setback – after all there had been not only two bad crop years, but a war, and the great influx of refugees from Bengal, the expenditure for which, coupled with food shortages, led to rapid inflation and eventually forced a major cut in public expenditure in 1973/4. But, although the situation was more acute for these reasons, it was not easy to be sure that, were they not present, everything would be vastly better. The recognition that existing policies were inadequate began in mid 1974 when the Government began to seek ways to encourage the private sector, and even to change its mind about private foreign investment, as well as to rethink economic strategy in the light of the world oil price increases.

We have stressed the underlying problems afflicting industry because they are often insufficiently appreciated. If one were to judge by much commentary both in the press, Indian and foreign, and in the literature, most of the ills of Indian development, and especially of industrial development, could be attributed to restrictions placed on the private sector. This is a view we do not share, not because the policies towards the private sector are universally well judged, but because other things are more important. The problems to which we refer are after all part of what constitutes under-development. The restrictions on the private sector are also understandable from other points of view – two in particular. One is the scarcity of resources: given the acute scarcity of almost all commodities, something has to be done to ensure that their use satisfies social needs – this would not happen in India if the market were left to itself since the given distribution of incomes would yield a product mix with an excessive weight in favour of the consumption needs of the rich. The other is rather specific to India – manufacturing has for decades been dominated by large conglomerate corporations of which the best known are the Tata and Birla groups. These conglomerates, or 'large houses' as they are called, produce wide ranges of unrelated commodities; they also have enormous social and economic power extending to the press, to the bureaucracy and to Parliament. Much of India's industrial legislation has been designed specifically to curb these companies' growth and influence, though in practice they have proved highly successful in manipulating the administrative procedures.

The major instrument of industrial planning in the private sector has been the Industrial Licensing Policy which requires governmental sanction for any investment over a certain size. In the nature of things this policy has been more useful in discouraging investments the government did not want than in promoting those that it did. It has also led to delays and uncertainities for businessmen wishing to extend existing capacity or to make new starts. Private foreign investment has also been disciplined by a policy which has endeavoured to keep out investments other than those which cannot be carried out with domestic resources – today that means almost everything except the manufacture of products of very advanced technology. This policy also has had its defects, since it in effect granted licensed monopolies to foreign companies in some fields, while protecting domestic industry from competition in others. Both these sets of policy instruments were essential to a government with the aims supported by the dominant political groupings in India; but all could have been better designed.

A key decision in any economic system which relies on incentives is what to leave to the price mechanism and fiscal policy and what to administer. The framing of such decisions in India has lacked judiciousness and incorporated some undue optimism about the ability of its administrators to judge commercial issues skilfully. As far as the 'large houses' are concerned the problem has been that they were and are the motive force of much of private industry; at any one time a high proportion of investment licence applications pending originate with them. The necessity was to leave these dynamic entrepreneurs freedom to proceed where their expertise warranted and the economy needed, while encouraging them to leave peripheral interests aside, and coping with their undue social and political influence by more appropriate means; only recently have any such measures been attempted; in the past the 'large houses' have been fairly successful in getting their way despite the legislation which has hindered the less powerful much more. And many of the controls on industry and imports have shifted the attention of the 'market' to other fields – to the influencing of favourable decisions or to the black market. There must be *some* rate of domestic tax or of import duty sufficient to compensate the government for uses of resources it considers out of keeping with its social philosophy. All too often the black market allows others to collect the scarcity value of commodities which should accrue to the government revenues. Greater pragmatism could have improved – could still improve – many areas of policy.

Much the same is true for private foreign investment. There are many dangers for a developing country in admitting private foreign investment without careful limitation.[9] At the very least there is a distinction to be made between investments which bring in large amounts of capital, transfer useful technology, train local personnel, contribute significantly to exports and employment and reinvest a respectable share of their profits; and those which raise a large amount of their capital in the host country, import little technology (or just a prestigious brand name), do not train people or export their products, and repatriate most of their profits. A pragmatic policy towards private foreign investment would attempt to limit admission to foreign companies which were likely to make a positive contribution to the economy. Few developing countries have such a policy; the combination of ideological standpoints, domestic interests and lack of understanding of the behaviour of private corporations has commonly led either to insufficient or excessive restrictions. India has yet to find an appropriate middle path. In particular the rule of 'more than 50 per cent domestic participation in equity' – a rule adopted in many developing countries – is inappropriate as a blanket measure; if an investment is harmful to the economy, it is no virtue that domestic capital has more than 50 per cent participation – and if the investment is beneficial, it may not matter that foreign ownership exceeds 50 per cent. We have also to refer to public sector industry which has had a disappointing record. In addition to suffering from the troubles which afflict industry in general there have been cases of exceptionally poor management and faulty technical design – and some enterprises which should probably never have been built in the first place. The country in some periods has imported steel with scarce foreign exchange while many of its steel plants were producing well below capacity; innumerable difficulties have produced the same damaging consequences in the fertiliser industry. And the investments in such plants as Heavy Electricals Limited, Bhopal, and the Heavy Engineering Corporation, Ranchi, have yielded little positive return.[10] One must not make the mistake of thinking that such phenomena are not to be found in the private sector. But most of public sector industry represents vast quantities of capital with regrettably low yields – a tragedy in this capital-scarce country. The Plans always concentrate on new investment – but it would be a major achievement to obtain respectable levels of capacity utilisation with much of existing investment.

In 1974 if further signs were needed that a radical break was necessary with past conceptions of economic policy, they were not hard to find. Yet the Fifth Plan, as originally published, contained many features of previous ones. The new Plan was particularly notable for an increase in the rigour and sophistication of the underlying economic model. And it contained a major new departure, an attempt – distinctly courageous in its political implications – to calculate the consequences of the shifts in the distribution of incomes which the Plan proposed. Yet the assumptions about the availability of resources, and the possibility of reducing the country's dependence on aid while maintaining a high rate of growth, were once more doubtful even before the rise in oil prices. The latter was a blow so crippling as to make nonsense of the Plan. To continue 1973 levels of oil imports at 1974 prices added about $1,000 million to India's import bill – at a time when imports were already squeezed drastically and what remained were essential to the economy. This represented about one-third of India's foreign exchange – and for nothing, simply absorbed by a price increase.[11]

And there was still one blow to fall. Assisted as she was by some favourable price movements for exports, some modest credits from the oil exporters and a small increase in aid, India might have weathered the storm in 1974 – not at the planned rate of growth, but without the total dislocation that the oil-price rise seemed to indicate. But when a combination of floods in some areas and droughts in others ruined the crop, on top of all the other difficulties, India was faced with trying to buy some 5 – 10 million tons of foodgrains on an international market already tight. With the price of imported wheat in the region of $150 a ton, this represented a final bitter stroke that laid waste India's hopes for the Fifth Plan before it had even begun. However the financial year 1974/5 did not end in complete disaster: a good *rabi* crop brought the total of foodgrains output to 104 – 5 million tonnes and the combination of higher foreign aid, credits from some oil-exporting countries and the diversion of a substantial amount of sugar production into the export market enabled the economy to avoid the worst. A similar combination of circumstances, a good *kharif* crop of 70 million tonnes and high inflows of foreign aid left India in a reasonable short-term position at the end of 1975. But the debts assumed to permit this did not leave much promise of any rapid progress towards greater self-sufficiency.

This and other indications of a new realism were visible in the revised version of the Fifth Plan which was published towards the end of 1976. The Plan no longer foresaw any swift approach to 'self-reliance', and official statements began to be warmer towards the continued receipt of foreign assistance. Ironically the short-term prospects for the economy had by then improved so much that the immediate case for more aid began to be somewhat difficult to argue. Two recent phenomena started to make themselves felt in the balance of payments: the strong performance of Indian exports and the remarkable growth of remittances from Indians living overseas. The latter resulted in part from new regulations permitting foreign residents to hold convertible currency in Indian banks and from favourable exchange-rate movements, but in part from successful action against smuggling and illegal foreign exchange dealing. The reported volume of remittances was in excess of $1 billion in a single year. This combined with increased aid flows more than offset the modestly growing trade deficit – for, despite substantial export growth, adverse price trends made imports grow even faster. The overall result in 1976 was an almost embarrassing growth of reserves to a figure in excess of $3 billion.

These encouraging trends in the balance of payments were matched by others. Reports from India's new oil-fields were better than expected and promised further support for the balance of payments. The inflation of the early 1970s was brought under control in 1975 and most of 1976 by a combination of greater food availability and cautious fiscal and monetary policies. Above all a stupendously good harvest of over 120 million tonnes in 1975/6 meant a return to real economic growth. The poor harvests of 1972/3 and the modest ones of the two following years had produced a lean period for the Indian economy. Indeed 1972/3 was a year of decline in real N.N.P.; and per capita N.N.P. fell not only in that year, but in 1971/2 and 1974/5 as well.[12] The return of more expansive prospects was thus very welcome. Nevertheless, the final version of the Fifth Plan, though bigger in rupee terms, was substantially smaller than the Draft in real terms – by some 12 – 15 per cent. N.N.P. growth of 5·2 per cent was projected; but even if achieved, with a poor start in 1974/5, despite 6 per cent growth in 1975/6, it would mean growth at a little less than 4·4 per cent for the Plan period as a whole and 2·4 per cent growth in income per head.

Several question marks still hover over the future of the economy. Its dependence on agriculture is clearly something that will continue for many years but that is a subject for later discussion. The industrial sector continues to present problems – the removal of two of the common constraining factors, shortage of agricultural supplies and foreign exchange, did permit some taking up of the slack and manufacturing output grew by some 10 per cent during 1976/7. But investment remained sluggish, especially in the private sector, leaving analysts to wonder whether political uncertainty was the cause or more fundamental factors: personal and corporate taxation and incentives; policy regulations or a mismatch between the pattern of demand and that of potential output which led to slow growth in demand for those products whose supply was capable of growing rapidly. And lying beneath all the issues of economic management were still the perennial problems of poverty and employment.

One of the main arguments of this book is that India's economic plans have consistently under-estimated the labour force growth which lay ahead. Even now that population growth is slowing down there will be little reduction in the growth rate of the population of labour force age. The industry based strategy always takes a large share of new investment for production which generates relatively little employment. The final

Fifth Plan could only disguise the conflict between its industrial goals and its ambitions – rather muted in comparison with those of the Draft – for employment and the welfare of the poor; part of the disguise was its excessively optimistic population projection. But the conflict is deeper and older than that: the tragedy of the Fifth Plan was that in its Draft form it gave promise for the first time of resolving it. Politics, the weather and external events put paid to those slender hopes.

As we have suggested one should not be mesmerised by the Plans and their fate; the economy has been making progress, in ways already described and others to be discussed below. Nevertheless the Plans have incorporated the ambitions of the government – ambitions which would not have made a vast difference in per capita terms even if fulfilled; the repeated defeat of these ambitions is therefore a serious matter. If one thing stands out with painful clarity, it is that the Plans over and over again have been frustrated by crop failures. The relations between population growth, planning and agriculture are so important that they will receive a section to themselves. But first we must turn to the relationships between population and economic growth.

MACROECONOMICS OF POPULATION

What role has population played in these twenty years of planning and of economic history? We have already seen (in Chapter 2) how gradual was the dawning in public apprehension of the seriousness of the population problem, how prior to the 1971 Census successive discoveries of the size of the population gave continual surprise. This had an influence on the Five Year Plans; targets were adjusted upwards to take account of newly expected increases in the population, and in retrospect the assessments of each Plan's shortcomings were all the more critical in the light of the increased numbers for whom employment had not been provided. In the eyes of some the rapidity of the increases in population even provided a reason for sacrificing social goals in the pursuit of economic growth – the situation was too serious to justify the diversion of resources for social justice or other growth-impeding ambitions.[13] Not a very good argument, as we shall see.

What did the growth of India's population contribute, positively or negatively, to the average rate of N.N.P. growth of approximately 3·6 per cent in the decades of the 1950s and 1960s? Until recently the literature of economic demography drew attention to two main relationships through which population growth affected the economy – what we may call the 'savings effect' and the 'composition of investment effect'. The former of these argues that savings are reduced by population growth because of the increase of the so-called 'burden of dependency': with high fertility, and declining mortality in younger and older age groups, the population acquires an increasing proportion of people in the non-working age groups relative to those of working age. Since all must consume while relatively fewer produce, consumption per head must rise (in the absence of increasing output per worker) and savings per head must fall – even if productivity is rising, savings are less than they would be with a smaller number of dependents per worker. The investment argument is simpler: it says that, with an increasing population, a share of investible resources has to be devoted to reproducing for additional people 'unproductive' facilities – particularly social overhead capital – which would be unnecessary if the population were not growing. The composition of investment is altered in an unproductive direction instead of additions to capital going to raise the productivity of the existing labour force.

Both these arguments have a certain logical validity though the conclusion that economic growth is slowed down by population growth only follows, in so far as they are correct, if there are no offsetting positive effects of population growth on the economy which is a possibility we will consider below. The main question about these arguments is their empirical significance. Thus even if it were true that there were less capital per head as population grew, and that the capital were less productively used and there were no offsetting effects, the magnitude of the loss of savings might be small and the diversion of investment similarly so. The few economists who have examined these relationships mathematically have generally considered them to be important. In 1958 a work of considerable academic distinction appeared which was one of the first books to give some solidity to the modern concern about population and its effects on the economy.[14] Its authors, Coale and Hoover, took India as their example for a model of population growth and economic development. They constructed alternative paths for the economy under differing assumptions about fertility and made two separate projections: one, covering a period of fifteen years, found G.N.P. to be 17 per cent higher at the end of the period with fertility declining (to 50 per cent of its initial level) than with fertility constant. This projection assumed changes in labour force growth to be relatively unimportant: most of the differences in numbers, being caused by lesser fertility, affected the population below working age; they also made long-term projections in which productive use of additional labour was postulated;[15] in one of these projections the number of equivalent adult consumers after 55 years of high fertility was double that of the reduced-fertility population and output per consumer was halved, so G.N.P. growth was much the same; this was the result with a pessimistic assumption about the productivity of labour and capital. With a more optimistic one – which the authors thought appropriate for India – total G.N.P. grew faster under high fertility, but not nearly enough to outweigh the growth of numbers: per consumer product grew by 170 per cent under reduced fertility compared with only 60 per cent without fertility decline.

Since Coale and Hoover wrote there have been several such models for a variety of countries.[16] In all of them positive contributions of population growth to the economy are relatively small, or non-existent, and the comparison of high and low fertility paths always shows greater growth of G.N.P. with the lesser rate of population growth. No one would be surprised to learn that *per capita* economic growth is lower if the population increases and does not make an economic contribution; that is an arithmetical truth. But the first appearance of the Coale-Hoover model did cause concern since it claimed to show reduced growth of *total* G.N.P. The subsequent models have evoked less interest; they all came to the same conclusion – and they all reached it because of the same two effects on savings and the composition of investment. Unfortunately for the theory we have strong reason to doubt the importance of these effects and also the theoretical framework in which they are set.

It seems quite likely that the effect on savings of the growing burden of dependency under high fertility has been exaggerated: it is obscure whether any form of savings other than household savings is much affected by differential population growth and that may be only modestly affected if the bulk of savings is carried out by a small wealthy class whose fertility is low, or if the costs of additional children are met out of consumption rather than savings to any considerable extent. Corporate savings and government savings can only be claimed without circularity to be affected in so far as population growth reduces overall economic growth by means other than savings reduction. (Government current expenditure is likely to increase at the expense of government investment, but that is really a 'composition' argument.) Over an extremely long period in which a very great shift in the dependency burden may occur there may be a distinct effect on savings; but in the relatively short run the effect may not be very large.[17] Total domestic savings in India have averaged a little less than 10 per cent of net domestic product annually since 1950, with about 60 per cent or 70 per cent of it in private household savings. The figure for total savings rises in good crop years, falls in bad ones: there is a negative correlation between savings and food prices as one would expect in a poor economy where food bulks large in most people's expenditure patterns. But public and corporate savings have fluctuated more than household savings.[18] The proportion of savings in the national income has fluctuated only moderately altogether around the 10 per cent figure – in recent years somewhat above it.

Between the Censuses of 1951 and 1971, approximately 187 millions were added to India's numbers. Of these the addition to the proportion of people outside the age group 15–64 was about 5·9 per cent, or about 32 million additional 'dependents'. If all these 32 million consumed one average income each at the expense of savings, the reduction of savings would indeed be enormous, since savings at 10 per cent of national income equals 54·8 million per capita incomes (given the 1971 population of 548 million). But first of all, as we noted in Chapter 2, children begin earning well before age 15; secondly dependents consume only a fraction of an average income; thirdly if household consumption is increased at the expense of household saving, some modicum of it flows into business and, via indirect taxes, government savings. The third of these effects is small since most of the additional consumption would be of food; the other two might reduce the 'savings cost' of the additional dependents by anything from one-half to three-quarters – but even the latter reduction would leave an amount equal to more than one-sixth of total savings.[19] Why therefore should we believe that the burden of dependency effect on savings has been exaggerated? The main reason is the *distribution* of savings. It is quite likely that the number of dependents grows faster among the poor than the rich, whose fertility is probably declining more rapidly than average. But even if the dependents were equally divided among income groups, the top 10 per cent of income earners probably account for the bulk of (monetised) household savings. Even they may reduce consumption as well as savings when they have additional children. The other 90 per cent have little choice but to cut down their consumption – this very probable truth is consistent with what we shall discover about consumption later in this chapter. Under these assumptions the savings cost of additional dependents might be quite inconsiderable.[20] Argument in this area is hazardous as the assessment of the effect depends on a number of empirical values of parameters which are more or less unknown for India.[21] But it is fair to say that the effect may be relatively minor.

Of course if there are more non-earning dependents, their consumption must come from somewhere and some part of it may be at the expense of savings. Our argument is just that something like a third of total monetised savings is not in the private domestic sector and that much of the consumption needs of additional dependents will be met out of reduced consumption by others, not out of savings. One could say that if the dependents were not there, the savings potential would be greater; but, as we saw when discussing the economics of family formation, one of the effects of children, in poor families at least, is to force parents to give up some of their own consumption – we cast some doubt on the possibility that if the children were not there, the parents would, or easily could, save more. The discussion so far is really all within this framework. In the macroeconomic picture, if in fact population growth leads to slower growth of total output, then one would expect a slower growth of savings – but once again, to avoid circularity, the negative impact of population on G.N.P. growth must be established independently of the savings effect. We shall proceed to other arguments about these relationships.

We have first to deal with the 'composition of investment' argument. As noted this says that as population increases, some part of investment has to go to reproducing 'unproductive' facilities for additional people or, if not wholly unproductive, relatively less productive. Population growth requires capital widening rather than capital deepening; it reduces the possibility of increasing productivity by providing more capital for each worker – instead additional workers force the available capital to be more thinly spread. This argument too turns out to be somewhat dubious as applied to welfare investment, though in a more general form it is quite correct.

In the first place if we look at these so called 'unproductive' or 'welfare' investments, they are things like schooling, health facilities and other forms of social overhead capital – urban infrastructure for example. But supposing we find that, given the extra population, there is a high return to educating them and helping to keep them healthy – then the real question becomes that of whether such educated and healthy people make a greater contribution to the economy than would be achieved by using the capital to raise the output of a smaller population. So the question in fact is whether additional people benefit the economy: but this is the question we started out to try to answer and therefore to label these investments 'unproductive' is to beg the question. Coale and Hoover take a more legitimate stance than the model builders who succeeded them, who commonly attribute no return at all to this 'diverted' investment; they put the case that, even if these investments are productive, they take several years to show any return and therefore will not be as effective as investment in say manufacturing industry. However even this may not be of major significance, as we argue below.

In the second place the shift in the composition of investment, even if deleterious, may not be very great – partly because the total of affected expenditures are themselves a small proportion of national income so that a population-induced increase in them will not make a huge difference – in one calculation based on Indian data a fertility path declining linearly to a 50 per cent reduction over fifteen years up to 1981 yielded a saving a government expenditures on health and education equal to 0·3 per cent of national income compared with constant fertility.[22] Partly the shift may be less great than was once postulated simply because population growth fails to induce it: the 'requirements' of the growing population are not met. Certainly one cannot mechanically relate to population increase expenditures under one or another head; some of them, especially education, may grow much faster than population. In many cases in India today the existing levels of provision are so far below what is required that additions to population growth make little difference – they affect the size of the backlog of unmet need rather than the level of expenditure.

In casting doubt on the major importance given to the savings and composition of investment assumptions in past models one should not deny them all validity. One cannot lightly dismiss these small fractions of national income; they add up to something significant and – since many many aspects of private expenditures are not included – it is not difficult to argue that they may be greater than some critics of the old view have claimed. Nevertheless it seems clear that one must look elsewhere for indications of major interference with economic performance. (Of course we are still talking of the growth of total income; it is very difficult to construct for a poor country in today's circumstances a demonstration that population increase does anything other than reduce the growth rate of per capita incomes, if only because of the increase in numbers.) There is undoubtedly one very important area that none of the existing economic-demographic models, incorporate, none at least known to the author. This too is a feature of the composition of investment though not of what has been called 'welfare' investment. It is a question of *the changing composition of the resource costs of producing basic consumption goods*. In the case of India the main area is agriculture.

The figures indicate that the growth of India's foodgrain output from the early 1950s up to the early 1960s was due about equally to increasing acreage under cultivation and increasing yields per acre. In the decade 1962/3 to 1971/2 acreage under foodgrains grew at only 0·7 per cent annually while yields per acre rose by 2·8 per cent per year.[23] These facts by themselves tell one little about inputs except that increasing acreage requires mainly irrigation and land improvement, which are quite labour intensive, and additional crop labour, while increasing yields may be due to increased labour or to improved seeds, methods of husbandry, fertiliser and irrigation.[24] The latter decade corresponds however with the advent of the 'package programme' and a considerable acceleration in the use of modern inputs. While these inputs have themselves been associated with increased demand for labour, they have begun to absorb increasingly large sums of capital and foreign exchange. The major new investments of fixed capital, apart from those in farm equipment itself, have been in power generation for tube-well pumps, and fertiliser plants. Provision of power and fertilisers for agriculture has absorbed, directly and indirectly, significant sums not only of capital but of foreign exchange, both for the capital goods themselves and the necessary raw materials as well as, in the case of fertilisers, direct imports of the finished product to supplement domestic production. These resources, to finance increases in agricultural production, are or will be considerably greater than any population-induced increments in welfare investment.[25]

The theoretical point being made here needs clarification before we go further. The proposition is that as long as a society can increase agricultural output by mainly labour-using means, the chief resource to feed the growing population is provided by the population itself; the capital required is mainly circulating capital, wage-goods to support the labour force. And the return on this investment is virtually immediate except in the case of major irrigation works. But a point is reached where required increases in agricultural output necessitate yield improving inputs which are expensive in both capital and foreign exchange and where the return to investment comes after a longer gestation period. That point differs for each country depending on the potential for acreage extension, soil and climate conditions, man/land ratios and changing techniques in agriculture. For India one such point seems to have come in the early 1960s. Just as the Coale-Hoover model argued that with slower population growth more capital would have been available for raising per worker productivity because of reduced welfare expenditures, so we argue that more capital and foreign exchange would have been available from reductions in the expenditure devoted to raising agricultural output.[26]

The composition of investment argument is really quite general: wherever population growth requires increased production which in turn requires investment, a lesser rate of population growth would release investible funds for use elsewhere. It is hard to understand why past models have concentrated on welfare investments unless it be the remains of prejudice about the productivity of service industries.[27] Food production is in fact the least postponable of all forms of population-related output needs. And if, as is suggested in the Indian case, agriculture enters a phase of fundamental alteration of the production function, or to put it in plainer English, of changing resource requirements for additional output, this can be a major burden of population growth.

Although there is a convincing case that the marginal cost of raising food output has been on the increase it does not follow from that alone that population growth has slowed down the growth of G.N.P. In the first place much of the increased investment in agriculture might have taken place even with slower population growth – it all depends on the period over which one compares the actual population increase with a hypothetical smaller one. Thus the agricultural output of 1970 would not have been greatly excessive for the population of 1960. It would have meant something over 2600 calories per head as opposed to about 2000 calories. Secondly it may be misleading to assume that diminishing returns in agriculture imply a slower rate of growth for the economy. Although the resource costs of producing wage goods have risen, as long as we do not know how far the economy is constrained by the shortage of wage goods, we do not know their implicit value in the growth process and we cannot confidently say – though we may suspect – that G.N.P. growth is suffering. Finally, on a somewhat separate point, we must not make Malthus's mistake and give credence to the view that rising costs are inevitable as far ahead as we can see: as noted below some potentially cost-reducing innovations in agriculture are on the horizon. (Though if, as some suspect, the 'green revolution' package has already reached its productive limits, the short-term problem could be considerable.)

Almost all the past models have cast the argument in terms of 'productive' versus 'unproductive' investment. At the least, so it was argued, 'welfare' investment has a delayed return compared with 'directly productive' investment in industry or agriculture. This itself may be questioned or at least qualified: for example if children enter the labour force at very young ages, the return to expenditure on primary education may come little less quickly than from the construction of a fertiliser plant. The same might be said for child nutrition programmes. But even if the case is granted, the approach is missing an important point – that much of the *productive* investment in some sectors would be unnecessary if the population grew more slowly. The further one looks into India's future, the more important this point becomes: there are probably increasing returns to scale in many aspects of welfare provision. In agriculture it is going to become increasingly expensive, for a time at least, to wring each extra ton of food out of the soil. The recent rise in oil prices has given an unexpected additional twist to this cost spiral. But, as we have argued above, the trend was already apparent. The question that we should be asking is what happens to the whole pattern of investment under alternative assumptions about fertility: the shifts between productive sectors as well as just the division between production and welfare and their effect on development. The biggest problem for India, if current trends continue, is the increasing share of the investible surplus that will be taken up by food needs. There are also very considerable problems of internal allocation between regions, given that increases in agricultural production are geographically con-centrated; the magnitude of required inter-regional transfers could reach politically troublesome dimensions.

Many have commented that the whole approach of these models has concentrated excessively on savings and investment which play only one of the important parts in the development process. The model builders would reply that they are abstracting from the other determinants of develop-ment to estimate the *ceteris paribus* effect of different fertility assumptions. Even for this purpose it is unfortunate that they have largely neglected the other most common economic element in development models, namely foreign exchange.[28] As we have noted this is becoming increasingly critical in Indian agriculture. There are also unexplored issues such as the competition created by the domestic demands of a growing population for exportable goods or the advantages for exports of cheap labour.

We have looked first at the influence of population growth on the Indian economy in the light of the main postulated relationships of economic theory; and we have found more important an aspect of simple classical economics, the increasing cost of food production on a fixed amount of land. In terms of the analysis in the first section of this chapter, in which it was seen how repeated crop failures frustrated economic plans, the potency of population growth as a negative factor in India's economic performance is clear. The same natural disasters of flood or drought are the more damaging as numbers grow; the growth in numbers has itself contributed to environmental damage, especially through reduction of soil-cover and consequent flooding. And the problems of feeding the growing population become immense: an increasing expenditure of scarce resources not only in investment, but in administration and research, is required simply to maintain levels of food availability. And when the weather fails the costs are enormous in terms of relief expenditure at home and food purchases abroad. The economy not only has to run in order to stand still – it has to run faster and faster. As population growth eases off – which it is beginning to do – the weight of these problems will slowly diminish; but they may well continue to be of major importance for several decades.

People are often perplexed as to why population growth is considered of doubtful economic value in many developing countries today whereas it is believed to have been positively helpful in the industrialised countries during the nineteenth and early twentieth centuries. A number of significant differences account for this. Perhaps most important the rates of population growth were much lower – in Britain, for example, the annual rate never exceeded 1·5 per cent and only rarely was as high as that. The European average, even when populations were growing rapidly in the nineteenth century, was closer to 0·7 per cent. These countries also had an outlet for excess population via migration – considerable in some cases such as Sweden. Certainly they did not experience population growth rates of 3 per cent or more as is common in the Third World today, or even India's 2·2 per cent. In addition the developed countries were relatively wealthy before they began to industrialise and could manage adequate rates of capital formation even while their populations were growing. They also had relatively easy foreign markets to export to, by competition or, if necessary, by imperialist power. And their economies were generating increasing demands for labour as the early industrialisation processes were highly labour intensive. Finally rates of growth of total product in nineteenth century industrialisation were of the order of 2–4 per cent a year, not fast enough to provide rapidly rising income levels at today's population growth rates in developing countries.[29]

India has none of the advantages possessed by the rich countries during industrialisation. In particular the economy has for long suffered from under-utilisation of labour. We shall see in the next section how difficult it is to measure, but its existence and considerable magnitude is undeniable. This provides the simplest case for finding population growth a burden rather than a benefit: where labour is scarce, and cooperant resources exist to employ it, additions to the labour force can be beneficial. But in India much of the additional labour shares out the available jobs with the results for the standard of living which we are about to explore. In addition the potential for travelling along the development path taken by the rich countries is ruled out in India's circumstances. If a modern industrial work-place costs $500, a country with income per head of $100 a year and a savings rate of 10 per cent requires the savings of 50 people to produce one such work-place. But if population grows at 2 per cent, 50 people become 51 after a year. Thus in an economy characterised by such parameters (not unlike India's) only the additions to population can be absorbed in modern employment with no possibility of taking up the backlog of unemployment or rapidly transferring an increasing share of agricultural workers into industry. Of course the proportion of the labour force engaged in industry does gradually grow, if all increments to the population or even a share of them greater than the existing share, become employed in industry. But this has hardly been happening in India hitherto.

Some assumptions underlie this last crude calculation: that all investment can be devoted to new industrial jobs (obviously untrue) and that $500 is the cost of a modern work-place. The latter is not true either, if one is thinking of modern industry where even in India's conditions, it may be more of the order of $2000. But each new urban industrial job may generate two jobs in service trades requiring little capital; and there are opportunities for small scale manufacturing which may require investment of less than $500 per head. If the total mix of investment is taken into account, it may not be too far off the average cost of an urban (as distinct from an industrial) work-place. The argument seems convincing: more accurate figures might show a lower cost of new urban investment per head, but also a share of total capital available for such investment well below 100 per cent: agriculture, irrigation, education and health alone account for at least 32 per cent.[30] Given her poverty and her population growth, India has no chance of transferring much of the growing labour force out of rural employment at any rapid pace. Over the years 1951 – 71 the proportion of the labour force engaged in agriculture has not in fact declined at all significantly, despite considerable expansion of the manufacturing sector.[31]

The impossibility of rapid industrialisation of the labour force is simply another (and more accurate) aspect of the 'capital-widening' argument referred to above; but, instead of concentrating on the diversion of investment into so-called unproductive uses, we are making the more obvious point that all investment has to be spread over larger numbers of people with the consequential difficulty of raising individual incomes. The income that can be produced by this growing population could grow more rapidly if there were positive offsetting effects: if proportionately more capital were being generated or technical progress were raising the productivity of labour and capital together. That the national income has been growing faster than the population since Independence is evidence that one or both of these effects have been present, albeit weakly. A further offsetting effect is contained in the possibility of shifting towards more labour-intensive methods of production for which there is still some scope in India.

An old argument for larger populations was that they provide opportunities for economies of scale in production. There are however no conceivable economies of scale for a population of 600 million which were not obtainable for 300 million. (Besides even if it were arguable that a bigger population yielded economic advantages, it would not follow that reaching that population at a rapid rate of population growth would still

yield higher individual incomes over time than a slower rate of growth.)
And we have observed a major source of diminishing returns to increasing
capital and labour in the fixed availability of land. If poverty does not
diminish as population grows, there is insufficient growth of demand for
goods in whose production scale economies are available.

As we have seen the case that rapid population growth reduces the rate
of capital formation has been exaggerated, but it is difficult to find any
grounds in India's circumstances for saying that it positively increases it;
and it is equally difficult to make out any case that technical progress has
been accelerated by population growth.[32] The conclusion that the growth
of income per head would have been faster over the last 25 years at a slower
rate of population growth is inescapable. Whether total G.N.P. would
have grown more rapidly, as the economic-demographic models would
have us believe, is rather more questionable; we have argued that the food
production problem gives some ground for believing this during the period
since 1966, and the existence of under-utilised labour casts doubt on the
productive value of continued increases in the labour force. To give a more
general answer for the whole period since Independence we would need to
know where the economy was on the 'production surface' at the beginning
of the period – to what extent in other words it has been possible for the
economy to make profitable use of additional labour by movement
towards the labour-intensive side of capital utilisation counteracting the
disadvantages of population growth. In the existing state of India's
economic statistics this is not measurable.

For the economist these possibilities are depicted in Figure 4.1. Labour
(L) is on the x axis, capital (K) on the y axis. The curves $Y_0 - Y_3$ are
isoquants showing the combination of labour and capital required to
produce given levels of output, each level a constant percentage above the
previous one. The isoquant map reflects a particular feature of the Indian
situation to which we drew attention above – constant returns to scale
prevail only to the left of the line OR; to the right of OR constant
proportionate increases in both labour and capital produce progressively
less additional output due to the fixed quantity of land. The curves also
become flatter to the right of the diagram reflecting the diminishing
usefulness of labour as population grows.

In terms of our argument for India the economy starts (Case I) with
capital stock K_0 and population L_0, producing output Y_0. At the end of the
first period, with capital and population growing to K_1 and L_1, output
reaches Y_1; in the second period, K_2 and L_2 do not suffice (by the
assumption of the last paragraph) to produce output Y_2 and, in the third
period, the economy, with the same percentage increase in the factors of
production, is even further from Y_3. Still in Case I, we compare the
economy's path with a constant percentage increase in population ($L_0 -
L_3$) and with diminishing population growth, $L_1' - L_3'$; the dashed lines
represent the alternative paths with the large dots marking the position

reached at the end of each period. The left-hand line shows lower total output with reduced population growth; but higher capital per worker and higher output per man.

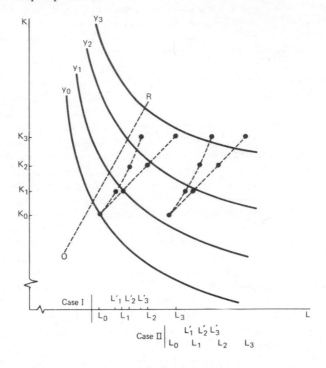

FIG. 4.1 Capital and labour

Compared with the Coale-Hoover model and similar analyses our isoquants have the same relative positions as theirs, ours because of fixed land, theirs because of reduced productivity of capital mainly for other reasons. Our diagram has population growth making no difference at all to capital formation: savings is carried on by the rich, perhaps, while the poor are responsible for all the increase in numbers – that could be one way of interpreting this assumption, which is a little extreme, but perhaps not excessively so over a short period. Case II represents a similar situation with the difference that capital per worker is lower throughout as the initial population is much greater. This has the effect that, at the end of the third period, the difference between total income with higher and with lower population is negligible as the isoquant on which lie the terminal points of the two expansion paths is almost flat: moving to the right on this diagram is akin to reaching the point where unemployment is so severe that additional labour by itself may add next to nothing to total output. As we have said it is extremely difficult to judge how far the Indian economy has gone in that direction. But the use of Cobb-Douglas functions in economic-demographic models commonly assumes that technology adjusts and full employment is maintained – in direct contradiction of much observation that technology fails to adjust and underemployment is widespread.

This diagram has only a crude illustrative purpose to show the consistency between the points we have been making. It is essentially a short term model, each 'period' corresponding to something like a decade. In view of that, as the purist would point out, smooth, continuous isoquants of the kind depicted are strictly a feature of longer-term models. However, within the periods in relation to the small alternative population sizes considered, neither this nor the assumption about constant capital increases seem unreasonable. Our tentative conclusion is that population growth in the post-Independence period as a whole has made a positive contribution to total G.N.P. growth, but less positive in the last decade; it has reduced the rate of per capita income growth; and, for the future, additions to the population will be of progressively little economic value, quite possibly of negative value – continuation of our isoquants to the right would show them turning upwards. Considerable light will be shed on all this discussion by an investigation of the distribution of income over this period, or the question of the 'condition of the people', to which we turn in the next section. But we must note here that the increase in the ratio of total income to population is slowed down far more by the rise in the denominator than by any effect its rise has on the numerator. Even in the Coale-Hoover model the difference between the high and low fertility paths over a 50 year period is 29 per cent in total income but 85 per cent in income per head.[33] Few would suggest that, if population growth were one percentage point less, aggregate income growth would be one point higher, but per capita income growth would be with no change in the growth of aggregate output.

If we may summarise the argument so far: the post-Independence period is too short for the savings effect and the composition of investment effect to have had more than a slight downward impact, if any, on the growth of total product though no doubt in a longer period their influence could be clearly seen. But per capita product is undoubtedly lower than it would have been had population been growing more slowly, for three reasons: firstly if fertility had been lower for a long period, the labour force would have been little smaller in size but the number of people it had to support would have been much smaller; secondly the amount of capital per worker would have been greater simply by reason of the smaller number of workers; finally the capital itself would have been more productive – the effect of diminishing returns in agriculture was equivalent to a lower average productivity of capital. All of these effects are likely to become more and more powerful as time goes on. They amount to little more than a spelling out of the ways by which, if population growth has no positive effects on per capita output, output per head grows faster if the number of heads grows more slowly. The additions to the population have however made some positive contribution to total product, but the degree to which they will continue to do so depends on the extent of unemployment and the rate at which India's economic problems multiply as the population grows.

All these considerations appear simply from the contemplation of the old fashioned factors of production, land, labour and capital. It is well-known however from innumerable examinations of the course of economic growth that changes in the quantity of labour and capital explain at most half of historical economic growth.[34] The other half is little understood but is connected particularly with changes in economic organisation and institutions and with changes in the labour force. To isolate the factors of labour and capital as though they were immutable ingredients added to the growth recipe in measurable amounts is a serious distortion; we have indulged in it for the sake of simplicity but it will not really do to say that all these other changes – including technical progress to which we have alluded – are wrapped up in the changing productivity attributed to labour and capital. If our concern is with the effect of population growth on economic performance, we should try to trace out the influence of that growth on productivity through all these other dimensions.

To do this is in fact impossible; the data, the concepts even, do not exist. The best we can do is to trace, without attempts at quantification, some of the possible arguments. An important one relates to the quality of the labour force. The faster the rate of population growth, the more rapidly rising the proportion of young people in the labour force. If young people are imbued with more modern attitudes, skills and adaptability, the average productive quality of the labour force may be thought to rise, rather as in a rapidly growing economy with a high rate of accumulation, the proportion of capital that is new, 'superior', capital increases faster – growth accelerates growth. Unfortunately while this could be true if the new labour force entrants were educated or trained better than, or even as well as, the old, the poverty of India's educational system is such as to negate most of the potential value of this effect: the limitations on resources are such that the proportions of those young people receiving better or even longer courses of education are very small.

The Fifth Five Year Plan quotes impressive figures for increases in enrolment in schools and colleges at all age groups. 84 per cent of those aged 6 – 11 are now enrolled in primary education; 36 per cent of those aged 11 – 14 in secondary and 4·4 per cent of the 17 – 23 age groups in higher education – double or treble the rates of twenty years ago. But the figures are belied by other observations: the literacy rate as measured by the censuses increased from 24 per cent in 1961 to 29·3 per cent in 1971; the wastage in education is enormous – one study found 60 per cent of children enrolled in primary schools left without achieving functional literacy;[35]

there is a tendency for enrolment figures to be artificially inflated in any case.[36] Decades of reports by official bodies lament the poor quality of education in India at all levels.[37] In general a much more important feature of population growth than the one under discussion here is the impossible demands placed upon the educational system by the growth of numbers. As noted earlier there is no mechanical relationship between educational expenditure and population growth and the former has in fact been rising, even in real terms, faster than the latter. But a large proportion of the additional expenditure has been going into higher education which has been growing disproportionately fast. No one can claim there is substantial evidence of any rapid improvement of the average educational attainments of labour force entrants. Instead the combination of poor educational standards in schools and universities, and the lack of employment opportunities for those who become educated, has obstructed the onset of what elsewhere seems to have proved an influential constraint on fertility – that process whereby the costs and rewards of education induce parents to have less children so that they can afford to educate them well. There is certainly a 'composition of investment' effect in education itself – if population were growing more slowly, many of the resources devoted to education could be used to improve its performance rather than spread its depressingly low standards over greater numbers.

Thus it is impossible to believe, even if the 'quality' of new labour force entrants is improving at all, that the economic contribution of rapid population growth through the process of labour force renewal outweighs the negative effects of that growth. Rather the economy remains such that most parents withdraw their children from education at a very early age in the hope that each child can contribute its pittance to the family income through (mainly unskilled) labour. In an interesting article,[38] Harvey Leibenstein has reviewed this and other neglected aspects of the economics of population growth; India's circumstances are just such as would in his view negate the potential positive value of population growth as far as concerns this phenomenon. Of the others – mostly negative – to which he draws attention, two are also suggestive for India: he cites a growing body of evidence that children with smaller numbers of siblings tend to have higher measured intelligence and better nutrition than those of larger families, other things being equal; longer age intervals between siblings also are associated with higher intelligence. This material too would suggest that lower fertility, not higher, is likely to have a beneficial effect on the productivity of the labour force.

Altogether we must note that per capita income has risen over the period under discussion and there is little reason to believe that it cannot continue to do so for a considerable time to come. But there are several reasons for concluding that per capita incomes would be able to grow more rapidly if the population were growing more slowly. In effect, instead of greater increases in individual consumption, the economy has to provide increases in capital simply to maintain the existing levels of consumption for the increasing numbers. Up till now we have been taking a simplistic view of the nature of capital as machinery and equipment and also labour embodied in land improvement. The rate of formation of this capital is typically greater than the rate of population growth in developing countries, as can be seen if one divides the aggregate savings and investment rate by the capital-output ratio. (For example if savings and investment are 12 per cent of total product and the capital-output ratio is 3, the capital stock is growing by 4 per cent.) This of course refers to reproducible capital.

Quite apart from the question of non-reproducible capital (land in particular) there are questions about certain items of consumption which should perhaps be regarded as investment – education for one. The more one puts into the 'capital' requirements for growing numbers, and the higher the capital-output ratio, the more consumption gains have to be foregone for capital growth as population increases. And the things that could be taken as entering into the determination of the capital-output ratio are very numerous. If one were to think of social and political unrest in this light (and who can deny that that has been a factor in determining the productivity of capital in India?), it would not be difficult to identify further adverse effects of population growth. It may be for example that instability is related to unemployment and the absolute number of the unemployed may matter more than the proportion. A city of 10,000 people with 1000 unemployed may be stable while one of 10,000,000 with 1,000,000 unemployed is far less so. But here we enter on the realm of the completely speculative and also on the subject matter of the final section of this book. Evidently one cannot hope to exhibit all the consequences of population change for economic growth. Certainly these deeper problems in the words of Simon Kuznets, the most distinguished of modern commentators on our subject, 'can hardly be explored by economic and quantitative analysis' – and that is the verdict of the economist who has done more than any other to provide that quantitative analysis himself wherever it *has* been possible.[39]

The notion of the economy coping with population increase by giving up a share of potential consumption gains for new capital requirements is a very aggregative one, as has been deliberately the approach of this section. We have now to consider how the economy's success or failure to deliver gains in consumption has fallen on different strata of society – the question, in an older phrase, of the condition of the people.

THE CONDITION OF THE PEOPLE

That there are a large number of very poor people in India does not require demonstration. That the number of them has been growing in the last decade is also almost certain to be true – to think otherwise one must believe that most of the extremely modest gains in average income per head has percolated down to the poorest members of society – as we shall see there is little reason to believe that. There are three somewhat separate questions however which deserve examination: (1) whether the distribution of income has improved or worsened in recent years; (2) whether the proportion of the population below some given poverty line has increased or decreased and (3) whether the incomes of the poorest deciles of the population have risen or fallen in absolute terms. Our general conclusion is that the direct evidence of personal income and consumption data does not yield a decisive answer to any of these questions. But we intend to look at a range of other evidence not always considered in this context; when we have reviewed it all it will prove difficult to escape the distinct impression that, as far as concerns those features of social and economic development other than family planning which affect fertility, the amount of progress being made is extremely small.

Before we look at the detailed evidence let us just record some of the aggregate and per capita performance figures of the economy for the decade between the last two censuses. India's N.N.P. in the financial year 1960/1 was Rs. 132,840 million; this rose to Rs. 342,530 million in 1970/1 (current prices) but only Rs. 188,760 million at 1960/61 prices. The 1961 census population was 439 million; at the 1971 Census it was 548 million. Adjusting those populations to the middle of the respective financial years, per capita real national income grew from Rs. 306·1 to Rs. 348·9. In terms of annual compound rates over the decade this represents just under 3·6 per cent N.N.P. growth, about 2·25 per cent growth in population and just over 1·3 per cent growth in real N.N.P. per head.[40]

Over the whole decade average income per head thus rose by 14 per cent. The first point to make is that if income were perfectly evenly distributed in 1960/1, it would have amounted to less than one rupee per head per day, little more than the bare minimum necessary for an adult to survive; though for a family of five with two adults and three children 4 to 5 rupees a day would have been rather better than marginal adequacy. (Of course N.N.P. is far from being completely devoted to personal consumption. Per capita private consumption is approximately 90 per cent of per capita N.N.P.) If further the 14 per cent increment were perfectly evenly distributed, it would be an extremely modest improvement for 10 years of development though perhaps not a discreditable one in view of the fact that the decade contained wars, major droughts and other setbacks, as well as a 109 million increase in the population. (Judging by the 1950s or the start of the 1970s there does not seem any reason to consider the decade of the 1960s as particularly unusual in any of its experiences.)

Clearly, on the basis of the aggregate figures, it is not hard to see that the increment over the decade available for redistribution was small and that, if there were even a moderate skewness of the distribution of the increment in the disfavour of the poor, the extent to which they could conceivably have benefited must be slender. And of course the beginning of the decade was not a situation of equality: in 1960/61 in fact two-thirds of the population had consumption expenditure below the average as we shall show below.

Estimates of personal consumption
In 1970 a study entitled *Poverty in India*[41] was published in New Delhi which attracted considerable attention. Its authors, V. M. Dandekar and N. Rath, concluded about the 1960s that the situation of the poor had not improved. Without the benefit of the 1971 Census they over-estimated population growth (as did most observers of India during the 1960s) and therefore under-estimated the growth of per capita consumption expenditure from national income statistics. However their main conclusions were based on household surveys and are not thus affected; they were – as far as concerns the 1960s – that 'the small gains have not been equitably distributed among all sections of the population. The condition of the bottom 20 per cent rural poor has remained more or less stagnant. The condition of the bottom 20 per cent urban poor has definitely deteriorated; and for another 20 per cent it has remained more or less stagnant.'

The survey data they relied on was most importantly the National Sample Survey (N.S.S.). The N.S.S. data are a sample of household consumption expenditures obtained by interview. Those for 1960/61 agree remarkably with the national income data at just over Rs. 276 per capita consumption. Unfortunately the N.S.S. data for 1967/8, the latest available to Dandekar and Rath, they found to be about 10·7 per cent under the national income figures for consumption per head in the same year – had the authors been dividing the total by a closer approximation to that year's population, which was smaller than they thought, the gap would have been even wider. Indeed, at constant 1960/61 prices, the N.S.S. estimate for 1967/8 is below the N.S.S. figure for 1960/61. They argue convincingly that the under-estimate is greatest for the rich under the N.S.S. procedures and revise the figures upwards (though it is arguable that the N.S.S. under-represents the very poorest also). But to do this requires making assumptions about the precise distribution of the discrepancy and, however plausible one finds their assumptions, they are based mainly on *a priori* argument and, since it is the change in distribution over time they were trying to measure, their general conclusion cannot be accepted. It is quite possibly correct but they have not demonstrated it to be so.

Perhaps the most commonly cited of their findings was not that about the changes over time but their estimates of the numbers living on inadequate diets at the beginning of the period (1961/2). They found this to be 38 per cent for the rural population and 46·5 per cent for the urban populations. Here unfortunately it is not so much that they failed to demonstrate their conclusions as that they used a faulty technique. They examined the quantities of various foods recorded as actually bought at different expenditure levels (again from N.S.S. data) and converted these into daily caloric intake. They then computed the numbers living on monthly expenditure below that at which a given number of calories was purchased and stated these numbers to be living on inadequate diets. The pitfalls in such a procedure are numerous, as readers of the section on nutrition in Chapter 2 will appreciate.[42]

We have criticised the calculations of Dandekar and Rath. Our reason for doing so is that they have been, and still are, widely quoted. But we do not wish to detract more than necessary from the value of their work. There are many important sections of their book which are not touched by the above criticisms. Above all, despite the fact that other serious studies had preceded theirs, their book was successful in penetrating the public consciousness and the issue of persisting poverty in India arrived fully on the platform of public debate and has not since left it.

Returning to our three questions in the first paragraph of this section we must take a look at some other views. In the first place there have been several efforts to estimate changes in the overall distribution of income or consumer expenditure over time[43] using measures of concentration, most commonly the 'Gini coefficient'; nearly all of these use N.S.S. data. Curiously enough, despite the widespread belief that income distribution has worsened in India, most of these studies show little alteration, or even some reduction in concentration, over the ten or fifteen years prior to 1970; estimates for consumption expenditures have in fact shown concentration somewhat more distinctly reduced than for incomes.[44] (These measurements were made in current prices; at constant prices the trend is less clear.[45]) Disaggregated for rural and urban populations, the calculations appear to show reduction of concentration in both consumption expenditure and incomes for rural areas; in urban areas concentration of incomes as measured, has increased while that of consumption has declined.

In our view none of these calculations have advanced us very far. Such changes as have been measured are small and, given the troubles of the data, not very trustworthy. These troubles are first of all in the N.S.S. themselves – we have already noted the incompatibility of one of them with national income data, although it is arguable that the latter themselves contain arbitrary elements and are at least as unreliable as the N.S.S.[46] But, quite apart from the common difficulties of all questionnaire-based data (especially on subjects where respondents may have reasons for tempering the truth), the N.S.S. figures are subject to certain special types of unreliability: consumer expenditure is estimated for households and an error in the estimate of the number of persons per household in various income or occupational categories can make a considerable difference to the estimate of per capita income or expenditure in those categories; there are doubts, as we have noted, about the representativeness of the samples as a whole, in particular about the extent of coverage of the poorest sections, and serious doubts about the consumption estimates of the rich; there are questions about estimation of income in kind – and so forth. For calculating measures of distribution, further problems arise: the choice of price deflators for money-value comparisons over time; the small number of income classes; the selection of the measures themselves – different ones give different results.[47] Altogether, if consistent and large changes in the measures of concentration were found, it might be possible to discount these awkward things but, as the changes found are small and not consistent, the difficulties in the sources must force us to conclude that we do not really know what is happening to overall distribution – not from these calculations at any rate.

We reproduce below a table which shows how little the N.S.S. fractile shares alter in *current* prices. The finding that the poorest 20 per cent of the population have about 7 – 8 per cent of total consumption is common to this and most other sources. The bottom line gives the Lorenz ratios.

TABLE 4.1 Percentage share of total consumption expenditure by fractile groups: rural India

Fractile group (1)	1956 – 57 (2)	1957 – 58 (3)	1960 – 61 (4)	1961 – 62 (5)	1963 – 64 (6)	1964 – 65 (7)	1967 – 68 (8)
Poorest 5%	1·36	1·37	1·46	1·35	1·51	1·47	1·48
5 – 10	1·89	1·88	1·94	1·87	2·07	2·01	2·02
10 – 20	4·67	4·67	4·80	4·84	5·07	4·99	5·01
20 – 30	5·75	5·62	5·80	5·71	6·14	6·07	6·08
30 – 40	6·70	6·61	6·74	6·81	7·15	7·05	7·09
40 – 50	7·74	7·66	7·65	7·94	8·17	8·11	8·13
50 – 60	8·91	8·75	8·77	9·16	9·33	9·51	9·29
60 – 70	10·35	10·11	9·99	10·59	10·72	10·67	10·68
70 – 80	12·21	11·98	11·71	12·53	12·43	12·45	12·46
80 – 90	15·11	14·84	14·78	15·43	15·08	15·18	15·15
90 – 95	9·55	9·48	9·53	9·69	9·27	9·36	9·37
Richest 5%	15·76	17·04	16·82	14·08	13·06	13·33	13·24
Concentration ratio	0·32	0·31	0·31	0·31	0·29	0·29	0·29

NOTE The different rounds of N.S.S. used for approximating the financial years are given below:

1956 – 57—11th and 12th rounds (August 1956 – February 1957, March – August 1957)
1957 – 58—13th round (September 1957 – May 1958)
1960 – 61—16th round (July 1960 – June 1961)
1961 – 62—17th round (September 1961 – July 1962)
1963 – 64—18th round (February 1963 – January 1964)
1964 – 65—19th round (July 1964 – June 1965)
1967 – 68—22nd round (July 1967 – June 1968)

SOURCE Minhas (1970).

Even if we were confident that concentration ratios were going down, and average inequality of distribution declining, we would anyway not know the answers to our second and third questions, namely whether the proportion under some poverty line was going up or down, or whether the incomes of the lower deciles were rising or falling in absolute terms. It is conceivable that the fall in the Gini coefficients is a true one, but this may reflect only increasing equality of distribution among the upper four-fifths (say) while the lowest fifth has lost some of its share. What has been happening to the poorest deciles?

Unfortunately most of the evidence is the same as that to which we have already referred – the N.S.S. surveys of household consumption expenditure or the national income data. Some additional information has however been applied to it. As far as our question (2) is concerned the first major salvo was fired by another distinguished Indian economist, B. S. Minhas:[48] he found the proportion below a 'poverty line' of Rs. 200 per capita per year at 1960/61 prices had fallen steadily from 52·4 per cent in 1956/7 to 37·1 per cent in 1967/8. As he said the problem in India is to differentiate the very poor from the not quite so poor – that is the purpose of the poverty line; he noted in a memorable phrase that the poorest 30 per cent 'seem to be in infernal destitution.' But his findings if accepted would give some encouragement that the pattern of Indian development was slowly yielding benefits to the worse off, if the trend could continue.

The only trouble is that his basic data were derived by applying the N.S.S. distribution *shares* to national income estimates of consumption: he was dubious of the magnitudes of N.S.S. consumption estimates. Virtually all writers except Dandekar and Rath have adopted the distribution pattern in the N.S.S., whatever they thought of the levels of expenditure indicated. But once one doubts the accuracy of the levels one may legitimately suspect biases in the distribution. The national income estimates of aggregate consumption are of course themselves not entirely immune to doubt. Perhaps the one author most responsible for disseminating a view opposite to that of Minhas is P. K. Bardhan who has written a series of articles claiming a worsening of the situation and in particular a sharp rise in the proportion below a particular line.

In one of his most substantial articles,[49] Bardhan, using a slightly lower 'minimum' line of Rs. 15 per month at 1960/61 prices found 38 per cent of the rural population below that line in 1960/61 and 58 per cent below it in the 1967/8. Most of this difference from Minhas's estimate is due to his basing himself on the N.S.S. data for the years in question. But Bardhan also carefully worked out consumer price indices for different fractile groups in the income distribution whereas Minhas used the national income price deflator to maintain the constancy in 1960/61 prices; Bardhan has shown convincingly that prices of the consumption goods of the rural poor rose faster than the national average (largely because the poor spend such a large share of their incomes on cereals, particularly coarse cereals, whose prices rose extremely rapidly during the period); thus, even if Minhas's basic data are accurate, the improvement he finds in the proportion above the minimum is exaggerated. But perhaps one finding above all others casts doubt on Bardhan's (1973) treatment of the data: that the proportion below the poverty line in the Punjab increased from 13 per cent to 33 per cent between 1960/61 and 1967/8. The Punjab is the one area in particular where one must expect most incomes to have risen as a result of the wheat revolution and other developments; even if distribution has worsened, as it probably has, and even if there has been an increase in the proportion of the poor, an addition of 20 per cent to the numbers below the minimum line is hardly credible. In fact the most careful manipulation of N.S.S. data yet attempted shows the proportion in the Punjab below a newly calculated poverty line to have risen from 18·2 per cent in 1960/61 to only 22 per cent in 1970/71.[50]

The difficulty of reaching conclusions on any of these issues is illustrated by a paper by Deepak Lal,[51] which courageously attempted to swim against the general current and show that, by some criteria at least, things were improving for the poor. In particular the proportion below the 'poverty line' had fallen. Whichever of three poverty lines were used, in five out of six States for which data were available (Maharashtra, Orissa, Punjab, Rajasthan, Uttar Pradesh) the percentage of agriculture labour households below the poverty line in 1956/7 declined by 1970/71. Only in Mysore had it risen. This was one of the first published papers to make use of the N.S.S. 25th Round[52] – most of the earlier debate had used 1967/8 as the terminal year. But it does not appear to be the 1970/71 data alone which gave Lal his result;[53] the substitution of 1956/7 data for the 1960/61 figures, which others (referred to above) had used, was also important. It appears that the proportion below the poverty line in 1956/7 was considerably higher than in 1960/61: thus comparisons with 1956/7 are more likely to look like improvements. For example Lal found the proportion in Uttar Pradesh had fallen from 73·6 per cent in 1956/7 to 51·3 per cent in 1970/71 whereas a comparison for the rural population as a whole based on 1960/61 data, in which the proportion below the poverty line was a little under 42 per cent, shows a deterioration.[54] (The 1970/71 proportion below the poverty line is much the same for the whole rural population as for agricultural labour households only.) As we have already noted Rajaraman's study found that the proportion below a (somewhat different) poverty line in the Punjab had risen since 1960/61 – and that did employ the 1970/71 data.[55]

We have had occasion both here and in Chapter 2 to express scepticism about the household expenditure data; here is another case in point where the critical question depends on assessing which of two surveys is the more reliable. The alternative is to believe that the proportion below a poverty line was high in 1956/7, very much lower in 1960/61 and somewhere in between in 1970/71. But if that is so, the swings probably do not reflect any significant trends. The figures are bound to improve in good crop years and worsen in bad ones. There is not enough difference between the harvests of 1956/7 and 1960/61 to explain the distributional changes between those years. But 1970/71 was a spectacularly good year – in terms of per capita output the highest in recent agricultural history. It seems that for these comparisons the choice of years strongly affects, if it does not wholly determine, the outcome. The issue is of major importance since it bears on the validity of India's entire economic strategy and the whole question of whether the kind of development which has been taking place has brought real gains for the poor or whether a wholly different approach is needed. Yet, on the basis of these sets of figures, it seems that no conclusion can be reached. It must be said though that whatever the *direction* of change, the 1970/71 data show that the extent of poverty was still very considerable: with a very low poverty line equivalent to Rs. 14·5 – 16 per capita per month in 1960/61, the proportion of agriculture labour households below the same line in 1970/71 (Rs. 25 – 31 at that year's prices) was almost 60 per cent in Maharashtra and Mysore, over 72 per cent in Orissa, 43·4 per cent in Rajasthan and 51·3 per cent in Uttar Pradesh.[56] Only in Punjab had the figure come down to a tolerably low level, 24·6 per cent; and, as noted, other studies suggested it had risen to such a level since 1960/61. The N.S.S. 27th Round for 1972/3 showed the proportion of households below a similar line to be over 40 per cent for India as a whole.[57]

Lal also estimated changes in the shares in income of particular deciles, rightly observing that the proportion below the poverty line test ignores the distribution of income of those below and above the line. He found that in all six States the lowest three deciles had gained – though so had the highest decile while the next three highest had lost. But, as we have already noted, other data for other periods indicate a different view. The picture as seen from the 1970/71 data seems better than that in the studies for the 1960s but, if that is mainly because 1970/71 was such a good year, the situation could well have worsened subsequently.

The evidence permits no lucid, ringing truths. So much depends on the credence we can given to the National Sample Surveys. On the one hand we have a large mass of data collected by a large variety of field staff and the data show reasonable internal consistency in many dimensions – the data for each State do not jump around much; the 'bad years' (droughts and so forth) show up somewhat as expected. On the other hand much of the actual practice of the field staff is known to be subject to error. It simply will not suffice for Bardhan (1973) to insist that N.S.S. consumption estimates are obtained 'by following a systematic and explicit procedure for canvassing information from a scientifically chosen sample of households' even if he qualifies his insistence by admitting that, being survey estimates, 'they might be subject to response bias.' It is of critical importance to his case that the biases be consistent in various dimensions and over time and that is something of which we cannot be sure. That the response bias in some N.S.S. data is very large is not hard to demonstrate.[58] When the changes that are being measured from uncertain data are small and result from a sequence of hazardous calculations, the proper attitude to adopt is one of scepticism.

What very few authors have taken quantitatively into account when manipulating prices is the effect on producer incomes. Minhas believed, in distinction from Bardhan, Dandekar and others, that agricultural labourers constituted only one-third of the rural poor and small farmers more than half; he also claimed that many even of the small farmers are not sellers of food and thus benefit from a situation where food prices rise faster than others. Given these complexities, together with the problems of evaluating labour incomes in money and kind and the dubious quality of the basic data, we have some doubts as to whether the modest trends in the well-being of the poor will ever be discoverable from large-scale surveys of the present character.

The price level changes are extremely important; the rise in prices affecting the poor was in the region of 100 per cent in the 1960s. It must make us suspicious of any claims of improvement in the condition of the poor unless we find evidence of substantial increases in pay. That leads us to yet another body of evidence – agricultural wages. Sadly this is yet another morass, and one from which the most determined researcher is likely to emerge with a general sense of analytical dismay and without much clear information. There are various sources of wage statistics.[59] They are subject (like all the data to which we have been referring) to particular problems about the estimation of income in kind, which is a large share of labourers' wages, and a range of other uncertainties. ('One well-known trap is that the village official [who reports on the wage] uses one price for converting payments in kind into money, and the economist another to convert the money rates back into real figures – by this process wages which have in fact been constant in real terms for decades can be converted into a falling or rising trend.' Dharma Kumar (1974).) The conversion of the money wage to the goods it can buy requires another statistical step which has its problems. Finally, when one has arrived at a notion of the real daily wage in a given area, one is still confronted with the employment data – how many people have been earning that wage and for how many days in the year?

After wading through a part of this morass we have come to the same conclusion as we do elsewhere. In the 1960s at least there were few parts of the country where the money wage rose more than the price index and many where it rose less; the trend in real wage rates including income in kind is pretty uncertain. Various data sources show great variability by region and District in the trend in days worked and in the numbers working them relative to the increase in the labour force. It is our impression that the demand for labour considerably increased in many of the 'green revolution' areas despite partial mechanisation of some labour tasks; how much of a net gain there has been for the inhabitants of these areas, after allowing both for the growth in the labour force in the areas themselves and increasing competition from migrant labour from elsewhere, we do not know. Where there have been no dramatic improvements in agricultural technology – much the majority of India's cultivated land – the possibility that things have improved is tenuous except where non-agricultural employment has made headway. The trend in real earnings for rural labour is quite obscure. One study has found an increase in real wages between 1954/5 and 1968/9 only in three Indian States, Kerala, Madras and Punjab, where over 14 per cent of acreage was under new seeds.[60] Lal however has suggested that this and studies with similar findings may be misleading: the data on which they are based – the Ministry of Agriculture's series *Agricultural Wages in India* – are unreliable and the choice of particular years biases the results, particularly because of the lag between wages and prices. He claims that N.S.S. data show that from 1956/7 to 1964/5 'real wages were constant or fell in 8 out of the 15 states of India, but in the following period . . . to 1970/71 they have risen sufficiently to offset the earlier decline.'[61] But, if the expenditure data are any guide, these increases in wage rates have not led to substantial increases in the real income of poorer households. This may be connected with the trends in employment – if unemployment or under-employment was increasing, that would offset to some extent such real wage increases as there were. Unfortunately the trends in employment are notoriously even more difficult to assess, as we shall now see.

Employment and unemployment estimates
For a long time economists and others have been unhappy about the usefulness of data on employment or unemployment available in India. The only series of any reliability in terms of numbers employed covered the 'organised sector' – large scale manufacturing enterprises and the public services; but these include less than 10 per cent of the total working population. If one were trying to measure the progress of the economy in terms of jobs provided, the problem was to know what was happening outside the organised sector (within it, jobs were growing faster than the population).[62] The National Sample Surveys and others tried to discover the extent of gainful employment in given occupations, usually by enquiring whether (or for how long) people had been gainfully employed during some reference period. But problems of the seasonality of employment, the known presence of multiple occupations, the definition of occupational categories and so forth, together with the sampling and other unreliabilities of the surveys and the difficulties of interpreting the findings rendered them seemingly unpersuasive for many purposes.

If you were trying to answer the question, how many additional jobs were being provided by the course of development, perhaps the most difficult aspect was the extent of under-employment. Thus, even if you knew accurately the number of people who had been 'gainfully employed' in each occupational category during the year, there was a major problem about the extent to which work – especially in rural areas – might simply be being shared out among increasing numbers of people or whether the work was truly productive. To put the question graphically, someone on a Calcutta street carrying half a dozen combs on a cardboard tray would make a positive appearance in the statistics for 'petty traders', or some similar category, provided he had sold a comb or two during the reference period, but the economic significance of his activity is doubtful. On the farm, it might be less income with less days worked per man, less hours per day, or the same hours and days, but less effort, which might or might not be compensated by other paid employment elsewhere. Altogether the overall employment surveys did not really tell you what was happening to total employment. In the Fourth Five Year Plan the Government of India stopped trying to estimate it.[63]

If you wished to measure *un*employment, and how it was changing, you had an additional difficulty. Not only did you not know the numbers employed or the change in those numbers; to measure unemployment you had also to know how many potentially employable people there were – the size of the labour force and its participation rate. Consideration of Indian labour – perhaps particularly the position of women in the labour force – and the large number of social and cultural traditions embodied in practice in the conditions of its hire, led many people[64] to question the value for India's circumstances of concepts of employment and unemployment which were defined for very different (largely Western) conditions.

All this had the effect – healthy in our view – of concentrating attention away from such estimates and onto the identification of the poor – who they were, where they were, what were their incomes and what could be done for them. However new work was published in the mid 1970s which undoubtedly puts the estimators of unemployment back in business and we shall borrow some of its observations to assist us in assembling our jigsaw puzzle of Indian living conditions. One of the authors, Amartya Sen, accepts the impossibility of finding a single statistic which will give a satisfactory measure of unemployment, which is, as he puts it, 'not one concept but a class of concepts.'[65] As he properly observes the multi-dimensionality of the concept is no reason for rejecting useful information. His approach is to look particularly at three aspects of employment – 'income', 'production' and 'recognition'. Does a person receive income in return for work? Does he or she contribute to output in the sense that total output would be reduced in the worker's absence? And does the worker regard himself or herself as employed or unemployed? Data on 'unemployment' is based on one or more of these concepts.

Thus a recent (1973) Committee on Unemployment estimated a total of 18·7 million unemployed persons in India in 1971 – their estimate in part used N.S.S. data from the 19th Round covering the years 1964/5.[66] Since the N.S.S. used 'seeking work' as well as 'gainfully employed' in their criterion this would in Professor Sen's terms be an estimate based on both 'income' and 'recognition' aspects. The census estimates of employment make use of similar concepts. On the whole both census and N.S.S. unemployment estimates have been regarded as unrealistically low – in particular the test for being 'gainfully employed' was very weak; none of their estimates of male unemployment, rural or urban, have reached as high as 4 per cent. And, since the criteria change from one period to another, the trend is difficult to discern from them. The Committee on Unemployment got the figure for total unemployment up to 10 per cent of the labour force for 1971 mainly by making one criterion more stringent: by including those who worked less than fourteen hours a week they added 9·7 million to the total of the unemployed. (The last clause of that sentence perhaps deserves an exclamation mark.)

Perhaps even more practical has been the work of Raj Krishna which has permitted an empirically useful re-interpretation of the N.S.S. employment data.[67] Basically Krishna has defined alternative concepts of employment or unemployment which correspond to some of the different categories of survey data. Thus a survey which asked about periods worked during the previous week would yield a different estimate of unemployment from one which asked about the previous year. If however one defines employment carefully in terms of persons and time worked and unemployment in terms of time, income, willingness to work and productivity, the different measures of unemployment can be sorted out. Thus the low census figures in the region of 1·0 per cent of the labour force unemployed represent what Krishna calls the 'usual status person rate' (Y.S.R.) – it is the number of people *usually* unemployed in the preceding year who are *usually* in the labour force. For rural areas these numbered 0·57 million persons in the 1961 Census and 1·82 million in 1971.

Krishna then defines the 'end of week stock rate' (W.S.R.): in the N.S.S. this was the number of people who did not work a single hour in the week but were seeking or available for work, as a proportion of all those who worked at least one hour or were seeking/available for work: in 1972/3, this proportion was 3·4 per cent for rural India, or 10·0 million persons. But perhaps the most revealing is the weekly 'person-day unemployment rate' (P.D.U.R.). The W.S.R. calculation required the respondent to record his 'activity' and, if he had more than one, to confine himself to his main activity. For the P.D.U.R., the respondent could answer for all activities; thus the finding is for the ratio of unemployed days per week (of those seeking/available or work) to the total of available days. This estimate gives the number of unemployed person-days per week as 121·45 million for 1972/3, or 17·35 million fully unemployed person-weeks of time per week: if this is taken as equivalent to persons unemployed, it comes to an unemployment rate of 6·83 per cent. It should be noted that each measure employs a different numerator *and* denominator and, given the kind of data, it is the P.D.U.R. that will show the highest of the three rates. But for India's circumstances it seems more appropriate than the other two, if what one is looking for is a measure which takes account both of multiple occupations and the individual's varying availability for work.

As Krishna observes, 'The distinguished statisticians and demographers who have been "improving" employment concepts used in successive surveys in India have seen to it that no economist should be able to compare, with strictly logical justification, the numbers generated after every "improvement" with previously collected numbers.' Nevertheless there were a few broadly comparable surveys which permitted him to reach tentative conclusions about trends in unemployment. By the Y.S.R. criterion the figures already cited from the 1961 and 1971 Censuses indicate a deterioration, the number of unemployed multiplying by more than 3 times; the N.S.S. 27th Round permits an estimate for 1972/3 higher yet at almost 2 million, though still a small percentage of the labour force. The numbers unemployed by the W.S.R. crterion fell from 8 million to 4·5 million in the 1960s before rising to 10 million in 1972/3. The P.D.U.R. rate for 1972/3 also represents 'a reversal of the declining trend of weekly unemployment and under-employment . . . in the sixties.' 1972/3 was a bad crop year – but there were only two really good years from 1970 to 1976 so that the first half of the 1970s cannot have been a good time for the rural poor in general. The story does not quite end there since these measures of unemployment are deficient in one particular: they all relate to labour availability in excess of actual employment but they do not indicate the *price* at which labour is available. For unemployment measurement one cannot be entirely happy with indications of labour's availability, lacking information of that labour's desired pay.[68] It is a well observed fact that rural works schemes have to offer a wage sometimes considerably in excess of what men are currently earning if they are to be induced to take on additional work. If they are to move substantial distances for different kinds of jobs, again they will expect pay much higher than they earn in the village. The reasons for this are numerous and range from the actual caloric cost of some forms of additional work to the costs of moving, or the value of formal or informal contractual or other arrangements which the worker would break if he went elsewhere, even if within the village he is 'available' for additional work.[69]

These insights are valuable, both for the planner concerned with employment generation and the interpreter of unemployment estimates. One cannot simply take availability for work as equivalent to unemployment. Nevertheless the trend in the P.D.U.R. rate would suggest that there has recently been an adverse trend in days worked even if wage rates have risen and it does not seem right to interpret this as an expression of labour's 'income-leisure preferences'. Similar evidence from village studies indicates a lack of improvement in employment prospects in the village, or in some cases substitution of female for male at lower wages, to the detriment of family income. It is probably safer to rest with a qualitative estimate of the widespread existence of surplus labour than to try to put a figure on it. Attempts to do so come to widely different conclusions depending on data and concepts. If labour surplus is calculated by the number of workers required to produce a given output compared with the numbers actually employed, the result – apart from lacking a wage dimension – is critically dependent on the norm of individual working days. Thus Sen outlines a set of assumptions under which surplus labour in 1971 could have been as high as 23·7 per cent of the labour force, giving 42·4 million unemployed 'in the production sense' in agriculture alone.[70] Other estimates[71] (including some of his own) have put the figure at a small fraction of that total and there is no way of concluding that any one of them is the 'right' figure.

Lastly one could use the 'recognition' aspect on its own. Using survey data from the N.S.S. 25th Round for rural workers and the live registers of the Employment Exchanges (which he argues are not worthless as data sources as has often been supposed) together with some plausible assumptions, Professor Sen comes up with a *minimum* estimate of those without work and actively seeking it between 19·9 – 21·3 million for 1971.[72] Whichever way one looks it appears that unemployment or under-employment are substantial, even if each measure has a different meaning. None of the measures discussed here tells one a great deal about poverty except for those which purport to show absolute worklessness among those wishing to work. For many of those who are employed, even fully employed, are desperately poor. This is why unemployment estimates are valuable for diagnosing aspects of poverty and for indicating policy measures to relieve it (and warning about some which will not) but do not say much about its extent. Nevertheless taken together with all the other indicators examined here they contribute to the general picture that builds up about the 'condition of the people'.

It seems that wherever one looks it is difficult to find any evidence of a trend of improvement for the poor. Their fate in rural areas, at least as measured by the N.S.S. or similar surveys, is bound up most importantly with the magnitude of the harvest and in urban areas, given the volume of migration and natural population growth, with the slow progress of manufacturing and service trades employment. The data on expenditure, income distribution, wages, prices and employment do not show any very distinct trend. But if the plight of the poor were really being alleviated, the fact might be expected to show up elsewhere than in comparisons over a period with a 'bad' year at one end and a 'good' one at the other. The available information tells one a great deal about who is poor and why they are poor and also that the poor are very numerous; but it does not indicate whether they are becoming proportionately less numerous or less poor. The information is of course highly aggregative; one is often tempted to leave the studies of the country as a whole or its individual States and look at villages in the hope that at least for those microcosms something approaching the truth might be arrived at. To that temptation we now succumb.

The process of rural change and the evidence of village studies

Having reviewed some of the aggregative evidence, we turn to village studies both to see what support they give to the general picture of poverty in India and to try to understand the processes underlying the distribution of incomes. Most of the 300 million additional people India has acquired since 1941 are in the villages of which there are about 600,000; the 'proportion urban' in the last three censuses has risen about 2 per cent per decade and is even now only about 20 per cent. What has happened to the economics of village life as a result of this growth in numbers and other changes in the economy and society?

Anyone who knows India's villages knows the meaning of scarcity. There are comfortable villages with many brick houses and visible prosperity for many or even most of the inhabitants – especially in the irrigated areas or those with assured rainfall. But the average is not like this – 75 per cent of India's cultivated land is 'dry' (though it does not carry 75 per cent of the population); the average village has very few if any wealthy men – mostly large landowners – a not very prosperous middle section and a mass of poor and very poor families, reliant at least in part on wages, with or without a small parcel of land – they live in dwellings of mud or other impermanent materials. In 1963 – 4, 8·4 per cent of the villages containing about one-fifth of the rural population (i.e. the larger villages) had a source of electricity; 40 per cent had no electricity within 15 kms; 25 per cent of villages had no qualified doctor within 15 kms, and only 3·4 per cent of them had a doctor on the spot (as opposed to a 'traditional' medical practitioner present in a large proportion of villages). About 45 per cent of the population in villages were more than 15 kms from a dispensary, health centre or hospital. Wells were the drinking water source for 65 per cent of villages; about 2 per cent had tap water.[73]

In recent years many of these things have improved. As many as 15 per cent more villages may now have electricity; the number of health centres has increased considerably; the number of villages with piped water-supply may have doubled (though still only about 5 per cent of all villages),[74] and so forth. When talking of economic progress one must not look solely at indicators of personal consumption expenditure. The ordinary person in today's villages is more likely to go to school, to possess or be able to listen to a radio, to have access to medical services, to have hope of surviving natural disasters, to be close to a paved road and inexpensive transport and, at least until recently, his life expectancy was rising and more of his children were remaining alive. Thus there have been welfare improvements offsetting reductions (or adding to increases) in consumption expenditure; perhaps they should be called 'overhead consumption'.

In a situation where most incomes are earned from the land, and most economically cultivable land has already been cultivated, the growth of population is bound to create pressure. Strangely we know very little about the effects of this pressure in any quantitative detail. There has been a great deal of subdivision of holdings through inheritance, but we do not really know for certain how far it has progressed. If there is one subject on which we may properly be doubtful about statistics, it is landholding.[75] Various village studies suggest a common pattern which certainly accords with other observations. The wealthier landowners are able to buy land and from one generation to another may well succeed in slowing down considerably the diminution of the estates they hand on to their sons.[76] The further down one goes into the size classes of holdings, the less available is this form of protection, and subdivision goes on up to and beyond the limit of holding size capable of supporting a family; with subdivision often goes fragmentation to provide the inheritors with shares of land of equal quality. Given the laws or rules of inheritance and continuing growth of population, this process can go on for a very long time since even families who have to rely on wage incomes commonly prefer some land to no land. When a point is reached where the family considers it would be totally uneconomic to subdivide further they may try to share the work and produce of an undivided holding; or a younger brother or two may go off, or be sent off, to earn a living in some other way, inside or outside the village. That point clearly has been reached in many villages; perhaps in most villages for some people.

This is the pure process of subdivision under population growth, abstracted from other economic events. But technical change takes place in agriculture and men are forced to borrow, for consumption or investment, and subjected to natural and man-made disasters. To pay off debt, or to acquire capital sums for different forms of investment, men sell their land. Those who are profiting from technical change or public investments which assist agriculture are in the best position to buy it. Two potential forces work in a different direction: land reform and land consolidation. The latter has reduced the problems of fragmentation in some parts of India; the former, as is well-known, has not achieved a great deal.

There remain the non-landowners: tenants and labourers. The prospects of tenants depend particularly on the value to the landowner of crop-sharing arrangements – we cannot pretend in this book to examine tenancy problems. The agricultural labourer's position depends on the changes in crop/labour requirements and in the acreage and pattern of cropping and the opportunities for non-farm employment – and of course the overall availability of labour seasonally and geographically.

How have these relations been working out in practice? The most interesting village studies are resurveys spanning a period of years. In a particularly careful and detailed one,[77] Scarlett Epstein has examined two villages in a district of Mysore, first in 1955 and again after an interval of almost fifteen years. (Before 1939 one village had acquired canal irrigation for much of its land; the other had not.) In both villages the wealthier farmers grew more prosperous and acquired more land, in the 'wet' village because they had more access to the irrigation water and because they could afford other inputs. In the 'dry' village the wealthier farmers could afford to sink tube-wells. The improvements in prosperity for the rest of the wet village were more modest or non-existent: some of the middle farmers did well, others were squeezed. For the labourers, some crops – sugar and paddy in particular – became more labour-intensive; the cropping pattern shifted in their favour also, as they became relatively more profitable. The net result was an increase over the fifteen years in the number of labour days demanded; but the population had grown, and available labour days had increased about as much as the demand for them, so that the proportion of employable labour days not employed – about one-third of the total – remained roughly constant. But for many labourers there was little increase in prosperity, even some decline – there was some sub-stitution of female for male labour (at lower wages) and many of the villagers complained of competition from migrant labour. And prices had risen steeply.

In the dry village the number of those worse off after fifteen years was considerable; many of the medium landholders could not make ends meet; labour days required did not grow in proportion to the increase in days available resulting from population growth, and labourers' real earnings fell. There was considerable net out-migration. The situation of the Harijans or scheduled castes, at the very bottom of the social scale, was appalling – few of them migrated: they could not hold out very long financially while searching for work outside the village; they had few job-providing connections outside; and they were discriminated against where jobs were available. Debt played its miserable part–a man could borrow Rs. 200 to help with a wedding or simply to survive in a drought year and be crippled for years to follow by paying interest at 20 per cent or very much more with little hope of repaying the principal: as we have seen from the income distribution figures above even Rs. 40 per year could be a sizeable fraction of many Indian incomes. Professor Epstein observed in the dry village a notable increase in contract labour – a wage of perhaps Rs. 150 a year, plus daily meals and clothing twice a year; a man could be forced into this either by debt or simply by the necessity of accepting basic security on the edge of the economic abyss.

We must emphasise that these are but two of India's 600,000 villages. We quote them not for their statistical significance but for their depiction of a process which may be characteristic; they illustrate some of the features of rural life which result in the distribution of income discussed from other points of view above. Of course it is the magnitudes that count; but, since these processes are so common, one must be able to point to fairly powerful opposing effects if one wishes to dispute the pessimistic view they present. We will return to this question; but first a glance at some of the salient features of other village studies.

Increasing landlessness has been noted in a number of surveys; studies of 'green revolution' areas have also shown a tendency towards disturbance of tenancies.[78] We have remarked on the increase in female wage employment in Professor Epstein's study; this occurs elsewhere too – to the extent that it substitutes wives' ill-paid for husbands' better paid labour, the consequences for income distribution are adverse. Some studies note the withdrawal of women of the richer classes from labour in the fields. A considerable presence of child labour has been observed, i.e. paid employment below the age of 12. Increasing indebtedness is extremely common among labourers (and among others too, but that is more likely to be productive debt). Where irrigation has arrived in the interval between surveys the more common finding is an increase in employment both absolutely and even relative to the increasing availability of labour within the village. Where employment has not so risen within the village compensatory work outside the village has often become available – but often not. A widening gap in prosperity between the bigger landowners and the rest is an extremely frequent phenomenon, whether or not the rest were getting better or worse off.[79]

The statistical value of these studies is obscure; it will become less obscure when the processing of statistical data from several hundred Indian village studies is more advanced under the Institute of Development Studies' *Village Studies Programme*.[80] We will content ourselves for now with some general observations. Village studies fall into two main groups – remote tribal villages and more ordinary ones. The latter (from which we have taken our observations) are about average in size but tend to be nearer to main roads and towns than the average. They cannot be said to constitute a random sample, though further investigation may show them to be on the whole better than average in certain respects and therefore indicative of what may be happening elsewhere. On one or two important subjects the results are pretty certain to be unsystematic – thus opportunities for paid employment outside the village may depend on the establishment of a factory nearby, a pretty random event for a small and unstratified sample of villages; and the effect of migrant workers on village incomes is also pretty random. However it should be possible to establish common characteristics of villages where given classes of events occur – where within-village employment rises faster than population or where the incomes of the poorest are rising, and so forth.

But, like all the data we have been examining, these too, though inconclusive, do little to relieve concern about the trends in living standards. The villages surveyed have not been deliberately chosen as below average villages, and it may be that they are better than average.

Certainly if the trends in the country as a whole were exhibiting a reduction of poverty, one would expect less of the resurveyed villages to demonstrate the opposite, in the absence of any indications that they were uncharacteristic. As we have stressed the important thing is the process of economic change where population is pressing on limited land. The tendency of that process to create increasing poverty is opposed by technical change and investment increasing agricultural productivity and also be increasing employment opportunities in manufacturing and services. But there is a lot of evidence that many of the sources of improved agricultural productivity have benefited the rich more than the poor, and the large landowner more than anyone else. And non-agricultural employment, while it has grown faster than the population, has not been growing fast enough to make much of a dent in the overall employment problem. Much of it, as in agriculture, pays very low wages which, because of the great excess in labour supply, have not been forced to keep pace with inflation.

The extensive literature on the 'green revolution' widely supports the view that it has worsened the distribution of income. We will not here enter other controversies about it, save to say that those who decry its social consequences have rarely given it the credit it deserves for having raised food output (and therefore benefited the poor) at a critical time. Nor do we comment on the mechanisation/employment debate other than to observe that existing studies are inconclusive about its net employment effects; agricultural mechanisation – in particular tractors – has in any case affected only a small fraction of India's rural areas. (See for example I.L.O. (1973).)[81] Over a longer period smaller farmers may profit more – they appear to put a higher proportion of their land under the new varieties, even if they come later to them, as Kumar (1974) observes.

Two words of caution are in order: connoisseurs of village study literature will be familiar with our story. Most of the resurveys to which we have referred have their second survey in the middle or late 1960s. Resurveys for earlier periods have also shown a tendency for worsening conditions. For example one in 1940 for twelve villages in the Madras area concluded that since 1920 'deterioration or stagnation in some vital points overshadows the definite improvements that have been made in some aspects of rural life.'[82] Food output was not keeping pace with population increase. Holdings had fragmented. Few wells had been sunk. There was little improvement in methods of cultivation. Draught cattle were inefficient, milk yields low; breeding methods and fodder production were unchanged. There was rapid growth of tenancy-at-will and casual labouring. Debt multiplied. Cooperative credit was tried – it failed. Water-supplies and their use were backward and unchanged. On the other hand there were better links to railways, trunk and leader roads improved, motor buses were running, education was spreading, interest rates were down, professional money lenders were turning towards genuine investment and some medical aid was available.

Indeed one can go back into the nineteenth century and find concern for population pressure on the land and all its effects. One is left in a quandary. Something we certainly observe is that the countervailing forces operating against deterioration are more powerful today and more widespread. But the population is growing more rapidly so that deterioration seems to be occurring nonetheless, or at least there is very little improvement. Is the village asymptotically approaching some limit of capacity to absorb additional people? If so what happens when the limit is reached?

In our view there is some limit, and it may be set by social and political institutions and their ability to absorb change rather than any technical agronomic or economic parameters. But given the number of things which can adjust – including, it must balefully be noted, the death rate – that limit may be quite a long way off: long enough indeed for the much needed arrival of India's demographic transition. The historical perspective is valuable – it restrains one from concluding that a process which has been operating in India for centuries is going to end with some sudden discontinuity; though it should not induce *excessive* restraint in this regard. There may be discontinuities near at hand. But, in the present state of knowledge, or rather ignorance, about what is happening now, it is beyond our analytical powers to determine how near.

We shall close this section with an instructive sample from the village literature – Gilbert Etienne's *Indian Agriculture: the Art of the Possible*.[83] Based on observations up to 1964 he concluded about subdivision of holdings that ' . . . the deadline has now been reached. The Khandoi peasants have . . . ten to fifteen years during which they must at all costs improve the yield of their land so that they will be able to live on less than two hectares.' On the population/agriculture balance he suggested 'The days are numbered for the farmers of Khandoi. The major part of the land yields a surplus which can be reinvested in order to increase production. In ten years' time, unless a new stage in the progress of farming has been reached, the increased population will absorb most of today's hard-earned surplus.' But with disarming honesty he added a note when the book was translated from the French original of 1966:

> '*Postscript.* – During a new visit in August 1967 I was struck by the fast growth of the economy. No less than eight private tube-wells had been installed since 1964. This means that only a very limited acreage is not under irrigation now and that most of the previous shortcomings of the irrigation system have been eliminated. In addition, new varieties of Mexican wheat are being used increasingly and yield an average of 2000 to 3000 kg/ha, a figure that can be increased still further.'

Khandoi it should be noted is in Uttar Pradesh, the Western, more prosperous part, where the 'green revolution' has spread widely.

Everything we have so far looked at gives inconclusive evidence about the change in the living conditions of the mass of the Indian people, although we have little reason to believe in any improvement during the last decade and a half in either the proportion above a minimum level, or the level of the lowest deciles, and some reason to believe in a worsening. The death rate is of interest as a general indicator of conditions – and, as we have seen in Chapter 2, the death rate appears to have reached a plateau below which it will only progress with a general rise in the levels of living of the mass of the people – and in bad years it may rise above it. The death rate provides still further tentative evidence of the failure of economic growth to alleviate poverty.

We have reached the end of this particular trail, or rather set of trails. We remain baffled by each. But the overall picture is fairly impressive. If some of the indications were misleading, we would expect one at least of the half-dozen types of evidence we have looked at to contradict the others. But little of it does. Though each body of evidence tells us nothing clearly they all point in the same direction. The various mechanisms at work in the economy have produced a kind of equipoise. Aggregate income grows, some get better off; if any of the gains, other than those in 'overhead consumption', have benefited the poorer half of the population, it is not very often discernible. How long this state of affairs can continue is an open question. In many ways that question may prove to be largely political. As such, it forms the subject matter for our final chapter.

FOOD, POPULATION AND RURAL DEVELOPMENT

Famines are not the result of the land's incapacity to cope with the increasing demand, but of the political chaos and physical oppression which invade the state in its decline.

Ibn Khaldun

Both from the point of view of the economy, and from that of the survival of the population, the volume of agricultural production, and particularly of foodgrains, is obviously a central question. For most of the post-Independence period the increase in foodgrains output has exceeded the growth of population – however that increase is measured. An official average rate calculated from 1960–61 to 1971–2 gives 2·64 per cent.[84] The rate depends very much on the period and the form of the curve chosen. We have fitted an exponential time trend from 1949–50 to 1973–4 (see Figure 4.2); it shows that foodgrains output had an average annual growth over the 25 years of 2·6 per cent.[85] The fastest annual rate of intercensal population growth has been just over 2·2 per cent between 1961–71. Does this mean that there is little cause for concern? Unfortunately, no.

The most general problem is the adequacy of the overall volume of the food supply for the needs of the population – but the simple matching of the volume of food output to the numbers to be fed is far from accounting

TABLE 4.2 (a) Agricultural Production (million tons)

	1955/56	1960/61	1965/66	1966/67	1967/68	1968/69	1969/70	1970/71	1971/72	1972/73	1973/74	1974/75	1975/76	1976/77
Foodgrains of which:														
Rice	69·38	82·21	72·35	74·23	95·05	94·01	99·50	108·42	105·17	97·03	104·66	101·06	120·8	117
Wheat	28·73	34·64	30·59	30·44	37·61	39·76	40·43	42·22	43·07	39·25	44·05	40·25		
Jowar	8·87	11·00	10·39	11·39	16·54	18·65	20·09	23·83	26·41	24·73	21·78	24·24		
Bajra	6·73	9·81	7·58	9·22	10·05	9·80	9·72	8·10	7·72	6·97	9·10	10·22		
Maize	3·46	3·29	3·75	4·47	5·19	3·80	5·33	8·03	5·32	3·93	7·52	3·23		
Other Cereals	9·86	10·71	10·09	10·36	13·56	11·58	12·24	14·42	11·56	12·24	12·21	12·72		
Pulses	11·73	12·75	9·94	8·35	12·10	10·42	11·69	11·82	11·09	9·91	10·00	10·40		

SOURCE Government of India, *Economic Survey 1975–76* (New Delhi: Ministry of Finance, Department of Economic Affairs (1976)). Figures for 1975/76 and 76/77 are estimates.

(b) Net Availability of Foodgrains (grams per person)

	1956	1961	1966	1967	1968	1969	1970	1971	1972	1973	1974	1975
Cereals	360·5	399·7	360·0	361·7	404·1	397·9	403·1	417·8	420·2	383·1	411·9	373·6
Pulses	70·4	69·0	48·2	39·7	56·0	47·3	51·9	51·3	47·1	41·4	40·9	41·7
Total foodgrains	430·9	468·7	408·2	401·4	460·1	445·2	455·0	469·1	467·3	424·5	452·8	415·3
Total population (millions)	397·3	442·4	493·2	504·2	515·4	527·0	538·9	550·8	562·5	574·2	586·1	597·9

SOURCE Government of India, *Economic Survey 1975–76*. Figures for 1967–75 are 'provisional.' Population figures are official mid-calendar-year estimates derived from censuses up to that of 1971. 'Net availability' is calculated from gross production in crop years (July – June) minus 12·5 percent (for feed, seed requirements, and wastage) plus net imports plus or minus changes in government stocks. Figures for stocks with traders, producers, and others are not known. '*Net availability*' *may therefore not equal consumption.*

for 'adequacy'. However, we shall start there. As can be seen from our Figure 4.2 and calculations there is little discernible positive trend in output per head of population; the average over the 25 years is marginally upward but only by about one-fifth of one per cent annually. Of course without the catastrophic years of 1965–6 and 1966–7 the trends would look better. But it is not easy to rule out those years as completely abnormal. They are exceptional as proportionate deviations from the trend, being both about 18 per cent below it, compared with other bad years, say 1957–8 which was 8 per cent below, or 1972–3 less than 7 per cent below trend; it is also exceptional to have two such appalling years in a row. But, if we are thinking about the prospects ahead, we cannot rule out such bad years as possible occurrences for the future.

It is interesting to compare the trend values given by the estimate from 1949–74 with the available figures for the 1970s up to 1977:

TABLE 4.3 Foodgrains output (in tonnes)

	1970/71	1971/72	1972/73	1973/74	1974/75	1975/76	1976/77	Average
Actual	108·42	105·17	97·03	104·66	101·06	120·8	117	107·73
'Trend'	98·04	100·58	103·20	105·88	108·63	111·45	114·34	106·02

As can be seen the actual series for foodgrains has on average been minutely above the estimated trend. After the good crop of 1970/71 the succeeding years had begun to give cause for concern that output growth might be falling off. Writing about India's food output often takes its tone from the current scene. Thus the mid 1960s were full of dire warnings. Then with the early success of the 'green revolution' optimism began to dawn and there was even concern about food surpluses and falling food prices. Taking a long view we could observe that the amplitude of fluctuations around the trend has not altered much but the floor and ceiling levels have both risen. Nevertheless there was a new wave of pessimism in the early 1970s despite the fact that deviations from the trend were smaller than at past crises.

Any assessment of future food prospects must first take account of possible changes in the natural environment. When bad crop years have occurred hitherto they have been due to two causes: drought or floods. There is some partial evidence of a worsening of rainfall trends over the last twenty years, possibly as part of very long swings in rainfall cycles, related to such distant causes as changes in the polar ice-cap.[86] There is also some evidence that the extent and frequency of flooding have been increasing.[87] The latter may have something to do with man-made causes. In North India at least the floods are commonly the result of an excessive rate of flow in the major rivers which are in turn partly related to deforestation in the Southern Himalayas and elsewhere – the reduction in ground cover

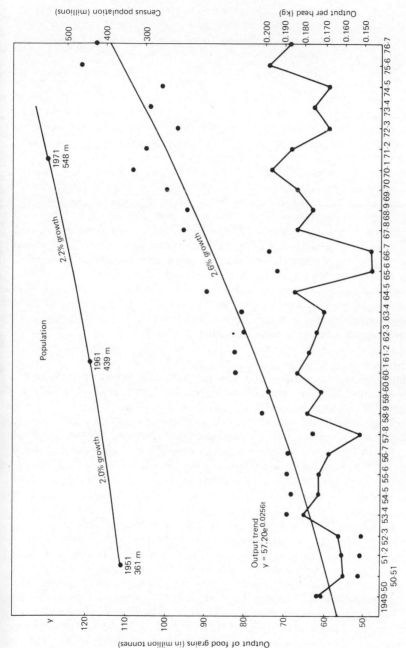

Fig. 4·2 India: Foodgrains and population

accelerates the flow of water down the slopes. Whether the observed reduction in average rainfall in some places is also due to the depletion of soil cover by over-grazing and deforestation is altogether more contentious; but if rainfall is worsening, for whatever reason, the outlook is grim.

These long-term considerations were not the cause of the pessimism of the early 1970s which lay rather in a number of factors, some of them international rather than domestic to India. In the wake of the oil price rises which began in late 1973 there followed an international shortage of fertilisers; India, a net importer of fertilisers, consequently suffered – every ton of fertiliser deficiency translates into a loss of several tons of grain. The 1974 crops further suffered both from drought and floods – the drought affecting not only irrigation water but the generation of electricity on which many farmers also depend for pumping. But what really made the situation so painful was the international food shortage. The latter had come about as a result of the depletion of U.S. reserves and bad harvests in the Soviet Union and elsewhere. India had come through the poor season of 1973 because of its own food reserves and a modest quantity of imports. In 1974 its own reserves were very low and imports were hard to come by – and, if available, at very high prices when the balance of payments was already hard hit. Finally we must note that if everything remains the same in percentage terms, a given proportionate shortfall in foodgrains means hardship for a larger absolute number of people.

This brings us to the key points: as so often in economic matters, attention is focussed on the aggregate while what count are both the aggregate and its distribution. The fact is that in current circumstances food output growing marginally faster than population is simply insufficient. There are two main components in the demand for food: income and population. One can work out food 'requirements' by multiplying the numbers of people by their average food needs. But what happens depends on the distribution of purchasing power in relation to supply. We have put the figures of output per head in our diagram; the per caput *availability* of foodgrains depends additionally on the amount of production needed for seeds, cattle-feed and that lost in various ways, together with the amount imported and the net change in stocks. But since so many people – nearly 70 per cent of the labour force – gain their living from agriculture, output per head has an important bearing on individual incomes. It also partially measures India's progress towards self-sufficiency in food. And because imports and stock changes are small relative to the total, there is a very high correlation between production and availability: imports and stock changes do little to iron out the fluctuations, as Table 4.2 shows.

India recently ended the period of the Fourth Five Year Plan (1969–74). In that Plan it was estimated that the income-elasticity of demand for foodgrains – the proportion of additional income that would be spent on additional food – was 0.8. With the growth of private consumption expenditure projected, food output had to grow at 4·7 per cent annually for the Plan to succeed and for stable prices to be maintained; growth higher than that was hoped for in order to reduce food imports. The actual out-turn of the Plan period with food output growing at something close to 3 per cent annually would thus have defeated virtually all the Plan targets even had nothing else gone wrong. Shortages of food have to be combated either by additional imports, which conflict with planned uses of foreign exchange, or by reductions of domestic expenditure – this last mainly in the public domain; the choice is thus to cut back the Plan, or to permit inflation which falls mainly on food prices.

It is the latter which demonstrates the misleading character of the relationship between population and total food availability. During the decade of the 1960s food prices rose by roughly 100 per cent. Total N.N.P. in constant prices was 42 per cent higher in 1970/71 than it was in 1960/61, but the availability of foodgrains had risen only 24·6 per cent. Had the gains in income been evenly distributed and the income-elasticity of demand for foodgrains of 0·8 applied, the food available should have risen by 0·8 times 42 per cent of 33·6 per cent. In other words the amount of food available had risen by almost one-third less than the amount needed to satisfy the demand that would have been generated by the increase in income during the decade, had that increase been evenly dis-tributed.

The calculation is gross; it assumes – probably rightly – that con-sumption grew at the same rate as national product. But it also assumes – as is not the case – that a uniform price for foodgrains prevails. This is not true across regions or other dimensions; most importantly the Government makes a considerable amount of food available through the Fair Price Grain Shops on ration cards, creating a two-tier price system for food which is designed to assist the poor. Many workers, especially agricultural labourers, are paid in kind as well as receiving a money wage. Thus these aggregate calculations give only a crude indication of the way in which the events of the decade affected the poor. Nevertheless they give further support both to the view that the plight of the poor has not been remedied and to the contention that food output, though 'keeping pace' with population growth, has not been adequate. It is not the poor whose growing incomes have been bidding up the price of food. If one looks at the price increases in food of the fifteen years prior to 1975/6, they were more like 150 per cent than 100 per cent, and this has inevitably born down painfully on the poor whose incomes in money and kind have not risen by such amounts. For 'adequacy', the availability of food must increase enough to match the share of the increase in incomes which will be spent on food *and* incomes must be in the hands of those who need more food. This has simply not been happening. The fluctuations in output and incomes are also important; not only do imports and stock changes fail wholly to make up the availability of food when output falls – nothing makes up for the loss of incomes in bad years. The 'food problem' has therefore really to be seen in the context of rural development generally.

Rural development

One of the proudest buildings in Malgudi was the Central Cooperative Land Mortgage Bank which was built in the year 1914 and named after a famous Registrar of Cooperative Societies, Sir _ _ _ _ _ _, who had been knighted for his devotion to Cooperation after he had, in fact, lost his voice explaining cooperative principles to peasants in the village at one end and to the officials in charge of the files at the secretariat end. It was said that he died while serving on a Rural Indebtedness Sub-Committee.

R. K. Narayan, The Financial Expert

It follows from the analysis of this and earlier chapters that a major improvement in agricultural performance is a necessity for almost everything we have been considering – to provide adequate food for the population; to create additional employment; to act as a brake on excessive rural-urban migration and to permit the expansion of the economy and a more soundly-based process of industrialisation. In the circumstances provided by such changes the demographic transition could itself be accelerated and it is difficult to imagine any other circumstances that will have this effect. What then are the possibilities for employment-oriented expansion in agriculture? And will India be able to feed its growing numbers for as long as they continue to grow?

At first sight one might be tempted to give discouraging answers to both these questions. A defender of Indian policies and performance hitherto would make the following case: 'In all our economic Plans we have estimated the likely increase in demand for food, based on estimates of need and allowing both for population growth, the maintenance of stocks and some improvement in nutritional standards. To plan for more than that would be to risk the creation of excess supplies and depressed prices for producers. We have provided in the Plans the resources we judged necessary to achieve these levels of output. But agricultural progress is difficult to achieve. We have tried every conceivable approach. But in the end, we depend on local administrations and the structure of social and economic interests at the local level. Where these have been favourable, or where the profitability of new measures has been overwhelmingly attractive, we have been successful. But this is far from universal. People tell us to put more resources into irrigation. Well, look at the Fourth Plan – we allocated Rs. 10,870 million to irrigation and flood control; that may have been only 4·4 per cent of Plan outlays but it represented a colossal task of implementation. The same is true in other departments of agriculture. We cannot usually complete all that we propose to do, let alone do more. And when you add to all our difficulties the unreliability of the weather – the monsoon of 1966 provided less than half the normal rainfall – you will appreciate that we are doing about as well as can be expected.'

There is a great deal in this defence even if it hardly fills one with optimism. It certainly is true that there is hardly any measure for agricultural change which has not been attempted in India. In the immediate post-Independence period reliance was placed mainly on the Community Development and Cooperative movements: the former had some impact on village improvement in the early days, but only a modest one on agricultural production, even after 1959 when its emphasis was shifted considerably in that direction. The latter was successful in some of its commercial activities and, in parts of the country, even in its intended primary function of providing credit, inputs, shared facilities and sales organisation for farmers; more commonly however the Cooperatives, like many of the Community Development institutions, have been dominated by the large landlords and served mainly their interests; as Daniel Thorner once remarked,[88] they became yet another form of the extended family in India. The next main thrust of agricultural policy was the Intensive Agricultural District Programme (I.A.D.P.), precursor of the 'green revolution'. Under this programme the new package of inputs was to be delivered in selected Districts; in the event the I.A.D.P. Districts do not seem to have done any better than other Districts,[89] but adoption of the new inputs – seeds, fertilizer, credit – spread rapidly, as far as wheat was concerned, wherever conditions were suitable.

The 'High Yielding Varieties Programme' for wheat has been the most dramatic success of post-Independence agriculture – as we have noted, not without its distributional disadvantages, but a major contribution to output in the late 1960s and early 1970s after several years of virtual stagnation in yields. The two questions for the immediate future of Indian agriculture are thus whether there are other technological improvements in the offing which, as it were, make the task of adoption relatively simple by dint of sheer profitability; and whether adequate progress can continue in less innovatory measures. As is well-known the main scope for new technology is in rice production where a breakthrough is hoped for comparable to that which altered the character of wheat production. But the problem seems more intractable. While almost the whole of North Indian irrigated wheatland is planted to one variety, *kalyan sona*, the diversity of conditions under which rice is grown demands a range of new varieties to be counted not on the fingers of one hand but in dozens. There are a number of new rice varieties but so far they have all had drawbacks of one kind or another. The first introduced, such as I.R.8, did produce considerable yield increases, but are very glutinous when cooked and do not fetch a high price although they are now being bought by those who cannot afford anything better in times of scarcity. Other varieties have shown insufficient resistance to field pests or diseases; or, bred for thin husks, they succumb to other pests in storage. Several locally bred varieties have done tolerably well in limited areas and the most promising current prospects lie with summer rice in Eastern India where groundwater is available and beginning to be developed.

New varieties of maize and pulses (with the exception of *bajra*, millet) have also made little lasting contribution to yield increases, largely owing to weak disease resistance. The difficulty of developing successful new strains of crops can hardly be exaggerated; nor should it be forgotton that, although the original strains came from Mexico, the main work of developing the new wheat varieties for adaptation to Indian conditions was done in India by Indian scientists. Nevertheless when one thinks of the difference made by the new wheats to the entire Indian economy one could wish for higher priority treatment of plant breeding research in India for crops other than wheat. The budget for research is not commensurate with the enormous promise in such expenditure. And there is a particular need for social science research directly related to plant breeding: the biological approach is still biased towards yield increase – while this is not in itself wrong, there are also opportunities to develop new varieties which may not necessarily yield more than old ones but for example have a shorter growing period and thus be more profitable to the cultivator. Plant breeding needs a greater orientation to maximising the cultivator's net income, which is by no means necessarily the same thing as maximising per acre yields with each crop planted.[90]

Among the factors contributing to the low productivity in agriculture the first place is occupied by insecure water-supply. Old and new varieties alike, especially when fertilisers are used, are responsive to well-regulated water. It is estimated that of a total of 138 million hectares of land under cultivation, some 82 million have good irrigation potential;[91] yet by the end of the Fourth Plan period (1969–74), only about 43·5 million hectares were actually irrigated. In the Fifth Plan (prior to the 1975 revision) the irrigation of a further 12·2 million hectares was provided for. It is not possible to insulate agriculture from variations in the monsoon anything like completely – apart from all else, when the monsoon fails, rivers, irrigation channels and underground water tables will themselves lack water. Nevertheless irrigation affords considerable protection against crop failure. It is clear that the value of irrigation investment has been under-estimated in the past: if the calculation looks only at the return in terms of additional agricultural output, it may not always seem particularly favourable by comparison with other investments. But the cost has also to be reckoned in relation to the price of food imports when domestic crops fail, and the waste of famine relief expenditure. When large areas of India spend more in a drought year on famine relief than on irrigation in the previous five years together, one senses that something is wrong – especially when the authorities are looking for employment-creating investments in rural areas. In fact both for major and minor irrigation there remains an enormous amount to be done; in the case of the latter there are large areas where the extent and character of underground water tables have not been surveyed – hydrological survey is in general an underdeveloped aspect of Indian agriculture. The full potential of existing irrigation schemes is far from being utilised and, as we have noted, in almost half the total irrigable area the main investments have yet to be made.

Another considerable area for useful change is that of tenurial and land reform. Where land is held on a share cropping tenancy and the landlord does not share the costs of production the tenant either has little incentive to raise productivity or, even if he has, inadequate resources and access to credit with which to do it. This is another of the important historical reasons for low productivity in agriculture. Given the state of land records we do not know for certain what share of land is held on various specific forms of tenancy let alone on what share of tenancies landlords participate in production costs, or tenurial disadvantages are in other ways mitigated. But it has been estimated that the amount of land held in tenancy is of the order of 25 per cent of all cultivated land and the proportion of tenancies which are of a character detrimental to productivity is thought to be large, if diminishing.[92] The amount of productive potential in land redistribution may actually be rather less than that to be expected from tenancy reform; the main purposes of land redistribution are equity and employment creation. This can be seen from the estimated distribution of landholdings: while it is true that a high proportion – possibly more than a half – of individual holdings suffer from size disabilities, the total area comprised by such holdings may be less than 20 per cent of all cultivated land[93] – the great majority of land (though not of holdings) is still in parcels of viable size. Nevertheless there is some gain in production to be expected from land reform.

It is now widely accepted that there is unlikely to be any considerable productive *cost* in land redistribution, in the long term at least (there may be some short term dislocation); studies since the 1950s have shown that only on the very smallest holdings is there any diminution of yield per acre; the greatest productivity is to be found not on the largest holdings but on medium sized ones. The most common explanation of this is that the smaller farms are more intensively worked and the size has to be very small indeed before this effect is outweighed by the disadvantages of smallness of scale.[94] It is also plausible that the larger holdings will have a higher proportion of land leased to tenants whose productivity is lower for reasons already noted. The combination of redistribution of large holdings, improved legal status of tenants and consolidation of fragmented holdings at the small end of the landholding scale could all make a possible contribution to per acre yields.

We have listed the main sources of potential agricultural progress. There are of course several others: the improvement of agricultural administration,[95] the expansion of credit, raising the quality of extension work, introduction of better farm management. There are also high-return investments to be made such as forestry, soil conservation, drainage, flood control, storage, marketing and processing of agricultural produce. With the exception of the new wheat varieties and above-average performance in other crops over limited areas, Indian yields are among the lowest to be found anywhere in the world; this itself indicates that there is ample scope for progress and it is clear that action on the fronts indicated could bring it about. The question is not so much whether it can be done but whether it will be done.

The first consideration relevant to that issue is whether the Government will make a much larger allocation of funds to agriculture. It is not a question of agriculture receiving say 80 or 90 per cent of productive investment; in any programme of agricultural expansion, transport, power and fertiliser production must all claim an important share of investment and these in turn necessitate related investments – quite apart from essential expenditures in other fields. But there is a considerable difference between an economic plan which speaks of food output growing at $4\frac{1}{2}$ per cent and allocates resources for it which, especially with only moderate determination to implement, on all historical evidence will not produce that growth, and a plan which starts off from the resolve to maximise rural employment and agricultural production and treats the rest of the investment pattern – strategic and other necessities apart – as a derivative. (It is not either a question of financial resources alone but also of giving to agriculture a greater share of the country's most able administrators.) The old arguments for import-substitution apply to such a strategy – the investment necessary to avoid having to import 5 million tonnes of food is likely to be smaller than that required for generating an additional net sum of $1 billion in foreign exchange – the potential cost of food imports in a bad year. And fields such as forestry have never been considered for their role in agricultural ecology instead of simply for the productive value of wood; where deforestation has been causing flooding the protective value of forestry investment is high. However, while we would argue that the return to investment in agriculture and related fields has been under-estimated even as measured by contribution to G.N.P., the case for a higher priority for agriculture does not rest on such arguments alone.

If the chief purpose of development is to generate higher incomes, it must presumably do so by benefiting those whose incomes are not already relatively high. It is now a commonplace observation that economic growth in many developing countries has brought little improvement of material conditions for the lowest income groups. The old argument that growth must come first and distribution later has largely been silenced; far from hampering growth indeed redistributive policies may make it happen more rapidly. And even if they do not, there are good grounds for adopting policies which maximise the rate of growth of the lowest income classes.[96] (These issues have been most cogently explored in a work jointly produced by members of the staff of the World Bank and the Institute of Development Studies in Sussex, *Redistribution with Growth*.[97]) Any such policies in India must be embodied predominantly in a rural strategy as we have argued – though that does not of course mean no policies for the acceleration of urban manufacturing employment. The urban poor will of course also benefit from increased output and reduced prices of agricultural commodities.

Although the case for 'agriculture first' is a strong one it by no means follows that it will be adopted. There are powerful interests pressing for continuation of the existing industrial priorities as reflected by the current distribution of Plan expenditures. And there will be those who argue that efforts to shift much greater resources into agriculture will be defeated by the nature of the agrarian problem itself – the very conditions which have defeated decades of attempts at accelerating rural development. These conditions are the social and economic structure of rural society and production and their relationship with Indian politics. The clearest case of this is land reform: the big landowners are well represented in the State governments whose constitutional responsibility it is to legislate land reform measures. For this reason most land ceiling legislation has left adequate loopholes to ensure that owners could maintain their large holdings under their own or their family members' names. Attempts to give tenants a more secure title to the land they work have been similarly thwarted when landowners consider them against their interests. Even if a tenant has improved rights at law, the landowner can threaten to dispossess him by force, by foreclosing debt, by involving him in legal proceedings which the landlord can and the tenant cannot afford and whose outcome the landlord may in any case be able to influence in his own favour. For these reasons a very large number of tenancies are on oral lease with no written agreement at all. The tenant knows where power lies and acquiesces; legal rights, even where they exist, are no help if they cannot be claimed. (It is interesting that the State which has done most for land and tenancy reform has been Kerala where also the extent of grassroots political organisation in the countryside is far greater than elsewhere.) We have already referred to the distortion of Community Development and Cooperative institutions by the interests of the powerful. These interests operate everywhere they can, perhaps most importantly among areas to which we have not yet alluded in this context – in water use. The big landowners not only have land of better quality; they are also more likely to have access to irrigation facilities, public or private; further it is usually important to have irrigation water turned on at the right time and the rich are more likely to enjoy the cooperation of the water engineer.[98] When there are new inputs, such as new seeds and fertilisers, the rich get them first; or, when they are in general demand but scarce, they obtain them when others cannot. And it is by no means always the case that they are paying higher prices which the less well-off cannot afford; on the contrary they often use their influence to appropriate a disproportionate share of subsidised inputs. They meanwhile provide credit to the less privileged at high rates of interest and use the power of the creditor to perpetuate their dominance. Debt is the key to many aspects of rural life.

The Government has made efforts other than through the Cooperative movement to improve rural credit, most notably by the nationalisation of domestic banks which had as one of its main aims the penetration of new strata of rural society with government credit. But its very success, including a high recovery rate of loans, indicates that it has not gone very far down the income scale: credit can only be recovered when there is collateral. Indeed it is commonly found that extending credit to very poor, indebted farmers within a stagnant rural economy is unlikely to produce much benefit. This has given rise to the slogan 'no loans without savings' – rural financial institutions which provide channels for the savings of the poor may be a prerequisite for satisfying their credit needs. And farm improvements which do not involve heavy prior cash investments are prerequisites for the poorer farmers being able to save.[99] The shortage of credit explains much rural behaviour – while investments exist with quite attractive rates of return in such things as storage facilities or improved farm equipment the investments are not made because there are other uses of funds with even higher returns: for the rich, lending to others at high rates once their basic family investments are taken care of; while the poor would use cheap credit to pay off old debts, or for consumption loans in hard times – such things as got them into debt in the first place.

One can see the prospects for rural development in terms of a minimum and a maximum strategy. The minimum strategy would accept the *status quo* and attempt development within it. Even here there is room for much movement with irrigation, new varieties, the use of price policy (especially to favour the growing of the most labour-intensive crops), rural works programmes – all the things which might be done to increase rural incomes and grow more produce while not necessarily making much impact on the distribution of incomes. Land consolidation would come into such a programme since it is something from which potentially all participants can gain – a positive sum game; and all the special schemes started in the early 1970s, suitably modified, directed at particular low income groups in rural areas.[100] The maximum programme would incorporate real implementation of tenancy reform and land redistribution, more fundamental measures for the provision of credit and services for small farmers (for even the most radical land reform would leave many holdings at sizes too small for economic ownership of some inputs), possibly new forms of organisation in which farmers could combine to promote the reduction of indebtedness if necessary by cancellation of debt. . . . In the maximum maximorum programme there would even be an end of caste, which is itself economically wasteful, requiring the duplication of some facilities, creating attitudes hostile to certain kinds of work and preventing valuable forms of cooperation. We discuss the politics of rural change in the last chapter. For now we conclude that there is much to be done without radical change which could have some impact on rural poverty. But the history of rural development hitherto has not yielded a very great deal for the poor and we suspect that, without radical change, whatever is done is likely to be less than is needed to accelerate the demographic transition.

Virgil was quite right to place Hunger and Poverty, personified, side by side in Hades – *malesuada Fames ac turpis Egestas*. There is no solution to the food and nutrition problem unless incomes as well as food output increase to meet the needs of the population. 1974 saw the most graphic demonstration of this with people dying of starvation actually in sight of rice which they could not afford to buy.[101] But the production question is important because it is involved in the question of the limits of population growth. (In principle if the food is there it may be possible to distribute it – though in practice this distribution depends on the Government's ability to procure food for low price distribution which is a politico-economic question. The sufferings of 1974 were in part due to the Government's inability to do just this, in the face of depleted stocks after the difficulties of 1973 and hoarding by farmers awaiting higher prices.) We shall not examine the problems of the immediate two or three years, but will confine ourselves to those of the medium term and the more distant future.

The food production aspect of population growth requires a period of sustained increase in food availability at the rate of about 4 per cent annually to allow for rising incomes, population growth and the backlog of unmet food needs. This rate would not be required indefinitely; if all went well there would first come a time when the income elasticity of demand for food went down to a very low level; and, when population ceased to grow, required growth in food output would be very modest. The Fifth Plan proposed growth targets of 4·7 per cent a year for agriculture as a whole which incorporated 4 per cent growth for food grains, 4·9 per cent growth for non-foodgrains and 5·8 per cent for livestock. If net sown area increases as planned, as a result of accelerated irrigation work, area growth could run at about one per cent a year (compared with 0·4 per cent currently). But not all of that increase in net sown area would be for foodgrains; indeed the Fifth Plan wants to reverse the trends of recent years in having non-foodgrains output move faster than foodgrains. Still yield increases of an average of 3 per cent a year have been sustained recently – thus even if most of the increase has to come from further improvements in yields, 4 per cent annual growth of foodgrains output does not seem over-optimistic. The scope for continuing expansion of wheat output at the recent pace may be limited but as we have noted there are good opportunities for expansion elsewhere. As well as a major programme of direct agricultural investment this will require heavy investment in power, fertilisers and other complementary inputs and infrastructural facilities[102] – but nothing beyond the country's capacity to afford provided, as we have said, that agriculture is given adequate priority.

One of the constraints on food output in 1974 was a shortage of fertilisers both in India and internationally. This added to the fears of famine often expressed in the press and elsewhere – but in fact the danger has been misunderstood and therefore exaggerated. The shortage had very little to do with the oil crisis; there is in fact an investment cycle in the world's fertiliser industry,[103] and the mid 1970s have stretched existing functioning capacity to the point of considerable increase in fertiliser prices. But capacity already under construction or complete which will come on stream in the current period will ease the situation. The situation could be eased still further if there were an international fertiliser pool which could transfer fertilisers to countries in need as recommended by the 1974 World Food Conference. The increment to food output from an additional ton of fertiliser is several times higher in developing countries than in the rich countries, simply because the latter are already closer to a maximum economic use of fertiliser, while the former are far below it. Thus India's fertiliser use is still only of the order of 2·5 million nutrient tons a year[104] or an average of less than 20 kg per hectare compared with more than 450 kg per hectare used in the world's most fertiliser-intensive agricultures such as the Netherlands and New Zealand, or close to 150 kg per hectare in the U.K. Provided complementary irrigation is available, there is obviously very considerable yield potential in additional fertiliser use especially with new fertiliser-responsive varieties.

Of the Fifth Plan's agricultural targets, the more difficult ones to meet are those other than foodgrains. Non-foodgrains yield growth has been in the region of one per cent annually in recent years; to bring output growth to the requisite 4·9 per cent per year, even if yield growth is doubled to 2 per cent, will require 2·9 per cent of that 4·9 per cent growth to come from increases in area – and that could only be obtained at the expense of foodgrains area unless large quantities of additional land are to be brought under the plough. There are also other problems of balance within agriculture: part of the increase in cereal production has been at the expense of pulses, the per capita availability of which has declined since the 1950s[105] – these have traditionally formed an important part of the diet of the poor being relatively inexpensive and also a good protein source. And there are regional and climatic area imbalances: it is much easier to raise yields on rain-fed and irrigable land. Yet much of India's land will never have good water-supply and, in the next years, considerable efforts of research and investment will have to be devoted to improving dry land agriculture – as indeed the Fifth Plan proposed.[106]

Altogether, while medium-term agricultural performance may not reach the targets of growth in excess of 4 per cent annually, there is good reason to be confident of the possibility of average growth in excess of 3 per cent – this would permit both some improvement in average nutrition and the building up of stocks to mitigate the bad years. Even this rate of growth requires continuing research and deployment of massive resources, but it is perfectly feasible – with the exception, we must remind ourselves, of any serious deterioration of average rainfall. The authors of *Famine 1975*[107] looked right in 1975 but wrong in 1976. If they do not continue to be wrong, it will either be the fault of the weather or of failures by the Government – it will not be the result of the inability of Indian soil to feed India's numbers. Our own conclusion is that the worst result in the rest of the 1970s with any likelihood of occurring is a continuation of the experience of its opening years – and that is, as we have suggested, quite bad enough with no reduction in mortality and little redress of acute poverty throughout the country. The best result would be the achievement of the Fifth Plan's targets and the continuation of similar progress for a further ten years after which a slower rate of increase could be adequate.

What of the longer-term future? Is India condemned to have its population growth one day drastically curtailed by tremendous mortality peaks stemming from gross inadequacy of food? We do not believe so: provided that technical progress plays the part that it has hitherto there seems no overwhelming reason to postulate any failure of agriculture on a grand scale. As we have noted, within the existing technology there is enormous scope for raising output. If food were distributed more equitably, it would in any case not have to rise so fast: in a 'good' year even today the per capita availability of food grains is not far below the minimum dietary requirements – it is owing to maldistribution that so many go hungry. But when all available irrigation water is utilised, fertiliser, pesticides and other current inputs are all used at maximum economic levels, existing plant varieties and farming practices are adopted – then a stage is reached at which additional yield must come from further technological advance. Such advance does not arrive automatically, as Swaminathan has underlined.[108] But it can be made to arrive and some of its character is already apparent. In the developed countries agricultural yields have been rising for at least the last eighty years[109] and few would suggest that they cannot continue to do so. India is nowhere near the state of productivity of the world's most advanced agriculture except in some of its wheat areas. And there are potential innovations that will almost certainly contribute to rapid improvement in future: it is remarkable how little is known about many aspects of the growth of plants, and soil chemistry and bacteriology and plant physiology contain considerable promise. The issue of nitrogen fixation alone shows this – research on the breeding of plants and the management of soils to enhance the plant's capacity to absorb nitrogen can on its own make a considerable contribution.[110] It may soon be possible to breed bacteria which will assist this process.[111] Altogether one can hope with good reason for continued progress in agricultural productivity for as long as population is likely to grow.

This is not the same thing as saying that India will never suffer food crises. The coincidence of bad weather conditions at home and shortages abroad occurred in 1974 and can do so again. And we emphasise that much depends on the continued and determined efforts of the Government, both directly in agricultural investment and research and indirectly in dealing with the adverse ecological consequences of population growth, most notably at present in forestry. Also the less that is offered by technical advances, the more necessary it will be to implement those reforms which are socially and politically most difficult for contemporary governments given their orientation and sources of support. And finally there are possible disasters other than the weather to which we have not alluded–plant diseases and pests in particular–which could wreak major havoc. All these dangers exist. But the balance of probability, at least until we are more certain about rainfall trends, seems to lie with at least a continuation of recent performance and an excellent possibility of improving on it. To take the dangers lightly would be to assist their realisation. But to predict an inevitable catastrophe in the food-population balance seems to be indulging a taste for the horrific rather than appreciating the lessons of history.

MACROECONOMICS OF DISTRIBUTION

We have already alluded to the case for redistributive growth. But it is worth a little more thought. It may be objected against the employment emphasis we have outlined that it raises current consumption at the expense of savings and therefore future growth. Part of the case in favour of our argument is that current consumption seems always to be being sacrificed for a future which never arrives. But there are grounds for believing that an emphasis of this kind will actually raise the long-run rate of growth of per capita incomes. The early stages of planning in India deliberately frustrated consumption – one of the alleged merits of the heavy industry strategy was that its products could not be consumed. But the combination of this strategy with the foreign exchange regime and industrial licensing policy has been to create a modern sector producing goods for the consumption of the rich, with mostly high pay for those employed in the sector and relatively little employment. Protection has further made the domestic more attractive than the foreign market with the result that India has been one of the low labour cost countries which has had little share in the enormous recent world growth of low labour cost exports. An export oriented strategy would have encouraged labour-intensive production. Even if India wanted heavy industry, it did not have to fabricate all the equipment for it domestically.

As noted there has been little change in the sectoral distribution of employment and the extent of unemployment. We have not attempted to assess how far this is due to population growth and how far to other things – that would be a vast if not impossible, enterprise. But we can give some idea of the policy choices that have caused the slow growth of employment. Undoubtedly the main one has been the pattern of investment stressing heavy industry and manufacturing. One study has examined the employment generated in India per unit of final demand in a 77-sector model of the economy. Of the first 30 sectors when all were listed in order of employment potential, 27 were agricultural.[112] Planners of the early Five Year Plans may have believed that they were creating less employment currently for the sake of more employment in the future – but that future has not yet come and indeed will not for many years. We have not attempted in this book so far to project the future growth of the labour force. We have projected the population of what might be termed labour force age, but to derive the future labour force from that is exceptionally hazardous. Many aspects of development affect the participation rate: they include education, urban development and employment opportunities themselves. In the course of India's development there might be some general expectation that participation rates would rise over all: the proportions kept out of the labour force by educational advance might increase, but this will mainly affect the under-15s who may be omitted from projections for the future. The main source of change could be in female participation as the change in female status and education is gradually reflected in the employment structure. (Participation rates of men in the main working age groups are already very high.) But for many women in rural areas withdrawal from the labour force is a sign of family prosperity and may to some extent balance increased participation by others. The observed changes in participation rates of course are strongly influenced by employment opportunities: while the measures commonly derive from surveys which ask whether people are working or seeking work, one cannot really tell how many more would be seeking work if there were more desirable jobs available.

Although the 1971 Census showed lower participation rates than that of 1961 definitional changes are almost certainly the reason. Thus the N.S.S. 27th Round (1972 – 3) showed rates higher than 1961.[113] It is reasonable to conclude that there has been no clear trend in the recent past and therefore our labour force projections will be based on constant age specific participation rates for both sexes. (The rates used are actually 1961 figures from the Dantwala Committee Report[114] adjusted to give the N.S.S. 29th Round total proportion in the labour force; the correspondence is so close that the adjustment is quite small.) The population projections used are those discussed in Chapter 2.

The effects of both fertility and mortality differences can be seen in these projections. The labour force is actually larger the smaller the population in 1976 and 1986 because higher mortality is reducing the labour force age group in the projections in which fertility is higher. But by 2001 it is Projection (c) which has the largest labour force. In fact there is very little difference in labour force growth in any of these projections; the main difference between them is in the base of the population pyramid, the

TABLE 4.4 Projected population and labour force 1976 – 2001

	Projection (a) $F_6 M_2$			Projection (b) $F_3 M_1$			Projection (c) $F_4 M_{1.5}$		
	Pop'n	Labour force	%	Pop'n	Labour force	%	Pop'n	Labour force	%
1976	619·2	248·8	40·2	619	248·1	40·1	617·7	248·3	40·2
1986	720·0	322·4	44·8	745	318·3	42·7	736·3	319·1	43·4
2001	859·2	429·4	50·0	921·9	428·5	46·5	886·7	432·1	48·7

number of children below age 15. A large share of the 2001 labour force is already born by 1976 and, since both mortality and fertility are lower in each successive projection, there is not a great difference in the increase in the size of the 15 plus age groups resulting from births during the projection period. Obviously in other possible projections these features could change; but the main lesson of the ones presented here is that likely reductions in population growth promise relatively little reduction in labour force growth. One would see more variation between projections which differed only in the fertility assumption. But even then, because of the past pattern of growth, the important fact would still remain, that labour force growth will exceed population growth for a substantial period. Thus in Projection (c) from 1996 – 2001 while population grows at 1·25 per cent annually, the labour force grows at 1·78 per cent; even in the implausibly optimistic Projection (a), for the same five years, population is growing at 1·2 per cent but the labour force by 1·51 per cent. (It should be stressed that we have only explored population variants, and thus it is mainly the *relative* magnitudes of labour force size that are of interest. A different time path for participation rates could alter the absolute size of the projected labour force considerably.)

The implications for the task of employment creation that lies ahead are somewhat daunting. Under any of these projections if all the increments to the labour force are to join the ranks of the employed, some 180 million jobs must be created in the twenty-five years from 1976 – 2001 or an average of 7·2 million jobs annually. Depending on one's estimate of the backlog of unemployment or under-employment, and the speed with which the backlog might be eliminated, this could rise to as much as 8 million or more annually. The time-path for this average does not alter much under any of the projections, though under Projection (c) the absolute annual increments to the labour force grow fastest and begin to fall off in 1991 – 6, while in Projection (b) they grow up till 1995 and only begin to decline thereafter. The higher the estimate of existing unemployment and the earlier the target of removing the backlog is set, the greater becomes the task for the immediate years.

The imperatives of employment creation give the clearest indications of the desirable directions for future economic strategy. Only in the twenty-first century will the numbers added to the labour force each year begin to fall off substantially. The only crumb of comfort is that, with a declining share of dependents in the population, a higher level of unemployment may be economically – if not politically – tolerable. But the needs of employment creation do appear more manageable as time goes on if the number of labour force entrants remains more or less constant or declines while economic capacity increases. The former results from our assumptions about population growth and labour force participation rates. But the latter rests on expectations that the future of economic growth is going to be like the past. There is no settled view among economists and others about the long-run prospects – opinions vary from the sanguine to the doom-laden. India will long require increasing foreign trade to complement its domestic resources. If for one reason or another the international economy does not continue to expand in a manner that permits this, India would face severe difficulties. There may also be difficulties arising from domestic constraints. We do not see much virtue in speculating about this more distant future. The debate surrounding the Club of Rome calculations suggests that the computer can be made to yield hopeful or hopeless answers depending on the assumptions of the programmer. But the next fifteen years look difficult enough and whatever is said now about the twenty-first century is not likely to remain valid by 1990. What we *can* say now is that the greater the success in improving the lot of the Indian poor in this century, the less rapidly their numbers are likely to be growing in the next.

The change in recent development thinking towards employment-oriented policies only rests in part on the recognition that economic growth in the Third World has done little for the poor and that past definitions of development have been weighted against them. There is also a belief that a reduction in growth previously attributed to high consumption policies may have been exaggerated. The actual impact on savings of the shift in incomes may be smaller than was once believed. The demand pattern likely to arise from a shift of consumption towards the currently poor could require less foreign exchange – their needs are for the types of goods which can be produced domestically. And the growing market for these goods could induce a more productive use of the savings that do exist – if there are profits to be made in supplying the consumption needs of the poor, the private sector would move in this direction. There are humane as well as economic arguments – even if there is some cost in terms of growth, it is arguable that a society which provides work for those who seek it makes people's lives more meaningful.

There is of course also a great deal to be said for utilising that society's most abundant resource – labour. For all these reasons the belief in employment-oriented strategies is not just the latest fashion in development studies but a fundamental change of approach whose full consequences have still to be elaborated. We have already referred to

Redistribution with Growth and will return to its political aspects in the next chapter. But in our view an important opportunity was missed in this work; while mentioning the population issue the book did not incorporate it fully into the rest of the analysis. This is unfortunate since there are few more important themes in development studies today than the uniting of the economic arguments about growth and distribution with the demographers' findings about the relations between income distribution and fertility. One must not exaggerate the potency of the latter. There is no guarantee that making the poor better off will lead to any rapid fertility reduction. But in any society where fertility is declining, it is hard to believe that improving the living conditions of the poor will fail to assist the acceleration of that decline.

Population growth in India itself works to worsen the distribution of incomes. If the poor have more children than the rich and their children, having a disadvantageous start in life, are more likely to be themselves poor than the children of higher income groups, that by itself constitutes a mechanism for worsening income distribution. More important however than any such abstract argument is the way in which such things work themselves out in the context of Indian society. We have tried to depict a process of this kind in our discussion of village behaviour above – pressure on the land, distribution through inheritance, and the creation of a growing class of landless families through excessive fragmentation, debt or disaster. (The cycle of deprivation is less complex for the urban poor and we shall not dwell on it.) It is a curious fact that little work has been done on the relations between population growth and land ownership – in all the research for this book the author has hardly come across a single valuable study devoted to the subject.[115] It would be interesting to know at what point in history villages in various regions ran out of unclaimed land to cultivate, when the squeeze of land shortage began and what manifold effects it has had. Certainly in parts of the sub-continent it began a long time ago – witnesses of the repeated cyclones in the Bay of Bengal might wonder why people live in such low-lying flood-prone areas as the Bengal delta: the answer is population pressure – but it began in the eighteenth century.[116]

The reversal of such processes is not just a matter of giving incomes to the poor, and certainly not necessarily one of giving them high incomes – rather, of creating the conditions of at least a minimally decent economic life, with better prospects of child survival, and an educational system that encourages less traditional attitudes and also is an important path to material rewards. Particularly important is the enhancement of the status of women – as long as women know little beyond the household and the family farm and have no independence of decision they are more likely to find fulfilment in childbearing. We think of policies for employment and distribution very much in this sense, not just as the creation of more cash and working hours for the wage earner. If better policies do succeed in these goals, the fact that they may involve some cost in terms of the growth of total incomes could become relatively insignificant: if fertility decline is accelerated, the growth in income per head could well be greater on the redistributive path than on the higher-total-income less-distribution path. If maximisation of the growth of per capita incomes is what is sought, distributive strategies may be more efficient than that prescribed by the old fashioned view of 'growth first and distribution later'.

It is important to realise how low the incomes of the poor are likely to remain even under optimistic assumptions and how this may be related to fertility levels. In our Projection $F_4M_{1.5}$ a total fertility rate of 2·5 is reached by 2001. This is not far from replacement fertility. But if national income were growing at 5 per cent a year in real terms for the thirty years prior to that, income per head under those population assumptions would grow at just under 3·4 per cent. If the poorest 40 per cent of population started at $55 per head in 1971, they would have $150 per head by 2001 with no change in income distribution. (For the sake of clarity we have rounded 1971 income per head to $100 and generously assumed the share of the four lowest deciles in total income to be 22 per cent.) For total fertility then to average 2·5 children per couple either the better-off classes would have to have fertility well below that level or the poor would have reached it at income levels which, by current international experience, have never been associated with such reproductive restraint. Even if the share of the poorest 40 per cent rose to 40 per cent of total income by 2001 – a highly unlikely eventuality – their per capita income would still be only $270.

This is merely an illustrative calculation but it is highly instructive for, whatever plausible assumptions one makes, the picture cannot be greatly altered. *If the demographic transition is to arrive at all soon in the poor countries of the world, it will be without the benefits of living standards remotely resembling those of countries where it has occurred already.* It would be very wrong to expect fertility in a single country over time to follow the kind of path relating fertility and income which might be derived from international comparisons at a point of time. This is not the case for mortality as has been shown: a country with $x per capita income can expect a higher life expectancy today than another at the same $x per capita income ten years ago. For the kinds of fertility decline projected in this book, the practice of birth control must make almost unprecedented progress at low incomes. The example of Kerala shows what is possible; but that example has long historical roots and must be widely repeated in India in a much shorter time if it is to be the pattern for the country as a whole. The reader who believes that even the high population projections of Chapter 2 are excessively pessimistic should reconsider them in this light.

Our common theme has been that it is not income itself that is associated with fertility decline so much as specific aspects of development; but higher incomes may be essential if those forms of development are to be widely enjoyed. (It is clear also that family planning programmes have a vastly greater part to play in bringing down fertility than they did in the historical transitions of the rich countries.) We can thus reaffirm the necessity for reducing the disparities in social advancement both between different classes in the population and different geographical regions. Failure to achieve this will leave both material and demographic backwardness among significant sections of the population and defeat any hopes of early stabilisation of its numbers.

CONCLUSIONS

Discussions of the impact of population growth on development often generate more heat than light. It seems wise therefore to state clearly the main points we have made, and also those we have not made. We have argued that the current rate of population growth is reducing the rate of growth of income per head but has not so far been responsible for any substantial reduction in the rate of growth of total income. We attribute to the additional population of the 1950s and 1960s some positive contribution to total income growth although, as the volume of under-employed labour increases, it has become harder to believe that such contribution is now at all sizable. And we have claimed that India has already run into diminishing returns in agriculture – perhaps only temporarily – which may already have affected the growth of total income adversely and certainly will if technology does not reverse the trend.

We have observed that the economy is failing to deliver the 'correlates of declining fertility' with any rapidity to the mass of the people – that nexus of better health, education and employment prospects which is the opposite of poverty. We have *not* argued that this failure is due more than partially to population growth itself. Poverty has been the common lot in India for centuries. And policies could have been pursued in the last twenty-five years – not to speak of the two hundred before – which would have made far greater inroads on poverty, even with population growing as it has been. In particular modern India has adopted industrial policies, a foreign exchange regime and an under-emphasized rural strategy which have resulted in grave inadequacies in employment creation. It would be absurd to deny that population growth has made India's difficult economic situation even more difficult – and this would have been so whatever the policies followed. And it would be less than just if we did not credit the Government with its truly immense achievements in making the progress that it has in the face of all the obstacles. But a major change of direction is needed if that progress is to be accelerated.

To say that diminishing returns in agriculture have been reached is not to say that India cannot continue to feed its growing numbers, only that doing so has become increasingly costly. The cost situation can be reversed by future technical change and, whether it is or not, there is no inherent reason for India to run into growing food shortages – though such shortages may recur because of deteriorating weather or because of insufficient research and investment in rural development, including those investments which protect against adverse weather. The food problem requires both the production of more food and its better distribution by putting more purchasing power in the hands of those who presently lack it. The population problem requires better health and education which also depend on income. The generation of employment is therefore the prime economic necessity; and, since the potential for creating urban industrial employment is limited, in the short run the case for a much greater stress on employment-oriented rural development is inescapable. The belief that this would reduce the growth of total income rests on arguments which are not entirely satisfactory. And, even if redistributive strategies do reduce total income growth, they are likely to have a compensating beneficial effect on the growth of per capita incomes by their impact on fertility.

5 The Future of Indian Society

> The evils which were endured with patience so long as they were inevitable
> seem intolerable as soon as a hope can be entertained of escaping from them.
> De Tocqueville, *L'Ancien Régime et la Révolution* (tr. Reeve).

Economic development of a kind which raises the material conditions of life not of some, but of all, has not been occurring in India. Government planning and policy have not brought it about; nor has it happened spontaneously. It is the thesis of this book that both the population and the development problems of India have essentially the same solution – employment-intensive growth which must in the early stages at least be predominantly rural. That this has been prevented fundamentally by the alignment of social, political and economic forces at every level in the country is neither a novel nor a radical thesis. Some would say it is not even a true one and would give more emphasis in explaining failures of development to such factors as religion, climate, native character and *mores*. But, while it is not possible to deny their relevance, few scholars who have examined Indian development in any depth would attribute the major share of causal significance to them.[1] Examples are not legion of Indian cultivators or businessmen voluntarily foregoing highly profitable opportunities free from excessive risk, in recent times at least. While popular views dwell on those aspects of the Hindu religion which stress resignation and self-denial, it is less often remembered that injunctions to asceticism are in the main confined to the later stages of life and that, in earlier stages, the search for prosperity is virtuous in the householder. Perhaps the major example of a cultural attitude inimical to development is the distaste for most forms of farm work of the Brahmin landowner which has led to much inefficiency and waste; but even that is set in perspective when one remembers that a huge share of non-Brahmin-owned land has long been and still is farmed under conditions of tenancy which offer little incentive to the tenant to make improvements. At higher levels of course politicians and administrators are not dominated by religious beliefs whatever else may motivate them. At the most one might say the prevailing culture leads to a certain lack of enterprise and initiative – but that too has an economic as well as a cultural explanation.

In pre-British times almost the whole Indian economy, apart from a small layer of craftsmen and merchants, consisted of an inefficient agriculture taxed by rulers and their minions to live in luxury, build monuments and fight wars. The British attempted, with little success, to create a landed gentry with a greater stake in agricultural efficiency; their reforms only modestly altered the lot of many of the tenantry. The abolition of the *zamindari* system by the Government of newly independent India reduced the holdings of the biggest landlords; those and other efforts of agrarian reform enlarged the class of small and middle peasants. But a large share of agriculture still presents the same picture of the exploiting landlord and the disadvantaged tenant and many of those who have their own land can only get credit to make improvement on punitive terms. As long as labour is cheap and land is scarce and expensive the big landowner can have his own way. It was into this socio-economic structure that the Government poured its resources with the Community Development and Cooperative movements; the landed interests controlled the *panchayats*, or village democracies, and the Cooperative administrations at the local level, and appropriated the lion's share of these resources for themselves. Where new productive inputs became more widely accessible, with output increasing greatly and labour becoming relatively scarce, many sections of the rural community prospered – these were the developments of the late 1960s in the main and of some irrigation work not associated with new plant varieties in earlier decades. But such has not been the experience of most of rural India.

In our discussion of the process of rural change, we expressed some puzzlement about how long various trends could continue including increasing fragmentation of holdings and landlessness, the worsening economic position of the poor both relatively, and for some it seems, absolutely, and the continuing growth of population with no fast-growing urban employment to absorb the rural excess. But this process has been going on for a long time. And since India's rural poor know very well who their oppressors are, one might wonder why they have not long ago risen up and done something about it themselves. Our first task in this chapter will be to consider the history of revolt in India. If those who govern do not improve the lot of the people, can the people create a government that will?

REVOLT AND REVOLUTION

Students of revolution have tried to discern the similarities in the revolutionary processes in various countries that have succeeded in forcing changes in the class basis of power.[2] One of the few things they are all agreed on is that misery itself does not generate revolution. 'It is not always by going from bad to worse that a country falls into revolution', as de Tocqueville said in a much quoted passage.[3] But certainly the succession of rural revolts that have occurred in India have been grounded in economic distress. Since distress is and has always been so widespread, what most requires explanation is why major rural revolts have been so few in number and so limited in their extent and results. In the nineteenth century there were hardly more than two of any consequence, the Deccan riots of 1875 and the Moplah Rebellions of 1836 – 98; in the twentieth century the most notable have been the Satara Rebellion of 1919 – 21; peasant revolts in Tanjore and Kerala; the Telangana incident and the Tebhaga and Naxalite movements in West Bengal. (We exempt from this list activities directed mainly against British rule some of which had the character of rural unrest, not least in association with the Mutiny of 1857.)

The so-called Deccan Riots took place in the districts of Poona and Ahmednagar and consisted mainly of attacks on the homes and property of money lenders. As such they have attracted the attention of historians as a genuine protest movement of the oppressed against their masters. On close examination they do not appear all that impressive, certainly not as precursors of a revolutionary tradition. The rioting was aimed most particularly at money lenders who were not of the local community, Marwaris and others; they were the work of ordinary cultivators with little organisation or leadership caught in the squeeze of new, excessive taxes imposed by the British, high prices of food and other commodities, and the failure of the money lenders to help them except on onerous terms. The rioters seemed to have had few goals other than to destroy the money lenders' written contracts – almost no one was hurt and no long-term demands were made. The movement stopped as rapidly as it started, though for decades afterwards it was well remembered and the British made some efforts – mostly vain – both in the Deccan and elsewhere to cope with the problems of rural credit.[4] The Moplah Rebellions in the Malabar District of Kerala were mainly Muslim tenant revolts against Hindu landlords. There were twenty-five separate episodes over a period of sixty years; landlords were killed as well as British officials and soldiers. While these revolts had their roots in exploitation they were particularly animated by communal feeling. This is one of the themes of Indian rural revolts, which only rarely absorbed people who had nothing in common but their oppression; they have nearly always contained elements of ethno-religious, nationalistic or tribal antagonism.

The nineteenth century saw many other forms of rural unrest of a minor character. Dacoits abounded, many of them with that 'Robin Hood' flavour of robbing the rich to help the poor identified by Eric Hobsbawm as a feature of numerous rural societies.[5] One of the best known was 'Honya's gang' which carried out its depredations in the Western Ghats in 1874. (It too was mainly supported by a tribal community.)[6] There were numerous other incidents of attacks on landlords, moneylenders and tax officials such as those by the Santals in Bihar in 1855, the Indigo Disturbances in Bengal of 1859 – 60 or the Punjab revolts of the 1890s.[7] Many of these took violent form after cultivators refused to pay rents or taxes and resisted attempts at coercion or alienation of land. Such episodes continued into the twentieth century. Examination of them is one of the main ways to understand the possibilities of radical change in India. We have given this section the title 'Revolt and revolution', the briefest way to characterise movements with limited objectives of revenge or redressal of grievances as opposed to those which aim to transform government and society. In a famous exchange Louis XVI said, when informed of the fall of the Bastille, *'C'est une révolte.'* *'Non, Sire'*, the Duc de la Rochefoucauld replied, *'c'est une révolution.'* The latter may have used the word more closely to its etymological origin related to natural phenomena, the movement of the planets. If that was all he meant, he was being unconsciously prophetic.[8] In the early twentieth century Indian peasants were still engaged in revolt.

An example is the Satara Rebellion of 1919 – 21. Satara District in Maharashtra became the focus of an anti-Brahmin movement and of the Satyashodak Samaj, an anti-religious group. Tenants and service castes, frustrated in attempts at rent strikes and other forms of non-cooperation, moved to other traditional measures, forcibly harvesting landlords' crops, looting and burning their houses, beating them and chasing them from the village. The landlords were Marwaris and predominantly Brahmins; the revolt was both over land and tenants' rights and the Brahmins' religious dominance and social and economic power, which was contested in cooperatives and local boards of the District. The presence of the Satyashodak Samaj was a new feature giving the peasants upper class and intellectual support. Like others the rebellion faded out, in this case without even any particularly strong government action.[9] During this same period serious disturbances occurred in Kerala. The following account is taken from Gough (1969).[10]

The first modern politically-sponsored revolt took shape under the Congress-Khilafat movement of 1920 – 21. Guided by the Indian National Congress and the Muslim League, Kerala's new middle class of students, rich peasants, middle ranking merchants, and professionals encouraged cultivators and handmill workers to engage in non-violent strikes and boycott of British goods. The goals were Home Rule for India and for Turkey, at that time struggling against European hegemony. The British responded with violent repression. At this, poor Muslim tenants, heirs of the nineteenth century rebels, organized in village assemblies round their religious leaders and with knives, spears, clubs and home-made firearms drove out or killed both Hindu and Muslim landlords, government servants, and police. Muslim leaders of middle peasant rank took over the government of 220 villages for several months. They killed five to six hundred landlords, police, and others who had aided the British military. Once violent revolt occurred, Congress leaders under Gandhi withdrew their support. The British defeated the movement and deported or executed many rebels. About 10,000 died in this rebellion.

It is from this era that rural – and urban – movements began to be associated with political forces acting on a wider political stage, mainly of course against the British in association with the Independence struggle until 1947. The Indian Left was divided between those who were willing to cooperate with the Congress Party and those who wanted not only Home Rule but radical change. In Kerala in particular Communists were active in stimulating peasant action in the 1930s and 1940s and disruption of the wartime State adminstration, except for the period after 1941 when the Soviet Union entered the war and Indian Communists agreed to collaborate with the British and the war effort. After Independence Communist-led agitations had limited successes in Tanjore and Kerala, for the first time with major participation by landless labourers, many of them harijans. Unions were formed and India's first rural strikes by labourers took place on cash crop farming estates in Kerala in 1947. In eastern Tanjore peasants drove out landlords and occupied several villages for a time in 1948. But now it was the Congress Government's turn to overcome subversion and by 1950 most of the revolts in South India were suppressed.[11]

The three most considerable of these more 'political' events were the Tebhaga, Telangana and Naxalite movements. The Tebhaga movement was an action of share croppers against landlords in Bengal, demanding a reduction of the landlords' share from one-half to one-third. It lasted from 1946 – 7 and was organised by the Communist dominated Kisan Sabha; the Government was forced to give some assurances to the share croppers, as many as 6,000,000 of whom in nineteen Districts may have been involved according to one account.[12] Peasant committees took power in many villages, administering justice and village affairs. But the movement collapsed in 1947 when the Government turned against it. Before the more recent Naxalite actions the most revolutionary peasant movement in India was that of Telangana, in Andhra Pradesh, which began in 1946. It had a guerilla army, also Communist organised, of about 2000 regulars and about 10,000 in village squáds at its height. Landlords and local bureaucrats were killed or driven out, land was seized and redistributed, peasant 'soviets' were established in villages and integrated with a central organisation controlling an area, according to Communist claims, of about 1500 square miles and 3000 villages. The movement was finally extinguished, not without difficulty, by the Indian army in 1951 but the spirit had gone out in 1948 when the army first intervened.

The events of the 1960s have been somewhat different in nature from those that came earlier. Before discussing them some conclusions can be drawn from those described already. We have not mentioned every single noteworthy occasion of rural revolt. A fuller list would include the

Champaran (Bihar) Satyagraha led by Gandhi in 1917 – 18; the successful Canal Cess Movement of 1939 and the *hat tola* (market levy) agitation of the same period (Bengal); a long series of small and unsystematic outbreaks of violence in Uttar Pradesh; the Warlis in Maharashtra in 1946 – 7. . . . But we have covered the main ones. There are two things to be explained. The number of rural revolts may be somewhat misleading; for most of the last century and a half the vast majority of India's villages have been untouched by organised action on the part of the oppressed. What accounts for this stability? And what accounts for those revolts which did take place? We could do worse than to start with some observations of Karl Marx. After quoting a long passage from an official report, describing the persistence of Indian village organisation through centuries of change, Marx described how British commercialism disrupted the villages' way of life which was based on agriculture and domestic crafts. 'English interference . . . by blowing up their economic basis . . . thus produced the greatest, and, to speak the truth, the only *social* revolution ever heard of in Asia.' What follows deserves quotation in full, with all its characteristic vigour and exaggeration:

> Now, sickening as it must be to human feeling to witness those myriads of industrious patriarchal and inoffensive social organizations disorganized and dissolved into their units, thrown into a sea of woes, and their individual members losing at the same time their ancient form of civilization and their hereditary means of subsistence, we must not forget that these idyllic village communities, inoffensive though they may appear, had always been the solid foundation of Oriental despotism, that they restrained the human mind within the smallest possible compass, making it the unresisting tool of super-stition, enslaving it beneath traditional rules, depriving it of all grandeur and historical energies. We must not forget the barbarian egotism which, concentrating on some miserable patch of land, had quietly witnessed the ruin of empires, the perpetration of unspeakable cruelties, the massacre of the population of large towns, with no other consideration bestowed upon them than on natural events, itself the helpless prey of any aggressor who deigned to notice it at all. We must not forget that this undignified, stagnatory, and vegetative life, that this passive sort of existence evoked on the other's part, in con-tradistinction, wild, aimless, unbounded forces of destruction, and rendered murder itself a religious rite in Hindustan. We must not forget that these little communities were contaminated by distinctions of caste and by slavery, that they subjugated man to external circumstances instead of elevating man to be the sovereign of circumstances, that they transformed a self-developing social state into never changing natural destiny, and thus brought about a brutalizing worship of nature, exhibiting its degradation in the fact

that man, the sovereign of nature, fell down on his knees in adoration of Hanuman, the monkey, and Sabbala, the cow.[13]

Virtually every author who has commented on the agrarian unrest of the nineteenth century agrees that its most general cause was the introduction under the British of new commercial relations in agriculture, as well as new economic impositions, which began to break up both the economic life and the social ties that had so long endured in rural India. What Marx most exaggerated was the degree to which the old order had been shaken. The British certainly introduced many radical changes making possible the sale of land, legalising new forms of tenure, introducing new cash crops, ruining the livelihood of domestic spinners and weavers and much more. But the social character of Indian villages absorbed a good deal of it. As the source quoted by Marx – a report to the British Parliament of 1812 – put it: 'The boundaries of the villages have been but seldom altered; and though the villages themselves have been injured, and even desolated by war, famine or disease, the same name, the same limits, the same interests and even the same families, have continued for ages. The inhabitants gave themselves no trouble about the breaking up and divisions of kingdoms; while the village remains entire they care not to what power it is transferred, or to what sovereign it devolves; its internal economy remains unchanged.' What Marx went on to say about the village permitting 'Oriental despotism' – the rule of the Moguls – has continued even up to the present; despite roads, railways and modern means of communication, villages remain very much self-contained. This has been a powerful factor in rural inertia. It is gradually ceasing to be so; but in the past rural agitation was very difficult to organise. This was not only true because of poor communications between villages; the village itself was also difficult to mobilise.

The bonds which held rural society together were not dissolved, as Marx expected, by the advent of the steam engine, Lancashire cottons or even a high-minded administration attempting to apply the principles of classical economics to Indian agriculture. The chief of them was, and still is, caste. Caste not only determines who a person may marry and take food with and with whom contact is not polluting; it is also strongly related to occupations. In Kerala and elsewhere tenant farmers of different castes even had different forms of tenancy.[14] Caste and economic status reinforced each other. The lowest castes saw themselves as inevitably fixed in their situation; religious sanction strengthened the deference of the lowly and the feeling of entitlement to deference of the superior. (In the first paragraph of this chapter the view was expressed, rather baldly, that religious belief has not been a major influence on modern development; to the extent that caste is to be thought of as religion that view obviously requires serious qualification.) For members of a lower caste to take arms against a higher required the severest goading; for different castes to unite in a common cause – when they had one – was extremely difficult. It is hard for outsiders to appreciate the significance of caste – those invisible barriers which hold people apart in an extreme form of human separation.

To the isolation of the village and the institution of caste must be added a third feature of rural stability: the extraordinary complexity of social and economic organisation resulting in a great diversity of interests. A close look at almost any part of rural India will usually discover a ramifying network of relationships in land ownership, tenancy rights, financial and social obligations, family ties and political connections. One of the principal inhibitions to organising the rural poor is that their economic interests are often opposed. Share croppers, small landowners and labourers may all be suffering at the hands of the bigger owners and money lenders but their sufferings may have different causes and different remedies. Within these crude groups there are further differentiations: some forms of relationship may connect the exploited with the exploiters. Few scholars have done more to draw our attention to the inappropriateness of many of our categories in trying to account for Indian realities than André Béteille; he has argued persuasively that if we were being careful, we would not even use the word 'peasant' to describe agriculturists in India.[15] His work and that of several others should make us very wary of any simple notions of oppressed and oppressors.[16] Certainly one may attribute to the complexity of 'interests' a share of the stability of the countryside; coupled with the rigidities of caste, it has created an effective barrier to spontaneous or organised revolt despite the burdensome and often cruel conditions of life of the great majority.

Yet revolts there have been, overcoming some or all of these obstacles, for a time at least. How are they to be explained? In the first place in many of them there were special reasons for solidarity among those involved. A large number of the events we have described were actions not of caste – or casteless–Hindus but a distinct minority groups in the population: tribals, or Muslims. The Telangana Movement also possessed special features: it was in part an uprising against the oppressive rule of the Nizam of Hyderabad whose refusal to join the Indian Union on Independence contributed a nationalist flavour to it; when the Nizam was forced to capitulate to the Congress Government in 1948 only the Communist guerillas fought on, revealing that revolutionary Communism itself had struck no deep roots in the area though the Communist Party did well in the four 'stronghold' Districts in the elections of 1952.[17] At the same time this was 'largely an anti-landlord movement of the agrarian masses';[18] it was the combination of exploitation and opposition to the Nizam on which the Communist leadership capitalised. Factors in the Tebhaga Movement were the aftermath of the 1943 famine which drew the educated middle class into contact with the cultivators; a drive against hoarders and blackmarketeers of food led by the Kisan Sabha, which had the support of the Government; participation by militant tribals and a change in the bargaining strength of the share croppers owing to death, migration and alternative employment opportunities created by the Japanese invasion of Assam and East Bengal.[19]

Other features of past centres of agrarian unrest have been suggested by Béteille.[20] He observed 'a high degree of concentration in the rice producing areas of East and South India'. Indeed most of the incidents we have discussed occurred in such areas, large parts of West Bengal and Kerala, more restricted parts of Andhra Pradesh and Tamil Nadu. As he notes these areas show a high pressure of population on the land. But so do others. What may distinguish many of the revolted areas is a very high proportion of tenants and landless labourers in the rural work force and characteristics of the landowners themselves. In his study of the Tanjore disturbances[21] Béteille notes that the earlier ones, to which we have already referred, were mainly directed at the problems of tenancy and those of the 1960s, to which we shall shortly come, with agricultural wages. Most of the disturbances in Tanjore occurred in the 'Old Delta', the eastern *taluks* of the District where the proportion of labourers is highest and its caste composition unusually homogeneous, with large majorities of harijans, compared with the Western, New Delta, where they are in a minority.[22] The fact that the labourers were united, and not divided by caste, is a rarity in India. The contrast between large landowners and other agricultural classes is and was much more glaring in the Old Delta than in the New; the result of those and many other differences which Béteille describes is that agricultural development and innovation has been able to take place with less tension in the New than the Old. Similar, though subtly varying, features can be observed more generally in other areas under discussion. In particular 'the areas which have a large proportion of agricultural labourers are also the ones where land is very unequally divided among those who operate it as either owners or tenants.'[23]

An important feature may be not just ownership and occupational divisions, but also the nature of work involved. Wet paddy cultivation is peculiarly unpleasant: it requires 'long hours of backbreaking work which might have to be performed for weeks together in mud or standing in water with the rain beating overhead. Those who work in the fields during the day are sometimes too exhausted to take the filth off their bodies at night and such people frequently suffer from recurring skin ailments during much of their lives.'[24] Not surprisingly owners of wet paddy land will avoid this kind of work; here is a point where caste, status, economic power and the 'material means of production' all bear on each other and the sharpest of distinctions is drawn between those who own and those who work the land. Where, as in wheat farming, most landowners do at least part of the work, the distinction is less sharp; and so as it happens are others, giving more continuous gradations of many categories of socio-economic relationships. But Béteille rightly warns us against any facile economic determinism; the same or very similar social and economic conditions have prevailed in other parts of India where no incidents have occurred. 'Sometimes people acquire a consciousness of their identity in spite of over-riding differences in their material conditions; at other times they fail to develop such a consciousness in spite of an identity of material con-ditions.'[25] Explanations should take account of the conditions of work and life, the consciousness of these conditions and the political organisation of that consciousness.

We have not yet brought out the significance of the last of those three elements. Indian Communism deserves a particular mention in this respect. Since Independence nearly all major actions of rural revolt and resistance have been Communist led as were some of those before. The existence of the Kisan Sabha and other Communist organisations has been a material factor in agrarian movements. But the discussion above underlines the need for judicious choice of circumstances in which to operate; indeed our discussion may convey a misleading impression since it covers only the events which have had, in their own terms, a degree of success the ones that, so to speak, take their place in the history books. There have been far more calls for action which never got anywhere, such as that in 1947 for armed uprisings all over India shortly after Independence. A prolonged hiatus occurred in the succession of agitations in the countryside – except for some episodes in West Bengal – from the early 1950s to the mid 1960s. After Telangana the Communist Party largely pursued a constitutional road achieving major electoral successes in Kerala and West Bengal (though these too were not left in peace by the Congress Government in New Delhi) and putting pressure on Congress for radical measures. This was only a recognition of realities: most Indians believed that their new Government would redress their wrongs. Besides the prospects for armed struggle were dim, with the Indian army to contend with and a benevolent national leader in Jawaharlal Nehru, who enjoyed tremendous support. Further even the Telangana movement at the end was being weakened by its own inner contradictions – the redistribution of land was not equally pleasing to all parties.

Growing tensions within the Communist Party during this period finally led to a split in 1964. The split expressed itself in attitudes to the Congress Party, the biggest faction believing the correct line was cooperation with it, since it stood against 'imperialism' and had many progressive views on domestic policy. The Communist Party of India (or C.P.I.) henceforward took this stand seeing its role as backing the Left inside Congress and opposing the reactionary elements within and outside Congress. The minority formed itself into the C.P.I. (Marxist); as far as it was concerned there was nothing progressive in the Congress Party and both it and anyone who collaborated with it were 'rightists'. It was the C.P.I. (M) which was successful in elections in Kerala and West Bengal – in the 1965 mid-term elections in Kerala some of their candidates stood for election from jail where many Communists, especially those suspected of pro-

Chinese sympathies, were sent as 'traitors' after the border war with China in 1962. (The C.P.I. was popularly identified as pro-Soviet which it largely was and is; the C.P.I. (M) as pro-Chinese, which was less accurate, as there were numerous differences between the C.P.I. (M) and the Communist Party of China (C.P.C.).) In the 1967 elections the C.P.I. (M) won 53 out of 133 seats in the State Legislature of Kerala and was the dominant party. In West Bengal it was second to Congress but formed a coalitition or 'United Front' with other opposition parties against the Congress Party which did not have an overall majority. There followed a succession of crises in Bengal with coalitions collapsing and reforming, punctuated with periods of President's Rule (the imposition of Central power provided for in the Constitution when members of the democratically elected State legislature cannot form a government). The C.P.I. (M) increased its number of seats at each election up to 1971 when Mrs Gandhi's Congress Party, in Bengal as almost everywhere else, swept the board.

The 1960s saw a renewal of armed struggle in the countryside which had been temporarily abandoned. Its most spectacular outbreak took a desperate form, though its origins were not new. The first even appears to have been a clash between tribal peasants and a landlord who had tried to evict a poor tenant by force in defiance of a court order in May 1967; other incidents followed: police sent in to restore order in another clash were ambushed and killed; another police squad took reprisals, killing women and children. The tribals then joined with local C.P.I. (M) leaders and took control of Naxalbari, a group of villages in Siliguri District, the northernmost part of West Bengal, and declared it a 'liberated zone'. The chief figure of the Communists in that part of Bengal was Charu Mazumdar, a real devotee of the Chinese view of revolution, at odds with the C.P.I. (M) leadership in Calcutta. The latter temporised over the events in Naxalbari for obvious reasons. The C.P.C. had no such doubts; 'Spring Thunder Breaks over India' proclaimed the *People's Daily*. Later articles in Chinese journals castigated the C.P.I. (M) for failing to support this genuinely revolutionary movement[26] thus antagonising the Government of India. Within fifty-two days of its beginning the rising was crushed by a police contingent with units of the Border Security Force. Several of the leaders were arrested and stayed in jail until 1969. The revolt was dead; but it gave birth to a new movement in India, the 'Naxalites', and later a new splinter of the Communist Party, the C.P.I. (ML), Marxist-Leninist, founded in 1969 and dedicated to 'armed struggle in the countryside and encirclement of the cities', the Chinese revolutionary programme and quickly recognised by the C.P.C.

After the rising in Naxalbari itself was put down the Naxalites at first confined themselves to organising meetings and strikes, gathering members and producing propaganda, apart from two abortive raids on police stations in Kerala and raids on landlords' property in Srikakulam (Andhra Pradesh). But after the release of Mazumdar, and with his urging, Naxalite activities began to acquire the character for which they have since been known. 'Armed struggle' was to take the form of direct attacks on 'class enemies'. This was the 'annihilation campaign'. The theory was that big landowners and other 'feudal elements' would be killed; others would take flight and the masses would be left in command of the land and the villages. 'The expectation was that killing a "hated oppressor" would receive the overwhelming support of the local people and would identify the movement with the poorer sections of the population.'[27] The latter would gradually take over the leadership of the movement from its – initially – middle class hands. From 1968 to 1970 the 'annihilation campaign' was in action. Many of the killings were of a deliberately grisly and sadistic character intended to inspire fear in others and encourage cooperation with the movement.

In some places this form of action supervened on others which had been going on earlier. Thus Naxalism came to Srikakulam District in Andhra Pradesh where hill tribes, or girijans, had been fighting government policies and local landlord oppression since 1959. We have observed the frequency of the presence of tribals in earlier revolts. They have long been a source of difficulty for the authorities. They do not take to regulation. They have been known to drive off census enumerators, vaccinators, family planning units and other inoffensive parties with bows and arrows. But this is in part due to their general hostility to governments, which in turn is due to treatment that has often been far from benevolent, including incursions on their way of life and their land – or land they regarded as theirs – by agricultural, forestry or military departments, as well as protection by the authorities of local landlords and money lenders who not only exploited them economically but frequently, as commonly happens to harijans and other weak sections of the community, ignored their legal rights. It is quite wrong to think of rural revolts as purely the 'have-nots' attempting to take away the property of the 'haves'; the 'have-nots' commonly start their action simply trying to obtain their legal rights of which local landlords, in league with political parties, police, even corrupt courts of law, conspire to deprive them. Altogether the position of India's tribal peoples bears many resemblances to that of the American Indians in earlier times, though they have not in modern times been subject to large-scale and ruthless slaughter. And the American Indians never had a communist party to take up their cause. With their readiness to resort to arms India's tribals were a natural focus for Naxalism; the movement indeed started with the Santals in Bengal.

After the suppression by police of the Srikakulam girijan movement, which had achieved some success in getting wages raised, crop-shares reduced and even some land freed from private mortgage or forestry restriction, the Girijan Sangham, as it had become, was ready to listen to Mazumdar's advice and a more militant guerilla phase in the movement began in November 1968, though the brutal killings which characterised Naxalism only started three months later. By mid 1969, some 500 – 700 square miles were claimed as 'liberated'. But then the State authorities began counter-action and within twenty months over 1500 arrests were made and over a dozen leading figures in the movement, which had itself claimed 54 'class-enemy' victims, killed. Little was left to fight on with by the end of 1970. Similar episodes took place in Midnapore District of West Bengal, in Muzaffarpur (Bihar) and a small one in Lakhimpur-Kheri (Uttar Pradesh), all with major tribal participation, all involving murders, crop and land appropriations and all shortlived.

The fact that the rural Naxalite movement was everywhere suppressed by state power may obscure the other reasons for its failure. It never acquired any significant following among the non-tribal rural classes. The landless and the other poor were repelled by the killings. 'In the absence of political propaganda the villagers saw in the campaign for the liquidation of class enemies nothing more than the murder of a co-villager by strangers . . .'[28] The Naxalite leadership rejected as 'economism' programmes which the poor could understand and which might actually help them. Instead they demonstrated their distance from them by talking a political language that had little meaning. As Dasgupta delicately says: 'Slogans like "China's Chairman is our Chairman" were . . . out of tune with the reality of the countryside.'[29] The movement was not linked with the masses. And in its next phase it began to look even more like a series of 'murders by strangers'. In 1970 its main focus was Calcutta and there followed a series of gruesome killings, many of them carried out by middle class teenagers attracted to Naxalism. Some were the work of criminals who either joined the movement, or just murdered people as if they had, settling scores and conducting what amounted to gang warfare in the streets. Even the rural killings included a share of middle peasants and others who could hardly be classed as major enemies of the poor. Urban deaths included a large number of C.P.I. (M) members as well as assorted civil servants and low-ranking policemen; no big businessmen or senior police officers were touched and several of the middle class 'annihilations' were of people who failed to pay up the 'protection' money demanded. In June 1971 President's Rule was again imposed in West Bengal. Within two months the Naxalites were totally defeated; this time the police were assisted by armed bands directed by Congress members. Many of the movement's active workers had by then defected, horrified by the course events had taken or realising that the end was near. Charu Mazumdar himself was arrested and died in police custody.[30]

If armed struggle is the path of the future, the Naxalites did not find the method of organising it. Local units were often at odds with their middle class or student leaders before they were forcibly suppressed. And selective violence without political preparation achieved the opposite of its aims, alienating both the poor and many of the middle class who despair of social progress through parliament and support revolutionary politics. The whole Naxalite episode cast discredit on the Left in general, especially when it appeared to incorporate factional fights between C.P.I. (ML) and C.P.I. (M). Theirs was not the only militant activity of the late 1960s and early 1970s, but it deserves emphasis as a significant failure. A list of other notable events starts with the Communist led agitations in Tanjore which began in 1967 – wage labourers were in dispute with landowners for higher pay and would strike after harvesting the paddy but before taking it to be threshed. There was a widely reported episode in which landowners set fire to labourers' huts and some forty men, women and children were burned to death. Action does not have to be illegal to attract a violent response. This period was notable also for a series of 'land grab' movements in the Gangetic plain; although quite widespread, they were more gestures than anything else. Bands of men would enter landowners' fields, occupy them and harvest the crops. But they were fairly easily driven off and there was little organised resistance. There were troubles once more in Telangana, the worst in 1969, but this time they had the nature of demands for economic and linguistic autonomy or at least for an end to what was regarded as discrimination against *mulkis*, inhabitants of the old Hyderabad State, who had been numerically overwhelmed when Hyderabad was incorporated into Andhra Pradesh; Naxalism appeared in Nalgonda District in Andhra but it did not get far.[31]

Revolutionary prospects

Many things are needed for a revolution. They include not only widespread dissatisfaction with the existing order of things and a sense that the existing government will not put them right, but also some belief in the possibility of an alternative which must be presented to the dissatisfied. Pre-revolutionary societies are usually characterised by deep class antagonisms; many revolutions have been particularly stimulated by a rising class frustrated by the curbs restraining them and the privileges of the old dominant classes. Since revolutions involve the overthrow of government, government must be vulnerable; in many past cases governments have been failing and inefficient and the governing groups losing faith in their ability to continue in power – although, in some twentieth century cases, the revolutionary movement itself has been the chief cause of downfall of a government that was not otherwise close to collapse. Disaffection of the intellectuals is a further common feature of pre-revolutionary conditions.[32]

If one asks which of these conditions are satisfied in India, the answer is that several of the main ones are not. There is no shortage of dissatisfaction and it would hardly be surprising if most people in India had lost all hope that Congress-style government would provide a significantly better future. But a credible alternative is not apparent. There are *theoretical* alternatives, but not a 'revolutionary project'[33] which has been put before the country and with which the great mass of the people can identify themselves. Internal antagonisms abound, but the extent to which they may properly be described as class antagonisms is a matter of doctrinal dispute which we are not qualified to resolve; as we have seen many groups with material interests in common do not possess solidarity and only rarely have they been able to join forces. The self-identification of a powerful class capable of overthrowing the existing order has yet to occur. Perhaps most important, government is not at all vulnerable – not at least as long as the military remains loyal; as we have seen the Central Government has without much trouble put down any opposition that seriously threatened the *status quo* even if it was an elected State government. Governing groups have not lost faith in themselves even if many outside have lost faith in them. Allegiance of intellectuals is difficult to assess. Until the events of 26 June 1975[34] one might have said that, although a large number had become convinced of the need for more radical changes, many of the best minds in the country were only disillusioned with the present incumbents and still believed in the ability of parliamentary democracy, with some changes of policy and implementation, to bring about desirable progress. Even if that belief was limited, it was strengthened by contemplation of the alternatives. Since the people who suffered most directly in the immediate aftermath of the Emergency were journalists and opposition politicians, who had most to gain from a resumption of liberal normalities, a belief that parliamentary democracy can solve India's problems may still be the majority view among intellectuals. Whether that belief will survive the uncertainties which resulted from the 1977 election remains to be seen.

The difficulties faced by a mass revolutionary movement in India seeking violent overthrow of the existing government are acute. If it is confined to a single locality, it will easily be put down by force. But to be more than local it must transcend not only the micro-social differences of caste and economic interest we have already discussed, but the very considerable linguistic and other differences that separate one part of India from another. We have already noted the narrow geographical confines of past agitations, their dependence on locally significant characteristics and their failure to spread even to linguistically similar neighbouring areas. It must be repeated that the huge majority of India's villages have for most of their history been undisturbed by political violence. The Naxalites and many other leaders have thought they were igniting the spark that would set India aflame, but the sparks have mostly fallen on damp and inert material and the few small fires which did catch were quickly smothered by the blanket of government power. No regime could resist a simultaneous rising by the people of India. But what can produce that?

The last time it happened – and also the first for that matter – was during the Quit India movement when the entire country seethed with disturbances. There was a common cause, a common enemy and inspired leadership in the person of Gandhi whose genius spoke to every Indian. General unrest is, from the revolutionary point of view, conspicuously lacking in India. If one thinks of Russia or China one is struck by this fact in particular; these countries were in a prolonged state of turmoil and not

only immediately prior to the revolutions themselves. Rather the revolutions seemed the culmination of a succession of blows against the
political structure. China's rural revolts prior to the Long March had a
depth and sophistication quite unlike those we have described in India;
they united different classes in the population and often had aims far
beyond the peasant interest incorporating idealistic demands for new
forms of government, universal equality, even women's rights. India has
not witnessed either a peasant movement on the scale of Pugachev's
Rebellion which came 140 years before the Russian Revolution but was
only the start of a long history of upheavals. India has not had this air of
continuing political crisis in the grassroots which threatens the very being
of the state in its existing form. The main threats have come from linguistic
separatism: forecasting the break-up of the Indian union was a favourite
theme of the commentators of the 1950s and early 1960s. But, while the
number of States has been added to since Independence, a mixture of
containment and concession has greatly weakened the force of centrifugal
tendencies.

Russia and China are not of course the only models. Mention of the Quit
India movement calls to mind a strand of the literature on revolution
which suggests that many countries have dissipated their revolutionary
potential in the fight against colonialism.[35] It is certainly true that national
governments based on independence movements which take power when
the colonial ruler departs are natural inheritors of the kind of unity and
popular enthusiasm which is needed for revolution. It is also true that the
anti-colonial struggle has brought revolutionary regimes to power, as in
Algeria or, in a more complex manner, Vietnam. But, if the boat was
missed, it may still come round again. The question is, if India's past does
not look like the prelude to revolution, does the future hold anything
different? Perhaps no countries are models for India. Revolution itself is a
variegated phenomenon and its analysts have found only limited uni-
formities, and rather more fundamental differences, among all its
specimens. India too has certain features peculiar to itself and need not be
expected to follow paths exemplified elsewhere.

The most signal peculiarity is undoubtedly the caste system. Since that
has already been identified as an obstacle to revolutionary change one
might ask whether its hold on individuals and society is likely to weaken.
There are many processes within society which have had the effect of
loosening caste ties.[36] But these are somewhat slow-moving. The Government also has comprehensive programmes to improve the lot of 'scheduled
castes' and reports regularly on their progress.[37] Jobs are reserved in
government offices, places at universities; more profound reforms are here
and there attempted. But the situation is only modestly affected. One of the
few who made a frontal assault on it was Gandhi himself who coined the
term 'harijan', or child of God, and openly performed the most unclean
tasks such as sweeping up excrement in public, trying by example to break

centuries of instinctive rejection and self-rejection. But it was an example
that few have followed. Even in some of the Communist-led agitations we
referred to in Tanjore in which harijans and other castes shared, the former
'acted separately, although in alliance'.[38] One cannot expect the very
gradual erosion of caste to accelerate unless it too is taken up as a political
cause. There are occasional signs that this may happen. For example
outbreaks of murders of landlords by untouchables and *vice versa* occurred in
Bihar in 1974 and 1975,[39] possibly Communist-inspired. There has also
been a militant movement to raise lower caste consciousness in Maharashtra, the so-called Dalit Panthers.[40] Whether this will prove a fruitful·
source of militancy remains to be seen. If it does, the authorities will have
no one to blame but themselves. It is their neglect of which others will be
taking advantage.

Another important feature of past stability identified above was the
complexity of economic interests; so a further question is whether India's
development is going to bring greater polarisation along any of the major
dimensions. One thing we can say with confidence is that not only the
number but the proportion of the landless is bound to increase. The process
of subdivision of holdings, though slow, must reach a limit. There is room
for further division of larger holdings, but not enough to give viable
holdings even to the present rural population. The size of holding which is
viable can be reduced by technical progress and greater intensity of
cultivation. But rural India will acquire something like 250 million more
people in the next thirty years. The existing agrarian structure is fairly
resistant to land redistribution; even if it becomes less so, nothing can stop
the growth of the landless classes until population itself stops growing.
Whether this is a destabilising development can be debated. Deference is
slowly vanishing from the countryside, together with many of the social ties
and forms of organisation which produced cohesion in the village of old. A
number of these, while exploitative, gave a degree of security. An example
is the *jajmani* system, under which services of various kinds were performed
by lower caste members for their patrons – this was not usually a simple
relationship of payment for services on a one-to-one basis, but a general
duty of provision by the patron and of work on various occasions by the
labourer, who might possess simple artisan skills. This system is very
gradually disappearing in North India where it has been widespread. But
whether social stability changes greatly as a result depends on many things.

It would seem inevitable that the rural poor will become better
organised. The fact that they have not been so hitherto is only in part
explained by the sorts of reasons we have already gone over. It is also true
that the political parties which stood to gain from doing so only very
belatedly turned to rural organisation. For much of their existence India's
Communist parties either pursued the 'parliamentary road' or concentrated on organising urban workers. The Congress party has mainly
relied on the big farmers to bring in the vote of those who depended on

them and has not really tried to base its electoral strength on the direct organisation of landless labour, poor tenants or smallholders. Politics, like development itself, has neglected the rural poor. But the omission is beginning to be made up as we have seen. If new forms of organisation secure better conditions for labourers and tenants, they could add to stability rather than detract from it. One of the features of rural life in recent years is that for very large numbers of people it has become less and less secure, partly because of the numbers thrown onto an uncertain labour market.[41] If there is genuine progress in rural development of course real incomes could rise, especially if the bargaining strength of the rural poor is improved by effective organisation and their rights begin to be respected. But many of those doing the organising will not have greater security for the organised as their ultimate objective; rather they will be aiming at laying a basis for militant action.

A great deal has been written on the connections between development and revolution, little of it to our purpose.[42] Long ago de Tocqueville observed that conditions had been improving until shortly before the French Revolution. Such ideas have been advanced by one side of the debate; it is not misery but the defeat of expectations which produces revolutions – they are most likely when a period of improvement is interrupted by sharp reverses, and their leaders may be found among a rising class whose path to further success is blocked by the *ancien régime*. The contrary view that development forestalls revolution by mitigating the conditions in which it breeds is perhaps the more popular. We have caricatured the opposing views; obviously no scholar has put forward anything quite so crude. But, however detailed one makes them, these theories are not very helpful other than to remind one of all the possibilities that can be expected. What the history of revolutions mainly teaches is that each one has been very particularly of its own time and place and the lessons of one case do not apply in another. In India there are far too many possible sources of change for any simple theory to yield intelligent predictions.

So far we have looked at revolutionary prospects arising from rural areas. It is easier to present a picture of urban India as a focus for future unrest. As we pointed out in Chapter 2 the absolute size of cities may be an important factor in their politics, other things being equal. A million unemployed in a city of ten million are likely to offer greater threats to the *status quo* than 10,000 in a city of 100,000. The sheer mass and accessibility of numbers of desperate men must inevitably pose growing threats to public order as India's cities expand unless conditions in them improve – perhaps even if they do. Once again however the distinction between revolt and revolution is pertinent. Cities may increasingly become the seats of militant agitation for better conditions and life in them progressively less pleasant for ordinary men and women. But what generates revolutions rather than revolts lies in the realm of factors we have yet to explore.

So far we have spoken of broad trends such as may underlie revolutionary change. But further conditions are necessary if the unrest which seems highly possible in India is going to turn into revolution. One of these is a revolutionary organisation capable of providing leadership for a mass uprising. So far the Indian Left has not given much sign of its capacity for this task. It has been divided, uncertain and frequently misguided, as the Naxalite movement showed. Above all perhaps it has not been very Indian. The various Communist parties have usually aligned themselves with one or other international movements, Moscow or Peking. This has been valuable to them for purposes of prestige and financial and other support. But it has not helped to create any kind of popular following – for that, the leadership must surely draw on Indian sentiment. It is to a specifically Indian ideology, relevant to India's circumstances and capable of arousing an emotive response among ordinary Indians, that any politician must look if he hopes for success. As we have observed the last person who achieved this was Gandhi – how extraordinary was the devotion he inspired is well-known: great enough to induce thousands of his followers to sit down unmoved under the flailing batons of British troops. It is India's tragedy that the national energies released under Gandhi's leadership were directed mainly against the colonial power and not against the oppressor within. Gandhi's conservative domestic policies – not least on the issue of land ownership – and rejection of modern technology in production could also never have satisfied for long either the developmental needs of the country or the ambitions of other powerful politicians that India should become a major force in the international arena.[43]

Undoubtedly, whatever leadership may arise, it would face formidable difficulties in the combination of the tremendous diversity of India's composite parts and the effectiveness of the physical power of the Central Government. Any local movement can be swiftly put down by police or the military; even a legally elected State government which is not to the Centre's liking can be subverted or constitutionally removed on pretexts which are not hard to invent or engender. Communications on major road and rail routes are good through most of India and army units are stationed all over the country and highly mobile. A repeat of anything like Mao's Long March is unthinkable in India. The only way a revolutionary movement could overcome the physical power of the Centre – unless the military were itself converted to the revolutionary cause – would be by a simultaneous uprising over very large areas of the country. But this is inherently unlikely. As we have seen there are relatively few historic seats of radicalism in India and there are special reasons for their having been such. Not only must radical movements be created in many new centres, if they are all to rise at once, their leadership must act in concert, transcending differences of language, ethnic composition, caste, regional and economic interests – something that has only been seen in the

Independence struggle itself. And that as we have said was a fight against a common, external enemy, with a simple objective, under charismatic leadership of a kind that appears only rarely in a country's history.

Most past revolutions have taken place not against mildly incompetent governments which were failing to solve difficult problems, but against deeply detested, tyrannical regimes whose rule was itself burdensome, as well as permitting oppressive practices by some classes against others and persecuting important minorities or even majorities. Another common feature has been the declining confidence of the regime in power in its capacity to continue to rule. Recent Governments of India have not been in the latter category: indeed for some tastes they have often shown an excess of confidence rather than a lack of it. Until the Emergency one could not have described them as tyrannical or burdensome. They may have been seen as inefficient and somewhat corrupt and capable of acting repressively against opponents, be they would-be leaders of rural revolts or railway trade unionists.[44] But they were undoubtedly regarded by many people, perhaps most, as being, for all their faults, as good as could be expected. The day-to-day administration of the country may have had much scope for reform, but it was not breaking down; many would say that, considering the magnitude of the country's problems and the political constraints within which government works, affairs were being managed tolerably well. If little was being done for the poor, their problems were intractable and had long been so.

The Emergency did not last long enough to provide great insight into public behaviour under authoritarian rule. There was undoubtedly much resentment of several features of the Emergency, not only censorship and the loss of legal and political rights or the enforced sterilisations in some areas of the country, but a whole range of high-handed actions by locally powerful officials and others whose normal powers to harass ordinary people were greatly enhanced by the conditions of the Emergency. There is no telling how long this state of affairs would have been tolerated; all we know is that in 1977, as soon as an opportunity was available to the electorate to express their views at the ballot-box, the Emergency and all that happened under it was decisively rejected. But there had not been much overt opposition except to the more aggressive moves of the sterilisation and slum clearance drives. Whether that opposition would have begun to build into a potent force, and whether indeed the fear that it might was a factor in the decisions to hold an election in 1977, is only speculation. Governments of any form can only go so far without the open or tacit consent of the governed. How close the Emergency had come to going too far we will never discover, but it is at least possible that another few years of it could have generated the conditions for violent opposition at the grassroots. At the same time one would expect an intelligent government to draw back from unpopular measures long before such conditions arose.

The last ingredient in revolutions is usually a crisis of some kind – wars, famines, political divisions inside the government. Only occasionally has the crisis been created by the revolutionary movement itself; much more commonly such movements aggravate and take advantage of difficulties besetting the existing regime from other quarters. It is certainly not difficult to imagine crises in India. But these are only precipitating factors in revolutions; if our analysis is correct, it is most unlikely in the next few years that there will be any national revolutionary force waiting for a crisis to create the circumstances in which it can topple the Government. The political evolution of India in the next decade or two is not presently imaginable in terms other than the possible forms of development of the existing system of government. To this issue we shall turn in the third section of this chapter. For now we conclude that most circumstances weigh against the possibility of any overthrow of government by a popular uprising. Coups, perhaps; mass revolutions, no. However closely one analyses this, one may still be left with a feeling that somehow or other, as India's problems pile up, there must be growing prospects for violent overthrow of governments by organised movements of the poor and the oppressed. If we are wrong in our belief that this is a long way off, we are at least in good company. Lenin himself at the end of 1916 thought the success of the Russian revolution was something he might not live to see.[45]

INDIA AND CHINA: CHINA'S POPULATION

There is, of course, the abstract possibility that the number of people will become so great that limits will have to be set to their increase. But if at some stage communist society finds itself obliged to regulate the production of human beings, just as it has already come to regulate the production of things, it will be precisely this society, and this society alone, which can carry this out without difficulty.

Engels, Letter to Kautsky, 1881.

There is a growing literature comparing contemporary India with China, which stems in part from a desire to see how successful a revolutionary society has been in coping with many of the same problems that India faces. The verdict many would reach has been that China is succeeding in several fields where India is not. The deeper question of how relevant any such comparisons may be has less often been raised, let alone answered. We will start with the population question; apart from anything else no assessment of China's economic progress is possible without an idea of the size and rate of growth of its population. Unfortunately that is not an easy thing to discover.

The benchmark of recent population figures is the 1953 Census result which counted 582·6 million people. Doubt has even been expressed about this figure and by Chinese sources at that: an official source gave a series of population figures for the years 1949 – 56 putting the 1953 numbers at

587·96 million.[46] Some have surmised that the 1953 Census, like many elsewhere, was an under-count, perhaps by as much as 5 per cent.[47] Although various sources – speeches of political leaders, newspaper and journal articles – give figures for subsequent years, there is only one further estimate since 1953 in which we may have tentative confidence as having probably resulted from a count of some sort and that is for the year 1964. The first evidence that there was a census in that year came from refugees reaching Hong Kong one of whom claimed even to know details of the census questionnaire.[48] But no total was announced. During 1967 and 1968, on the formation of the provincial Revolutionary Committees, the population of each Province was announced; the total comes to 712·32 million.[49] It is most unlikely that conditions during the immediately preceding years could have been favourable either to careful registration work or to the conduct of a census. It makes a good deal of sense to regard these figures as the results of the 1964 Census, yielding an average annual rate of growth since 1953 of 1·85 per cent. Corroboration was provided in 1972 by Chou En-lai who told a group of visitors that there had been a census in 1964, that it had found a population of about 700 million, growing at just under 2 per cent.[50] In 1966 also newspapers began to use the figure of 700 million when referring to the population total where previously they had used 650 million or 600 million.

For later figures we are on still shakier ground though in 1976 there was talk of a census being taken. In its absence observers have tried to employ figures, estimated or assumed, for birth and death rates. A widely accepted number is 800 million in 1970 given by Vice-Premier Li Hsien-nien in a remarkably candid statement in which he cited various figures produced by different agencies for their own purposes.[51] The 800 million figures gives a rate of growth of 2·0 per cent annually from that of 712 million for 1964. This rate of growth is itself uncertain and, if correct, compatible with a variety of pairs of birth and death rates which are uncertain too. There have been no published results of fertility enquiries since the foundation of the People's Republic. While the 1953 and 1964 population totals referred to above may be correct they are probably not the result of a constant annual rate of growth of 1·85 per cent. In the early 1950s successful public health campaigns and better food distribution must have brought down the death rate considerably below the pre-revolutionary level and could well have assisted an increase in the birth rate resulting in growth in excess of 2 per cent. The late 1950s and early 1960s were marked by food problems and tremendous strains in personal life during the period of the Great Leap quite possibly both raising death rates and reducing birth rates. The average figure of 1·85 per cent is thus quite plausible. We shall defer consideration of current vital rates until we have examined the 'planned birth' programme. But if one of its goals is achieved and a growth rate of 1·5 per cent reached by 1980, that would put the 1975 population close to 890 million.[52]

Ideology

The population question in China has been the subject of heated and frequently changing controversy. In the pre-revolutionary era, Malthusians and anti-Malthusians debated the pros and cons of population growth and the desirability of various means of fertility control. The early 1950s saw the beginnings of officially supported family planning services, but not much in the way of public discussion of the population issue until 18 September 1954 when Shao Li-tzu made an important speech at the First National People's Congress. The points he made were to set the tone for statements in favour of birth planning. It was a good thing to have a large population; but 'in an environment beset with difficulties, it appears that a limit should be set.' He was careful to dissociate himself from Malthusian thinking, to stress the health of mothers and children and to suggest a role for public services in giving guidance and supplying contraceptives. This line was endorsed by the Party journal *Study* (2 October 1955). On 16 September 1956, Chou En-lai supported family planning at the Eighth National Congress of the Communist Party of China 'to protect women and children and educate our younger generation in a way conducive to the health and prosperity of the nation.' On 27 February 1957 Mao himself made a statement to the Supreme State Council in which he described China's 600 millions as an asset, but noted that the growth of foodgrain output of only 10 million tons a year was barely sufficient for the needs of the growing population and that only 60 per cent of the youth of the country were placed in primary schools. Steps must be taken to 'keep our population for a long time at a stable level.'[53]

At this stage in the debate the standard-of-living argument became prominent. An editorial in the *People's Daily* on 7 March 1957 was headed 'It is Proper that We Appropriately Restrict Reproduction'; ten days later it carried a signed article entitled 'It is Necessary that We Appropriately Restrict Reproduction.' Other articles there and elsewhere stressed the difficulties of providing employment and raising labour productivity. As the Hundred Flowers period dawned some writers came out with outspokenly Malthusian views – a few subsequently were transferred from their posts as a result. The opponents of family limitation also became vociferous. Perhaps the most subtle ideological statement in favour of fertility control was produced by Wang Ya-nan, President of Hsiamen University, who attacked the Malthusian approach on the correct Marxian ground that population problems arose from particular social systems. However he continued, 'the elimination of the system of private property can only erase the population problem that it generates, . . . it does not root out population problems in general.' There can still be contradictions between the relations of production and the means of production. But in China it was no longer an antagonistic contradiction: the problem was that of an advanced social system constrained by backward means of production, the inheritance of pre-revolutionary history. In order to raise productivity population growth must be restricted; otherwise the rate of accumulation would not suffice.[54]

With the approach of the Great Leap, the opponents of population control enjoyed a temporary victory. It was obviously not consistent with the tremendous optimism about productive potential to suggest that there was any need for population control. Also production goals were so high that a very large share of the labour force was overworking, with the result that managers of economic units were unlikely to have perceptions of labour shortage. (Ironically however it is quite possible that the birth rate fell during this period as we shall suggest.) This period came to an end in the chastening atmosphere of shortages and social disruption. There was a last bout of opposition to population control during the Cultural Revolution. But the need for it was not publicly disavowed by the country's leaders. Family planning work did not stop completely; it was pursued but with varying intensity. While the population debate continued its fluctuations were more or less clearly related to changes in political and economic circumstances. To a lesser extent birth control activities followed these fluctuations, but they had a certain persistent momentum. Characteristically however it was not until the political forces of the country were aligned with the movement that these activities began to assume their present effective form.

The 'planned birth' programme

Early marriage is a poisonous gas exuded by the rotting corpse of capitalism.
Wall poster, 1960s. (Cited by Orleans (1972).)

In 1950 a Marriage Law was passed establishing a minimum age at marriage of 20 for men and 18 for women. An important aim of the law was to put an end to traditional arranged marriages and reduce women's economic dependence on husbands. Ever since the Revolution a great deal of effort has gone into improving the status of women, drawing them into the labour force and moving towards equality with men. Whatever other arguments in the population debate have come and gone, the improvement of women's and children's health and of women's social position has been a permanent aim constantly stressed in birth control propaganda even when other underlying motives have been at least equal in importance. In the early days family planning work was a function of the Health Ministry. As early as 1953 we find the State Council instructing the Ministry to 'help the masses to control reproduction' and approving the Ministry's revised regulations on birth control methods to be offered, including abortion. Many traditional methods were still in use at this stage including the swallowing of live tadpoles (now no longer encouraged, although as late as 1965 an article appeared complaining that its rejection had not been based on scientific evaluation). As with the beginnings of the

Indian programme there was public advocacy of birth control and scattered provision of services.[55]

Today the planned birth programme is an integral part of Chinese life. The transition to this situation started with the development of China's health system on its modern basis in the 1960s. After Mao's famous directive of 26 June 1965 ('in health work put stress on the rural areas') the formal organisation of medical services was developed from the barefoot doctor at the lowest level up through a referral system of clinics and mobile medical teams to the hospitals at the apex. The barefoot doctors were a product of the Great Leap period, but their full development and integration with the medical system came in the post-1965 era. There are now estimated to be more than a million of such grassroots health workers;[56] that means better than one per 1000 population. The result is that there now exists a health network with virtually complete coverage of the rural as well as the urban population.

But the crucial step which established the programme as it is today was still to come. After 1971 every revolutionary committee had a sub-committee for planned birth work at every level: from the provincial headquarters to the production team in rural areas and from the municipal to the street committees in urban areas. On these sub-committees were represented health service workers, members of the Women's Federation, the Young Communist League as well as of the revolutionary committees themselves. Their function is to 'help the masses to formulate their birth plans and follow this through.'[57] From 1971 – 2 onwards returning visitors described meetings of local groups to agree on who was to have babies in the coming year.[58] This method of 'birth-in-turn' planning seems to be spreading. It appears in many cases to be more a response to nationally established norms than an assessment by say the production team of the numbers of additional people it can support. No doubt these grassroots units are aware of the problem of their own numbers, but they also have national obligations such as the delivery of agricultural produce for consumption elsewhere. The presence of Party members in these sub-committees is not of itself evidence of the degree of political commitment to the aim of planned reproduction; its purpose is to assist the maintenance of enthusiasm for the programme and its adherence to national goals. There is no doubt however that official commitment at the highest level is very strong.

The main principles of planned birth work are three: (i) to raise the age at marriage to 28 for men and 25 for women in urban areas and in rural areas to 25 and 23; (ii) to encourage a birth interval of five years after the first child and (iii) to promote a norm of two children per couple in urban areas, three in rural areas. There does not appear to be any universal 'target setting'; a typical directive instructs 'leading comrades' to 'strive hard to accomplish outstanding results.'[59] But visitors have often found spokesmen referring implicitly or explicitly to some or other of the above three principles or to yet other goals, such as a birth rate of 15 per 1000.

In the small group meetings of which we have spoken preference may be given among those wishing to have an additional child to parents whose last child was born more than four years earlier. Other targets cited are for overall growth rates of numbers in local communities and organisations reflecting a national objective which has been quoted of achieving a growth rate of 1·5 per cent per year by 1980 and one per cent by the end of the century if not sooner. Late marriage has been an important part of the programme encouraged both by active propaganda and by economic circumstances the direction of labour and the shortage of new housing make it quite difficult for young people to marry and set up house together. But social pressure exercised particularly through small group motivation work is the main instrument of the programme. There is little mention either of incentives for small families or sanctions against large ones. At one time there was a positive incentive to have children in the shape of the grain allowance – a full adult allowance used to be given for every family member – but nowadays children are only granted a fraction of the adult allowance. Withholding of the grain allowance after the third child was tried in places, but has been denounced as 'non-socialist'.[60]

All main modern methods of birth control are currently available in China though there are no statistics giving the extent of use of the various methods. Sterilisation, male and female, has been available since the 1950s. At first men complained on grounds that it made them 'impotent', but this has been countered with propaganda on the sexual equality theme; husbands should not place all responsibility for birth control on their wives.[61] The I.U.D. has been in use since the mid 1960s. There is little evidence about retention rates, but the method is officially regarded as fully satisfactory.[62] Abortion is available on demand and China has pioneered some relatively simple aspiration devices (although the very simplest technology is now used in the West – we do not know whether it has been adopted in China).[63] Development of orals has impressed foreign observers most of all. There was little discussion about them in the country prior to 1969, but they were at work developing their own production from indigenous raw materials and the state of the art is now highly advanced including a preparation fixed on water-soluble paper (22 doses on a perforated sheet) which has been praised for its low cost and simple manufacture. Domestic production is now claimed to be adequate for tens of millions of women.[64]

All methods are for the most part distributed by the health network. Visitors have often – though not universally – found that chemists' shops in urban areas did not carry supplies except in bulk quantities for health workers. There is some mystery about the extent of sexual activity outside marriage. Extramarital pregnancy seems to be extremely rare and much frowned upon and contraceptive instruction is often observed to be given to married couples only after the birth of the first child. The spate of early marriages during the Cultural Revolution[65] may suggest that many young people would prefer an earlier start to sexual life, but at least until the practice of contraception is more widely and regularly adopted, and the small family norm accepted everywhere, the currently recommended pattern is unlikely to change. How unmarried young people feel about this, no one seems to have been able to ascertain.

Future prospects

Assessing China's demographic prospects is no easy matter. We are not sure of any base year figure for the total population and there are no reliable national figures for current birth and death rates. The United Nations gave a birth rate of 33 and a death rate of 15 as averages for 1965 – 74. Published figures for death rates in several Chinese cities are compatible with an overall figure of this magnitude or below it. Some of them indeed are so low that Western observers have cast doubt on their accuracy. Death rates between 6·5 and 9 per 1000 were given for several major cities in the late 1950s[66] and in the region of 5 or 6 per 1000 currently.[67] When one considers that the death rate in Hong Kong was 5·2 in 1972 or 5·4 in Singapore in 1970[68] and further that, in addition to a young age structure, health conditions in Chinese cities are at least the equal of such places, there are no good reasons for rejecting these estimates. As Salaff observes 'death rates and morbidity rates for some cities and communes which come from several journals are internally consistent, and therefore falsification would have had to permeate every public health unit at all levels.'[69]

By comparison with India one would certainly expect China to have very low mortality. Public health campaigns have been conducted not only against the major communicable diseases, but against flies and other disease-carrying insects and vermin.[70] As Joshua Horn once remarked it is not true that there are no flies in China; but the few that there are have a very brief expectation of life.[71] Food availability per head is very considerably above that in India and there is every reason to believe that distribution both geographically and by persons is very much more even. Considerable gains in height and weight of children have been observed by anthropometric measurement between 1930 and the mid 1950s.[72] Community involvement in programmes to improve hygiene, sanitation and water-supply is at a high level. The medical network and pervasive health education activities have undoubtedly been highly effective. It would appear that, for most people, most of the conditions of good health have been created. And they have been there for some time. The big pest and public health campaigns were in the 1950s; the system of medical services was mainly created in the 1960s.

All this does not solve the question of the actual level of mortality. A figure of 11 per 1000 was given for 1958.[73] In that year the urban population was approximately 14 per cent of the total;[74] if urban mortality was say 7 per 1000, a level of about 12 for rural mortality is implied. These figures seem to be on the low side; to the extent that they are based on registration data there are grounds for suspecting them. For the present period unfortunately we do not have a figure even for the rural-urban distribution of population. There has however been considerable effort to restrain urban growth in recent times. If one assumes the present urban proportion is 15 per cent and accepts the figure of 5 per 1000 for urban mortality, then, even if the rural death rate is double the urban, the death rate over all is only a little over 9 per 1000. This figure is roughly equivalent to that of present day Sri Lanka and may not be wide of the mark. But we should not pretend to 'know' the level of current mortality.[75]

If we could accept such a mortality figure, and we knew the rate of growth of the population, we could derive the birth rate – if it were 2 per cent, the birth rate would be just under 30 per 1000. But we do not know the current growth rate either so this route of birth rate estimation is barred. The last official figure for the birth rate was 24 per 1000 in 1958 from the same source as the death rate; it too is possibly doubtful. The one thing we can be fairly confident about is that the birth rate has been declining in recent years. Although no overall figures are available, reports for a large number of small communities indicate a moderately widespread adoption of modern contraceptive methods.[76] And the efforts to raise the marriage age and the age of first birth appear to have paid off at least in some areas. One study – self-confessedly short of perfection from the point of view of sampling theory – showed men aged 25 – 29 having their first child 3·5 – 4·5 years later than men in their early 40s; the median age was 27 – 28.[77] If the birth rate was in the mid 30s a decade ago, as scholars seem to believe, it is credible that it has now reached or passed below 30; though whether the extremely low birth rates recently cited[78] from Chinese sources for particular localities are either true themselves, or more than isolated instances, is impossible to judge. All one can say is that if the birth rate in China is not yet in the 20s, it must soon arrive there. The planned birth movement is not in fact equally stressed everywhere; in border areas and among minority communities it is not at all actively pursued.[79] And official sources frequently make clear that, particularly in rural areas, progress is difficult and far from uniform. But with the entire weight and energy of China's political and administrative structures behind it in most of the country, and with the exceptional degree of social control that prevails there, even something so intractable as fertility must be expected to yield to the forces of persuasion.[80]

The following chronology setting the fluctuating fortunes of the movement against other events is reproduced from Pi-chao Chen:[81]

1958	Great Leap; communisation; drought and food crisis	Official promotional programme called off; individuals free to practice contraception

1962	Improved economic conditions; rustication of urban youths initiated	Second campaign resumed; late marriage strongly pushed; abortion approved; sterilisation and I.U.D. promoted
1966	Cultural Revolution; disruption, especially in cities	Confusion and *de facto* neglect of planned birth programme; health services in rural areas expanded
1969	Political order restored	Programme reactivated; oral pills certified; extension work intensified
1971	Decisions to promote birth planning as highest priority nationwide	Free planned birth services initiated; pressures against early marriage and excess childbearing; network of local services expanded; small group motivation and planning innovated

Some authors have tried to relate changes in vital rates to this chronology too, suggesting that birth and death rates were falling prior to 1958, the former as a result of urbanisation, labour direction and so forth, the latter responding to public health programmes; and that mortality rose and birth rates fell further in the disturbed 1959–62 period and then respectively fell and rose once more with the end of the crisis and the numerous early marriages of the Cultural Revolution period.[82] While these general directions of change may be correct there is little basis for putting magnitudes on the changes. It is doubtful that the planned birth movement had much impact on birth rates prior to 1969. The current programme is very much a creature of the post-1971 initiatives which were themselves a reflection of the slow progress earlier.

Population size
Until another census is taken we remain rather in the dark about the present size of China's population and its rate of growth. If the 800 million figure growing at 2·0 per cent is realistic, we reach 887 million by 1975. Further assuming that the targets of a 1·5 per cent growth rate by 1980 and a 1·0 per cent rate by 2000 are met, one would come to 1019 million by 1985 and 1087 million by 1990.[83] But all these figures are conjectural and the 1970 total itself derives from the '1964' figure and an assumed growth rate. It is very easy to change the total for 1964 and the growth rate thereafter to arrive at numbers as much as 50 million more than the 800 million employed for 1970; one could produce smaller numbers too. Thus, while we regard these figures up to 1970 as plausible, they are no more than that; and even if the growth targets are reached or exceeded, the true

population total as we look towards the end of the century may be considerably greater than estimated. It is very important when examining China's economic performance to remember that, in so far as it is population growth against which judgement is made, the population figure for any year has a range of uncertainty as great as 50 million or even more.

Perhaps most interesting from the point of view of comparison with India is that so many factors regarded as contributing to high fertility in India were present in the China inherited by the Revolution: high mortality, early marriage, preference for sons, low status of women, lack of education, desire for old age security. With every one of these conditions contemporary China has contended and made progress.

India and China: economic performance
Making economic comparisons of India and China has of late become something of an industry, if as yet a small scale one.[84] Its main motive does not always seem to have been the search for truth by dispassionate enquiry. Rather radical economists have tried to demonstrate the superiority of a revolutionary society; Indian nationalists sought to dispel the implications of invidious contrasts; cold-warriors attempted to belittle Chinese achievements.[85] The last feature is disappearing, as studies of China have begun to show greater signs of objectivity, even those emanating from sources that in earlier days might have been expected to show the opposite.[86] But a clear picture of China's economic performance is hard to obtain even for those whose main aim is to produce one. Whatever the Chinese economy is good at, the generation of definitive statistics is not its *forte*.

As with any other country estimates of economic growth depend on the period examined. For China however there has until recently been little choice; some figures regarded as reliable were available for 1952 and 1957, but after that there was a hiatus until 1970. Most growth rate figures use those terminal dates. The majority of estimates put annual G.D.P. growth rates between 4 and 6 per cent for 1952 – 70 and somewhat lower for 1957 – 70. One author, rather obviously in the Indian nationalist tradition,[87] makes the figure 2·6 per cent for 1952 – 70 and 1·7 per cent for 1957 – 70. His work has however been seriously criticised.[88] But so have the 1970 figures themselves, the main basis of which is a statement of Chou En-lai in conversation with Edgar Snow – the figures are very hard to interpret with certainty.[89] Official data for India suggest that Indian total product grew at 3·7 per cent in 1952 – 70, and at 4 per cent in 1957 – 70. But why should precisely those years in India be chosen for the comparison? One could with good reason choose other 18- or 13-year periods. It does appear possible that China's total product growth was slightly faster than India's over precisely those periods, but given all the uncertainties of the data, as well as the question of the choice of periods, it may not be too meaningful to dwell on it. And obviously in view of what we have said about population data for China there is still less point in trying to determine what has been happening to per capita product in the two countries: population growth rates in India and China probably did not differ over the period enough to alter the comparison yielded by the rates for total product.

The picture is not much clearer for agriculture or industry on their own. China's total output of foodgrains (usually defined to include sweetpo-tatoes and other staples) has fairly consistently been about double that of India. It has had its good and bad years–the bad particularly from 1959 to 61 – and some rather poor years recently in terms of growth. Once again the rate of growth can be raised or lowered by suitable choice of periods; but in agriculture there are not many claims that China's growth performance exceeds India's – in fact some of the committed China enthusiasts concede a faster agricultural growth rate to India since the 1960s.[90] Nor would anyone challenge that output per head in China has on average been above that in India – a fact not wholly attributable to the revolution since grain yields in China have been higher than India's for many decades. Few commentators however have tackled the question of whether China, in keeping a higher level of output and productivity increasing at a similar or slightly lower rate, is doing better or worse than India. China's average yields for foodgrains were double those of India in 1950 and rice yields more than treble. There was not much additional acreage to be brought under the plough in China after 1949 as there was in India during the 1950s. Thus virtually all China's agricultural growth has been by productivity increase; since it began at a higher level as well it is arguable that this represents the greater achievement.[91]

There is some consensus that in industrial growth, China's record has been superior to that of India both in its rate of increase and its character. Progress has been uneven as is well known and was even poor in the Great Leap and Cultural Revolution periods. But if one looks back to 1950, one finds a remarkable similarity in the situations inherited by India and China at Independence and Liberation: indices of output per head in physical terms in coal, steel, cement, electric power, chemical fertilisers, cotton cloth and yarn and crude oil were extremely close for the two countries; but China has in the ensuing twenty-five years acquired a lead in all of them and a considerable one in most cases.[92] One might add that the advances in these sectors are especially promising from the point of view of future industrial growth. Many sources express the opinion that pro-duction is more 'efficient' in China although the evidence for this seems rather casual. A much quoted source claiming the superiority of Chinese management[93] has been rightly criticised as being based on a series of very brief visits to a small number of plants, selected far from randomly, where interviews were conducted via interpreters.[94] Regrettably much of the India-China comparison work is of this kind. Nevertheless the pace of industrial growth in China is accepted as having been sustained at a level of about 8 per cent annually up to the early 1970s, with excellent long-term prospects,[95] while India's industry as we have seen has really been struggling. Unless India changes its ways it is difficult to believe that China's planned industrial expansion will not continue to be more effective than India's inefficient public sector and rule-bound private sector, even if there are as yet no detailed studies which conclusively prove it. China has also one great advantage which owes nothing to politics – self-sufficiency in oil, on which India has to spend a large share of its scarce foreign exchange, although here too it must be said that the delays tolerated by the Government of India in the development of such oil reserves as the country possesses have been lamentable.

As suggested, in the present state of research, not a great deal is to be gained from these aggregate comparisons. Even if everything were growing faster in China than in India, one might remain unimpressed. What matters after all is the quality of life and, so far as the economy is concerned, the distribution of its benefits. Once again there is a notable absence of statistical data for China; we have spent some time examining the trend in personal income distribution in India without any conviction of the high quality of the data. But at least there are data, and enough from a variety of sources which can partially be used to cross-check each other, so that one may feel a certain respect for the empirical mosaic that is put together. For China the figures do not even have this degree of adequacy. We are mostly dealing with qualitative information from sources of uncertain objectivity and occasional quantitative data based on very small samples. For all these cautions it must be said that, in terms of equality, there is less doubt about China's relative superiority than in the question of growth rates.

There is perhaps one dimension in which China's record is little if at all better than India's – that of regional equality. The need to maximize agricultural production has – just as in India – led to the highest rates of agricultural growth being maintained in areas of highest productivity. While marketing and price policies redistribute food output the regional distribution of production is changing only slowly.[96] In industry all societies face difficulties in encouraging dispersion: there are almost always good economic reasons for the clustering of industrial development and agriculture and industry are often mutually sustaining. The development of small scale rural industry is thought to have been fairly effective in recent years in China – certainly more so than the often ill-judged initiatives of the Great Leap – but this has had more effect on the balance within regions than between them. There has also been considerable stimulation of small town development to countervail the big urban centres. The rural-urban dimension is one in which China has had some success in moving towards equality as compared with India. Wage differentials between rural and urban occupations have been narrowing (since the 1960s at least; they were widening in the 1950s). In general China has controlled the rural-urban drift only in part by administrative fiat; it has done a great deal to improve the economic situation of rural life by spreading health and education and social facilities, but also by encouraging rural incomes to rise while restraining the growth of urban incomes.[97] India as we have seen has made little progress in any of these directions except in parts of one or two States.

Perhaps the greatest interest attaches to the question of personal incomes. There can be little doubt that the range of incomes between the highest and the lowest paid in locally comparable situations is exceptionally low in China. It is practically impossible in the Chinese system for anyone to earn an income very much above the average; and even if he or she did, there would not be a great deal that could be bought with it. The few luxury consumption goods that can be found for sale are offered at punitively high prices. In industry the usual ratios of highest to lowest paid observed are of the order of 4 or 5:1; in agriculture the absence of private property with huge variations in landholdings eliminates the main source of rural maldistribution of income. There certainly are differences, and quite large ones, between some production units and others – explained by differences of skill, resources, quality of land and so forth. Most payment within the production team is according to work and teams are permitted to do well if circumstances permit. Between the highest paid urban official and the lowest paid worker in manufacturing there are income ratios of 8 : 1 or even more; for agriculture it is hard to cite a figure – the gap between the best paid in the best units and the worst paid in the worst may be quite wide. Neither the taxation nor price or marketing systems are used with strong progressivity to equalise income levels between units. However part of income is always according to need; there is a basic grain ration and there are collective welfare funds for the old, the sick, the disabled and for orphans. In addition health and education facilities are very widely available for all – perhaps still with some leeway to be made up in the difference between rural and urban, but in most respects markedly in advance of the distribution of incomes and welfare services to be found in India.[98] There is no evidence of anything in China resembling the differences between richest and poorest in India with thousands of rupees per month contrasted with hundreds per year; and enough has already been said about the distribution of India's education and welfare services.

Doubt is sometimes expressed about whether China has really been so successful in abolishing basic destitution. It is said that much of the evidence comes from returned visitors, but these visitors have travelled only selectively and vast areas of the the country are not open to visitors at all. While this is true it must be remembered that many of the areas where foreigners may not go are not the poorest, but among the richest parts in China such as the province of Setzuan. Undoubtedly there are parts of China where life is not as good as in the more prosperous parts of India; there may even be pockets of really poor people. But the idea that the kind of widespread, severe poverty that exists throughout India can also be found in China, and is just concealed by travel restrictions, scarcely bears examination. No evidence has ever been found to suggest this, and given the number of people with a vested interest in demonstrating the case if it were true, one might expect it to have been discovered by now if it existed. Returning foreigners are not the only source of evidence other than official statistics. Although some regions are better off than others and some are politically less stable than others – probably the main reason for re-strictions on foreign travellers – there is no suggestion that the revolution has not reached any part of the country or that there are major areas where there is a different system of economic organisation from that which has been documented in places that are open to inspection. There is no reason to believe that the many dozens of major cities, small towns or villages that have been visited are all 'showplaces' and the rest of China is seething with misery. (At the worst, even if there were showplaces, it would be pleasant if India could boast even one city that is clean, easy to get about in and without poverty.) Mortality data, school attendance figures, figures for health service personnel and a great variety of other indicators suggest that, while China may have some relatively backward parts, similar equality of distribution is common to them all so that, where standards are somewhat lower, they are lower for everyone and basic minimum standards are in normal times more or less universal. (And Chinese officials are apologetic about those differentials that do exist; they are part of the transitional phase of socialism – in the passage to true communism material incentives are supposed to disappear altogether.)

If this is substantially true as we believe and not, as some would have it, the delusions of romantic Maoists, another point is added to the growth rate debate. For if there really is some trade-off between growth and distribution, and China's growth rates are roughly comparable to those of India while distribution is better, then China's is once again the more significant performance. The comparison is reasonable from several points of view: China in 1949 was as replete with social and economic problems as India. Its cities had similar extremes of wealth and squalor and its countryside of domination and oppression. Perhaps the one initial advantage which China had over India – and it is of some importance – was the existing base of higher agricultural productivity. This has made the task of accumulation compatible with providing material sufficiency for the whole population – though obviously the latter depended heavily on the achievement of a high degree of equality in distribution. Be that as it may and granting that it does not excessively undermine the merit of China's relative performance, we still have two questions to ask: what have been the costs of the 'Chinese road'? And is it conceivable that India could go along it in any case? For if it could not, perhaps the whole undertaking of the comparison is misguided.

The most obvious 'cost' of China's revolution was the violent death of large numbers of landlords and other 'class enemies' – numbers that have been estimated in seven figures. More generally not only deaths were involved but the painful disruption of innumerable lives. It is beyond human capacity to say whether anything can balance against such 'costs'. One's view would depend very much on who one was. Most of us who merely contemplate such terrible events have never suffered the extremes of experience which drive men to act in them. It is a curious fact about Western morality that we tend to view with much greater horror suffering deliberately inflicted than that which the *status quo* simply permits to occur. No doubt this is due to our conceiving of morality almost uniquely in terms of individual responsibility. If one man dies by another's hand, without extenuating circumstances of war, wrong, passion or derangement, it is abhorred. If one man dies of hunger while his neighbour eats enough for two, that too is abhorred, but is part of the way things are; not all would condemn the neighbour, even if he could have helped and chose not to. Certainly many such neighbours do not condemn themselves. According to a celebrated authority we are all, or nearly all, such neighbours. In some calculus of mortality it is rather likely that the Chinese revolution has minimised the number of deaths; the number of lives saved has greatly exceeded the number prematurely extinguished, if one thinks of the numbers dying of starvation, disease or violence in pre-revolutionary China. But only for a utilitarian, and a rather narrow-minded one at that, would such an observation suffice for judgment. The broader felicific calculus, the question of whether the sum of human welfare has risen or fallen, is harder to work out; and even if the answer were clear, the non-utilitarian would not be obliged to follow it.

Life is still hard for most people in China today. Material conditions, though adequate, are austere. A great deal of what might otherwise be leisure time is taken up with meetings, ideological and educational activities. It is an exceptionally disciplined society. Possibly the aspect of both India and China in which comparison is most difficult is the question of freedom. As is well known the Chinese system operates with a high degree of social control. Revolutionary ideology governs virtually every aspect of life, in education and at work, in the village and in the city street. Yet it would be wrong to exaggerate the extent of this discipline to the point of describing it as regimentation. Within the framework laid down by the authorities a wide range of issues are left to the initiative and decision of subordinate groups, particularly those affecting work and social planning. Forms of organisation are designed for participation and productive units are encouraged to be as self-sufficient as they can. The result is that many ordinary Chinese men and women have considerable influence over decisions affecting their personal lives, even if they cannot greatly influence the rules, the priorities, the general context within which the decisions are taken.

To many who live in a more responsively democratic society that might seem a high price to pay even for the undoubted benefits it brings in the way of equality and material progress. But how responsive is democracy in India and what is the extent of freedom there? After the political crisis in mid 1975 which seriously weakened – however temporarily – the Parliamentary system at the centre, many argued that Indian democracy had always been something of a sham and those events only served to demonstrate its true character. We would not go so far. Being subject to re-election is a powerful restraint on the governing class. The Indian electorate has frequently demonstrated the wisdom of its choices and undoubtedly values the opportunity for continued expression of them. Freedom of the press, and freedom in general to criticise publicly the government of the day, is something whose value becomes the more obvious the more a country is deprived of it. Yet, as we have seen in earlier parts of this book and as we shall argue in the next two sections, there are patent defects in Indian society which obstruct the protection of human rights – the lower a person is in the social hierarchy, the more he or she would feel the truth of that fact. And many of the institutions which are essential complementary parts of Parliamentary democracy and which in other democratic countries permit the majority to influence events extensively and also minorities not to be overwhelmed, are in India too weak for the purpose.

A good issue for comparison is the situation of women in the two countries. In India middle class women can rise to the top in every walk of life, be it business, academe, administration, public services or politics. As in most male-dominated societies they are not proportionately represented at the highest levels, but they are powerfully represented and they take their place with greater ease and greater acceptance by the opposite sex than is common in many Western countries. But for most women the opposite is the case; they are still chattels and virtual slaves in the lower reaches of society, working for little reward and with far less educational or other opportunities than men. They do not even have the advantage of living longer as they do in almost all other countries. In China tremendous efforts have been made to release women from their traditional subjection. Their presence in high positions, though also not proportionate to their numbers, is well beyond mere tokenism and, at every level of society, they are encouraged to participate fully in every activity and crèches and other facilities are widely available to assist them. Many problems remain. Few communes as yet give work-points (in relation to which wages are paid) for domestic work, of which women do the major share even if they have full time jobs. There are unresolved ideological questions such as whether women will be fully liberated by the 'normal' development of socialism or whether they need special attention – it is a question of whether the oppression of women is wholly, or only partly, a feature of the class struggle. Reading about the situation of women in China one has a sense of energetic social engagement, of movement and change.[99] In India these problems are low on the agenda and the status of women is altering almost imperceptibly slowly.

This is the kind of contrast which it is important to examine: it shows up the aridity of the comparison of growth rates. If one really wished to do justice to the China-India question, one would compare some other things: research and technology, the quality of education, cultural facilities, leisure, prospects for the future. . . . It is not a foregone conclusion that China would 'win' in every single one. We stated at the outset of this section however that there was some question as to the relevance of the whole comparison enterprise. For China's achievements are mainly a product of its revolution. If such a revolution is unthinkable in India, the value of looking at its results becomes uncertain.

We have already suggested that for many reasons – military, geographical and other – a violent upheaval such as culminated in China's Liberation in 1949 is unlikely in India for several years at least. But even if we were wrong about this, there would still remain doubts as to whether China's type of revolutionary society could be transplanted to such different soil. One might doubt indeed whether it could be transplanted anywhere. It is arguable that the success of the social organisation which has evolved in China has depended in many ways on features of the culture and history of its people peculiar to that country or, put another way, that the leaders of the revolution have been particularly skilful in adapting the development of a revolutionary society to forms which its people would find acceptable and satisfying. Even if the power of those who stand in the way of radical change in India was eliminated, it might prove more difficult to produce satisfactory forms of social organisation which would carry forward essential processes of development. One cannot easily imagine what those forms might be – anyone of revolutionary sympathies in India is deluding himself if he thinks the institutions of China, or any other country – can be transferred to India as they stand. A change in the power structure is a necessary but not sufficient condition for other desirable changes. How amenable are the inheritors of millennia of Hindu culture to a highly disciplined, cooperative, materialist life and how will they be organised? We would repeat whatever the nature of change in India, it must be of a character suited to the country's culture and history. There are no decisive grounds for thinking that Chinese institutions will work there any better than British ones.

People in India must find it galling to be told again and again by their own or by foreign scholars how much better China is doing in this respect or in that. We feel somewhat apologetic for adding our own chip to the pile of comparisons. The appeal of making them is obvious. China and India achieved independence from foreign domination at almost the same time. They are both sub-continental powers with vast populations. Their starting resource base was similar – though not identical – as was the extent of deprivation and inequality. China has shown that many of the problems India faces can be solved or at least addressed with promise of success. China may indeed have much to teach India besides the uses of revolution. But China is not India and China has had a revolution of a kind which we believe is not likely to occur in India. The nature of any revolution which might succeed there is obscure and its preconditions therefore cannot be specified. Nor is China's future, any more than that of other countries, assured of stability and calm. There are periodic worries about the food situation,[100] about employment problems, about renewed possibilities of political strife. As the Soviet Revolution approaches its sixtieth birthday one can only reflect on the distance by which it falls short of the expectations of its creators. Marx proposed a society of omnicompetent men, classless, pursuing not material incentives but social cooperation and achieving the greatest possible fulfilment of human potential. The odds are rather against any country realising this dream. But the Chinese revolution has made a principle of defeating the odds and no one can say that they will not.

FUTURE PROSPECTS

It could be said that much of this book describes a country piling up combustible social material and then expresses, when it comes to the revolutionary issue, some confidence in the ability of the central authorities to forestall any conflagration. Growing landlessness, decline of caste conformities, rising expectations with no fulfilment, employment problems for educated and uneducated alike, social oppression for many, an economy which grows only modestly and in which increasing numbers compete for a share of material prosperity while much of its growth accrues to those already well off – these could certainly be the conditions in which movements for violent change would flourish. If the centre *can* prevent it, that is mainly because of its physical power and the scattered nature of the forces which oppose it. This need not remain so far all time; but for some time at least, if there is going to be change, it seems far more likely that it will be brought about by alterations in the behaviour of those who are already powerful rather than by power being wrested from their hands by those who presently lack it. For that reason India's political future for the next decade or two must mainly be studied from the viewpoint of the evolution of the present system of government. The great question is whether the antagonisms in the Indian polity can be resolved by any plausible evolutionary process – for if they cannot be resolved, they surely cannot be forever contained.

In a study of the workings of India's democratic system,[101] the late A. H. Hanson and Janet Douglas speculated about its future. Many had thought democracy would not last prior to the 1971 election; the Congress majority was steadily diminishing and the future had begun to look unstable since there was no natural successor to Congress. Rather, if Congress lost its overall majority, it would have remained the largest party, but coalition politics would have taken over. Mrs Gandhi's landslide victory in 1971 changed all that. Opposition parties were pulverised – some hardly managed to retain any seats in the Delhi Parliament. Nevertheless the future of democracy still did not seem assured. If the tendency, marked in the 1960s, for political power to become dispersed to the State capitals continued, new stresses and strains could appear for politicians at the Centre. If new regional groupings became strong, these strains might intensify. In any case, the authors asked, was democracy capable of 'providing the most appropriate political environment for the huge developmental tasks which the country inevitably faces'[102] – a question they have not been alone in asking.

That the future of India's political system depended so heavily on the fate of one party was understandable. And, as in many countries which achieved independence after the World War II, the question arose whether the party which led the independence movement would be capable of maintaining power once the unifying independence struggle was won and its achievements had receded into history. Congress had certainly lasted longer than many African or Asian nationalist parties and, just when it seemed it might be going the way of those others, Mrs Gandhi's victory appeared to give it a new lease of life. There was considerable euphoria in India in 1971. Not only was the viability of its political system apparently demonstrated but Mrs Gandhi's campaign, run on the slogan of *garibi hatao* or getting rid of poverty, promised a new deal for the poor at long last, and her majority was crushing enough to suggest that it would also be possible for a government to do all the things that were necessary but, from a weaker position, politically difficult. These hopes came to nothing. In 1975 people were wondering how four years of power had passed with so little to show for them. They were not it must be said easy years – few are in India. In 1971 there was the Bangladesh War and the refugee problem it created. There were poor harvests in 1973 and 1974 and 1972 was not much better. There was the oil crisis and the problems with the Fifth Plan that we have already described. But somehow the feeling remained of a political opportunity wasted.

In 1975 the problems seemed to be coming to a head. Stories of corruption have always circulated in India, but in the early 1970s some of them were well attested enough to be reported in the press – mostly connected with dubious methods of collecting funds for the Congress Party. There were also numerous alleged cases of favouritism in the award of contracts, personal profiteering from public enterprises, connivance at crime – enough to gather a wide assortment of public sympathisers around the veteran J. P. Narayan in an anti-corruption campaign, directed particularly at the Delhi Government, but not only that – Narayan had for many years based himself in Bihar where the State Government had perhaps the worst record of any State in India. Further trouble for Congress came in the Gujarat State election where Mrs Gandhi and other Congress leaders campaigned for the local candidates who were defeated. Finally in June a lawsuit brought by one of Mrs Gandhi's opponents accusing her of election malpractices reached a judgment against her: the actual malpractices were very slight (some graver charges were not upheld by the court). But the judgment had the effect of denying Mrs Gandhi her parliamentary rights.

It was thought in many quarters that Mrs Gandhi would abide by the decision and await the result of her appeal to the Supreme Court. But that was not to be. On 26 June came the famous Declaration of Emergency; many of Mrs Gandhi's opponents (including some in her own party) were placed under detention; press censorship was instituted. Parliament passed various measures to permit Mrs Gandhi to continue legally as the Prime Minister. The reasons for the Declaration have never been made entirely clear. The formal reason was that the safety of the country was threatened by internal disturbances. The Government claimed that there was a conspiracy against it, but the conspirators were never named and no evidence was adduced. To the outsider it was not obvious that the situation was so far out of hand that it could not have been met without the extraordinary powers of the Emergency. Some have argued that the main threat was to Mrs Gandhi's own position – she faced opposition among a substantial section of her own party as well as the Narayan movement and opposition parties in the States. Possibly she was uncertain of the pliability of any politician who might take her place while the appeal judgment was awaited. The decline of her support among Congress M.P.s must also have caused her concern. 'India's crisis or Indira's crisis?' wrote one commentator.[103] The question mark remains; perhaps historians will remove it – we cannot. Eventually the Supreme Court upheld her appeal (though not Parliament's attempt to place her above the Law). As 1975 drew to a close detainees began to be released, the censorship regulations were relaxed – but not removed – and observers began to wonder what the new 'normality' was going to consist of. The Prime Minister did not make it especially easy to divine. She told one audience that India must be democratically governed, another that in the past there had been an excess of freedom.[104] The people needed a sense of 'discipline' inculcated into them.[105] A new regulation announced that the Government would be empowered to rearrest prisoners after their term was up for the same offence; another defined a new censorship code for the press. And many of the detainees remained unreleased. If democracy was to be restored, it would evidently be on conditions imposed by those in power.

The events of 26 June were unforeseen. Many scenarios had been prefigured for the development of Indian politics, but this was not one of them. The favourites have been the fragmentation of the Union by centrifugal tendencies in the States and various developments of the multi-party system at the Centre – polarisation or splitting.[106] There were even expressions of faith in the continuance of things more or less as they were.[107] But if unforeseen, the events in retrospect did not completely seem out of character with what had gone before. Many signs had shown an increasing authoritarianism in the practice of government. Reports by Amnesty had spoken of untried political prisoners in excess of 15,000 in India well before 1975.[108] Many of them were Naxalite suspects, but many were just members of parties – especially Left parties – opposed to Centre or State Governments. Stories of torture were becoming more frequent. In fact one of the pieces of news to pass the Censors in 1975 was a directive by the Union Home Minister to State authorities not to torture prisoners.[109] The Central Reserve Police and other organs of State intelligence and security seemed to be ramifying and growing. The exceptionally harsh measures used in breaking the railway strike have already been referred to. Manipulation of State Governments by the Centre to instal leaders favourable to the ruling party was another feature of the times. Hanson and Douglas observed in 1971 a 'growing tendency of Mrs Gandhi's government to treat the Constitution as something that can be, and ought to be, manipulated for party political advantage.'[110] This was *à propos* the imposition of Presidential Rule in U.P. in 1970.[111]

That was written in the context of an account of the increasing lack of respect for the Constitution evident in opposition politics. It brings us more nearly up to date: for that was also the nature of Mrs Gandhi's case for the Emergency. Both inside and outside the Delhi Parliament the power of the Constitution to govern political behaviour was on the wane. Some of the accusations against the J. P. Narayan movement itself were far-fetched. But things were certainly being done and tolerated in public life that reflected no credit on Congress or opposition. What was strange was the emergence of Mrs Gandhi as the champion of integrity and order since she had herself been associated with some of the ills of the past and was soon to show her own lack of enthusiasm for the Constitution. However the new broom began by sweeping at least superficially clean. Tax inspection became more rigorous. Many blatant smugglers and black marketeers were jailed. Officials in fear of their jobs were ordered to be punctual and obeyed. Bureaucratic decision processes were said to be speeded up. But the real mettle of the new order, for such it was, could not be tried so quickly. Not long after the proclamation of the Emergency came the announcement of a programme for socio-economic reform. Described as the 'twenty point programme', the measures included such important matters as implementation of land reform legislation and reduction of rural debt by new credit agencies.

None of these announced measures were new – indeed they were positively ancient. They represented a good share of the body of reforms that any non-totalitarian observer would prescribe as the basic necessities for remedying the lot of the poor. Yet their announcement was not greeted with instant enthusiastic belief. Rather they sounded much like the professions of intention to restore democracy usually uttered by military dictators after a coup, the necessary rhetoric of political drama. Least convincing of all was the suggestion that, now the opposition was broken, these valuable measures could at last be carried through. The opposition to Mrs Gandhi's government had had very little power after the 1971 election. As has always been obvious the majority of rural reforms of the kind were opposed most of all by supporters of Mrs Gandhi's Congress. The only State governments which have achieved much in the way of land reform have been those of Kerala, where there is an effective grassroots organisation of the landless classes, and Tamil Nadu, where caste politics have weighed against landlords. Elsewhere, not only in this most contentious issue but in any other adversely affecting the landed interest, few State Governments which have attempted major change have lasted long. It was not untutored cynicism, but appreciation of the nature of interests in so much of the Congress party, that made for doubt about 'implementation of land reform legislation'.

By early 1977 after new elections had been announced pessimistic expectations about possible economic benefits of the Emergency seemed justified. The economic situation as a whole had improved, but that was due either to the good harvests of 1975/6 and 1976/7, the improved foreign exc'.ange situation or to policy measures most of which pre-dated the Emergency. The main specific actions which did benefit the poor somewhat and could be credited to the Emergency regime included a very modest amount of land distribution, some cancellation of rural debt (not usually backed by extension of credit) and a certain degree of success in discouraging grain hoarding. India's first post-Independence experiment in authoritarian rule seemed to show that, just by reducing the freedoms of the political opposition and the press, little difference was made to the features of the domestic power structure which obstructed radical change. One might add from the opposite standpoint that the suppression of strikes, which had a temporary effect of improving industrial performance, did not look a viable policy either even under the Emergency: towards the end of 1976 industrial action, especially among mill-workers, was beginning to increase in militancy.

But towards the end of 1976 authoritarianism still seemed well entrenched. A series of amendments to the Constitution were passed severely reducing the power of the courts and the rights of individuals. The press remained effectively silenced as a source of critical discussion of the Government's behaviour. Elections, already nearly a year overdue, were postponed for a further year. And then, within weeks of the latter's being announced, the Prime Minister made an extraordinary *volte-face* and changed her course. Elections followed in March 1977 with well-known results: the political demise for the time being at least of Mrs Gandhi and her son Sanjay, the demotion of Congress to minority status, the end of the

Emergency and the coming to power of a coalition of mainly Centre-Right parties.

The meaning of these events must depend more than a little on interpretations of why the elections were called in the first place and of why Congress lost so heavily. It is arguable on the first point that growing domestic pressures were causing the regime to seek renewal of the legitimacy of its rule, but it is equally arguable that the desire for renewal was wholly cosmetic and could have been indefinitely postponed – only serious miscalculation about the prospects of winning induced Mrs Gandhi to take to the polls. On the second a major factor in the Congress defeat was the unity of the opposition during the election; by a series of mutual agreements not to oppose each other, the opposition parties fielded 1000 fewer candidates in 540 seats than they had done in 1971. Congress had never received much more than 40 per cent of the popular vote and might have been defeated in earlier years by a unified opposition. Undoubtedly though the disastrous showing of Congress has also to be accounted for by its alienation of a large share of public sympathy.

A question for this book must obviously be how far the sterilisation issue was important in the election. The Emergency had many unpopular features: from the removal of civil liberties and the raising of land taxes to the unchecked high-handedness of police and local officials in innumerable spheres of life. Yet there are serious grounds for singling out the sterilisation drive as among the most potent causes of the forfeit of popular support by the Congress party. In all the States where sterilisation excesses were reported on a wide scale Congress was radically defeated; indeed Mrs Gandhi's supporters only managed to do at all well in the South where the sterilisation drive was not said to be unusually forceful. The main exception to this general hypothesis is West Bengal where Congress was also soundly defeated, though not apparently with any background of family planning excesses. But one need not seek a unique and universal principle which will explain the election results of all the States. There are several potential explanations of the Bengal result including the manipulation of State politics by the Centre and the suppression of the traditionally strong labour movement.

The attribution of causes in the 1977 election can only be surmised in the absence of the careful research which will no doubt appear in due course – these pages were written shortly after the election results were known. But there is reason to believe the above assessment. We have already described the hostility generated by the sterilisation drive in the States surrounding New Delhi, suggesting that it might not have been able to continue even had there been no election in 1977. A wide variety of Indian and foreign press reports during the election campaign indicated that it was very much an issue – as the authorities themselves admitted both by the announcement of the ending of the drive and the cancellation of most of its measures in the early days after the election was proclaimed as well as by a series of remarkable apologies in campaign speeches by senior Congress politicians. It is difficult to account in any other terms for the result in Uttar Pradesh, one of the States most marked by sterilisation incidents, where Congress, powerfully dominant before, lost every single seat including, by large margins, those of Mrs Gandhi and her son – the latter strongly identified personally with compulsion in family planning. What seems most surprising in retrospect, even though few had predicted the extent of the defeat, is not that Mrs Gandhi lost but that she had been confident of winning. Perhaps historians will conclude that this was the first election in the world in which family planning was a – if not the – deciding factor.

With the 1977 election a new class of politicians came to power after thirty years of Congress rule. At its outset the prospects for the new Government were uncertain – how stable it would be, what kinds of policies it would pursue. But though differing noticeably in many of their attitudes from the Congress of old, the new breed of politicians will essentially be operating the same system of government that prevailed before the Emergency and will be subject to the same social and economic pressures as their predecessors. With the end of Congress rule it is appropriate to return to our earlier general question and ask how far, under a democratically elected government, one can expect the types of change which will benefit the poor.

As was discussed in Chapter 4 there is not a unique choice, either you help the poor or you do not, and such and such are the necessary steps. There is a range of policy measures which increase in potential benefit to the poor only roughly as they increase in political difficulty. Our case has been that policy has rested too near the bottom of the range ignoring even some of the measures which were politically feasible. The future of Indian politics depends considerably on the distance up this range that the economy is able to travel. In so far as stability depends on satisfying the needs of the poor one can only speculate whether that will be achieved by any measures short of the most difficult. Conceivably a policy which only generates a modest improvement in employment, security and living standards could have significant political dividends. But it may be more realistic to think that radical measures are necessary; the question then becomes one of assessing how they may be achieved. If the overthrow of the existing power structure by a mass uprising is ruled out, what are the other possibilities?

We may look again at the prospect for land reform or other radical change under the existing system. It might have been reasonable to imagine after the 1971 election that the new situation favoured radical change. Had not Mrs Gandhi won mass support and was it not to a considerable degree divorced from the landowning class who in the past had 'delivered' the rural vote? Perhaps. But to rest there would be superficial. For Congress members have to be elected in the countryside and it is to the wealthy farmers that they must look for campaign funds and much else; in return they use their influence to further the farmers' interests. Much legislation on agrarian matters is reserved by the Constitution for the State assemblies where the members not only represent but frequently are wealthy farmers. 'Scratch a politician and you find a landowner' as the saying goes. Thus asking an unreformed Congress to push through a serious land reform was rather like asking bears to distribute their honey.

But the situation was clearly little changed by the Emergency; the regime either had no serious intention of carrying out its land reform promises or, despite its enormous powers, was unable to proceed even if it wished to. The interesting question is whether any elected government similar to those of recent years will be in any different position. If the new 1977 Government were to proceed to implement land ceiling legislation or other radical measures of rural reform, it would be a real break with the past; on the Government's early showing that did not look likely. Indeed the electoral platforms of some parties in the alliance were quite strongly big farmer oriented.

The Emergency and its aftermath is exceptionally difficult to analyse in any common political categories. Those who see historical events entirely in terms of class conflict could make out a case that the Emergency was a collapse of the post-colonial order which was gradually ceasing to satisfy the main class interests. In particular the industrial *bourgeoisie* wanted greater freedom from government control, the landlord interest greater security against threats to its continued political power and material prosperity. Some would see that collapse as 'inevitable' – parliamentary democracy was not resolving but sharpening the conflicts between straightforward material interests or power groupings at regional levels. Such truth as there would be in such an account – and it could not be dismissed out of hand – does not weigh too heavily against the facts which militate against it. In the first place it is not at all obvious what class interest 'won' with Mrs Gandhi's takeover. Many of the most vocal supporters of the Emergency came from the business world and the landowning class. But the Emergency did not favour business unduly: there were tax concessions, but coupled with a drive against tax-evasion and the 'black money' economy. As for industrial policy there were few major changes and those that were introduced pre-dated the Emergency. There was much talk of greater freedom for private capital, domestic and foreign, but little action. Delegations of U.S. and U.K. industrialists visited India in 1976 exploring the alleged new atmosphere for private investment from overseas but found little had changed. By 1977 the failure of domestic capital to invest in Indian industry was becoming something of an embarrassment to the Government – clearly the Emergency had not provided a climate of business confidence and equally clearly many sections of business were unhappy with the Emergency.

For industry the Emergency promised beneficial change and did not deliver it; for the landlord class diminution of power and an attack on material interests was promised – little of that was delivered either. The Government led by Morarji Desai may change the balance of concern to a greater stress on agriculture and give vent to expressions of Hindu nationalism more vocal than anything heard before in government circles, but it gave no signs in its early days of radical intentions that might lead to a new deal for poor people. In most of India it is not Congress alone but all the main non-Communist parties that have strong links with landowners. They cannot presently calculate that the support of the landed interest can be dispensed with. And if they could, but landowners resisted measures of reform, force would be required to push them through. It is this last consideration that makes land-redistribution or similar measures under the present form of government seem even more unlikely. The instruments of State power – army or police – are just as much a part of the existing social order. As noted above, even to secure legal rights less threatening than land-distribution, the weaker sections of society have throughout most of India had an uphill struggle; they have often preferred not to cause trouble by insisting on their rights. When they have, they have rarely found allies in the police and the judiciary. The army has never been called in to back such legislation; any attempt to employ it in this way would also be dangerous; senior army officers are themselves often major landowners or belong to families with large landholdings. One must conclude that, if improving the lot of the poor requires redistribution of land or tenancy reform, it is unlikely to occur rapidly or on any major scale under the existing balance of social forces.

That balance can change and in various ways short of a mass based revolution. The possibilities can only be sketched here. In the first place there is organisation of the rural poor – landless labourers, small farmers or other groupings. Such organisations may be perfectly legal and con-stitutional, but the greater the threat they offer to the *status quo*, the more obstacles will be placed in the way of their development. No one who knows of the early days of the trades union movement in Europe or America need have any illusions about the difficulties involved. Neverthe-less attempts to foster such organisations must be an important strand in the future of Indian politics. A second possibility is the advent of a more radical government by election. This is obviously connected with the first possibility. Organisation of the rural poor could have an effect on electoral politics. It is even imaginable that a majority party could begin to shift its traditional bias and seek support among the rural masses. That party could also become radicalised from within by the advent into positions of power within the hierarchy of more radical members whose constitutencies have a different class basis from those of the current incumbents. A third possibility is a military takeover. Although this is occasionally discussed in the press and elsewhere little is really known to the public of the political complexion of the military. There has not been much indication hitherto of anything other than complete loyalty of the armed forces to the government of the day and total subservience to the civilian arm. It is not impossible that somewhere in the country a group of young officers has pondered on the seizure of power from the politicians. But they would face formidable difficulties if they tried it. The army is widely dispersed in a number of powerful units. As long as senior officers remain committed to the civilian government – and the Prime Minister has a major say in their appointment, so that commitment remains highly probable – a military coup can hardly come about. Pay and conditions for the ordinary serviceman are good especially by comparison with the poverty from which so many of them come. Of course it is not unknown for armies to receive a political education when they are called into actions that pit them against civilian populations – in the twentieth century this has usually been overseas in colonial situations. Such things as the rising power of police or other paramilitary forces may also create rivalries and jealousy among military officers. But on the basis of its public image at least such developments in the Indian forces appear thoroughly implausible at present.

To return to the question from which we began, namely are the conflicts of Indian society likely to be resolved by non-revolutionary means – the answer must be that they can be, to some extent, but whether they will be depends on the degree to which government and politics themselves change. As far as concerns the alleviation of povery there are policy measures that a government such as the present one can take without political difficulty; many of them were described in Chapter 4. We would not go as far as some in the explanation of all failures of policy in class terms. But while such measures could provide a greater sufficiency of material things for the mass of ordinary people they would not by any means resolve all conflicts. We tend to be mesmerised by poverty and think of its existence as the main threat to stability. Men and women also seek equality. Even if there are no strong centrifugal tendencies, there are certainly regional power struggles of individual States against the Centre for resources or against each other; different communities, corporate groups and individuals seek increased power. The greatest problem caused by authoritarian regimes is that they force opposition politics into clandestine and conspiratorial forms. If the regimes in addition have no mass base, they plant the seeds of their own downfall. The latter is true for parliamentary democracies too. As was discussed above misery alone is not the begetter of revolutionary change.

It must be said that if one were forecasting the trend of Indian politics in the next two decades, none of these catastrophic eventualities would bulk very large. It is perhaps an illusion of the Left that things must always move in a leftward direction. The tendency of recent years was towards increasingly authoritarian government. No one can be certain that the ending of the Emergency has permanently reversed that tendency. As everyone knows democracy requires not only elections but many countervailing institutions to ensure the fairness of the elections themselves, the rights of minorities, the responsiveness of the Government to criticism, the prevention of abuses of power and position, even the pursuit of the interests of the majority who vote the Government into office. Recent events have shown such institutions to be extremely weak in India. True the judiciary at the highest levels proved to be a bulwark of the Constitution and of liberal rights up till 1976 – then the constitutional amendments undermined even that. But at lower levels it is only in theory that all are equal under the law. The Indian press could not always be relied on to be solidly responsible or universally outspoken; under the Emergency it was powerless to criticise at all. The Delhi Parliament has not been tremendously responsive to public opinion; the State Assemblies even less so – indeed for long periods, especially in the late 1960s, the shameless opportunism of their members, most notoriously shown in frequent 'floorcrossing', made a mockery of democratic procedure. Nevertheless in pre-Emergency India there were at least some limits to the extent of malfeasance or nonfeasance which individuals or governments could get away with without being exposed, and some pressure on them at least to try to fulfil their electoral pledges.

An authoritarian government in India may be able to silence irresponsible opposition and carry out valuable but unpopular measures without too much fear of adverse reaction. But good government needs criticism, just as it needs legitimate means of reconciling conflict. Above all in India it needs to hear the voice of the poor. One may have doubts about the ability of democratic government to succeed in the 'huge developmental tasks which the country . . . faces.' But the main developmental task is the mitigation of poverty; that is something in which authoritarianism alone does not promise success. If our analysis is correct, benefits for the poor are likely to be modest under regimes cast in recent moulds whether more or less authoritarian. However this is not at all to say that the 1977 election had no significance. To the class-interest theoretician it may merely have exchanged one set of *bourgeois* rulers for another demonstrating at most some interesting 'contradictions' within the *bourgeoisie*. But it seems to have demonstrated other things as well – in particular a new independence on the part of the electorate. Analyses of Indian elections have often spoken of local interests capable of 'delivering' the vote, especially in rural areas. Yet on this occasion, despite what must often have been strong pressures to support Mrs Gandhi's regime, many tens of millions of men and women said 'No' with resounding conviction. (That the election was, with only a few blemishes, a fair one is also highly creditable in the circumstances – by any standards, and even more so by those of other countries in Asia.) What is needed for the health of India's democracy is a government whose survival, or chances of re-election, depends on progress in meeting the needs of the poor. One may read the 1977 election as signifying that the mass of the public will not again accept the cynical defeat of its expectations. But it has yet to be seen whether the new Government justifies such a hopeful interpretation or whether it will be left to future ones to succeed where it will fail.

In the spring of 1977 we write at a time of great uncertainty for Indian politics. With the eclipse of Congress an era has ended and it is not obvious what will take its place. After the euphoria of the removal of an oppressive regime has dissipated, the strains of a multi-party coalition seem bound to emerge with no settled directions in view. The Emergency seems to have shown that India can only be governed by processes which resolve its conflicts in the open. Those who predict a quick reintroduction of authoritarian rule are surely reckoning without the deep hostility it has been shown to engender. But all the political problems of Indian society remain to be solved. We hope to have shown that apocalyptic talk has little basis for the near term and that the main future of India's politics lies in the evolution of its multi-party electoral system. One of the main hopes for a positive evolution lies in the political awareness which the 1977 election has made apparent. Change through swift eruption, if it does not come through slow evolution, cannot be ruled out forever. The centuries old passivity of India's rural masses cannot now be taken for granted; the continuing quiescence of urban society even less so. A crisis or combination of crises, international hostilities, food shortage, communal troubles, could unsettle the Centre and provide an occasion for a challenge to its authority. But there must be a considerable future for the present combination of the power of the Centre and the relative inertia of the rest. That power is very considerable; one can only hope, without much confidence, that it will be used with greater effect in the interest of the poor than has been the case in the past.

CONCLUDING OBSERVATIONS

> There is no going back,
> For standing still means death, and life is moving on,
> Moving on towards death. But sometimes standing still is also life.
>   John Ashbery, *The Double Dream of Spring*

The main purpose of this book has been to provide a detailed account and analysis of India's population as it has affected and been affected by the process of economic development. An attempt to summarise it therefore goes rather against its spirit. However, if the trees have been the chief subject, the wood deserves a few broad brush strokes. The framework of the argument is as follows: Population growth has helped to make difficult any substantial progress in material living conditions for the majority of India's people. At the same time, with growing numbers, a better economic record could have been achieved if different policies had been adopted or even if the policies chosen had been pursued more effectively. In many other countries in the past birth rates have declined in response particularly to education, urbanisation, industrial growth, reduced infant and child mortality, improvements in employment opportunities and the status of women. Family planning assists the decline of fertility where these things are occurring and may even do so to a limited extent where they are not. Fertility in India is going down as a result of both of these general societal changes and the work of the family planning programme. But the failure of development to accelerate the spread of these 'correlates of fertility decline' – which are to be thought of as parts of a social process rather than as factors which necessarily affect fertility by themselves – has meant that progress has been extremely slow.

If India's demographic transition is to be speeded up, it will have to be by a process somewhat different from that experienced in the advanced countries. Industrial development is not likely on economic grounds to involve any fast-growing share of the population. But it is possible for India to improve employment prospects, health, education and social equality even without rapid change in the sectoral balance of the economy. If that were to happen, the family planning programme could make greater headway despite the unsatisfactory state of contraceptive technology. There are also some trends which may change the perception of the economic usefulness of children, especially growing land shortage; if more were known about the importance of the economic motive in fertility, such trends could be taken into account in predicting future fertility decline. And even in existing conditions India's family planning programme could be somewhat more effective.

A good deal of emphasis has been given to the role of social structure in shaping the character of economic development. At the highest level, while the framers of successive Five Year Plans have expressed sympathetic views regarding the 'weaker sections', the conduct of economic policy has been mainly in the hands of those for whom the welfare of small farmers, tenants, landless labourers or urban workers outside the modern sector has not been the first priority. Down through all levels of economic organisation from Central Government to the village we have observed how the less well-off are almost always at a disadvantage in claiming a share of the benefits of development. Measures have either not been designed to help them in the first place or, when they have, the existing power structure has thwarted much of any potential benefit they contained. Some scepticism about the extent to which future policies will be better designed to help the poor, or better executed, is inevitable unless either there is some alteration in social relationships or the powerful feel sufficiently threatened to act more decisively in favour of the lower income groups. There must be expectations of increasing efforts to mobilise those sections of the population politically; but a successful revolutionary assault by them against the existing power structure seems at present a very remote possibility. The

Declaration of Emergency of June 1975, and the election of 1977 which succeeded it, however, introduced new elements of uncertainty into Indian politics and made alternative political developments more than usually difficult to forecast.

The above three paragraphs summarise the thread of argument that runs through this book. In the remaining ones certain features of our study are brought out for particular attention together with one or two topics not discussed elsewhere. A major ambition was to place the population problem in perspective. Although the eventual population size India will reach is very large one should be trying to discover how its future will differ from the past. What will be the difference between the passage from 300 to 600 million in the last thirty-five years and that from 600 to one billion, which may occur in a shorter time, although population will be growing more slowly? We must admit that we have not provided any definitive answers to that question – perhaps nobody can. Expert opinion suggests that the food problem is not insoluble – which is not the same as saying that it will be solved. We have pointed to forestry and soil conservation generally as a serious danger area which has not been adequately catered for. We have not really gone deeply into the question of long-term water availability and use; we know of no such studies and to make one ourselves was not possible. There is an enormous volume of unutilised irrigation potential, but the effects of utilising it require investigation. There is the whole question of the trends in rainfall about which again there is no certainty. To other environmental problems such as water and air pollution we have given little space – these are of course affected as much by income growth and technological choice as by population increase, if not more. The one situation which we have suggested may be subject to a genuine size threshold, though of a social character, related to economic conditions, is urban growth. But in general we have not been able to identify any area that presents an unambiguous likelihood of catastrophe. Rapid population growth is not a time bomb but a treadmill. It postpones the day when most people in India can enjoy an agreeable life; but that day could be brought nearer or postponed still further by many other things besides demographic change.

Many people who make dire predictions about the ecological future do so out of genuine concern; others seem to be doing no more than cashing in on the public's seemingly inexhaustible appetite for nightmares. There are opposing 'no-problem' or 'the market will adjust' schools whose optimism cannot be shared either. It is more honest to admit that we do not know what the future holds; that it will be good or bad depending on some things that are within human control and others that are not. The business of the academic observer is to point to the areas where action is most needed and also – and this is one of our self-confessed aims – to create a climate of opinion for balanced judgement about future development. Pessimism sometimes seems to come purely from false images of the future and hasty generalisation. Bad analogies are often made with the behaviour of animals. One author whose views have achieved a certain currency concluded after making a careful study of mice in cages that humans would breed up to the point of 'standing room only'.[112] Possibly we move too easily from large numbers to simplistic thought. The phrase 'one billion people in India' may conjure up all manner of misleading pictures. One should be careful to think of these numbers as being arrived at both very gradually and over a very large expanse of space. The gradualness leaves room for innumerable processes of adjustment, and so does the spatial dimension. All these extra millions arrive not in huge crowds springing up overnight in city centres, but in small numbers each year in half a million villages and on the edges of towns and suburbs. To a very considerable extent one can answer the question, what does the future hold for India, with the observation that the future has already arrived. It is sad enough to contemplate an India continuing to make the modest progress we have seen hitherto; there is no need to invent speculative disasters.

The international community

An important part of our analysis has been that the *rate* of population increase, though certain to remain substantial, is probably past its maximum; for some time to come we expect the birth rate to decline more rapidly than the death rate. A more sophisticated economy and a more slowly growing population should make possible the achievement of greater gains in individual living conditions. Doubts that these will in fact materialise stem from three sources: the imponderables of the physical environment alluded to above, of the future of the international economy and of domestic developments. Next to nothing has been said in this book about the role of the international community for various reasons. The focus of so much writing on India has been the foreign aid programme, the role of foreign capital and trading arrangements. If they have been neglected here it is not because they are unimportant. We have chosen to concentrate on internal problems because that is where the theme of population mainly leads. But an account of India's development is incomplete without some reference to its international background. There is a considerable literature laying much of the blame for 'underdevelopment' on the rich countries; indeed the term has for some commentators virtually come to mean a condition inflicted on the poor countries by the rich.[113] In our opinion such a case cannot be made out for India with anything like the same force as might apply in several African and Latin American countries. That is not to say that the international community has been immensely helpful to India – far from it.

India has at times received quite large amounts of aid, even exceeding $1 billion in a year on occasion. But while it has received more genuine aid in absolute amount than any other country, in relation to the size of its population there are few developing countries that have had less. This is not surprising; if all aid were equally divided on a per capita basis, there would be little left over for other countries – India's population is, after all, about equal to the combined populations of the whole of Africa and South America.[114] If there is ever any temptation to feel that aid has not lifted India out of its difficulties, one should always bear in mind that it has never amounted to more than a few pence per head and, in the years when it was greatest, much of it was food aid replacing some of what the droughts had taken away. Nevertheless there are other measurements of aid which indicate how important it has been to the Indian economy, even if small relative to the country's needs. Aid has averaged between 10 and 15 per cent of annual investment and reached far higher percentages in some years of India's foreign exchange availability – as much as 50 per cent or more. Given the crucial nature of the foreign exchange constraint in the country's growth process, its significance should not be minimised. Undoubtedly too without food aid, especially in the crisis years of 1966–7, there would have been cruel hardship in many parts of the country.[115]

In recent years there has been increasing talk of 'disillusionment' with aid both in India and in the capitals of the lending countries. The dissatisfaction in India has had many strands. There is the powerful appeal of nationalism and self-respect that makes many Indians wish to see the end of aid. Such sentiments took root particularly in the mid 1960s when devaluation appeared to have been forced on the Government by the Aid-India Consortium; their intensification was fostered by the U.S.A.'s use of withdrawal of aid as an instrument of pressure, both in the drought crises of the late 1960s and at the time of the Bangladesh War. An equally potent cause for dissatisfaction with aid was the modest levels to which it fell in the early 1970s; when 'aid' was referred to above the figures were for gross aid – the inflow of disbursed funds. Over a long period the inflow was large relative to the outflow of debt repayments on past aid. Current aid to India from the Consortium is on very easy terms. But the aid loans of the 1950s and early 1960s were on much harder terms – these loans were becoming due in the early 1970s and debt service mounted to levels over $600 million. At this time the gross inflow was down to amounts in the region of $900 million.[116] The net inflow at its lowest was little more than $300 million in a year and, since debt service has to be paid in free foreign exchange while aid is hedged about with all manner of conditions which reduce its value, it is hardly surprising that questioning of the worthwhileness of aid became commonplace. The Draft Fifth Plan, like its predecessor, saw the budgetary future as containing the elimination of net aid; the Approach Document for the Fifth Plan was called 'Towards Self Reliance'[117] and ministerial pronouncements of the time echoed the theme.

It was never clear whether talk of self-reliance reflected a real determination or just the acceptance of a trend. One might have thought it was also a self-fulfilling prophecy; if the Indian Government spoke of self-reliance, would not 'aid-weary' governments in the Consortium eagerly help them to that end? In fact this has not happened. If net aid was falling in the early 1970s, it was partly because of the phasing out of food aid, but partly also because of declining non-food aid. The latter was however mostly the result of frictions between the United States and India; it was declining U.S. aid that brought the total down while in fact other Consortium members, not least the World Bank and the International Development Association, were making considerable increases in their lending. In fact self-reliance is both a genuine ambition of many responsible Indian officials as well as a position necessary to adopt for domestic political reasons. At the same time, in the practical difficulties faced by the economy, the early achievement of self-reliance was never likely to have the highest priority. The sensitivities have on the whole been appreciated on both sides; aid had risen substantially since its low ebb in the early years of the decade and the Government of India, apart from refusing food aid for a period, has never turned down an offer of genuinely concessional assistance. With the change in aid policies after the 'oil crisis', promising more aid to the poorer among the developing countries and to those most seriously affected by the oil price increases, India stands to benefit from increased aid flows for the time being and in the final Fifth Plan ambitions for self-reliance were muted.

Aid is however not the most important aspect of India's international economic relations. Unlike the case of some countries where the 'dependency' or 'neo-colonialism' issues are of major significance, private foreign investment is no longer a powerful factor in India either. The inflow of new investment is small as is the outflow on private account. Foreign firms have played, and still play, a considerable part in industry. But they are not an overwhelming presence as they are in say Brazil or, to a somewhat lesser extent, Kenya. Part of the radical thesis about the role of aid and foreign investment is of course not just the economic effects but their influence on the structure of power relationships in the recipient country; the involvement of India in these aspects of the international economy, so the argument would run, maintains the power of the *bourgeois* elite and assists the continuation of policies which carry forward *bourgeois* ambitions rather than the interests of the mass of the people. This thesis, like others which have their origins in the contemplation of U.S. relations with Latin America or those of Britain or France with some African countries, is not wholly convincing as applied to India. That is not because there is no coincidence of interests among the Indian ruling elite, aid-giving governments and business, domestic and foreign – on the contrary. But in this grouping the foreign interests are relatively minor. If one were to imagine a major reduction in the role of aid and foreign investment in India, one would not predict as a result a great subsequent radicalisation of Indian politics. The landed interests and domestic capital are the leading actors on this stage; aid and foreign investment may be part of the supporting cast, but the play would not stop, nor the theatre crumble, without them.

Much more important to the Indian economy than either aid or foreign investment is trade. The bulk of India's available foreign exchange today is earned by exports which have exceeded $4 billion since 1974.[118] Chapter 4 looked at some of the domestic aspects of exports and export policy. But this is where the international community is most open to criticism. The potential markets for many of India's manufactures are protected by high tariffs; even primary products, such as tea, are subject to indirect taxes in some countries. The various ways in which developing countries are at a disadvantage in international trade have been widely discussed.[119] Redressing them is a part of the activities conducted under the heading of the 'New International Economic Order' in the United Nations and elsewhere.[120] This case certainly applies as much to India as to other Third World countries. In some respects indeed India has been worse off than many others. On Britain's accession to the European Economic Community for example various trading arrangements of value to India were damaged. The British Government was active in making the Lomé Convention, the treaty which governs the E.E.C.'s relations with associated Third World countries, a more generous document than the Yaoundé Convention which preceded it. But while most countries previously connected with Britain were thus brought into – on the whole – advantageous relations with the E.E.C. several, including India, were left out.[121] India has had to pursue its economic interest *vis à vis* Europe in a special commission set up for the purpose. As noted India was also one of the countries most heavily hit by the oil price increase, whilst benefiting little from the commodity boom which preceded it since most of the other commodities whose prices rose were not those of main interest to India. Although suffering with other Third World countries from the systematic disabilities they encounter in international trade, India has not profited much from those few beneficial arrangements that have been established while some of the blows handed out by world markets have struck exceptionally hard. The country's problems are very far from being all of its own creation.

It is a curious fact that so much of the attention of the mass media in the West is given to aid when Third World problems are discussed. This may be in part because the most obvious thing the individual can do to assist the poor overseas is to give money through some voluntary agency, and analogously the most direct assistance governments give is through concessional lending. We do not share the hostility towards aid – not the current character of aid to India at any rate – expressed by some authors of both Left and Right.[122] But we would be seriously blinkered if our eyes were fixed on aid, which does on the whole assist development, while neglecting all the other things the rich countries do which actively hinder it, whether they be adverse trading arrangements, the transfer of inappropriate technology, the deleterious features of the operations of multi-national corporations,[123] even, on occasions, the direct inhibition of desirable political change. The public has been so little educated on the true nature of relations between rich and poor countries that it is in fact very difficult for individuals – or governments – to become involved in activities other than those connected with aid, if they wish to be of practical assistance to the Third World. That educative process deserves a major increase of attention.

This is not to imply that aid is not worthwhile. It may not be adequate to transform the situation of the Third World, but it does make a valuable contribution in many countries, India among them. We would hope indeed that this book will assist the removal of some of the arguments often heard against aiding India – that India is a 'bottomless pit' where aid will be swallowed up without trace or that the Government is so incompetent and corrupt that aid achieves nothing or ends up in the pockets of officials. Such arguments are without serious foundation. As we have seen developments in the immediate future can make a big difference to the country's long-term prospects. India's future may be one of a large population with low incomes, but the numbers will be greater or smaller, and the material conditions better or worse, depending on what is achieved now. The more aid can assist these achievements, the better. As far as competence or corruption is concerned India's governments have a better record than those of many developing countries. There are no known cases of serious misappropriation of aid funds in India though they have not been unknown elsewhere. And India does have reasonably coherent development policies, if not as thoroughgoing as could be desired, and a reasonable capacity to carry them out. India will be a major force in the international arena for the rest of history. Its government may not always act as others would like – few governments do. But on virtually all grounds on which aid is proffered, India has a strong case and should continue to be treated accordingly. As the preceding paragraphs make clear however there is a need for action on many fronts other than aid. Innumerable disadvantages confront the Third World in their efforts at development. Until the governments of the rich countries do more to rectify them, their professions of concern at the existence of world poverty will continue to sound hollow. And population growth as we have seen is intimately connected with that poverty. It is not even logical for rich country governments to send delegations to Bucharest who speak of the need for reducing rates of population growth and then instruct their delegates to UNCTAD not to give too much away. But that is what they do.

Most of what we have said here refers to the role of the developed market economies. What of the Socialist countries – is their record any better? Recent years have seen a marked increase in trade between India and the European Socialist countries; it rose from 0·5 per cent to over 18 per cent of India's total trade in the twenty years from 1952/3.[124] At the same time aid from the Socialist bloc did not increase at anything like the rate of Consortium assistance. But aid and trade with the Socialist countries are much more closely allied. This results from the condition that all settlements are made in rupee terms, both for aid and trade, so that debt repayments or trade imbalances will all be reflected ultimately in the flow of goods. The value of this trade and aid have been questioned. On the trade side it has been said that sales to Socialist countries divert goods which could have been exported for hard currencies; that some Indian exports are later dumped by the Socialist countries in world markets to India's cost; or that the prices arranged for Indian goods have been low while those for imports from the Socialist bloc have been high. The most careful examination of these issues that we know finds these criticisms valid only to a modest degree; 80 per cent of this trade is real, additional trade.[125] Socialist aid has similarly been criticised for being on hard terms, excessively project tied, and for supplying high priced and inappropriate equipment. In fact its record on these scores is on the whole neither better nor worse than that of other donors on average.[126]

Trade and aid with the Socialist countries have had certain special advantages. One of these obviously is rupee settlement itself, if one accepts the argument that indirect hard currency costs are limited. Both trade and aid have to some extent been put on a long-term footing giving some continuity and permitting India to plan accordingly. Aid was often available for public sector manufacturing enterprises at a time when Consortium assistance was not (nowadays it is). On the other hand the development of these relationships has not been easy. In 1968, on the morning of the opening of the New Delhi UNCTAD meetings, the Soviet Union achieved a notable public relations success as newspaper headlines announced 'U.S.S.R. to Purchase 10,000 Railway Wagons Made in India'. In fact for several years trade delegations came and went without arranging any deal for the wagons. The Soviet Union for some time was trying to induce India to buy some of its less economical passenger aircraft; India wanted materials that were not in excess supply in the Soviet Union such as non-ferrous metals. But gradually over the years a certain harmony of interests has come about with the Socialist countries buying an increasing share of Indian manufactures in their imports from India. For its part India purchases a large proportion of its defence material from the Bloc – a consideration which probably outweighs all other defects in economic relationships as far as India is concerned. The biggest aid donor, the Soviet Union, has not in fact provided India with as much aid as has the United Kingdom let alone the U.S.A. But the combination of arms supplies and powerful political support in the international arena have brought the Socialist countries into ever closer liaison with India. This, as the Government of India no doubt recognises, can also be helpful in India's relations with the West.

India's problems

It is clear enough that, while the international community can do much to ease India's path, most of the burdens must be shouldered by India itself as they always have been. All the various policy aspects of India's development touched on in this book will not be rehearsed here. Most of them were summarised at the ends of Chapters 3 and 4. We wish in closing to reflect on one main theme. In so far as 'development' means not the modernisation of society by acquisition of the trappings of industrialism, but improving the lot of the great majority of the people, India's key development problem is to improve the utilisation of labour – to employ more labour, make it more productive and reward it more adequately. As we and others before us have found, that is not likely to come about as the result of a conventional strategy concentrating on traditional notions of investment allocation – not of course that investment allocation has nothing to do with it. All economic activity affects employment: not just the creation of new workplaces by new investment, but increases in wheat yields or shifts in cropping patterns. But there is a limit to what investment allocation or pricing and taxation will achieve by themselves. As is evident from so many examples the official encouragement of an activity which could benefit the poor is no guarantee that it will do so. Whether it be irrigation, agricultural extension, health services or urban settlements, the 'weaker sections' are so often passed by.

A large proportion of the problems, for rural India at least, are best considered at the village level. It is there that the imbalances of social and economic power begin. Yet as we have observed again and again it is there that the problems have to be solved. Village water-supplies will not be renovated by centrally supplied funds for many decades; by village self-help they could be quite rapidly. Central or State health services will not reach the rural poor for a very long time; 'health by the people' could do so more quickly. While many developmental resources must come from taxation outside the village a large share of what is needed lies in the village itself – the labour and the means to make it productive. Even the population question itself may find its answer in this context: perhaps only when communities work for the collective good and take responsibility for their own numbers will those numbers be sensibly regulated by voluntary means.[127] As it is, life in the village is not cooperative but competitive. And the rich appropriate both externally supplied and internal resources; they benefit most from subsidised irrigation and credit. They lend not to enrich but to impoverish their fellows and to enhance their own estates. If all the inhabitants of the village were to cooperate for their mutual advancement, many of them other than those in the very poorest villages could solve most of their own problems.

That is not the way things currently work. The appeal of revolution is that it removes the main obstacles to this cooperation – the vested interests which prevent the sharing of wealth and work for the common good.

Among possible futures for India's rural poor three main variants could be categorised. One would be to continue as at present with little if any improvement for the poor. A second would be an 'allocation' strategy which concentrated more on investments, technologies and price and fiscal incentives which encourage labour-intensive production, perhaps even with some modest redistribution of assets. These possibilities are not to be sniffed at – many might feel they are the most that can be expected, perhaps more than can be expected. The third possibility is one of more thorough-going change; it would require not only the allocative measures of the second, but a fundamental change in the social structure such that resources were used to the maximum extent for the common good.

It is only under the third of these that real redistributive growth can be imagined; the other alternatives are either stagnation or minor changes promising at best only slight improvements for the poor. Yet the prospects for this 'thorough-going change' do not appear very bright at present. In principle one could imagine it happening by peaceful means; a leader of Mahatma Gandhi's stature and charisma could persuade the better-off to use their resources for the benefit of others which would in many ways be to their own advantage. But such an eventuality, though conceivable, seems rather far-fetched, and the history of those idealistic movements which have tried such a path – that of Vinoba Bhave for example – is not impressive in terms of major alteration of social behaviour. As we have observed the peasant revolution which might bring it about also seems a distant prospect. That is why for the time being one looks for change mainly to the present system of government. Here yet again the future of 'thorough-going change' looks dim: if our analysis is correct, the existing constellation of social and economic forces does not appear ready to produce widespread concessions on a large scale. It seems to be the case that Indian politics has produced a balance of forces that cannot solve its main political problem – the ending of deprivation.

Yet if this problem is not solved, or even relieved, it is hard to imagine the present system of government remaining unchanged for very long. One should not under-estimate the power of governments to deal repressively with discontent; yet if discontent continues to intensify, fostered by under-ground political movements or even the unfulfilled promises of politicians, the forces of repression will gradually become incapable of containing it. Somehow real human needs must be met. There is more than one way in which this can come about. A left-wing view would maintain that there are no alternatives to revolution; that the existing socio-economic system has run out of potential for progress and will collapse out of its own contradictions to be replaced, after conflict, by the revolutionary order. But that view rests on a limited appreciation of the capacity of such an economy to change and an optimistic one of the probability of revolution. It cannot be proved incorrect; but history is full of unfulfilled prophecies of the downfall of systems. At the same time, it may be excessively optimistic to hope that desirable change can come without pain. The history of economic development shows that it can sometimes, but it takes many decades and the poor are not indefinitely patient.

Most people would agree on the kinds of change needed in India if poverty is to be ended. But there is far less agreement on the nature of the process that would induce such change or the likelihood of its occurrence. We would reiterate what we said above: whatever that process it will be Indian in character and appeal, something that the foreigner is ill-placed even to attempt to describe. Certainly there is something distasteful in the situation of the Western scholar, safe in his university library, preaching revolution for other people. Our book has tried to trace the connections between population change, the economy and society. It is for those who live with these problems to find their solution. If we have the right to lecture anyone it is our own people whose high standard of living rests to a degree on the poverty of the Third World, and our own governments, which offer modest assistance and much obstruction to the development of the Third World in general and of India in particular.

India's population will stabilise, if at a high level. Its problems will be little different, except in scale, from those of many other, smaller societies. We can do a great deal to make their future more comfortable and less dangerous. Or we can turn our backs hoping the problems will go away and leave us untouched. They will not.

Appendix A
Demographic Glossary

In the course of the book various demographic terms are employed with a reference to this appendix at their first appearance. Demographers have evolved various measures of populations to take account of subtleties of population arithmetic which cruder measures omit; they have also worked out particular techniques of estimation based on the forms in which population data are available. We define here, with brief explanation, the most common terms. The reader who wishes to go deeper is referred to standard texts such as Barclay (1958) or Cox (1970); the mathematically inclined will appreciate Keyfitz (1968). Where it is appropriate typical 'high' and 'low' rates of the more common of the various measures are given as an indication of the normal ranges to be found – they should not be thought of as the known extremes of the measures.

Age distribution: The number or proportions of people in a population according to age group. The commonest age intervals employed are for 5 or 10 years, though for very precise calculations single years are sometimes used. The age distribution for a population is commonly depicted on a diagram giving numbers of males and females in each age interval. Successive age distributions reflect the history of a population. Thus a war in which a large number of men aged 20 – 30 are killed will show up for decades afterwards, both in the subsequent age groups which they themselves would have entered had they not been killed, and by the absence of the number of children they would have fathered. Much of the mathematics of demography is concerned with distinguishing between those changes in the population which are due to alterations in the age distributions (or age structure, as it is sometimes called) and those which are due to other things.

Age specific: Specific to given age intervals. Thus while in demographic parlance 'mortality', say, is an average per 1000 for the whole population, 'Age specific mortality' is the number of deaths per 1000 people of a given age, whether for 5 or 10 year groups, or for each individual year. Age specific mortality could remain constant while total mortality changed because of a shift in the age distribution; similarly with age specific fertility.

Birth rate or *Crude birth rate*: The number of live-births per 1000 population. This is a common measure; when the crude death rate is subtracted from it, it gives the rate of population growth or crude rate of natural increase. But it is rightly called 'crude' for the reason that it does not exhibit what is happening to child-bearing habits. Thus the birth rate can change because the age distribution changes or because the marriage rate changes without any change in the number of children married couples are having. Very often it is the latter that people are interested in. For this and other reasons, different measures are also used: see Fertility below, and Gross and Net Reproduction Rates. 14 – 20 per 1000 are common 'low' birth rates, 35 – 45 per 1000 common 'high' rates.

Cohort: Usually 'birth cohort' or 'marriage cohort' – a group in the population (usually numbering 1000, 10,000 or 1,000,000) such as those born or married in a given year whose experience is examined over subsequent years.

Expectation of life: The mean number of years that would be lived by a person experiencing the age specific death rates prevailing at a given time, measured from a particular year of life. For example the expectation of life at birth in 1971 is the mean number of years someone would live from age 0 if at each year he/she was subject to the age specific death rates of 1971. Note that this is a summary measure of mortality in the 1971 population, *not* the number of years someone born in 1971 can expect to live: at age 20 he/she will be subject to the 1991 mortality rate for that age not the 1971 rate.

Fecundity: The physiological capacity for persons or couples to produce live-born children.

Fertility: A measure of the number of live children born to individuals, couples or populations. The most common measurements used are the General Fertility Rate and Total Fertility Rate (q.v.) to be distinguished from Fecundity (q.v.).

General fertility rate: The number of live-births per 1000 women of reproductive age, generally taken to be 15 – 44 or 15 – 49.

Gross reproduction rate: Most commonly the mean number of female children born alive to women passing through the reproductive period and experiencing the age specific rate for female births at each age, assuming no mortality before the end of the reproduction period.

Infant mortality: The number of deaths of live-born children prior to completion of the first year of life, per thousand children born alive. An infant is defined as a child in his or her first year of life. The distinction is sometimes made between the 'correct' and 'conventional' infant mortality rates – the 'correct' rate is established by counting, out of 1000 particular children born, the number who die before reaching their first birthday – that is to say, following a cohort of 1000 live-born children through their first year. The 'conventional' rate is obtained by observing the number of infant deaths in a calendar year per 1000 live-births in that year. Thus the conventional rate includes in the numerator deaths of children who may have been born in the previous year, while the denominator includes only children born in the year of measurement. But it is usually a close approximation to the correct rate and is easier to obtain. 'Low' national rates are 12 – 25 per 1000; 'high' are 75 or more per 1000 live-births. In particular localities such as urban slums rates may reach 200 or more per 1000 live-births.

Marital fertility rate: The number of live-births per 1000 married women of reproductive age.

Mortality: The liability to death in a population. The word is often loosely used more or less interchangeably with the (crude) Death Rate. It does not have a precise meaning distinguished from the C.D.R., as fertility is distinguished from the Crude Birth Rate.

Net Reproduction Rate: As the Gross Reproduction Rate with the important exception that women at risk *are* assumed subject to prevailing mortality within the reproductive period. The N.R.R. thus measures the replacement rate of females in the population and thus its capacity for growth.

Parity: The number of live-births a women has had.

Parity progression ratio: The probability that a couple will progress from parity n to parity n + 1.

Reverse survival method: A technique for estimating population numbers in earlier years from figures for a given year by the use of mortality data – e.g. if there were *x* males of age 10 – 15 in 1971, given the death rates to which male children were subject in the previous decade, the numbers aged 0 – 5 in 1961 can be estimated.

Stable population: A population with indefinitely unchanging age specific birth and death rates – to be distinguished from a stationary population (q.v.).

Stationary population: A population with unchanging age specific birth and death rates *and* an age distribution such that the total size of the population is also unchanging. (Both this and the stable population are hypothetical constructs used in demographic analysis.)

Total Fertility Rate: Loosely the total number of children born to women who live through the reproductive period. More precisely the mean parity of women passing through the reproductive period and experiencing the given age specific fertility rates at each age assuming no mortality until the end of the reproductive period. (As such the T.F.R. equals the sum of the age specific fertility rates.) 5 – 7 are high values, 1·5 – 3 low ones.

Appendix B

THE WORLD'S COUNTRIES – CRUDE BIRTH AND DEATH RATES, 1970

Region and country	Crude birth rate	Crude death rate	Region and country	Crude birth rate	Crude death rate
I. *East Asia*			29. Turkey	39·5	12·8
1. Japan	19·1	6·9	30. Israel	27·1	6·4
2. Korea	28·2	9·2	31. Cyprus	21·4	7·0
3. China (Taiwan)	28·1	5·5	V. *Western Europe*		
II. *South Asia*			32. Germany (F.R.)	13·2	10·2
4. India	38·8	15·4	33. France	16·6	11·9
5. Pakistan	43·3	15·7	34. Netherlands	18·6	8·5
6. Bangladesh	43·5	21·2	35. Belgium	14·5	11·4
7. Iran	45·3	15·1	36. Austria	15·1	12·8
8. Afghanistan	44·9	25·3	37. Luxembourg	13·5	12·0
9. Sri Lanka	31·0	7·8	VI. *Southern Europe*		
10. Nepal	43·2	22·0	38. Italy	13·7	9·0
III. *Southeast Asia*			39. Spain	19·7	8·3
11. Indonesia	47·1	18·3	40. Yugoslavia	17·5	8·3
12. Vietnam	33·5	13·2	41. Portugal	17·9	10·1
13. Philippines	44·7	10·6	42. Greece	17·3	8·9
14. Thailand	32·1	9·3	VII. *Northern Europe*		
15. Burma	39·1	16·3	43. United Kingdom	16·3	11·3
16. Malaysia	37·0	9·3	44. Sweden	13·8	10·7
17. Laos	41·6	16·0	45. Denmark	14·6	10·1
18. Singapore	23·4	5·2	46. Finland	13·8	8·6
19. Khmer Republic	41·7	14·3	47. Norway	16·4	10·3
IV. *Southwest Asia*			48. Ireland	21·8	10·7
20. Iraq	48·8	14·2	49. Iceland	20·1	7·7
21. Syria	46·9	14·0	VIII. *Western Africa*		
22. Lebanon	27·2	12·8	50. Nigeria	49·7	23·8
23. Jordan	48·8	14·4	51. Ghana	48·0	16·6
24. Kuwait	50·2	21·5	52. Upper Volta	49·0	28·2
25. Saudi Arabia	49·9	21·5	53. Mali	49·4	25·7
26. Yemen A.R.	49·7	21·5	54. Ivory Coast	45·8	21·7
27. Yemen P.D.R.	49·5	21·5	55. Senegal	46·2	21·8
28. Oman	49·5	21·4			

Region and country	Crude birth rate	Crude death rate	Region and country	Crude birth rate	Crude death rate
56. Guinea	46·9	24·1	90. Botswana	44·0	21·1
57. Niger	51·9	22·2	91. Swaziland	51·4	22·1
58. Sierra Leone	44·8	21·7	**XIII. Northern America**		
59. Dahomey	50·5	24·4			
60. Togo	50·5	24·4	92. United States	18·4	9·9
61. Liberia	45·2	22·5	93. Canada	17·1	7·6
62. Mauritania	44·9	21·7	**XIV. Tropical South America**		
63. Gambia	43·2	22·4	94. Brazil	37·1	8·8
IX. Eastern Africa			95. Colombia	44·2	10·4
			96. Peru	41·7	10·4
64. Ethiopia	43·8	24·2	97. Venezuela	40·2	7·6
65. Tanzania	47·1	20·9	98. Equador	43·9	10·7
66. Kenya	47·6	16·2	99. Bolivia	44·0	18·1
67. Uganda	43·0	16·4	100. Guyana	38·1	7·6
68. Malagasy Republic	49·7	22·1	**XV. Middle America**		
69. Malawi	49·0	23·8	101. Mexico	43·5	8·8
70. Zambia	43·1	18·9	102. Guatemala	46·0	13·9
71. Rwanda	51·4	22·3	103. El Salvador	40·1	11·9
72. Burundi	47·9	24·2	104. Honduras	50·0	16·4
73. Somalia	46·9	22·2	105. Nicaragua	42·0	14·7
74. Mauritius	26·9	7·4	106. Costa Rica	33·2	6·6
X. Middle Africa			107. Panama	37·1	8·4
75. Zaire	45·8	21·8	**XVI. Temperate South America**		
76. Congo (P.R.)	45·3	21·8	108. Argentina	22·8	8·3
77. Cameroon	44·1	21·9	109. Chile	31·5	9·2
78. Chad	47·6	23·7	110. Uruguay	20·9	8·7
79. Central African Republic	47·2	24·2	111. Paraguay	44·9	9·6
80. Gabon	33·8	23·4	**XVII. Caribbean**		
81. Equatorial Guinea	34·6	21·0	112. Haiti	47·0	18·6
XI. Northern Africa			113. Dominican Republic	48·4	14·0
			114. Jamaica	33·2	6·6
82. Egypt	43·8	15·3	115. Trinidad & Tobago	20·3	5·9
83. Sudan	48·7	17·1			
84. Morocco	49·1	15·2			
85. Algeria	48·6	15·2	**XVIII. Oceania**		
86. Tunisia	41·8	14·1	116. Australia	20·6	8·2
87. Libya	45·4	14·6	117. New Zealand	22·3	8·0
XII. Southern Africa			118. Fiji	33·0	4·8
88. South Africa	36·0	14·3	**XIX. European Socialist Countries**		
89. Lesotho	38·5	19·8	119. Albania	33·1	8·1

Region and country	Crude birth rate	Crude death rate	Region and country	Crude birth rate	Crude death rate
120. Bulgaria	16·3	9·4	**XX.** *Other countries not*		
121. Czechoslovakia	18·8	11·5	*listed above*		
122. Germany (D.R.)	10·6	13·7			
123. Hungary	15·0	11·8	127. China	33·0	15·0
124. Poland	17·4	8·0	128. Cuba	28·3	5·5
125. Romania	18·1	19·8	129. Korea (D.P.R.)	38·8	11·2
126. U.S.S.R.	17·7	8·7	130. Switzerland	13·6	8·8

SOURCES 1–118, I.B.R.D. *Population Projections for Bank Member Countries*, (Washington D.C., 1973). The I.B.R.D. uses the *U.N. Demographic Yearbook* statistics except where they have more recent census or other data, 119–130, U.N. op.cit. (1973). Some small countries are not listed. The figures for India are at variance with those we describe in Chapter 2. The figures for China are from *U.N. Demographic Yearbook* (1974) and are averages for 1965–74.

Notes

CHAPTER I

1. Bernier (ed. of 1968). Bernier's spelling of 'Dehli' for Delhi has been modernised.
2. Francisco Pelsaert, quoted in Davis (1951).
3. Quoted in Kiernan (1969).
4. Nikitin (ed. of 1958).
5. Pran Nath (1929).
6. Russell (1969).
7. Das Gupta (1972).
8. Moreland (1920).
9. Das Gupta (1972) and references there cited.
10. Bishop Heber for example – see Heber (1828) – or even Thomas Bowrey in the seventeenth century – Bowrey (ed. of 1905). Bengal was found by many earlier writers to be very well off. It certainly exported food to the rest of India in the nineteenth century.
11. See Ingalls (1968).
12. Census of India (1911).
13. Davis (1951).
14. Davis (1951).
15. Chandrasekhar (1972).
16. Boner (1955).
17. Mill (1873).
18. For a profound examination of Malthus and his frequently restated views, set in the context of the intellectual life of his times, the reader is referred to Eversley (1959). See also Glass (1960).
19. See e.g. Coale (1973).
20. Cipolla (1962).
21. Lassen (1965) quoted by Wrigley (1966).
22. Hollingsworth (1969). See also Razzell (1974).
23. Glass (1950).
24. Useful if inconclusive discussions of the various problems can be found in Glass and Eversley (1965), Flinn (1970), Habakkuk (1971), Chambers (1972).
25. Krause (1958).
26. Hollingsworth (1969).
27. See Appendix A.
28. See, for example, Hobsbawm (1957), Hartwell (1961), Inglis (1971).
29. Hirst (1953).
30. Biraben (1975).

31. Jutikkala *et al.* (1971).
32. Cited in Smout (1969).
33. McKeown *et al.* (1962). On smallpox Razzell (1974) is more convincing.
34. McKeown *et al.* (1962). Much of the case presented by these authors is generally accepted though, as we note below, it requires qualification.
35. McLaughlin (1971), Renbourn (1972).
36. Rowntree (1901). See also Townsend (1970).
37. Briggs (1963). See also Rosen in Dyos *et al.* (eds.) (1973).
38. Blythe (1969). But see also Drummond *et al.* (1957) which claims that working class nutrition at the end of the Victorian era, though poor, was better than ever before. Razzell (1974) argues that there was possibly a worsening of nutrition in the first half of the nineteenth century – but this is based on aggregate production statistics of uncertain reliability and omits imports of food. His emphasis on improved personal hygiene as a factor in mortality decline in this period is credible however and a valuable corrective to the McKeown and Record thesis.
39. McKeown *et al.* (1962).
40. Grigg (1958).
41. Cassel (1971).
42. Wrigley (1969). In 1841 urban expectation of life at birth was lower than rural. While the average for England and Wales was about 40 years, it was 35 in London, 25 in Liverpool and 24 in Manchester. See U.N. (1973), p. 133.
43. Rowntree (1901).
44. Smout (1969).
45. For a general review of the relations between mortality and development see Preston (1975).
46. Himes (1936).
47. Hajnal (1965), Laslett (1969).
48. Paradoxically the age at marriage could fall after a great mortality crisis since the departed left empty jobs and homes for young husbands to move into.
49. Cox (1972).
50. Van de Walle (1972).
51. Stott (1969). See also *Journal of Biosocial Science* (1970), *passim*.
52. Wrigley (1969).
53. Laslett (1971).
54. See Laslett (1969), Wrigley (ed.) (1972).
55. Wrigley (1966).
56. Vaizey, in Henderson (1966).
57. There is more than a trace of this solecism in Adelman's article (*op.cit.*).
58. Hawthorn (1970).
59. Prest (1972).
60. Demeny (1968).
61. It must not be thought that the process of women's emancipation in nineteenth century England was uniformly favourable to the practice of contraception. On the contrary, for a time at least, many Victorian feminists saw contraception as a permit for husbands to subject wives to their 'bestial desires' without fear of the consequences. (Banks (1964). Also on this subject see O'Neill (1969).)

62. London School Board (1904), Reeves (1894), Rubinstein (1969).
63. E.g. Banks (1954).
64. E.g. Demeny (1968).
65. Bourgeois-Pichat (1951), Braudel *et al.* (1970).
66. Biraben (1972).
67. Braudel *et al.* (1970) (author's translation).
68. Ibid.
69. Henry (1965).
70. For the role of prices in the Paris insurrections of the Revolution, see Rudé (1970).
71. Braudel *et al.* (1970).
72. Montyon (1778).
73. Biraben (1972).
74. Biraben (1966).
75. Montyon (1778).
76. Chamoux *et al.* (1969).
77. Lachiver (1969).
78. Ganiage (1963).
79. Braudel *et al.* (1970), Biraben (1966).
80. Blacker (1957).
81. Bourgeois-Pichat (1951).
82. Van de Walle (1972).
83. *Ibid.*
84. Spengler (1942).
85. Taeuber (1958).
86. Taeuber (1960).
87. Wilkinson (1965).
88. Taeuber (1958).
89. Taeuber (1958), Muramatsu (1971).
90. Dore (1959), Muramatsu (1971).
91. Muramatsu (1971).
92. Davis (1963).
93. Muramatsu (1971). Currently over 75 per cent of contraception in Japan is by means other than abortion.
94. See also Biraben (1969).
95. Van de Walle *et al.* (1967), Coale (1969).
96. See e.g. Baster (1972) which demonstrates something of the wide variations in socio-economic conditions which can coexist with given levels of fertility.
97. The developing countries on the diagram with birth rates between 25 and 36 and death rates below 16 are: South Korea (2), Taiwan (3), Sri Lanka (9), South Vietnam (12), Thailand (14), Mauritius (74), Chile (109), Jamaica (114), Fiji (118) and China (127). Recent figures would place other countries in it too, some noted in the text.
98. For a variety of references see Cassen (1976). On the relations between development and mortality see especially Preston (1975), also Lefebvre (1976) who concluded (p. 1297) that 'Economic progress does not seem to have played a major part in increasing longevity in developing countries' – not with progress measured by per capita income at least.
99. Brown (1976).

100. Kirk (1971), Boyer *et al.* (1975). For a general survey including the role of family planning in recent Third World fertility decline, see Veron (1976).
101. See Chapter 5, where China's population is discussed in detail.
102. U.N. (1973), (1977).
103. Kirk, *op. cit.*
104. E.g. Kocher (1973), Rich (1973).
105. E.g., for education, Miro *et al.* (1968) or more generally Kamerschen (1971) who suggests that a particularly significant factor may be the mother's educational level.
106. See e.g. CELADE (1972), Kirk (1966). The degree of religious observance is measured by such things as frequency of church attendance or taking communion.

CHAPTER 2

1. Agarwala (1973).
2. Wattal (1916).
3. Malaker (1972).
4. Agarwala (1965).
5. Chidambaram and Zodegekar (1969).
6. Das (1969).
7. Talwar (1965). For additional, similar findings see Agarwala (1973).
8. Agarwala (1973). Strictly speaking the census estimates quoted from this source are not averages of observed rates in a given year but are calculations from a 'synthetic cohort'. The method – explained in the source – is adopted because the census does not record age at marriage which has to be calculated from data on age, mortality and proportion married.
9. For references, see Mandelbaum (1974). One might also note the following: 'It is obvious that after one's children are fairly grown up, it is not seemly to go on producing more offspring since this leaves a bad impression on the minds of the older children.' Thus Gandhi in *Navajivan* (9 February 1926), reprinted in Gandhi (1962).
10. In addition to items cited above, the *Mysore Population Survey* (U.N., 1961) showed those marrying at age 18 – 21 had 1·2 children less than those marrying between 14 – 17. For further references, see Venkatacharya (1971); Malaker (1972); Jain (1975).
11. Agarwala (1965).
12. See Gulati (1969); Kale (1969); Das Gupta (1974).
13. See Mandelbaum and references there cited.
14. Mandelbaum (1974).
15. Gideon (1962).
16. Repetto (1972).
17. O.R.G. (1971).
18. Sarma and Jain (1974) examining mainly the O.R.G. data.
19. Ibid.
20. Heer and Wu (1974).
21. See e.g. Kosambi (1965). There are even those, such as some Jain sects, for whom celibacy is important.

22. For an excellent survey, see Visaria (1974) on whom we mainly rely here.

23. Perhaps more caution is due in attributing any major influence to the decline of Hindu opposition to widow remarriage. There is evidence that young widows with less than three children can and do remarry; the opposition is strongest among high caste Hindus; see Dandekar (1974).

24. Mukerjee (1961) and Driver (1963) found only slight reductions in the number of children born alive to primary-educated men or women compared with illiterates. In U.N. (1961) little such differential was found for Bangalore city. Agarwala (1973) refers to a National Sample Survey study for 1960 – 1, which we have not seen, with similar findings.

25. See for example Farooq and Tuncer (1974) on Turkey; for Latin America, Miro and Mertens (1968). Compare these with recent censuses for Kenya, Botswana and elsewhere in Africa where commonly women with primary education have more children than those with none.

26. Husain (1972).

27. Sarma and Jain (1974); O.R.G. (1971). See also Jain (1975).

28. O.R.G. (1971).

29. Jain and Sarma (1974).

30. Mandelbaum (1974). On this topic his account is the most interesting in the literature for India.

31. Dhagamwar (1974). This distinguished work deals particularly with the legal sale of women in India and their status in personal law but it has much of value to say on the role of Indian law in social oppression generally.

32. All figures on literacy here are from the 1971 Census. At the opposite end of the spectrum in India, see Nair (1974) for some interesting suggestions about the role of education in Kerala.

33. See e.g. U.N. (1961); Cassen (1968) and sources there cited; Rele (1974).

34. Studies in Bombay, Calcutta and Delhi show fairly high rates of ever-use of contraception. One would not necessarily expect the same progress in other urban areas.

35. See pp. 229ff.

36. Schultz (1974) and others of his studies there cited. Other studies, especially in African countries, have not always borne out these relationships which are in fact most complex. See Cantrelle *et al.* (1975) and other papers from that seminar.

37. Schultz and Da Vanzo (1970).

38. See note 36.

39. For numerous references and a careful discussion see Taylor *et al.* (1976).

40. Wyon and Gordon (1971).

41. In many parts of India the woman returns to her parents' home to bear the child and remains there for a considerable period of the child's infancy – a period which is reduced if the child dies. The typical birth interval is usually put at about thirty months – see Jain (1975).

42. G.o.I. (1974a).

43. Mamdani (1972).

44. Wyon and Gordon (1971).

45. W.H.O. (1973a).

46. E. g. Ohlin (1969).

47. Mueller (1976) quotes from an unpublished paper by Visaria employing

1961 Census data alleging labour force participation of 2 per cent for males and one per cent for females in the age group 5 – 9. Although the Census used a generous definition of participation (at least one hour a day of regular work outside the home), such figures are frankly incomprehensible to anyone who has travelled extensively in India. A study of the brass industry in Moradabad (U.P.) showed 50 per cent of the labour force in the age group 6 – 16 (personal communication, S. Abrahams).

48. Mueller (1976).

49. Fogel and Engerman (1974).

50. Symbolically the present value of 'earnings' is $PV = \sum_{t=1}^{\infty} (Y_t - C_t)(1+r)^{-t}$

where Y is the child's income, C consumption costs and r the discount rate.

The present value depleted for mortality is $PV_m = \sum_{t=1}^{\infty} P_t(Y_t - C_t)(1+r)^{-t}$

where P_t is the probability of the child being alive in year t. Obviously since $P_t < 1$, $PV_m < PV$.

51. Agarwala (1973). The figures are for the decade 1951 – 61 and may be a little lower today. We use this age group for illustration. According to Agarwala the mean age at widowhood of women widowed by age 54 was 34 in the decade 1951 – 61.

52. May and Heer (1968).

53. Another way of treating this would be to say that the discount rate applicable in present value calculations to earnings in parents' old age may be very low, even negative; i.e. the present value of Rs. x in year t may be Rs. $x(1-r)^{-t}$. But the same effect may be captured in the utility function.

54. Lorimer (1967); Ruprecht and Jewett (1975).

55. Indeed there is some (modest) evidence that fertility may be lower in nuclear families – see Nag (1965). (Also Mandelbaum (1974) touches on this subject.) Perhaps the greater security of the joint family is outweighed by 'modernisation' factors in the nuclear family.

56. Neher (1971) has produced a model in which he assumes a maximum sustainable rate of per capita income growth over time depending on the rate of growth of capital and population. He explores the 'Golden Rule', that each generation of parents procreates for future generations as it would have liked past generations to have procreated for itself. In this model the pensions motive coupled with a relative lack of concern for future generations produces population growth in excess of the 'Golden Rule' rate, i.e. forcing per capita income growth below the maximum sustainable rate.

57. Hardin (1968) quoting 'Two Lectures on . . . Population' by W. F. Lloyd (1833). The tragedy in question concerned the grazing of sheep on common land; while it paid each sheep farmer to let the marginal sheep on to the commons, if everyone did likewise, over-grazing resulted. J. S. Mill in his *Principles of Political Economy* discusses the effect of various agricultural systems in different countries on the usefulness of children to farmers.

58. See e.g. Sen (1967).

59. See Mandelbaum (1974) and further references there.

60. Mehta (1974). See also Leibenstein (1974) where a theoretical account of this phenomenon is offered: over time increases in income are associated with declining fertility because people aspire to the behaviour patterns of social classes higher than their own, but within a social class at any given time the

wealthier members may have more children than the less well-off in the same class.

61. G.o.I (1974*d*).
62. For a review see Piepmeier (1973).
63. Cassen (1976) lists further references.
64. The majority of K.A.P. studies only interview women and the issue of differential husband-wife attitudes to family size has been little studied in India. Das (1972) suggested that illiterate urban women wanted fewer children than illiterate urban men. In general though women in Indian surveys have been less exposed than men to family-planning propaganda. For other references see Pareek and Rao (1974) pp. 57ff.
65. Some recent studies suggest that population pressure at village level – resulting from mortality decline – is beginning to make itself felt; but not necessarily inducing any rapid resort to fertility control. See several studies in the Institute of Development Studies (Sussex) population project under Scarlett Epstein; or Poffenberger (1975; 1976).
66. G.o.I. (1945). See also Aykroyd (1974). But for a more penetrating analysis, see Sen (1976).
67. Davis (1951), citing the 1901 Census report.
68. Census (1951).
69. Hirst (1953).
70. Ibid.
71. Parkinson (1963).
72. McLaughlin (1971). See also Renbourn (1972).
73. Seal (1960).
74. Cavenaugh (1971).
75. Learmonth (1958).
76. Datta (1966); Chandrahas and Krishnaswami (1971).
77. Learmonth (1958).
78. Choudhury (1963).
79. Seal and Patnaik (1963); G.o.I. (1969).
80. Hirschhorn and Greenough (1971).
81. Davis (1951). The reliability of these statistics is of course doubtful and probably worse than that of plague statistics.
82. Banks (1961).
83. G.o.I. (1972*b*).
84. Bencic and Sinha (1972).
85. Hirschhorn and Greenough (1971).
86. G.o.I. (1972*b*).
87. Wyon and Gordon (1971).
88. Figures were given at a conference in Shillong in February 1974 attended by delegates from India, Bangladesh and W.H.O., and reported in various newspapers, e.g. *The Times* (14 February 1974). And see Sharma *et al.* (1974).
89. *The Times* (18 September 1975). By the end of 1977 it appeared that the disease had indeed been eliminated.
90. Newman (1965).
91. Ibid.
92. Frederiksen (1966) and references in Newman (1970).
93. Newman (1970).

94. Gray (1974). This work in the author's judgement is methodologically superior to all the previous attempts to isolate the effect of malaria from other health-related factors.
95. Cf. Krause (1958); McKeown and Record (1962) and Razzell (1974); also Stolnitz (1965).
96. Learmonth (1958).
97. Ibid.
98. W.H.O. (1971).
99. Johnson (1966).
100. G.o.I. (1972*b*).
101. Lamba (1971).
102. Dhir *et al.* (1969).
103. W.H.O. (1973*b*); Rao (1973).
104. Sehgal *et al.* (1973); Sharma *et al.* (1973).
105. Rao (1973).
106. For some surveys see Bruce Chwatt (1974), Giamiccia and Hempel (1972); Scholtens *et al.* (1972).
107. Quoted in Davis (1951).
108. I.C.M.R. (1959).
109. G.o.I. (1972*b*).
110. Fox (1962).
111. See a report in *The Hindu*(6 May 1973) reproduced in *Indian Journal of Tuberculosis* XX 2 (1973) (unsigned). The article reports a submission to Parliament of the data in question which we have not been able to find. The article suggests that 'no evidence of increasing incidence' of tuberculosis is not a satisfactory outcome for all the effort that has been put into the National Tuberculosis Control Programme and notes a proposal of the Tuberculosis Association of India for a new national survey to assess the prevalence of the disease and examine possible modifications of the control programme. See also Lotte (1971) for comparative material for Europe.
112. Banerji (1971).
113. See White *et al.* (1972) though most of the epidemiological studies cited are for rural Africa where mortality is very high and its sources very numerous. Obviously too if there are several water sources and only some are improved, the prevalence of water-borne and water-related diseases may not change much. A controlled study by the Planning Research and Action Institute (Lucknow) claimed reduced incidence of diarrhoeas, typhoid fever, scabies and trachoma due solely to water-supply improvement in villages of Uttar Pradesh in the late 1960s. (P.R.A.I. (1969).)
114. Blyn (1966).
115. Dewey (1974).
116. The only anthropometric study for the pre-independence period known to the author – pointed out to him by Dr J. Powles – is Madhavan *et al.* (1964) which examined the height and weight of railway workers, born approximately between 1928 and 1937, at age 26–35 and found them taller and heavier than those aged 36–45, i.e. born in 1918–27. But, as the study notes, recruiting standards on the railway may have risen!
117. Ghai *et al.* (1970).
118. Rao *et al.* (1969).

119. E.g. Rao *et al.* (1959); Grewal *et al.* (1973); Levinson (1974); and other references in this section. I.C.M.R. (1961) reviewed a large number of surveys conducted prior to 1961 and concluded that weaknesses of sampling technique etc. rendered most of them useless for 'any' purpose.

120. I.C.M.R. (1974). It should be noted that even this excellent report may not be statistically representative of India as a whole; it covers rural areas near Hyderabad, New Delhi and Poona and urban or 'semi-urban' populations in Bombay, Calcutta and Vellore. Also four of the six surveys are confined to low income groups, two to 'low and middle' groups. The results are very like those in other studies, but villages more remote from urban centres are studied only relatively rarely and might if fully represented show conditions to be worse than those reported in the I.C.M.R. survey.

121. Personal communcation, M. C. Swaminathan.

122. P.N.D.P. (1974).

123. For a survey see e.g. J. Cravioto and E. De Licardie, 'The effects of malnutrition on the individual', in Berg *et al.* (1973).

124. Sommer and Lowenstein (1975).

125. Observation of the *growth* of individual infants and children is of course a well established and valuable indicator of child development related to nutrition and in common use throughout the world, but it is not a practicable method for nationwide surveys of nutritional status.

126. I.C.M.R. (1972).

127. Vijaraghavan *et al.* (1971).

128. Levinson (1974).

129. U.N. (1976).

130. Clark (1972); Sukhatme (1973).

131. Merewether (1898).

132. I.C.M.R. (1968; see also the same publication for 1958). The 1968 recommendations were republished in 1974 without change.

133. W.H.O. (1973*a*). This source also gives a table of the Harvard Standards, Annex 1.

134. Ibid., Annex 4.

135. Ibid., pp. 37–8.

136. Gopalan and Raghavan (1969); I.C.M.R. (1972). We employ the latter's figures which are far more detailed. The data in both sources are for the mid 1960s.

137. W.H.O. (1973*a*), Table 27.

138. Jelliffe (1955).

139. See e.g. Achar and Yankauer (1962); Vijaraghavan *et al.* (1971).

140. I.C.M.R. (1972), Table 60.

141. Fomon (1974) on U.S. infants; the British data were supplied to us by Mary Griffiths of the London School of Hygiene and Tropical Medicine from a study in preparation (they show a considerable drop since the classic study by Widdowson (1947)); data for U.S. girls from Peckos and Ross (1973). The U.K. household figures are from U.K. (1974).

142. National Institute of Nutrition (1972).

143. F.A.O. (1971) for the 1964–6 figures; for the remainder, Sukhatme (1973).

144. Sukhatme (1973); Clark (1972).

145. Reutlinger and Selowsky (1976). The equations used are (col. 1)

$C = -997 + 663$ lnY, (col. 2) $C = 491 + 332$ lnY. (The parameters for elasticities were derived at a level of calorie requirements slightly higher than the 2000 calories assumed above.) The data for income distribution are from an unpublished study by P. K. Bardhan and K. R. Ranadive cited in the same source. The estimate of 13 per cent of income enjoyed by the poorest 30 per cent compares closely with the Draft Fifth Plan figure of 13·64 per cent of total consumption by the poorest 30 per cent.

146. In 1975 the N.S.S. prepared for the F.A.O. calorie and protein consumption data by income groups for the various States: e.g. G.o.I, (1975). But no breakdown by population percentages can be deduced from the figures: the proportion of *households* at each level can be determined from what has been published but, without more detail about the sample frame, one cannot derive population proportions. Thus in the sample of 938 households for Bihar, 69 had per capita consumption of 1211 calories per day and 152 had 4949 (sic) per day per consumer unit. The average for Bihar as a whole is given as 2732 calories per consumer unit. (*Op. cit.* Table 3.0/R, p. 25.)

147. Rajagopalan (1974).

148. Ibid., p. 14.

149. Hindustan Thompson Associates (1972).

150. Cited by Reutlinger and Selowsky (1976).

151. Gopalan and Rao (1970) as cited by Levinson (1974).

152. Bardhan (1973).

153. See Ghosh (1976); Levinson (1974) etc. Wyon and Gordon (1971) report the effects of giving solid food as well as breast milk to infants: despite consequent diarrhoea, not one of the 147 children in the study area receiving solid food died in the 6th–9th month, while about 4 per cent of the 531 children not receiving solid food died. In the fourth and fifth trimesters of life the death rate of those not on solids was 3 times, in the sixth 4 times, and in the last three months of the second year, 10 times the death rate of those receiving solids and milk.

154. For numerous references on those and other aspects of nutrition, see Swaminathan (1976).

155. The fundamental work on this question was by Indian scholars, e.g. Sukhatme (1970). The position described here is accepted by the I.C.M.R. – see e.g. I.C.M.R. (1974) – but not followed in all its nutrition work by various Government of India agencies – see Chapter 3.

156. See Rosa and Turshen (1970); Wishik (1972). For a more general survey and bibliography, including materials on developed countries, see U.S. National Academy of Sciences (1970) and for more detailed information, Schofield (1972).

157. Rosa and Turshen (1970).

158. Gopalan (1961); Shankar (1962). Jelliffe in the W.H.O. *Bulletin* for 1962 also suggests that malarial infection of the mother can result in a small foetus.

159. Wyon and Gordon (1971).

160. Gordon *et al.* (1964); W.H.O. (1965); Scrimshaw (1970).

161. See the life-table, p. 116.

162. Puffer and Serrano (1973).

163. The information is given in the Pocket Book of Population Statistics (G.o.I. (1971*a*)). In some other sources, such as the One-per cent Sample Data

(G.o.I. (1971*b*)), the population 0 – 9 is given undivided reflecting the fact that the Registrar General's Office had not at the time decided what to do about the discrepancy.

164. G.o.I. (1971*a*). Our calculation here is just a rough estimate. We give our more careful estimate below.

165. Brass *et al.* (1968). The Post Enumeration Check of which we speak below also found the volume of under-counting greatest in this age group.

166. Cassen and Dyson (1976).

167. Rele and Sinha (1973). One or two of the combinations of assumptions they examine with alternative methods of estimation yield slightly higher birth rates in the 1960s, in the region of 43 or more.

168. Adlakha and Kirk (1974).

169. Coale (1971).

170. G.o.I. (1974*a*).

171. Agrawal (1969); Ramabhadran and Agrawal (1972); Lingner and Wells (1973).

172. The Post Enumeration Check has been conducted for the last three censuses; it involves a professional recount in selected census Areas; see G.o.I. (1973*b*).

173. Adlakha and Kirk (1974) were apparently unaware of the Post Enumeration Checks – 'no direct data on under-count or over-count of the censuses of India are available'. They also had 'no information on the validity of the S.R.S. estimates'.

174. For additional reasons to doubt the inclusiveness of the 1971 Census see Visaria (1971) with comments by Raghavachari (1971) and Srinivasan (ibid.) and a reply by Visaria (ibid.).

175. Soni (1975); Brass (1968); Coale and Trussell (1974).

176. Dyson (1975); Cassen and Dyson (1976).

177. Gray (1974).

178. Adlakha and Kirk (1974).

179. Rele and Sinha (1973).

180. Adlakha (1972). His views are of course taken account of in Adlakha and Kirk (1974).

181. G.o.I. (1972*a*).

182. See footnote 171.

183. The reader requiring further details of the life-table is referred to Dyson (1975) and Cassen and Dyson (1976). Suffice it to say here for the specialist that we employed an African Standard model from the Brass logit life-table system with appropriate alpha and beta for males and females, with allowance for female mortality becoming lighter than male after the main reproductive years.

184. G.o.I. (1974*a*).

185. Cassen and Dyson (1976).

186. G.o.I. (1974*c*).

187. Bose (1967). It is very common for women to marry someone from another village and, when this happens, it is almost always the woman who moves. In some parts of India a man is traditionally expected to marry a woman from outside his village.

188. Zachariah and Ambannavar (1967). The figures are calculated by the authors for the areas defined as 'urban' in the 1961 Census. Care is needed as the

definition changed in 1961 in a manner that excluded many places defined as urban in 1951. To qualify as a town in 1961 a place had to satisfy four conditions: (i) density at least 1000 per square mile; (ii) three-quarters of the working population engaged in non-agricultural occupations; (iii) total population at least 5000; (iv) possession of certain urban characteristics and amenities. (The definitional problem is amply discussed in Bose (1973), Chapter 2. As Bose frankly notes there is no definition of 'urban' valid for every time and place – it is to some extent a term of art.) All figures in this chapter where possible employ the 1961 definitions, with prior census figures recalculated accordingly: the new definitions exclude many places which were previously counted as urban.

189. Between 1961 and 1971 the total number of internal migrants grew from 134 million to 166 million: – an increase of 23·88 per cent, comparable to the increase in total population. The proportion of those in the category of rural-urban migrants rose from 14·5 per cent to 15·0 per cent. However the proportion of urban-to-rural migrants rose even more, from 3·6 per cent to 4·9 per cent. Thus this measure does not show any increase of net rural-urban migration as a proportion of all migrants or of the population. The alert reader will note that such figures give net rural-urban migrants in 1951 – 61 of the order of 10·9 per cent of all migrants, approximately 14·8 million people or almost three times the number estimated by Zachariah and Ambannavar (1967). The census number refers to *life-time* migrants, that is in this context all those enumerated in urban areas at the census who were born in rural areas, whereas Zachariah and Ambannavar's number is an estimate of those who migrated during the decade 1951 – 61 and remained in urban areas, net of those who departed for rural areas. The new questions on migration included in the 1971 Census should throw further light on this topic, but the data are not yet available.

190. N.S.S. Number 53 (1962) quoted in Bose (1973). The proportion of females in these categories for the big cities comes to 3·5 per cent while those coming 'on marriage' or 'with earning members of the household' come to 57·8 per cent, categories which account for 11·2 per cent of the males. Another study based only on seven States found 75 per cent of males migrating for economic reasons (Kumar (1967)).

191. Todaro (1969; 1973).

192. Connell *et al.* (1974).

193. Gosal (1967).

194. Bose (1973). Bose also shows that rural-urban migrants in the year 1960/61 were twice as numerous as the annual flow which would account for the volume of migrants with residence-duration of five years. (This is another topic on which the migration questions in the 1971 Census may shed some light.) It should be noted, however, that reporting of residence duration suffers from the same digital preference and other defects as census age data and all estimates based on them are suspect.

195. In 1968 the author was told by a bank official in Calcutta that his bank had received over 4000 applications for an advertised position as bank clerk, including more than 100 with higher degrees. On the general subject of 'escalation of educational qualifications', see Dore (1976).

196. Government of West Bengal (1966). It is possible that the growth figures for

1931–41 are somewhat inflated; allegedly the 1941 Census was affected by communal rivalry to increase representation. See Visaria, P. 'The reliability of census data . . .', in O.E.C.D., *National Accounts of Asian Countries* (Paris, 1972).

197. The migration and natural increase estimates for 1951 and 1961 are from Zachariah (1968) and those for 1971 from Joshi and Joshi (1975). In the latter net migration is derived from an estimate of natural increase which is then subtracted from the increase in total population as given by the Census. Since the Joshis' mortality estimates use an all-India life-table, they may have over-estimated mortality and consequently over-estimated the volume of net immigration. The error is not likely to be large however in relation to other possible errors–in the estimates of births and indeed the Census estimate itself.

198. Patel (1974).

199. Joshi and Joshi (1975). This work contains a valuable critique of India's past employment policies and analysis of the urban employment problem which complements our account of rural employment in Chapter 4.

200. Bose (1973).

201. Bose (1973). Kannada is mainly spoken in Karnataka (earlier Mysore).

202. Moorehouse (1971).

203. For a review of recent developments since the main Calcutta Metropolitan Development Plan see Lubell (1974). In view of the quotation with which this section opened we should note in particular that three new bridges over the Hooghly are planned, one already under construction.

204. Sivaramakrishnan (1974).

205. G.o.I. (1969).

206. Visaria (1969).

207. G.o.I. (1969).

208. Coale and Hoover (1958).

209. Raghavachari (1974).

210. I.B.R.D. (1972).

211. Frejka (1973).

212. For fertility we employed the method devised by Coale and Trussell (1974); for mortality the logit life-table system developed by Brass (1968). On these and most other points further detail and explanation can be found in Cassen and Dyson (1976).

213. See Bourgeois-Pichat and Taleb (1970).

CHAPTER 3

1. See Thapar (1963) and Samuel (1966) for historical details.
2. Visaria and Jain (1976). Expenditure in 1973/4 was cut to Rs. 535 million.
3. Blaikie (1975).
4. Elder (1974).
5. See Chapter 2 on the economics of family formation.
6. The term 'loop' is sometimes used as a generic name for the I.U.D.; it is also used to denote a specific variety or family of varieties of the device such as 'loops and spirals' in distinction from other forms.

7. Many have accused foreign advisers of over-persuading Indian authorities about the suitability of the I.U.D. in a mass programme. Undoubtedly some excessively enthusiastic advice was given, but that does not wholly absolve from responsibility those who accepted the advice. This issue is referred to later.

8. See the report of the Second Mission, U.N. (1969).

9. Here and elsewhere in the text, unless otherwise indicated, we adopt performance figures (suitably rounded) as published in G.o.I. documents, in this case G.o.I. (1975*d*). See also Table 3.1. For 1975/6 figures various newspaper reports and unpublished Ministry data have been used.

10. W.H.O. (1968).

11. Davies (1972). The copper I.U.D.s do appear to inhibit blastocyst implantation, see Tatum (1972).

12. Orlans (1975). See also Huber *et al.* (1975) and, for an earlier view, Tietze (1970*a*). Some materials on the Copper-T in India can be found in Hefnawi *et al.* (1975).

13. Tietze (1970*b*).

14. Tietze (1970*b*); Bernard (1971).

15. Davies (1972).

16. Zipper *et al.* (1971); cf. also Tatum (1972).

17. Kandaurova, V. *et al.* (1970). (See also ibid. February 1971 and November 1971 – from which the quotation is taken, translated by the author – and February 1972.)

18. Malgouyat (1970).

19. Bernard (1971); Snowden *et al.* (1973).

20. Davies (1972).

21. N.I.F.P. (1971*a*).

22. Government of Turkey (1971).

23. Sun (1971); cf. Freedman *et al.* (1972).

24. E.g. Bhandari (1967); Bhinder (1969); Devi *et al.* (1969); Kashyap (1971); P.R.A.I. (1969).

25. Research Triangle Institute (1970). A very similar rumour-based wave of removals in Singapore in 1966 is reported by Wolfers (1970).

26. O.R.G. (1971).

27. Some of these studies are referred to in these notes. Little purpose would be served in citing more of them. One convenient source is Kumar (1971) which lists and gives a brief account of 127 of them. On some important aspects, see C.F.P.I. (1969) and N.I.F.P. (1973).

28. Dandekar *et al.* (1971).

29. Laumas (1969).

30. W.H.O. (1966).

31. U.N. (1969).

32. E.g. Ward and Simmons (1968).

33. In a study of the carefully documented Singapore programme a distinct difference in expulsion rates was observed between Indian/Pakistani acceptors and those of Chinese or Malay origin. As the study commented this difference (unlike that in removal rates which was also observed) 'cannot be explained save by reference to genuine physical or physiological peculiarites.' The programme in question used only one I.U.D., the Lippes 'D'. See

D. Wolfers and S. S. Ratnam, 'Follow-up study of inserted women' in Wolfers (1970) (also published in Zatuchni (1970)).

34. This has been studied in places other than India – for example in Singapore (see Wolfers (1970)) where no relationship was found and in Taiwan, where there appears to have been a *negative* correlation between I.U.D. continuation and education. It has been explained there on the grounds partly that the well-educated 'having more family planning alternatives available to them, are less disposed to persist with the I.U.D. in the face of side effects' and partly that 'some of the tendency for wives of educated husbands to have higher expulsion and removal rates depends on their being younger on average than wives of less educated husbands.' (This comes from a study by Potter quoted in Watson (1970).) It does also seem to be the case that the more educated of those who discontinue adopt other contraceptive methods thereafter. These aspects of the Taiwanese experience are of doubtful relevance to India.

35. Mahajan (1966). The author does not state any reasons for omitting the other nineteen trials from his survey. (The Indian Council of Medical Research published a report entitled *Clinical Trials of I.U.C.D. in India* in 1968 which may shed further light on the matter. This publication however has eluded search at the time of writing.)

36. Cited in Mahajan (1966).

37. Several hospital-based programmes have had reasonable success with the I.U.D. in India as has the post-partum approach generally (though not with *immediate* post-partum insertion of the I.U.D.). See Zatuchni (1970) and particularly the paper there by Phatak and Chandorkar.

38. The author wrote in 1967 that the possible rate of expansion of the programme was a question of balancing risks. Measures which could help to spread family planning faster risked disrupting the programme if there was even a small proportion of failures. (Cassen (1968).) He was however in the comfortable position of not having to decide where the correct balance of risk lay. A member of the first U.N. Mission – who asked not to be named – told the author that the Health Minister at the time, Sushila Nayar, favoured a very cautious launching of the I.U.D. at selected centres, with simultaneous monitoring, and that it was another Mission member who persuaded her after day-long discussions to abandon these careful plans. It has been suggested in the text that there were however quite careful deliberations on the Indian side. But understandably this whole episode left the Government suspicious of foreign 'experts' in family planning. They were all too often expert in their own fields but knew little about India.

39. Gould (1969).

40. Wortman (1975).

41. G.o.I. (1970). For a general bibliography see Kumar (1972).

42. We were grateful to Dr Pai who conducted us on a 'family planning tour' of Bombay in 1970; his later turn towards authoritarian solutions was not in evidence then.

43. Banerji (1973).

44. Krishnakumar (1972).

45. Soni (1975).

46. E.g. G.o.I. (1974).

47. See Table 3.1 below (p. 171).

49. As long ago as 1966 a study observed 67 per cent of vasectomised patients in one area to be ineligible i.e. sterile, unmarried, widowed, separated or with wives over the age of 45. Let it be said that studies on camps have shown very much lower levels of ineligibility, largely due to improved screening. It is significant that this study, which became mysteriously unobtainable in India after publication, recommended even then that the motivator's fee be abolished. (P.R.A.I., (1966).)

50. Wortman (1975).

51. Gupta (1973).

52. Franda (1972).

53. Jain (1973).

54. Dumm *et al.* (1974).

55. Franda (1972).

56. In the *Khanna Study* for example over 10 per cent of a sample of 1765 pregnancies terminated in abortion. The authors note that figures of 20 per cent and more have been observed elsewhere but, as they say, information on the subject is 'grossly inaccurate'.

57. For references and a modestly annotated bibliography, see Karkal (1970).

58. Van der Vlugt and Piotrow (1974). See also Kleinman (1972).

59. Sadashivaiah *et al.* (1971). One study (Majumdar *et al.* (1972)) has shown somewhat better continuation rates than others but the reasons are not obvious. For another, less optimistic study, see N.I.F.P. (1971*b*) (also C.F.P.I. (1970)).

60. Wortman and Piotrow (1973).

61. The W.H.O. conducted trials in Chandigarh and Bombay, with results in Bombay as good as those anywhere but poor continuation rates in Chandigarh. However re-examination of the evidence shows that physical side-effects were identical in both places; what needs explaining is why tolerance of the side-effects was so much better in one case than the other. If that were satisfactorily investigated, Depo-Provera might be shown to be a useful adjunct to India's family planning techniques in appropriate circumstances. See Benagiano *et al.*, forthcoming. More generally see Rinehart and Winter (1975).

62. For a survey of work in India, see Virkar (1973).

63. *Nature* (13 December 1974) as reported by Nature-Times News Service.

64. Duncan *et al.* (1973); Segal and Tietze (1971); W.H.O. (1973).

65. Gould (1975). The drug operates by suppressing the hormone secreted by the early embryo, preventing menstruation and otherwise inducing conditions necessary for pregnancy to continue.

66. *Chinese Medical Journal* (March 1975). This method seems not yet to be known in the West, see Abbott *et al.* (1975).

67. Berelson (1975).

68. *Times of India* (13 February 1973). 'Bombay, 12 February: Jagatguru Shankaracharya of Puri has appealed to the Centre to reconsider its family planning. He said that the All-India Anti-Family Planning Action Committee, which has decided to start an agitation, should refer the problem of "genocide of Hindus" to the United Nations, start a signature campaign, fasts and padyatras. The family planning programme would result in "Hindus

becoming a minority in their own homeland" he added.'

69. Lack of political support by national leaders has been advanced as a partial cause of the slow progress of family planning – see Finkle (1971). More generally, see Smith (1973).

70. Schwarz (1975) in an interview with the Minister.

71. Ibid.

72. Agarwala (1972); Misra (1973); Vig (1972).

73. In I.B.R.D. (1974), Annex B.

74. Jain and Sharma (1974).

75. Ibid.

76. Enke (1960; 1966).

77. Simmons (1971); Zaidan (1971).

78. Cassen (1976).

79. Robinson and Horlacher (1971), for example.

80. Seal and Bhatnagar (1974).

81. Seal (1974).

82. Soni (1975).

83. As presented, for example, in Wolfers (1969); Bean and Seltzer (1968); Potter (1969); Chandrasekaran and Hermalin (1976).

84. We have employed a marginal savings rate of 0·15 and an incremental capital-output ratio of 2. The methodology of the calculation is identical to that in Cassen (1968) where a variety of combinations of parameters were explored with similar results – except that, with a rather low ($10) cost per prevented birth, the differential in income per head was rather greater in the comparison of family planning with other investment. In that work we were also rather optimistic about the number of births a family programme in India might have succeeded in preventing during the last decade.

85. Simmons (1971) and Enke (1960), respectively.

86. G.o.I. (1976*b*).

87. Ibid.

88. The measures differed from State to State but with a considerable over-all similarity. See on Andhra Pradesh, *Times of India* (23 September 1976); West Bengal, *The Statesman* (17 June 1976); Himachal Pradesh, *Hindustan Times* (5 June 1976); Tamil Nadu, *Times of India* (22 October 1976); Madhya Pradesh, *Hindustan Times* (30 June 1976) etc. These sources also give other measures adopted by the States.

89. This was the declared policy of the Tamil Nadu State Government – see *Times of India* (22 October 1976). It has also been the policy of the New Delhi Municipal Council and was said to be a factor in the Turkman Gate incident in Delhi when a confrontation leading to some loss of life occurred after a slum area around the Jama Masjid was cleared.

90. *New York Times* (28 October 1976).

91. See interview with Dr Karan Singh in *People*, vol. 3, no. 4 (1976). This issue of *People* contains a full account of the original Maharashtra bill.

92. *Times of India* (8 November 1976).

93. Mrs. Gandhi, in reply to a question as to whether the sterilisation drive had been a mistake, said: 'The mistake was that it was left to officials largely, instead of citizens taking up and persuading people. The government's policy was not coercion at all. Somehow there was sort of both things – on the one

side perhaps over-zealousness of people thinking they would each compete with the other in doing more, and sometimes people doing things deliberately in order to make the Government and the programme unpopular.' (B.B.C. Television Interview, 21 July 1977.)

94. See interview in *People*, Vol. 3, No. 4(1976), p. 18.
95. It was a feature of the new measure that for the first time it made breach of the law a 'cognizable' offence, i.e. one for which the transgressor can be arrested without a warrant. But whether, if it remains in force, there will be any new willingness to prosecute remains to be seen.
96. Blaikie (1975).
97. Visaria and Jain (1976).
98. G.o.I. (1975*b*).
99. I.E.M.R. (1976). This source simply tabulates Centre and State budgets by various heads of expenditure.
100. G.o.I. (1973).
101. G.o.I. (1972).
102. G.o.I. (1974), p. 264.
103. G.o.I. (1976*a*), p. 82.
104. I.E.M.R., (1976).
105. G.o.I. (1976*a*), p. 83.
106. G.o.I. (1972); cf. also Chuttani (1973).
107. See e.g. W.H.O. (1975*a*).
108. G.o.I. (1975*a*).
109. G.o.I. (1975*b*).
110. G.o.I. (1975*c*).
111. The best known of these is the Jamkhed scheme in Maharashtra; the numerous others include Palghar and Kasa (also Maharashtra); the Indo-Dutch project near Hyderabad (Andhra Pradesh); the Tilonia development project (Rajasthan); Kottar (Tamil Nadu). Larger and better known research projects such as Project Poshak, Narangwal, Khanna etc. have also investigated the potential of a variety of health and nutrition delivery systems.
112. Cited in an unsigned Medical Education column, *E.P.W.* (24 January 1976), p. 92.
113. Obviously many villages would require public assistance but not to the tune of $2,500 million.
114. W.H.O. (1965).
115. Desai and Gaikwad (1971).
116. Rajagopalan (1974).
117. CARE (1975).
118. G.o.I. (1976*a*).
119. I.C.M.R. (1966).
120. An effective rural health service of the kind described here – which almost certainly has to be related to rural development more generally – appears to be the only way in which all the necessary components of better health can be diffused at a reasonable cost. It has other cost advantages too. Villagers do in fact spend quite large sums on health out of their own pockets – about 2 per cent of expenditures according to N.S.S. data – either on travel to distant health facilities or on locally available 'traditional' practitioners. They could

afford to support a community health programme which met a large proportion of their needs within the village; indeed individual financial contributions, however small, are usually thought a desirable feature of these programmes as they encourage participation and interest and may help to overcome the suspicions that 'free' services sometimes induce.

CHAPTER 4

1. The Legislative Council in 1933 recommended setting up a Committee 'to draw up a five years' plan of economic development' for the United Provinces. For a history of the beginnings of planning in India and much else see Hanson (1966).

2. Quoted in Hanson (1966). For detailed discussions of many aspects of Indian policy in the post-Independence era see particularly Bhagwati and Desai (1970) and Streeten and Lipton (eds) 1968; and for the theory that underlay much of the economic plans, Bhagwati and Chakravarty (1969).

3. Mahalanobis was the senior professor at the Indian Statistical Institute; a physicist turned economist, his views, partly shaped by Soviet theory and practice, were tremendously influential. In fact the quantitative assumptions needed in his model to demonstrate the primacy of heavy industry were never spelled out; it would have required a careful assessment of the possibilities of real resource conversion both domestically and in foreign trade which was never attempted. (See Bhagwati and Chakravarty, 1969.)

4. The Consortium is an association of Western aid-giving countries under the chairmanship of the World Bank. The Consortium's role in 'promising' aid to support the devaluation was ill-advised since it was not within its power to coerce member countries to fulfil their undertakings.

5. See the introduction to the Fourth Five Year Plan and discussion of agriculture below. The Plan documents referred to in these paragraphs are G.o.I. 1951, 1956, 1961, 1966, 1967, 1968, 1969, 1973.

6. G.o.I. (1975a). For comparison, industrial production grew at a steady 8–10 per cent annually during 1960–5. As far as exports were concerned one must remember the devaluation of the rupee after it was floated in 1972 and the considerable share in these years of aid-financed exports to Bangladesh.

7. Another way of describing this, or part of it – and one more common in the economic literature of planning – is as the 'problem of wage goods'. It is interesting that this crucial aspect of economic policy has received relatively little attention; in the two works by Bhagwati and others cited in note 2 for example it receives only a cursory mention and then mainly with reference to the 'transformation problem', i.e. the question of the other factors, involved in using labour, even if adequate wage goods exist, to promote increased industrial production.

8. The allocation of these scarce goods is only partially achieved by licensing; importers go to curious lengths to obtain licences, sometimes without even any intention of using them for production. Many importers find it more profitable to sell than to use the imports and an extensive black market performs the rest of the allocative function – a sad reflection on the Government's policies. More generally on foreign exchange policies, see Bhagwati *et al.* (1975).

9. See, for an account of the earlier post-Independence period, Kidron (1965). For a view of the behaviour of the major oil companies towards India see Tanzer (1969). For an approach to selectivity in policies towards private foreign investment see Lal *et al.* (1975).

10. See Bhagwati and Desai (1970).

11. See House of Commons (1974).

12. G.o.I. (1975*a*).

13. See Hanson (1966) citing various writers commenting on the Third Five Year Plan, especially pp. 216–7.

14. Coale and Hoover (1958).

15. By means of a Cobb-Douglas production function. (Ibid., pp. 321ff.)

16. See e.g. Hoover and Perlman (1966); Ruprecht (1967); Walsh (1971). A similar statement, without a model, can be found in Demeny (1969).

17. See on this subject in general U.N. (1973) and Bilsborrow (1973). We do not refer in the text to the problem of 'non-monetised savings', i.e. those savings which reflect the incorporation of labour into productive assets without any market transaction taking place. The main example of this is unpaid family labour used for improving the family farm. This form of savings may well rise with population growth; its cost to the economy depends on the availability of alternative employment. The value of this form of saving and investment in India is more or less unknown. It is estimated nowadays by assumption – see G.o.I. Reserve Bank, *Bulletin*, various issues.

18. Reserve Bank, *op. cit.* The measurement of public and corporate savings is undoubtedly more accurate than that for household savings and none are very accurately known.

19. For the figures in this paragraph 15–64 is taken as the working age group by Coale and Hoover. The proportions to the total population are taken from census figures (unsmoothed). There are various ways of assessing the consumption of non-adults. Coale and Hoover, counting an adult as 1, take children as 0·5 of an 'equivalent adult consumer'. Kleiman (1966) suggests figures which we may round up to 0·15 for ages 0–4, 0·3 for ages 5–9, 0·45 for ages 10–14 and 0·85 for ages 15–19. Obviously the cost of the burden of dependency varies greatly with the assumed consumption of the dependents. Little actual data exists to give us a reliable set of figures for India. Further the numbers outside some given age range do not constitute the total of dependents; even within the working age range many are dependents – a customary figure for the participation rate in India is 0·6 of the population of working age. But these dependents may not change in proportion to the labour force as population grows. Assumptions somewhat different from these are adopted in our labour force projections later in this chapter.

20. If only 10 per cent of the additional dependents (i.e. children of the rich) reduced total household savings *and* half the consumption costs of these children came out of their parents' consumption and each child is half an 'equivalent adult consumer', the savings cost would come to 0·8 million per capita incomes or about 1·5 per cent of total savings. (We confine this extreme calculation to the notes rather than the text – it is a thoroughly dubious one.) It might be thought that the poor can dis-save by going into debt; but, given village money-lending interest rates, they are soon consuming less than before they borrowed and total consumption in the village may actually fall,

depending on the money lenders' savings propensities. The author has explored some of these relationships in an (as yet unpublished) model. Data on personal savings are rare and unreliable; such as they are they support the view expressed here, e.g. N.C.A.E.R. (1965), which found net dis-saving on the part of the poorest 60 per cent of rural population; the top one per cent of households accounted for 59 per cent of positive net savings (see vol. II, p. 95).

21. Bilsborrow (1973) produces illustrative calculations for a country in the $200 per head income range, based on typical estimated empirical values, and suggests a realistic result for a 3 per cent increase in the dependency ratio of a reduction of savings by 1·9 per cent. Kuznets (1974) showed that the difference between a one per cent and a 3 per cent population growth rate could be accommodated by a reduction of 12·5 per cent in consumption per adult consumer unit for a typical developing country. If one were comparing not one per cent and 3 per cent but 1·5 per cent and 2 per cent, i.e. feasible ranges of population growth rate reductions, the amount would be much smaller. In India of course any reduction in consumption is painful; or, if the consumed resources were to come out of savings, they would be a significant fraction of savings. But this calculation too suggests that one should not exaggerate the population effect on growth.

22. See Sinha (1973) and Cassen (1973) for more detailed examination of these points.

23. Minhas and Vaidyanathan (1965); G.o.I. (1972). Both production and acreage figures are subject to error; nevertheless one can have confidence in there having been a major difference between the two decades, if not in its precise magnitude. The figures are on an all-India basis; there is of course considerable local variation in the patterns of acreage and yield growth. Also, if the overall figures are broken down crop by crop, it is clear that a good part of the difference between the decade is due to shifts of acreage from one crop to another.

24. On economic grounds one might doubt that increased yields were due to additional labour alone, since labour has always been relatively abundant, so that one could expect yield-increasing applications of labour to have been exhausted. That may however be an argument of undue neoclassicism. Apart from other consideration there is new knowledge even in farming with traditional implements and seed varieties. We should qualify what is said here and shortly about irrigation by recalling that some major irrigation works in this period have not used labour-intensive construction techniques and all have had long gestation periods. But feeder canals etc. *are* labour intensive.

25. For some idea of the capital and foreign exchange costs involved we offer the following. Although the figures are uncertain they indubitably constitute magnitudes out of all proportion to the savings and composition of investment effects. Unfortunately there appear to be no reliable figures for fertiliser investment; the expected source (*Fertiliser Statistics*, Fertiliser Association of India) gives figures for 'outlay' of the industry without adequate indication of what that covers. One can also make inferences from official statements on the public sector such as the Annual Reports of the Bureau of Public Entreprises, Ministry of Finance. The deficiency of data for investment in the private sector makes estimation impossible – during the period 1967–72 it has been as important as the public sector. A figure for fertiliser plant of about 2·9–5

per cent of total annual investment in the economy during that period seems approximately the right order of magnitude. The figure for Central investment in fertilisers in the Draft Fifth Plan was Rs. 11490 million out of a total for major public sector industries of Rs. 70290 million (excluding replacement and inventories) or 16·3 per cent. (G.o.I. (1973c) vol. 2, p. 140.) Fifth Plan investment targets were later revised downwards but fertiliser investments will have higher priority than others; the failure to carry out this investment will have serious consequences over the longer run. *Imports*: From statistics of the Directorate General of Commercial Intelligence we can derive import figures for fertilisers and fertiliser raw materials as follows: 1968/9 $264 million: 1969/70 $157 million; 1970/71 $133 million; 1971/2 $150 million; 1972/3 $181 million (1973/4 $250 million estimate). As a guide India's annual exports during the period averaged about $2,000 million so that those imports averaged only a little less than 10 per cent of exports. This does not exhaust the foreign exchange cost of fertilisers as much of the plant and equipment going into India's industry is imported. Total imports of finished plant and machinery have averaged over $250 million a year during the same period and the fertiliser industry accounted for a substantial share of it, much of it paid for by aid.

Some figures on power are given in Henderson (1975): agriculture in 1960/61 absorbed electricity measured as 0·8 million tons of coal equivalent, compared with 4·5 million tons in 1970/71; the figures for oil are 2·7 million and 4·5 million respectively. The difference in foodgrains output between the two dates is 32 per cent. For agricultural production as a whole growth was almost identical – the index for 1970/71 is 131·4 with the three years 1959/60 – 1961/2 as the base = 100 (see G.o.I., 1975a).

It could be objected that the changeover to a capital and foreign-exchange-intensive agriculture was not a necessity and that acreage could have been extended and yields raised using more labour and domestic resources. Many observers though would dispute such a judgement – it is discussed later in the chapter. We can at least say that this was the direction taken by the economy even if other directions might have been possible.

26. This point is hardly taken care of in the Coale-Hoover model by their allowance of a small annual rise in the capital/output ratio. As in so many details in their impressive book, they foresaw the possibilities. They judged that of increments in total output only 25–30 per cent would be agricultural goods and that the low capital output ratio in agriculture was likely to continue. They did note ((1958) p. 199) that 'As development proceeds, the capital costs of further irrigation and land-improvement projects, and in general of programs for stepping up agricultural yields, will probably be larger in relation to results.' But their calculation over fifty years did not allow for so great a change to arrive so quickly. (Strictly speaking Coale and Hoover employ not a capital/output ratio, but a relationship, called 'R' in their model, between 'development outlays' and output.)

27. Clive Bell has suggested to the author that it has more to do with the fact that growth models of that period were dominated by a neoclassical approach which neglected the increasing costs of additional land, and which also neglected the complementarity between investments.

28. Economics might suggest to some that 'capital' will serve as a proxy for

'capital and foreign exchange' – after all is there not *some* exchange rate at which a country can sell abroad enough of its domestically produced goods to earn the foreign exchange it needs? And is not the only problem therefore one of saving to reduce sufficiently the consumption of domestically produced goods? To our knowledge the theoretical conditions for the existence of such an exchange rate have not been established and are unlikely, in so far as one can imagine them, to obtain in practice. In any case if one is using 'capital' as a proxy for 'capital and foreign exchange', the 'capital'/output ratio must be raised to allow for the fact. (For some empirical evidence on population induced domestic consumption of exportable commodities see Nayyar (1976).)

29. See Kuznets (1974).

30. See G.o.I. (1974*a*) Table 2.4. If even 60 per cent of capital were available for creating new jobs in manufacturing, and the cost of a work-place were only $300, our calculation above would remain unchanged: the savings of fifty people would finance one work-place. Of course, as per capita income grows, if the real cost of a work place remains constant, it will gradually become possible to shift people out of rural employment. But the pace must be extremely slow. A rise in the savings rate and a concentration of investment in small-scale manufacturing could alter these parameters; but there are limits to the latter – even the small scale sector requires complementary investments in power, transport and other less labour-intensive overheads. The *lowest* figure for capital per head in a survey of small-scale industry was about $300; the average much higher: N.C.A.E.R. (1972). For earlier works which reached these same general conclusions see Khusro (1962) and Rao (1960). Further the *consumption* as well as the investment costs of manufacturing may be higher: though the size of the wage differential between agriculture and industry is disputed, as is also the issue of whether the differential is matched (and explained) by higher productivity – see Horowitz (1974).

31. Krishnamurty (1974) adjusts the census figures for changes in definitions and finds the share of the male working force engaged in agriculture to be 69·3 per cent in 1951, 68 per cent in 1961 and 66,–67 per cent in 1971. Indeed he suggests the employment structure has changed very little since 1911.

32. Subramaniam Swamy counters such arguments with the panacea of improving technology: but while it is true that technological improvements in agriculture have given the lie to Malthus, in that food output can grow faster than population, this is not the same as demonstrating that there is no such thing as diminishing returns to fixed land. There is such a thing and we believe India has reached it. Swamy also cites the misleading argument that a larger population would yield greater numbers of gifted individuals to make contributions to knowledge. There may indeed be potentially gifted individuals in the additions to the population – but so there·are in the existing population; while only 29·6 per cent of the population can read and write, the volume of human intellect already unexploited makes it wholly absurd to call for still more. Swamy's other 'benefit' of population growth is that a large population guarantees demand for the nation's output. (Swamy (1974).) India's problem however has rarely been one of deficient demand in the post-Independence period – and if it were, deficit financing could always be resorted to. Such arguments have appeared elsewhere, and others too,

attributing alleged advantages of population growth even in India's circumstances – see for example Clark (1968). They appear to the author to possess little merit; they can appeal, if to anyone, only to those who give priority to goals other than that of improving the material conditions in which most Indians live. Clark in particular indulges in a remarkable piece of *post hoc ergo propter hoc* reasoning: setting side by side figures for population and total output during periods when both were rising, he attributes the growth of output to that of population by pure juxtaposition.

33. Coale and Hoover (1958). For the argument in the text see also Cassen (1968).
34. See Kuznets (1974) *passim*. Though see Star (1974).
35. A.E.R.C. (1971).
36. Sen (1970).
37. E.g. G.o.I. (1966*b*).
38. Leibenstein (1971).
39. Kuznets (1974) and others of his works there cited.
40. G.o.I. (1973*a* and *c*).
41. Dandekar and Rath (1970).
42. Bardhan (1974) repeats this error – see Chapter 2.
43. For a review of the literature and references other than those cited below see Kumar (1974) and Bardhan, P. K., 'The pattern of income distribution in India,' in Bardhan and Srinivasan (1975).
44. Kumar (1974).
45. Bardhan (1974) in footnote 4.
46. *Ibid.*
47. See, for example, Ranadive (1971). For a discussion of the significance of different possible measures of concentration see Sen (1973*a*).
48. Minhas (1970).
49. Bardhan (1973); see also *idem* (1970*a*).
50. Rajaraman (1974).
51. Lal (1976*a*).
52. G.o.I. (1974*b*). The 1956/7 data are from the Second Agricultural Labour Enquiry.
53. The 1970/71 data do show improvement over those for 1967/8; the latter year was one of rapid inflation and, as Lal observes, there is a lag between rural price and wage increases which by 1970/71 had been made up.
54. See Nayyar (1976).
55. Rajaraman (1974).
56. Lal (1976*a*).
57. Cited in Krishna (1976).
58. For an example see G.o.I. (1970*a*). It contains a table for 1964/5 (p. 9) showing infant mortality *rising* steadily with incomes: 38·38 for the class with monthly expenditure level Rs. 0 – 11 and 259·98 in the monthly expenditure class Rs. 43 and above. The notes quaintly comment: 'this may be possibly due to under-reporting of infant deaths in the lower expenditure classes.'
59. See Bardhan (1970*b*); Kumar (1974).
60. Herdt and Baker (1972).
61. Lal (1976*a*).
62. G.o.I. (1973*a*).

63. See in particular G.o.I. (1970*b*).
64. Not least Myrdal (1968).
65. Sen (1975). The scope of this work is far wider than is suggested by the sections of it to which the present paper refers.
66. G.o.I. (1973*b*).
67. Krishna (1976).
68. Once again Deepak Lal, 1976(b) has challenged the common view by claiming that, when such information is considered, the belief in voluminous surplus labour in rural India is upset. Taking data from the N.S.S. 25th Round which asked questions about the wage at which people would move outside the village for full-time employment, he estimates a labour supply curve. Since it has no flat segment – and only if more labour is available at the same wage would some purists agree to the existence of surplus labour – he concludes that the true extent of under-employment is modest. This surely takes a reasonable point too far; there are a variety of other interpretations of the data.
69. See e.g. G.o.I. (1967*b*) and (1970*b*), p. 163.
70. Sen (1973*b*).
71. Reviewed in Krishna (1976).
72. Surveys have shown that a proportion of those on the registers have existing employment; but only by the (weak) N.S.S. test. A 1970 survey showed 45 per cent on the registers to be educated to matriculation standard or above (most of them male) – this is much higher than the urban average, suggesting that the registration system is biased against the uneducated and therefore under-estimates urban employment. Besides, the number from the registers contributes only about one-fifth of the total estimated unemployed of 19·9 – 21·3 million. (The number on the live registers was 4·2 million in March 1971; it was 8·2 million by October 1973.) See Sen (1973*b*) and (1975).
73. G.o.I. (1970*c*).
74. G.o.I. (1973*c*).
75. Particularly since the period of modern land reform legislation and its evasion, whatever may be reported about ownership of land conceals much of the truth.
76. Mukherjee (1971). This work shows an increase of land per household in the hands of the richest at the expense of others between 1922 – 42.
77. Epstein (1973).
78. There was a large increase in the proportion of agricultural labourers in the labour force according to the 1961 and 1971 Censuses; but the definitions of 'labour force' and 'cultivator' were changed in the 1971 Census in such a way as would reduce 'cultivators' and increase 'labourers' so that too much weight cannot be given to the figures. (See G.o.I. (1971).) Thus 43 per cent of the total population were 'workers' in the 1961 Census and only 34 per cent under the tighter definitions in 1971; agricultural labourers were 18·87 per cent of workers in 1961 and 29·98 per cent in 1971. The absolute number of 'agricultural labourers' was 31·5 million in 1961, 47·3 million in 1971; this 50 per cent rise can only partly be explained by definitional changes. We can get rid of part of the definitional problem by looking at the numbers in the 15 – 59 age group which were 235 in 1961 (53·6 per cent of the total population) and 285 million in 1971 (52 per cent of the total) – an increase of 21·3 per cent in

the size of the age group; agricultural labourers as defined in 1961 were thus 13·4 per cent of the 15–59 age group in 1961 and as defined in 1971, 16·6 per cent of the age group in 1971. See further, 'Trends in rural unemployment in India, Two Comments' (P. Visaria and S. K. Sanyal) in *E.P.W.* 29 January 1977.

79. Most of the items in this paragraph are taken from *resurveys*, with the second survey in the late 1950s. For references see Connell (1973); also see next note. This particular bibliography covers over 300 village studies for India, the majority of which are *not* resurveys. It is for that reason that we refer in the next paragraph to the sample of village studies as 'small'. See also Moore (1974).

80. The *Village Studies Programme* (under the general guidance of Michael Lipton) is surveying some 2000 village studies from a variety of countries. About 1000 of them are for India. A publications programme has begun to make bibliographies and surveys on various topics – migration, nutrition, labour utilisation, agricultural subjects etc. – available to the public. Data from the studies is being tabulated for statistical use; some work with the data is already nearing completion – e.g. a study on migration, supporting the statement we make in the section on migration in Chapter 2 concerning the relationship between maldistribution of land and out-migration.

81. See also N.C.A.E.R. (1973) which shows a general increase in the employment of hired labour per acre on mechanised land and of male family labour on holdings above and below the size class 10–30 acres. There was displacement of male family labour within that size class. The study was for District Muzaffarnagar, Western U.P. On the other hand Wills (1971) suggests the possibility of considerable displacement of hired labour.

82. Thomas and Ramakrishnan (1940).

83. Etienne (1968).

84. G.o.I. (1973*c*).

85. Data for this calculation and for Figure 4.2 come from G.o.I. (1972) and (1975*a*). The equation fitted was log $Y = a + bt$, where Y is annual foodgrains output. A linear trend gave a slightly lower rate of growth, at 2·43 per cent. There is no 'correct' way to measure this average growth. For a discussion of the debate on the possible methods and their implications see Dey (1975).

86. Winstanley (1973). See also Calder (1974) and Lamb (1972).

87. Singh (1973) gives estimates of flood damage in U.P. alone of Rs. 18·5 crores in 1968/9, 42·2 in 1969/70; 73·97 in 1970/71, and Rs. 400 crores in 1971/2. Forestry outlay for U.P. in 1971/2 was Rs. 2·51 crores.

88. Thorner and Thorner (1962).

89. Brown (1967).

90. Lipton (1974).

91. Fourth Five Year Plan. (G.o.I. 1969.)

92. Khusro (1973). See also Ladejinsky (1964).

93. Khusro (1973).

94. When technology is changing it may be that improvements are first adopted on larger holdings and it could be observed temporarily that yields were higher on larger holdings for that reason. The 'accepted view' to which we refer holds for identical technology at all farm sizes, and identical quality of

land and other inputs – the pure effect of size, in other words. The first sources for data on this topic were the Farm Management surveys of 1954/5 to 1958/9 (G.o.I. 1954–9); more recent studies showing similar results are cited in Khusro (1973).

95. Hunter (1970) and Hunter and Bottrall (eds) (1974) are among the better studies on this topic. They point in particular to the multiplicity of agencies involved in the administration of Indian agriculture at all levels and suggest a variety of approaches for improving on current practices.

96. For the philosophical and welfare grounds see Rawls (1971).

97. Chenery *et al.* (1974).

98. For discussions of equity and administration in water use see Chambers (1974) and Vander Velde (1971).

99. Hunter and Bottrall (1974).

100. On consolidation see Minhas (1970). The schemes referred to comprise a number of programmes initiated in the early 1970s attempting to benefit the rural poor: a scheme for Marginal Farmers and Agricultural Labourers (M.F.A.L.) and the creation of a Small Farmers Development Agency (S.F.D.A.); the Drought Prone Areas Programme (D.P.A.P.) and the Crash Scheme for Rural Employment (C.S.R.E.). No detailed evaluation of those schemes have been published though they have been criticised, e.g. by Sen (1975). But they have all had partial success (Minhas, 1972). They have also demonstrated the need for preparation of any such programmes to be carried out at the local level, taking account of the immense variety of needs and conditions. The S.F.D.A. attempted to do for smaller farmers what earlier programmes had done for the larger ones, particularly by the provision of credit for small improvements and purchases – but it has proved difficult to overcome the disadvantages of very small size with minute doses of credit and other forms of assistance and the requirement for new forms of cooperation has been made apparent. The M.F.A.L. was a programme of schemes of income supplementation for farmers with holdings below viable size and for the landless. The D.P.A.P. lacks in particular well designed economic and technological 'packages' suitable to the needs of dry area farming – their absence reflects the prolonged neglect of research for farming in these conditions. The C.S.R.E. has run into various problems, not least the fact that labour is not always forthcoming even when a wage higher than that existing locally is offered: an old problem (see G.o.I. 1967b) and one which is now being studied, together with other findings in the light of the C.S.R.E. experience, in the Pilot Intensive Rural Employment Projects – a 3-year scheme to examine the best methods of creating rural employment based on trials in fifteen development Blocks. The future of such schemes is uncertain. In 1977 the Planning Commission was working on a new comprehensive rural development strategy. The government in the mid 70s appeared to regard such programmes as relatively low priority 'welfare' measures rather than the core of its economic strategy–so at least it seems correct to infer from the fate of the 'minimum needs programme' proposed in the early versions of the Fifth Plan, sacrificed when the economic troubles of 1974 required cuts in the Plan.

101. Schwarz (1975).

102. Swaminathan (1973). Kirit Parikh has carried out a study investigating the feasibility of a three-fold increase in agricultural output by 2001, required by

extreme assumptions about population and income growth. India was divided into agro-climatic zones and no further irrigation was assumed apart from schemes already planned for implementation by 1980. The main new input was fertiliser, plus appropriate development of new seeds to prevent fall-offs from presently attainable yields. Crop response to fertiliser was estimated from current actual yields, not experimental best practice performance. Trebling of food output required reaching 20 million tonnes of chemical nutrients (N, P and K) by 2001, not an impossible goal; altogether, with the exception of certain crops such as cotton, the author concluded that agriculture could bear the strain of rapidly growing population and incomes (his 'high' population for 2001 was 1127 million, higher than our highest projection F_1M_3); with more modest assumptions both about population and income growth (per capita expenditure grew at 3·37 per cent, 4·3 per cent and 5·3 per cent in the three decades from 1971 respectively, in his high growth projection) the situation appeared manageable for all crops. The study did not investigate other constraints such as water use; nor did it estimate the total resource cost of these agricultural requirements. But it bears out what others have claimed, that India's food problems *can* be solved. (See Parikh, 1973.)

103. Allen (1974).
104. The last figure we have for fertilizer availability was for 1972/3: 1·7 million tons of nitrogen, 0·5 million of phosphates and 0·3 million of potash (G.o.I., 1974a). In the case of N, more than one-third, and P, nearly two-thirds were imports and for K, 100 per cent is imported. India has yet to find domestic deposits of potassium; but production of N and P will expand considerably in the next few years.
105. G.o.I. (1974a). See also Narain (1972).
106. For elements of a dry farming programme see Jodha (1972).
107. Paddock and Paddock (1968). This work claimed that India was so hopelessly condemned to starvation that the country was not worth aiding and should be 'written off' by the international community.
108. Swaminathan (1973).
109. Hayami and Ruttan (1971).
110. Nutman (1974).
111. The Nitrogen Fixation Unit at the University of Sussex has already solved some of the fundamental scientific problems in this field, though practical applications may be many years away.
112. Hazari and Krishnamurty (1970); see also Sethuraman (1974).
113. G.o.I. (1975b).
114. G.o.I. (1970b), p. 166. The figures include rates for the 64-plus population.
115. Kumar (1975) showed that there was little if any increase in inequality of land distribution in Madras Presidency between 1853 and 1947. Our conclusion earlier in this chapter that the process of subdivision was slower for large holdings than small would imply increasing inequality. Population growth has accelerated since 1947 and there has ceased to be additional land to be brought under cultivation. The quality of contemporary holding size data might still hinder detection of the present direction of change in distribution; many large holdings would now be reported as split up which are not so in fact.
116. Nicholas (1962).

CHAPTER 5

 1. For a dismissive discussion of such cultural causes of non-development by a relatively conservative author see Moore (1966).
 2. A short bibliography of general works of this kind would include Brinton (1952); Dunn (1972); Forster and Greene (eds) 1970; Rudé (1966); Wolf (1971). Also valuable is Kumar (ed.) 1971, both for its readings from earlier and better known writers and its thoughtful introduction.
 3. See e.g. Kumar (1971), p. 43.
 4. Kumar (1965); Catanach (1966 and 1970); Charlesworth (1972). The causes and nature of the Deccan Riots are a subject of dispute as a reading even of these four sources will make clear. For example, while they began in areas where taxes had been increased, they spread to others where they had not, so the role of the tax increase is obscure.
 5. Hobsbawm (1969).
 6. Catanach (1966).
 7. See e.g. Chaudhuri (1955); Desai (1969).
 8. The exchange is cited and set in its context by Kumar (1971), p. 35.
 9. Omvedt (1973).
10. Gough (1969), p. 531.
11. Gough (1969); Alavi (1965).
12. See 'Peasant associations and class structure' in Béteille (1974) discussing a study in Bengali by Abdullah Rasul. Also H. D. Malaviya, 'Agrarian unrest after Independence' in Desai (1969); and Alavi (1965).
13. Marx, 'The British Rule in India', *New York Daily Tribune*, 25 June 1853, reprinted in Marx and Engels, undated, pp. 19–20.
14. Gough (1969).
15. See his U.G.C. National Lectures nos 2 and 3. 'The Study of Peasant Communities', and 'The Concept of Peasant Society', Béteille (1973).
16. See, for example, his account of the *jotedars* of Bengal, 'Class Structure in an Agrarian Society: the case of the Jotedars' in his 1974 work already cited.
17. Dasgupta (1974). This work also contains a brief history of the Communist revolutionary movement in India.
18. Forrester (1970), p. 11. This source also suggests that there was resentment in Telangana of 'immigrant' farmers from neighbouring districts who took advantage of new irrigation works when the resident farmers were slow to do so.
19. Alavi (1965).
20. 'Causes of agrarian unrest' in Béteille (1974).
21. 'Agrarian relations in Tanjore District', ibid.
22. Ibid., Table II, p. 166; an unfortunate misprint has reversed the words 'majority' and 'minority' in the second paragraph of p. 165.
23. 'Agrarian relations . . . ' *op. cit.* p. 189.
24. Ibid., p. 191.
25. Ibid., p. 192.
26. Dasgupta (1974). This is the only detailed account of the movement and we rely on it extensively here.
27. Ibid., p. 41.

28. Ibid., p. 58.
29. Ibid., p. 59.
30. Ibid.
31. Forrester, *op. cit.*
32. See the works cited in footnote 2 above for general discussions.
33. The phrase is from Dunn (1972).
34. We refer to the declaration of emergency by Mrs Gandhi on that date, the character and consequences of which are discussed below.
35. See, e.g. Zartman (1970).
36. Srinivas (1966); Bailey (1957).
37. For a particularly full and interesting report, see G.o.I. (1969).
38. Gough (1969), p. 533.
39. See Busquet, G., 'La renaissance d'une guerilla maoiste traduit un malaise paysan', *Le Figaro*, 30 May 1975.
40. See d'Monte, D., 'The Dalit Panthers', *The Guardian*, 1 March 1974.
41. Béteille (1974) makes a considerable point of the extent to which increasing numbers of rural inhabitants are losing old forms of security and moving into more uncertain conditions.
42. See several of the works listed above; and Davies (1962); Hoselitz and Weiner (1970); and Huntington (1968).
43. Moore (1966) has a long section entitled 'India: The price of peaceful change', in which he comments on the connections between the urban *bourgeoisie* and the rural masses via Gandhi's non-violent campaign in the Quit India movement. One of the 'prices' of peaceful change he identifies was this very conservatism.
44. In 1974 railway unions struck for a 75 per cent pay increase; the Government broke the strike by a punitive series of arrests and dismissals. It was a situation reflective of many of India's problems: the Government was in no position to meet the railwaymen's demands. It was generally accused of acting feebly in domestic politics. Yet the extremely tough action against the railway unions met little but criticism.
45. See reference to Lenin's 'Lecture on the 1905 Revolution' cited in Kumar (1971), note 110, p. 68.
46. *Tung-chi kung-tso* (Statistical work) no. 11, June 1957, cited in Orleans (1972).
47. Paillat and Sauvy (1974).
48. Nakano (1968).
49. Ibid. for the detailed figures, or Aird (1974).
50. Chen (1973).
51. Orleans (1972).
52. Yeh and Lee (1974).
53. Tien (1973).
54. Ibid.
55. Ibid.
56. See sources cited in Rifkin, S., 'Health care for rural areas', in Quinn (ed.) (1973).
57. Chen (1974).
58. The first such report to our knowledge was by Han Suyin (see Suyin, (1973)) but there have been many since.

59. Chen (1974).
60. Ibid. For a different view, but concentrating mainly on the earlier period, see Salaff (1972).
61. Tien (1973).
62. Orleans (1973).
63. Draper *et al.* (1971).
64. Djerassi (1974*a*).
65. Chen (1974).
66. Salaff (1973). The U.N. figures are from U.N. (1974*a*).
67. Orleans (1972).
68. Paillat and Sauvy (1974).
69. Salaff (1973).
70. Ibid.
71. At a lecture attended by the author in August 1974; Joshua Horn is the author of *Away with All Pests.*
72. Salaff (1973).
73. In *Ten Great Years* (Pekin, 1960) cited by e.g. Paillat and Sauvy (1974).
74. Tien (1973).
75. Paillat and Sauvy's guess is 8 per 1000 (1974).
76. Chen (1973); Djerassi (1974*b*).
77. Tien (1974). (Abstract in *Population Index*, July 1974.)
78. Ibid.
79. Idem (1973).
80. Faundes and Luukkainen (1972) estimated that one-third of couples of reproductive age were current users of contraception. They do not give the basis for their estimate; but if true, taken with the late age at marriage one would expect a birth rate of 30 per thousand or less.
81. Chen (1974).
82. Yeh and Lee (1974) citing Aird.
83. Yeh and Lee (1974).
84. See for example Byres and Nolan (1976); Chen and Uppal (1971); Harris (1974); Klein (1965); Lateef (1976); Malenbaum (1959); Raj (1967); Swamy (1973).
85. There is a rather unedifying exchange between Richman (1975); Weisskopf (1975) and Desai (1975) showing something of the first two of these tendencies. On the changing character of Chinese studies in general see Gittings (1976). As examples of work not based on any extreme of benevolence towards China see citations of Aird or Orleans above.
86. See, for example, many of the papers in U.S. Congress (1975).
87. Swamy (1973).
88. Perkins (1974). See also papers by Ashbrook and Nai-Ruenn Chen in U.S. Congress (1975).
89. Lateef (1976).
90. See, e.g., Weisskopf (1975).
91. Byres and Nolan (1976).
92. Ibid.
93. Richman (1975).
94. Lateef (1976).
95. U.S. Congress (1975). In fact Chinese industry had a poor year in 1977.

96. Byres and Nolan (1976).
97. Ibid.
98. These differences are reported in most of the sources referred to above.
99. See Croll (1974).
100. See *The Times*, 11 November 1975, reporting a debate about the size of the 1975 foodgrains crop. If the lower of the official figures announced is correct (264 million tons), the problem of the slow growth of agriculture is still present. But a higher figure of 274 million has also been claimed.
101. Hanson and Douglas (1972).
102. Ibid., p. 211.
103. Morris-Jones (1975).
104. Ibid.
105. See Mrs Gandhi's interview with Maurice Edelman, *The Times*, 14 November 1975.
106. Harrison (1960); Segal (1965); Hanson and Douglas (1972).
107. See, e.g., evidence of M.Weiner and M. F. Franda in U.S. Congress (1973).
108. Amnesty (1974, 1975).
109. Morris-Jones (1975).
110. Hanson and Douglas (1972) p. 49.
111. There was much other evidence of a deepening political and economic crisis prior to June 1975. For an account of it, and a statement of the view that the Emergency was not the only possible response, see Morris-Jones (1977).
112. Calhoun (1970). (Other work suggests that study of captive animals is not even a good guide to animal behaviour in the natural habitat, let alone to human behaviour—e.g. Sadleir (1969).) For a much more sophisticated view of population and social pathology, see Olin (1972).
113. See, for example, Leys (1975); Rhodes (1970).
114. The 1973 population of Africa was 374 million, that of South America 206 million, or 580 million altogether, compared with India's 575 million. (U.N., 1974*b*).
115. We will not attempt here to resolve the debate about the pros and cons of food aid. We believe both the price-disincentive and inflationary effects to have been exaggerated (for an excellent analysis, see Isenman and Singer, 1975). There is a case however for the view that successive governments would have had to make greater efforts in agriculture in the 1950s and 1960s had they not been able to rely on the prospect of food aid.
116. See O.E.C.D. (1974) and earlier volumes.
117. G.o.I. (1972). There was a similar document for the Third Plan – See G.o.I. (1961).
118. G.o.I. (1975). Since foreign exchange shortage is treated as a key problem for the economy throughout this book, a comment is due on the strong reserve position of 1976 and 77. As noted, a new element in the situation was a major inflow of remittances by overseas workers. But there was also some compression of imports after the 1973 oil crisis, and the economy had been operating at a low level of activity. In 1976 there were many calls for expansion in the light of the comfortable state of food stocks and foreign exchange. But by late 1977, no major expansion had been set in motion. The Janata Government had yet to formulate a clear economic programme which would take advantage of import capacities. This was one of the main short-

run macro-economic problems. But for the longer term, any sustained growth which might relieve unemployment and poverty would soon encounter the foreign exchange boundary.

119. For a review of the literature, see Evans (forthcoming).
120. See U.N. (1975).
121. Tulloch (1973).
122. See, e.g., Hayter (1971); Payer (1974); Prabhat Patnaik in Blackburn (1975); Bauer (1971).
123. For a recent examination related to the Andean Pact countries see Vaitsos (1974).
124. Nayyar (1975).
125. Ibid.
126. Chaudhuri (1975).
127. McNicoll (1975) discusses some aspects of this view in an interesting paper. See also Mukherjee (1976).

Bibliographies

CHAPTER I

Adelman, I., 'An econometric analysis of population growth', *American Economic Review* (June 1963).

Banks, J. A., *Prosperity and Parenthood* (London, 1954).

Banks, J. A. & O., *Feminism and Family Planning in Victorian England* (Liverpool, 1964).

Baster, N. (ed.) *Measuring Development: The Lack of Adequacy of Development Indicators* (London, 1972).

Behrman, S. J., L. Corsa and R. Freedman, (eds.), *Fertility and Family Planning: A World View* (Ann Arbor, 1969).

Bernier, F., *Travels in the Mogul Empire 1656–1669* (New Delhi, 1968).

Biraben, J. N., 'L'évolution de la fécondité en Europe occidentale', Council of Europe, *Conférence Démographique Européenne* (Strasbourg, 1966).

Biraben, J. N., 'Quelques précisions sur l'année "cheval et feu"', *Notes et Documents* (I.N.E.D., 1969).

Biraben, J. N., 'Certain demographic characteristics of the plague epidemic in France, 1720–22', in Glass and Revelle (eds.) (1972).

Biraben, J. N., *Les Hommes et la Peste en France et dans les Pays Européens et Méditerranéens*, Vol. I (Paris, Hague, 1975).

Blacker, J. G. C., 'The social & economic causes of the decline in the French birth rate at the end of the eighteenth century', Ph. D. Thesis (London University, 1957).

Blythe, R., *Akenfield* (London, 1969).

Boner, H. A., *Hungry Generations: the Nineteenth-Century Case against Malthusianism* (New York, 1955).

Boughey, A. S., *Ecology of Populations* (New York, 1973).

Bourgeois-Pichat, J., 'The general development of the population of France since the eighteenth century', *Population*, 1951, reprinted in Glass and Eversley (eds.) (1965).

Bowrey, T., *Countries Round the Bay of Bengal, 1669 – 79*, ed. Temple (Cambridge, 1905).

Boyer, P. and A. Richard, 'Eléments d'analyse de la transition démographique', *Population* (July – October, 1975).

Braudel, F. and E. Labrousse, *Histoire Economique et Sociale de la France, Tome II (1660–1789)* (Paris, 1970).

Briggs, A., *Victorian Cities* (London, 1963).

Brown, L. R., *World Population Trends: Signs of Hope, Signs of Stress*, Worldwatch Paper No. 8 (Washington D.C., 1976).

Carleton, R. O., 'The effect of educational improvement on fertility trends in Latin America', *Proceedings of the World Population Conference* (New York, 1967).

Cassel, J., 'Health consequences of population density and crowding', in U.S. National Academy of Sciences (1971).

Cassen, R. H., 'Population and development: a survey', *World Development*, (October – November 1976).

CELADE, *Fertility and Family Planning in Metropolitan Latin America*, Centro Latino-americano de Demografia and Community and Family Study Center (Chicago, 1972).

Chambers, J. D., *Population, Economy and Society in Pre-industrial England* (London, 1972).

Chamoux, A and C. Dauphin, 'La contraception avant la révolution française: l'exemple de Châtillon-sur-Seine', *Les Annales* (May – June 1969).

Chandrasekhar, S., *Infant Mortality, Population Growth and Family Planning in India* (London, 1972).

Cipolla, C. M., *The Economic History of World Population* (Harmondsworth, 1962).

Coale, A. J., 'The decline of fertility in Europe from the French Revolution to World War II', in Behrman *et al.* (eds) (1969).

Coale, A. J., 'The demographic transition reconsidered', I.U.S.S.P., *International Population Conference*, vol. 1 (Liège, 1973).

Cox, P. R., *Demography* (Cambridge, 1972).

Das Gupta, A., 'Study of the historical demography of India', in Glass and Revelle (eds) (1972).

Davis, K., *The Population of India and Pakistan* (Princeton, 1951).

Davis, K., 'The theory of change and response in modern demographic history', *Population Index*, vol. 29, no. 4 (1963).

Davis, K., 'Population policy: will current programs succeed?' *Science*, no. 3802 (10 November 1967).

Demeny, P., 'Early fertility decline in Austria-Hungary: a lesson in demographic transition', *Daedalus* (1968) (reprinted in Glass and Revelle (eds) (1972)).

Dore, R. P., Review of Taeuber (1958), in *British Journal of Sociology*, September 1959.

Drummond, J. C. and A. Wilbraham, *The Englishman's Food*, rev. ed. (London, 1957).

Dyos, H. J. and M. Wolff, (eds), *The Victorian City: Images and Realities* (London, 1973).

Eversley, D. E. C., *Social Theories of Fertility and the Malthusian Debate* (London, 1959).

Flinn, M. W., *British Population Growth 1700 – 1850* (London, 1970).

Ganiage, J., 'Trois villages d'Ile-de-France en XVIIIe siècle', I.N.E.D., *Cahier* no. 40 (Paris, 1963).

Glass, D. V., 'Gregory King's estimates of the population of England and Wales, 1695', *Population Studies*, vol. VIII, no. 4 (March, 1950).

Glass, D. V. and E. Grebenik, *The Trend and Pattern of Fertility in Great Britain*, H.M.S.O. (London, 1954).

Glass, D. V., 'Population growth, fertility and population policy', address to The British Association (Section N) (6 September, 1960).

Glass, D. V. and D. Eversley (eds), *Population in History* (London, 1965).

Glass, D. V. and R. Rèvelle, (eds), *Population and Social Change* (London, 1972).

Grigg, E. R. N., 'The arcana of tuberculosis', *American Review of Tuberculosis*, vol. 78 (1958).

Habakkuk, H. J., *Population Growth and Economic Development since 1750* (Leicester, 1971).

Hajnal, J., 'European marriage patterns in perspective', in Glass and Eversley (eds) 1965.

Hartwell, R. M., 'The rising standard of living in England 1800 – 50', *Economic History Review* (1961).

Hawthorn, G., *The Sociology of Fertility* (London, 1970).

Heber, R., Bishop of Calcutta, *Narrative of a Journey through the Upper Provinces of India . . . 1824 – 25*, 3rd ed. (London, 1828).

Heer, D. M., 'Economic development and fertility', *Demography*, vol. iii, no. 2 (1966).

Henderson, P. D. (ed.), *Economic Growth in Britain* (London, 1966).

Henry, L., 'The population of France in the eighteenth century', in Glass and Eversley (eds) 1965.

Himes, N. E., *Medical History of Contraception* (New York, 1963) (1st ed. 1936).

Hirst, L. F., *The Conquest of Plague* (London, 1953).

Hobsbawm, E. J., 'The British Standard of Living, 1750 1850', *Economic History Review* (1957).

Hollingsworth, T. H., *Historical Demography* (New York, 1969).

Hopkins, K., 'Contraception in the Roman Empire', *Comparative Studies in Society and History* (October 1965).

Ingalls, D. H. H. (tr.), *Sanskrit Poetry from Vidyakara's 'Treasury'* (Harvard, 1968).

Inglis, B., *Poverty and the Industrial Revolution* (London, 1971).

Journal of Biosocial Science, *Biosocial Aspects of Human Fertility*, supplement no. 3 (1970).

Jutikkala, E. and M. Kauppinen, 'The structure of mortality during catastrophic years in a pre-industrial society', *Population Studies* (July 1971).

Kamerschen, D. R., 'The statistics of birth rate determinants', *Journal of Development Studies* (April, 1971).

Kiernan, V. G., *The Lords of Human Kind* (London, 1969).
Kirk, D., 'Factors affecting Moslem natality', in Berelson *et al.* (eds) *Family Planning and Population Programs* (Chicago, 1966).
Kirk, D., 'A new demographic transition?' in U.S. National Academy of Sciences (1971).
Kocher, J., *Rural Development, Income Distribution and Fertility Decline*, Population Council (New York, 1973).
Krause, J. T., 'Changes in English fertility and mortality 1781 – 1850', *Economic History Review* (1958).
Lachiver, M., *La Population du Meulan du XVIIᵉ au XIXᵉ Siècle* (Paris, 1969).
Laslett, P., 'Size and structure of the household in England over three centuries', *Population Studies* (July 1969).
Laslett, P., *The World We Have Lost* (London, 1971).
Lefebvre, A., 'Nombre de médecins et espérance de vie', *Population* (November – December 1976).
London School Board, *Final Report* (London, 1904).
Mallik, M. C., *Orient and Occident: A Comparative Study* (London, 1913).
Matras, J., 'The social strategy of family formation: some variations in time and space', *Demography* (1965).
McKeown, T. and R. G. Record, 'Reasons for the decline of mortality in England & Wales during the nineteenth century', *Population Studies* (November 1962).
McLaughlin, T., *Coprophilia* (London, 1971).
Mill, J. S., *Autobiography* (London, 1873).
Miro. C. and W. Mertens, 'Influences affecting fertility in urban & rural Latin America', *Milbank Memorial Fund Quarterly* (July 1968).
Montyon, A.-J.-B.-R. A., Baron de, *Recherches et Considérations sur la Population de la France* (Paris, 1778).
Moreland, W. H., *India at the Death of Akbar* (London, 1920).
Muramatsu, M., *Country Profiles – Japan*, Population Council (New York, 1971).
Nikitin, A., *Khozhenie za Tri Morya 1466–73* (Moscow, 1958).
O'Malley, L. S. S., *Modern India and the West* (London, 1941).
O'Neill, W. L., *The Woman Movement* (London, 1941).
Parkinson, C. N., *East and West* (London, 1963).
Petersen, W., 'The demographic transition in the Netherlands', *American Sociological Review* (1960).
Pran Nath, *A Study in the Economic Condition of Ancient India*, Royal Asiatic Society (London, 1929).
Prest, J., *Lord John Russell* (London, 1972).
Preston, S. H., 'The changing relation between mortality and economic development', *Population Studies* 29 (2) (July 1975).
Razzell, P. E., 'An interpretation of the modern rise of population in Europe – a critique', *Population Studies* 28 (1) (March 1974).
Reeves, J., *Recollections of a School Attendance Officer* (London 1894) (1913 ed.).

Renbourn, E. T., *Materials and Clothing in Health and Disease* (London, 1972).

Rich, W., *Smaller Families through Social and Economic Progress*, Overseas Development Council (Washington D.C., 1973).

Rowntree, B. S., *Poverty: A Study of Town Life* (London, 1901).

Rubinstein, E., *School Attendance in London, 1870 – 1904* (Hull, 1969).

Rudé, G., *Paris and London in the 18th Century* (London, 1970).

Russell, J. C., 'The population of Hiuen Tsang's India (A.D. 629–645)', *Journal of Indian History* (August, 1969).

Smith, A., *The Wealth of Nations* (London, 1776).

Smout, T., *History of the Scottish People* (London, 1969).

Spengler, J. J., *French Predecessors of Malthus* (Duke University Press, 1942).

Stott, D. H., 'Cultural and natural checks on population', in Vayda (1969).

Taeuber, I. B., *The Population of Japan* (Princeton, 1958).

Taeuber, I. B., 'Japan's demographic transition re-examined', *Population Studies* (July 1960).

Thomas, Dorothy S., *Social and Economic Aspects of Swedish Population Movements, 1750 – 1933* (New York, 1941).

Townsend, P., *The Concept of Poverty* (London, 1970).

U.N., *The Determinants and Consequences of Population Change*, vol. I (New York, 1973).

U.N., *Levels and Trends of Fertility throughout the World, 1950 – 70*, Dept. of Economic and Social Affairs, Population Studies no. 59, ST/ESA/Series A/59 (New York, 1977).

U.S. National Academy of Sciences, *Rapid Population Growth* (Johns Hopkins University Press, 1971).

Vaizey, J., 'Education, training and growth', in Henderson (ed.) (1966).

Van de Walle, E., 'Marriage and marital fertility', in Glass and Revelle (eds) (1972).

Van de Walle, E. and J. Knodel, 'Demographic transition and fertility decline: the European case', I.U.S.S.P., *Sydney Conference* (1967).

Vayda, A. P. (ed.), *Environment and Cultural Behavior* (New York, 1969).

Veron, J., 'Niveaux nationaux de natalité et politiques de limitations des naissances', *Population* (November – December, 1976).

Watt, R., *An Inquiry into the Relative Mortality of the Principal Diseases of Children in Glasgow* (reprinted) (Glasgow, 1888).

Weintraub, R. E., 'The birth rate and economic development', *Econometrica* (October 1962).

Wilkinson, T. O., *The Urbanization of Japanese Labor 1868 – 1955* (Amherst, 1965).

Wrigley, E. A., 'Family limitation in preindustrial England', *Economic History Review* (April 1966).

Wrigley, E. A., *Population and History* (New York, 1969).

Wrigley, E. A. (ed.), *Nineteenth Century Society* (London, 1972).

CHAPTER 2

Achar, S. T. and A. Yankauer, *Indian Journal of Child Health*, vol.11 (1962).

Adlakha, A. and D. Kirk, 'Vital rates in India 1961–71 estimated from 1971 census data', *Population Studies*, vol. 28, no. 3 (November 1974).

Agarwala, S. N., 'Effect of, a rise in female marriage age on birth rate in India', *World Population Conference* (Belgrade, 1965).

Agarwala, S. N., *India's Population Problems* (Revised 1st Edition) (New Delhi, 1973).

Agarwal, B. L., 'Sample registration in India', *Population Studies* (November 1969).

Ambannavar, J. P., *Long term prospects of population growth and labour force in India* (Ford Foundation, Second India Studies, Bombay, 1975).

Aykroyd, W. R., *The Conquest of Famine* (London, 1974).

Banerji, D., 'Tuberculosis: a problem of social planning in India', National Institute of Health & Education, *Bulletin*, 4, 1(1971).

Banks, A. L., 'Religious fairs and festivals in India', *The Lancet* (21 January 1961).

Bardhan, P. K., 'On the incidence of poverty in rural India', *E.P.W.*, Annual Number (February 1973).

Bardhan, P. K. and T. N. Srinivasan (eds), *Poverty and Income Distribution in India* (Indian Statistical Institute, New Delhi, 1975).

Bencic, Z. and R. Sinha, 'Cholera carriers and circulation of cholera vibrios in the community', *International Journal of Epidemiology*, vol. 1, no. 1 (1972).

Berg, A. *et al.* (eds) *Nutrition, National Development and Planning* (M.I.T., 1973).

Blyn, G., *Agricultural Trends in India 1891–1947* (Philadelphia, 1966).

Bose, A., 'Migration streams in India', I.U.S.S.P., *International Population Conference* (Sydney, 1967).

Bose, A., (ed.) *Patterns of Population Change in India, 1951–61* (New Delhi, 1967).

Bose, A., *Studies in India's Urbanization, 1901–1971* (New Delhi, 1973).

Bose, A., P. B. Desai, A. Mitra and J. N. Sharma (eds), *Population in India's Development 1947–2000* (Delhi, 1974).

Bourgeois–Pichat, J. and S. Taleb, 'Un taux d'accroissement nul pour les pays en voie de développement en l'an 2000: rêve ou réalité', *Population* (September–October 1970).

Brass, W. *et al.*, *The Demography of Tropical Africa* (Princeton, 1968).

Bruce-Chwatt, L. J., 'Twenty years of malaria eradication', *British Journal of Hospital Medicine*, vol. 12, no. 3 (September 1974).

Cantrelle, P., B. Ferry and J. Mondot, 'Relationships between fertility and mortality in tropical Africa', Paper for C.I.C.R.E.D. Seminar on infant mortality in relation to the level of fertility (Bangkok, May 1975).

Cassen, R. H., 'Population control: aims and policies', in Streeten *et al.* (eds) (1968).

Cassen, R. H., 'Population and development: a survey', *World Development* (October–November 1976).

Cassen, R. H. and T. Dyson, 'New population projections for India', *Population and Development Review*, vol. 2, no. 1 (March 1976).

Cavenaugh, D. C., 'Specific effect of temperature upon transmission of the plague *bacillus* by the oriental rat flea *X. cheopis*', *American Journal of Tropical Medicine & Hygiene*, vol. 20, no. 2 (March 1971).

Chandrahas, R. K. and A. K. Krishnaswami, 'Flea fauna on domestic rodents in some areas of the South Indian plague focus', *Indian Journal of Medical Research*, vol. 59, no. 11 (November 1971).

Chidambaram, V. C. and A. V. Zodegekar, 'Increasing female age at marriage in India and its impact on the first birth interval: an empirical analysis', I.U.S.S.P. *International Population Conference* (London, 1969).

Choudhury, D. S., 'Investigation on the reappearance of suspected human plague in Madras State', *Indian Journal of Malariology*, vol. 17, no. 4 (December 1963).

Clark, C., 'Extent of hunger in India', *E.P.W.* (30 September 1972).

Coale, A. J., 'Constructing the age distribution of a population recently subject to declining mortality', *Population Index*, 37, no. 2 (1971).

Coale, A. J. and P. Demeny, *Methods of Estimating Basic Demographic Measures from Incomplete Data*, U.N. Manual IV (New York, 1967).

Coale, A. J. and E. M. Hoover, *Population Growth and Economic Development in Low Income Countries* (Princeton, 1958).

Coale, A. J. and T. J. Trussell, 'Model fertility schedules: variations in the age structure of childbearing in human populations', *Population Index* (April 1974).

Connell, J., B. Dasgupta, R. Laishley and M. Lipton, 'Migration from rural areas: the evidence from village studies', *Discussion Paper*, no. 39 (Institute of Development Studies, Sussex, 1974).

Dandekar, K., 'Fertility, its control and future prospects', in Bose *et al.* (eds) 1974.

Dandekar, V. M. and N. Rath, *Poverty in India* (Ford Foundation, New Delhi, 1970).

Das, N. C., 'A note on the effect of postponement of marriage on total fertility and female birth rate', I.U.S.S.P., *International Population Conference* (London, 1969).

Das, N. P., 'Factors related to knowledge, family size preference, practice of family planning in India', *Journal of Family Welfare*, 19, 1(1972).

Das Gupta, M., 'Factors affecting age at marriage in India' (London School of Economics, 1974 (unpublished)).

Datta, S. P., 'Rodent and flea survey of Poona Camp', *Bulletin of the Indian Society for Malaria and Communicable Diseases*, vol. 3, no. 44 (1966).

Davis, K., *The Population of India and Pakistan* (Princeton, 1951).

Dewey, C., 'The agricultural statistics of the Punjab, 1867–1947', *Bulletin of Quantitative and Computer Methods in South Asian Studies* (March 1974).

Dhagamwar, V., *Law, Power & Justice* (Bombay, 1974).

Dhir, S. L. *et al.*, 'Focal outbreak of malaria caused by *P. malariae* in Tumkur District, Mysore State', *Journal of Communicable Diseases*, vol. I, no. 2 (1969).

Dore, R. P., *The Diploma Disease* (London, 1976).

Driver, E. D., *Differential Fertility in Central India* (Princeton, 1963).

Dyson, T., 'India's population: an analysis of its size, age-structure, fertility and mortality', *Discussion Paper*, no. 72 (Institute of Development Studies, Sussex, 1975).

E.P.W., *Economic and Political Weekly* (Bombay).

F.A.O. *Food Balance Sheets*, 1964–66 Average (Rome, 1971).

Farooq, G. M. and B. Tuncer, 'Fertility and economic and social development in Turkey: a cross-sectional and time series study', *Population Studies* (July 1974).

Fogel, R. W. and S. L. Engerman, *Time on the Cross* (Boston, 1974).

Fomon, S. J. *Infant Nutrition*, 2nd ed. (Philadelphia, 1974).

Fox, W., 'The chemotherapy and epidemiology of tuberculosis, some findings . . . from the Tuberculosis Chemotherapy Centre, Madras', *The Lancet* (1 September 1962).

Frederiksen, H., 'Determinants and consequences of mortality trends in Ceylon', *Public Health Reports* 76 (1961).

Frederiksen, H., 'Determinants and consequences of mortality and fertility trends', *Public Health Reports*, 81 (1966).

Frederiksen, H., 'Malaria eradication and the fall of mortality', *Population Studies* (March 1970).

Frejka, T., *The Future of Population Growth–Alternative Paths to Equilibrium* (Population Council, New York, 1973).

Gandhi, M. K., *True Education* (Ahmedabad, 1962).

Ghai, O. P. *et al.*, 'Nutritional assessment of preschool children in a rural community', *Indian Journal of Medical Research* (November 1970).

Ghosh, S., *Feeding and Care of Infants and Young Children* (U.N.I.C.E.F., New Delhi, 1976).

Gideon, H., 'A baby is born in the Punjab', *American Anthropologist*, 64 (1962).

G.o.I. (Government of India) *Final Report* (The Famine Enquiry Commission, Madras, 1945).

G.o.I. *1961 Census: Life Tables 1951–60*, Census of India 1961 (Office of the Registrar General, New Delhi, 1964).

G.o.I. *Report on the Population Projections worked out under the Guidance of the Expert Committee set up by the Planning Commission*, Office of the Registrar General (New Delhi, 1969).

G.o.I. *Principal Causes of Death in India*, Sen Gupta, S. K. and P. N. Kapoor, Central Bureau of Health Intelligence, Technical Studies Series 1, no.

13 (Ministry of Health, New Delhi, 1970).

G.o.I. *Pocket Book of Population Statistics* (Office of the Registrar General, New Delhi, 1971*a*).

G.o.I. 1971 Census: One-per cent Sample Data, mimeo (Office of the Registrar General, New Delhi, 1971*b*).

G.o.I. 1971 Census–*General Tables* vol. I (Office of the Registrar General, New Delhi, 1971*c*).

G.o.I. 'Measures of fertility and mortality in India', Sample Registration, *Analytical Series*, no. 2 (Office of the Registrar General, New Delhi, 1972*a*).

G.o.I. *Report on Survey of Causes of Death 1969* (Office of the Registrar General, New Delhi, 1972*b*).

G.o.I. *Sample Registration Bulletin*, Vol. VII, 3–4 (joint issue) (Office of the Registrar General, New Delhi, July–December 1973*a*).

G.o.I. Post Enumeration Check, Preliminary Results, Census of India, mimeo (Office of the Registrar General, New Delhi, 1973*b*).

G.o.I. *Draft Fifth Five Year Plan 1974–79* (Planning Commission, New Delhi, 1973*c*).

G.o.I. *Sample Registration Bulletin* VIII(1) (Office of the Registrar General, New Delhi, April 1974*a*).

G.o.I. *Weekly Epidemiological Record* XXVIII 39 (Directorate General of Health Services, New Delhi, October 1974*b*).

G.o.I. *Age and Life Tables* (one per cent sample), Census of India 1971, Series I. India, Miscellaneous Studies, Paper 2 of 1974 (Office of the Registrar General, New Delhi 1974*c*).

G.o.I. *Towards Equality*, Report of the Committee on Status of Women in India (Ministry of Education & Social Welfare, New Delhi, 1974*d*).

G.o.I. *Calorie and Protein content of Food Items Consumed Per Diem Per Consumer Unit in Rural and Urban Areas of Assam and Bihar*, National Sample Survey, 26th Round, July 1971–June 1972, no. 258/1 (Department of Statistics, Ministry of Planning, New Delhi, 1975).

Gopalan, C., 'Maternal and infant nutrition in underdeveloped countries', *Journal of the American Dietetic Association*, 39 2 (August 1961).

Gopalan, C., 'Observations on some epidemiological factors . . . of Protein-Calorie Malnutrition', in Von Muralt (ed.) (1969).

Gopalan, C. and K. V. Raghavan, *Nutrition Atlas of India* (National Institute of Nutrition, Hyderabad, 1969).

Gordon, J. E., M. Behar and N. S. Scrimshaw, 'Acute diarrhoeal disease in less developed countries' (3 articles), *Bulletin*, 31 (1–7) (W.H.O. 1964).

Gosal, G. S., 'Redistribution of population in Punjab 1951–61', in Bose (ed.) (1967).

Government of West Bengal, *Basic Development Plan for the Calcutta Metropolitan District, 1961–1986* (Calcutta Metropolitan Planning Organisation, Calcutta, 1966).

Gramiccia, G. and J. Hempel, 'Mortality and morbidity from malaria in countries where malaria eradication is not making satisfactory progress', *The Journal of Tropical Medicine and Hygiene* (October 1972).

Gray, R. H., 'The decline of mortality in Ceylon and the demographic effects of malaria control', *Population Studies* (July 1974).

Grewal, T., T. Gopaldas and V. J. Gadre, 'Etiology of malnutrition in rural Indian preschool children (Madhya Pradesh)', *Journal of Tropical Pediatrics and Environmental Child Health*, 19, 3 (September 1973).

Gulati, S. C., 'Impact of literacy, urbanization and sex-ratio on age at marriage in India', *Artha Vijnana* (December 1969).

Hardin, G., 'The tragedy of the commons', *Science* (13 December 1968).

Heer, D. and H. Wu, 'The effect of infant and child mortality and preference for sons upon fertility and family planning behaviour and attitudes in Taiwan', 1974, in Kantner, J. F. (ed.), *Population and Social Change in South East Asia* (forthcoming).

Hindustan Thompson Associates, *A Study of Food Habits in Calcutta* (U.S.A.I.D., Calcutta, 1972).

Hirschhorn, N. and W. B. Greenough, 'Cholera', *Scientific American* (15 August 1971).

Hirst, L. F., *The Conquest of Plague* (London, 1953).

Husain, I. Z., 'Educational status and differential fertility in India', in Husain (ed.) (1972).

Husain, I. Z. (ed.), *Population Analysis and Studies* (Bombay, 1972).

I.B.R.D., *Population Projections for Bank Member Countries*, K. C. Zachariah and R. Cuca (International Bank for Reconstruction and Development, Washington D.C., 1973).

I.C.M.R., *Tuberculosis in India–a sample survey*, (Indian Council of Medical Research, New Delhi, 1959).

I.C.M.R., *Dietary Allowances for Indians*, Special Report Series, no. 35 (Hyderabad, 1960).

I.C.M.R., *Review of Nutrition Surveys Carried Out in India*, Special Report Series, no. 36 (New Delhi, 1961).

I.C.M.R., *Dietary Allowances for Indians*, Special Report Series, no. 60 (Hyderabad, 1968).

I.C.M.R., *Growth and Physical Development of Indian Infants and Children*, Technical Report Series, no. 18 (New Delhi, 1972).

I.C.M.R., *Studies on Pre-school Children*, Report of the Working Party of the I.C.M.R., Technical Report Series, no. 26 (New Delhi, 1974).

Jain, A. K. and D. V. N. Sarma, Some explanatory factors for statewise differential use of family planning methods in India, mimeo (Population Council, New York, 1974).

Jain, S. P., *Demography: A Status Study on Population Research in India*, vol. II (Family Planning Foundation, New Delhi, 1975).

Jelliffe, D. B., *Infant Nutrition in the Subtropics and Tropics*, Monograph Series, no. 29 (W.H.O., Geneva, 1955).

Johnson, D. R., 'Status of malaria eradication in India 1965', *Mosquito*

News, 25, 4 (December 1965).

Johnson, D. R., 'Malaria eradication achievements in India', *Proceedings of the New Jersey Mosquito Extermination Association*, 53rd Meeting (1966).

Joshi, H. and V. Joshi, *Surplus Labour and the City: A Study of Bombay* (O.U.P. India, 1975).

Kale, B. D., 'Contours of female education and age at marriage in urban India: a district level study', *Journal of the Institute of Economic Research* (Dharwar, July 1969).

Klein, I., 'Malaria and mortality in Bengal, 1840–1921', *Indian Economic and Social History Review* (June 1972).

Klein, I., 'Death in India', *Journal of Asian Studies* (August 1973).

Klein, I., 'Population and agriculture in Northern India, 1872–1921', *Modern Asian Studies*, 8, 2 (1974).

Kosambi, D. D., *Ancient India* (New York, 1965).

Krause, J. T., 'Changes in English fertility and mortality, 1781–1850', *Economic History Review*, 2nd Series, vol. XI (1958).

Kumar, J., 'The pattern of internal migration in India', I.U.S.S.P., *International Population Conference* (Sydney, 1967).

Lamba, J. S., 'Recrudescence of malaria in Punjab and Haryana', *Armed Forces Medical Journal* (1971).

Learmonth, A. T. A., 'Medical geography in India and Pakistan: a study of twenty years' data for the former British India', *Indian Geographical Journal*, XXXIII 1 and 2 (1958).

Leibenstein, H., 'Socio-economic fertility theories and their relevance to population policy', *International Labour Review* (May–June 1974).

Levinson, F. J., *Morinda: An Economic Analysis of Malnutrition among Young Children in Rural India*, Cornell/M.I.T. International Nutrition Policy Series (Cambridge, Mass., 1974).

Lingner, J. W. and H. B. Wells, 'Organization and methods of the dual record system in India', Laboratories for Population Statistics, *Scientific Report Series*, no. 9 (University of North Carolina, October 1973).

Lorimer, F., 'The economics of family formation under different conditions', World Population Conference 1965, *Proceedings*, vol. II (New York, 1967).

Lotte, A., *Epidémiologie de la Tuberculose et Défaillances de la Lutte Anti-tuberculose chez l'Enfant* (W.H.O., Geneva, 1971).

Lubell, H., *Calcutta: Its urban development and employment prospects* (I.L.O., Geneva, 1974).

Luce, R. D. and H. Raiffa, *Games and Decisions* (New York, 1957).

Macdonald, G., *The Epidemiology and Control of Malaria* (London, 1963).

McKeown, T. and R. G. Record, 'Reasons for the decline of mortality in England and Wales during the nineteenth century', *Population Studies* (November 1962).

McLaughlin, T., *Coprophilia* (London, 1971).

Madhavan, S., R. Singh and M. C. Swaminathan, 'Secular changes in height and weight of Indian adults', *Indian Journal of Medical Research* (June 1964).

Malaker, C. R., 'Female age at marriage and the birth rate in India', *Social Biology* (September 1972).

Mamdani, M., *The Myth of Population Control* (London and New York, 1972).

Mandelbaum, D., *Human Fertility in India* (University of California, Berkeley, 1974).

May, D. A. and D. M. Heer, 'Son survivorship motivation and family size in India: a computer simulation', *Population Studies* (July 1968).

Mehta, R., 'White collar and blue collar family responses to population growth in India', Paper presented to the Wingspread Conference on Social and Cultural Responses to Population Change in India (Racine, Wisconsin, November 1974).

Merewether, F. H. S., *Through the Famine Districts of India* (London, 1898).

Miro, C. and W. Mertens, 'Influences affecting fertility in urban and rural Latin America', *Milbank Memorial Fund Quarterly*, vol. XLVI, no. 3, part 2 (1968).

Moorehouse, G., *Calcutta* (London, 1971).

Mueller, E., 'The economic value of children in peasant agriculture', in Ridker, R. G. (ed.), *Population and Development: The Search for Selective Interventions* (Baltimore 1976).

Mukherjee, R. K., *Social Profiles of a Metropolis* (Bombay, 1961).

Nag, M., 'Family type and fertility', World Population Conference, *Proceedings* (Belgrade, 1965).

Nair, P. R. G., 'Decline in birth rate in Kerala', *E.P.W.* Annual Number (February 1974).

National Institute of Nutrition, National Nutritional Monitoring Bureau, I.C.M.R., *Plan of Operation* (Hyderabad, 1972).

Neher, P. A., 'Peasants, procreation and pensions', *American Economic Review* (June, 1971).

Neher, P. A., 'Peasants, procreation and pensions: a reply', *American Economic Review* (December 1972).

Newman, P., *Malaria Eradication and Population Growth* (Michigan, 1965).

Newman, P., 'Malaria control and population growth', *Journal of Development Studies*, 6, 2 (1970).

Ohlin, G., 'Population pressure and alternative investments', I.U.S.S.P. *International Population Conference*, vol. III (London, 1969).

O.R.G., *An All India Survey of Family Planning Practices* (Operations Research Group, Baroda, 1971).

Pakrasi, K. *et al.*, 'The relationship between family type and fertility', *Milbank Memorial Fund Quarterly*, 45, 4 (October 1967).

Panikar, P. G. K., 'Economics of nutrition', *E.P.W.*, Annual Number (February 1972).

Pareek, U. and T. V. Rao, *A Status Study on Population Research in India*, vol. I Behavioural Sciences (Family Planning Foundation, New Delhi, 1974).

Parkinson, C. N., *East and West* (London, 1963).

Patel, S. B., 'The Future of Bombay–an alternative approach to urban planning', in Bose *et al*. (eds) (1974).

Payne, P. R., 'Characteristics and use of nutritional indicators and criteria for their selection', Background paper for F.A.O./W.H.O. Expert Committee on Methodology of Nutritional Surveillance (1975).

Peckos, P. S. and M. I. Ross, 'Longitudinal study of the caloric and nutrient intake of individual twins', *Journal of the American Dietetic Association*, 62 (April 1973).

Piepmeier, K. B. and T. S. Adkins, 'Status of women and fertility', *Journal of Biosocial Science*, no. 5 (1973).

P.N.D.P., *Nutrition in Punjab*, Punjab Nutrition Development Project, Government of Haryana–CARE (Chandigarh, 1974).

Poffenberger, T., *Fertility and Family Life in an Indian Village*, Michigan Papers on South and South East Asia (University of Michigan, Ann Arbor, 1975).

Poffenberger, T., *The Socialization of Family Size Values: Youth and Family Planning in an Indian Village*, ibid. no. 12 (1976).

P.R.A.I., *Induced Change in Health Behaviour*, Study of a pilot environmental sanitation project in Uttar Pradesh (Planning Research and Action Institute, Lucknow, 1967).

Puffer, R. R. and C. V. Serrano, 'Patterns of mortality in childhood', Report of the inter-American investigation . . . , *Scientific Publication* no. 262 (W.H.O./Pan-American Health Organization, Washington D.C., 1973).

Raghavachari, S., 'Provisional population totals of the 1971 Census', Comment I, *E.P.W.* (9 October 1971).

Raghavachari, S., 'Population Projections, 1976-2001', in Bose *et al*. (eds) (1974).

Rajagopalan, S., *Tamil Nadu Nutrition Project*, Report to F.A.O. Regional Seminar (New Delhi, 14 February 1974).

Ramabhadran, V. K. and R. D. Agrawal, 'A preliminary note on missing of vital events in Indian Sample Registration Scheme', *Sample Registration Bulletin* (January–March 1972).

Raman, M. V., 'A demographic profile of Calcutta', in Bose *et al*. (eds) (1974).

Rao, K. S., M. C. Swaminathan, S. Swarup and V. N. Patwardhan, 'Protein Malnutrition in South India', *Bulletin*, 20, 603–9 (W.H.O. 1959).

Rao, N. P. *et al*., 'Nutritional status of preschool children of rural communities near Hyderabad city', *Indian Journal of Medical Research* (November 1969).

Rao, T. R., 'Reflections on malaria eradication in India', *The Journal of*

Communicable Diseases (September 1973).

Razzell, P. E., 'An interpretation of the modern rise of population in Europe–a critique', *Population Studies* (March 1974).

Rele, J. R., 'Trends in fertility and family planning', in Bose *et al*. (eds) (1974).

Rele, J. R. and U. P. Sinha, 'Birth and death rates in India during 1961–70–a Census analysis', *Demography India*, II 2 (December 1973).

Renbourn, E. T., *Materials and Clothing in Health and Disease* (London, 1972).

Repetto, R., 'Son preference and fertility behaviour in developing countries', *Studies in Family Planning* (August, 1972).

Reutlinger, S. and M. Selowsky, 'Malnutrition and poverty', *Occasional Paper*, no. 23, (World Bank Staff, Washington D.C., 1976).

Robinson, W. C., 'Peasants, procreation and pensions: a comment', *American Economic Review* (December 1972).

Rosa, F. W. and M. T. Turshen, 'Fetal nutrition', *Bulletin* (W.H.O., 1970).

Ross, W. C., 'The epidemiology of cholera', *Indian Journal of Medical Research*, 15, 951–64 (1928).

Ruprecht, T. K. and F. I. Jewett, *The Micro-economics of Demographic Change* (New York, 1975).

Sarma, D. V. N. and A. K. Jain, Preference about sex of children and use of contraception among women wanting no more children in India, mimeo (Population Council, 1974).

Schelling, T. C., 'On the ecology of micromotives', *Public Interest*, no. 25 (Fall 1971).

Schofield, S., The nutritional status of children: evidence from village studies, mimeo (Institute of Development Studies, Sussex, 1972).

Scholtens, R. G. *et al*., 'An epidemiologic examination of the strategy of malaria eradication', *International Journal of Epidemiology*, 1, 15–24 (1972).

Schultz, T. P., 'Fertility determinants: a theory, evidence, and an application to policy evaluation', *Reports*, no. R–1016–RF/AID (Rand Corporation, Santa Monica, January 1974).

Schultz, T. P. and J. Da Vanzo, 'Analysis of demographic change in East Pakistan', retrospective survey data, *Reports*, no. R–564–AID (Rand Corporation, September 1970).

Scrimshaw, N. S., 'Synergism of malnutrition and infection: evidence of field studies in Guatemala', Goldberger Lecture, *Journal of the American Medical Association* (June 1970).

Seal, S. C., 'Plague', *Bulletin* 23 (W.H.O., 1960).

Seal, S. C. and K. C. Patnaik, 'A short study of plague in Madras and Mysore with reference to plague in India', *Indian Journal of Medical Research*, 51 (1963).

Sehgal, P. N. *et al*., 'Resistance to chloroquine in *Falciparum* malaria in

Assam State, India', *The Journal of Communicable Diseases* (December 1973).

Sen, A. K., 'Isolation, assurance and the social rate of discount', *Quarterly Journal of Economics*, LXXXI 1 (February 1967).

Sen, A. K., 'Famines as failures of exchange entitlements', *E.P.W.*, Special Number (August 1976).

Shankar, K., 'The dietary intake and nutritional status of pregnant and nursing women in Hyderabad', *Indian Journal of Medical Research* (January 1962).

Sharma, M. I. D. *et al.*, 'Effectiveness of drug schedule being followed under the National Malaria Eradication Programme, India, for radical cure of *vivax* malaria cases', *The Journal of Communicable Diseases* (December 1973).

Sharma, M. I. D. *et al.*, 'National smallpox eradication programme in India–progress, problems and prospects', *The Journal of Communicable Diseases* (September 1974).

Sivaramakrishnan, K. C., 'Calcutta 2001: triumph by survival', in Bose *et al.* (eds) (1974).

Sommer, A. and M. S. Lowenstein, 'Nutritional Status and mortality: a prospective validation of the QUAC stick', *American Journal of Clinical Nutrition*, 28 (March 1975).

Soni, V., 'A demographic analysis of the sterilisation programme in the Indian States, 1957–73', Ph.D. Thesis, University of London (1975), unpublished.

Stolnitz, G. J., 'Recent trends in mortality in Latin America, Asia and Africa', *Population Studies* (November 1965).

Streeten, P. and M. Lipton, *The Crisis of Indian Planning* (London, 1968).

Sukhatme, P. V., 'Incidence of protein deficiency in relation to different diets in India', *British Journal of Nutrition*, 24 (1970).

Sukhatme, P. V., 'The calorie gap', *Indian Journal of Nutrition and Dietetics*, 10, 198 (1973).

Swaminathan, M. C., 'Nutrition in India', in *Community Nutrition*, ed. J. Greaves (New York, 1976).

Talwar, P. P., 'Adolescent sterility in an Indian population', *Human Biology*, vol. 27, no. 3 (September 1965).

Taylor, C. E., J. S. Newman and N. U. Kelly, 'The child survival hypothesis', *Population Studies* (July 1976).

Todaro, M. P., 'A model of labor migration and urban unemployment in less developed countries', *American Economic Review*, 59, 1 (1969).

Todaro, M. P., 'Rural-urban migration, unemployment, and job probabilities', Paper for International Economic Association Conference, (Valescure, 1973).

U.K. Ministry of Agriculture, Food and Fisheries, *Household Food Consumption and Expenditure, 1973* (H.M.S.O., London, 1974).

U.N., *The Mysore Population Study*, ST/SOA/Series A (New York, 1961).

U.N., Department of Economic and Social Affairs, *Poverty, Unemployment and Development Policy: A case study of selected issues with reference to Kerala* (New York, 1976).

U.S. National Academy of Sciences, *Maternal Nutrition and the Course of Pregnancy* (Committee on Maternal Nutrition, Washington D.C., 1970).

Vaidyanathan, K. E. (ed.), *Studies on Mortality in India* (Gandhigram, 1972).

Venkatacharya, K., 'Impact of postponing marriages on India's birth rate', *Artha Vijnana*, 13, 3 (September 1971).

Vijaraghavan, K., D. Singh and M. C. Swaminathan, 'Heights and weights of well-nourished Indian school children', *Indian Journal of Medical Research*, 59, 648 (1971).

Visaria, L., 'Religious differentials in fertility', in Bose *et al.* (eds) (1974).

Visaria, P. M., 'The sex ratio of the population of India and Pakistan and regional variations during 1901–61', in Bose (ed.) (1967).

Visaria, P. M., 'Mortality and fertility in India 1951–61', *Milbank Memorial Fund Quarterly*, 47, 1 (January 1969).

Visaria, P. M., 'Provisional population totals of the 1971 Census', *E.P.W.* (17 July 1971).

Visaria, P. M., Review of Mamdani, 1972, in *Population Studies* (July 1975).

Von Muralt, A. (ed.), *Protein-Calorie Malnutrition* (New York, 1969).

Waterlow, J. C., 'Some aspects of childhood malnutrition as a public health problem', *British Medical Journal*, 4, 88–90 (12 October 1974).

Wattal, P. K., *The Population Problem in India* (Bombay, 1916).

White, G. F., D. J. Bradley and A. U. White, *Drawers of Water* (Chicago, 1972).

W.H.O., 'Nutrition & Infection', *Technical Report Series*, no. 314 (Geneva, 1965).

W.H.O., *Case Studies in the Epidemiology of Malaria* (Geneva, 1971).

W.H.O., 'Energy and Protein Requirements', Report of a joint F.A.O./ W.H.O. *ad hoc* expert committee, *Technical Report Series*, no. 522 (Geneva, 1973*a*).

W.H.O. 'Malaria eradication in 1972', *Chronicle*, 27, 12 (December 1973*b*).

Widdowson, E. M., *A Study of Individual Children's Diets*, (Medical Research Council, London, 1947).

Wishik, S., 'Nutrition, family planning and fertility', U.N. Protein Advisory Group, *Bulletin*, vol. II, 4 (1972).

Wyon, J. B. and J. E. Gordon, *The Khanna Study: Population Problems in the Rural Punjab* (Harvard, 1971).

Zachariah, K. C., *Migrants in Greater Bombay* (Bombay, 1968).

Zachariah, K. C., and J. P. Ambannavar, 'Population redistribution in India: inter-state and rural-urban', in Bose (ed.) (1967).

CHAPTER 3

Abbott, J. *et al.*, 'Sex preselection–not yet practical', *Population Reports*, Series I, no. 2 (May 1975).

Agarwala, S. N., 'A study of factors explaining variability in family planning performance in different States in India', International Institute for Population Studies, *Proceedings of the 1972 All-India Seminar on Family Planning Problems in India* (Bombay, 1972).

Banerji, D., 'Health behaviour of rural populations', *E.P.W.* (22 December 1973).

Banerji, D., 'Social and cultural foundations of health services systems', *E.P.W.* Special Number (August 1974).

Bang, S., 'Korea: the relationship between I.U.D. retention and check up visits', *Studies in Family Planning*, 2, 110–12 (Population Council, May 1971).

Bean, L. L. and W. Seltzer, 'Couple years of protection and births prevented: a methodological examination', *Demography*, 5, no. 2 (1968).

Behrman, S. J., L. Corsa and R. Freedman (eds), *Fertility and Family Planning: A World View* (Ann Arbor, 1969).

Benagiano, G. *et al.*, 'Multinational comparative clinical, evaluation of . . . injectable contraceptive steroids . . . ', *American Journal of Obstetrics & Gynaecology*, forthcoming.

Berelson, B., *The Great Debate* (Population Council, Occasional Paper, New York, 1975).

Berg, A. R. and J. Muscat, *The Nutrition Factor* (Washington D.C., 1973).

Bernard R. P., 'Factors governing I.U.D. performance', *American Journal of Public Health*, 61, 559–67 (March 1971).

Bhandari, V., 'Study of I.U.C.D. acceptors in rural areas around Delhi', *Family Planning News*, VIII 10 (October 1967).

Bhinder, G., 'Report of studies on I.U.C.D. at Irwin Hospital . . . ', in C.F.P.I. (1969).

Blaikie, P. M., *Family Planning in India: Diffusion and policy* (London, 1975).

C.F.P.I., Adoption of a new contraceptive in urban India, Central Family Planning Institute, *Monograph Series*, No. 6 (New Delhi, 1969).

C.F.P.I., 'A report on the oral pill pilot project clinics in India', Central Family Planning Institute, *Technical Papers*, no. 9 (New Delhi, 1970).

CARE, *Project Poshak: An integrated health-nutrition macro pilot study for preschool children in rural and tribal Madhya Pradesh* (New Delhi, 1975).

Cassen, R. H., 'Population control: aims and policies', in Streeten and Lipton (eds), *The Crisis of Indian Planning* (London, 1968).

Cassen, R. H., 'Population and development: a survey', *World Development* (October–November 1976).

Chandrasekaran, C. and A. Hermalin (eds), *Measuring the Effects of Family Planning Programmes on Fertility*, I.U.S.S.P. (Dolhain, Belgium, 1976).

Chuttani, C. S., 'A survey of indigenous medical practitioners in rural areas of five different States in India', *Indian Journal of Medical Research*, 61, 6 (June 1973).

Dandekar, K. and S. Nikam, 'The loop–what did fail?' *E.P.W.* (27 November 1971).

Davies, H. J., 'I.U.C.D.s: present status and future prospects', *American Journal of Obstetrics and Gynecology*, 114, 88–92 (1 September 1972).

Desai, G. V. and V. R. Gaikwad, 'Applied nutrition programme: an evaluation study', Indian Institute of Management (Ahmedabad, 1971).

Devi, P. K. *et al.*, 'Complications of I.U.C.D. with special reference to abnormal vaginal bleeding', in Laumas (ed.) (1969).

Dumm, J., P. Piotrow and J. Dalsimer, 'The modern condom', *Population Reports* Series H, no. 2 (Washington, D.C., May 1974).

Duncan, G. W. *et al.* (eds), *Fertility Control Methods* (New York 1973).

Elder, R. E., 'Targets versus extension education: the family planning programme in Uttar Pradesh, India', *Population Studies*, 28, 2 (July 1974).

E.P.W., *Economic and Political Weekly* (Bombay).

Enke, S., 'The gains to India from population control: some money measures and incentive schemes', *Review of Economics and Statistics*, 42, 3 (1960).

Enke, S., 'The economic aspects of slowing population growth', *Economic Journal*, 76, 301 (1966).

Finkle, J. L., 'Politics, development strategy and family planning programmes in India and Pakistan', *Journal of Comparative Administration*, 3, 3 (November 1971).

Franda, M., 'Marketing condoms in India: the Nirodh program', American Universities Field Staff, *South Asia Series*, XVI 8 (1972).

Freedman, R. *et al.*, 'Fertility trends in Taiwan 1961–70', *Population Index* (April–June 1972).

Gould, D., 'Patients or guinea pigs?' *New Statesman* (9 May 1975).

Gould, K., 'Sex and contraception in Sherupur: family planning in a Northern Indian village', *E.P.W.*, 4, 1887 (1969).

G.o.I., *Family Planning Programme: An Evaluation*, Government of India, Planning Commission, Programme Evaluation Organisation (New Delhi, 1970).

G.o.I., *Tables with Notes on Villages and Towns in India: Some Results*, National Sample Survey, no. 196, 22nd Round, 1967/8 (New Delhi, 1972).

G.o.I., *Pocket Book of Health Statistics 1973*, Central Bureau of Health Intelligence, Ministry of Health and Family Planning (New Delhi, 1973).

G.o.I., *Draft Fifth Five Year Plan 1974–79*, Planning Commission (New Delhi, 1974).

G.o.I., *Health Services and Medical Education: A Programme for Immediate Action*, Report of the Group on Medical Education and Support

Manpower, Ministry of Health and Family Planning (New Delhi, 1975*a*).

G.o.I., *Agenda Item No. 1*, Report on Medical Education and Support Manpower, Ministry of Health and Family Planning (1975*b*).

G.o.I., *Integrated Child Development Services Scheme*, Department of Social Welfare, Ministry of Education and Social Welfare (New Delhi, 1975*c*).

G.o.I., *Family Planning–programme Information 1974/75*, Ministry of Health and Family Planning (New Delhi, 1975*d*).

G.o.I., *Fifth Five Year Plan*, Planning Commission (New Delhi, 1976*a*).

G.o.I., *National Population Policy*, Statement by Dr Karan Singh, Ministry of Health and Family Planning (New Delhi, April 1976*b*).

Government of Turkey, *Turkish I.U.D. Retention Survey, 1969*, Ministry of Health (Ankara, 1971).

Gupta, D. R., 'The battle of the population bulge', International Planned Parenthood Federation, Victor-Bostrom Fund, *Report*, no. 18 (Washington D.C., 1973).

Gwatkin, D. R., *Health and Nutrition in India*, Ford Foundation (New Delhi, 1974).

Hawkins, D. F., 'Complications with I.U.D.s', *British Medical Journal*, ii, 381 (1969).

Hefnawi, F. and S. J. Segal, *Analysis of Intra-uterine Contraception*, (Amsterdam, 1975).

Hermalin, A. I. *et al.*, 'Motivational factors in I.U.D. termination: data from the second Taiwan I.U.D. follow-up survey', *Journal of Biosocial Science*, 3, 351–75 (October 1971).

Huber, D., *Health Aspects of Oral Contraceptive Use*, London School of Hygiene and Tropical Medicine, mimeo (1973).

Huber, S. C., P. T. Piotrow, F. B. Orlans and G. Kommer, 'I.U.D.s reassessed – a decade of experience', *Population Reports*, Series B, no. 2 (Washington D.C., January 1975).

I.B.R.D., *Village Water Supply & Sanitation in Less Developed Countries*, Research Working Papers (Washington, D.C., March, 1974).

I.B.R.D., *Population Policies and Economic Development*, International Bank for Reconstruction and Development (Washington D.C., 1974).

I.C.M.R., *Review of Work Done on Rural Latrines in India* (Indian Council of Medical Research, New Delhi, 1966).

I.C.M.R., *Report on Clinical Trials of I.U.C.D.* (Indian Council of Medical Research, New Delhi, 1968).

I.E.M.R., *Analysis of Expenditures on Social Sectors*, Institute of Economic and Market Research, for I.B.R.D. (New Delhi, 1976).

Jain, A. K., 'Marketing research in the Nirodh program', *Studies in Family Planning* (Population Council, New York, July 1973).

Jain, A. K. and D. V. N. Sharma, 'Some explanatory factors for statewise differential use of family planning methods in India', Population Council, mimeo (New York, 1974).

Johannisson, E., 'Recent developments with intra-uterine devices', *Contraception*, 8, 2 (August 1973).

Joy, J. L., 'Food and nutrition planning', *Journal of Agricultural Economics* (January 1973).

Kandaurova, V. *et al.*, [Family planning with the I.U.D. in rural areas], [Clinical effectiveness of I.U.D., &c.], *Akusherstvo i Ginekologiya* (Moscow, March 1970, February 1971, November 1971, February 1972).

Karkal, M., *A Bibliography of Abortion Studies in India* (International Institute for Population Studies, Bombay, 1970).

Kashyap, P. *et al.*, 'Continuation rates of use with . . . polygon (M) and Lipps Loop (B)' *Indian Journal of Medical Research*, 59, 660–70 (April 1971).

Kleinman, R. L., *Induced Abortion* (International Planned Parenthood Federation, London, 1972).

Krishnakumar, S., 'Kerala's pioneering experiment in massive vasectomy camps', *Studies in Family Planning* (Population Council, New York August 1972).

Kuder, K., 'Clinical experience with the I.U.C.D. in the international field', *Proceedings of the 6th All-India Conference on Family Planning* (New Delhi, 1968).

Kumar, A., *An Overview of I.U.C.D. Studies in India* (International Institute for Population Studies, Bombay, 1971).

Kumar, A., *An Overview of Sterilisation Studies in India* (ibid., 1972).

Kunders, P. *et al.*, 'Clinico-histopathological aspects of I.U.C.D.', *Journal of Obstetrics and Gynaecology, India*, 20, 117 (1970).

Laumas, K. R. (ed.), *I.U.C.D.: Review of Research Work in India* (Indian Council of Medical Research, New Delhi, 1969).

Mahajan, B. M., 'On certain aspects of clinical trials on I.U.C.D. in India', *Economic Affairs* (Calcutta, November 1966).

Majumdar, M., B. C. Mullick, A. Moitra and K. T. Mosley, 'Use of oral contraceptives in urban, rural and slum areas', *Studies in Family Planning* (Population Council, New York, September 1972).

Malgouyat, R., [Five years' experience with the I.U.D.], *Gynécologie Pratique*, 21, 481–7 (Paris, 1970).

McNicoll, G., 'Community-level population policy: an exploration', *Population and Development Review*, 1, 1 (Population Council, New York, September 1975).

Melton, R. J., *et al.*, 'Pill versus I.U.C.D.: continuation rates of oral contraceptives and Dalkon shield in Maryland clinics', *Contraception* (1971).

Mills, W., 'Further experience with I.U.C.D.s' *Lancet*, 2, 291–3 (31 October 1970).

Misra, B. D., 'Family planning: differential performance of States', *E.P.W.* (29 September 1973).

N.I.F.P., *Director's Report 1970–71* (National Institute of Family Planning,

New Delhi, 1971a).

N.I.F.P., 'The oral pill pilot project in India: report of an acceptor follow-up study', National Institute of Family Planning, *Technical Papers*, no. 16 (New Delhi, 1971b).

N.I.F.P., 'Post insertion contraceptive and fertility behaviour of I.U.C.D. acceptors', *Technical Papers*, no. 18 (New Delhi, 1973).

O.R.G., *An All-India Survey of Family Planning Practices* (Sponsored by Ministry of Health and Family Planning), (Operations Research Group, Baroda, 1971).

Orlans, F. B., 'Copper I.U.D.s—Performance to Date', *Population Reports*, Series B, no. 1 (Washington D.C., December 1975).

P.R.A.I., *A Qualitative Study of Vasectomy in a District of Uttar Pradesh*, Planning Research and Action Institute (Lucknow, 1966).

P.R.A.I., 'A follow-up study of 117 acceptors of I.U.C.D., in two research blocks of Lucknow District' (Planning Research and Action Institute, Lucknow, mimeo, 1969).

Potter, R. G., 'Estimating births averted in a family planning programme', in Behrman *et al.* (eds) (1969).

Rajagopalan, S., *Tamil Nadu Nutrition Project*, Report to F.A.O. Regional Seminar (New Delhi, 14 February 1974).

Rao, K. G., 'Rehabilitation of the loop in India – an appraisal for developing a new approach' (Carolina Population Center, mimeo, October 1970).

Rao, K. G., 'Has I.U.C.D. been a failure? A second look at the loop programme' (Carolina Population Center, mimeo, February 1971).

Repetto, R., 'Son preference and fertility behaviour in developing countries', *Studies in Family Planning* (Population Council, August 1972).

Research Triangle Institute, 'Topical investigation and analysis of rehabilitating the loop in South Asia', mimeo (North Carolina, 1970).

Rinehart, W. and J. Winter, 'Injectable Progestogens', *Population Reports*, Series K, no. 1, (Washington D.C.., March 1975).

Robinson, W. C. and D. E. Horlacher, 'Population growth and economic welfare', *Reports on Family Planning*, no. 6 (Population Council, New York, 1971).

Sadashivaiah, K. *et al.*, 'The oral pill programme', *Journal of the Christian Medical Association, India* (April 1971).

Sadashivaiah, K. *et al.*, 'Evaluation of intra-uterine conception in selected mission hospitals in India', *Journal of Biosocial Science* (July 1973).

Samuel, T. J., The development of India's policy of population control', *Milbank Memorial Fund Quarterly*, 44 (1966).

Schwarz, W., 'Karan Singh: India's new start in family planning', *People*, 2, 1 (1975).

Seal, K. C., 'Evaluation of national family planning programme in India', *Studies on Population and Family Planning in India* (Planning and Evaluation Division, Department of Family Planning, Ministry of Health and Family Planning, New Delhi, 1974).

Seal, K. C. and N. K. Bhatnagar, 'On method of assessment of overall impact of family planning programme on fertility', *Studies on Population and Family Planning in India* (Planning and Evaluation Division, Department of Family Planning, Ministry of Health and Family Planning, New Delhi, 1974).

Segal, S. J. and C. Tietze, 'Contraceptive technology: current and prospective methods', Population Council, *Reports on Population/Family Planning* (July 1971).

Simmons, G., *India's Investment in Family Planning* (Population Council, New York, 1971).

Singh, B. R. *et al.*, 'A study of the use and effectiveness of intra-uterine device in Allahabad district', *Indian Journal of Public Health*, 16, 47-50 (April 1972).

Smith, T. E., *The Politics of Family Planning* (London, 1973).

Snowden, R. *et al.*, 'Social and medical factors in the use and effectiveness of I.U.D.s', *Journal of Biosocial Science*, 5, 31–49 (January 1973).

Soni, V., 'A demographic analysis of the sterilisation programme in the Indian States, 1957–73', Ph.D. Thesis, University of London (1975) unpublished.

Stephen, J., 'Cuba and Chile: differing philosophies in health care', *World Medicine*, vol. 10, 15 (7 May 1975).

Sun, T. H., 'Birth control experience in Taiwan', *Contraception* (April 1971).

Takulia, H. S., C. E. Taylor *et al.*, *The Health Centre Doctor in India* (Baltimore, 1967).

Tatum, H. J., 'Intra-uterine contraception', *American Journal of Obsetetrics and Gynecology*, 112, 7 (1972).

Thapar, S., 'Family planning in India', *Population Studies* (July 1963).

Tietze, C., 'Experience with new I.U.D.s', *Contraception* (January 1970a).

Tietze, C., 'Evaluation of I.U.D.s: 9th progress report of the Cooperative Statistical Program', *Studies in Family Planning* (Population Council, July 1970b).

U.N., *An Evaluation of the Family Planning Programme of the Government of India* ST/TAO/IND/50, United Nations (Bureau of Technical Assistance Operations, New York, 1969).

Van der Vlugt, T. and P. T. Piotrow, 'Pregnancy Termination', *Population Reports*, Series F, no. 3 (Washington D.C., June 1973).

Van der Vlugt, T. and P. T. Piotrow, 'Uterine aspiration techniques', *Population Reports*, Series F, no. 3 (Washington D.C., 1974).

Vig, O. P., 'An application of path analysis to study variation in acceptance of the family planning performance in India, 1966–71', International Institute for Population Studies, *Proceedings of the 1972 All-India Seminar on Family Planning Problems in India* (Bombay, 1972).

Virkar, K. D. *et al.*, 'Long acting injectable therapy for fertility control',

All-India Conference on Reproduction and fertility, Indian Council of Medical Research, Technical Report Series, no. 21 (New Delhi, 1973).

Visaria, P. and A. K. Jain, *Country Profile: India* (Population Council, New York, May 1976).

Ward, S. and G. B. Simmons, 'Preliminary report of a rural loop retention survey' (University of California (Berkeley), mimeo, 1968).

Watson, W. B., 'Post-acceptance experience and duration of use of contraception', in Zatuchni (ed.) (1970).

Webster, F. L., 'I.U.C.D.s in general practice', *Practitioner*, 205, 20–9 (July 1970).

White, G. F., D. J. Bradley and A. U. White, *Drawers of Water: Domestic water use in East Africa* (Chicago, 1972).

W.H.O., *Integration of Mass Campaigns against Specific Diseases into General Health Services*, Technical Report Series no. 294 (Geneva, 1965).

W.H.O., *Basic and Clinical Aspects of I.U.D.s*, Technical Report Series no. 332 (Geneva, 1966).

W.H.O., *Intra-uterine Devices: Physiological and Clinical Aspects*, Technical Report Series no. 397 (Geneva, 1968).

W.H.O., *Advances in Methods of Fertility Regulation*, Technical Report Series no. 527 (Geneva, 1973).

W.H.O., *Health by the People*, ed. K. W. Newell (Geneva, 1975a).

W.H.O., *Promoting Health in the Human Environment*, A review based on the Technical Discussions held during the Twenty-seventh World Health Assembly, 1974 (Geneva, 1975b).

Wolfers, D., *Post-partum Intra-uterine Contraception in Singapore* (Amsterdam, 1970).

Wolfers, D., 'The demographic effects of a contraception programme', *Population Studies* (March 1969).

Wortman, J., 'Vasectomy–What are the Problems?' *Population Reports*, Series D, no. 2 (Washington D.C., 1975).

Wortman, J. and P. T. Piotrow, 'Vasectomy–Old and New Techniques', *Population Reports*, Series D, no. 1 (Washington, D.C., 1973).

Zaidan, G. C., *The Costs and Benefits of Family Planning Programs*, World Bank Staff, Occasional Paper, no. 12 (International Bank for Reconstruction and Development, Washington D.C., 1971).

Zatuchni, G. I. (ed.), *Post-partum Family Planning* (New York, 1970).

Zipper, J., H. J. Tatum, M. Medel, L. Pastene and M. Rivera, 'Contraception through the use of intrauterine metals. 1, Copper as an adjunct to the "T" device,' *American Journal of Obstetrics and Gynecology*, 109, 5 (March 1971).

CHAPTER 4

A.E.R.C., *Primary Education in Rural India – Participation and Wastage*

(Agricultural Economics Research Center, Delhi University, 1971).

Allen, G. R., *Fertiliser estimates*: notes for a discussion at I.D.S./O.D.M. conference on South Asian Food Prospects (I.D.S., Sussex, November 1974).

Ambannavar, J. P., *Long-term Prospects of Population Growth and Labour Force in India* (Ford Foundation, Second India Studies, Bombay, 1975).

Bardhan, P. K., 'On the minimum level of living of the rural poor', *Indian Economic Review*, April 1970*a* (with a further note, ibid., April 1971).

Bardhan, P. K., ' "Green revolution" and agriucultural labourers', *E.P.W.*, Special number (July 1970*b*) (with a correction in *E.P.W.*, 14 November 1970).

Bardhan, P. K., 'On the incidence of poverty in rural India', *E.P.W.*, Annual number (February 1973).

Bardhan, P. K., 'Life and death matters', *E.P.W.*, Special number (August 1974).

Bardhan, P. K. and T. N. Srinivasan (eds), *Poverty and Income Distribution in India* (New Delhi, 1975).

Berg, A., *Famine Contained: Notes and Lessons from the Bihar Experience*, Brookings Reprint 211 (Washington D.C., 1971).

Bhagwati, J. N. and S. Chakravarty, 'Contributions to Indian economic analysis: a survey'. *American Economic Review*, Supplement (September 1969).

Bhagwati, J. N. and P. Desai, *India: Planning for Industrialisation* (London 1970).

Bhagwati, J. N. and T. N. Srinivasan, *Foreign Trade Régimes and Economic Development: India*, N.B.E.R. Special Conference Series, vol. VI (New York, 1975).

Bhalla, G. S. *et al.*, *Changing Structure of Agriculture in Haryana* (Department of Economics, Punjab University for Government of Haryana, Chandigarh, 1972).

Bilsborrow, R. E., 'Fertility, savings rates and economic development in less developed countries', in I.U.S.S.P., *International Population Conference*, vol. I (Liège, 1973).

Bose, A., P. Desai, A. Mitra and J. M. Sharma (eds), *Population in India's Development* (New Delhi, 1974).

Brown, D., 'The Intensive Agricultural Districts Programme and agricultural development in the Punjab, India', *Economic Development Report*, no. 79 (Center for International Affairs, Harvard, 1967).

Calder, N., *The Wealth Machine and the Threat of Ice* (B.B.C., London, 1974).

Cassen, R. H., 'Population control: aims and policies', in Lipton and Streeten (eds) (1968).

Cassen R. H., 'Population growth and public expenditure in developing countries', in I.U.S.S.P., *International Population Conference*, vol. I (Liège, 1973).

Chambers, R., 'The organisation and operation of irrigation: an analysis of evidence from South India and Sri Lanka', Project on agrarian change in rice-growing areas of Tamil Nadu and Sri Lanka, Seminar (St. John's College, Cambridge, mimeo, December 1974).

Chaudhuri, P. (ed.), *Aspects of Indian Economic Development: a book of readings* (London, 1971).

Chaudhuri, P. (ed.), *Readings in Indian Agricultural Development* (London, 1972).

Chenery, H., M. S. Ahluwalia, C. L. G. Bell, J. H. Duloy and R. Jolly, *Redistribution with Growth* (London, 1974).

Clark, C., *Population Growth and Land Use* (London, 1968).

Coale, A. J. and E. M. Hoover, *Population Growth and Economic Development in Low Income Countries* (Princeton, 1958).

Connell, J. *Labour Utilisation: a Bibliography of Village Studies*, Part A (Institute of Development Studies, Sussex, mimeo, 1973).

Dandekar, V. M. and N. Rath, *Poverty in India* (Ford Foundation, New Delhi, 1970).

Das, P. K., *The Monsoons* (London, 1972).

Demeny, P., 'The economics of population control', I.U.S.S.P., *International Population Conference* (London, 1969).

Dey, A. K., 'Rates of growth of agriculture and industry', *E.P.W.*, Review of Agriculture (June 1975).

Epstein, S., *South India: Yesterday, Today and Tomorrow* (London, 1973).

E.P.W., *Economic and Political Weekly* (Bombay).

Etienne, G., *Indian Agriculture: the Art of the Possible* (University of California, 1968).

Frankel, F., *India's Green Revolution: Economic gains and political costs* (Princeton, 1971).

G.o.I. (Government of India), *First Five Year Plan, 1951–56* (Planning Commission, New Delhi, 1952).

G.o.I., *Second Five Year Plan, 1956–61* (Planning Commission, New Delhi, 1956).

G.o.I., *Third Five Year Plan, 1961–66* (Planning Commission, New Delhi, 1961).

G.o.I., *Age Tables*, Census of India (Office of the Registrar General, New Delhi, 1963).

G.o.I., *Annual Plan 1966–67* (Planning Commission, New Delhi, 1966a).

G.o.I., *Education and National Development* (Education Commission, New Delhi, 1966b).

G.o.I., *Annual Plan 1967–68* (Planning Commission, New Delhi, 1967a).

G.o.I., *Report on Evaluation of Rural Manpower Aspects* (Planning Commission, Plan Evaluation Organisation, New Delhi, 1967b).

G.o.I., *Annual Plan 1968–69* (Planning Commission, New Delhi, 1968).

G.o.I., *Fourth Five Year Plan, 1969–74* (Planning Commission, New Delhi, 1968).

G.o.I., *Tables with Notes on Differential Fertility and Mortality Rates in Rural and Urban Areas of India*, National Sample Survey, no. 186, 19th Round, 1964–5 (New Delhi, 1970*a*).

G.o.I., *Report of the Committee of Experts on Unemployment Estimates* (known as the Dantwala Committee Report) (Planning Commission, New Delhi, 1970*b*).

G.o.I., *Tables with Notes on Indian Villages*, National Sample Survey, no. 172, 18th Round, 1963–4 (New Delhi, 1970*c*).

G.o.I., *Provisional Population Totals*, Paper 1 of 1971–supplement, Census of India (New Delhi, 1971).

G.o.I., *Estimates of Area and Production of Principal Crops in India* (Ministry of Agriculture, Directorate of Economics and Statistics, New Delhi, December 1972).

G.o.I., *Economic Survey 1972–73* (Ministry of Finance, Department of Economic Affairs, New Delhi, 1973*a*).

G.o.I., *Report of the Committee on Unemployment*, (known as the Bhagavati Committee) (Department of Labour and Employment, New Delhi, 1973*b*).

G.o.I., *Draft Fifth Five Year Plan 1974–79*, 2 vols (Planning Commission, New Delhi, 1973*c*).

G.o.I., *Agricultural Situation in India* (Directorate of Economics and Statistics, Ministry of Agriculture, New Delhi, August 1973*d*).

G.o.I., *Economic Survey 1973/4* (Ministry of Finance, Department of Economic Affairs, New Delhi, 1974*a*).

G.o.I., *State Samples*, National Sample Survey, no. 230/1, 25th Round (New Delhi, 1974*b*).

G.o.I., *Economic Survey 1974/5* (Ministry of Finance, Department of Economic Affairs, New Delhi, 1975*a*).

G.o.I., *Employment-Unemployment Profile for India: a Preliminary Study* . . . , National Sample Survey, no. 255, 27th Round, 1972–73 (New Delhi, 1975*b*).

G.o.I., *Fifth Five Year Plan* (Planning Commission, New Delhi, 1976).

Griffin, K., *The Green Revolution: an Economic Analysis*, U.N.R.I.S.D., Report no. 72.6 (Geneva, 1972).

Hanson, A. H., *The Process of Planning* (O.U.P., London, 1966).

Harpstead, J. D., 'High lysine corn', *Scientific American* (August 1971).

Haswell, M., *Economics of Development in Village India* (London, 1967).

Hayami, Y. and V. Ruttan, *Agricultural Development* (Baltimore, 1971).

Hazari, B. and J. Krishnamurty, 'Employment implications of India's industrialisation: an input-output analysis', *Review of Economics and Statistics*, LII 2 (1970).

Henderson, P. D., *India–the Energy Sector*, I.B.R.D. (Washington D.C., 1975).

Herdt, R. W. and E. A. Baker, 'Agricultural wages, production and high yielding varieties', *E.P.W.* (25 March 1972).

Hoover, E. M., and M. Perlman, 'Measuring the effects of population control on economic development', *Pakistan Development Review* (1966).

Horowitz., G., Wage determination in a labor surplus economy: the case of India', *Economic Development and Cultural Change*, 22, 4 (July 1974).

House of Commons, *The Oil Crisis and Third World Development*, Report no. 230 (Select Committee on Overseas Development, 1974).

Hunter, G., *The Administration of Agricultural Development: lessons from India* (London, 1970).

Hunter, G. and A. Bottrall (eds), *Serving the Small Farmer: Policy choices in Indian agriculture* (Overseas Development Institute, London, 1974).

I.L.O., *Mechanisation and Employment in Agriculture: Case Studies from Four Continents* (International Labour Office, Geneva, 1973).

Jha, P. S., 'Two decades of planning: case for new priorities', *Times of India* (11 January 1975).

Jodha, N. S., 'A strategy for dry land agriculture', *E.P.W.*, Review of Agriculture (25 March 1972).

Joy, J. L., 'Food and nutrition planning', *Journal of Agricultural Economics* (January 1973).

Khusro, A. M., *Economic Development with No Population Transfers* (Delhi, 1962).

Khusro, A. M., *Economics of Land Reform and Farm Size in India*, Studies in Economic Growth, no. 14 (Institute of Economic Growth, Delhi, 1973).

Kidron, M. *Foreign Investment in India* (London, 1965).

Kleiman, E., 'Age composition, size of households, and the interpretation of per capita income', *Economic Development and Cultural Change*, 15, 1 (October 1966)..

Krishna, R., *Rural Unemployment–a Survey of Concepts and Estimates for India*, World Bank Staff, Working Paper no. 234 (Washington D.C., 1976).

Krishnamurty, J., 'The structure of the working force of the Indian Union, 1951–1971', Paper presented to the Fourth European Conference on Modern South Asian Studies (University of Sussex, July 1974).

Kumar, D., 'Changes in income distribution and poverty in India: a review of the literature', *World Development* (January 1974).

Kumar, D., 'Landownership and equality in Madras Presidency, 1853–54 to 1946–47', *Indian Economic and Social History Review* (July–September 1975).

Kuznets, S., *Population, Capital and Growth* (London, 1974).

Ladejinsky, W. I., *A Study on Tenurial Conditions in Package Districts* (G.o.I., Planning Commission, New Delhi, 1964 (?)).

Lal, D., 'Agricultural growth, real wages and the rural poor in India', *E.P.W.*, Review of Agriculture (June 1976*a*).

Lal, D., 'Wages and surplus labour', *World Development* (October–November 1976*b*).

Lal, D. *et al.*, *Appraising Foreign Investment in Developing Countries* (London, 1975).

Lamb, H. H., *Climate: Present Past and Future* (London, 1972).

Leibenstein, H., 'The impact of population growth on economic welfare–non-traditional elements', in U.S. National Academy of Sciences (1971).

Lipton, M., *Plant breeding policy*: Notes for discussion at I.D.S./O.D.M. conference on South Asian Food Prospects, (I.D.S. Sussex, November 1974).

Lipton, M., *Why Poor People Stay Poor: Urban Bias and World Development* (London, 1976).

Mehra, S., 'Surplus labour in Indian agriculture', *Indian Economic Review* (April 1966) reprinted in Chaudhuri (1972).

Mellor, J. W., T. Weaver, U. J. Lele and S. R. Simon, *Developing Rural India* (New York, 1968).

Minhas, B. S., 'Rural poverty, land redistribution and development strategy', *Indian Economic Review* (April 1970).

Minhas, B. S., 'Rural development for weaker sections; experience and lessons', *Commerce* (14 October 1972).

Minhas, B. S. and A. Vaidyanathan, 'Growth of crop output in India, 1951–4 to 1958–61', *Journal of the Indian Society of Agricultural Statistics*, XVII, no. 2 (1965) reprinted in Chaudhuri (1972).

Moore, M. P., 'Some economic aspects of women's work and status in the rural areas of Africa and Asia', Paper presented to the Seminar on Participation of Women in Development (Peterhouse, Cambridge, March 1974).

Mukherjee, R., *Six Villages of Bengal* (Bombay, 1971).

Myrdal, G., *Asian Drama* (London, 1968).

Narain, D., 'Growth and imbalances in Indian agriculture', *Journal of the Indian Society of Agricultural Statistics*, XXIV 1 (June 1972).

Nayyar, D., *India's Exports and Export Policies in the 1960s* (Cambridge, 1976).

Nayyar, R., Wages, employment and standard of living of agricultural labourers in Uttar Pradesh, India, mimeo (I.L.O., 1976).

N.C.A.E.R., *All India Rural Household Survey* (National Council of Applied Economic Research, New Delhi, 1965).

N.C.A.E.R., *Study of Selected Small Scale Industrial Units* (New Delhi, 1972).

N.C.A.E.R., *Impact of Mechanisation in Agriculture on Employment* (New Delhi, 1973).

Nicholas, R. W., Villages of the Bengal Delta: a study of ecology and peasant society (Ph.D. thesis, microfilm, University of Chicago, 1962).

Nutman, P. S., *Biological Nitrogen Fixation*, Paper delivered to the I.D.S./O.D.M. Conference on Food Prospects for South Asia (I.D.S. Sussex, November 1974).

Paddock, W. and P., *Famine 1975* (London, 1968).

Parikh, K., 'India in 2001', in A. J. Coale (ed.), *Economic Aspects of Population Growth* (London, 1976).

Rajaraman, I., Poverty, inequality and economic growth: rural Punjab

1960–61 to 1970–71 (Ph.D. thesis, Cornell University, 1974).

Ranadive, K. R., 'Distribution of income–trends since planning', Paper presented to the Seminar on Income distribution (Indian Statistical Institute, New Delhi, 1971).

Rao, V. K. R. V., 'Population growth and its relation to employment in India', in S. N. Agarwala (ed.), *India's Population–Some Problems in Perspective Planning* (Delhi, 1960).

Rawls, J., *A Theory of Justice* (Harvard, 1971).

Ruprecht, T. K., 'Fertility Control, investment and per capita output: a demographic-econometric model of the Philippines', I.U.S.S.P. Conference, *Contributed Papers* (Sydney, 1967).

Schwarz, W., 'India, Pakistan, Bangladesh', *Guardian Weekly* (4 January 1975).

Sen, A. K., *The Crisis in Indian Education*, Shastri Memorial Lecture (New Delhi, 1970) reprinted in Chaudhuri (1971).

Sen A. K., *On Economic Inequalities* (London, 1973a).

Sen, A. K., *Dimensions of Unemployment in India*, Convocation Address (Indian Statistical Institute , Calcutta, 1973b).

Sen, A. K., *Employment, Technology and Development* (Oxford, 1975).

Sethuraman, S. V., 'Employment and Labor productivity in India since 1950', *Economic Development and Cultural Change* 22, 4 (July 1974).

Singh, G. N. 'Intersectoral linkages of forestry development', *Indian Forester*, 99, 4 (1973).

Sinha, J. N., 'Macro-models and economic implications of population growth', I.U.S.S.P., *International Population Conference*, vol. I (Liège, 1973).

Star, S., 'Accounting for the growth of output', *American Economic Review* (March 1974).

Streeten, P. and M. Lipton (eds), *The Crisis in Indian Planning* (London, 1968).

Swaminathan, M. S., 'Population and food supply', *Yojana* (New Delhi, 26 January 1973).

Swamy, S., 'Population growth and economic development', in Bose *et al.* (eds) (1974).

Tanzer, M., *The Political Economy of International Oil and the Underdeveloped Countries* (Boston, 1969).

Thomas, P. J. and K. C. Ramakrishnan, *Some South Indian Villages: A Re-Survey* (University of Madras, 1940), quoted in Haswell (1967).

Thorner, D. and Thorner, A. *Land and Labour in India* (Bombay, 1962).

U.N., *Determinants and Consequences of Population Change*, vol. 1 (United Nations, New York, 1973).

Vander Velde, E. J., *The Distribution of Irrigation Benefits: A Study in Haryana, India* (Ph.D. thesis, University of Michigan, 1971).

Walsh, B. T., *Economic Development and Population Control: A fifty year projection for Jamaica* (New York, 1971).

Wills, I. R., 'Green revolution and agricultural employment and incomes in Western U.P.', *E.P.W.* Review of Agriculture (March 1971).

Winstanley, D., 'Recent rainfall trends in Africa, the Middle East & India', *Nature*, 243, 464 (1973).

CHAPTER 5

Aird, J. S., 'Population estimates for the provinces of the People's Republic of China', U.S. Social and Economic Statistics Administration, Bureau of Economic Analysis, *International Population Reports*, Series P–95, no. 73 (Washington D.C., 1974).

Alavi, H., 'Peasants and revolution', in R. Miliband and J. Saville (eds), *Socialist Register* (London, 1965); also reprinted in Desai (1969).

Amnesty, *Short Report on Detention Conditions in West Bengal Jails* (Amnesty International, London, September 1974).

Amnesty, *Annual Report* (London, 1975).

Arendt, H., *On Revolution* (London, 1963).

Bailey, F. G., *Caste and the Economic Frontier* (Manchester, 1957).

Bauer, P. T., *Dissent on Development* (London, 1971).

Béteille, A., U.G.C. National Lectures (University of Delhi, mimeo, 1973).

Béteille, A., *Studies in Agrarian Social Structure* (London, 1974).

Blackburn, R. (ed.), *Explosion in a Subcontinent* (Harmondsworth, 1975).

Brinton, C., *The Anatomy of Revolution*, 2nd edition (New York, 1952).

Byres, T. and P. Nolan, *India and China Compared: 1950–1970* (Open University, London, 1976).

Calhoun, J., 'Population', in A. Allison (ed.), *Population Control* (Harmondsworth, 1970).

Catanach, I. J., 'Agrarian disturbances in nineteenth century India', *Indian Economic and Social History Review*, III 1 (March 1966).

Catanach, I. J., *Rural Credit in Western India 1875–1930* (Berkeley, 1970).

Charlesworth, N., 'The myth of the Deccan Riots of 1875', *Modern Asian Studies*, 6, 4 (October 1972).

Chaudhuri, P., 'East European aid to India', *World Development*, 3, 5 (May 1975).

Chaudhuri, S. B., *Civil Disturbances during the British Rule in India 1765–1867* (Calcutta, 1955).

Chen, L., 'Population planning in China', Speech of the Chinese delegation at the International Conference on Population Planning, *Pakistan Economic and Social Review*, 11, 3 (Autumn 1973).

Chen, Pi-Chao, 'China's population program at the grass roots level', *Studies in Family Planning* (Population Council, New York, August 1973).

Chen, Pi-Chao, 'The "Planned Birth" program of the People's Republic of China, with a brief analysis of its transferability' (Asia Society,

SEADAG, New York, mimeo, 1974).

Chen, K.-I. and J. S. Uppal (eds), *Comparative Development of India and China* (New York, 1971).

Croll, E., *The Women's Movement in China: a selection of readings 1949–73* (Anglo-Chinese Educational Institute, London, 1974).

Dasgupta, B., *The Naxalite Movement* (New Delhi, 1974).

Davies, J. C., 'Toward a theory of revolution', *American Sociological Review*, 27, 1 (February, 1962).

Desai, A. R. (ed.), *Rural Sociology in India*, 4th edition (Bombay, 1969).

Desai, P., 'Discussion of Richman, 1975, and Weisskopf, 1975', *American Economic Review* (May 1975).

Djerassi, C., 'Fertility limitation through contraceptive steroids in the People's Republic of China', *Studies in Family Planning* (Population Council, New York, January 1974*a*).

Djerassi, C., 'Some observations on current fertility control in China', *China Quarterly*, 57 (March 1974*b*).

Draper, W. H., E. Snow *et al.*, *Population and Family Planning in the People's Republic of China* (Victor-Bostrom Fund Committee and the Population Crisis Committee, Washington D.C., Spring 1971).

Dunn, J., *Modern Revolutions* (Cambridge, 1972).

Engels, F., 'Letter to Kautsky, 1 February 1881', in R. L. Meek (ed.) *Marx and Engels on Malthus* (London, 1953).

E.P.W., *Economic and Political Weekly* (Bombay).

Evans, D., 'Unequal exchange–a survey', Institute of Development Studies (Sussex), Discussion Paper (forthcoming).

Faundes, A. and T. Luukkainen, 'Health and family planning services in the Chinese People's Republic', *Studies in Family Planning*, 3, 1 (July 1972).

Forrester, D. B., 'Subregionalism in India: the case of Telangana', *Pacific Affairs*, XLIII 1 (Spring 1970).

Forster, R. and J. P. Greene (eds), *Preconditions of Revolution in Early Modern Europe* (Baltimore and London, 1970).

Gittings, J., *How to Study China's Socialist Development*, Communication no. 117, (Institute of Development Studies (Sussex), 1976).

G.o.I., Government of India, *Towards a Self-Reliant Economy: India's Third Plan 1961–66* (Planning Commission, New Delhi, 1961).

G.o.I., *Report on Scheduled Castes and Tribes* (Ministry of Home Affairs, New Delhi, 1969).

G.o.I., *Towards Self-Reliance: Approach to the Fifth Five Year Plan* (Planning Commission, New Delhi, 1972).

G.o.I., *Economic Survey 1974/5* (Ministry of Finance, Department of Economic Affairs, New Delhi, 1975).

Gough, K., 'Peasant resistance and revolt in South India', *Pacific Affairs*, XLI 4 (Winter 1968–9).

Hanson, A. H. and J. Douglas, *India's Democracy* (London, 1972).

Harris, N., *India-China: Underdevelopment and Revolution* (New Delhi, 1974).

Harrison, S., *India, The Most Dangerous Decades* (Princeton, 1960).

Hayter, T., *Aid as Imperialism* (Harmondsworth, 1971).

Hobsbawm, E. J., *Bandits* (London, 1969).

Hoselitz, B. F. and M. Weiner, 'Economic development and political stability', *Dissent*, XX 2 (1970).

Huntington, S. P., *Political Order in Changing Societies* (Yale, 1968).

Isenman, P. J. and H. W. Singer, *Food Aid: Disincentive Effects and their Policy Implications*, Communication no. 116 (Institute of Development Studies (Sussex), 1975).

Klein, S., 'Recent economic experiences in India and China–another interpretation', *American Economic Review* (May 1965).

Kumar, K. (ed.), *Revolution* (London, 1971).

Kumar, R., 'The Deccan Riots of 1875', *Journal of Asian Studies*, 24, 1 (August 1965).

Lateef, S., *China and India: Reassessing the Conventional Wisdom*, Communication no. 118 (Institute of Development Studies (Sussex), 1976).

Leys, C., *Underdevelopment in Kenya* (London, 1975).

Malenbaum, W., 'India and China: contrasts in development performance', *American Economic Review* (June 1959).

Marx, K. and F. Engels, *The First Indian War of Independence 1857–1859* (Foreign Languages Publishing House, Moscow, undated, based on Russian edition of 1959).

McNicoll, G., 'Community level population policy: an exploration', *Population and Development Review*, 1, 1 (September 1975).

Moore, B., *Social Origins of Dictatorship and Democracy* (New York, 1966).

Morris-Jones, W. H., 'India's crisis, or Indira's crisis?' *The World Today* (November 1975).

Morris-Jones, W. H., 'Creeping but uneasy authoritarianism: India 1975–6', *Government and Opposition* (Winter 1976/7).

Mukherjee, R., *Family and Planning in India* (New Delhi, 1976).

Nakano, K., 'The population of mainland China and its recent trends' (Population Problems Research Council, Tokyo (English translation circulated by U.N.), mimeo, 1968).

Nayyar, D., 'India's trade with the Socialist countries', *World Development*, 3, 5 (May 1975).

O.E.C.D., *Development Cooperation*, Efforts and Policies of the Members of the Development Assistance Committee, 1974 Review (Organisation for Economic Cooperation and Development, Paris, 1974).

Olin, U., 'Population pressure and revolutionary movements', in R. S. Parker (ed.), *The Emotional Stress of War, Violence and Peace* (Pittsburgh, 1972).

Omvedt, G., 'The Satyashodak Samaj and peasant agitation', *E.P.W.* (3 November 1973).

Orleans, L. A., *Every Fifth Child: the population of China* (London, 1972).
Orleans, L. A., 'Family planning developments in China, 1960–1966', abstracts from medical journals, *Studies in Family Planning* (Population Council, New York, August 1973).
Paillat, P. and A. Sauvy, 'Population de la Chine. Evolution et perspectives', *Population* (May–June 1974).
Payer, C., *The Debt Trap* (Harmondsworth, 1974).
Perkins, D. H., 'Issues in the estimation of China's national product' (Harvard University, mimeo 1974).
Quinn, J. R. (ed.), *Medicine and Public Health in the People's Republic of China* (U.S. Dept. of Heatlth, Education and Welfare, National Institutes of Health, Washington D.C., 1973).
Raj, K. N., *India, Pakistan and China: Economic Growth and Output* (Bombay, 1967).
Rhodes, R. L. (ed.), *Imperialism and Underdevelopment* (New York, 1970).
Richman, B. M., 'Chinese and Indian development: an inter-disciplinary environmental analysis', *American Economic Review* (May 1975).
Rudé, G., *Revolutionary Europe, 1783–1815* (London, 1966).
Sadleir, R. M. F. S., *The Ecology of Reproduction in Wild and Domestic Mammals* (London, 1969).
Salaff, J. W., 'Institutionalised motivation for fertility limitation in China', *Population Studies*, 26, 2 (July 1972).
Salaff, J. W., 'Mortality decline in the People's Republic of China and the United States', *Population Studies*, 27, 3 (November 1973).
Segal, R., *The Crisis of India* (London, 1965).
Sen Gupta, B., *Communism in Indian Politics* (New York, 1972).
Srinivas, M. N., *Social Change in Modern India* (Berkeley, 1966).
Stone, L., 'Theories of revolution', *World Politics*, 18, 2 (January 1966)
Suyin, H., 'Population growth and birth control in China', *Eastern Horizon*, XII 5 (1973).
Swamy, S., 'Economic growth in China and India 1952–1970: a comparative appraisal', *Economic Development and Cultural Change*, 21, 4, Pt. II (July 1973).
Tien, H., *China's Population Struggle: Demographic decisions of the People's Republic 1949–1969* (Ohio State University Press, Columbus, 1973). See also review symposium in *Demography*, 11, 4 (November 1974) and author's reply *ibid*.
Tien, H., 'Planned reproduction, family formation and fertility decline', Paper delivered to the Population Association of America (New York, mimeo, April 1974).
Tulloch, P., *The Seven Outside* (Overseas Development Institute, London, 1973).
U.N., *Demographic Yearbook* (New York, 1973, 1974a).
U.N., 'Fertility trends in the world', *Conference Background Papers* for U.N.

World Population Conference, E/Conf. 60/CBP/16 (New York, 3 April 1974*b*).

U.N., 'Resolution adopted by the General Assembly', *Development and international economic cooperation*, A/Res/3362 (S-VII) (New York, 19 September 1975).

U.S. Congress, *Hearing before the Subcommittee on the Near East and South Asia of the Committee on Foreign Affairs* (House of Representatives, Washington D.C., 31 October 1973).

U.S. Congress, *China: a Reassessment of the Economy*, A compendium of Papers submitted to the Joint Economic Committee, Congress of the United States (Washington D.C., 10 July 1975).

Vaitsos, C., *Intercountry Income Distribution and Transnational Enterprises* (Oxford, 1974).

Weisskopf, T. E., 'China and India: contrasting experiences in economic development', *American Economic Review* (May 1975).

Wolf, E. R., *Peasant Wars of the Twentieth Century* (London, 1971).

Yeh, K. C. and C. Lee, 'Communist China's population problem in the 1980s', *Rand Papers*, P-5143-1 (Rand Corporation, May 1974).

Zartman, W., 'Revolution and development: form and substance', *Civilizations*, XX 2 (1970).

Index